Knowledge in a Social World

Knowledge
in a
Social World

ALVIN I. GOLDMAN

CLARENDON PRESS · OXFORD

*This book has been printed digitally and produced in a standard specification
in order to ensure its continuing availability*

OXFORD
UNIVERSITY PRESS

Great Clarendon Street, Oxford OX2 6DP

Oxford University Press is a department of the University of Oxford.
It furthers the University's objective of excellence in research, scholarship,
and education by publishing worldwide in

Oxford New York

Auckland Bangkok Buenos Aires Cape Town Chennai
Dar es Salaam Delhi Hong Kong Istanbul Karachi Kolkata
Kuala Lumpur Madrid Melbourne Mexico City Mumbai Nairobi
São Paulo Shanghai Taipei Tokyo Toronto

Oxford is a registered trade mark of Oxford University Press
in the UK and in certain other countries

Published in the United States
by Oxford University Press Inc., New York

© Alvin I. Goldman 1999

The moral rights of the author have been asserted
Database right Oxford University Press (maker)

Reprinted 2003

ISBN 0-19-823820-7

To my brother Malcolm
whose intellectual challenges kindled my early curiosity

PREFACE

This is the best of times, or this is the worst of times, for the social pursuit of knowledge. Optimists point with pride to the World Wide Web and the Information Superhighway. They exult in the fact that with every new photograph from the Hubble Space Telescope we get more precise information about distant galaxies and greater insight into the origin of the universe. When have we been better endowed with information and knowledge? Pessimists point to more worrisome conditions. Broadcast political news in America increasingly comes in bite-sized morsels, and the average citizen has been shown to have sparse political knowledge. Ownership and control of news outlets increasingly reside in a few powerful media conglomerates. A small number of industrial corporations have more public communications power than any private businesses have ever possessed in world history (Bagdikian 1997: ix–x). On this scenario we seem perilously close to an Orwellian nightmare. How should these dramatically divergent perspectives be reconciled? Just how good or how bad are the prospects for knowledge in contemporary society?

This book does not provide an inventory of the current conditions for knowledge. It does, however, explore the ways that human knowledge can be increased via social transactions, whatever the present starting point happens to be. It is a cliché that ours is an information age; certainly it is an era in which issues of knowledge and information bombard us from every direction. What is missing, however, is a general theory of societal knowledge. What exactly is knowledge, as opposed to ignorance and error, and how can social factors contribute to its growth? This book attempts to construct such a theory. It lays philosophical foundations for a social theory of knowledge, and it assesses particular practices and institutions in terms of these foundations. It might be viewed as a philosopher's contribution to the shaping of an information-rich society.

This project falls within the subfield of philosophy that is standardly called "epistemology," but the project aims to widen epistemology's vista. Traditional epistemology has long preserved the Cartesian image of inquiry as an activity of isolated thinkers, each pursuing truth in a spirit of individualism and pure self-reliance. This image ignores the interpersonal and institutional contexts in which most knowledge endeavors are actually undertaken. Epistemology must come to grips with the social interactions that both brighten and threaten the prospects for knowledge. Although initial steps in the social direction have been taken in recent years, the present book aims to

construct a unified framework and a more detailed agenda for this epistemological expansion.

There is another reason to pursue this project. Many academic corridors are
flooded by the fashionable currents of postmodernism and (radical) social
constructionism, which purport to be replacements for traditional epistemology. These movements are appropriately sensitive to social factors in thought
and discourse, but they repudiate the hallmarks of traditional epistemology:
the quest for truth, reason, and objectivity. They imagine that social factors
necessarily cripple the prospect of anybody ascertaining truth at all; the very
intelligibility of objective truth or knowledge is denied. These misguided ideas
have led to rampant relativism in fields outside of philosophy, including law,
history, education, cultural studies, and science studies. Many philosophers
serenely dismiss these movements with the wave of a hand, but their influence has serious consequences and should not be taken lightly. Worries on this
score have been expressed by Farber and Sherry (1997) concerning the law,
and by Appleby, Hunt, and Jacob (1994) concerning history. Analogous concerns led the physicist Alan Sokal to effect a celebrated spoof of cultural studies by publishing an article full of gibberish (Sokal 1996a) in a leading
postmodern journal. He wanted to demonstrate the total absence of intellectual standards in this academic subculture (Sokal 1996b). While Sokal's spoof
was cunning and amusing, we also need sustained, philosophical responses to
these movements. Portions of this book undertake this task.

In contrast to relativism and anti-objectivism, I maintain that social practices can make both positive and negative contributions to knowledge. The
task is to show just which social practices, under what conditions, will promote knowledge rather than subvert it. The notion that positive epistemic
value can flow from social interchange appears in at least two recent epistemological works: C. A. J. Coady's (1992) book on testimony and Philip
Kitcher's (1993) book on the philosophy of science. These comprise perhaps
the closest neighbors to the present essay. Each of these works, however, has
a fairly restricted scope compared to the wide domain carved out here.
Although testimony is a core example of a social practice, it is not the only
social practice that deserves attention from epistemology. Similarly, although
science is the most dissected arena in which social ingredients influence epistemic outcomes, it is by no means the only such arena. Journalism, law, politics, and education are also crucial domains in which accuracy of judgment
and communication should be a desideratum, and in which the impact of different institutional practices needs to be explored.

Because this book offers take-home messages not only for philosophers but
for practitioners of many disciplines—lawyers, political scientists, communication theorists, economists, and educators—I have tried to keep it as accessible as possible. Although philosophical issues are explored in depth,
technicalities are avoided wherever possible and the essential ideas are
explained from scratch. Still, some readers may wish to skip the denser philo-

sophical material. Chapter 2, on truth, is the most difficult chapter but the most easily omitted. Non-philosophers can bypass it without significant loss.

I have been pondering these issues, learning new subjects, and gathering material for this book for over twenty years. Research support has fortunately come my way from several national funding sources, to which I am most grateful: the Center for Advanced Study in the Behavioral Sciences, the John Simon Guggenheim Foundation, the National Humanities Center, and the National Science Foundation (grant number SES-8204737). In 1975–6, at the Center for Advanced Study in the Behavioral Sciences, I framed the conception of epistemology as a multidisciplinary enterprise with two main parts: individual and social. Individual epistemology should be linked to the cognitive sciences, and social epistemology should be linked to those social science and policy disciplines that study knowledge in its social and institutional contexts. At first I envisioned a single book that would synthesize both individual and social epistemology, but that was clearly unrealistic. So the first half of the project was published as *Epistemology and Cognition* (Goldman 1986), a book-length treatment of epistemology and cognitive science. The connection between individual and social epistemology was briefly sketched there (and mentioned earlier in Goldman 1978). Beginning in 1987, a series of social epistemology articles appeared that were ultimately transmuted into chunks of the present book: Goldman 1987, 1991, 1994*a*, 1994*b*, 1995*a*, 1995*b*, Goldman and Shaked 1991*a*, Cox and Goldman 1994, Goldman and Cox 1996, and Talbott and Goldman 1998.

Work on this book *per se* began in the fall of 1994, partly with the support of the University of Pittsburgh's Center for Philosophy of Science. Later institutional support came from the University of Arizona's Udall Center for Public Policy Studies. An invitation to give the Earl and Edna Stice Lecture at the University of Washington provided an opportunity to float the general plan of the book. Drafts of various chapters were subsequently read to philosophy departments at Princeton University, the University of Utah, the University of Oklahoma, and the University of Glasgow, and to law school forums at Yale University, the University of Arizona, and the University of California, Berkeley. Helpful comments were received from audience participants in all of these venues.

I have been the beneficiary of diligent work and sage advice from many research assistants, graduate seminar participants, and colleagues in both my own and other departments. The most sustained research assistance came from Joel Pust, who carefully read early drafts of many chapters and offered incisive suggestions throughout. Tim Bayne contributed invaluable advice on later versions of all the chapters, plus dedicated pursuit of bibliographical details. Mark Wunderlich worked on Chapter 10, and his formal insights were especially helpful. As readers of the manuscript for the press, William Alston and an anonymous referee offered many good pointers on quite a range of chapters. It is difficult to recall everyone whose suggestions and criticisms changed the course of the book, but here are some that stand out in my mind: on Chapter 1, James Conant, Melissa Berry, and Holly Smith; on Chapter 2, Marian David; on Chapter 3, Peter Godfrey-Smith, Dave Truncellito, and Mark Wunderlich; on Chapter 4, Kurt Meyers, Shaughan Lavine, Moshe Shaked, and Todd Stewart; on Chapter 5, Scott Jacobs and Sally Jackson; on Chapter 6, Holly Smith, Carla Stoffle, Martin Fricke, Peter Ludlow, and Don Fallis; on Chapter 7, Jules Coleman and Brad Thompson; on Chapter 8, Shaughan Lavine and Moshe Shaked; on Chapter 9, Brian Leiter and David Golove; on Chapter 10, Brad Jones, Tom Christiano, and Dave Schmidtz; and on Chapter 11, Harvey Siegel, Scott LaBarge, and Yetta Goodman. Warm thanks go to all of these informants and critics. The undetected and unexcised errors, as usual, must be assigned to the author. Finally, I wish to thank my editor Peter Momtchiloff for more than the usual amount of valuable advice and encouragement.

A.I.G.

CONTENTS

PART THREE   SPECIAL DOMAINS

PART ONE

Foundations

ONE

Epistemology and Postmodern Resistance

1.1 *Truth seeking in the social world*

"ALL men by nature desire to know." So said Aristotle (1924: Book I) and he was right. Information seeking is a pervasive activity of human life. We scan the horizon to see if rain is imminent, we watch the news to learn who has been elected, and we listen to the traffic report to anticipate delays in our drive to work. Our interest in information has two sources: curiosity and practical concerns. The dinosaur extinction fascinates us, although knowing its cause would have no material impact on our lives. We also seek knowledge for practical reasons, as when we solicit a physician's diagnosis or compare prices at automobile dealerships. What we seek in all such cases is true or accurate information, not misinformation. No newspaper reader wants the sports page to misreport outcomes or the financial section to falsify market transactions. We commonly seek the truth, or a close approximation to the truth.

A familiar type of social interaction highlights the fact that truth is what we are after. Question asking is a universal feature of human communication and the prototype of a truth-seeking practice. The primary purpose of asking a question is to learn the answer, the true answer, from the respondent. In asking someone for the time, or the location of the nearest post office, a questioner evinces a desire to know something she does not already know. There are exceptions to this pattern. Teachers and quiz-show hosts pose questions when they already have the answer. Survey researchers simply want their respondents' opinions, true or false. These are nonstandard cases, however. The normal purpose of question asking is to learn a truth from the respondent. The truth motive explains why questioners direct their interrogatories at authoritative informants. If I want to know when the next faculty meeting is scheduled in my department, I will ask the department head or the secretary because *they* (probably) know the answer. I will not ask my children, my doctor, or a random pedestrian on the street.

Although question asking is interpersonal, truth seeking is not universally or necessarily social. To gauge the probability of rain, I can personally check the sky rather than listen to a weather forecaster. An enormous portion of our truth seeking, however, is either directly or indirectly social. It is directly social when one verbally requests information from others, or consults written texts. It is indirectly social when one's current activity, albeit autonomous, exploits intellectual skills acquired from others, through formal or informal education. The social dimensions of knowledge are dramatized by modern society, which teems with information-dispensing enterprises ranging from newspapers and libraries to the World Wide Web. Complex societies delegate knowledge-gathering and knowledge-disseminating missions to many specialized agencies. Justice systems are instituted to determine who perpetrated crimes or torts; census takers are appointed to obtain population statistics; and schools are established to transmit knowledge. These activities and enterprises form the starting point of social epistemology as here conceived.

Traditional epistemology, especially in the Cartesian tradition, was highly individualistic, focusing on mental operations of cognitive agents in isolation or abstraction from other persons. Roughly this traditional pursuit is what I have called *individual epistemology*. I have no general objection to individual epistemology; indeed, it was the subject I explored in the predecessor of this volume, *Epistemology and Cognition* (Goldman 1986). But given the deeply collaborative and interactive nature of knowledge seeking, especially in the modern world, individual epistemology needs a social counterpart: *social epistemology*. That is the topic of the present book.[1]

In what respects is social epistemology social? First, it focuses on social paths or routes to knowledge. That is, considering believers taken one at a time, it looks at the many routes to belief that feature interactions with other agents, as contrasted with private or asocial routes to belief acquisition. This "social path" dimension is the principal dimension of sociality that concerns me here. Second, social epistemology does not restrict itself to believers taken singly. It often focuses on some sort of group entity—a team of co-workers, a set of voters in a political jurisdiction, or an entire society—and examines the spread of information or misinformation across that group's membership. Rather than concentrate on a single knower, as did Cartesian epistemology, it addresses the distribution of knowledge or error within the larger social cluster. Even in this second perspective, however, the knowing agents are still individuals. Third, instead of restricting knowers to individuals, social episte-mology may consider collective or corporate entities, such as juries or legisla-

---

[1] The contrast between individual and social epistemology, plus the way I charac-terize individual epistemology, may make it sound as if mental operations fall outside the province of social epistemology. That is not so. As we shall see, especially in Ch. 4, the way an agent reasons from the reports, testimony, and arguments of others belongs to the field of social epistemology. In a sense, then, individual and social epistemology are not sharply exclusive branches of epistemology. I am indebted on this point to Corlett 1991. However, the bulk of the practices subsumed under social epistemology fall outside individual epistemology.

tures, as potential knowing agents. This third approach will occasionally be taken in this volume, but only rarely.[2]

Having said a few words about the social dimension of social epistemology, let me now say a few about its *veritistic* dimension, that is, its orientation toward truth determination. Veritistic epistemology (whether individual or social) is concerned with the production of knowledge, where knowledge is here understood in the 'weak' sense of *true belief*.[3] More precisely, it is concerned with both knowledge and its contraries: *error* (false belief) and *ignorance* (the absence of true belief). The main question for veritistic epistemology is: Which practices have a comparatively favorable impact on knowledge as contrasted with error and ignorance? Individual veritistic epistemology asks this question for nonsocial practices; social veritistic epistemology asks it for social practices. This book is an essay in social veritistic epistemology.

A brief glimpse of the book's contents should help put some flesh on this abstract skeleton.[4] Part One (Chapters 1–3) formulates and defends my general approach, contrasting it with other conceptions of social epistemology. Chapter 1 confronts and rejects reasons for scoffing at truth and denying the very possibility of its attainment. Chapter 2 dissects the truth concept in greater philosophical depth, and then the basic structure of my approach is detailed in Chapter 3.

Part Two (Chapters 4–7) examines generic social-epistemic practices, which cut across specialized domains. Chapter 4 considers simple reports or testimony about allegedly observed events. What reporting practices would be most beneficial, and how can hearers make positive veritistic use of speakers' reports? Chapter 5 analyzes the more complex speech practices of arguing and debating. Rules for debate are examined, and we explore how conformity with such rules can promote the goal of truth. Chapter 6 looks at the effects of technology and economics on the feasibility and scope of information dissemination. How does the electronic revolution affect prospects for human knowledge? How does the financing of the mass media constrain their role in the advancement of knowledge? Chapter 7 examines the role of "gatekeepers" of communication. What framework for speech regulation or deregulation would maximally foster the spread of knowledge? The free market for ideas is often touted as the best framework for knowledge maximization. Is it the best?

Part Three (Chapters 8–11) canvasses four specialized domains in which knowledge quests are crucial. Chapter 8 examines science, with specific atten-

---

[2] Since it plays a very minor role in my project, I shall not give any account of the metaphysical status of collective entities or of belief as the state of a collective entity. For one treatment of this topic, see Gilbert 1989.

[3] Beginning in Ch. 3 I shall broaden the inquiry so as to encompass degrees of belief (subjective probabilities) and degrees of knowledge. For the moment, however, I keep things simple by restricting attention to unqualified, flat-out belief.

[4] The synopsis that follows is not intended to be exhaustive. It generally presents only representative topics from each chapter.

tion to scientific authority and the assignment of professional credit. Chapter 9 looks at the truth-determining capacities of the law. It compares the prospects for truth determination under the common law system and the civil law system, and asks how the management of expert testimony can best promote truth determination. Chapter 10 targets a prominent topic in modern political science: the role of information in democracy. What types of information do voters need for democracy to succeed, and which institutional practices would foster optimal voter knowledge? Finally, Chapter 11 concerns education. What is the proper role of truth in systems of education, and which kinds of classroom and policymaking procedures can best cultivate knowledge in the long run?

The reader may wonder at this point how veritistic social epistemology can plausibly be applied to law or democracy. After all, knowledge and error-avoidance are not the only pertinent criteria for appraising these institutions' practices. This point is entirely correct, so I need to explain more precisely the mission of veritistic epistemology. Veritistic epistemology is a specialized subject, analogous to environmental studies and nutritional studies. Neither epistemology nor these other fields tries to fix correct social policies "all things considered." Each is dedicated to a special social value, one circumscribed kind of thing that people and institutions take an interest in. Environmental studies examines the impact of policies specifically on environmental integrity. Nutritional studies examines the impact of food content and diets specifically on health. The distinctive value of each field need not be exhaustive, supreme, or paramount; that does not invalidate the mission or integrity of the subject. Even if taste sometimes trumps health in the larger scheme of things, the nutritional effects of what you eat are worth studying. Analogously, the knowledge impact of various policies is worth determining even if that impact is trumped, in certain spheres, by other values. For example, the exclusionary rule that bars the admission of illegally obtained evidence might be acceptable, all things considered, even though it reduces the amount of knowledge obtained at trial. We need not resolve the problem of how, exactly, to prioritize plural values. As long as multiple things are valued, a sensible division of labor will ordain special fields of study, each dedicated to variables that augment or diminish the incidence of a selected type of good or bad. Veritistic epistemology is such a special field, where the selected good is knowledge and the selected bads are error and ignorance.

Social veritistic epistemology bears certain resemblances to familiar segments of social science, but its distinctive features must not be overlooked. Social veritistic epistemology does not merely seek to describe social practices that are actually in place, nor to trace their historical development. It has the distinctive *normative* purpose of evaluating or appraising such practices on the veritistic dimension, that is, in terms of their respective knowledge consequences. Practices currently in place will be veritistically good or bad in varying degrees; they will rarely be ideal. To investigate prospects for improvement, social epistemology must be prepared to transcend previously realized practices. It must be ready to consider the probable veritistic properties of practices that have not yet been, but might be, adopted. Thus, veritistic epistemology tackles the admittedly nontrivial task of assessing both actual and possible practices in terms of their foreseeable informational bounty.

1.2 Veriphobia

Having outlined my veritistic approach to social epistemology, I must hasten to observe that the playing field of social epistemology has been substantially preempted by world views quite opposed to the veritistic conception. I allude to such views as social constructivism, postmodernism, pragmatism, cultural studies, and critical legal studies. Although writers of these persuasions rarely use the phrase "social epistemology," they engage in projects that bear a superficial similarity to mine.[5] However, they all share a deep skepticism or utter repudiation of truth as a viable criterion for studying epistemic phenomena. They would raise a suspicious and even scornful eyebrow at any serious attempt to wield the concept of truth. I think they suffer from an affliction that may be called *veriphobia*. Although veriphobes differ from one another in the details of their preferred methodologies, they share the idea that the study of social "knowledge" should be confined to the interpersonal and cultural determination of belief: not true or false belief, just plain belief. When veriphobes talk of "knowledge," they do not refer, as I do, to *true* belief, but to something like institutionalized belief. They deliberately bracket questions of truth and falsity, holding that nothing legitimate can come of any attempt to draw distinctions in those terms. Whereas *epistemology* derives from the Greek word *episteme*, meaning knowledge, their enterprise is better classified as social *doxology*, from the Greek word *doxa*, meaning opinion or belief (whether true or false).[6]

A clear preference for social doxology over social epistemology is expressed by Steven Shapin, in a book with the intriguing but misleading title *A Social History of Truth* (Shapin 1994). In the first chapter Shapin takes issue with "a special community of language-users called 'academic philosophers'" who want to mark a distinction between what is true and what is merely taken to be so (1994: 3). He calls this a "restrictive" notion of truth, and pleads for a more "liberal" sensibility in which truth is simply *accepted belief* (1994: 4). After all, says Shapin, historians, cultural anthropologists, and sociologists of

---

[5] One of these writers, Steve Fuller, used the phrase "social epistemology" as the title both of one of his books (Fuller 1988) and of the journal that he has edited.
[6] This proposed use, of course, is unrelated to the religious use of the term "doxology."

knowledge are interested in understanding cultural variation in belief. Since truth on the "restrictive" approach cannot vary across communities, a liberal approach to truth is needed to accommodate these disciplines. So truth is defined, for Shapin's purposes, as accepted belief.

I have no quarrel with intellectual history, cultural anthropology, or the sociology of knowledge. They are perfectly legitimate disciplines understood as Shapin describes them, as explorations of social forces that influence the development and variation in belief. But why tamper with the word "true" to accommodate these disciplines? We already have such words as "belief" and "opinion," and these disciplines can ply their trades with these and kindred terms. They need no spurious help from a bogus use of "truth." The expressions "true belief" and "accepted belief" are simply not equivalent. There are (and were) innumerable accepted beliefs that are not true, for example, that the sun revolves around the earth. Why propose this revisionary sense of "true" when there is already a perfectly good word for the concept Shapin needs, namely, "belief"? Shapin defends his use of "truth" as more "tolerant" (1994: 5) than the restrictive use, presumably because it is less prone to invite invidious judgments among different communities or cultures. But if Shapin expects his favored disciplines to abstain from veritistic appraisals of different communities, let their practitioners simply use the words "belief" and "opinion" rather than "truth." Certainly history, cultural anthropology, and sociology of knowledge should not be deprived of the belief concept. But that does not mean that the ordinary ("restrictive") concept of truth should be replaced by, or confused with, the belief concept.

Unless true opinion is distinguished from opinion *per se*, we cannot draw the palpable distinction between normal, truth-seeking questioners, and survey researchers who merely want respondents' opinions.[7] Unless we avail ourselves of the so-called "restrictive" use of "true," this important distinction will be lost. Retention of this sense of truth does not stem from intolerance; it stems from a sensible desire to keep a valuable tool in our conceptual toolkit.

The distinction between truth and belief can be illustrated by the concept of a valid argument. According to the standard definition, an argument is *valid* just in case its conclusion must be true if its premises are all true. Here is an example:

> Premise 1: If it rained, then the street are wet.
> Premise 2: The streets are not wet.
> Conclusion: It did not rain.

If the premises are both true, the conclusion must be true as well. So the argument is valid. Suppose, however, that "true" is replaced by "believed" in the

---

[7] Of course, many survey questions concern the respondents' preferences rather than beliefs. It suffices for my purposes to focus on the latter.

foregoing definition. This yields a new definition of what we might call "balidity": an argument is *balid* just in case its conclusion must be believed if its premises are all believed. Is the indented argument balid? No. The two premises can both be believed without the conclusion being believed; in particular, if the believer is unappreciative of the logical relation between the premises and conclusion. Thus, if we substituted "belief" for "truth" everywhere, we would be forced to abandon the standard distinction between valid and invalid arguments, and make do with a different distinction between balid and inbalid arguments.

Shapin says that nothing in his book is intended to be an argument against the legitimacy of the restrictive concept of truth (1994: 4). Perhaps, then, he would not oppose (veritistic) social epistemology, but would simply prefer social doxology. Other theorists, however, certainly take a critical stance toward anything akin to veritistic social epistemology. They not only prefer doxology to veritistic epistemology, but challenge the very viability of the latter. I begin this book, therefore, with replies to many of their predictable objections. The remainder of this chapter looks at a sampling of probable misgivings, especially ones originating in postmodern quarters (where the term "postmodern" is understood loosely). Adherents of postmodernism now comprise a populous camp in the general vicinity of social epistemology, and they dismiss invocations of truth as naive and antiquated. This chapter therefore undertakes a minesweeping operation, to clear the territory of (many of) their objections. Also addressed are related worries of nonpostmodern philosophers. A more detailed and philosophically nuanced discussion of truth is undertaken in Chapter 2. Finally, the general contours of veritistic social epistemology are presented in Chapter 3, where I elaborate its structure and mission, critically examine rival conceptions of social epistemology, and reply to additional concerns.

1.3 *Six criticisms of truth-based epistemology*

Purveyors of anti-truth hostility are legion, but it is tricky to pinpoint their theses and arguments. Veriphobic arguments often evaporate like mist when examined in the full light of day. Nonetheless, I assemble six types of criticisms that are either expressly stated or strongly intimated in veriphobic writings. Some objections draw on well-known and hotly debated theses on which there are massive literatures. These literatures cannot be addressed here with anything approaching thoroughness, so I shall confine myself to selected arguments and comparatively brief replies. Because this book primarily aims to construct a positive epistemology rather than a critique of opposing voices, I restrict ground-clearing discussions to the first two chapters (plus bits and pieces of later chapters). Here, then, are six criticisms extracted from the literature. Although there is some overlap in the stated criticisms themselves, my replies will be fairly separate. In the case of several objections, a central critical theme is embellished by a family of variations.

(1) There is no such thing as transcendent truth. What we call "true" is simply what we agree with. So-called truths or facts are merely negotiated beliefs, the products of social construction and fabrication, not 'objective' or 'external' features of the world.

(2) Knowledge, reality, and truth are the products of language. There is no language-independent reality that can make our thoughts true or false.

(3) If there were any transcendent or objective truths, they would be inaccessible and unknowable by human beings, hence unavailable for any practical epistemological purposes.

(4) There are no privileged epistemic positions, and no certain foundations for beliefs. All claims are judged by conventions or language games, which have no deeper grounding. There are no neutral, transcultural standards for settling disagreements.

(5) Appeals to truth are merely instruments of domination or repression, which should be replaced by practices with progressive social value.

(6) Truth cannot be attained because all putatively truth-oriented practices are corrupted and biased by politics or self-serving interests.

1.4 *The argument from social construction*

Let me repeat the first criticism, to have it directly before us.

(1) There is no such thing as transcendent truth. What we call "true" is simply what we agree with. So-called truths or facts are merely negotiated beliefs, the products of social construction and fabrication, not 'objective' or 'external' features of the world.

This is a bundle of claims culled from a variety of sources. What they all deny is that truth is transcendent, in the sense that truths exist or depend on the nature of "reality" rather than on human persuasion. This is a criticism of veritistic epistemology because it presumes that truth does indeed depend on reality, which is what the present criticism disputes. In other words, veritistic epistemology requires some sort of correspondence conception of truth, at least a conception compatible with correspondence intuitions about truth.

In addition to rejecting transcendent truth, criticism (1) proposes an alternative theory of truth, roughly what is known as the "performative" theory. On this theory, calling a statement "true" is just a way of concurring with it. As Richard Rorty (1991: 24) puts it, "true" is merely a compliment we pay to statements we find good to believe. Truth is not a property possessed by beliefs in virtue of some relation they bear to "worldly" facts that stand outside of discursive practices.

The performative theory, however, is off the mark, as I shall briefly indicate here before returning to the subject in Chapter 2. There are many cases in which "true" does not express agreement or concurrence with any particular statement. For instance, if Frankie says there is left-over stew in the refrigerator and Johnnie says there isn't, I might comment, "Either Frankie or Johnnie said something true." But I may have no opinion as to which one is right, so I am not agreeing with either Frankie's or Johnnie's statement. Another flaw in the performative theory is that "true" can be used to ask questions as well as express agreement, as when one says, "Is Melanie's contention true?" Here one seems to be asking about the relation between Melanie's statement and an objective state of affairs, not just looking to compliment a statement. Performative theorists are right, of course, to the extent that someone who believes a statement to be true is prepared to agree with others who might assert it. This does not imply, however, that *all one does* in calling a statement "true" is signal a willingness to agree with others.

The suggestion that "true" merely signals belief, or a willingness to agree, fits the last sentence of (1), which says that truths are merely negotiated beliefs. The palpable error in this theory, construed as an account of the ordinary meaning of truth, can be highlighted by again considering questions. No matter how well a belief has been negotiated, or how deeply entrenched, institutionalized, or "stabilized" it is, we can always intelligibly ask, "But is it really *true*?" Mere entrenchment or institutionalization—in George Orwell's (1949) totalitarian society of *Nineteen Eighty-Four*, for example—would not resolve the issue of truth. As Hilary Putnam (1978: 108–9) observes, if "true" simply *meant* "stably believed," it would be pointless to say, "I grant that *P* is stably believed, but is it true?" Since such a question always does have a point, truth cannot be equated with stabilized or institutionalized belief.

A somewhat different version of an agreement or consensus theory of truth is also endorsed by Rorty. In other passages he writes of the "homely use of 'true'" to mean "what you can defend against all comers" (Rorty 1979: 308), and elsewhere suggests that "*S* knows that *P*" is a "remark about the status of *S*'s reports among his peers" (1979: 175). A brief formulation of the theory might be: truth is what peers let you say. This formula led one wag to pen the following limerick about Rorty:

> "Truth is what peers let you say,"
> It was false said at the APA,
> And so Richard Rorty
> Changed peer groups at forty;
> Now his statements get truer each day.[8]

---

[8] The author of this limerick is Dean Zimmerman. "The APA" refers to the American Philosophical Association, most of whose members would probably *not* consent to this theory of truth. Rorty's move from the philosophy department at Princeton University to the English department at the University of Virginia undoubtedly put him in a milieu more receptive to his theories.

Did Rorty's statements really become truer when he changed peer groups? The poet obviously does not think so; nor do I. Peer acceptance of one's statements might make one happy, but it does not make those statements more or less true.[9]

A consensus theory of truth seems wrong from the start, at least as an account of our ordinary concept. Not only does the truth of a proposition not require total consensus, it does not require anybody at all to believe it. Consider a proposition that asserts the existence of a huge ridge beneath the oceans (the Mid-Oceanic Ridge) and of a deep canyon (the Great Global Rift) that runs the length of the ridge and right along its center. Had the history of geological science been different, had the sea floor not been explored so extensively, no human being (or other intelligent creature) might now be aware of these formations. Nonetheless, a proposition asserting their existence would still be true. Similarly, if nobody had ever formed a belief in the double helical structure of DNA, it would still be true that DNA has a double helical structure. Such examples refute the attempt to equate truth with actual belief. Can a belief theory of truth be salvaged by appeal to future rather than current beliefs? Charles Peirce hoped to accomplish this in saying, "The opinion which is fated to be ultimately agreed to by all who investigate is what we mean by truth" (1931–5: 5.407). But surely this is not what we *mean* by truth. Even if a truth is formulated and investigated, there is no metaphysical guarantee that every investigator will be persuaded of it. Furthermore, even if all who investigate *will* converge on a given opinion, that does not make it true. Perhaps all the intelligent creatures who ever investigate a certain astronomical event that occurs at one end of the universe live at this end of the universe, and their evidence about the event, as it happens, is misleading. They might all converge on the same opinion, although it is erroneous. The conviction that convergence coincides with truth is the faith of optimists, not part of a proper definition of truth.

Until now my replies have assumed that critics wish to equate the ordinary sense of "true" with mere belief. But there is an alternative line that social constructivists may prefer. They might concede that ordinary thought admits the possibility of truth without consensus, but why should ordinary thought go uncontested? An analogy can be drawn here with moral language. The philosopher J. L. Mackie (1977) conceded that people regularly assume there are moral facts, but he disputed this widespread assumption. He denied the existence of "worldly" moral facts, finding them "queer" and unlike well-behaved physical facts. Metaethical theorists of this sort are called "error theorists." Analogously, social constructivists like Bruno Latour and Steve Woolgar (1986) seem to be error theorists about (unobserved) scientific objects or facts. Latour and Woolgar admit that scientists believe in objective scientific facts, but they

---

[9] For a pragmatist like Rorty, happiness (or the like) is all that matters. But whether or not truth "matters," it should not be equated with peer acceptance.

themselves reject these entities. All that really exists are sets of beliefs or inscriptions that scientific actors distribute within a social network.

Latour and Woolgar's theoretical vacillations make interpretation somewhat difficult. Near the beginning of their book, they adopt an agnostic position about the allegedly external entities or facts that scientists purport to discover (1986: 31). If they maintained this agnosticism throughout they could not be error theorists, because agnosticism consists in neutrality, which is incompatible with denial. In subsequent passages, however, Latour and Woolgar depart from their initial neutrality. They explicitly affirm that facts (or truths) are "constituted" or "fabricated" when statements come to be accepted, or no longer contested. They explicitly deny what scientists proclaim, namely, that scientists discover entities with independent, "out there" existence.

[I]n situations where a statement is quickly borrowed, used and reused, there quickly comes a stage where it is no longer contested. Amidst the general Brownian agitation, a fact has then been constituted. (1986: 87)

Despite the fact that our scientists held the belief that the inscriptions could be representations or indicators of some entity with an independent existence "out there," we have argued that such entities were constituted solely through the use of these inscriptions . . . [W]e do not conceive of scientists . . . as pulling back the curtain on pregiven, but hitherto concealed truths. Rather, objects (in this case, substances) are constituted through the artful creativity of scientists. Interestingly, attempts to avoid the use of terminology which implies the preexistence of objects subsequently revealed by scientists has led us into certain stylistic difficulties . . . We have therefore found it extremely difficult to formulate descriptions of scientific activity which do *not* yield to the misleading impression that science is about *discovery* (rather than creativity and construction) . . . [T]he formulations which characterize historical descriptions of scientific practice require exorcism before the nature of this practice can be best understood. (1986: 128–9)

Clearly, then, Latour and Woolgar deny the existence of "out there" truths or facts. The language of "truth" or "fact" is only legitimately applicable to accepted statements of the community of scientists, that is, to consensual beliefs. This is explicitly stated elsewhere by Woolgar: "[T]here is no object beyond discourse . . . the organization of discourse *is* the object. Facts and objects in the world are inescapably textual constructions" (1988: 73). The question is: What arguments do Latour and Woolgar offer to support their claim? What warrants them in denying the existence of scientific facts (or entities) independent of the negotiated agreements of scientists?[10]

---

[10] In some passages Latour and Woolgar suggest a weaker position. For example, they write: "We do not wish to say that facts do not exist nor that there is no such thing as reality . . . Our point is that 'out-there-ness' is the *consequence* of scientific work rather than its *cause*" (1986: 180–2). The last sentence seems to imply that there *is* "out-there-ness," which is inconsistent with the passages quoted in the text that imply the *nonex-*istence of independent, "out-there" (scientific) facts or entities. My criticism in the text

Apparently, Latour and Woolgar think that sociological analysis establishes the case for the nonexistence of independent scientific facts.

More recently, sociologists of science have convincingly argued the case for the social fabrication of science . . . But despite these arguments, facts refuse to become sociologized. They seem able to return to their state of being "out there" and thus to pass beyond the grasp of sociological analysis. (1986: 175)

So Latour and Woolgar's argument for the nonexistence of "out there" facts is supposedly based on sociological analysis. The question is: How does this argument from sociological analysis proceed?

Observe that their conclusion, that there are no external (scientific) facts, is what philosophers call a *negative existential* statement. Other statements of this genre include "There are no witches" and "There are no ghosts." Similarly, although the neuroendocrinologists studied by Latour and Woolgar posit the independent existence of certain hormones, Latour and Woolgar deny their existence. They regard the scientists' posits as just a "mythology" (1986: 54). The problem is: How can sociological analysis alone justify the negative existential conclusion "There are no (external) hormones"? Perhaps the form of inference they employ is a variant of "inference to the best explanation" (Harman 1965). Today we deny the existence of witches because all the phenomena that once seemed to indicate the existence of witches can now be explained without this hypothesis. The best explanation of those phenomena allows us to dispense with witches. Latour and Woolgar may be arguing that the "observable" phenomena they study, namely, agreement and disagreement among scientists, can be fully and satisfactorily explained by social acts of argumentation and negotiation (triggered, perhaps, by outputs of experimental apparatus). "External" scientific entities like hormones or chemical structures are not needed for a satisfactory explanation, so we should deny their existence.

Can sociological analysis alone provide a satisfactory explanation of scientific agreement and disagreement? For argument's sake, let us grant that social discourse and negotiation provide at least a *partial* explanation of scientific opinion formation. The proximal or immediate causes of scientists' beliefs, in other words, are acts of verbal argumentation. What about the distal or more remote causes of these beliefs, however? Couldn't they include "external" microentities (ones that either match or mismatch the scientists' descrip-

focuses on the latter, more extreme, claim, which I believe is Latour and Woolgar's main position. Philip Kitcher (1993: 165–7) addresses a weaker interpretation, under which Latour and Woolgar allow that scientists engage in causal interaction with something beyond themselves but merely deny that their beliefs are causally affected by these interactions. In reply, Kitcher constructs an ideal experiment which, if performed, would undoubtedly show that people's beliefs *would* be affected by inputs from external, asocial nature. Kitcher's hypothetical experiment is a good antidote, I agree, to the weaker claim, but I think that, on the whole, Latour and Woolgar mean to endorse the stronger claim.

tions)? This is just what realist scientists and philosophers maintain, and they would add that such entities are needed for a *full* explanation of observable phenomena, including the observed inscriptions on scientific recording devices.

To elucidate this realist response, let me introduce the following notation, which fits the neuroendocrinology case studied by Latour and Woolgar:

C = a nonobservable chemical structure, such as Pyro-Glu-His-Pro-NH_2;

T = traces on a recording apparatus, such as a myograph, a gamma counter, or an amino acid analyzer;

P = perceptual observations of T by scientists;

N = negotiatory or argumentative acts by scientists;

B = belief states of scientists, e.g., the belief that TRF (thyrotropin releasing factor) is Pyro-Glu-His-Pro-NH_2.

According to Latour and Woolgar, the following diagram depicts an adequate causal explanation of the production of B, the belief states of scientists. (Arrows represent causal-explanatory relations.)

$$T \longrightarrow P \longrightarrow N \longrightarrow B$$

Moving backward from "B" in the diagram, we see that belief states are (partly) caused by negotiatory acts, negotiatory acts are (partly) caused by the perceptions of recording device traces, and these perceptions are (partly) caused by those traces. This exhausts the set of causal or explanatory factors that Latour and Woolgar seem to acknowledge. Omitted from the set are any microentities like chemical structures.

Realists might accept Latour and Woolgar's positive explanatory story *as far as it goes*. They could agree that all of these factors have causal and explanatory relevance. However, they wish to supplement the list of causal-explanatory factors. In Latour and Woolgar's story, T goes uncaused or unexplained; but doesn't it stand in need of explanation? The proper explanation, say scientific realists, is one invoking some sort of chemical microentities that must have given rise to the observed recording traces (or inscriptions) under the experimental conditions. This is depicted in the following, expanded diagram:

$$C \longrightarrow T \longrightarrow P \longrightarrow N \longrightarrow B$$

By acknowledging the existence of the unobservable entities, C, we provide a better, more complete, explanation of the events in question than Latour and Woolgar provide. This explanation, of course, would invoke precisely the kind of "out there" entities that Latour and Woolgar reject.

To demonstrate the plausibility and legitimacy of expanded causal explanations, let me switch examples. Suppose that Jones suffers a head injury on a particular occasion, and we seek a causal account of this event. Initially, we point to the fact that a ceiling beam collapsed and struck him on the head. This looks like a very satisfactory explanation, which might be diagrammed as follows:

Ceiling beam collapse $\longrightarrow$ Head contusion

Does the fact that we have a satisfactory explanation of this sort exclude a more complete explanation? Certainly not. We might also seek an explanation of why the ceiling beam collapsed, and the answer might be: there was an earthquake. We could then expand our causal-explanatory diagram as follows:

Earthquake $\longrightarrow$ Ceiling beam collapse $\longrightarrow$ Head contusion

The fact that the first diagram is correct *as far as it goes* does not preclude the second diagram from also being correct. The moral for the Latour and Woolgar case is obvious. The mere fact that negotiatory acts play a role in the formation of scientific belief does not preclude the possibility of a more complete explanation, and such an explanation might ultimately invoke "external," "out there" entities of the sort Latour and Woolgar dislike.

The crucial dispute is between neuroendocrinologists and sociologists like Latour and Woolgar. The former claim that the best explanation of the observed trace-patterns of recording devices (T) is the existence of certain chemical substances (C). The sociologists dispute this. With what epistemic warrant, however, do sociologists join issue with the neuroendocrinologists? Sociologists may be experts on causal links between negotiations and beliefs, but they have neither evidence nor expertise about the links between chemical substances and recording-device traces. How could sociological information possibly shed light on this question? On the subject of chemistry, therefore, sociologists are well advised to hold their tongues. But since they are in no position to deny the existence of chemical microentities, they are unwarranted in saying that scientists "fabricate" such entities when they hypothesize them. Consensual *belief* in such entities may indeed be produced by human interaction. But the entities themselves, if they really exist, are not produced by human interaction. Furthermore, unless the sociologists can establish that the entities do not exist, unless they can establish these negative existential statements, the term "fabrication" is misleading because it suggests the construction of a fiction. My contention is, precisely, that they have failed to establish the negative existential statement.

A final difficulty for the social constructivist account of factuality is the infinite regress it generates, as pointed out by Arthur Fine (1996). According to constructivism, the truth of a statement P consists in there being a consensual belief in P by a community. But wherein consists the truth that there is a consensual belief in P? According to the theory, it must reside in yet another level of consensual belief, namely, belief in a proposition P^*, where P^* is the proposition that there is a consensual belief in P. Once again we must ask wherein the truth of P^* consists. According to constructivism, its truth must reside in still another consensual belief, this time a belief in the proposition P^{**}: that there is a consensual belief in P^*. Obviously, an infinite regress is generated. If there is any truth of the constructivist sort, there must be infinitely many levels of consensus. Surely, however, people are incapable of so many levels of belief! So there cannot be any truths or facts of the constructivist sort.

Constructivists might reply that their theory of truth is not intended to apply to truths about consensus. These truths, they might hold, are a special, privileged case. They have an "intrinsic" reality independent of agreements about them. In this fashion, constructivists might seek to escape the threat of a regress by seeking refuge in realism about consensus. But why should anyone accept realism about consensus (i.e., realism about belief states) if realism is rejected for chemical structures? This is just half-baked metaphysics. Social constructivists, I fear, have not really reflected systematically on these ontological questions.[11]

1.5 *Language and worldmaking*

The most pervasive source of social constructivism within postmodernism, perhaps, is its obsession with language as the great determiner, the determiner of both knowledge and reality. The dominance of language is encapsulated in Jacques Derrida's dictum: "The text is all and nothing exists outside of it" (1976: 158). It is also found in frequent assertions that truth can never be independent of language. Truth is said to be an "effect of discourse" (Flax 1990a: 35), or "a product of our willing bewitchment by language" (Norris 1988: 188). At a symposium on sexuality, one postmodern anthropologist suggested that if a particular language lacks the word for "orgasm," the people speaking the language cannot possibly experience anything like an orgasm (de Waal 1996: B1). (This remark led the assembled natural scientists to wonder whether, without a word for "oxygen," people could breathe.)

This obsession with language as the determiner of knowledge and reality leads to the second line of criticism of veritistic epistemology, which I formulated as follows.

(2) Knowledge, reality, and truth are the products of language. There is no language-independent reality that can make our thoughts true or false.

The first point to notice is that postmodernists tend to conflate knowledge, reality, and truth. These must be kept distinct. It is far more plausible to regard

---

[11] I do not wish to claim that all social constructivists, much less all researchers in science studies, hold the radical position I am criticizing. Some may hold more moderate positions. But only the radical position described here poses a potential roadblock to my veritistic project, so that is the position that has occupied my attention.

knowledge and thought as products of language than reality or truth, as I shall argue below. Even with respect to knowledge and thought, however, the significance of language has been oversold. The case for a more limited role for language is persuasively presented by Steven Pinker (1994: ch. 3), a case that I briefly sketch below.

The thesis of linguistic determinism antedates postmodernism, starting as early as the famous Sapir–Whorf hypothesis (Sapir 1921) that people's thoughts are determined by the categories made available in their language. One example is color. The linguistic determination thesis holds that people divide the color spectrum by the inventory of color words in their language. In fact, the reverse seems to be true: the way we see colors determines how we learn words for them. For one thing, speakers of different languages unanimously pick the shades of the eight-crayon Crayola box—the fire-engine reds, the grass greens, the lemon yellows—as the best examples of their color words, as long as the language has a color word at all in that part of the spectrum. This suggests that color "preferences" stemming from what we *see* shape the color vocabularies of languages. Languages do differ in their numbers of color words, but there seems to be an orderly progression based on which colors are perceptually most salient. Two-color languages have words for black and white, three-color languages have black, white, and red, and so on. In a clinching experiment by Eleanor Rosch (Heider) with the Dani of New Guinea, a people speaking one of the black-and-white languages, the Dani were found to be quicker at learning a new color category that was based on fire-engine red than a category based on an off-red (Heider 1972). That they could learn a new color category at all shows that the ability to *think* or *represent* color categories is not exhausted by prior linguistic vocabulary, and that a certain previously unlabeled shade was more easily learned than another suggests that they already had a language-independent preference for the former shade, presumably based on a nonlexicalized perceptual experience.

The independence of thought and language is attested by many other phenomena. In a recent book, Susan Schaller (1991) tells the story of Ildefonso, a 27-year-old deaf immigrant from a small Mexican village who lacked any form of language whatsoever—no sign language, no writing, no lip reading, no speech. When Schaller became his volunteer teacher, Ildefonso quickly showed her that he had a full grasp of number (he learned to do addition on paper in three minutes), and demonstrated numerous other dimensions of intelligence. Experimental work in cognitive science also demonstrates language-independent thought. Karen Wynn (1992) has experimentally demonstrated that five-month-old babies—obviously prelinguistic creatures— can do simple forms of mental arithmetic, such as add one and one, or subtract one from two. Other experimental research, by such pioneers as Roger Shepard and Stephen Kosslyn, has shown that adults (and presumably children) solve certain kinds of tasks using wordless imagery (Shepard and Metzler 1971; Kosslyn 1980). Furthermore, studies of first-language acquisition raise questions about the categories babies possess and the thought operations they must engage in *before* knowing any (natural) language. In learning their first language, babies learn its grammatical properties. But how could they mentally represent these grammatical properties unless they can already represent such linguistic categories as noun, verb, verb phrase, and so forth? And how could they choose among alternative possible grammars, based on what they hear, if they did not already possess reasoning procedures? Thought must ontogenetically precede language.

Finally, everyday experience plus a little reflection show that language does not exhaust thought. We have all had the experience of finding that a sentence we had just uttered or written does not convey exactly what we meant to say. To have that feeling, there must be a "what we meant to say" that is different from what we said. Sometimes, moreover, it is not easy to find *any* words that adequately convey what we meant (Pinker 1994: 57–8). Confirmation of this comes from reflecting on ambiguity. Below are some delicious headlines cited by Pinker (1994: 79) that actually appeared in newspapers:

> Child's Stool Great for Use in Garden.
> Stud Tires Out.
> Iraqi Head Seeks Arms.
> Columnist Gets Urologist in Trouble with his Peers.

Each headline contains at least one word that is ambiguous. But surely the original thought underlying the word was not ambiguous, for the writers of the headlines knew which of the two senses they had in mind. If there can be two thoughts corresponding to one word, however, thoughts can't be words. In short, postmodernists need to moderate their claim that language is the great determiner of thought, for that unqualified view is simply false.

What about language and reality? Postmodernists seem to be old-fashioned idealists or solipsists, at least according to what they say. Some of them simply deny the existence of the external world. Their behavior, however, belies what they write. Why do they bother to write or give lectures at all if they do not believe that other people exist (including their bodies) and can read the (physical) books that they publish? Many postmodernists, moreover, are activists whose theory is motivated by interest in social change. Their aim is not only "to interpret daily life but to transform it" (Huyssen 1986: 157–8). But what is there to transform if there is no reality? So I shall not waste space defending the reality of the external world, since I am unpersuaded that postmodernists sincerely deny it.

Assuming, then, that there is some kind of reality, the question is whether we, our language, or our epistemic practices *make* or *create* the world in which we live. Some such thesis has been defended even by eminent philosophers such as Nelson Goodman. Goodman says that people make reality, or "make worlds," by drawing certain boundaries rather than others.

Now as we thus make constellations by picking out and putting together certain stars rather than others, so we make stars by drawing certain boundaries rather than others. Nothing dictates whether the sky shall be marked off into constellations or other objects. We have to make what we find, be it the Great Dipper, Sirius, food, fuel, or a stereo system. (Goodman 1984: 36)

An apt rejoinder to Goodman is given by John Searle (1995: 165–6). When Goodman claims that we draw boundaries around objects, there is no way to understand this claim unless it presupposes some reality on which we draw the boundaries. No boundaries can be drawn unless there is a pre-existing territory on which to draw them.

The really crucial point, however, as Searle points out, is that people do not so much fix the *world* (or *reality*) as they fix the categories for classifying the world.

Conceptual relativism, properly understood, is an account of how we fix the applications of our terms. What counts as a correct application of the term "cat" or "kilogram" or "canyon" . . . is up to us to decide and is to that extent arbitrary. But *once we have fixed the meaning of such terms in our vocabulary by arbitrary definitions, it is no longer a matter of any kind of relativism or arbitrariness whether representation-independent features of the world satisfy those definitions, because the features of the world that satisfy or fail to satisfy the definitions exist independently of those or any other definitions* . . . Contrary to Goodman, we do not make "worlds"; we make *descriptions* that the actual world may fit or fail to fit. But all this implies that there is a reality that exists independently of our system of concepts. Without such a reality, there is nothing to apply the concept to. (Searle 1995: 166; emphasis in the original)

Similar points, I may add, apply to questions about truth and knowledge. Neither people nor their language literally create truths.[12] They merely create *candidates* for truth value, which features of the world render true or false. A helpful metaphor here is racetrack betting. At the track you make an arbitrary choice of whether to bet at all, whether to bet on a particular race, and, if so, which horse to bet on. All of this is up to you. But once you make your choice, whether you win or lose is not up to you (unless you can fix the race). That is up to the horses and jockeys. The parallel is obvious. It is up to you which propositions to entertain or contemplate for possible belief or acceptance. It is equally up to you (though not usually a matter of deliberate voluntary control) whether to go ahead and believe such a proposition. Once you form a belief, though, its "success" or "failure" is not up to you; that is up to the world, which in general is independent of you.

I said above that language does not literally create truths, but this calls for minor qualification. The statement is right insofar as the correctness or incor-

---

[12] One possible exception to this are "analytic" or verbally stipulated truths such as "A bachelor is a man who has never been married." Other possible exceptions are discussed in the next paragraph.

rectness of linguistic descriptions depends on what holds or transpires in the portions of the world described. On the other hand, descriptive uses of language are themselves events *in* the world, which commonly have causal effects. Descriptions or assertions can have the effect of persuading hearers of their contents, which can lead to small-scale or large-scale world changes, such as career shifts or political revolutions. These might be described as cases in which linguistic acts indirectly bring about truths. Occasionally, linguistic acts make their own contents true, as when telling someone she will win her tennis match so bolsters her confidence that she does win. Even in such cases, however, the linguistic act does not directly confer truth on its content. It is still the portion of the world predicted that directly confers truth or falsity on the prediction's propositional content. It just so happens, in self-fulfilling prophecies, that the predictive act causally influences the truth-conferring portion of the world.

In a significant sense, then, only the world confers truth and falsity. There is, nonetheless, something correct in constructivist claims. The thought contents we consider and accept are rarely "given" to us by the (nonhuman) world. They result from our own biological resources and linguistic activities; in that sense, they are human constructs or products. Since knowledge involves belief, and belief is in contents that are so constructed, there is merit to the claim that knowledge is (partly) a social construct. But since knowledge is *true* belief, knowledge also involves truth; and what is true, as we have seen, is not a human construct as opposed to being of the world. Hence, it is wrong to say that knowledge is *merely* or *entirely* a human construct. Similar points pertain to postmodern claims that knowledge is always "local," "contextual," or "situated" rather than timeless or universal. Knowledge partly consists of belief, and belief is always local or situated because it is always the belief of a particular knower or group of knowers who live at particular points in time. But knowledge also partly consists of truth, and when a fully determinate proposition is true, it is true for all time, not just at particular times or places. The proposition that there is a cup on the kitchen table at such-and-such an address at noon, Greenwich Mean Time, October 18, 1997, is either timelessly true or timelessly false. Similarly, the proposition that African slaves were brought to the Americas between the sixteenth and nineteenth centuries is true for all time. Its truth value does not change as a function of the locale of a given believer. In this sense, truth is not something local or situated or socially constructed.

Another correct point stressed by certain constructivists is that people are often unaware of the fact that their concepts are socially constructed. They mistakenly suppose that these concepts track "natural" properties rather than socially constructed ones. Many feminist writers—for example, Sally Haslanger (1993, 1995)—argue that the concept of gender is constructed roughly as follows. The ideal of Woman is an externalization of men's desire; so-called Woman's Nature is what men find desirable. This ideal is projected onto individual females and regarded as intrinsic and essential to them. What Haslanger and other feminists claim is that the social construction of the concept of Woman's Nature is an occurrence that has not been generally understood or appreciated (prior to the advent of feminism). People have mistakenly supposed that the concept of Woman's Nature simply mirrors a natural kind. This feminist story of social construction is eminently plausible but does not conflict with anything I am suggesting. I would put the point this way. The crucial feminist propositions make assertions about how certain concepts or ideals historically emerged or were created. It is very credible that these propositions are true, but if so, they are made true by historical features of the world. Once again, it is worldly facts that confer truth, in this case worldly facts concerning the development of certain concepts and language.[13]

1.6 *The unknowability criticism*

If truth is something "of" the world rather than "of" the knower, if it is transcendent rather than immanent, can we know it? This is a further pervasive worry of veriphobes, a worry articulated in the third postmodern criticism given above:

(3) If there were any transcendent or objective truths, they would be inaccessible and unknowable by human beings, hence unavailable for any practical epistemological purposes.

Is this a serious ground for worry? That depends on what is meant by "transcendent" and what is meant by "knowable." We cannot settle this issue without considering possible definitions of these terms and their implications.

I propose to distinguish two possible meanings, or definitions, of "transcendence," one yielding a concept of radical transcendence and the second a concept of moderate transcendence.

Radical transcendence: A state of affairs is radically transcendent just in case it is utterly and in principle unknowable by human beings.

Moderate transcendence: A state of affairs is moderately transcendent just in case its obtaining is logically independent of anybody's believing that it obtains. It could obtain even if nobody believed it did, and somebody could believe it obtained without that belief (logically) guaranteeing that it did.

I do not hold—nor do many realists hold—that truth in general is radically transcendent. Simply because a state of affairs is objective or external to the

---

[13] Haslanger herself does not attempt to use the constructivist story to undermine the worldliness of truth. On the contrary, she tends to favor an objectivist conception of reality.

mind does not imply that it is utterly and in principle unknowable. Demonstration of this point, however, must await clarification of the "knowledge" concept (see below).

I do maintain, however, that most states of affairs are moderately transcendent. For instance, take a state of affairs consisting of there being a quart of milk in the refrigerator. This is a state of affairs that (logically) *could* obtain even if nobody believed that it did. Of course, this is not likely to happen. Usually quarts of milk arrive in a refrigerator only when somebody puts them there, and usually such people believe that they are there. But it is "logically" possible for such a state of affairs to obtain without anybody believing that it does. Perhaps the person who places it there, the chief user of the refrigerator, was misleadingly assured that it was a fake milk container, really holding eggnog or beer instead. Nor does he believe that anything else in the refrigerator is a quart of milk. Thus, there *could* be a quart of milk in the refrigerator without anybody believing it. Conversely, somebody could believe that such a state of affairs obtained without thereby guaranteeing that it did. The same refrigerator owner might believe that there is a quart of milk in the refrigerator because he put one there, straight from the supermarket, only an hour ago. He might be wrong, however, either because it *was* a fake, or because, unbeknownst to him, his teenage son drank it up. Ordinary states of affairs, then, typically qualify as moderately transcendent.

Does moderate transcendence imply unknowability? That depends on what is meant by "know." I shall distinguish two main senses of "knowledge": *strong* knowledge and *weak* knowledge (S-knowledge and W-knowledge). Most of the philosophical literature on knowledge is addressed to S-knowledge. It assumes that S-knowledge consists of true belief plus some additional element or elements, such as justification or warrant for the belief, and the exclusion of alternative possibilities. According to an extreme view, an agent cannot know a proposition P unless P is true and the agent believes it on the basis of evidence that excludes *all* rival possibilities to P. Let us call knowledge fulfilling this extreme condition "superstrong" knowledge (SS-knowledge). It is obvious that SS-knowledge is rarely attained. You might truly believe that there is a quart of milk in your refrigerator, but does your evidence exclude all rival possibilities? If you are not pouring from the container right now, but are seated in your study, how does your evidence exclude the possibility that your son removed the container from the refrigerator? Even if you are looking into the refrigerator at the moment, can you exclude the possibility that somebody has substituted an empty (opaque) milk container for the full container that was there ten minutes ago? Even if you seem to be actively pouring milk from a milk container right now, does your evidence exclude the possibility that you are suffering a massive hallucination, or being deceived by a Cartesian demon? In light of such scenarios, most philosophers agree that SS-knowledge is largely unattainable.

It does not follow, however, that regular old S-knowledge is unattainable.

Maybe S-knowledge does not require that *all* (logical) possibilities be excluded by the knower's evidence. Perhaps knowledge requires that only a narrower range of possibilities be excluded, possibilities that are "serious," "realistic," or genuinely likely to transpire.[14] On this kind of approach, the possibilities of a Cartesian demon or a massive hallucination do not have to be excluded, because they are not realistic or likely enough. Perhaps even the other scenarios, the theft and substitution scenarios, are not likely enough to be serious rivals. In that case, one could have S-knowledge of the state of affairs in question.

Volumes of philosophical literature have been devoted to theories of S-knowledge. Although the debate continues, it is widely accepted that S-knowledge is feasible for external, or moderately transcendent, states of affairs. In particular, there is nothing about the assumption of objectivity or externality of states of affairs that precludes the possibility of knowing them. Some new argument by postmodernists or veriphobes would be needed to show that moderately transcendent states of affairs are S-unknowable, but no such argument has been offered.

The present book, however, will have nothing to say about S-knowledge. It is devoted entirely to the prospects for W-knowledge, which is simply *true belief.* One reason I focus on W-knowledge is to circumvent the intricate issues that surround the notion of S-knowledge. Addressing those issues would demand a major digression from the main thrust of the book. A second and more important reason is that people's dominant epistemic goal, I think, is to obtain true belief, plain and simple. They want to be *informed* (have true belief) rather than *misinformed* or *uninformed.* The usual route to true belief, of course, is to obtain some kind of evidence that points to the true proposition and away from rivals. But the rationale for getting such evidence is to get true belief. Hence, the entire focus of this book is on W-knowledge.[15]

Is there an ordinary sense of "know" that corresponds to true belief, or have I invented it? I believe there is an ordinary sense. In one sense of "*X* knows that *P*," it is synonymous with "*X* is aware that *P*" (or "*X* is apprised of *P*"), a sense that ignores justification. Suppose it is given that *P* is true, and we wonder whether Jane is aware of it. The only question that needs to be resolved is whether she believes *P*. If she does, she is aware of it; if she doesn't, she is unaware of it. The issue of justification or evidence is irrelevant. "Know" can be used similarly. If we wonder whether Jane knows that *P*, again given its truth, the only issue to be settled is whether she believes it. She knows if she

---

[14] This is the theme of theories of knowledge that take either the subjunctive conditional, "relevant alternatives," or "tracking" approach. See Dretske 1969, 1981, Goldman 1976, 1986, and Nozick 1981: ch. 3.

[15] Although I focus in this work on the weak sense of "knowledge," I do not deny that "know" is often used to express the strong sense of knowledge. This is, apparently, denied by Crispin Sartwell (1992), who unqualifiedly equates knowledge with true belief.

does believe it, and is ignorant (does not know) if she does not believe it. The issue of justification, or its ilk, is again out of the picture. Here is another example. The sentence "You don't want to know what happened while you were gone" seems to mean: You don't want to have the truth about what happened in your belief corpus. It does not seem to require the translation: You don't want to have a *justified* belief in the truth about what happened. So I believe there is an ordinary sense of "know" in which it means "truly believe." If I am wrong about this, however, I am prepared to proceed cheerfully with weak "knowledge" as a term of art (or technical term).

Having clarified what sense of "knowledge" concerns me here, let us return to the issue of (moderate) transcendence. Is moderate transcendence a threat to W-knowledge? Not at all. The mere fact that a state of affairs *could* obtain without being believed to obtain, or *could* be believed to obtain without obtaining, does not put it beyond the pale of knowability, especially in the weak sense of "knowledge." What is required for W-knowledge, after all, is that a person *actually believes* that a certain state of affairs obtains and it *does* obtain (it is true that it obtains). This is a fairly easy standard to meet, and the mere objectivity or externality of a state of affairs does not pose an insuperable hurdle. The fact that it is possible to be mistaken, as moderate transcendence implies, does not stand in the way of its *also* being possible to get it right (believe truly). Of course, there are some states of affairs to which it is difficult for most people to gain epistemic "access." This includes many of the states of affairs which science tries to investigate. As a general matter, however, externality *per se* is not an insurmountable barrier to W-knowledge.

Looked at one way, in fact, it is comparatively easy to attain W-knowledge; at least, for *somebody* to attain W-knowledge. Consider two people, Seth and Beth, reflecting on the question of whether there is life outside our solar system. Seth forms the belief that life outside our solar system does exist, whereas Beth forms the belief that no such life exists. *One* of them must have W-knowledge on this topic.[16] This is not intended as a proof that W-knowledge is always a snap. Nonetheless, the sweeping claim of criticism (3), that transcendent truths are unknowable for human beings, hardly applies to W-knowledge and moderately transcendent truths. W-knowledge is a goal within

---

[16] But, you may ask, does either Seth or Beth *know* that he or she knows? Perhaps not, but failing to know that you know does not preclude knowing. First-order knowledge does not require second-order knowledge. Anyone tempted to insist on the principle that knowledge of level N demands knowledge of level $N + 1$ should notice that such a principle leads to an infinite regress, because second-order knowledge would require third-order knowledge, and so on. It is unlikely that anybody has such an infinite corpus of knowledge. Notice that I say that first-order knowledge does not *require* second-order knowledge. This does not mean that second-order knowledge is impossible, or even particularly difficult. In fact, second-order *weak* knowledge is not much harder to attain than first-order *weak* knowledge; you just have to believe that you truly believe that P when you do truly believe it. I don't think that such a higher-order belief is automatic, but neither is it particularly difficult for anyone with the concept of belief.

human reach, which makes it a suitable topic for the discipline of social epistemology.

Some postmodern writers sound their loudest alarms for a special class of putative truths, namely, "grand narratives," metanarratives, or master narratives, which offer large-scale generalizations about history, culture, and social life (Lyotard 1984). Nothing I have said about the feasibility of W-knowledge is intended to guarantee the knowability of propositions or theories of such grand design.[17] It is misleading, however, to suggest that the failure of "grand narratives" spells doom for all types of knowledge quests. Each category must be considered on its own merits. We must also bear in mind the possibility that some categories of thought or discourse do not admit of genuine truth or falsity at all. Especially in such areas as normative ethics and aesthetics, it is notoriously controversial whether statements in those areas can be bearers of truth values. I shall remain largely neutral on this issue, that is, neutral about the precise scope of truth-valuable domains. It suffices for purposes of this book that many domains of human thought *do* admit of truth or falsity. If there are exceptions to this rule, that does not stop epistemology dead in its tracks.

1.7 *The denial of epistemic privilege*

Rorty's *Philosophy and the Mirror of Nature* (1979) is a widely cited attack on epistemology of the sort undertaken here. A centerpiece of that book is chapter 4, "Privileged Representations," which attacks the notion that some propositions, beliefs, or epistemic positions are more privileged than others. Invidious distinctions between beliefs or epistemic positions have indeed typified traditional epistemology, which has usually held that some beliefs are justified or warranted whereas others are unjustified or unwarranted. Rorty means to deconstruct this entire "problematic" by attacking the very notion of a privileged representation. This and related themes lead me to the fourth criticism of veritistic epistemology:

(4) There are no privileged epistemic positions, and no certain foundations for beliefs. All claims are judged by conventions or language games,

---

[17] This is not to say that I deny the W-knowability of all metanarratives. Veritistic epistemology might itself be a metanarrative, the feasibility of which I endorse. Of course, veritistic epistemology as a general project is not committed to any particular claim about which practices maximize knowledge. But it does suggest that some practices are veritistically better than others and it encourages the attempt to identify the better ones. I see no a priori reason to deny the possibility of knowing which practices are veritistically better than others. Furthermore, if the claim that certain practices are veritistically better than others is metanarrative, why isn't the denial of this sort of claim equally metanarrative? Yet postmodernists themselves are committed to such a denial. So the rejection of all metanarrative is not a sustainable position.

which have no deeper grounding. There are no neutral, transcultural standards for settling disagreements.

Rorty's critique of epistemic warrant or privilege, however, is strikingly abortive. He simply ignores most theories now under serious consideration. He pays almost exclusive attention to a single historical theory that once enjoyed popularity but was long since exploded, as everybody in the field knows. All the currently respected theories, on the other hand, are treated as if they did not exist.

What Rorty attacks is the classical doctrine of infallibilist foundationalism, which is a doctrine about epistemic *justification* or *warrant* for a belief.[18] Originally developed by Descartes, this doctrine held that all warranted belief rests on infallible foundations, a special class of beliefs that are absolutely certain and cannot be mistaken. Possible examples of such foundational beliefs are "I now experience a reddish appearance" and "All squares have four sides." The first illustrates the category of beliefs about the empirically "given," and the second illustrates the category of "analytic" truths. For a variety of reasons, including a critique of the given by Wilfrid Sellars (1963) and of analyticity by Willard van Orman Quine (1953), most epistemologists have given up infallibilist foundationalism. Rorty is right that this is a dubious doctrine, but for epistemologists this is old news (and it was old in 1979).

Meanwhile, epistemologists have not been standing around shedding tears for infallibilist foundationalism. They have developed a variety of theories of warrant or justification, and although no recent theory has emerged as a clear winner, there are many strong candidates. Rorty simply ignores this entire field, somehow assuming that the refutation of infallibilist foundationalism is the only needed *coup de grâce*.

This is not the place for detailed exposition of alternative theories of justification, but a brief mention of three leading candidates should convey a rough feel for the territory. First, there is fallibilist foundationalism. This view agrees with traditional foundationalism in claiming that some beliefs (the foundational ones) obtain initial warrant on their own, not from other beliefs. This independent infusion of warrant, however, can be overridden. According to fallible foundationalism, foundational beliefs are neither infallible nor certain. A second candidate theory is coherentism, which denies that there are any special foundational beliefs with independent justification. Instead, according to coherentism, all justified beliefs obtain their justification by virtue of cohering, or meshing, with the rest of the agent's belief system.

---

[18] There is another doctrine of "foundationalism" that Rorty and others attack, namely, the doctrine that philosophy can be a "founding" discourse for all other disciplines. This sense of foundationalism, unfortunately, is not systematically distinguished from foundationalism as a theory of justified belief. I shall not discuss this sense of "foundationalism" because I am not committed to it. The doctrine, as I understand it, postulates a kind of autonomy for philosophy that I do not accept.

Rorty's neglect of coherentism is particularly mysterious because he endorses Quine's "holism" which is simply a version of coherentism. He somehow classifies holism as an anti-epistemology doctrine, rather than a theory of justification.[19] A third theory of justification is reliabilism, which was only taking shape when Rorty was writing *Philosophy and the Mirror of Nature*. In its simplest form, reliabilism says that a belief is justified in case it is produced by reliable psychological processes, where "reliable" means "produces mostly truths." Like fallible foundationalism and coherentism, reliabilism requires neither infallibility nor certainty. Since Rorty registers no objections to these kinds of theories, a blanket refutation of "privileged representations" has hardly been achieved. It is like damning an entire political party by exposing the doctrine of its single most radical sect.

The postmodern rejection of epistemic privilege is not wholly rooted in displeasure with Cartesian epistemology. Much of it has a political cast. The language of "privilege" is the language of rank and honor, especially *unearned* rank and honor, which has a nasty anti-egalitarian odor. But we are not here talking about political status, rights, or liberties. The theory of justification is concerned with the circumstances in which a person has sufficient evidence or epistemic access to a state of affairs to be entitled to hold a certain belief about it. Manifestly, epistemic access to a given state of affairs is not the same for all people and all times. It can vary from time to time and from person to person, as a function of perceptual, memorial, and inferential circumstances. For example, consider the layout of buildings at a certain university, say the University of Heidelberg. Petra might now be justified in believing that such-and-such is the building layout at the University because she personally studied there, observed this layout on many occasions, and remembers it well. But Petra did not always have this evidence for the layout. Before she ever visited Heidelberg or heard it described, she had no basis for believing anything about the specific arrangement of buildings. Similarly, if Stefan never visited Heidelberg, nor heard specifics of the building layout described, he would also lack epistemic grounds for believing anything about the layout. This difference in epistemic state between Petra and Stefan, however, has no implications whatsoever of a moral or political nature. It is pointless to deny the palpable difference in epistemic condition out of a misguided desire to avoid all invidious distinctions between people.

Certain rather different strands of contemporary antijustificationism can be traced to Ludwig Wittgenstein. Wittgenstein's influence filters through the idea that justification is merely a matter of convention, which has no rational grounding. Intellectual authorization is a matter of language games, and the choice of language games is simply a matter of local custom. Here is a passage from Wittgenstein that suggests this idea:

---

[19] "A holistic approach to knowledge is not a matter of antifoundationalist polemic, but a distrust of the whole epistemological enterprise" (Rorty 1979: 181).

You must bear in mind that the language-game is so to say something unpredictable. I mean: it is not based on grounds. It is not reasonable (or unreasonable). It is there—like our life. (1969: para. 559)

This theme is adopted by many Wittgenstein interpreters, who dispute any attempt to base rules on anything, especially considerations of truth. For example, Gordon Baker and Peter Hacker write:

Philosophy is purely descriptive. It clarifies the grammar of our language, the rules for the construction of significant utterances whose violation yields nonsense. Explanation would be possible only if it made sense to get behind these rules and supply a deeper foundation. But there is no behind, and rules are not answerable to reality in the currency of truth. Any deeper explanation would simply be another rule of grammar standing in the same relation to the use of expressions as the rules it allegedly explains. Therefore philosophy must be flat. This insight shapes the whole of Wittgenstein's philosophy. (1985: 22)

This sort of theme runs through the second sentence of our criticism (4), which reads: "All claims are judged by conventions or language games, which have no deeper grounding."

This thesis about justification is pretty dubious. Careful reflection on judgments of justification suggests—as reliabilism maintains—that a belief is considered justified if it is arrived at by processes or practices that the speaker (or the community) regards as truth conducive. Beliefs formed by perception and retained by memory, for example, are viewed as justified because perception and memory are considered reliable, whereas beliefs formed by wishful thinking or hasty generalization are viewed as unjustified because wishful thinking and hasty generalization are thought to be unreliable (Goldman 1992: chs. 6, 7, 9). Thus, judgments of justification are not without grounding, nor are they purely conventional. They are grounded precisely on appeals to truth conduciveness. Furthermore, there seems to be nothing *arbitrary* in a concept of justification tied to truth conduciveness. Given people's interest in truth, it is relevant to classify beliefs in terms of whether they were formed by truth-conducive processes or non-truth-conducive processes. After all, those formed by truth-conducive processes are more likely to be true, and those formed by non-truth-conducive processes are less likely to be true.

Many contemporary writers tend to confuse justification with interpersonal agreement. Where there is no agreement, and no basis for settling disagreement, justification or rationality are thought to be impossible. Without neutral, transcultural principles for settling disagreements, prospects for an "objectivist" epistemology founder. But this view elevates agreement to an exaggerated epistemic position. An ability to elicit agreement is neither a necessary nor a sufficient condition of justification.

To demonstrate the nonnecessity of agreement, consider Heather and her headache. Heather currently has a headache, and is amply justified in believing that she has one. But Heather recently exhibited a deceptive streak in her conduct. She persistently lied about her health, and her friends and acquaintances now distrust her reports on this subject. Thus, Heather cannot get anyone else in her community to accept the proposition that she has a headache. Nonetheless, *she* is justified in believing that she has one.

To demonstrate the nonsufficiency of agreement for justification, consider charismatic Karen, who is gifted and personable enough to persuade anyone of anything she says. It does not follow that Karen is justified in all her beliefs. She might have a very foolish and unjustified belief yet be capable of getting people to agree with it by sheer force of personality.

Postmodernists not only think that agreement is necessary for justification, or at least rationality; they also think that the prospects for agreement are dim, because there are no transcultural principles for settling disagreements among different communities. Inspiration for this idea is often ascribed to Thomas Kuhn (1962), who says things like the following:

> As in political revolutions, so in paradigm choice—there is no standard higher than the assent of the relevant community. To discover how scientific revolutions are effected, we shall therefore have to examine not only the impact of nature and logic, but also the techniques of persuasive argumentation within the quite special groups that constitute the community of scientists. (1962: 94)

But wholesale denial of common criteria for theory choice is apparently not what Kuhn intended, despite this interpretation by numerous epigones. Elsewhere (Kuhn 1977) he has insisted that there are common criteria in science, even transparadigm criteria. There he presents five characteristics— accuracy, consistency, scope, simplicity, and fruitfulness—which provide the "shared basis for theory choice" (1977: 322). So Kuhn is far from denying transparadigm criteria for scientific judgment. Other writers, however, such as Barry Barnes and David Bloor, unequivocally maintain that "there are no context-free or super-cultural norms of rationality" (1982: 27).

Before examining this position, let us distinguish (1) the ultimate aim of epistemic practices from (2) the specific methods adopted in pursuit of that aim. I wholeheartedly grant that different methods are adopted by different communities; that is beyond dispute. It is far less clear that the bases for adopting such practices are so disunified, at least insofar as they have a genuinely epistemic or intellectual aim. The unifying aim, I suggest, is the pursuit of true belief. Both Galileo and the Church aimed at true belief, or knowledge, only the latter insisted on consulting scripture (or ecclesiastical authorities) to determine truth, while the former advocated experiment and observation. It will be replied that it is incredibly naive to suppose that all epistemic agents actually aim at truth or knowledge. Isn't it all too common to masquerade or parade oneself as committed to truth, though one's real aims are entirely different? Granting this point, we must probe more deeply. Why do epistemic agents parade their favored methods or practices under the banner of truth? The obvious explanation is that others will deny epistemic authority to a method unless they are persuaded, rightly or wrongly, that it meets the standard of truth conduciveness. In other words, truth conduciveness is the presumptive ground for epistemic authorization. That is why agents peddle their epistemic practices as instruments of truth even when their hidden agenda may be different. That is why Lenin named his propagandizing newspaper *Pravda* (truth).

Epistemic practices differ so dramatically throughout history and across cultures that it is often hard to credit the notion that these practices were commonly motivated, or at least rationalized, by truth considerations. Nonetheless, I believe that such motivations and rationalizations were in fact quite extensive. This is not to deny the pursuit of power across human culture and history, but that should not blind us to a coexisting interest in truth, however poorly it may have been pursued by our present lights. Let me trace a few examples of this theme in unlikely or little-discussed quarters.

A first example is the practice of torture in medieval European legal procedure. To enlightened modern eyes, torture is such a ridiculous method of truth determination that it is hard to imagine it might seriously have been so conceived. However, a brief review of its history, based on a treatment by John Langbein (1980), suggests precisely this. In 1215 the Roman Church effectively destroyed the older modes of legal proof such as trial by battle or by ordeal. The new law of proof, however, aspired to achieve the same level of certainty as had been accorded to the earlier methods. The Italian Glossators who designed the system entrenched the rule that conviction for serious crimes had to be based upon the testimony of two unimpeachable eyewitnesses. Alternatively, an accused could be convicted if he voluntarily confessed to the offense. The trouble with the early thirteenth-century proof system, however, was that the standard of proof was so high that it was difficult to obtain convictions of the guilty. That is one way to "miss" the truth. Bound by the weight of tradition, how could the standard be adjusted? The confession rule invited a subterfuge. When there was already strong evidence against a suspect, although less than two eyewitnesses, torture was authorized in order to obtain a confession. Torture was permitted when a so-called "half proof" was established against the suspect, meaning either one eyewitness or circumstantial evidence of substantial gravity. If a suspect was caught with a bloody dagger and stolen loot from a murdered man's house, each of those "indicia" would be a quarter proof, which together constituted half proof, and this was sufficient for torture. Confession under torture was not grounds for conviction since it was considered involuntary. The suspect was convicted only if he ("voluntarily") repeated the confession at a hearing held a day or so later. In this fashion the prohibition against circumstantial evidence was overcome, and the authorities found a way which, by their lights, did a better job at obtaining accurate judgments. Bizarre as we now find it, the method of torture seems to have been motivated by a concern for truth, constrained by the requirement that new procedures comply with tradition.

Let me turn from this historical case to contemporary crosscultural considerations. Postmodernists often imply that truth and reason are the special obsessions of white Europeans, or perhaps white European males, implying that other cultures do not partake of this value. Some evidence belying this claim comes from linguistics. A widespread concern for matters of evidence and reliability (truth conduciveness) seems to be present in all languages. Moreover, in a certain range of languages drawn from quite different families, *grammar* requires that the warrant for a claim be indicated by citing a channel of evidence, such as perceptual evidence, testimonial evidence, or inferential evidence (Chafe and Nichols 1986, Willett 1988).

Next I wish to marshal evidence from a valuable survey of epistemological anthropology by James Maffie (1995). Focusing on African sources, Maffie establishes that truth is a central concern of many cultures including prescientific ones. The research of Onyewuenyi (1991), Oruka (1990), and Tempels (1969) shows that various African ethnophilosophies conceive of knowledge in terms of truth. Other studies suggest that the desire for truth occupies a central role in workaday cognitive practices such as magic, divination, and religion. Maffie quotes Turner as saying:

[A]ll societies develop a need both for revelation and divination and construct appropriate cultural instruments for satisfying these needs . . . Man cannot tolerate darkness; he must have light, whether it be the sunlight of revelation or the flaring torch of divination. (Turner 1975: 29)

Horton (1982) claims that African and non-African cultures use magic, religion, and divination to discover the underlying system of natural and supernatural forces with the hope of successfully predicting and intervening in this system. Central to their endeavors is the belief that practical success turns upon truthful apprehension.

Frazer (1959) distinguishes theoretical from practical aspects of magic, where the theoretical aspect strives for understanding of the laws of contact and similarity governing the world. Magicians believe that one must first correctly apprehend these laws before successfully manipulating them with spells, incantations, and rites. Mistaken notions yield misguided practice. Religious practices are likewise truth oriented, according to Frazer. Truth is necessary for practical success, since false notions incur divine wrath.

Divination seeks information about things past, future, or otherwise hidden from ordinary perception. Peek argues that African diviners "exhibit an intense need to know the true reasons for events" (1991: 194). The Temne regard divination as a matter of "splitting truths from darkness" (Shaw 1991). Turner writes that modes of divination are regarded as both lie-detecting and truth-discovering instruments, which people use in order to undertake remedial measures or to restore individual or collective peace of mind (1975: 209).

Finally, we should not fail to observe that in contemporary South Africa a Truth and Reconciliation Commission has been established by the post-apartheid government to bring out the truth about atrocities committed by all sides in the struggle over white rule. This too illustrates the interest of Africans—including indigenous Africans—in learning truths.

There is ample evidence, then, that truth is a vital concern of humankind across history and culture, not an idiosyncratic concern of modern white Europeans. Despite the heterogeneity of truth-pursuing practices and the diversity of questions to which true answers are sought, a single concept of truth seems to be crossculturally present. It is eminently reasonable, then, for a discipline to be devoted to the systematic and critical evaluation of truth-oriented practices.

1.8 *The argument from domination*

It is time to turn to the fifth criticism of veritistic social epistemology, which was:

(5) Appeals to truth are merely instruments of domination or repression, and should be replaced by practices with progressive social value.

This kind of critique (at least its first clause) is most intimately associated with Michel Foucault, but it is echoed by many movements, including postmodern feminism. Focusing on the human sciences, Foucault (1979) contended that the sciences of man arose from practices of social domination, including "carceral" practices involving prisons and punishment and sexual confessional practices involved in psychotherapy and medical procedures. The interest in knowledge was driven by concerns for management and power:

I am not saying that the human sciences emerged from the prison. But, if they have been able to be formed and to produce so many profound changes in the episteme, it is because they have been conveyed by a specific and new modality of power . . . [which] required definite relations of knowledge in relations of power . . . Knowable man (soul, individuality, consciousness, conduct, whatever it is called) is the object-effect of this analytic investment, of this domination-observation. (1979: 305)

The criminal, for example, was conceptualized as a type that needed to be understood by the newly emergent sciences of psychiatry and criminology. Knowledge was essential to rehabilitate the criminal, so that what had been primarily a legal and political matter became invested with new dimensions of scientific knowledge, which served the end of "bio-power." As Hubert Dreyfus and Paul Rabinow summarize the idea:

Political technologies advance by taking what is essentially a political problem, removing it from a realm of political discourse, and recasting it in the neutral language of science. Once this is accomplished the problems have become technical ones for specialists to debate. In fact, the language of reform is, from the outset, an essential component of these political technologies. Bio-power spread under the banner of making people healthy and protecting them. When there was resistance, or failure to achieve its stated aims, this was construed as further proof of the need to reinforce and extend the power of the experts. A technical matrix was established. By definition, there ought to be a way of solving any technical problem . . . We are promised normalization and happiness through science and law. When they fail, this only justifies the need for more of the same. (1983: 196)

Foucault and his followers are not the only ones to highlight scientific abuses in the interest of political or social power. Postmodern feminists argue that the ideal of rationality—and with it, presumably, the goal of truth—is really a masculine ideal, advanced as a vehicle for marginalizing, dominating, and silencing women, who by nature, it was alleged, do not partake of rationality. The ideals of rationality and objectivity have only been used to sustain the inequality of power between males and females (Fraser and Nicholson 1990, Flax 1990*b*).

There are three lines of reply to this critique. First, the fact that appeals to truth are used as instruments of power or domination does not imply that truth is either nonexistent or deserving of neglect. Most of these appeals, in the domains just surveyed, were false, inaccurate, and even fraudulent. The way to combat such appeals is to *correct* the errors and inaccuracies. Stephen Jay Gould (1981) has traced the pockmarks of bias that have contaminated the history of intelligence measurement. Starting with the nineteenth-century "science" of craniometry, continuing through the twentieth-century measurements of IQ, including the flawed and finally fraudulent work of Cyril Burt, and persisting today with the dubious analyses of Herrnstein and Murray (1994), this area has been badly contaminated with personal and cultural prejudice.[20] But Gould rightly presumes the meaningfulness of such concepts as error, inaccuracy, and distortion, all of which presuppose a concept of objective truth. He also plausibly assumes that errors can be corrected.

Similarly, many feminist theorists reject the veriphobic and anti-objectivist aspects of postmodern feminism. Two important alternatives to postmodern feminism are feminist empiricism and feminist standpoint theories.[21] Feminist empiricists maintain that sexism and androcentrism are identifiable biases of knowers that can be eliminated by stricter application of scientific and philosophical methodologies. Feminist standpoint theorists reject the notion of an "unmediated" truth (which they associate with empiricism), and emphasize the role of social position in shaping understanding. However, they argue that the social position of the oppressed can pierce ideological obfuscation and facilitate a correct understanding of the world.[22]

[20] For a critique of Herrnstein and Murray, see Block 1995.
[21] For a discussion of these variants of feminism, see Hawkesworth 1989. A more complex classification of varieties of feminism is provided in Tong 1989. I am indebted to Melissa Berry for helpful advice about the feminist literature.
[22] Three examples of feminist standpoint theory are Harding 1991, Hartsock 1983,

Indeed, if one examines debunkings of truth on the grounds that truth claims merely cloak a drive for domination, almost all of these debunkings themselves depend on truth claims! Unless there is truth in Foucault's story that the human sciences arose, at least in part, out of motives to control, administer, and dominate, why should we pay it any attention? Presumably Foucault did not mean to write historical fiction, or why did he expend effort documenting his allegations? And if it was fiction, why should we agree with him that knowledge and power are inextricably intertwined? We need true evidence to persuade us of a tight connection between knowledge and power, and Foucault provides evidence. Apparently, he does so because he contends that there is truth in his claim. Admittedly, Foucault tries to avoid this consequence by denying that he is propounding a "theory." He says that he offers an "interpretation" of events, not a "theory." In Foucault 1979 he holds out no promise of a better, more "objective" social science. His method has been called "interpretive analytics" (Dreyfus and Rabinow 1983: 183), perhaps to distance it from truth-oriented science. But if his analysis contains no true propositions, why should we find it instructive or appealing? If it is false—or even truth-valueless—that truth appeals are tools of oppression, criticism (5) carries no weight or significance.

The need to base political progressiveness on truth is equally pressing in other domains. Historical truths about racism underpin claims to compensatory justice. Allegations of rape, domestic violence, and sexual harassment must not be mere fictions if they are to be cited in support of political action. This is clearly explained by Mary Hawkesworth:

> The victim's account of these experiences is not simply an arbitrary imposition of a purely fictive meaning on an otherwise meaningless reality. . . . [I]t would be premature to conclude from the incompleteness of the victim's account that all other accounts (the assailant's, defense attorney's, character witnesses' for the defendant) are equally valid or that there are no objective grounds on which to distinguish between truth and falsity in divergent interpretations. (1989: 555)

Similarly, I would argue that Catharine MacKinnon's (1989) critique of traditional rape law would be best articulated in terms of the *falsity* of men's beliefs about women's practices of consent to intercourse. MacKinnon argues that traditional rape law reflects a male perspective, but that men do not

and Jagger 1983. The formulation given at this point in the text is that of Hawkesworth. Here is how Harding articulates her conception of standpoint epistemologies: "The standpoint epistemologies . . . call for the acknowledgement that all human beliefs—including our best scientific beliefs—are socially situated, but they also require a critical evaluation to determine which social situations tend to generate the most objective knowledge claims. They require . . . a scientific account of the relationships between historically located belief and maximally objective belief. So they demand what I shall call *strong objectivity* in contrast to the weak objectivity of objectivism and its mirror-linked twin, judgmental relativism" (1991: 142). Though Harding is cautious about truth, standpoint epistemology under her formulation has nonnegligible points of similarity to veritistic social epistemology.

understand women. "Men . . . define rape as they imagine women to be sexually violated through distinguishing that from their image of what they normally do . . . But men are systematically conditioned not even to notice what women want" (MacKinnon 1989: 181). The best way to formulate MacKinnon's critique (though not MacKinnon's own explicit formulation) is to say that traditional laws or legal procedures concerning rape have rested on falsehoods men believe. This formulation presupposes a distinction between truth and falsity.

Other central theoretical arguments in feminism rely essentially on causal or historical truth claims. For example, as we saw in Section 1.5, feminist theories frequently assert that traditional norms for women (norms for being emotional, nurturing, and cooperative, for example) did not arise from veridical observations of natural, intrinsic features of human females that distinguish them from males. Rather, these norms arose from gendering: from the social creation or construction of certain roles. The classification of features as masculine or feminine is derivative from, and depends upon, the entrenchment of prior social—rather than natural—practices. Clearly, these causal claims are either true or false. If they are false, many feminist theories deserve far less credence than their proponents maintain. If they are true, these same theories become much more important. Thus, the strength of the theories depends essentially on the truth values of the causal claims. Theoretical feminists cannot afford to abandon truth.

Moving to my second line of reply, consider how implausible it is to advance the domination thesis in connection with *all* truth claims. Can one seriously maintain that every factual statement in everyday life cloaks a desire for domination, even such statements as "There's a coyote behind that bush," or "Your friend Molly called this afternoon"? Even Foucault does not venture this far. He restricts his theses to those "dubious" disciplines which have come to be called the human sciences, and exempts the "nondubious" sciences (physics, biology, and so forth) from his strictures (see Dreyfus and Rabinow 1983: xxiv, 206). Actually, even the generalization about the social sciences is too broad. If domination is equated with centralized control of individuals, economics does not belong on the list. The chief policy message of much of economics since Adam Smith has been the virtue of decentralized, free market association rather than organized state control. In any case, only a segment of truth discourse is alleged to be an instrument of domination, so it makes little sense to issue a general prohibition against truth claims. And if there is no general prohibition against truth claims, there is surely a place for truth-oriented epistemology, which concerns itself with the promotion of true claims (and beliefs) as contradistinguished from the false.

This second reply eases us into the third. Even if the truth concept has sometimes been used as a weapon of coercion or domination, should it be banned from use altogether? Truth claims, like knives, can sometimes be used for lethal purposes, as when one culture claims cognitive superiority over another and uses this claim to justify political or economic domination. But knives are not always or normally used for lethal purposes, and truth claims are similarly not normally so employed (Schmitt 1995: 231–2). Furthermore, even when one society does seek to intervene in another on grounds of cognitive superiority, the principal complaint should be against the intervention *per se*, not against the cognitive claim (although the latter might also be misguided). The issue becomes stickier when truth claims are claims to *moral* truth, and I shall not try to adjudicate this issue. Whether morality is a domain of "correspondence" truth, or truth at all, I leave unaddressed. But if the claim is one of superior scientific knowledge, for example, such a claim might be warranted in itself, but could not justify any form of oppression, domination, or imperialism. If it were said that American students know less mathematics than students of many other countries, this might have to be conceded, because this is what recent test scores show. But this would hardly justify military intervention on the part of other countries.

1.9 *The argument from bias*

The final criticism of veritistic epistemology was as follows:

(6) Truth cannot be attained because all putatively truth-oriented practices are corrupted and biased by politics or self-serving interests.

The argument seems to rest on two assumptions: that all belief is driven by motivational biases, and that there is always a conflict between these biases and the pursuit of truth. Both assumptions are highly questionable.

As a preliminary matter, we must distinguish belief from behavior, including speech behavior. When (6) talks of the unattainability of truth, it presumably refers to belief rather than behavior. It says that truth cannot be attained—that is, believed—because people's beliefs are swayed by their own politics and interests. This assumes that belief is controlled by one's motives, a claim that is open to challenge. Philosophers have long pointed out that belief is not *voluntary* in the way that behavior is voluntary. You can decide to lie about something if it suits your interest, but you cannot so easily decide to believe or disbelieve something. If the *New York Times* reports the defeat of your favorite political candidate the morning after the election, you cannot simply choose to disbelieve the story. I am not saying that personal motives never influence belief, only that their impact is indirect and not always determinative. (For further discussion see Section 8.3.)

The second assumption of criticism (6) is that personal motives invariably run counter to getting the truth. This premise is also wildly implausible. Although *speaking* the truth may sometimes cut against one's interest, it is less common for *knowing* the truth to do so. As argued in Section 1.1, people frequently have an interest in knowing the truth. If I suffer an accident and need an emergency room, it serves my interest to know the location of the nearest emergency room. It is possible, of course, that the pervasive corruption of truth contemplated by (6) is chiefly a matter of interest-distorted speech. But even if speakers' assertions were systematically distorted by interests, hearers need not always be duped. Dupery would only follow if hearers were universally gullible. The allure of generalizations like (6) arises from preoccupation with political domains, where the best case can be made for conflict between interest and truth (at least truth *speaking*). But epistemology is concerned with all domains, and facile generalizations based on a restricted sector of domains cannot be accepted. Of course, many workers in the sociology of science think that (6) applies even in science. This view will be scrutinized in Section 8.10, where I shall argue that there is no necessary conflict between private interests of scientists and the search for truth. A few remarks should be added here, however, about the inconclusiveness of most treatments of this topic.

Many writers appeal to Kuhn and Quine as having clinched the case for a sociopolitical analysis of science. Sandra Harding, for example, writes that "in effect, [Kuhn] showed that all of natural science was located inside social history . . . [A]ny theory can always be retained as long as its defenders hold enough institutional power to explain away potential threats to it" (1992: 582). Similarly, Quine's thesis of the underdetermination of theory is often cited as license for a noncognitive, sociopolitical analysis of science. However, in addition to doubts about the underdetermination thesis itself (see Section 8.5), it is quite unclear that logical gaps between theory and evidence must be filled by motives and interests (see Laudan 1990, Slezak 1991). Although Kuhn pressed the case for the incommensurability of paradigms, he himself seemed to lean toward cognitive explanations of paradigm choice; for instance, the prior entrenchment of a paradigm among older practitioners.

Many case studies within the field of science studies aim to show that politics and/or interests played a crucial role in the development and acceptance of scientific ideas. Such case studies cannot support (6), however, without establishing that politics or interests were causally efficacious for scientific beliefs, not merely temporally coincident with them. But causal efficacy requires the counterfactual thesis that the beliefs would not have occurred had the politics or interests of the situation been different.[23] Case studies, being mere chronologies, can seldom establish such a counterfactual.[24]

Furthermore, although case studies sometimes make a plausible case for the role of politics and interests in the initial development of certain ideas, it is

---

[23] This claim about causal efficacy oversimplifies a bit, but the nuances are not germane to the present discussion.

[24] Cassandra Pinnick (1994) makes the general point that the Strong Programme in the sociology of science cannot establish the causal efficacy of sociopolitical allegiances through historical case studies. Paul Roth and Robert Barrett (1990) show how a specific well-known work in the sociology of science, Pickering (1984), fails to establish the causal efficacy of its favored social factors.

rarely shown that the acceptance of these ideas—especially over a long period of time—stemmed from similar motivations. This leaves the evidence for the interests theory much weaker than it may appear. Consider Donald Mackenzie's study of the history of statistics (1981).[25] In turn-of-the-century Britain, Mackenzie relates, there was a social program of eugenics, intended to improve the genetic composition of the human race. Measures were proposed to promote the fertility of "better types" (the "fit") and diminish the birth rate among the "inferior" (the "unfit"). Tax incentives and family allowances were proposed to encourage a high birth rate among the professional class. Eugenics identified "civic worth" with "mental ability," thought to be an inherited characteristic of each person. Only those who possessed a high degree of this natural characteristic could survive the demands of a professional training, and thus the professional class could be seen as naturally superior. Francis Galton, who lived his life among Britain's intellectual elite, explicitly wrote in terms of replacing religious authority with a "scientific priesthood." Mackenzie shows how Galton developed a set of concepts in mathematical statistics to deal with the variability of human characteristics in order to support eugenics.[26] A similar thesis is developed by Mackenzie in tracing Karl Pearson's contributions to statistics.

One question I would raise here concerns the contrast between Galton and Pearson's initial proposals and the continued acceptance of these statistical ideas (about regression and correlation in bivariate normal distributions) over a long period of time. Suppose Mackenzie is right that interests drove Galton and Pearson to think up and deploy their statistical techniques. Galton and Pearson, however, are no longer with us, and, as Alan Chalmers (1990) points out, their techniques have a far wider range of application than human heritability. It seems extremely unlikely that the continued acceptance of these techniques, applied by many practitioners to a vast array of problems, can be explained in terms of the same sorts of politics or interests that motivated Galton and Pearson. Certainly Mackenzie has not established this. Since we are interested not simply in the creation of a scientific method but in a community's long-term commitment to it, the history of Galton and Pearson does not go far in settling the matter. Thus, even in this promising case for the interests theory, the evidence falls far short of supporting thesis (6).

It should also be mentioned that Mackenzie presents this example in support of a 'strong' version of sociology of science which holds that social influences can affect the content of even *good* science, not just *bad* science. In this case, the pieces of mathematical statistics that emerged were significant contributions, genuine advances in knowledge. This serves to undercut criticism

[25] For a useful summary of Mackenzie's work, see Chalmers 1990.
[26] Interestingly, Mackenzie disavows the claim that Galton's motive was a desire to advance professional interests. This, he claims, "is dubious" (1981: 51). But Galton's eugenic thought, says Mackenzie, was a celebration of the work of the professional elite.

(6) rather than support it. It shows that politics and interests do not inevitably hinder truth attainment, but can sometimes promote it.

This is an atypical feature of Mackenzie's case studies, however. Proponents of the interests approach to science studies commonly seek to show how interests corrupt or threaten the quality of science, as criticism (6) maintains. The trouble is that their selection of cases is frequently biased. They do not publish randomly selected scientific episodes, but mainly ones that are grist for their mill. Good scientific methodology does not sanction an inference to a generalization like (6) on the basis of a deliberately skewed set of cases. (Admittedly, their own bias in the selection of cases may be a confirming instance of the very pattern asserted in thesis (6). But although their own bias is one instance of the pattern, it is hardly sufficient evidence of its universality.)

The argument from historical case studies also poses a problem of reflexivity. If truth is unattainable, as (6) contends, then how can we hope to attain the putative truth that (6) itself asserts? If everyone is thoroughly biased by politics and interests, the proponents of thesis (6) must themselves be biased, so how can we trust their historical studies? In short, (6) seems to be self-defeating.

To summarize, all the central arguments against veritism that spring from postmodern and constructivist quarters have failed. This does not mean that no additional problems lurk in the wings, but I have replied enough to this genre of objections. In the next chapter, I address another central question for any veritistic program: What, exactly, is truth?

TWO

Truth

2.1 *Approaches to the theory of truth*

G IVEN the centrality of truth to the present project, greater scrutiny of
this elusive concept is now in order. The first chapter disposed of a few
misconceptions, but this one undertakes a more fine-grained analysis of truth,
addressing the tangled philosophical controversy that surrounds this concept.
I shall ultimately propose a theory—rather, the sketch of a theory—within the
correspondence tradition, but I shall also suggest that some elements of the
deflationary approach may be acceptable to adherents of correspondence.

What is the aim of a theory of truth? Not to list all the truths, nor a large
number of them. The primary aim is to explain what is *meant* by "truth," what
is said of a proposition in saying (rightly or wrongly) that it is true. In other
words, the primary aim of a truth theory is to define the phrase "true," or say
how it functions in language. An alternate or secondary project in the theory
of truth is to say something about the nature of truth, something about the
truth property (if it is a property) shy of giving a definition. "Water is H_2O"
does not provide a definition of "water," but it is certainly informative about
it. Similarly, there might be informative things to say about truth that do not
constitute definitions. Until the final section of the chapter, however, I shall
concentrate on the quest for a definition of "true."

Another historically prominent mission concerning truth is the attempt to
provide a *criterion* or *test* of truth, that is, a practical guide for telling which
propositions are true. Though easily confused with our stated goal, this mission is entirely independent of the definitional project. Just as the theory of
truth does not aim to list the true propositions, so it does not seek a method
of telling which ones are true. That is the task of another sector of epistemology: the theory of evidence, justification, or truth determination. These theories try to say when it is appropriate to accept a proposition as true, or how to
go about determining the truth or falsity of a proposition. No doubt these are
central parts of epistemology. But here we focus on a prior question: what does
it even mean to say (or believe) of a proposition that it is true? To highlight
the difference, consider the following contrast. One might understand perfectly what steroids are without knowing how to establish that an athlete had
taken them. A second person might not even know what it means to take

steroids, or what steroids are. The latter needs clarification of a more fundamental kind, which may not broach the question of *tests* for steroid use.
Similarly, the aim of the theory of truth is to elucidate the meaning of truth
without trying to identify tests for truth, or modes of determining a proposition's truth-value. It is assumed, of course, that people have an implicit or
intuitive understanding of the meaning of "true." We seek a theory that makes
more explicit this intuitive understanding.

Perhaps the most natural and popular account of truth—acknowledged to
be such even by its critics—is the *correspondence theory*. According to a standard version of this theory, a proposition (or sentence, statement, belief, etc.)
is true just in case there exists a fact or state of affairs that corresponds to it
(Russell 1912, Wittgenstein 1922, Austin 1950). While many philosophers
find this thesis unexceptionable in itself, they complain that it is incomplete
and/or unilluminating unless it can be supplemented with accounts of what
"facts" are and what the "correspondence" relation consists in. Unfortunately,
satisfactory accounts of "fact" and "correspondence" have proved elusive.
Opponents of the correspondence theory complain that "worldly" facts are
dubious entities and that correspondence is a metaphysically mysterious relation. A subsidiary complaint about the correspondence theory (anticipated in
Chapter 1) is that it makes truth too remote and inaccessible to mere human
mortals. These complaints have propelled philosophers to seek alternative
theories and many have been proposed. I shall review the chief alternatives in
the field before finally returning to the correspondence theory.

2.2 *Instrumentalism and relativism*

The *pragmatist* or *instrumentalist* theory tries to bring truth down to earth by
linking it to the results of action. An important feature of true beliefs is that
they usually lead to desirable outcomes. If I want to attend a certain lecture
tonight, a true belief about the lecture's location can serve me better than a
false belief. Instrumentalism elevates this feature into a definition, saying that
a proposition is true just in case it would prove useful to those who believe it.
Clear statements of instrumentalism were given by William James:

Those thoughts are true which guide us to *beneficial interaction* with sensible particulars . . . (1909: 51)

The possession of true thoughts means everywhere the possession of invaluable
instruments of action. (1975: 97)

[*I*]deas . . . become true just in so far as they help us get into satisfactory relations with
other parts of our experience. (1975: 34)

In short, James's theory seems to be:

(I–1) A proposition is true if and only if it is useful to believe it, that is, useful to the prospective believer.

The first objection to instrumentalism, promptly raised by its critics, is that even false beliefs can be useful, as when inaccurate self-opinions carry the ego through the pitfalls and thickets of life. Equally fatal to instrumentalism is the fact that true beliefs sometimes breed unhappiness, or even disaster. I may be better off not knowing what certain people think of me than believing the bitter truth. So the link between truth and instrumental utility is not a necessary one. Thirdly, (I–1) has the unacceptable property of allowing both a proposition and its negation to be true (Kirkham 1992: 96–7). Let *P* be: "Smith is better at her job than her co-workers." It is useful for Smith to believe *P* because it promotes self-confidence; so by (I–1) *P* is true. But the negation of *P*, "Smith is not better at her job than her co-workers," is useful for Smith's co-workers to believe, so (I–1) apparently deems it true as well. No satisfactory theory, however, can allow both a proposition and its negation to be true.

Instrumentalism might escape the last dilemma by going relativist about truth. Instead of allowing propositions to be true or false *tout court*, instrumentalism might insist on relativizing truth to individuals: a proposition may be true *for* one person but not for another. In the above example *P* would be true for Smith but not true for a co-worker Jones, and conversely in the case of not-*P*. The trouble is that the ordinary use of "true" is not relative in this way; although relativizations do occur in the speech community (for example, among undergraduates), it is a corruption of the usual sense of "true." "*P* is *true for me*" means "*P* is true by my lights," that is, "I *take P* to be true," or "I *believe P.*" These statements, however, withdraw any claim to genuine truth by signaling that *P* is (just) one's personal opinion. Our subject, however, is not personal opinion but actual truth; on that subject relativism is misguided.

This line of argument might not persuade relativists. Conceding that truth is *commonly* thought to be absolute, they might insist that the ordinary view is confused or misguided. (This would be an "error theory" of the sort described in Chapter 1.) All truth is really relative. Although it is colloquial to say "*X* is true," I should really say "*X* is true relative to Alvin Goldman" or "*X* is true relative to William James." As Hilary Putnam points out (1981: 121), however, we can also ask whether these relativized statements are true or false. Consider statement *Y*: "*X* is true for Alvin Goldman." A total relativist must say that there is no absolute truth or falsity to *Y*; whether *Y* is true is *itself* something relative. In other words, we have to ask whether *Y* is true relative to this or that person, for example, whether a proposition *Z*, such as "*Y* is true relative to Bill Clinton," is true. But repeated application of this point launches an infinite regress. As Putnam rightly observes, our grasp on what relativism even means "begins to wobble" (1981: 121).

To avoid relativism, one might formulate instrumentalism in terms of what is instrumentally valuable to all, not just to the prospective believer. This would yield:

> (I–2) *P* is true if and only if believing *P* would have net benefit for all concerned.

An immediate problem of interpretation arises: Whose belief in *P* is in question? Jessica's believing *P* might be beneficial for all concerned whereas Jason's believing *P* might have dramatically different consequences. Whose belief is the relevant one? One possible answer is: *everyone*'s believing *P*. In other words:

(I–3) *P* is true if and only if everyone's believing *P* would be beneficial for all concerned.

Although (I–3) averts any ambiguity, it is just plain wrong. Given the mischief of nuclear power, it might be beneficial if everyone—including all potential warmongers—believed that there is no such thing as nuclear power; but that does not suffice to make it true that there is no such thing as nuclear power.

2.3 *Epistemic approaches to truth*

A second approach to truth is the *epistemic* or *verificationist* approach, which equates the truth of a proposition with the existence of evidence or justification for that proposition. Since it is proper to affirm a proposition's truth precisely when we have good reasons, evidence, or justification for believing it, why not simply equate truth with such evidence? This was apparently John Dewey's idea in his "warranted assertibility" theory of truth (1938, 1957).[1]

The first objection is that the epistemic approach seems to conflate the two problems distinguished earlier: *defining* truth versus providing a *test* for truth. The epistemic theorist, however, might spurn this supposed distinction, claiming that all we do when we call a proposition true is say that there is evidence or warrant for it. This defense is unpromising. A proposition might not be true although someone has excellent evidence for it, if only because evidence can in general be defeated or undermined by further evidence. Thus, evidence or justification is not sufficient for truth. Similarly, evidence for a proposition is not necessary; there might be truths concerning distant galaxies for which we possess no evidence, but they are truths nonetheless. The last point is worth expressing slightly differently. Although scrupulous people will only assert things when they have ample evidence, one *can* make assertions on no evidence at all. With luck, moreover, it is possible to assert truths in this fashion. Thus, truth cannot be equated with possession of evidence.

These are a few of the serious problems facing the epistemic approach to truth. The approach has many variants, however, so it cannot yet be dismissed. Before proceeding to further variants, let us reflect on the range of possibilities. Notice that "is true" is a one-place predicate, whereas the epistemic

---

[1] Brandom (1994: 286) interprets Dewey to have offered warranted assertibility as a replacement for the truth concept rather than an analysis of it. I shall not try to assess this interpretive claim.

predicates "is justified" and "is warranted" are really three-place predicates. It is incorrect to say that a proposition P is justified *tout court*; rather, since evidence-possession for P can vary from person to person and from time to time, we must speak of P being justified for a person at a time. This poses problems for attempts to analyze truth in terms of justification or evidence, since truth is not relativized to persons or times. The problem might be solved through appropriate quantification over persons and times; the question is whether any quantification gets matters right. For example, one might try existentially quantifying over persons and times, yielding:

(E–1) P is true if and only if there is a person X and a time t such that X is justified in believing P at t.

Suppose "justified" is understood in a weak sense, implying that justification for P may be defeated or undermined by further evidence (perhaps all empirical justification is of this sort). This means that Mario might be justified in believing (an eternal or time-indexed) proposition P on Monday and justified in believing not-P on Tuesday. According to (E–1), both P and not-P would be true, an intolerable result.

Can "justified" be understood in a strong sense, so as to foreclose the preceding possibility? There are two problems. First, it is not clear that there is an acceptably strong sense, especially for empirical propositions (we shall return to this below). Second, even if there is such a sense, it will rarely be satisfied, so very few propositions will be either true or false (this assumes that falsity is defined as somebody sometime being justified in believing the negation). This entails far too frequent violation of the bivalence principle to be plausible.

Several historical theories of truth are variants of the epistemic approach and face similar problems to (E–1). One is the coherence theory, which says that a proposition is true just in case it coheres with a relevant system of other propositions. Which system? The system of the person who believes the proposition? What shall we say when there are two or more believers of the proposition whose respective systems of belief are otherwise quite different? We might next try existential quantification:

(E–2) P is true if and only if there is some person X and some time t such that P coheres with the rest of the propositions X believes at t.

Definition (E–2) suffers the same fatal flaw as (E–1): both a proposition and its negation could satisfy it, since P might cohere with one person's system of beliefs and not-P with a second person's system. The same problem is also encountered by a universally quantified version:

(E–2′) P is true if and only if for every person X who believes P at some time t, P coheres with the rest of the propositions X believes at t.

It is possible that P coheres with the belief systems of all who believe P, and not-P coheres with the belief corpora of all who believe not-P. In addition,

(E–2′) is far too restrictive. Surely the truth of *P* cannot be disqualified simply because one individual who believes it has a body of evidence that fails to cohere with it (or even coheres with its negation). Is there an "ideal" body of evidence against which *P*'s coherence might be tested (Rescher 1973, Rosenberg 1980)? It is just not clear how an ideal body of evidence should be specified.

Another historical version of the epistemic approach is that of Peirce (1931–5), whose theory was mentioned in Chapter 1. Here are two passages that state his view:

The opinion which is fated to be ultimately agreed to by all who investigate is what we mean by truth. (1931–35: 5.407)

The truth of the proposition that Caesar crossed the Rubicon consists in the fact that the further we push our archaeological and other studies, the more strongly will that conclusion force itself on our minds forever—or would do so, if study were to go on forever. (1931–5: 5.565)

Peirce might qualify as an epistemic theorist because he identifies truths with propositions that would be believed if people gathered enough evidence through investigation. As remarked earlier, however, there is no guarantee that people would believe the truth even if they investigated indefinitely. Some truths may be so well camouflaged by misleading evidence that people would never uncover them. And there might be truths on which beliefs never converge despite continued investigation; there might be persistent dissent, or waves of consensus oscillating in different directions. It is noteworthy also that Peirce's theory does not make truth very accessible, contrary to one of the motivations behind the epistemic approach. If truth is what would be believed at the "end" of inquiry, how does this help us right now to distinguish truth from falsehood?

Putnam (1981: 55) has proposed an account in the spirit of Peirce's "limit" idea. According to this proposal, *P* is true if and only if *P* would be justified under ideal epistemic circumstances. In other words, as William Alston reformulates it (1996: 204):

(IJC) To say of a belief that it is true is to say that it would be justifiable in a situation in which all relevant evidence (reasons, considerations) is readily available.

Notice that this proposal, like Peirce's, would not help make truth more accessible, as epistemic theorists commonly hope. Under (IJC), truth would be accessible to creatures in ideal epistemic circumstances, but since ordinary mortals are never in ideal epistemic circumstances, how can it help them?

What about the tenability of (IJC)? Alston points out several problems with the proposal, but I shall concentrate on one. Can the notion of justification in an epistemically ideal situation be defined or explained without using the notion of truth? If it cannot, if one needs the truth concept to define justification in an ideal situation, then one cannot turn around and define truth in terms of justification in an ideal situation, as (IJC) tries to do. This would be a form of definitional circularity. But in fact the truth concept is needed to define ideal justification.[2] First, it is difficult to provide an adequate account of epistemic justification without invoking the notion of truth, as a substantial literature strongly suggests. Second, although there are some approaches to justification that refrain from invoking truth, these would not suit the purposes of securing the match endorsed by (IJC), namely, a match between truth and justification in an epistemically ideal situation. For example, consider a "deontological" conception of justification according to which a belief's being justified amounts to a believer's not violating any intellectual obligations in holding the belief. Merely failing to violate intellectual obligations would not guarantee truth, even with all relevant evidence. For example, one might be psychologically and/or methodologically deficient, so that one could form false beliefs even if one did everything, cognitively, that could be reasonably required of one. To avoid this possibility, a defender of (IJC) would have to build truth conducivity into the concept of justification, or into the concept of all relevant evidence. This, then, would generate the threatened circularity.

It is noteworthy that Putnam himself has apparently recanted this epistemic approach to truth. He describes himself as having made a "long journey from realism back to realism" (Putnam 1994: 494). This journey, he says, has brought him back to the familiar: "truth is sometimes recognition-transcendent because what goes on in the world is sometimes beyond our power to recognize, even when it is not beyond our power to conceive" (1994: 516).

A final example I shall consider of an epistemic approach to truth is that of Crispin Wright (1992). Although Wright claims that a plurality of truth predicates are possible, a "minimal" truth predicate, he says, must involve a condition of warranted assertibility. Although he admits that truth and assertoric warrant diverge in extension, he claims that they have the same (epistemic) "normative force" (1992: 18). How does he arrive at this thesis? Starting with a disquotation schema, "'P' is true if and only if P," Wright says that the right-hand side of the schema ("P") says something about "proper assertoric use," namely, "warranted assertibility." Therefore, he concludes, the left-hand side must also say this. But here already is his first and basic misstep, as Alston points out (1996: 218–19). The right-hand part of the disquotation schema says nothing about proper assertoric use or warranted assertibility. Take a particular instantiation of the schema: "It is true that sugar is sweet if and only if sugar is sweet." The proposition on the right-hand side attributes sweetness to sugar; it is about sugar, a foodstuff. It says nothing whatever about warranted assertibility, or about when it is proper to believe the proposition. There is

---

[2] I made this point myself in Goldman 1986 (147), but Alston (1996: 204–8) has a much better and fuller discussion of it.

nothing in its content that even hints at the concept of positive epistemic status. A young child, for example, could easily understand the content of "sugar is sweet" without having the concept of epistemic warrant or justification.[3]

Wright proceeds to propose a minimal conception of truth as involving an epistemic notion he calls *superassertibility*:

> A statement is superassertible ... if and only if it is, or can be, warranted and some warrant for it would survive arbitrarily close scrutiny of its pedigree and arbitrarily extensive increments to or other forms of improvement of our information. (1992: 48)

It seems unlikely, however, that superassertibility captures the content of any truth predicate.[4] Although some critics have argued that superassertibility does not suffice for truth,[5] the problem I discern is its excessive strength. It requires that (after some point) some warrant for a true statement would survive arbitrarily close scrutiny and arbitrarily extensive increments in information. Does any statement meet that stringent condition? What is implied is that some warrant could never be defeated, even by misleading evidence. That seems clearly wrong. Almost any evidence could be at least misleadingly defeated, for instance, by indications that you were hallucinating the evidence, by a false but credible claim that your informant was lying, and so forth. Wright's definition registers an unfounded optimism that a true statement would (after some point) always encounter a favorable evidential climate, at least for some of its warrant, as it is exposed to more and more evidence. I fail to see how this ungrounded optimism is an improvement over Peirce.

2.4 *Realisms, antirealisms, and truth*

There is a great deal of confusion between debates over the nature of truth and debates over doctrines called "realism" and "antirealism." In this section I distinguish controversies over truth from controversies concerning realism. I borrow heavily from William Alston (1996), and commend his entire book for a more detailed excursus into these issues.

Metaphysics addresses the question of what is real. For any number of candidate entities, metaphysicians may argue about whether or not they are real,

---

[3] In fact, I would add, it is doubtful that the concept of epistemic warrant can be applied intelligibly to a sentence or proposition all by itself. As emphasized earlier, such an attribution only makes sense relative to a specified agent and time.

[4] Of course, Wright imposes some additional conditions for an admissible truth predicate, what he calls "platitudes" about truth. But those can be taken for granted in the discussion that follows.

[5] See Horgan (1995: 133–4), who provides an envatted brain case as a counterexample to Wright's thesis. However, Horgan appeals to a different and weaker definition of superassertibility, which Wright offers later in his book.

that is, whether or not they exist. Among the many entities subject to such disputes are propositions, numbers, God, moral properties, motion, and time. Metaphysicians also question whether the target entities have the *kind* of existence or character they are commonly thought to have. Antirealism comes in two forms. Either it flatly denies the existence of one of these types of entities, or it tries to give a non-standard or non-commonsensical account of what its nature consists in. Historically, the second antirealist approach usually takes the form of some sort of "reduction"; for example, reducing physical objects to actual and possible sense data, reducing mental states to behavioral dispositions, or reducing numbers to set-theoretic constructions. In each of these areas, realism asserts the reality of the entities in question and/or asserts that these entities have the "standard" form of existence rather than the "reduced" form.

What is the relation between metaphysical theories on these topics and the theories of truth? As Alston nicely puts it,

Though a particular realist or antirealist metaphysical position . . . has implications for what propositions are true or false, they have no implications for what it is for a proposition to be true or false. (1996: 78)

Consider a form of antirealism according to which there are no moral properties. It may follow from this doctrine that no proposition ascribing moral rightness to some action is true. So an antirealist doctrine can have implications for the truth status of certain propositions. But that does not turn this antirealist doctrine into a theory of truth. It is quite silent on the general question of what makes propositions true. It may presuppose an understanding of truth, but it does not contribute to it. It does not, for example, take a position as between a correspondence and a deflationary account of truth.

The same point holds for reductionist versions of antirealism. Consider the reductionist doctrine of phenomenalism (or idealism), which says that physical objects such as chairs and tables are just complexes of actual or possible sense data in people's minds. This is completely neutral on questions about the theory of truth, for example, about whether a correspondence theory, a deflationary theory, or some form of epistemic theory is correct. One can consistently be a correspondence theorist and still embrace phenomenalism. A correspondence theorist, for example, would just maintain that physical object propositions are true or false according to whether they correspond or do not correspond to the realm of sense data.[6]

Until now I have addressed *metaphysical* realism and antirealism. But under the influence of Michael Dummett, "realism" and "antirealism" have come to denote *semantical* doctrines, doctrines about the source or nature of meaning. According to what Dummett calls "antirealism," the meaning of a statement

---

[6] See Horwich 1996 for further endorsement of the thesis that the realism/antirealism debate is independent of theories of truth.

is to be given in terms of the conditions it would take to *verify* it, that is, the conditions under which we are able to *recognize* it as true. This contrasts with a realist approach to meaning like Frege's, according to which the meaning of a statement is to be given in terms of the conditions under which it would be true. As it stands, these are theories about *meaning*, not about *truth* (although at least realism makes pivotal use of the concept of truth). As in the case of the metaphysical issues concerning realism and antirealism, here too we should regard the semantical approaches labeled "realism" and "antirealism" as completely disjoint from the problem of truth theory.

The issue is clouded somewhat, however, by the fact that, in some places, Dummett also introduces verificationist or assertibilist concepts in discussing truth. For example, he writes:

[T]he notion of truth, when it is introduced, must be explained, in some manner, in terms of our capacity to recognize statements as true, and not in terms of a condition which transcends human capacities. (1976: 116)

Here we have the endorsement of a genuine theory of truth, an epistemic theory of truth. But insofar as Dummett restricts himself to his standard formulations of realism and antirealism, they are doctrines about meaning in general rather than truth.

Since semantical doctrines are separate from doctrines about truth, it may seem unnecessary for me to say anything substantial here about semantical realism and antirealism. However, the reader might feel that my opposition to an epistemic approach to truth would be significantly diluted if a verificationist or epistemic approach to meaning, of the sort Dummett favors, turned out to be correct. This is not right. Just as the correspondence theory of truth, for example, is compatible with antirealist metaphysics, so it is compatible with verificationist semantics (Alston 1996: 123–6). Nonetheless, let me say a few words in criticism of this semantical doctrine.

Putnam (1994) puts his finger on the nub of the error in semantic verificationism:

What is mistaken about verificationism is the claim that the meaning of an expression like "things too small to see with the naked eye" depends on there being methods of verifying the existence of such things, and the related claim that the meaning of such an expression changes as these methods of verification change (for example, with the invention of the microscope). (1994: 502)

The phrase "too small to see with the naked eye" was intelligible before the invention of the microscope, and its meaning did not change when the microscope was invented.

Other fundamental problems with semantic verificationism are identified by Alston, but I shall mention just one of these. As Quine has long emphasized, no statement can be subjected to observational test all by itself. Conditions of empirical verification can usually be derived from a statement only in conjunction with other statements. This means, however, that verification conditions cannot be parceled out to statements one by one; but this is just what Dummett's approach requires.[7]

Leaving Dummett, let me turn now to Wright (1992), who discusses truth in the same breath as realism. Like Dummett, Wright is interested in the question of which areas of discourse (for example, morals, comedy, aesthetic value, numbers) should be classified as "realistic" and which should be classified as "antirealistic." He proposes to draw these distinctions in terms of the kinds of truth predicates that apply to these discourses. According to Wright, there is a multiplicity of possible truth predicates, which can be categorized in terms of "epistemic constraint," "the Euthyphro contrast," "cognitive command," and "wide cosmological role." These distinctions of Wright's are unquestionably interesting, but do they distinguish types of *truth* (or truth predicates)? Indeed, has Wright offered a convincing argument for the claim that there are multiple meanings of "true"?

When a word is genuinely multivocal, there are usually clear-cut signs of this multivocality. For example, a meaning that the word has in certain uses would be anomalous in other uses. But Wright does not offer this kind of evidence, so I am inclined to agree with Paul Horwich (1993: 28) that there is just one concept of truth, just one truth predicate. As Horwich points out, the fact that different domains involve different types of truths (for instance, truths about mind-dependent objects vs. truths about mind-independent objects) does not imply that there are different concepts of truth, any more than the fact that people in different countries drive on different sides of the road implies that they have different concepts of *left*.[8] Thus, Wright's effort to distinguish different discourses on some realism/antirealism continuum (or set of continua) may have nothing to do with truth.

2.5 Deflationism

I turn now to what is certainly a contender for a theory of truth, indeed, what I regard as the second-best contender (after correspondence) for a satisfactory theory of truth, namely, *deflationism*. Deflationism is really a family of theories, which jointly hold that it is a mistake to suppose that sentences using the word "true" involve the predication of a property (or a "substantive" property) to propositions or anything else. The flavor of deflationism can be conveyed

---

[7] Dummett (1976: 111) makes a perfunctory acknowledgement of this point, as Alston indicates, but he does not take account of it systematically.

[8] Similarly, Sainsbury (1996) argues cogently that although it is one thing for a tree to exist, another for a sensation to exist, and yet another for a number to exist, these differences do not show that "exists" is ambiguous. If we consider the schema, "What is it for a . . . to exist?", we will indeed get different answers depending on how the blank is filled. But the explanation of this should be in terms of the different fillings, not in terms of different senses of "exist."

by an early form of it, the "redundancy theory." The *locus classicus* of the redundancy theory is F. P. Ramsey's claim: " 'It is true that Caesar was murdered' means no more than that Caesar was murdered" (1978: 44). So the redundancy theory says that there is no difference in content between (the assertion of) "It is true that *P*" and (the assertion of) "*P*." More generally, deflationism says that "true" mainly functions as a convenient linguistic device, rather than expressing a deep metaphysical relation between statements and the world. As a notational convention, let us use angled brackets "⟨" and "⟩" surrounding an expression to refer to the proposition picked out by the contained expression. So "⟨*P*⟩" refers to the proposition that *P*. Then deflationism says (roughly) that "true" in "⟨*P*⟩ is true" has no separate function; "*P*" and "⟨*P*⟩ is true" make the same assertion. The function of "true" in "That is true," uttered right after someone else has just asserted ⟨*P*⟩, is to assent to that very assertion, which would otherwise have to be done by repeating what the first person said. So "true" is a convenient device, but it does not add new "content." This is just the bare bones of the deflationary approach. It must be expanded to handle embedded uses of "true" such as "If it is true that Johnny plans to resign, then we need a new candidate," where the speaker does not endorse the antecedent. But deflationists have ostensibly promising ways of complicating their accounts to accommodate such cases.

Although the foregoing articulates the motivating spirit behind deflationism, the approach has several varieties which I shall discuss under three headings: *performative theories*, *disquotationalism*, and *minimalism*. My discussion will be conducted in two stages: I first present the distinguishing features of these versions and then raise difficulties confronting each variety.

The performative theory, which we met in Chapter 1 as Rorty's theory (or one of them), was first articulated by P. F. Strawson (1950) and A. J. Ayer (1963). They contended that truth ascriptions are performative utterances, much like "I promise to . . ." and "I do" (when uttered at the appropriate moment in a marriage ceremony). The theory claims that to utter the sentence "What Percy says is true" is not to *say* anything at all but to *do* something: to agree with Percy. It is the performance of a speech act other than *making a statement*; namely, the act of agreeing. The performative theory may be analogized to the expressivist conception of ethical sentences. Acts of calling something true are compared to acts of calling something good, which praise an object rather than describe it as possessing a certain property. Performative theories not only deny that truth is a property but offer an alternative, expressivist account of truth talk.

Disquotational theories are equally inclined to deny that truth is a property, but they do not give a performative account of truth talk. Rather, especially in Quine's version, they see "true" primarily as a device for semantic ascent—a device for talking about snow or whiteness by talking about sentences that are about snow or whiteness. Quine's view is that for simple sentences like "Snow is white," the perfect theory of truth is what Wilfrid Sellars has called the disappearance theory: " 'Snow is white' is true" can simply be replaced by "Snow is white" (Quine 1971: 11). But there are places, Quine adds, where we are impelled by certain technical complications to mention sentences. For example, when we want to generalize on such sentences as "Tom is mortal or Tom is not mortal," "Snow is white or snow is not white," and so on, we ascend to talk of truth and of sentences, saying "Every sentence of the form 'P or not-P' is true." Truth talk is thus a very handy device but in principle dispensable.[9]

Another prominent version of disquotationalism is the *prosentential* theory of truth developed by Dorothy Grover, Joseph Camp, Jr., and Nuel Belnap, Jr. (1975). Their theory takes its starting point from anaphoric uses of pronouns. Pronouns of "laziness," for example, acquire their referents from antecedent expressions, as "he" and "her" do in the sentence "Bob is happiest with Mary, and I think *he* will marry *her*." Proverbs operate similarly, such as "did" in "Mary ran quickly, so Bill *did* too." Grover, Camp, and Belnap go on to suggest that there is such a thing as a prosentence: "so" is sometimes used this way, as in "I don't believe Rachel is sick, but if *so*, she should stay home." They suggest that prosentences of laziness derive their propositional content from antecedent sentences. For example, in the following dialogue,

> BETTY: My sister finds humid weather debilitating.
> JANET: If *that is true*, she should move to a drier climate.

the phrase "that is true" in Janet's statement acquires its entire propositional content from Betty's statement. So "that is true" should be thought of as standing in for "my sister finds humid weather debilitating," and not as *adding* any independent new content (Grover 1992: 13). The suggestion is that phrases like "It's true" and "That's true" can generally be treated as prosentences. Grover, Camp, and Belnap contend that "is true" is not a real predicate and does not express a genuine property. It just enables people to repeat other contents in a shorthand fashion.[10]

A third form of deflationism is minimalism, a variant developed by Paul Horwich (1990). Unlike other deflationists, Horwich does not deny that "is true" is a predicate and therefore expresses a property; he just denies that it expresses a substantive, complex, or naturalistic property. On the positive side, Horwich's theory resembles other forms of deflationism in resting on the simple equivalence schema:

(T) $\langle P \rangle$ is true if and only if P.

---

[9] The reader will notice that I have not tried to formulate a full definition of truth in the disquotational mode. That is because such a definition is quite difficult to construct and open to many difficulties; see David 1994: ch. 4.

[10] This is just a heuristic sketch of the prosententialist approach. It does not address the treatment of "is true" in quantificational sentences, for example.

His minimalist theory (MT) simply consists of all instances of (T); that is, every substitution instance of (T), or T-sentence, is an axiom of MT. Observe that minimalism is a very large theory, indeed infinitely long. For any proposition ⟨P⟩, whether expressible in any natural language or not, there is a biconditional of the form (T) that is part of, that is, an axiom of, the theory. Although Horwich admits that his theory, being infinite, is not explicitly formulable, he claims that it nonetheless provides a satisfactory and economical explanation of all the facts involving truth. For example, the theory explains why the proposition that snow is white follows from the two premises "Everything Bill asserted is true" and "Bill asserted that snow is white." Without the aid of any truth theory, the two premises imply "It is true that snow is white." Theory MT contains the proposition "It is true that snow is white if and only if snow is white," and so enables us to deduce that snow is white. Since this and other examples demonstrate that MT is explanatorily adequate, according to Horwich, the search for any deeper principles governing truth is pointless. Horwich goes on to contend that MT constitutes a correct definition of "true," and that a person's understanding of the truth predicate consists in his disposition to accept, without evidence, any instantiation of schema (T).

With this brief summary of the three views in hand, let us now see how they fare under critical scrutiny, starting with the performative theory. First, as Strawson is aware, "is true" figures in a variety of expressions other than simple ascriptions. It occurs in questions of the form "Is it true that . . .?" and in conditionals of the form "If it is true that . . . then . . .," for example. To handle such cases, Strawson expands his theory, saying that "is true" can also function, like the adverb "really," as an expression of surprise, doubt, or disbelief (1964). This raises many problems. First, it appears that Strawson does not have *one* theory about "is true," but several. Second, as Peter Geach anticipated (1960), the following argument becomes invalid on Strawson's theory by virtue of committing the fallacy of equivocation, because the first "is true" is an expression of doubt, while the second is an expression of agreement (or the like):

> If *X* is true, then *P*
> *X* is true
> Ergo, *P*

Indeed, as Richard Kirkham adds, since "*X* is true" is supposed to be an action rather than a statement, it cannot even qualify as a premise (1992: 309). But we know that the argument is valid, so there is something badly wrong with the theory. Horwich makes a similar point (1990: 40). If apparent truth predications are non-statemental speech acts, how can we make sense of the inference from "Oscar's claim is true" and "Oscar's claim is that snow is white" to the conclusion "Snow is white"? Finally, whereas the performative theory claims that "is true" is used to endorse a proposition *rather than* to describe it, these types of speech acts are not really mutually exclusive. One might

endorse a proposition *by* ascribing a property to it, so the performative potential of "is true" does not exclude the possibility that it also expresses a property.

I turn next to disquotationalism. The nub of disquotationalism is the claim
that a sentence like " 'Snow is white' is true" means nothing more nor less
than "Snow is white," which is obtained from the longer sentence by deleting
the words "is true" and removing the (single) quotation marks. The first problem with this approach concerns indexicals, demonstratives, and other terms
whose referents vary with the context of use. It is not the case, for instance,
that every instance of "I am hungry" is true if and only if *I* am hungry. And
there is no simple way to modify the disquotational scheme to avert this problem (Horwich 1992: 513).

The second problem with disquotationalism is the *counterfactual problem*,
first identified by Casimir Lewy (1947). There is actually a substantive difference in meaning between "Snow is white" and "'Snow is white' is true," as
revealed by their different truth-values in some counterfactual situations.
John Etchemendy (1988) puts the point this way:

["Snow is white"] makes a claim that depends only on the color of snow; ["'Snow
is white' is true"], on the other hand, depends on both the color of snow and the
meaning of the sentence "Snow is white." For this reason the states of affairs
described can vary independently: "Snow is white" might have been false, though
snow was still white; if, for instance, "snow" had meant *grass*. And conversely,
snow might not have been white, though "Snow is white" was still true; say if
"snow" had meant *vanilla ice cream*. (1988: 61)

Another way of explaining the counterfactual problem is in terms of the following pair of counterfactual sentences:

> If we had used "snow" differently (for example, to mean *grass*), "Snow
> is white" would not have been true.

> If we had used "snow" differently (for example, to mean *grass*), snow
> would not have been white.

According to disquotationalism, these two sentences should be equivalent,
because "'Snow is white' is true" is supposed to be equivalent to "Snow is
white." But these two sentences are clearly not equivalent; the first is true
whereas the second is false, as Frederick Schmitt points out (1995: 132–3).

The third problem for disquotationalism is the *bivalence problem* (Horwich
1990: 80). Bivalence is the principle that every proposition is either true or
false (a proposition that is not true must be false). Disquotationalism is committed to bivalence, as the following argument shows. First, disquotationalism identifies falsehood with the absence of truth. Once one identifies "'Snow
is white' is true" with "Snow is white," there does not seem to be any room
for distinguishing between "is false" and "is not true." Assuming, then, that
"⟨P⟩ is false" is equivalent to "⟨P⟩ is not true," we can use the principle of con-

traposition to infer the equivalence of "⟨P⟩ is not false" and "⟨P⟩ is not not true." Now from the denial of bivalence, namely, "⟨P⟩ is not true and not false," we can deduce a contradiction: "⟨P⟩ is not true and ⟨P⟩ is not not true." Since the denial of bivalence implies a contradiction under disquotationalism, the latter is committed to bivalence. But bivalence is a mistaken principle, since vague propositions, for example, admit of truth-value gaps. In the case of men with borderline baldness, it is neither true nor false to say that they are bald. Disquotationalism suffers, then, from this commitment.[11]

Deflationists are not unaware of these problems, and indeed Hartry Field (1994*a*, 1994*b*), working as a deflationism sympathizer, has proposed solutions to all three problems. It is questionable, however, just how satisfactory these solutions are. Since they are rather technical, and since other problems I shall pose below strike me as more severe, I will not attempt to assess their adequacy.

Prosententialism is a highly ingenious theory, but it faces many serious difficulties, as shown by W. Kent Wilson (1990). For example, anaphoric devices, even lazy ones, do not generally assume the meaning or content of their antecedents (although they do assume their referents). Many nominal anaphors have meaning that their antecedents may not have, as in:

> *Leslie* was a wonderful colleague, but *he/she* was a very private person.

> We're not leaving *the Chancellor*'s office until *the bastard* talks with us.

In the first sentence, the meaning of the pronoun "he" or "she" indicates gender whereas the proper name "Leslie" does not. In the second sentence, "the bastard" obviously has a different meaning from "the Chancellor" although one is an anaphor of the other. The question is why a prosentence should assume the meaning or propositional content of its antecedent although other proforms do not. Another problem raised by Wilson concerns the following example:

> *A*: Colorless green ideas sleep furiously.
> *B*: That's not true.

We don't understand what *A* has said because *A*'s utterance is anomalous. We do understand what *B* has said, however, and indeed it seems to be true. But it is hard to square this with the prosentential theory, since the content of *B*'s utterance, according to the theory, is entirely dependent on the content of *A*'s. Wilson adduces numerous other problems facing prosententialism, which Grover admits are "daunting" (1992: 20).

I turn now to Horwich's minimalist theory. The first problem emerges from

---

[11] Some have tried to support bivalence by claiming that vague sentences are either true or false; we just can't say which (Horwich 1990: 80–7, Field 1986: 68–70). Schmitt (1995: 137–41) argues persuasively, however, that this reply is weak.

close attention to a problem Horwich himself addresses (1992: 511–12). An important property of truth talk is its ability to say things about propositions that are designated indirectly. Suppose you are told that Einstein's last words expressed a claim about physics, an area in which you think he was very reliable. Unknown to you, his claim was the proposition that quantum mechanics is wrong. What conclusion can you draw? Well, asks Horwich, which proposition is the object of your belief, when you believe that Einstein's last words expressed a truth of physics? Not the proposition that quantum mechanics is wrong, because by hypothesis you are unaware that this is what he said. It must be something equivalent to the infinite conjunction:

> If what Einstein said was that $E = mc$, then $E = mc$, and if what he said was that quantum mechanics is wrong, then quantum mechanics is wrong, . . . and so on.

This fits Horwich's theory well, of course, because his theory says that our understanding of the truth predicate consists in the disposition to accept any instance of the T-schema. Field (1994*a*: 264) gives the same answer to a precisely similar problem, showing how disquotationalism would also handle it. Suppose that we remember that someone said something false yesterday but can't remember what it was. What we are remembering, says Field, is equivalent to the infinite disjunction of all sentences of the form "She said '*P*', but not-*P*."

Can this infinite conjunction or disjunction reply handle these types of cases? No. It does not solve what I shall call the *belief-content* problem. Consider a minor variant of Horwich's case. Suppose Judith is told that Einstein's last utterance was a sophisticated claim about physics. Judith believes that this last utterance was true, but since she knows virtually no physics, she also believes that what Einstein said was utterly beyond her grasp. So she says, sincerely, "What Einstein said is true, but I am sure it is beyond my grasp." What is the propositional content of Judith's belief when she assents to "What Einstein said is true"? Of course, it is not the content of what Einstein actually said, since Judith does not know what that was. Could it be the kind of infinite conjunctive proposition proposed by Horwich? This infinite conjunction will not work, because it includes many elements, like ⟨$E = mc^2$⟩, that Judith does not grasp. But every content of a person's belief, and every constituent of the content of her belief, must be something that the believer does grasp! Believing a proposition presupposes that the believer grasps the (whole) proposition. Notice that I am not here objecting to the infinite, list-like character of minimalism, though that may well be objectionable. Rather, my objection is that the sort of conjunctive proposition Horwich commends to us would contain many things ungrasped by Judith, yet they must be grasped if they are elements of the proposition that is the genuine content of her belief.

What the minimalist needs to locate is a (propositional) content for Judith's belief such that (A) Judith grasps it, and (B) it fits the minimalist requirements. Could it be a finite conjunction of those physics propositions that Judith *does* grasp? No, because such a conjunction will not include the proposition Judith is alluding to (in her definite description), so it will not be equivalent to what she asserts or assents to. For example, let all the physics propositions Judith does grasp be $\langle P \rangle$, $\langle Q \rangle$, . . ., $\langle Z \rangle$, which do not include the one Einstein said. Then the Horwichean conjunction involving these propositions, namely, "If Einstein said P, then P, and if Einstein said Q, then Q, . . ., and if Einstein said Z, then Z," will be true, because the antecedents of the conditional conjuncts are all false. The proposition Einstein actually asserted, however, might be false, and hence the proposition Judith believes, expressed by the utterance "What Einstein said is true," would also be false.[12]

The natural interpretation of Judith's situation is that she refers to a sentence Einstein uttered (or a proposition expressed by his sentence) via a content that she grasps; for example, the concept expressed by the description "what Einstein said." The question then is: What is the remaining content of the proposition she believes, the content expressed by "is true"? It looks as if this content must be (1) some general concept, (2) a concept that Judith grasps, and (3) a concept that yields a proposition to which she assents. For example, things proceed smoothly if this concept is the general concept of corresponding with reality. But this is just the sort of proposal deflationists are at pains to deny. They mean to deny that "is true" expresses any such concept or property (or, in Horwich's case, any "substantive" property). We are then left, however, with no clear account of what thought content Judith grasps, or entertains, when she (sincerely) utters, "What Einstein said is true."

A second objection with a very similar thrust has been lodged against Horwich's minimalism by Anil Gupta (1993). Definitions that explain our understanding of a word or concept, says Gupta, have the following feature. If one lacks knowledge of parts of the definition, one will have less than a full grasp of the meaning of the definiendum; the greater the lack, the lesser the grasp (if meaning is grasped at all). Suppose, for instance, that the Peano axioms are taken to be a definition of the notion of number. Then if one lacks knowledge of the first axiom, or lacks the concept of identity, one will have less than a full grasp of the notion of number. Recall now that according to Horwich, our understanding of the notion of truth (or, more precisely, "true proposition") consists in our disposition to accept, without evidence, all biconditionals of the form (T). Can this list of biconditionals, asks Gupta, play the required role?

None of us has more than a minute fraction of the concepts employed in the biconditionals, yet we have a good understanding of the concept of truth. Similarly, we lack a disposition to accept the vast majority of the biconditionals, but this casts

---

[12] Thanks to Joel Pust for assistance with this paragraph.

not the slightest doubt on our understanding of truth . . . [P]erfect possession of the disposition requires possession of all the concepts. But this is not a requirement for a perfect understanding of the meaning of "true." (1993: 366)

The biconditionals, says Gupta, are particular in character. They explain the notion of truth proposition by proposition, using massive conceptual resources, namely, the resources required to express *all* of the infinitely many propositions. Our understanding of truth, by contrast, has a general character. We seem to possess rules that enable us to understand truth attributions even when truth is attributed to propositions beyond our conceptual ken, for example, abstruse propositions of physics, as in the previous example. Hence, Gupta argues, our understanding of truth does not *derive* from the biconditionals, but only (at most) *leads* to them. A very natural hypothesis (though not one that Gupta himself advances) is that it derives instead from the understanding of a general relation like correspondence to reality.

There are additional problems confronting deflationism (see David 1994, Schmitt 1995, and Alston 1996: sec. 1. xi), but those already discussed are crippling enough to deflationism and sufficiently suggestive of correspondence that we should turn to the latter with hopeful anticipation.

2.6 *The correspondence theory*

Let me now offer a sketch of the version of the correspondence theory that I find congenial. This sketch will admittedly leave many major issues unresolved, but it may still point in a helpful direction. As previously noted, the root idea of the correspondence approach is that truth involves a relation to reality. I would add another ingredient, namely, that items are candidates for truth only if they (purport to) *describe* reality. A desire or a wish, if fulfilled, may have an appropriate correspondence relation to reality in the sense that (a portion of) reality matches or realizes the desire's content. But such a desire or wish is not called "true" because it represents what the subject *wants* reality to be like, rather than how the subject *depicts* reality. Similarly, an imperative sentence like "Go to the store" may correspond with reality if the addressee complies with the order, but we would not call such an imperative "true." As John Searle puts it (1983: 7), these attitudes or utterances have the wrong "direction of fit" to qualify as true. They have a "world-to-mind" (or "world-to-utterance") direction of fit rather than a "mind-to-world" (or "utterance-to-world") direction of fit. Thus, a theory of truth should involve the requirement that the truth bearer should *describe* reality. This, coupled with our earlier discussion, invites the following theory:

(DS) An item X (a proposition, a sentence, a belief, etc.) is true if and only if X is descriptively successful, that is, X purports to describe reality and its content fits reality.

This is in the general vicinity of William Alston's "minimal realist" theory of truth, which he states (in its basic form) as follows:

A statement is true if and only if what the statement says to be the case actually is the case. (1996: 22)

Alston declines to call his theory a version of the correspondence theory, but he also says that it may be thought of as an "inchoate correspondence theory" (Alston 1996: 37). That might be a good characterization of (DS) as well. A full theory of this kind would spell out when an item has descriptive content, what determines its specific content, and what the relation of "fittingness" consists in. These questions all go beyond the scope of my investigation, partly because they cross over into the territories of metaphysics, philosophy of mind, and philosophy of language that could not be addressed here even if I were ready to address them.

My theory is a descriptive-success theory, hence the label "DS." Discussions of truth often overlook the fact that "true" is a success word. It characterizes sentences, propositions, beliefs, and so forth as being descriptively successful. Calling a belief "true" is very much like saying that a goal is "fulfilled," or that a plan is "executed." All these terms imply that some sort of goal, undertaking, or function has been accomplished. What distinguishes "true" from "fulfilled" or "executed" is that "true" is a term of *descriptive* appraisal. People sort or segregate entities or actions into various categories of success and failure, as a function of whether they live up to the primary aim or function associated with them. Truth and falsity are categories for sorting descriptive projects into successes and failures. Since a content is descriptively successful if and only if it fits reality, correspondence to reality is exactly what descriptive success consists in.[13]

Linguistic evidence that supports my version of the correspondence approach comes from related senses of the word "true." In particular, consider the sense of "true" that means *faithful*. We speak of a "true friend," of being "true to one's word," and of being "true to one's cause." In all these cases, "true" expresses a *relation* of faithfulness or fidelity between a person and another object. Other phrases, such as "true to life" and "true to form," apply to actions or representations that conform to, or are faithful to, some standard. I suggest that the descriptive-success sense of "true" is related to the faithfulness sense of "true." Descriptive success is faithfulness to reality.[14] It

---

[13] Of course, propositions and sentences do not have goals or aims, despite the fact that they are called "true." The thrust of my account, however, is that the root notion of truth is applied to assertion and belief, in which a speaker or subject does have a (default) goal, namely, to describe or represent reality. Propositions and sentences can be considered true (or false) in a derivative fashion, even when they are not believed or uttered by any goal-possessing subject.

[14] About a year after writing this passage, I discover that Wilson espouses a similar idea. Wilson writes: "A representation is true if it is faithful to the world or to an appropriate object in it, or to some standard envisaged or accepted . . ." (1990: 30). Wilson

features a relation between the descriptive item and (some segment of) reality. Thus, the basic intuition of the correspondence approach, that (descriptive) truth involves a relation to reality, is correct.

My invocation of reality brings into focus an important feature of the correspondence theory, which distinguishes it from its competitors. This is the claim that truth requires "*truth makers*": worldly entities of some sort that *make* propositions or other truth bearers true. Obviously, the success of a content in "fitting" reality depends not just on the content but on the portion of reality that it purports to describe. The truth maker element of the correspondence theory, however, is one of its features that invites the most criticism. The standard candidate for truth makers are facts, and the usual form of the correspondence theory says that there is a distinct fact for each true proposition or sentence. "Caesar crossed the Rubicon" is made true by the fact that Caesar crossed the Rubicon, "Abraham Lincoln was assassinated" is made true by the fact that Abraham Lincoln was assassinated, and so forth. Since facts seem to have similar grain and structure as sentences, they seem to be "sentence-shaped pieces of nonlinguistic reality" (Rorty 1991: 4). Such entities, though, are highly dubious. Are there pieces of reality with the same structures as negations, disjunctions, conditionals, existential quantifications, and so forth? Worse yet, classical versions of the correspondence theory, such as those offered by Wittgenstein (1922) and Bertrand Russell (1912), talk of propositions or sentences as "picturing" or "mirroring" the facts. They hold that a truth bearer is true just in case it has a structural isomorphism to a fact, where the parts of the former mirror the parts of the latter in the way that a map mirrors portions of the world. Critics find this ontology highly objectionable, as this passage from Quine indicates:

What on the part of true sentences is meant to correspond to what on the part of reality? If we seek a correspondence word by word, we find ourselves eking reality out with a complement of abstract objects fabricated for the sake of the correspondence. Or perhaps we settle for a correspondence of whole sentences with *facts*; a sentence is true if it reports a fact. But here again we have fabricated substance for an empty doctrine. The world is full of things, variously related, but what, in addition to all that, are facts? They are projected from true sentences for the sake of correspondence. (1987: 213)

In my view, the correspondence theory need not be saddled with sentence-like facts, or facts at all for that matter.[15] Indeed, it is not entirely clear that

also adduces similar examples of truth (and falsity) talk that support the fidelity construal of truth: "Tyler's novel is true to life," "imagine a true red," and "Rodney flew false colors" (1990: 30).

[15] Although I presently wish to avoid commitment to facts as the relata of correspondence, a correspondence theory in which facts are the truth makers has been cleverly defended in recent papers by Sommers (1994, 1997). Sommers disambiguates different senses of the term "fact" and argues that although facts in the relevant sense are not "in" the world, they have reality as properties "of" the real world.

the correspondence theory requires a unique category of objects to serve as truth makers. Perhaps some propositions are made true by concrete events, whereas other propositions are made true by relations among abstract entities. As long as anything that makes a proposition true is part of reality—construed as broadly as possible—this fits the correspondence theory as formulated by (DS). For purposes of analogy, consider the theory of reference. There is no assumption in the theory of reference that only one category of objects can be referred to. All manner of "objects"—not just substances but trajectories, sounds, manners, and amounts—can be referred to. Why, in the case of truth theory, must it be assumed that only one category of things must serve as truth makers?

Even when we focus on a particular category of possible truth makers, moreover, we run into metaphysical controversies over their nature. In the domain of events, some metaphysicians take events and actions to be "fine-grained" entities of a roughly factlike nature (Kim 1993, Goldman 1970, 1994c). Other theorists hold a deliberately unfactlike interpretation of events and actions, slicing them more "coarsely" (Davidson 1980). Each kind of theory, however, countenances events as pieces of reality, things in the world, and each kind of theory might regard them as candidates for truth makers. Consider a case in which the following propositions are all true:

(A) John ran this morning.
(B) John ran for 40 minutes this morning.
(C) John ran eight miles this morning.
(D) John's legs moved with a sequence of angular momenta m_1, m_2, m_3, etc.

According to a coarse-grained approach, a single event—John's run—could be said to make each of these propositions true.[16] According to some versions of the fine-grained approach, there were four different events, and different ones could be said to make the four propositions true. A full account of truth makers, then, would require us to settle this sort of metaphysical dispute. But that is the kind of metaphysical detail about truth theory that lies outside the scope of this work.

Of course, if a coarse-grained metaphysics of truth makers were adopted, the relation of correspondence certainly would not be a one–one relation, as classical versions of the correspondence theory maintain. As illustrated in the previous example, a coarse-grained theory of truth makers would imply that one and the same event could make many different propositions true. This is

---

[16] In suggesting that a coarse-grained theory could count its favored type of events as truth makers, I am not claiming that all proponents of a coarse-grained theory of events would endorse them as truth makers. In particular, Davidson would not; see Davidson 1980.

perfectly acceptable, however, because the correspondence theory is not wedded to one–one correspondence. If repudiation of a one–one relationship makes the "correspondence" label seem inappropriate, I am happy to abandon this label, which in any case suffers from its historical formulations. The crucial thing to retain is the commitment to truth makers, an element that deflationism and other rival theories either reject or ignore.

Given the possibilities being floated here, it should be clear that the correspondence theory is not necessarily committed to sentence-like truth makers, such as disjunctive truth makers, conditional truth makers, and so forth. Suppose there was a run by John this morning but no run by Sally. What makes the disjunctive proposition (E) true?

(E) Either John ran this morning or Sally ran this morning.

The correspondence theory need not say that it is a disjunctive fact: the fact that either John ran this morning or Sally ran this morning. It can say that it is John's run that makes (E) true. So the correspondence theory is not necessarily saddled with the worrisome types of entities that historical versions of it seemed to invoke. However, I shall not try to settle all the metaphysical questions that arise concerning truth makers.

Whatever the truth makers are, a correspondence theory is in a better position than deflationism to explain the sense in which a factually defective discourse could be defective. This problem for deflationism is stressed by Paul Boghossian (1990). Boghossian suggests that deflationism cannot even make sense of the widespread view that certain regions of assertoric discourse, such as moral, aesthetic, or counterfactual discourse, have only an expressive rather than a fact-stating role. Boghossian argues that on the deflationary construal of truth, mere significance and declarativeness suffice for truth conditionality, leaving no real space for factual defectiveness. This problem is readily solved by the correspondence theory, for under this sort of theory, appeal can be made to the absence of the requisite worldly entities that would serve as truth makers for the domain of discourse in question.

Some will object that the (DS) theory is wholly trivial and platitudinous. *Every* approach to truth could concede what (DS) asserts. Since it provides no further details, moreover, it is totally uninformative and unilluminating. My first reply is that it should not be an embarrassment for a theory of truth to be platitudinous. Truth is a very familiar and basic concept, and a correct formulation of its meaning might well be expected to sound familiar and straightforward.

My second reply is to reject the suggestion that (DS) is trivial or uninteresting on the grounds that every approach to truth concedes it. On the contrary, the meaning of "true" specified by (DS) is not one that other approaches do or can accept. So it is certainly not trivial. Like other versions of the correspondence approach, (DS) implies that truths arise from (or supervene on) reality-based truth makers. Its appeal to truth makers, however, or the particular types of truth makers, contrasts with each of the other approaches to truth. Let us review this in detail.

Deflationism is deliberately silent about reality-based truth makers. It is precisely intended to give the meaning of "true" *without* invoking any sort of relation to a truth maker. This conflicts with the meaning that (DS) attaches to "true." Epistemic theories might be construed as invoking truth makers, but if so, their truth makers consist in epistemic states (actual or hypothetical) of believers. Such states or conditions are indeed parts of reality, but in general they are not those parts of reality that make the content descriptively successful. Rather, they are events of *verifying* that the content is descriptively successful.[17] Similarly, instrumentalism might be construed as countenancing truth makers. The truth makers of instrumentalism, however, would not be things that confer *descriptive* success on a truth bearer; they are things that contribute to *instrumental* success. These rival approaches, then, do not accept what (DS) proposes. So there is nothing trivial or uncontentious about the (DS) theory.

A different type of criticism would object to (DS)'s employment of concepts that themselves presuppose the truth concept. For example, (DS) presupposes that some items have meaning or descriptive content. According to many writers on truth, however, the concept of meaning or content should not be presupposed by a theory of truth because the chief purpose of a theory of truth is to provide the groundwork for a semantical theory (Brandom 1994). This objection raises large issues in philosophical methodology, which cannot be adequately canvassed here. Suffice it to say, for present purposes, that I agree with Alston (1996: 260) that truth should be viewed as a *postsemantic* concept. In other words, it is only after a proposition or other meaningful truth bearer is (somehow) identified that the question of the bearer's truth-value can be raised. The theory of truth, as here conceived, is concerned with the question of what makes a bearer have one particular truth-value rather than another. That question is independent of how the bearer comes to have the meaning or content that it does.

A few virtues of the (DS) theory can now be displayed. Since the (DS) theory regards truth as a property or relation, it is obviously quite distinct from the performative theory. Nonetheless, it easily explains the initial attractiveness of the latter. The (DS) theory explains why simple truth ascriptions are acts of endorsement because when you call a sentence or belief descriptively successful, you in effect give it your endorsement, or agree with it. This does not mean that you fail to make a statement, as the performative theory contends;

---

[17] A verificational semanticist might say that these epistemic parts of reality *are* what fit or exemplify the propositional contents. But this theory would combine a verificationist semantics with a correspondence theory of truth.

rather, the speech act of endorsement piggybacks on the speech act of making a statement.

The (DS) theory can also explain the appeal of disquotationalism while showing why it is wrong. It is wrong, as we have seen, because " 'Snow is white' is true" is not meaning-equivalent to "Snow is white." The (DS) theory can account for this by pointing out that " 'Snow is white' is true" characterizes something (namely, "Snow is white") as being descriptively successful, whereas "Snow is white" does not characterize anything as being descriptively successful. Nonetheless, the (DS) theory can also explain why " 'Snow is white' is true" is extensionally equivalent to "Snow is white." Take any instance of the equivalence schema (T), for example,

(S) "Snow is white" is true iff snow is white.

It can be derived from (DS) together with the meaning or content of the quoted sentence. Given the content that the English sentence "Snow is white" actually has, this sentence is descriptively successful if and only if snow is white. Thus, the material equivalence holds.

The (DS) theory also contrasts sharply with minimalism, since it gives a brief and simple definition of "true" and has no need for the infinitely many axioms invoked by Horwich. This accords with Gupta's point that we seem to understand "true" by means of a very economical set of conceptual resources, not the massive conceptual resources demanded by minimalism. It also readily explains what Judith believes when she believes that Einstein's last claim is true: she believes that his claim is descriptively successful. This is a very simple content, not the infinitely long content that would be required by minimalism.

Observe that the (DS) theory is entirely neutral on the question of what "reality" consists in, as a proper theory of truth should be. As noted earlier, a theory of truth should be capable of accommodating not only physicalist and dualist metaphysics but even idealist metaphysics, and (DS) has these capabilities. It is worth noting that the idealist J. M. E. McTaggart was also a correspondence theorist of truth, though he regarded facts as ideal entities, or spiritual substance (McTaggart 1921). I do not myself, of course, wish to endorse idealism. I emphasize this feature of (DS) only to reiterate the point of Section 2.4 that theories of truth should be neutral with respect to the metaphysical realism/antirealism controversies. The (DS) theory possesses this virtue of neutrality.

Although the (DS) theory leaves many issues unresolved, its virtues persuade me that the venerable correspondence approach is basically on the right track. That is what I shall assume in the remainder of this book. As a postscript, however, I shall close this chapter by noting the possibility of a *partial compromise* between correspondence and deflationism.

Foundations

2.7 Partial compatibility between correspondence and deflation?

The theory of truth is a very tangled topic. Without retracting my preferred
view, I nonetheless acknowledge the possibility that some form of deflationism might manage to evade the problems posed in Section 2.5. It cannot be
denied, moreover, that there is a great deal of elegance in disquotationalism,
prosententialism, and minimalism. I can also imagine strides in grammatical
theory that would further enhance the strength and attractiveness of prosententialism. I therefore want to close by pointing out that the possible future
success of such theories would not spell doom for the principal ideas of correspondence.

Most brands of deflationism have two parts, a positive part and a negative
part. The positive part is the substantive portion of the theory that explains
what the word "true" means, or how it functions in the language, for example,
as a device for semantic ascent, as a prosentence-forming operator, or what
have you. The negative part is the "commentary" portion that rejects certain
elements of the correspondence approach, for example, the claim that each
truth is made true by the existence of a corresponding fact. What I wish to
point out is that the positive part of deflationist theories is often compatible
with elements of correspondence, even if the negative part is not. So one
might adopt one of these positive theories without giving up on correspondence, particularly the existence of robust, worldly truth makers. Admittedly,
the part of deflationism that invites the label "deflationary" is typically the
negative part. If that part is omitted, the remaining doctrine might not deserve
the label. Be that as it may, all I am saying is that the positive, constructive
portions of deflationary theories are often compatible with the critical elements of correspondence.

However, as Marian David has observed (in a personal communication),
since each version of the correspondence theory gives a meaning for "true"
and each version of deflationism gives an *incompatible* meaning for "true," it
is hard to see how any two such approaches can be reconciled. What can be
suggested, however, is that a correspondence approach to truth might capture
some non-definitional *fact* about truth even if some hypothetical deflationist
formula gives the uniquely correct *meaning* of truth. I anticipated this possibility already in remarks at the beginning of the chapter. Although the definition of "truth" was presented as the primary aim of a truth theory, a
secondary aim was contemplated of specifying the nature of truth, or some
facts about the truth property. I now point out that the correspondence idea
might be introduced in the secondary project even if it is rejected in the *definition* of "truth."[18]

---

[18] Actually, for purposes of this book, I could accept an even more modest role for
correspondence. It suffices for present purposes that only in some, not all, domains of
discourse does truth involve correspondence to reality. It might be conceded, for

The general idea of compatibility between deflation and correspondence is explicitly acknowledged by at least one leading deflationist, Paul Horwich, and hinted at by at least one other. Here is a passage from Horwich that clearly articulates his stand on this issue:

> Admittedly, minimalism does not *explain what truth is* [by reference to correspondence]. But it does not deny that truths *do* correspond—in *some* sense—to the facts. And it does not dispute the existence of relationships between truth, reference, and predicate-satisfaction. Thus we might hope to accommodate much of what the correspondence theorist wishes to say without retreating an inch from our deflationary position . . .
> The line of thought leading to the correspondence theory begins with the innocuous idea that whenever a sentence or proposition is true, it is true *because* something in the world is a certain way—something typically external to the sentence or proposition. For example, . . . "Snow is white" is *made true by* the fact that snow is white. These observations are perfectly consistent with minimalism . . . Thus we can be perfectly comfortable with the idea that each truth is made true by the existence of a corresponding fact. (1990: 110–12)

I interpret Horwich to be saying that his official minimalist theory of "true," given by the equivalence schema (T), is *silent* and hence *neutral* about whether propositions are made true by things in the world. There are properties of truth not mentioned by the equivalence schema, among them the property that sentences or propositions are made true by elements in the world. Obviously this is something perfectly compatible with the correspondence theme I have stressed.

Horwich is not the only (so-called) deflationist who says things that are music to the ears of a correspondence theorist. Here is Quine, an arch-deflationist:

> [A philosopher] is right [to think] that truth should hinge on reality, and it does. No sentence is true but reality makes it so . . . [T]he truth predicate serves . . . to point through the sentence to the reality; it serves as a reminder that though sentences are mentioned, reality is still the whole point. (1971: 10–11)

This too echoes the idea that what make sentences true are worldly truth makers. How is this compatible with disquotationalism? Although "is true" is just a logical device of semantic ascent, according to Quine, which adds no new substantive content to ordinary indicative statements, such statements are already about reality. Since sentences already aspire to describe reality, it is

example, that in some truth-valuable domains such as mathematics, logic, and modality, no good sense can be made of a "reality" that true items must fit. Nonetheless, correspondence might be required in other areas of truth talk, including propositions about the physical world and human affairs. I do not advocate this position, but it is certainly a fallback option.

reality that renders their descriptive mission a success or a failure. The truth operator just inherits this property.[19]

To summarize, I believe that the various rivals of the correspondence theory are subject to crippling objections, so that the correspondence theory, while requiring further metaphysical clarification, is still the best bet. But even if some form of positive deflationism can surmount its obstacles and be rendered fully attractive, this would not force us to relinquish the basic correspondence idea that what *makes* sentences or propositions true are real-world truth makers. The tenability of this basic idea is all that is required for the veritistic epistemology I shall develop in the remainder of this book. Actually, it might be argued that the epistemological project of the book is compatible even with full-fledged deflationism. The only requirement is that epistemic, pragmatic, and relativist theories of truth be excluded. This is a possible alternative position available to me, which I shall not try to settle definitively. Officially, I shall proceed on the assumption that some form of the correspondence theory is correct. But little will be said, in the rest of the book, on the subject of truth theory. Anyone who wishes to interpret the remainder of the project in deflationist terms will find few if any obstacles to that interpretation.

[19] A third deflationist who sometimes sounds like he is disclaiming a conflict with correspondence is Robert Brandom (1994). Interpretation of Brandom's position is a subtle matter, however, for he does deny a "robust" correspondence between claims and facts (1994: 330), and his treatment usually seems to exemplify the epistemic approach, as when he says, "Being true is then to be understood as being *properly* taken-true (believed)" (1994: 291).

THREE

The Framework

3.1 *Alternative conceptions of social epistemology*

CHAPTERS 1 and 2 laid the foundations for a veritistic approach to social epistemology. People have interests, both intrinsic and extrinsic, in acquiring knowledge (true belief) and avoiding error. It therefore makes sense to have a discipline that evaluates intellectual practices by their causal contributions to knowledge or error. This is how I conceive of epistemology: as a discipline that evaluates practices along truth-linked (veritistic) dimensions. Social epistemology evaluates specifically social practices along these dimensions.

This chapter articulates the framework of veritistic social epistemology in greater detail. Before turning to that task, however, let me consider some rival conceptions of social epistemology, to see why they are less appealing than veritism. These competitors fall under three headings: (A) *consensus consequentialism*, (B) *pragmatism* or *utility consequentialism*, and (C) *pure proceduralism*.

3.1.A *Consensus consequentialism*

This approach would replace the truth-linked outcomes of veritism (true belief, false belief, and so forth) with agreement and disagreement. Instead of evaluating social practices in terms of their veritistic outcomes, it would evaluate them by their tendencies to promote agreement or disagreement. It assumes that the aim of intellectual practices is not to produce true belief, but simply consensus, so practices are better to the extent that they promote consensus and worse to the extent that they promote dissensus.

Many writers on argumentation, dialogue, public reason, and the public sphere may appear to share this fundamental idea, including Jürgen Habermas (1984, 1990, 1996), John Rawls (1993), Bruce Ackerman (1989), and Frans van Eemeren and Rob Grootendorst (1984). They propose consensus as the chief aim of dialogical activities, or public debate. Thus, Habermas writes: "Thus all arguments . . . require the same basic form of organization, which subordinates the eristic means to the end of developing *intersubjective conviction* by the force of the better argument" (1984: i. 36; emphasis added). This approach has a plausible ring to it, since when we argue with one another, we typically try to get the interlocutor to agree; and the job of mediators is to help arguing parties settle their dispute or reach agreement. A second argument for agreement-based evaluation would appeal to science. Philosophers of science often cite objectivity in the sense of *intersubjectivity* as the distinguishing mark of science. Bayesians, for example, sometimes defend their method as the proper method of science because its repeated use allegedly breeds convergence toward the same subjective probabilities or degrees of belief (Earman 1992: 137–8). These perspectives lend support to consensus consequentialism, but they do not provide convincing reasons to substitute consensus for knowledge as the basic value in epistemology.

Several of the abovementioned writers approach the topics of discourse and public debate primarily from the vantage point of moral, social, or political philosophy. Rawls's conception of "public reason" is expressly tailored to the political context, and his treatment of the "objectivity" of reason in terms of mutual agreement is precisely addressed to *practical* reasoning, that is, moral or political reasoning (Rawls 1993: 116–20). Similarly, much of Habermas's writing, and specifically his notion of the public sphere, is dedicated to the theory of democracy. Here it is unsurprising that agreement should be highlighted. Whether or not contractarianism is the best approach to justice or political legitimacy, it is undeniable that one aim of social discourse is to make collective plans for coordinating action and organizing society. In this context, proposals and procedures that elicit agreement from all parties are desirable. But our main topic is not political philosophy or political discourse.[1] Epistemology is interested in knowledge, and most knowledge is not concerned with establishing principles of government that everybody can find legitimate or binding. So political philosophy's reason to be concerned with agreement is not a reason for epistemology to focus on agreement. In any case, the primary species of "agreement" appropriate to political philosophy is not agreement in *belief* but agreement in *action commitments*. The latter certainly falls outside of epistemology (at least as concerns its principal end).

If we concentrate on discourse in the factual realm rather than discourse for the sake of coordinating action or organizing society, it seems clear that consensus is not the sole or primary aim. Three examples will illustrate how little value is accorded to the production of agreement *per se*. A totalitarian practice of state-controlled news and the suppression of all countervailing views might be very effective in an Orwellian society, effective, that is, in producing massive (if not unanimous) agreement. But who would consider this an epistemically appropriate practice? Similarly, if the sole aim of trial pro-

---

[1] Chapter 10, of course, is dedicated to the realm of politics. But that is because, as we shall see, democracy also has an interest in knowledge in the sense of true belief, not merely agreement and mutual commitment on courses of action.

ceedings were to promote agreement, an ideal jury-selection procedure might be one that is deliberately biased toward one party, chosen, let us say, at random. Such a biased procedure might select a jury composed exclusively of the selected party's loyalists and friends. This procedure would certainly foster juror agreement, but intuitively it is absurd. A third example has a similar flavor. Suppose beliefs could be induced by pills, and specific beliefs could be induced by adjusting the pills' chemistry. Would the following be a good method of scientific theory acceptance? Take all rival theories and let one be chosen at random. Then adjust the pills' chemistry to that theory and have scientists in the field swallow them. This would vastly simplify the conduct of science, and would be wonderfully efficient at manufacturing scientific agreement. Yet it is obviously a ridiculous scientific method. If agreement were the sole aim of science, however, why would anything be wrong with it?

These objections only succeed, of course, against *pure* consensualism. If we consider a modified theory that makes epistemic propriety a matter of the *rational* promotion of agreement, for example, these criticisms will not apply. Presumably, totalitarian news control, deliberately ordained bias, and randomized chemical control of belief do not satisfy the standard of *rational* agreement promotion. This new suggestion, however, moves us away from a purely consequentialist approach—where the consequence is agreement or disagreement—toward a proceduralist approach. So I shall return to the rationality criterion under heading (C), which addresses proceduralism.

For now, let us concentrate on pure consensus consequentialism. The illusion that science and factual discourse aim at agreement might be fostered by the fact that agreement is often sought and used in intellectual life. First, when we argue, we try to persuade others to share our beliefs. Second, when we form beliefs, we frequently rely on the consensus of others to guide us. These phenomena might give the impression that agreement is central. On closer inspection, however, it is clear that the real goal is true belief rather than agreement, at least when the goals are purely intellectual. When I try to persuade others of my beliefs, it is because I take my beliefs to be true and want my audience to share those truths. Not all attempts at persuasion, of course, stem from genuine conviction in the thesis advanced; they often have entirely different and unscrupulous motives. Where persuasion attempts are grounded in ulterior motives, however, the goal is not purely intellectual. In the second case, where agreement is used as evidence to settle belief, one is pursuing truth for oneself, and the agreement of others is simply taken as *diagnostic* of truth. Agreement, however, is not always diagnostic of truth. If I know that the subjects of a psychological study have all been exposed to the same compelling illusion, or that certain people have all read the same political exposé by a certain scurrilous author, I will not accept their rendering of the facts simply because they agree. Thus, the notion that agreement is the fundamental aim or guide in matters intellectual is surely an illusion.

3.1.B *Pragmatism, or utility consequentialism*

As a program for social epistemology, pragmatism is the view that social belief-causing practices should be evaluated by the amount of utility (happiness, desire satisfaction, value realization) that they would produce. Just as act utilitarianism says that acts should be evaluated by their utility outcomes and rule utilitarianism says that rules should be evaluated by their utility outcomes, so pragmatism or epistemic utilitarianism would say that epistemic practices should be evaluated by their utility outcomes. This approach could be erected into a general framework for social epistemology.

One thing that attracts certain theorists to pragmatism is despair over truth. Correspondence truth appeals to a mind–world relation, and theorists skeptical of such a relation regard veritism as unpromising. "Success" construed as goal fulfillment, desire satisfaction, or value realization ostensibly involves something firmer than truth, so it has its initial attractions. It takes little reflection to realize, however, that pragmatism so construed offers no improvement for anyone worried about the mind–world relation. The notions of desire satisfaction and goal fulfillment are as deeply immersed in the waters of correspondence as the concept of truth. There is a precise analogue between a belief being true and a desire or goal being fulfilled. In both cases there is a relation between mental states and reality. Only the "direction of fit" is different.[2] Any hope of escaping this sort of relation is no reason to prefer pragmatism to veritism.

The most explicit recent defender of pragmatism, Stephen Stich (1990), encounters exactly this problem in arguing for pragmatism over a truth-based epistemology. Stich's central objection to a truth-based epistemology is that there are rival candidates to the aim of true belief—what he calls true* belief, true** belief, and so forth—and no reason to prefer plain old true belief to the others. Stich's argument rests on the claim that true* belief, true** belief, and so on represent alternative mapping functions from beliefs construed as brain-state tokens (mental sentences) to truth conditions, functions that are just as legitimate as the commonly sanctioned one. If this were right, however, a precisely analogous problem would apply to pragmatism. There would be equally legitimate alternatives for the mapping function from desire states to conditions of fulfillment (or satisfaction), and we would have no reason to heed the aim of ordinary desire fulfillment as compared with desire fulfillment*, fulfillment**, and so forth. Moreover, since having a reason to prefer something, according to pragmatism, depends on that thing's best satisfying one's intrinsic desires, if there are alternative accounts of satisfaction (namely, sat-

---

[2] Beliefs aim to fit an antecedently existing world; they have a "mind-to-world" direction of fit. Desires aim to have the world fit them; they have a "world-to-mind" direction of fit. If fitness is lacking in the first case, the belief needs adjusting. If fitness is lacking in the second case, the world needs adjusting. See Searle 1983: 7–8.

isfaction*, satisfaction**, and the like) and hence alternative accounts of what one intrinsically desires, it is impossible to have a determinate reason to prefer one thing rather than another.[3] Thus, pragmatism would run afoul of precisely the same problem as the truth approach, assuming that the latter is a bona fide problem.

In fact, the truth approach does not have a bona fide problem, as Alston makes abundantly clear (1996: 258–61). Stich purports to identify a superabundance of different truth-like relations, with no principled way to choose among them. But the alternative interpretation functions he considers are not different truth relations; they are merely different ways of assigning propositional contents, that is, truth conditions, to bearers of such contents. Truth *conditions* only constitute the semantic content of a belief; they do not specify a truth relation. The truth relation is the relation that determines the truth *value* for a proposition given the proposition's content (or truth conditions) plus the actual state of the world. Stich goes no distance toward showing that there are many truth-like relations comparable to the standard one. As Alston puts it, Stich is flying under false colors. He purports to display an uncomfortably large array of choices between different truth-like relations, but actually he presents only different ways of assigning meanings or contents to brain states.

This point is important for assessing the force of Stich's critique of the veritistic approach. He criticizes the idea that true belief should be intrinsically valued on the grounds that it is not clear why we should intrinsically prefer it to true* belief, true** belief, and so on. Similarly, he criticizes the idea that true belief is instrumentally valuable because it isn't clear that it is instrumentally preferable to true* belief, true** belief, and so on. But once we see that true*, true**, and so forth are not genuine truth-like relations, these criticisms evaporate.

Stich offers an additional reason, however, for challenging the instrumental value of true belief, a reason that does not rest on the alleged multiplicity of truth-like relations. He claims that it isn't clear that true belief is generally better than *false* belief at achieving our goals. That true belief is not *always* a better means to our goals than false belief is illustrated by his example of a man who dies in a plane crash (Stich 1990: 122–3). Such a man would have been better off with a false belief about his flight time rather than a true belief, because a false belief would have kept him from boarding the flight. Stich continues: "it would be no easy matter to show that believing the truth is *generally* (or even occasionally!) instrumentally optimal" (1990: 124).

Contrary to what Stich here implies, there is an important class of propositions for which it is certainly true that believing the true members of this class leads to goal fulfillment. Consider the class of means–ends propositions,

---

[3] Thanks to Joel Pust for this sentence's formulation of the problem.

which take the general form, "If I adopt means M, then I will achieve end E." Assume that the agent values E more than anything else in the picture, that she is in a position to adopt means M if she chooses to do so, and there is no other means M^* that she believes would achieve end E. Then if the agent believes the means–end proposition, she will adopt means M. Furthermore, if this means–end proposition is *true* and M is adopted, it follows necessarily that goal E will be achieved. So if she believes the means–end proposition and it is true, goal E will be fulfilled. This tight connection between true belief and goal fulfillment does not hold, of course, for all true beliefs, only for beliefs in means–ends propositions. But there is also a general relationship in this direction to the extent that beliefs of all sorts inferentially feed into means–ends beliefs. So contrary to Stich, there is a systematic, though not invariable, pattern of links connecting true belief to goal fulfillment.[4]

---

[4] Paul Horwich (1990: 45–6) generalizes this point about means–ends propositions from categorical belief to degrees of belief. Horwich's demonstration can be rendered as follows (where I adopt my own notation and fill in a number of details that Horwich leaves implicit). Suppose an agent is given a choice between actions X_1 and X_2, and the possible outcomes of these actions are exhausted by the mutually exclusive outcomes $O_1, O_2, \ldots$ Let $V(O_1), V(O_2), \ldots$ be the values that the agent places on these outcomes, and let $B(O_j/X_i)$ be the degree of belief that the agent attaches to the conditional proposition, "If the agent did X_i, then outcome O_j would result." Next let $p(O_j/X_i)$ be the objective probability that attaches to this same conditional proposition. (Here I go beyond Horwich's language; he does not talk explicitly of objective probabilities.) Now let $V(X_i)$ be the objective prospective value of the agent's performing X_i. This is written as follows:

$$V(X_i) = [V(O_1).p(O_1/X_i)] + [V(O_2).p(O_2/X_i)] + \ldots$$

Finally, let $EV(X_i)$ be the agent's expected value from performing X_i.

$$EV(X_i) = [V(O_1).B(O_1/X_i)] + [V(O_2).B(O_2/X_i)] + \ldots$$

Assuming that agents always act so as to maximize their expected value, Horwich proves that the closer the agent's degrees of belief are to the truth, that is, to the objective probabilities, the more likely it is that her choice of action will be correct, that is, the better her choice of action will be given the objective probabilities. To illustrate the idea, suppose that the objective probabilities are either 1 or 0. Then the objectively more valuable action is the one that would lead, with probability 1, to the more valued outcome. That objectively more valuable action is more likely to be chosen the closer the agent's degrees of belief are to 1 where the objective probabilities are 1.

These ideas may be illustrated with the following example. I am considering a business deal and my options are to accept the deal (X_1) or to reject it (X_2). The possible outcomes of these actions are: reap a bonanza (O_1), suffer a financial disaster (O_2), or break even (O_3). The utilities I assign to these outcomes are +1,000,000, −1,000,000, and 0 respectively. Suppose that the objective probability of a disaster if I accept the deal is 1, whereas the objective probabilities of the other two outcomes if I accept the deal are each 0. The objective probability of breaking even if I reject the deal is 1, and the objective probabilities of the other outcomes if I reject the deal are each 0. Calculations show that −1,000,000 is the objective prospective value of acceptance and 0 is the objective prospective value of rejection. So the objectively better choice is rejection. Under what degrees of belief would I be led to this superior choice? I will certainly be led to it if my degrees of belief match the objective probabilities. I will also be led to it if I have correct degrees of belief associated with rejection and semiaccurate degrees of belief associated with acceptance, for example, a .50 degree of belief that acceptance would lead to disaster and .25 degrees of belief associated with each of the other two outcomes. In

However, we should not rest our defense of veritism wholly on the instrumental value of true belief. As argued earlier, true belief is also sometimes valued intrinsically. Our desire to know what caused the dinosaur extinction is not merely a means to fulfilling some further desire. Second, even when it is not valued purely for its own sake, truth is often *constitutive* of certain values rather than merely instrumental to them. In the law, for example, it is a prime value of the system that it seeks to convict only the guilty, that is, the *truly* guilty. To satisfy this value, it is necessary for factfinders to make accurate determinations of who is and who is not guilty; that is, it is necessary to form true beliefs. (This theme will be developed in Chapter 9.) Similarly, in many walks of life we wish to honor or reward people for deeds they actually performed, not for fictional accomplishments. So award selection committees need to form true beliefs about who genuinely performed deserving actions.

Finally, only a little reflection is needed to reveal that, contrary to pragmatism's intent, allegiance to a social epistemology based on pragmatism would actually constrain people to concern themselves with truth. After all, what would pragmatism require when applied to social epistemology? It would require people to choose those social practices that best promote whatever it is that they intrinsically value. But how are the right practices to be chosen? They will only be chosen (or are most likely to be chosen) if people have *true beliefs* about the consequences of the various practices. If people have significantly mistaken beliefs about those consequences, they will choose the wrong practices, the ones that will not maximally promote their values. So whatever people intrinsically value, choosing the best practices that conduce to those values requires true belief. To paraphrase Hilary Kornblith (1993: 371), people who care about acting in ways that further the things they care about have pragmatic reasons to favor epistemic practices that are effective in generating truths, whether they otherwise care about truth or not.

3.1.C *Proceduralism*

The three approaches we have considered thus far, including veritism, are all species of consequentialism. Are there approaches that eschew consequences and fasten on the intrinsic merits of intellectual practices to judge their epistemic worth or propriety? There are such approaches in the literature, but none, I shall argue, is an adequate candidate for a comprehensive social

---

this scenario, $-250,000$ is the expected value of acceptance whereas 0 is the expected value of rejection. So I would still choose rejection, the objectively superior action, even with these semiaccurate degrees of belief. However, if my degrees of belief were totally inaccurate—for example, if I had degree of belief 0 for the proposition that acceptance would lead to disaster—I would make the inferior choice. So in general it is better to have accurate rather than inaccurate degrees of belief (vis-à-vis means–ends propositions).

epistemology. Moreover, few of these approaches remain *purely* procedural when examined carefully.

One nonconsequentialist criterion, mentioned earlier, is rationality. An initial problem with this proposal is its ambiguity, or indeterminacy. Which epistemic practices, exactly, qualify as rational? That is a longstanding debate, and the prospects for resolution are not bright unless one turns to consequentialist considerations. Consider Bayesianism, for example.[5] While it has many advocates, it also has its detractors (see Earman 1992). How should its claim to epistemic rationality be settled? It is unlikely to be settled without turning to consequentialist criteria. Indeed, when asked to defend their approach, Bayesians commonly offer consequentialist rationales, such as Dutch Book theorems. These theorems show that if you violate probabilistic coherence, you are liable to suffer monetary losses from betting, and monetary losses presumably cause disutility. So this kind of rationale falls under pragmatism, a species of consequentialism. Other defenses of Bayesianism point out that Bayesian methods ultimately lead different users to probabilistic convergence, or lead in the limit to truth. These defenses are also in the spirit of consequentialism—consensus consequentialism in the first case and veritism in the second—rather than pure proceduralism.

Another fundamental problem with the rationality criterion is limited scope. There are many social intellectual practices that a wide-ranging social epistemology should hope to assess, and the rationality criterion seems incapable of offering insight about them. Consider simple speech acts in which speakers deliver reports or testimony to hearers. Which of these reports are epistemically proper or improper? Unlike formal argumentation using premises and conclusions, there is no obvious standard such as logical validity by which to judge whether a simple statement is rational. Is it rational to deliver a report if and only if one believes it? In what sense of rationality does this precept allegedly follow? Another problem for social epistemology is the allocation of speech opportunities under limited-capacity communication channels. How would the rationality criterion generate any evaluations or guidance in this arena?

One clear example of a rationality approach to social epistemology is that of Keith Lehrer and Carl Wagner (1981). They consider cases in which inquirers assign credal trust or "respect" to one another's opinions. Each person, they argue, should update his opinion on a target question to reflect other people's opinions on the same question, as a function of the degree of trust accorded to those other people. Lehrer and Wagner contend that rationality demands a series of iterated opinion changes on the part of each inquirer.

[5] Is Bayesianism a *social* practice? Not in general, I agree. But when applied to the task of making inferences from the reports or testimony of others, it does qualify as a social practice. So it will be treated in Chapter 4.

Under very weak conditions, a series of appropriate changes by all inquirers leads toward consensus (as proved by De Groot 1974). Although this might appear to be a form of consensus consequentialism, Lehrer and Wagner do not rationalize their proposed procedure by appeal to consensus. They defend it on grounds of intrapersonal *consistency*, and simply demonstrate that consensus follows as a byproduct.

Although this is a genuine example of pure proceduralism, it seems inadequate as a comprehensive basis for social epistemology. Many important social activities performed by scientific and other communities cannot be addressed within this framework, such as coordinated evidence gathering, proposing and rebutting arguments, allocating speech opportunities, and creating incentives for research and investigation. In short, the vast majority of social practices that belong under social epistemology fall outside the purview of this approach. Even in the domain of reasoning from the opinions of others, their proposal is limited. It does not address the general question of how to assess the expertise or competence of others, but simply adopts subjectively chosen assessments as givens. So it is really a proposal for a specific inferential practice, not a general framework for social epistemology on a par with veritism.

A different procedural approach to social discourse is due to Habermas, especially in his more recent writings. This procedural approach is well encapsulated by Seyla Benhabib:

[T]he model of practical discourse developed in this ethical theory is a radically proceduralist one. It views normative dialogue as a conversation of justification taking place under the constraints of an "ideal speech situation." The procedural constraints of the ideal speech situation are that each participant must have an equal chance to initiate and to continue communication; each must have an equal chance to make assertions, recommendations, and explanations; all must have equal chances to express their wishes, desires, and feelings; and finally, within dialogue, speakers must be free to thematize those power relations that in ordinary contexts would constrain the wholly free articulation of opinions and positions. Together these conditions specify a norm of communication that can be named that of *egalitarian reciprocity*. (1992: 89)

Note first that this procedural approach of egalitarian reciprocity is restricted to practical discourse, or normative dialogue. This restriction makes it unsuitable for the purposes of a general social epistemology, which certainly encompasses discourses of a purely factual, nonnormative kind. Could this restriction simply be dropped? It could be, but the result would hardly generate intuitively suitable norms for social epistemic practices. A fair chunk of public speech is transmitted over one-way communication channels; for example, news reports delivered over radio or television. Since these forums typically offer no opportunity for listeners to engage in dialogue, they violate the terms of Habermas's ideal speech situation. Is there really anything epistemically faulty in this kind of discourse practice? I think not. Where political decisions are to be made, equal opportunity to voice one's opinion may well be in order. But this does not apply to the transmission of news. Similarly, consider scientific and academic journals that publish only specialized work by highly trained researchers. Is this an objectionable discourse practice because not everyone has an equal chance to make assertions? Surely not. Interpreted literally, then, Habermas's approach to discourse lacks the requisite scope for social epistemology; and if it is straightforwardly generalized, it implies counterintuitive judgments.

A final example of a procedural approach is a set of criteria proposed by Helen Longino (1990) for the social practice of science, criteria which contain some Habermasian overtones. Longino stresses objectivity as the principal aim of science, and states four criteria by which objectivity should be measured:

Scientific communities will be objective to the degree that they satisfy four criteria necessary for achieving the transformative dimension of critical discourse: (1) there must be recognized avenues for the criticism of evidence, of methods, and of assumptions and reasoning; (2) there must exist shared standards that critics can invoke; (3) the community as a whole must be responsive to such criticism; (4) intellectual authority must be shared equally among qualified practitioners. (1990: 76)

As presented here, Longino's criteria seem to be selected for their intrinsic merits. Examined more carefully, however, Longino's treatment turns out to have consequentialist contours, and a deeper analysis would warrant specifically veritistic foundations.

At the beginning of her chapter on values and objectivity, Longino characterizes objectivity as "the willingness to let our beliefs be determined by 'the facts' or by some impartial and nonarbitrary criteria rather than by our wishes as to how things ought to be" (1990: 62). Longino proceeds to emphasize how objectivity requires the avoidance of partiality or subjective preference, and argues that this avoidance is best secured by criticism from the scientific community, which is precisely what her four criteria are intended to promote. It seems clear, then, that her general methodological framework is a consequentialist one: the virtue of various social practices is their tendency to promote greater impartiality and nonarbitrariness.

Perhaps this should lead us to posit a new kind of consequentialism, one that assigns fundamental epistemic value to impartiality and nonarbitrariness. But I believe that the desirability of these traits is instrumental in character. Partiality and arbitrariness tend to breed falsehood and error, whereas impartiality and nonarbitrariness foster accuracy and truth. So although Longino does not say so, the ultimate rationale for her favored social practices seems to be veritistic in character.

This concludes my review of some leading candidates for an alternative approach to social epistemology. All are found wanting, and in several cases their flaws point to the importance of veritistic factors. Thus, the initial attractiveness of veritism, explained at the beginning of Chapter 1, has now been confirmed.[6]

3.2 *Employing veritism*

We have seen the weaknesses of veritism's rivals, but what of veritism itself? Does it not also suffer from inherent weaknesses, albeit of a different nature? In this section and the next, I examine two fundamental types of worries people might have about veritism. This section addresses the problem of employing the norm of veritism, and the next section examines the problem of circularity.

Under veritism we are asked to select the social practices that would best advance the cause of knowledge. How is that selection to be made? How is the standard of veritistic value to be employed? Don't people need prior intellectual practices to employ it? How should *these* practices, in turn, be selected? Can any of them guarantee that the practices selected with their help will indeed be veritistically good? Can they guarantee that disputes or disagreements over veritistic merit will be settled? If guarantees of these kinds cannot be offered, what good is veritism?

First, let us introduce a bit of notation and terminology. Call the set of practices from which veritism wishes to make a selection the *target* practices. Call the practices used to select among the target practices the *selection* practices. The problems raised in the previous paragraph, then, include the following: (1) Which selection practices should be used to choose among the target practices? (2) Is there any guarantee that the selection practices will accurately

---

[6] It is worth mentioning some recent approaches to epistemology that are even more "deeply" social than mine. They are, from my perspective, *social* approaches to *individual* epistemology. I have in mind Richard Miller (1995) and Bruce Brower (1996). Both Miller and Brower claim that norms for evaluating (what I would call) individual belief-forming practices arise from cooperative activity (Miller) or a social contract (Brower) in the pursuit of truth. Both approaches are clearly social and also clearly veritistic. Because of their veritistic orientation, I do not see them as rivals to my form of veritism. Moreover, I do not interpret them as full-scale social epistemologies in my sense because they do not deal comprehensively with social or interpersonal practices but at most with the practice of relying on the assertions of others. In fact, they deal heavily with individual practices such as perceptual belief formation.

Note that a variety of other social approaches within philosophy are not addressed here because their sectors of philosophy lie outside of epistemology. They may be in the neighborhood of epistemology, even relevant to epistemology, but not epistemology *per se*. For example, there is Saul Kripke's (1982) interpretation of Wittgenstein on rule-following that emphasizes community practices. And there is Robert Brandom's (1994) account of assertive content in terms of the social practices of giving and asking for reasons. I take these projects to be semantical, and therefore not forays (primarily) into epistemology. No doubt there are significant connections between epistemology and semantics, but it would take us too far afield to consider these relationships.

identify the veritistically best target practices? (3) Is there any guarantee that the process of selection will lead different veritistic theorists to agree on the choice of target practices?

Obviously, when people *first* engage in veritistic selection, selection practices must be deployed that have not previously been subjected to veritistic analysis. That just trivially follows from the assumption that this is the first exercise of veritistic selection. The enterprise of veritistic analysis, then, must begin through the medium of heretofore unanalyzed selection processes. Whether these selection processes are native, untutored practices or refined, culturally acquired practices, they could be veritistically deficient. Notice, however, that there is no difference on this score between veritism and any of its rivals. If the standard of evaluation for social epistemology were, for example, consensus consequentialism rather than veritism, it would still be necessary to utilize some sort of selection procedures to decide which practices are optimal according to the consensus consequentialist criterion. Whichever selection practices are used, they could be veritistically deficient.[7] They could lead people to suppose that certain target practices are optimal promoters of consensus when in fact they are not. Thus, other standards or criteria of social-epistemic evaluation are also in danger of being misused, just like veritism.

Clearly, there is no logical guarantee that the veritistic enterprise—that is, the enterprise of *trying* to identify veritistically desirable social practices—will succeed. But the absence of guaranteed success is no count against veritism as compared with its rivals. Like any enterprise, the project of veritism could fail; but unless one is a total defeatist, that is not much of a reason against trying.

Similar points apply to the problem of reaching consensus on the veritistically best practices. There is no guarantee that two people who both try to identify the veritistically best practices will agree. If their initial selection practices differ and they staunchly resist change, they might easily select different target practices. This applies equally, however, to veritism's rivals. People seeking to identify *pragmatically* best practices could easily disagree, especially if their selection practices differ. In fact, for any enterprise of an intellectual nature, shared goals offer no guarantee of agreement on the best means to those goals. Potential disagreement is a fact of life all enterprises must live with; it is not a peculiar disability of veritism.

Having conceded the possibility of pessimistic scenarios, let me now illus-

---

[7] It might be argued that if consensus consequentialism is the correct standard of epistemic goodness, appliers of it should not seek to identify practices that *truly* satisfy it but only practices about which there is *consensus belief* that they satisfy it. Intuitively, however, this seems wrong. A genuine proponent of consensus consequentialism should seek to identify practices that accurately (truly) satisfy it. I view this as an additional hint that consensus consequentialism is misguided: its own application (tacitly) invokes the standard of veritism.

trate how veritistic epistemology might prosper: how improved social practices can, at least in principle, be identified, and how agreement can be reached even by parties who initially use different selection practices. I shall proceed with the help of an extended example involving a theorem about expert opinions.

Suppose that a local weather bureau wishes to establish the veritistically best practice for predicting the weather. It has five weather forecasters available and wishes to "pool" or amalgamate their daily judgments about the next day's weather into a single prediction by the bureau, and they wish to maximize the bureau's forecasting accuracy. What social practice of amalgamating the experts' opinions is veritistically best? To make the case more concrete, suppose that two of these forecasters each has a 90 percent success rate in making categorical predictions of rain versus nonrain, and the other three have a 60 percent success rate each. These numbers are assumed to represent their propensities or competences in forecasting, not simply their past track record. Finally, assume that the forecasters' judgments are reached independently, and that the two possibilities, rain or nonrain, are a priori equally likely. How should their daily predictions be pooled to arrive at the bureau's judgment? (I shall assume that this judgment constitutes a "belief" on the part of the weather bureau construed as a corporate entity.)

At least three possibilities present themselves. The first is *unweighted majority rule*: the prediction favored by a majority of the experts should be the bureau's prediction (belief). This yields a probability of correctness for the bureau of .877. A second possibility is *dictatorial rule*: let the bureau adopt the prediction of its most competent expert. In the present case of a tie for maximal competence—the two experts with 90 percent accuracy—the bureau chooses one of the two at random and lets his or her judgment constitute the bureau's judgment. This would yield a correctness probability for the bureau of .900. A third scheme would use *weighted voting*. A theorem due to several independent authors (Shapley and Grofman 1984, Nitzan and Paroush 1982) says that a maximally truth-conducive weighting scheme is one that assigns a weight w_i to each expert i that satisfies the following formula:

$$w_i \propto \log \left(p_i / (1 - p_i) \right)$$

where pi represents the probability that expert i makes a true prediction. In the present example, one weight assignment that would conform with this rule is: .392, .392, .072, .072, .072. That is, the higher voting weight, .392, is given to each of the two forecasters with 90 percent accuracy, and the lower weight, .072, is assigned to each of the three forecasters with 60 percent accuracy. (This might seem like a large differential between the two levels of expertise. Notice, however, that the forecasters with 60 percent accuracy perform only slightly better than chance.) Using a weighted voting scheme with these weights, and letting the weighed vote of the five forecasters determine the bureau's own judgment, the bureau's probability of correctness is .927. This is veritistically better than the .900 accuracy of dictatorial rule and the .877 accuracy of unweighted majority rule. How does the weighted voting scheme manage to improve on the opinion of a single maximally competent expert? Because it implies that the joint opinion of the two most competent experts is followed whenever they agree, but when they disagree the opinion of a majority of the remaining experts is followed. In general, having the bureau follow this weighted voting scheme is the veritistically best practice available to it (when competence information is available about the individual experts). In a second interpretation of the rules, they might be interpreted as the best way for an otherwise uninformed bystander (rather than a corporate entity like the weather bureau) to form his or her belief on the subject. The same scheme is still the best.

Let us now ask how someone might arrive at the view that the weighted voting practice is veritistically optimal, or at least better than its two rivals. First, someone might use mathematics to prove a theorem establishing this proposition, or might read someone else's proof. Either would be a selection practice that would correctly yield a choice of this target social practice (the weighted voting practice). Second, someone might begin with a selection practice at variance with the weighted voting scheme (in its second, individualized interpretation). For example, suppose Felix initially follows a practice of majority rule: he personally accepts whatever a majority of the experts concur on, without attempting to weight their opinions. However, most of the experts Felix has consulted on the subject of amalgamating expert opinion say (without providing a proof) that the weighted voting scheme is veritistically optimal. So Felix switches to this practice. Someone else, Désirée, initially follows the selection practice of dictatorial rule. On any subject, Désirée identifies the person who (in her opinion) is the most expert on the subject, and then accepts whatever that person says. In her case, the chosen expert says that weighted majority rule is veritistically optimal. So Désirée also switches to this practice. These examples illustrate three things: (1) People can sometimes successfully identify veritistically good target practices. (2) People can start with one practice as their selection practice, and then use it to endorse a rival target practice. (3) People can start with interpersonally different selection practices but wind up agreeing on the optimal target practice. Thus, both success (accuracy) and agreement are possible in the veritistic enterprise.[8]

---

[8] I hasten to acknowledge that although the weighted voting scheme is optimal *when the competences of experts are accurately known*, the italicized condition may be met only infrequently. There may be relatively few occasions, then, on which this practice or scheme can feasibly be implemented.

3.3 *Veritism and circularity*

The next problem on our agenda is epistemic circularity. Fundamentally, the problem is whether one can have grounds for believing that practices have good veritistic properties without implicitly relying on those selfsame practices. Now social practices do not confront the threat of circularity in the same direct way that certain individual practices do. But readers might feel that if there is a serious circularity threat to individual practices, the entire veritistic program is endangered. So I begin with the circularity problem facing individual practices.

Suppose I wish to assess the reliability of sense perception, that is, to determine whether sense perception usually delivers true beliefs. The most obvious way to do this is to appeal to what William Alston calls the "track record" of sense perception: how frequently it delivered true beliefs in the past (Alston 1989, 1993, 1994). A track-record argument would be an argument of roughly the following sort:

On occasion O_1, person S_1 perceptually formed the belief that P_1, and P_1 was true.
On occasion O_2, person S_2 perceptually formed the belief that P_2, and P_2 was true.
. . .
Therefore, sense perception is a reliable source of belief.

Such a track-record argument for the reliability of perception, however, tacitly appeals to sense perception itself. This is because a proponent of this argument could only learn the cited premises—which assert the truth of certain beliefs—by using sense perception. If vision once produced a belief that a certain salt shaker is taller than its companion pepper shaker, the only way to determine the truth of this belief is to apply vision (or some other sense modality) once again. A track-record argument does not involve the standard form of circularity, which philosophers call *premise circularity*, because the conclusion—"Sense perception is a reliable source of belief"—does not appear as an explicit premise in the argument. But in *using* perception to determine the truth of the beliefs cited in the premises, one *presupposes* the truth of this conclusion. This kind of circularity is called *epistemic circularity*.

It is important to distinguish *direct* and *indirect* (epistemic) circularity. Direct circularity holds of a practice if it is impossible to validate the reliability of that practice using other practices only.[9] I would say that vision is not directly circular because, on many deliverances, at least, it can be validated by touch. But vision might still suffer from indirect circularity, because vision itself is one of the practices that might have to be used to validate any practice

---

[9] When this holds, Alston (1993: 14) calls the practice a *basic* practice.

that validates it, for example, touch or hearing, if the validation problem is pressed deeply enough.

How worrisome are the properties of direct and indirect circularity? It takes but a little reflection to realize that these traits are necessarily going to hold of *some* practices, no matter what people's cognitive endowments may be like. This seems guaranteed by the assumption that basic cognitive endowments must be finite in number. If the number of practices is finite, there cannot be an infinite sequence of practices $\pi_1, \pi_2, \pi_3, \ldots$ such that the reliability of each practice πi can be validated by the use of some other practice πi_{+1} without ever "circling back" to π_1. As long as the number is finite, some sort of "circling back" is necessary, either circling back to the practice itself, or circling back to other practices which themselves can only be validated by direct or indirect circling. But if this is just a matter of logical necessity (given finite resources), how troubling should it be? Not terribly, in my opinion.

To see why, let us look more closely at direct circularity. As Alston points out, not every doxastic practice involves direct circularity (what he calls *basicness*). Consider, for example, the very "narrow" practice that takes something's looking like a peach as input and takes the belief, "That is a peach," as output. This practice is not directly circular, because one can use touch to determine whether objects judged by this practice to be peaches really are peaches. One need not use the selfsame practice. Similarly (although Alston does not emphasize this), no practice associated with a specific sense modality—vision, audition, olfaction, and so forth—incurs direct circularity. It is only when this set of practices is grouped into the "superpractice" *sense perception* that one gets a practice that incurs direct circularity. (In some cases, though, gerrymandering is not needed; memory, for example, has the trait of direct circularity.) Once again, however, it is a trivial fact that *some* practices must have the trait of direct circularity, especially if "superpractices" are allowed. Consider the widest possible superpractice: *human cognition* (engaging in belief formation via some human method or other). Obviously, humans cannot mount any effective track-record argument for the reliability of *human cognition* without using *human cognition*. The analogue holds for any cognitive creature X. For consider the superpractice X *cognition*. Obviously, Xs will be unable to mount any effective track-record argument for the reliability of X *cognition* without using X *cognition*. Once we appreciate these necessary facts, does it still seem like an epistemological catastrophe that *some* practices should be directly circular? Not to me.

Why should recognition that epistemic circularity is logically necessary (for *some* practices) reduce its sting? Consider an analogy. One might initially be upset to learn that some people in a given population have below average incomes. However, it merely follows necessarily from the definition of "average" that some people will have below average incomes—as long as incomes are not all identical. The same holds of any population measure whatsoever. Once this definitional necessity is recognized, one can appreciate that the existence of below average incomes is not in itself a source of concern (at least if perfect equality of incomes is assumed to be unfeasible). Of course, *large* income disparities are a legitimate matter of concern, but large disparities are not definitionally necessary. Analogous reflections can eliminate or reduce worries about epistemic circularity.

We should not be wholly mollified, however, until we examine the assumptions that underlie circularity threats. What perturbs people, undoubtedly, is the apparent worthlessness of any directly circular defense of a practice's reliability. If practice π is used to check on previous reports of practice π, and if it says that all or most of the original reports were true, such evidence is assumed to be worthless.[10] It does nothing, allegedly, to support the reliability of π. This is the kind of thinking that makes direct circularity so troubling. But it is mistaken.

The first point to notice is that neither vision nor any other perceptual practice is destined to rubber-stamp its previous judgments. Each new visual sighting is a separate and independent test of the judgment rendered by a previous sighting. This should serve as a partial antidote to the notion that a repetition of the original judgment is evidentially worthless. Since such repetitions are not a foregone conclusion, they are not trivial or worthless findings, in the way that a second copy of the same newspaper (to use Wittgenstein's example) is bound to replicate a first copy. In general, vision does not remember what it saw earlier, and it is not determined, like a scheming witness, to keeps its story consistent. It is quite capable of rendering conflicting reports. This is especially true because subsequent visual checks may be from closer proximity, or from a different angle, than an earlier sighting. It is perfectly *possible*, then, for vision to issue discrepant reports. If, instead, a corroborating report is delivered, that has some significance.

Alston notes that massive internal *in*consistency demonstrates the *un*reliability of a practice (1993: 134–7), but he does not seem to think that internal consistency lends genuine self-support.[11] On one prominent approach to evidence, however, a case can be made that self-corroboration of the kind described above does provide *some* evidential support for a practice's reliability. Specifically, a Bayesian analysis of the situation supports this claim.

Suppose that the report initially given by vision is that the sole object on the table is a peach. And suppose that the perceiver puts on his glasses, moves closer to the table, and vision renders the same report again. What is the likelihood that it would deliver the same report twice if it were mistaken both

---

[10] See Markus Lammenranta (1996), for example. He quotes a passage from Thomas Reid expressing a similar worry: "If a man's honesty were called into question, it would be ridiculous to refer it to the man's own word, whether he be honest or not" (Reid 1983: 276).

[11] Alston does identify *some* kinds of significant self-support (1993: 138), but he appears to regard these forms of self-support as evidentially unhelpful for purposes of establishing reliability (1993: 139).

times, and there is no peach on the table? One possibility, of course, is that vision is unreliable and errs in the same way twice. There are, however, different possible variants of unreliability stories, and these are worth distinguishing. One possible source of unreliability is an evil demon who ensures that there are no physical objects but who systematically deceives the senses in a massively coherent fashion. Under this scenario, it is indeed highly likely that even if there were no peach on the table (and no physical objects in general), vision would render the same report twice (thereby preserving coherence). I grant that repetition of the original visual report does nothing to preclude or disconfirm this scenario of systematic unreliability. However, the prior probability of this scenario may be extremely low.

Another range of unreliability scenarios would have vision being much less systematic. It might give merely random reports, or it might be highly susceptible to local variables that warp its judgment. Under all of these unsystematic scenarios, it is unlikely to make the same mistake twice, especially under different viewing conditions. If there is no peach on the table but a different object instead, it might see it as a peach under one viewing condition, but why would it continue to see it as a peach a second time, especially under different viewing conditions? And if we go beyond a single corroboration to numerous corroborations, it is highly unlikely that unsystematically unreliable practices would keep delivering the *same* mistaken reports. It is analogous to the improbability that numerous independent witnesses to an event would all make the same error.

With respect to these forms of unreliability, we can now apply Bayes' Theorem. (For readers unfamiliar with Bayes' Theorem, a formulation and extended illustration of it are given in Chapter 4.) Bayes' Theorem implies that if a possible outcome has a high likelihood given one hypothesis and a low likelihood given a competing hypothesis, then actually observing that outcome boosts the posterior probability of the high-likelihood hypothesis relative to the low-likelihood hypothesis. For example, if drawing a red ball from a certain urn is highly likely on the hypothesis that the urn has property F and very unlikely on the hypothesis that the urn has property G, then actually drawing a red ball from the urn boosts the posterior probability that the urn has property F as compared to the hypothesis that it has property G. Applied to our case, I claim that a visual corroboration of vision's first report is more likely on the hypothesis that vision is reliable (and both reports are correct) than it is likely on the hypothesis that vision is (unsystematically) unreliable (and both reports are false). Again, this is because an unreliable practice is not so likely to issue in the same mistaken judgment twice (or three or four times). As long as the likelihood of the corroboration is higher given the reliability hypothesis than given the (unsystematic) unreliability hypothesis, corroboration events provide evidence in favor of reliability.

Let me be clear about my claim. I am not claiming that a corroboration event supports the reliability hypothesis in comparison with the systematic unreliability (evil demon) hypothesis. But such differential support is not a necessary ingredient of my argument. As long as corroboration events lower the posterior probability of some of the unsystematic unreliability hypotheses, that leaves room for raising the posterior probability of the reliability hypothesis. This suffices to show that self-corroboration provides *some* evidence for reliability, without, of course, "proving" reliability.

Our entire discussion of circularity has concerned individual practices, because it is quite unclear that any social practices are threatened with either direct or indirect circularity.[12] The issue is relevant to the veritistic project for social practices, however, because selection practices include perception and memory, which do confront the circularity problem. If the reliability of such selection practices is questionable, this raises doubts about the social project. We have seen, however, that there are ways of meeting the challenge(s) of epistemic circularity. Moreover, whatever remains to be said about these deeply gnarled issues at the foundations of epistemology, does anyone seriously propose that we cease all attempts to assess social practices with the help of perception and memory? Does anyone propose that from this day forward we should cease regarding perception as more reliable than idle speculation? Should we uproot the legal practice of admitting testimony from eyewitnesses and replace them with idle speculators who never had perceptual access to the events being litigated? No sensible person would propose this. So although the final word on the epistemic status of basic individual processes is yet to be written, we should not hesitate to go forward in a veritistic spirit.

3.4 *Veritistic value*

It is time now to provide more specifics about veritistic evaluation. I have said repeatedly that veritistic social epistemology aims to evaluate social practices in terms of their veritistic outputs, where veritistic outputs include states like knowledge, error, and ignorance. What I am contemplating, then, is an evaluative structure of two parts. States like knowledge, error, and ignorance have *fundamental* veritistic value or disvalue. Practices have *instrumental* veritistic value insofar as they promote or impede the acquisition of fundamental veritistic value. The structure here is perfectly analogous to the structures of consequentialist schemes in moral theory. One type of state, such as happiness or utility, is taken to have fundamental or intrinsic moral value, and other items, such as actions, rules, or institutions, are taken to have instrumental value insofar as they tend to produce (token) states with fundamental value.

---

[12] Some would say that it threatens the practice of accepting testimony, on the ground that the reliability of testimony cannot be established by independent practices. This is controversial, however; see Chapter 4.

In approaching the analysis of belief states with fundamental veritistic value, we have two main options. (Henceforth "veritistic value" will be abbreviated as *V-value*.) First, we can use the traditional classification scheme which offers three types of credal attitude toward a proposition: believe it, reject it (disbelieve it), or withhold judgment. I call this the *trichotomous* approach. Second, we can allow infinitely many degrees or strengths of belief, represented by any point in the unit interval (from zero to one). I call this scheme the *degree of belief* (DB) scheme. On this approach, degrees of belief are equated with subjective probabilities. For example, a degree of belief (or level of confidence) of .65 in a given proposition is a subjective probability of .65 for that proposition. Admittedly, it is not entirely obvious or uncontroversial that degrees of belief can be equated with subjective probabilities. But it is so convenient for theoretical purposes that I shall proceed on this assumption.[13]

There is no entirely unproblematic method of mutually translating the trichotomous scheme and the DB scheme. For example, should plain "belief" in the trichotomous scheme be translated as "DB 1.0"? That would be misleading, since not all belief involves total certainty. Should "withholding judgment" (or having no opinion) be translated as "DB .50"? Again, this is an imperfect translation. Although no perfect translations are known to me, my V-value assignments will sometimes appear to presuppose certain equivalences. This is more a matter of convenience than a matter of conviction that there are perfect equivalences here.

In constructing a model of V-valuable states, it is helpful to use a *question-answering* model. It may not be possible to adhere to this approach systematically throughout the book, but it provides the most satisfactory theoretical framework. In a question-answering model, agent S's belief states (of either the trichotomous or the DB kind) have value or disvalue when they are responses to a question that *interests S* (or, more generally, when other agents are interested in S's knowing the answer). Interest comes into the picture for the following reason. Suppose S is ignorant about all of the following matters: What is the 323rd entry in the Wichita, Kansas, telephone directory? Who placed sixth in the women's breast stroke at the 1976 Summer Olympics? What was the full name of Domenico Scarlatti's maternal grandmother? Does S's ignorance on all of these matters constitute, or even contribute toward, the impoverished V-condition of his credal corpus? Does such ignorance imply that his

---

[13] In place of "point" probabilities, which might be too precise to capture fuzzy belief states, one might adopt a classification scheme of confidence *intervals*. However, the subjective probability (degree-of-belief) scheme is simpler and more convenient, and there will be enough complexities of other kinds on our hands to dictate a preference for simplicity on this score. I have previously expressed some worries about the psychological plausibility of subjective probabilities (Goldman 1986: ch. 15). Although I do not retract those worries entirely, some sort of levels-of-confidence scheme is needed for people's credal psychology. Subjective probability is a tolerable idealization for these purposes.

credal state should receive a low V-value, or V-ranking? If *S* is totally uninterested in these questions, I am inclined to say that his knowing no answers to them does not count against the V-value of his belief states. (At any rate, if neither *S* nor anyone else has such an interest—where interest remains to be defined—then this should not lower the V-value of his belief states.) In short, V-value should always be assessed relative to *questions of interest*. Sometimes the questions that interest a person are only implicit rather than explicit or fully conscious.[14] But implicit questions are fine as far as my analysis is concerned.

Suppose, then, that *S* has an interest in a yes/no question: "Is it the case that *P*?" I shall abbreviate such a question as: Q(*P/−P*). Then we can assign the following V-values to the three possible states in the trichotomous scheme. If *S believes* the true proposition, the V-value is 1.0. If he *rejects* the true proposition, the V-value is 0. And if he *withholds judgment*, the V-value is .50. The first state constitutes *knowledge*, the second *error*, and the third *ignorance*. As shorthand, we may write:

V-value of B(true) = 1.0
V-value of W(true) = .50
V-value of R(true) = .0

("B" stands for "believe," "W" for "withhold," and "R" for "reject.") Notice that I have said nothing about *S*'s attitude toward false propositions. I shall assume throughout that if someone believes a proposition *P*, then he rejects its negation, not-*P*, and vice versa. So there is no need for additional principles concerning falsehoods. Someone might suggest assigning V-credit for *error avoidance*—rejecting a falsehood—in addition to credit for true belief. If we assume *P* is true, *S* would get credit of 1.0 for believing *P* and additional credit of 1.0 for rejecting not-*P*. But this is "double counting," which seems inappropriate.

Veritistic analysis, as I present it, focuses on *changes* in V-value over time. Suppose, for example, that *S* becomes interested in Q(*P/−P*) at time t_1, and at that time his credal state is W(*P/−P*). That is, he withholds judgment, or has "no opinion," on whether *P* is true or not. At t_1, then, his V-value vis-à-vis Q(*P/−P*) is .50. At t_2 he forms a belief in *P*, that is, his credal state is B(*P*). What is his V-value at t_2 vis-à-vis Q(*P/−P*)? If *P* is true, his V-value is 1.0. If *P* is false, his V-value is 0. (If he believes *P*, he rejects not-*P*; and if *P* is false, not-*P* is true. By rejecting the truth—not-*P*—he gets a V-value of 0 on this question.)[15] Thus, by changing his belief state from no opinion at t_1 to belief in *P* at t_2, he either

[14] For a discussion of implicit questions, see Larry Wright 1995.
[15] As in this example, I shall typically assume bivalence. This is an assumption of convenience. A more complex scheme would have to be adopted if bivalence were rejected as a working principle. As indicated earlier, however, we shall have enough complications without adding the denial of bivalence to our list.

improves or worsens his V-value with respect to the question $Q(P/-P)$, depending on whether P is true or false.

Now consider V-values in the DB scheme. Let us assume that at t_1, when S first takes an interest in $Q(P/-P)$, his DB in P is .33. At the later time t_2 his DB in P is increased to .75. How is the V-value of his DB affected? V-value assignments under the DB scheme are very straightforward, following the simple principle that any DB in a truth has the same amount of V-value as the strength of the DB. In other words,

$$\text{V-value of } DB_X(\text{true}) = X.$$

Suppose, then, that P in the above example is true. Then P's V-value with respect to $Q(P/-P)$ is .33 at t_1 and .75 at t_2. This is a gain in V-value of .42. If P is false, then P's V-value with respect to $Q(P/-P)$ is .67 at t_1 and .25 at t_2. This is because his DB vis-à-vis the truth of not-P was .67 at t_1 and .25 at t_2. This is a loss in V-value of .42.

The foregoing concerns the V-evaluation of belief states. Now let me turn to the V-evaluation of practices. The theoretical discussion will be conducted in terms of practices generally, whether individual or social practices, though subsequent developments will of course highlight social practices. As I have said, practices are to be V-evaluated instrumentally, in terms of their causal contributions toward belief states with various V-values. Suppose that question Q_1 begins to interest agent S at time t_1, and S *applies* a certain practice π to question Q_1. The practice might consist in a certain perceptual investigation, such as visually scanning the environment, or it might consist in asking a friend for information and drawing a conclusion from her response. One possible result of the practice is to change S's state of belief (vis-à-vis question Q_1) at time t_2. If the result of applying π is to increase the V-value of the belief state from t_1 to t_2, then π deserves positive credit. If the result of applying π is to decrease the V-value of the belief state from t_1 to t_2, then π deserves negative credit (discredit). If there is no change in V-value, π deserves neither credit nor discredit in connection with this application.[16]

In evaluating a practice, we are not interested, of course, in its application

---

[16] In previous writings (Goldman 1986, 1987) I employed the veritistic notions of *reliability* and *power*. Roughly, reliability measures the tendency of a practice to produce beliefs that are true a high percentage of the time. Reliability thereby ignores "no opinions," or withholdings of judgment, since only the ratio of true to false *beliefs* determines reliability or unreliability. Power is the tendency of a practice to produce belief in true answers to questions of interest. This measure effectively takes account of no opinions. When a practice leaves an agent in credal limbo on a question of interest, that counts against its power, because the practice fails to produce a belief in the true answer. The theoretical analysis in this chapter abandons the terms "reliability" and "power," but those concepts are reflected or encapsulated in the proposed veritistic measure. The present veritistic measure is slightly closer to the power measure, except that ignorance (no opinion) has a smaller negative impact on V-value than error (false belief), as it should.

to just a single question. We are interested in its performance across a wide range of applications, both actual and possible. This inevitably introduces a certain amount of vagueness: exactly which applications are relevant? First, the class of cases must be sufficiently varied so that they reflect the sorts of questions to which the practice is intended to be applicable. Second, they must be the sorts of questions and situations people typically encounter. In other words, even when we consider hypothetical applications, they should be similar to real-world applications, not bizarre applications in a "far out" possible world.

Why should merely possible, as opposed to actual, applications be considered at all? Veritistic social epistemology seeks to assess not only the practices currently employed by people and communities, but to inquire whether there might be better practices to replace those presently in use. This means that practices must be evaluated that, so far, have no track record at all. To evaluate such hitherto undeployed practices, one must consider how they *would* perform in a range of possible applications. In other words, we must consider their veritistic "propensities," not just their veritistic "frequencies." In fact, the same point holds of practices that do have a prior track record. Whatever that track record is, it may be partly due to various accidental features, which are not firm guides to the future performance of the practice. Here again we must consider possible as well as actual applications. Needless to say, it is not easy to determine the prospective performance of a practice. It cannot be determined by direct empirical observation, only by theoretical considerations, typically conjoined with background empirical information. This makes the task of veritistic epistemology extremely difficult.

The implementation of veritistic epistemology is difficult for still another obvious reason. In defining the V-values of belief states and (derivatively) of practices, I assumed that the beliefs have objective truth-values. This assumption does not imply, however, that those truth-values are *known* to the veritistic theorist, or that they are easy to ascertain. A practice's V-properties are what they are, whether or not they are known to the theorist.

If they are not known, though, of what use are they? Why bother with such abstract definitions if V-performance cannot be determined? My measures of V-value are intended to provide *conceptual* clarity, to specify what is *sought* in an intellectually good practice, even if it is difficult to determine which practices in fact score high on these measures. Conceptual clarity about desiderata is often a good thing, no matter what hurdles one confronts in determining when those desiderata are fulfilled. An analogous situation is encountered in creating and filling positions in a business or organization. Clearly specifying the desired qualifications of a job-holder is highly desirable, however tricky it may be to identify an applicant who best satisfies those qualifications. Similarly, we want clear specifications of what it means for a practice to be V-valuable, however difficult it may be to identify the practices that actually exemplify this virtue.

Let me return now to measures of a practice's V-value. Suppose the range of pertinent applications of the practice has been settled. Theoretically, then, we can take the *average* (mean) performance of the practice across those applications as a measure of its V-value. If on average the practice increases the V-values of the user's belief states, the practice has *positive* V-value. If on average it decreases the V-values of the user's belief states, the practice has *negative* V-value. And if on average it leaves the V-values of the beliefs unchanged, the V-value of the practice is neutral. As we shall see, matters are somewhat more complicated than this proposal acknowledges. Nonetheless, this is a good general guide to the spirit of my approach.

The previous paragraph considers the V-value of a practice all by itself, rather than by comparison with any rival practice. This is an *absolute mode* of V-evaluation. In addition to this absolute mode, there is also a *comparative mode* of V-evaluation. In the comparative mode, we compare one practice, π, with an alternative practice, π', which would tackle the same set of intellectual tasks in a different way. In the comparative mode, we ask which is V-better: π or π'? One virtue of the comparative mode is that it makes selection of the precise class of possible applications of the practice somewhat less pressing. For certain practices, whether they earn a positive or negative average V-value may hinge on which applications are chosen. But the comparative mode may avoid this issue, as long as the *same* range of applications is used for any pair of practices being compared.

Let me be more specific about the comparative mode of evaluation, focusing on a single application. The idea is to take an agent with a particular question, Q, and to ask what changes did result or would result in the V-value of his beliefs (vis-à-vis Q) when he applied, or if he were to apply, each practice to Q. What change occurs if π is applied, and what change occurs if π' is applied? If the change resulting from π is V-better than the change resulting from π', then the former is V-better than the latter in this application. For some pairs of practices, it may be possible to say that one practice is systematically better than the other across any plausible range of cases. The exact range of cases, then, need not be settled. Of course, the same might be true in the absolute mode of evaluation. It might be possible, for certain practices, to say that those practices have positive V-value on average, no matter what range of applications is selected. Examples of both kinds will be presented in Chapter 4.

A simple example will put a little flesh on this abstract skeleton. A military general wants to know whether the enemy is preparing to launch an attack. He has five soldiers to employ as scouts. One possible practice is to send all five scouts in a single direction to reconnoiter and report their findings. A second possible practice is to send each of the five scouts in different directions, and have each report what he sees. On the assumption that the enemy could attack from any of several directions, the general could not expect to be so lucky as to send the five-person team in the actual direction of attack. So the second practice is clearly V-preferable. Reports of the *scattered* five scouts would, on average, yield more increases in question-relevant knowledge than reports of the *concentrated* group of five. Of course, special circumstances might upset this comparison. Perhaps single scouts would be spotted and picked off by enemy troops before they could report to home base, whereas a team of five would survive to communicate whatever intelligence they gathered. Barring this kind of scenario, however, the practice of scattering the scouts is clearly the V-better practice.

A minor permutation of the preceding case calls attention to another variable of interest to veritistic epistemology, namely, the *speed* of knowledge acquisition. A team of five scouts need not restrict its explorations to a single direction. The team can sequentially search all of the same directions as the distributed scouts could search. The time difference, however, seems critical here. As long as each of the scattered scouts is a viable entity, they can collectively acquire and report the same information much more rapidly than a sequential search by a five-person team. Even if the general's belief state, after receiving all reports, enjoys the same V-increase under both practices, this increase will obviously come *sooner* under the second practice. That is an informational advantage. Although I shall take account of speed in a few applications in this book, generally speaking it will not loom large in my treatment.

Up to this point, I have concentrated on the impact of a practice on a single credal agent. For many purposes of social epistemology, however, we should consider the impact of a practice on a community of agents. Many social practices aim to disseminate information to multiple agents, and their success should be judged by their propensity to increase the V-values of many agents' belief states, not just the belief states of a single agent. Thus, we should be interested in the *aggregate* level of knowledge of an entire community (or a subset thereof). The theoretical analysis of aggregate V-value is moderately straightforward. I shall discuss it solely within the DB classification scheme.

Consider a small community of four agents: S_1–S_4. Suppose that the question of interest, again, is $Q(P/-P)$, and that P is true. At time t_1, the several agents have DBs vis-à-vis P shown in the table below. Practice π is then applied, with the result that the agents acquire new DBs vis-à-vis P at t_2, as shown in the table.

	t_1	t_2
S_1	DB(p) = .40	DB(P) = .70
S_2	DB(p) = .70	DB(P) = .90
S_3	DB(p) = .90	DB(P) = .60
S_4	DB(p) = .20	DB(P) = .80

What is the aggregate level of V-value in this community, and how does it change over time? A simple measure of aggregate V-value is the group's *mean* V-value. At t_1 the group's *mean* DB in P, the true answer to $Q(P/-P)$, is .55, so

.55 is their aggregate V-value at t_1. At t_2 the group's mean DB in the true answer is .75, so that is their aggregate V-value at the later time. Thus, the group displays an increase in its aggregate V-value of .20. Since, by hypothesis, this increase is attributable to the application of practice π, that practice displays positive V-value in this application. The mean is not the only possible measure of aggregate V-value (or knowledge). Another possible measure is the root mean square, or some sort of weighted average.[17] These measures all share the property that if some individuals' V-values rise and no individuals' V-values decline, the aggregate V-value rises.[18] The mean is a simple, convenient, and familiar measure, but mathematically inclined readers may prefer one of the other measures in its place.

3.5 *Complications: interests, attribution, and questions*

This section confronts a number of complications arising from the theoretical framework proposed in the preceding section. I begin with the concept of "interest" in a question, and the role this should play in our framework.

3.5.A *Interests*

The only interest that figured prominently in the foregoing discussion was the interest of the credal agent. But veritistic evaluation, especially in *social* epistemology, need not be confined to the agent's interest. Institutions, for example, sometimes have an interest in certain of their actors becoming informed on certain questions. It is appropriate for veritistic analysis to assess how well the institution's practices serve this end, whether or not individual players are personally interested in the questions. The legal system takes an interest in having juries render accurate judgments; so the system is interested in having jurors form true beliefs about matters litigated before them. Jurors may personally be indifferent to these questions. They may not care whether they get correct answers; but the legal system does care (see Chapter 9). Similarly, it may be important to democracy as an institution that its citizenry be well informed (see Chapter 10), even if individual citizens have scant desire for political information. In short, veritistic evaluations can be made relative

---

[17] The root mean square is given by the expression:

$$\sqrt{\frac{\sum_{i=1}^{n} a_i^2}{n}}.$$

[18] Thanks here, and in the previous note, to Shaughan Lavine.

to institutional interests as well as the interests of credal agents individually.

I turn next to the definition of "interest," restricting discussion for brevity to the interest of the credal agent. There are three relevant senses of "interest." One measure of a question's interest is whether the agent actively finds it *interesting*, that is, has an aroused curiosity or concern about the question's answer. Such concern can arise from intrinsic fascination or from recognition of the potential practical value of knowing a correct answer. A second measure of interest is dispositional rather than occurrent. Many questions *would* be interesting to a person if he/she only thought of them, or considered them, although no such thought or consideration has in fact occurred. Such dispositional interest should also be counted in assessing a question's "importance" or "significance" for that person. A third sense is more broadly dispositional: what would interest the agent if he or she knew certain facts. Students might take no active interest in a certain topic, yet such knowledge may be objectively *in* their interest because it is relevant to matters in which they do take an interest.

Now that we have widened the ambit of interests that might make a question ripe for veritistic analysis, we must decide the exact role that the concept of interest should play. I shall discuss two options: a *pervasive* role and a *moderate* role. A pervasive role might go so far as to use the degree of interest in a question to give an overall weighting to an agent's veritistic success, and to the V-performance of a practice as well. If an agent gets high V-scores on the questions that interest her most, does she not deserve high veritistic ratings? Higher than those of an agent whose best veritistic scores come on questions of relatively less interest to him? And couldn't a similar idea apply to practices? There are at least two problems with these proposals. First, one person's questions of interest might be easier to answer than those of a second. The fact that the first scores higher on the set of questions that interest *her* does not demonstrate superior intellectual skill. Second, the intensity of interest a person takes in a question may reflect factors that do not properly belong in an epistemological analysis. The magnitude of interest may depend on the person's financial or mortal stake in the question. But that does not mean that his succeeding or failing to answer those questions correctly should loom disproportionately large in an epistemic analysis. This would lead down the path toward abandoning the specialized, veritistic mission of epistemology in favor of a more purely pragmatic enterprise. However, a good epistemic practice should not be indifferent to the relative amounts of interest that a given agent takes in different questions. A social practice that systematically delivers information on topics of mild interest to an agent while regularly concealing or masking evidence on topics of core interest is an epistemically unsatisfactory practice.

I shall therefore assign interests a moderate role in my framework. If a certain question fails to interest an agent in any of the three senses of "interest," and fails to interest any other pertinent body, there is no basis for rendering a

V-analysis of his credal performance vis-à-vis that question. V-analysis is appropriate, however, whenever any of the indicated sorts of interests come into play. Moreover, sensitivity to relative amounts of interest should play a modest role in assessing a practice's epistemic credentials.

Before leaving this topic, let me say a few more words about a community's interest in its members getting good V-scores with respect to certain questions. In some cases, a community may want all of its members to have certain information, for example, information about how to avoid communicable diseases. In other cases, it may only be important that certain team members each have the specific knowledge required for proper execution of his or her tasks. In the navigation of a ship, different members of the team have different tasks, for instance, taking visual bearings (Hutchins 1996). Each must get answers to certain timely questions as the ship moves along, but not all team members need have answers to the same questions. Information must be distributed to the people with a "need to know"; it does not have to be shared by all. A veritistically good practice for such an enterprise would promote the required distribution of knowledge, even if that does not translate into a high average knowledge across the whole team (on any given question). Similarly, a President, Congressperson, or other decision maker cannot be expected to know all details of every issue they confront. As long as aides responsible for a given topic have pertinent information on that topic, and have appropriate communication channels to the decision maker, that structure of information distribution may suffice. A community should not be downgraded veritistically for failure to distribute *all* knowledge to *all* of its agents.

3.5.B *Practice application and causal attribution*

I turn now to an entirely different issue. In discussing the V-evaluation of practices, I made extensive use of the notion of *applying* a practice to a question. In some cases, this relation is clearly and unambiguously exemplified. The inferential response of a hearer to a speaker's testimony (discussed in Chapter 4) is a clear case of applying a certain inferential practice to a certain question. For other social epistemic practices, however, it is less clear-cut when they are "applied" to a question. Consider a standing legal practice of admitting expert testimony into evidence under certain circumstances. Suppose that a defendant faces specified charges in a jury trial, and a particular expert witness influences the jurors' beliefs with her testimony. Does the standing legal practice, or rule, that allowed this influential piece of expert testimony to be heard have a causal impact (albeit an indirect one) on the jurors' beliefs? Certainly. This is an example of the sort of social practice that should be analyzed under the program of veritistic social epistemology. Can it be said, however, that this practice was *applied* to the question at hand? Perhaps; but it might be regarded as somewhat ambiguous. The point I want to make is that the notion of practice application should be understood broadly. Whenever a practice has indirect effects on credal changes, whenever belief-influencing transactions take place under the aegis of a practice, I shall count that as an instance of practice "application."

As the last example illustrates, belief changes are frequently caused by multiple practices. In this example beliefs are causally influenced by three (types of) practices: (1) the inferential practices of the credal agents—here the jurors; (2) the speech practices of the speaker—here the expert witness; and (3) the communication-control practice that allowed the speaker to communicate with these credal agents—here the evidentiary rule governing expert testimony. One might worry about how causal attributions should be doled out to these various practices. This problem in causal analysis is noted by Nicholas Rescher (1977: 29) in a similar epistemological context; he calls it the *problem of attribution*.

The problem of attribution might seem to pose a difficulty for my approach, since this approach proposes to assign a veritistic propensity to each practice considered singly. But if credal changes are the joint products of multiple practices, rather than of single practices in isolation, how can a single practice be assigned a determinate veritistic measure? A belief change that occurs on a particular occasion cannot be pinned exclusively on a single practice. So how can a practice that played some causal role be assigned credit or discredit for the change? Should it receive "partial" credit? If so, how can partial credits be assigned? One possible strategy is to abandon the project of appraising practices one by one and replace it with the strategy of evaluating *systems* of practices (as was proposed in Goldman 1986: ch. 5). An alternative strategy, which is the one I favor here, is to appraise single practices *against the background* of the remaining system.

To assess a specific legal rule of evidence, for example, we would consider the differences in belief changes that would result from its adoption or non-adoption, taking as *fixed givens* the other current evidential rules, the inferential practices of jurors (insofar as these can be specified), the rules for cross-examination of witnesses, and so forth. It may be impossible, on this approach, to associate with a given practice π its own unique set of credal changes. Ideally, however, we can compare the credal outputs of the entire system *inclusive* of practice π with its credal outputs *exclusive* of π. Then we can say that π is beneficial or detrimental to the aim of knowledge (given the rest of the system). This is roughly what I called, in Section 3.4, the absolute mode of evaluation. We can also compare π to alternative practices π', π'', and so forth by asking how the entire system would perform if these alternative practices were substituted for π. This is the comparative mode of evaluation. Such comparisons are all we need for veritistic purposes. Another advantage of the comparative focus is the following (also mentioned in Section 3.4). There is admittedly some looseness in selecting the questions on which a practice should be assessed. If we adhere to the comparative mode of evaluation, however, we just have to ensure that any two rival, or alternative, practices are compared relative to the same questions.[19]

3.5.C *Other types of questions*

My earlier discussion dealt entirely with yes/no questions, but many other types of questions also interest credal agents and they require a little different treatment. At a minimum, they cast a slightly different light on some decisions made earlier.

Consider how-questions, what-questions, who-questions, where-questions, and why-questions. These questions do not wear all their possible answers "on their sleeves." In fact, they do not wear *any* of their possible answers on their sleeves. Suppose I hear a strange noise outside, with no tell-tale characteristics, and I ask, "What made that noise?" The possible answers to this what-question are legion. No specific partition of possible answers comes with the question. For questions like this, unlike yes/no questions, the credal agent cannot be expected to have a probability distribution over possible answers that sums to 1.0. In the noise example, there might be four causes that come to my mind as remotely possible, but all of them might be assigned very low probability. Where N is the noise I heard, and A_1–A_4 are possible answers, my subjective probability distribution (set of DBs) might look something like this:

$$A_1 \ (W \text{ caused } N): .08$$
$$A_2 \ (X \text{ caused } N): .05$$
$$A_3 \ (Y \text{ caused } N): .06$$
$$A_4 \ (Z \text{ caused } N): .02$$

It will be replied that there is another possible answer, "None of the above," that would also receive some probability assignment, and since the sum of the probabilities assigned to A_1–A_4 is .21, this answer should presumably receive a probability assignment (a DB) of .79. Then the sum of probabilities assigned to all answers is 1.0. But, I reply, this "answer" is not really an answer to the what-question in the same sense as the $A$is are. It does not name a particular cause. In general, in the case of what-questions, why-questions, and so forth,

---

[19] One apparent danger in the present proposal, pointed out by Joel Pust, is that we might get stuck in "local maxima." A given practice might be good relative to the set of practices currently in place, but the whole system might be improved if many practices were changed simultaneously. This worry is readily resolved, however. We can appraise not only single practices but also *n*-tuples of practices—pairs of practices, triples of practices, and so forth—by asking what the veritistic results would be if we *concurrently* adopted certain *n*-tuples while holding the remainder of the system fixed. This parallels a procedure I proposed elsewhere for the comparative measurement of *social power*, involving the abilities of multiple individuals to obtain desired outcomes. See Goldman 1992: chs. 13, 14.

knowing that something is *not* an answer is not equivalent to knowing an answer (knowing of a possible answer that it is the correct answer).

The problem with this class of questions is that a credal agent is in danger of earning *zero* V-credit according to our analysis! In the noise example, if none of the considered answers is true, there is *no* true answer to the question to which I assign nonzero probability. Hence, my V-value on this question is zero. Does that seem right? It might seem to be an uncharitably low assignment, because at least I have wisely assigned very low probabilities (DBs) to four incorrect answers. Shouldn't that earn me *some* positive V-credit?

My solution to the problem is this. First, we should gracefully accept the result identified in the previous paragraph: zero V-credit on this question. This solution has the virtue of reflecting my failure, in the hypothesized example, to generate a correct answer.[20] Thinking up good candidate answers is often a major component of an intellectual task. A large part of science is devoted to the task of hypothesis generation. In the context of social epistemology, one of the principal underlying rationales for the "free market for ideas" has probably been the notion that an open market for ideas allows numerous hypotheses to be floated, and solving problems often requires good hypotheses.[21] So we should be content with the judgment that someone who fails to come up with a true answer to a question deserves a zero V-rating on that question.

We lack a fully satisfactory solution to the problem, however, unless we appropriately honor the fitting assignment of low probabilities to the false answers A_1–A_4. One possibility is to reconsider the previously dismissed proposal of giving credit for error avoidance. But this proposal would involve giving high levels of credit for the low probabilities assigned to each of A_1–A_4. That would inadequately reflect my poor performance on the cited question. A preferable solution is this. Simply take note of the fact that I do have true answers, or high DBs, for the following yes/no questions: "Was W the cause of N?", "Was X the cause of N?", "Was Y the cause of N?", and "Was Z the cause of N?" In each case, I assign a high probability to the answer, ". . . was *not* the cause of N." In each case, this answer is correct. So there are several yes/no questions to which I would receive a high V-rating. But I continue to receive a zero V-rating for my performance on the what-question "What was the cause of N?" This seems to capture the crucial intuitions about the case and similar such cases. So our approach comes through with flying colors, so long as the entire range of questions is fully considered.[22]

---

[20] The question "What made that noise?" does not have a uniquely correct answer because there could be many correct classifications of the object or event that caused the noise. The example assumes, however, that I do not think up *any* correct classification for the cause of the noise.

[21] For further discussion of the free market for ideas, see Chapter 7.

[22] There is still a residual problem, as Pust points out. If high DBs in propositions of the form '. . . is *not* the cause of N' yield high V-credit on the corresponding yes/no questions, won't someone get intuitively excessive amounts of credit for generating lots of

This completes my presentation of the basic framework of veritistic social epistemology. I have tried to keep the framework relatively simple and unembellished, so as to facilitate its application to a variety of domains. Given the complexity of social life, complications enough will appear in each of the domains to be examined. A relatively simple and uncluttered framework will smooth the path to analytical progress.

outlandish hypotheses to which he wisely attaches a low probability? Despite his failure to generate a true answer to the what-question, such a person might (counterintuitively) get more total V-credit than someone who, without wasting time considering false hypotheses, immediately generates a correct answer to the what-question and assigns it a high probability.

One way out of this problem is to distinguish *primary* and *subsidiary* questions, and to attach greater weight to the former. Pursuing the present example, the what-question is obviously the primary question facing the cognizer, and the yes/no questions concerning all of the generated hypotheses are subsidiary questions. Intuitively, more V-credit should be given for true answers to the primary question than for true answers to the subsidiary questions. It is not obvious, however, exactly how to quantify these matters. In general, I have not developed a full-fledged "calculus" of V-value here. What has been developed, however, should suffice for purposes of the book. Further refinements might be added in the future.

PART TWO

Generic Social Practices

FOUR

Testimony

4.1 *The social spread of knowledge*

CHAPTER 3 erected the evaluative framework of veritistic social epistemology, thereby completing Part I of this book. Part II begins the examination of social practices by considering practices of wide applicability,
practices that cut across content areas. This chapter examines the most elementary and universal social path to knowledge: the transmission of observed
information from one person to others. More generally, it considers observers
who decide whether and what to report, and receivers who decide what credence to place in reports they receive.

I begin with a seemingly trivial question: Does a high level of social knowledge require a high level of social interaction? If we mean by "high level of
social knowledge" a high aggregate of knowledge among the members of a
community, the answer is: not necessarily. In principle an impressive aggregate of knowledge might be acquired if each member independently explores
and discovers the facts of interest. A hallmark of human culture, however, is
to enhance the social fund of knowledge by sharing discovered facts with one
another. Communication is an efficient mode of increasing knowledge
because information transmission is typically easier, quicker, and less costly
than fresh discovery. Even in the animal kingdom, important information
such as the presence of food or predators is conveyed to conspecifics by signals, alarms, or, in the case of honeybees, incredibly detailed descriptions. The
honeybee's complex dance specifies the distance to food, its location, and its
quality.[1] Since not every member of a community observes each fact other
members observe, there is room for veritistic improvement through communication. Not every discoverer, of course, chooses to disseminate her newly
won knowledge to others. Nor is every report or item of testimony a sincere
and veridical report. So let us consider the kinds of practices that might contribute to increases in knowledge through testimony.

Four stages of testimony-related activity are relevant to the ultimate level

---

[1] For an excellent survey of the literature on animal communication, see Hauser
1996. Analysis of the honeybee language is due to the pioneering work of Karl von Frisch
(1967).

of socially distributed knowledge: (1) discovery, (2) production and transmission of messages, (3) message reception, and (4) message acceptance. The first stage, discovery, occurs when a group member observes one or more facts.[2] For the moment I assume that the observed facts are indeed facts, that is, true. Endowed with this information, the potential informant moves to the second stage of activity: deciding *whether, what, how,* and *to whom* to communicate. On the "whether" dimension, there are the options of remaining completely silent or of communicating something about one or more of the observed facts. If the choice is to communicate, two sets of options arise concerning the "what" dimension. First, the communicator must select which of the observed facts to communicate. If she just observed ten truths[3] but it is not feasible to communicate each of them, she must decide which subset to report. Second, for each of the observed truths, there is the option of reporting it sincerely versus the option of distorting or falsifying it. The third dimension is "how" to communicate. More than one medium of communication may be available, and the media may differ, for instance, in terms of their likelihood of reaching the intended audience. So choices must be made. Finally, on the "to whom" dimension, the observer needs to select the targeted audience for the selected messages. To which individuals should the various messages be directed? Are there potential receivers that the reporter wants to *prevent* from receiving the messages? Choices along the four dimensions may be interdependent. The chosen medium or manner of transmission might constrain how many messages can be sent. The audience targeted for the messages may influence their contents, and vice versa.

If an observer remains totally silent, there is clearly no testimonial increment in the aggregate of knowledge. Assume, however, that one or more messages are sent; then the next stage is reception. Are the messages actually received, who receives them, and are they properly understood?[4] Attempts at communication may succeed in varying degrees. Reports may reach a larger or smaller proportion of the intended audience. If a report reaches nobody, it will neither increase nor decrease the level of aggregate knowledge. Once a message is received by one or more hearers, the fourth stage of the process

---

[2] Although discovery is here portrayed as an individual practice, it need not be a purely individualistic affair. The technical resources for investigating *P*, and even the concepts needed to understand *P*, may have been acquired from others. Nonetheless, though the individual may have been *prepared* or *equipped* for her discovery by the assistance of others, the discovery is still the achievement of that individual rather than others.

[3] It is not easy, of course, either practically or theoretically, to individuate and count the number of truths gleaned in a given observation or series of observations. My assumption that there is a determinate number of such truths is merely an expository convenience.

[4] In what follows I take proper understanding largely for granted, although this is a nontrivial task for the receiver and one that much occupies the psychology of language comprehension.

kicks in: the acceptance stage. Each receiver must adopt a credal attitude toward the report: believe the reported proposition, reject it, withhold judgment, or assign some intermediate degree of belief. If all of the reports are sincere and hence true (given the assumed accuracy of the observations), and if some receivers increase their belief in the reported propositions as a result of the messages while none of them lowers their belief, then the social aggregate of knowledge increases. Moreover, the larger their increases in belief, the greater the increase in the social aggregate of knowledge.[5]

Even this rather abstract characterization of testimonial activity allows us to deduce certain things about the veritistic impact of various message production and transmission practices. As an analytical device, assume first that a given communicator intends to send only sincere (and hence truthful) reports, and that the same audience will receive and fully believe any message she transmits. Given these assumptions, which reports will produce the largest positive changes in V-value? First, good reports will be on topics that interest the audience. This follows from the fact that there is V-value only when learners have an interest in what they learn.[6] Second, since increases in V-value are maximized by having the largest belief increments in truths, the best reports are those for which the audience initially has the lowest degrees of belief. Initially low DBs leave more room for larger increases. Under what conditions can prior DBs be expected to be low? When the following three conditions are satisfied: (1) the occurrence of the reported event or fact is not predictable from background information, (2) audience members do not themselves observe the reported event or fact, and (3) audience members have not already received reports of the event from other communicators. Intriguingly, this combination of features almost defines what is commonly understood as a "newsworthy" event. First, such an event must be of interest to hearers. Second, it must not be a readily predictable event; the rising of the sun is not newsworthy. Third, the message must not be "stale" at the time of report, that is, already well disseminated to the bulk of the audience.

Even this brief overview makes it obvious that different speaker practices can have significantly different veritistic effects. In the remainder of this section, I explore a few selected issues concerning speaker practices. After this section, however, the chapter turns to hearer practices.

I began the discussion of testimony by assuming that reporters' observations are accurate, but that assumption, clearly, is often violated. False reports can issue from observational error. A second source of inaccurate testimony is dishonesty or insincerity, which can be prompted by a variety of incentives the speaker might have for deception. Similar incentives can lead a potential informant to prefer silence to either disclosure or mendacity. In fact, it is not

---

[5] At least this holds when the reports interest the hearers; but the fact that they bother to receive and mentally process the reports may already imply interest.

[6] Here I ignore the possible interest of other parties or institutions.

obvious what generally motivates knowledgeable agents to disseminate their knowledge. The conveyance of information, it appears, generally profits the receiver rather than the communicator. So wherein lies the motivation or incentive for informed agents to disseminate their knowledge?

According to one view, people have a natural, default disposition to speak the truth, to express their beliefs honestly and sincerely. This view was articulated by the Scottish philosopher Thomas Reid:

The wise and beneficent Author of nature, who intended that we should be social creatures, and that we should receive the greatest and most important part of our knowledge by the information of others, hath, for these purposes implanted in our natures two principles that tally with each other.

The first of these principles is, a propensity to speak truth, and to use the signs of language, so as to convey our real sentiments. This principle has a powerful operation, even in the greatest of liars; for, where they lie once, they speak truth a hundred times. Truth is always uppermost, and is the natural issue of the mind. It requires no art or training, no inducement or temptation, but only that we yield to natural impulse. Lying, on the contrary, is doing violence to our nature; and is never practiced, even by the worst of men, without some temptation. Speaking truth is like using our natural food, which we would do from appetite, although it answered no end; but lying is like taking physic, which is nauseous to the taste, and which no man takes but for some end which he cannot otherwise attain. (1970: 238–9)

Reid's hypothesis is a motivation-innateness hypothesis. Although he focuses on a propensity toward truth as opposed to falsehood (honesty as opposed to deception), the innateness hypothesis may also include a propensity toward revelation as opposed to silence. Evidence about the animal world points toward innate propensities of this kind, though the detailed story is undoubtedly complex. Marc Hauser (1996: 413) indicates that the ubiquity of predation exerts strong selection pressures for an evolved mechanism of warning, of sounding an alarm when a predator is in the vicinity. The existence of such mechanisms is borne out by a vast empirical literature, covering a wide variety of species. Domestic chickens, for example, issue alarm calls when detecting a hawk (or what they think is a hawk). In general, more alarm calls are produced to conspecific audiences than to audiences of another species, and fewer alarm calls yet are produced when there is no audience at all (Hauser 1996: 577–8). In human beings, of course, the range of information that the species is capable of expressing and is apparently disposed to express is vastly greater. And it is plausible that people too have an evolved disposition toward truthful revelation or dissemination. It is equally obvious, however, that people often have motives for silence or deception. Such behavior is present even in animals. Although chickens and rhesus monkeys commonly signal their conspecifics when food is discovered, they sometimes withhold this information from their troop (Hauser 1996: 581).

If an innate disposition toward truthful revelation can be overridden by conflicting incentives, how can a society increase the amount of truthful revelation so as to enhance veritistic outcomes? Offers of reward and threats of punishment are obvious techniques. Informal rewards to communicators seem to be part of many, if not all, human cultures. Such informal rewards may consist in smiles of appreciation, or heightened respect and status conferred on informants. Informal rules of information sharing may exist in conversational settings. If you share your gossip with me, I am expected to reciprocate. Each person profits by exchange of goods "in kind." Punishment can also be employed. If a spy withholds information from his handler, who subsequently learns of the concealment, punishment will probably be inflicted. Even animals punish their conspecifics when information is withheld. Retaliatory behavior has been observed in honeybees, birds, horses, and a variety of primates (Hauser 1996: 582). In modern human society, news dissemination has become a more formal economic activity, in many cases a major profit-making enterprise.[7]

In addition to motivating potential speakers via reward and punishment, there are other ways to help speakers increase their potential contribution to veritistic improvement. Assuming a speaker's good veritistic intent, her ability to realize this intent depends on what she knows about her audience. A speaker can make better report selections, for example, if she knows which topics interest her audience. Why waste time and effort reporting facts that don't concern them? Another helpful item of knowledge for the speaker is the audience's prior credal state vis-à-vis the information available for report. If most of the audience already has (and believes) certain information, no veritistic gain will accrue by repeating it. Given time and resource constraints on communication, it is veritistically preferable to report previously unknown facts, or, even better, facts about which false opinions are rife. In other words, *surprising* information is the most valuable to transmit.

Potential reporters can learn about their audience's prior informational states if audience members direct queries at them. By verbally querying $Q(P/-P)$, a person tells a potential informant two things: (1) that he is ignorant of $Q(P/-P)$, and (2) that he is interested in $Q(P/-P)$. This indicates that an authoritative report of either P or not-P would yield a substantial veritistic increase for that receiver. The opportunity to query potential informants is therefore a valuable contribution to veritistic enhancement, and communication formats that enable such querying activities are, in this respect, superior to ones that do not.

Another type of knowledge reporters should have is which channels and styles of communication are most likely to reach the intended audience, especially in a timely fashion. Both knowing about communication channels and

---

[7] Michael Bloomberg became an overnight billionaire by providing a digital news service for financial managers.

knowing the habits of one's audience can be relevant. If Emilio never reads his e-mail, or regularly allows it to accumulate for weeks on end, it is pointless to send him information via e-mail—at least when he needs the information promptly.

Another category of veritistic assistance is communication technology. More powerful technologies of communication offer expanded opportunities for message transmission, enabling audiences to learn things they would not otherwise learn. Historically, the printing press, the telegraph, the telephone, and radio and television are the most dramatic examples. On the contemporary scene, of course, the major revolution is digital technology, which will be examined in Chapter 6.

Thus far we have looked at communication decisions from the perspective of a single source. But a full veritistic analysis should consider the effects of multiple communication sources. If many sources amplify the volume of their messages in order to maximize their audience size—if they flood the landscape with billboards and fill the mail boxes with junk mail—receivers cannot process all the transmitted messages. The resulting glut of messages must be filtered, and the filtering choices may not be veritistically optimal.[8]

Earlier in this discussion I introduced the assumption that receivers would believe any message they receive and process. This assumption, however, must now be relaxed. Receivers have an option of believing, disbelieving, or assigning some intermediate level of belief to any message received. Even if audience members receive true reports whose contents they do not already fully believe, there will be no increase in V-value unless the reports induce some of them to increase their levels of belief. What can truthful speakers do to make their reports more credible to hearers than they otherwise might be?

There are two types of skepticism receivers might have about a speaker or her report. First, receivers might worry about the source's competence to make an accurate observation or interpretation of the alleged state of affairs, especially in a technical subject matter. To combat such possible skepticism, a speaker might enhance her credibility by issuing "signals" of observational competence. She might accompany her report with a display of certification, such as a professional degree or license. She might wear a professional uniform (a physician's white coat, for instance), or use professional jargon that signals technical expertise.

The second category of possible skepticism concerns the reporter's honesty rather than competence. What strategies can combat this type of skepticism? In face-to-face communication, the speaker's style of delivery can powerfully influence credibility: her tone of voice, her facial aspect, and her body language. Another element is the speaker's prior pattern of (verifiable) truth telling. By telling truths in the past, a speaker establishes a reputation for hon-

---

[8] The filtering problem will be addressed in Chapter 6 in the context of electronic communication.

esty that can promote credibility on each new occasion. Another strategy is to inform hearers of how to authenticate one's report if they question it. Other witnesses of the reported event might be identified who could be consulted for confirmation. Openly exposing oneself to refutation can inspire confidence in one's veracity.[9]

Unfortunately, many of these efforts to enhance credibility can be duplicated or approximated by deceptive and even incompetent reporters. Inevitably, the task of deciding how much confidence to place in a report falls to each hearer. It is time to turn, therefore, to the sorts of hearer practices that can promote V-value. In contrast to this section—which provides little more than a laundry list of possible speaker practices—the remainder of the chapter explores at some depth the receiver's task of assessing message credibility. Under what circumstances should a receiver accept a report, reject it, or accord it a specific degree of belief?

4.2 *A Bayesian inference practice*

The veritistic merits of a hearer acceptance practice cannot be assessed in isolation from the reporting practices that it complements. This point can be appreciated by reflecting on results from game theory. A particular strategy for playing a certain game can be very successful when pitted against a second strategy but much less successful when used against others (Axelrod 1984). Similarly, a given message-acceptance strategy may be veritistically successful when used in the environment of certain reporting practices but unsuccessful in response to different reporting practices.

Consider the simple acceptance practice of BLIND TRUST, which is to believe every report or piece of testimony you hear.[10] BLIND TRUST is an excellent acceptance practice if it complements a reporting practice that generates only truths, in other words, if it is used in an ideal reporting environment. An ideal reporting environment is one in which speakers never misperceive, misremember, or deliberately distort the facts. Unfortunately, there is no realistic prospect for such infallibility and scrupulous honesty. So

---

[9] The devices of "signaling" and establishing a reputation are intensively studied in the economics of information. (The seminal work on signaling is Spence 1974; for discussions of reputation in game theory, see Rasmusen 1989.) The directions taken by economists are somewhat different, though, from the applications I suggest in the text. In any case, there is no space here to canvass this massive literature.

[10] BLIND TRUST cannot be implemented in all environments while remaining consistent, because receivers may receive contradictory messages from different speakers. To cope with this problem, redefine BLIND TRUST as the practice of accepting the most *recent* report received on a topic. If one speaker reports P and a subsequent speaker reports not-P, the user of BLIND TRUST will initially believe P and then switch to belief in not-P.

we need to ask how BLIND TRUST would fare in other reporting environments. Clearly, it is not optimal in *every* possible reporting environment; in a speech environment where every report is false, BLIND TRUST is terrible.[11] The optimal strategy in that environment is BLIND CONTRATRUST, that is, believing the negation of every report. Is there any acceptance practice that is optimal in *all* reporting environments, in other words, better in each reporting environment than every other acceptance practice would be? As in game theory, the answer appears to be "no."

In light of this situation, how should social epistemology proceed? First, it might recommend a certain reporting practice and then recommend an acceptance practice that would optimally complement it. But there is no guarantee that speakers would adopt the recommended reporting practice. Should hearers be counseled to adopt the complementary acceptance practice even if reporters are using practices at variance with the recommended one? Surely not. Alternatively, social epistemology might take the *de facto* distribution of reporting practices as a given, for good or ill. An acceptance practice should be crafted that would complement the existing distribution of reporting practices. Since different reporting practices might be used in different contexts— one practice when reporting the weather and a different practice when declaring one's annual income to the revenue service—perhaps epistemology should advise hearers to vary their acceptance practices as a function of those different contexts. But should social epistemology take on the assignment of trying to describe the *de facto* reporting practices in every social niche and sector of discourse? From a practical point of view, this would be excessive. Even I, whose aspirations for epistemology might strike some as grandiose, am not prepared to ask *that* much of it.

Here is a more modest project for the epistemology of testimonial acceptance. Instead of seeking an optimal acceptance practice, either for every possible reporting environment or for the actual reporting environments, let us adopt a *satisficing* approach. Let us seek a veritistically *good* practice, even if it is not the *best* practice relative to this or that reporting environment. We confine ourselves, then, to the absolute mode as contrasted with the comparative mode of veritistic evaluation (recall Section 3.4). A good practice is one that produces veritistic improvements *on average*, over a range of actual and possible applications. In fact, I think we shall be able to identify a reception practice that is objectively likely to produce *some* veritistic improvement—not necessarily the largest amount of improvement—in any reporting environment. Even this may seem like an impossible dream; but there is such a practice, as I shall demonstrate.[12]

The practice I have in mind is a version of Bayesian inference supplemented

---

[11] It is debatable whether universal false reporting is logically possible. For purposes of illustration, however, this issue can be ducked.

[12] To say that there *is* such a practice is not to say that it is easy to implement.

with an additional requirement. Is Bayesian inference a *social* practice? As a general inference principle it does not qualify as social, but when applied to the reports or testimony of other *people*, I count it as a social practice. The use of Bayesian inference in testimony has been nicely described by Richard Friedman (1987). Friedman's concern is legal testimony, especially legal rules concerning hearsay. For the purposes of this chapter, however, I focus on the general Bayesian analysis of testimony, without restriction to the specific problem of hearsay or even the legal context more generally. In the present section I explain the Bayesian approach and its intuitive appeal. In the following section I offer a *veritistic* rationale for deploying the Bayesian practice (suitably augmented).

In expounding Friedman's application of Bayesianism to testimony, the cases to be described are ones in which a witness testifies in court to a fact which he allegedly observed personally. Before turning to such cases, however, consider a nontestimonial application of Bayes' Theorem. Mornings in the city of Omphalos are either cloudy or not cloudy, and afternoons are either rainy or not rainy. Suppose we arrive in Omphalos on a rainy afternoon, and wish to estimate the probability that the morning was cloudy. Given the afternoon rain, what is the probability that the morning was cloudy? That is, what is p(CLOUDY given RAINY)? Two (equivalent) forms of Bayes' Theorem are given in equations (4.1) and (4.2):

(4.1) p(CLOUDY given RAINY) =

$$\frac{p(\text{RAINY given CLOUDY}) \times p(\text{CLOUDY})}{p(\text{RAINY})}$$

(4.2) p(CLOUDY given RAINY) =

$$\frac{p(\text{RAINY given CLOUDY}) \times p(\text{CLOUDY})}{p(\text{RAINY given CLOUDY}) \times p(\text{CLOUDY}) + p(\text{RAINY given NOT-CLOUDY}) \times p(\text{NOT-CLOUDY})}.$$

These can be rewritten using the slash notation (" / ") for "given":

(4.1′) p(CLOUDY/RAINY) = $\dfrac{p(\text{RAINY/CLOUDY}) \times p(\text{CLOUDY})}{p(\text{RAINY})}$

(4.2′) p(CLOUDY/RAINY) =

$$\frac{p(\text{RAINY/CLOUDY}) \times p(\text{CLOUDY})}{p(\text{RAINY/CLOUDY}) \times p(\text{CLOUDY}) + p(\text{RAINY/NOT-CLOUDY}) \times p(\text{NOT-CLOUDY})}.$$

Friedman explains Bayes' Theorem in terms of "routes" from one "place" to another. Figure 4.1 shows that the route to RAINY could have been through

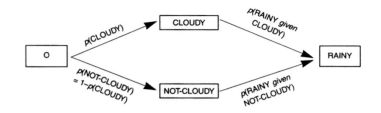

FIG. 4.1. Probabilistic routes to rain

(Reprinted by permission of The Yale Law Journal Company and Fred B.
Rothman & Company from *The Yale Law Journal*, Vol. 96, page 671.)

either CLOUDY or NOT-CLOUDY. The task is to estimate "retrospectively"—
that is, given RAINY—the probability of the actual route having been through
CLOUDY. As equation (4.2) indicates, this probability can be calculated from
four other values: (a) the prior probability of CLOUDY, (b) the prior probability of NOT-CLOUDY (= 1 − prior probability of CLOUDY), (c) the conditional
probability of RAINY given CLOUDY (also called the *likelihood* of RAINY given
CLOUDY), and (d) the conditional probability of RAINY given NOT-CLOUDY
(the *likelihood* of RAINY given NOT-CLOUDY).

Precisely the same treatment applies to cases of testimony. Here the
observed "outcome" (analogous to RAINY in the previous example) is the fact
that a witness testifies that a particular fact X occurred. Call this testimonial
event "TESTIMONY(X)." The problem for each juror in the courtroom is to
assess the probability that X actually occurred—for example, that the defendant actually committed the alleged crime—in light of TESTIMONY(X) plus
other evidence. Obviously, jurors are not expected to place blind trust in the
testimony of witnesses. They have to weigh such testimony along with other
evidence they have at their disposal: other evidence introduced in court plus
general world knowledge. According to Bayes' Theorem, however, the probabilities relevant to determining the probability of X given TESTIMONY(X) are
specified as follows:

(4.3) $p(X/\text{TESTIMONY}(X)) =$

$$\frac{p(\text{TESTIMONY}(X)/X) \times p(X)}{p(\text{TESTIMONY}(X)/X) \times p(X) + p(\text{TESTIMONY}(X)/\text{NOT-}X) \times p(\text{NOT-}X)}.$$

As shown in equation (4.3), the four relevant values to use in determining the
probability of X in light of TESTIMONY(X) are (a) $p(X)$, the prior probability
of X occurring, (b) $p(\text{NOT-}X)$, the prior probability of X not occurring (= 1 −
$p(X)$), (c) the conditional probability of the witness testifying to X, given that

X did occur (the *likelihood* of the testimony to X, given X), and (d) the conditional probability of the witness testifying to X, given that X did not occur (the *likelihood* of the testimony to X, given not-X).

Clearly, the probability of a given witness being truthful or accurate is not the same for all reports. For some subject matters of report, a witness may have an incentive to misrepresent the facts; for other subject matters, she may not. Someone may have no reason to report that it rained yesterday if it didn't, but may well have reason to report "The check is in the mail" even if it isn't. Thus, the conditional probability of her *saying* the check is in the mail (even) if it isn't may be high. Similarly, in a particular legal case, the witness may or may not have an incentive to lie about what she observed. Equally, her particular viewing circumstances may have made it more or less difficult to observe the fact in question. So a juror trying to assess the probative impact of an item of testimony should take account of the particulars of the case in order to assess all four values, including the two likelihoods. Once these probability values are assessed, Bayes' Theorem indicates how they should be combined to reach an estimate of the probability of X in light of TESTIMONY(X).

Let us consider more closely the role of the likelihoods, in particular, a certain term often used in probabilistic analysis, the *likelihood ratio*. The likelihood ratio, for an evidentiary proposition Y, is the quotient

$$(4.4) \qquad\qquad \frac{p(Y/X)}{p(Y/\text{NOT-}X)}.$$

It specifies whether the truth of Y is more or less likely given the truth of X as compared with the falsity of X—and by how great a factor. If the probability of the evidentiary proposition Y is greater given X than given NOT-X—that is, if the likelihood ratio is greater than one—then the evidence has positive probative value (for X). If the probability of the evidentiary proposition Y is less given X than given NOT-X—that is, if the likelihood ratio is less than one—then the evidence has negative probative value. In our cases of testimony, the evidentiary proposition Y is the proposition that a certain witness testifies to X (in a certain manner) (= TESTIMONY(X)). If such testimony is more likely on the assumption that X did occur than it is on the assumption that X did not occur, then Bayes' Theorem implies that the posterior probability assigned to X, once the testimony is heard, should be higher than the prior probability. Furthermore, as the likelihood ratio increases more and more (away from one), the change in probability arising from the evidence will be more dramatic (for a fixed prior). Thus, for a piece of testimony to be as probative as possible, one would like a witness whose credibility is as high as possible on the topic in question: one for whom the likelihood of accurate testimony is much higher than the likelihood of inaccurate testimony.

Friedman applies route analysis to the case of testimonial evidence. Figure

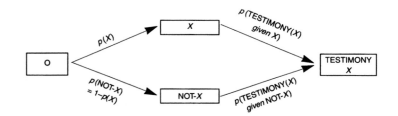

FIG. 4.2. Simple probabilistic routes to testimony

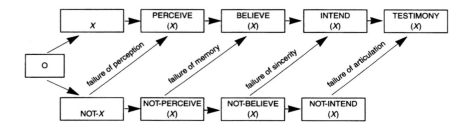

FIG. 4.3. Complex probabilistic routes to testimony

(Figs. 4.2 and 4.3 reprinted by permission of The Yale Law Journal Company and Fred B. Rothman & Company from *The Yale Law Journal*, Vol. 96, pages 677, 687.)

4.2 is a simple diagram illustrating how TESTIMONY(X) can emerge from a path involving X or, alternatively, from a path involving NOT-X. Figure 4.3 is a more complex diagram showing several ways it can transpire that a witness's testimony is inaccurate. It is customary in the legal literature to speak of four testimonial capacities, referred to by such labels as "perception," "memory," "sincerity," and "articulateness." Accurate testimony depends on the satisfactory operation of all four capacities. In route analysis terms, this means that for events to go from a fact X to accurate testimony to X by a witness, they must first go from X to PERCEIVE(X) (the witness perceived X), then to BELIEVE(X) (the witness remembered, and so now believes, X), then to INTEND(X) (the witness sincerely intends to declare X), and only then to TESTIMONY(X) (the witness testifies articulately to X). (See Figure 4.3.) This is called the "truth path" to TESTIMONY(X). A variety of other routes, however, might pass through NOT-X and lead to TESTIMONY(X). The witness might correctly perceive NOT-X, for example, at the time of its occurrence, but forget it by the time of his declaration. In a different route, the witness might perceive NOT-X and still remember it at the time of his declaration, but lie about it. Friedman shows how to analyze these complexities in Bayesian terms, but I shall not pursue the details that occupy him.

Many readers, either familiar or unfamiliar with Bayesianism, might find the Bayesian analysis of testimony intuitively congenial. But how, it might be asked, does this bear on the search for a *veritistically* meritorious acceptance practice? People familiar with standard treatments of Bayesianism might be especially perplexed, because Bayesians rarely rationalize their approach in veritistic terms. In the next section, however, I shall show how and why the use of Bayes' Theorem can be a veritistically desirable practice in testimonial inference.

4.3 *A veritistic rationale for Bayesian inference*

We saw earlier that many report-acceptance practices would be veritistically good in certain speech environments but poor in others. This was true, for example, of BLIND TRUST. What I shall show about Bayesian inference is that, when certain additional conditions are met, it has veritistic merit in *any* report environment. The kind of veritistic merit I have in mind is not so strong as to guarantee any particular level of knowledge. All that can be said for the practice concerns its *positive* veritistic effect: its ability to raise the user's degree of knowledge vis-à-vis the target (reported) proposition. Actually, the claim is even weaker than the previous sentence suggests. Use of Bayes' Theorem will not always raise the user's degree of knowledge; but, under conditions to be specified, it is *objectively likely* to raise his degree of knowledge. This is a significant property, which should certainly not be belittled.

The reader must be forewarned, however, that there is no free lunch. Veritistic attainments do not come free, or even cheap. As the saying goes, "garbage in, garbage out." Good inference procedures alone do not guarantee veritistically good outputs; one also needs good factual inputs. What I am leading up to is readily illustrated by deductive reasoning, allegedly the "class act" of inference procedures. No deductive method can pledge to a reasoner that its use will guarantee true conclusions. Only a more modest claim can be made: true conclusions will follow if the reasoner's *premises* are true. As the usual formula has it, deduction "carries truths into truths," that is, carries true premises into true conclusions. If one begins with false premises, all bets are off.

If this is the strongest claim that can be made on behalf of deductive inference, more can hardly be expected from inductive or probabilistic inference. One should be pleased to find any analogous property in the latter domains. Precisely such an analogous property is what Bayesian inference can be shown to possess, under assumptions to be specified. In particular, what I shall show (roughly) is that when a reasoner starts with *accurate likelihoods* (analogous to true premises), it is objectively probable that Bayesian inference will increase his degree of knowledge (truth possession) of the target proposition. More precisely, after using Bayes' Theorem, the objectively expected degree of truth possession (or V-value) associated with the reasoner's posterior DB will be greater than the objectively expected degree of truth possession (or V-value) associated with the reasoner's prior DB. I shall explain this general result, plus a second, related result, and show how they apply to the domain of testimony. The general theorems to be given were formulated and proved by Moshe Shaked, based on a framework and related conjectures by the present author.[13]

Consider a witness's testimony that he personally observed X, where X might be the presence of a campsite at a certain location, or the perpetration of a criminal act by a certain individual, or any other such singular event or state of affairs. The question before the reasoner is whether or not X is true $(Q(X/-X))$: whether there is such a campsite at the specified location, or whether the individual in question did commit the criminal act. If X is true and the reasoner has a DB of 1.0 in X, then the reasoner has a maximum degree of knowledge or truth possession vis-à-vis $Q(X/-X)$. If NOT-X is true (X is false), and the reasoner has a DB of .7 in X—hence, assuming probabilistic coherence, a DB of .3 in NOT-X—then her degree of knowledge or truth possession vis-à-vis $Q(X/-X)$ is .3. Now assume that, prior to hearing any testimony, a juror has a DB of .2 in X. The problem is how to change her DB in response to the testimony so as to increase her degree of truth possession or V-value. We shall see that if the reasoning juror meets certain conditions, the Bayesian method will, on average, produce an increase in truth possession or V-value.

As seen earlier, the reasoner's subjective estimates of the likelihoods play a crucial role in Bayesian inference. If the reasoner's subjective likelihood ratio is greater than 1.0, her use of Bayes' Theorem will lead her to revise upwards her DB in X. If her subjective likelihood ratio is less than 1.0, she will revise downwards her DB in X. In the first case, she thinks it more likely that the witness testifies to X given the truth of X than it is that he testifies to X given the falsity of X. In the second case, she reverses the relative magnitudes of the likelihoods. Admittedly, in a testimony example, it would be a somewhat bizarre witness who is more likely to testify to X given its falsity than given its truth. But in other types of examples (not involving testimony), the likelihood ratio can easily go in either direction: greater than 1.0 or less than 1.0. Moreover, if we allow specifications of *manner* or *demeanor* of testifying—not merely "testifying to X" versus "not testifying to X"—there may be certain manners of testifying to X that are more likely given the falsity of X than given its truth.

---

[13] See Goldman and Shaked 1991*a*, reprinted in Goldman 1992: ch. 12. The proofs of the theorems appear in the Appendix of the 1992 reprinting only. Some mathematical generalizations of these results appear in Goldman and Shaked 1991*b*, of which Shaked is the primary author.

Now the crucial assumptions for obtaining our results are twofold. First we assume that each likelihood has an *objective* magnitude. In the testimony example, this means that there is a specific objective probability that this particular witness would testify to X given (the truth of) X, and a specific objective probability that this witness would testify to X given NOT-X. This sort of assumption is admittedly open to challenge. There is little agreement among philosophers about when, or under what precise conditions, statements have determinate objective probabilities. But at least in testimony cases it looks as if jurors, for example, work hard at trying to get *accurate* estimates of such probabilities, which seems to presume objective facts concerning such probabilities. If the witness in fact has very strong incentives to lie about X, this seems to make it objectively quite probable that she would testify to X even if it were false. If the witness has no such incentives, nor any disabilities of perception, memory, or articulation of the sort relevant to the paths in Figure 4.3, then the objective probability of her testifying to X even if it were false seems to be much lower. In any case, the theorems to be formulated below depend on objective likelihoods. It seems plausible that any mathematically *provable* generalization about the veritistic properties of a practice will require some sort of assumptions, and this is the sort of assumption required here.[14]

Now if a reasoner makes poor or perverse estimates of the likelihoods, she can hardly expect to benefit veritistically from the witness's testimony. If, for example, she thinks it more likely that he would testify to X in the observed manner if it were false than if it were true, but the reverse is actually the case, she cannot expect her use of Bayes' Theorem to increase her degree of truth possession (or V-value) vis-à-vis $Q(X/-X)$. This is where the analogy with deductive reasoning enters the picture. If a reasoner begins with false premises, she cannot expect deductive inference to lead her to new truths. Similarly, if a probabilistic reasoner begins with inaccurate likelihoods, she cannot expect the Bayesian method to improve her V-value vis-à-vis the target question. So let us ask what the Bayesian method will do if the reasoner has *accurate* likelihoods, that is, if her subjective likelihoods match the objective likelihoods. Here is where we locate our mathematical results. If subjective likelihoods match objective likelihoods, use of Bayes' Theorem leads to an objectively expected increase in degree of truth possession (V-value). In other words, under these conditions a Bayesian practice exhibits positive V-value.

Rather than state the theorem precisely at the outset, as custom dictates, let me walk through a single example. When the reader has a feel for the territory, the theorem will be more comprehensible. Assume as before that a witness testifies to the occurrence of some event X, and the question is whether X really occurred. Further assume that the testimony might take any of four

---

[14] It is quite possible, however, that theorems similar to the ones presented here can be obtained for intervals rather than point probabilities. So the assumption of objective point probabilities may not be crucial.

forms, combining both content and demeanor: (1) testimony that X occurred, delivered with confidence, (2) testimony that X occurred, delivered nervously, (3) testimony that X did not occur, delivered with confidence, and (4) testimony that X did not occur, delivered nervously. I shall label these, respectively: (1) $T_C(X)$, (2) $T_N(X)$, (3) $T_C(\text{NOT-}X)$, and (4) $T_N(\text{NOT-}X)$. A set of such possible outcomes should be both mutually exclusive and jointly exhaustive. Although this set is not logically exhaustive (the witness might not testify at all), I shall assume that it exhausts the relevant probability space.

Next let us make some assumptions concerning the *objective* likelihoods, the conditional probabilities of getting each of the foregoing testimonial outcomes given either that X occurred or that it did not occur. The matrix below represents the set of likelihoods for the imagined case. Each cell in the matrix presents the objective likelihood of the testimonial outcome of the column given the target event specified in the row. For instance, the cell in the upper leftmost corner says that the likelihood of the witness testifying confidently to X given that X actually occurred is .60, and the cell in the upper rightmost corner says that the likelihood of the witness testifying nervously to NOT-X given that X actually occurred is .20.

	$T_C(X)$	$T_N(X)$	$T_C(\text{NOT-}X)$	$T_N(\text{NOT-}X)$
X	.60	.10	.10	.20
NOT-X	.10	.20	.60	.10

Notice that the likelihoods in each row sum to 1.0. This reflects the assumption that the listed outcomes exhaust the probability space. X and NOT-X, of course, also jointly exhaust their probability space.

As theoreticians, we want to consider the possibility that either X or not-X is true (actually occurred), and we want to see what will happen to a Bayesian reasoner's degree of truth possession under either assumption, once she observes the witness's testimony. Recall that we are also assuming that our Bayesian reasoner has accurate subjective likelihoods. This means that her subjective assignments of the conditional probabilities for each cell coincide precisely with the objective likelihoods. In other words, the foregoing matrix represents the reasoner's subjective likelihoods as well as the objective likelihoods. We do not assume, however, that the reasoner begins with a particularly good or bad estimate of the truth or falsity of X. Indeed, our analysis will show that wherever she starts—whatever her *prior* probabilities for X and for NOT-X—application of Bayes' Theorem to derive a *posterior* probability in light of the witness's testimony leads to an (objectively) expected *increase* in her truth possession. (More precisely, this holds so long as her prior probabilities are neither 0 nor 1.0, and the likelihood ratio is not identical to 1.0.) In other words, if X is true, it will lead her, on average, to have a higher degree of belief in X; and if NOT-X is true, it will lead her, on average, to have a higher degree of belief in NOT-X.

Let us first see how a reasoner will change her DBs in X and in NOT-X once she observes the witness testify. For illustrative purposes, I assume that her initial DB in X, prior to hearing this witness's testimony, is .20, and her prior DB in NOT-X is $1.0 - .20 = .80$. This is an arbitrary choice, and the theorem to be presented holds for any prior whatever (other than 1.0 and 0). But I shall work through the case of $p(X) = .20$. We have already learned that changes in DB dictated by Bayes' Theorem depend heavily on the likelihood ratio. When this ratio is greater than one—the likelihood for X exceeds the likelihood for NOT-X—there will be an increase in DB for X and a decrease in DB for NOT-X. Conversely, when this ratio is less than one—the likelihood for X is smaller than the likelihood for NOT-X—there will be a decrease in DB for X and an increase for NOT-X. Thus, looking at the matrix given above, it is obvious that testimony $T_C(X)$ and testimony $T_N(\text{NOT-}X)$ will each raise the DB for X and lower the DB for NOT-X, because the first likelihood ratio is $.60/.10 = 6$, and the second likelihood ratio is $.20/.10 = 2$. Conversely, testimony $T_N(X)$ and $T_C(\text{NOT-}X)$ will each lower the DB for X and raise the DB for NOT-X, because the first likelihood ratio is $.10/.20 = .50$, and the second likelihood ratio is $.10/.60 = .167$. However, we cannot infer from this information alone whether the changes in DB are likely to constitute increases or decreases in amounts of *truth possession* (and hence V-value) on the part of the reasoner. That is the principal question to be addressed.

To answer this question, we need to calculate more precisely the magnitude as well as the direction of the reasoner's DB-changes in response to each of the different testimonial outcomes. This can be computed by applying Bayes' Theorem to the reasoner's prior DBs for X and NOT-X and her subjective likelihoods. Her subjective likelihoods, recall, are given by the matrix, because they are assumed to coincide with the objective likelihoods. To guide our computations, here again is Bayes' Theorem, written in notation suitable to our purposes. "E" represents the target event (either X or not-X) and "T" represents the item of testimony that serves as new evidence.

$$(4.5) \quad p(E/T) = \frac{p(T/E) \times p(E)}{p(T/E) \times p(E) + p(T/\text{NOT-}E) \times p(\text{NOT-}E)}$$

Suppose that $T_C(X)$ occurs; how will the reasoner change her DB in X? The relevant numbers here are the two priors, $p(X) = .20$ and $p(\text{NOT-}X) = .80$, plus the two likelihoods in the leftmost column of the matrix, .60 and .10. Filling in the values on the right-hand side of the equation, we have:

$$(4.6) \quad \frac{(.60) \times (.20)}{(.60) \times (.20) + (.10) \times (.80)} = \frac{.12}{.12 + .08} = \frac{.12}{.20} = .60.$$

This means that the reasoner's posterior DB after observing $T_C(X)$ would be .60. So, if the first type of testimony is heard, she will be led to increase her

DB from .20 to .60, a DB increase of .40. By similar calculations, we determine that the following DB movements would ensue from the four types of testimony:

$T_C(X)$: from .20 to .60, an increase of .400
$T_N(X)$: from .20 to .111, a decrease of .089
$T_C(NOT-X)$: from .20 to .04, a decrease of .160
$T_N(NOT-X)$: from .20 to .333, an increase of .133

We next ask whether these changes would be increases or decreases in *truth possession* (V-value). This depends, of course, on whether X or NOT-X is actually true. First let us assume that X is true. In that scenario, the foregoing DB increases are increases in V-value as well, and the DB decreases are decreases in V-value. So let us ask: If X is true, what are the (objective) probabilities of these positive and negative changes in V-value occurring? The objective probabilities are given by the objective likelihoods, which are the numbers in the top row of the matrix. Thus, if X is true, we can calculate the *expected change in V-value* as follows:

(4.7) $ECVV(X) = .60(+.400) + .10(-.089) + .10(-.160) + .20(+.133)$
$= +.2417.$

So the objectively expected change in V-value, if X is true, is *positive*! To be sure, there are some possible developments that would lead the reasoner to make DB changes that constitute decreases in V-value. On average, however, there is an expected increase in V-value.

Precisely the same result holds under the scenario in which NOT-X is true. We have already calculated what DB changes would occur for X if each of the different types of testimony were given. Precisely opposite changes take place in DB changes for NOT-X, which are the relevant DBs to consider in the scenario in which NOT-X is true. Thus, in the case of $T_C(X)$, where the reasoner's DB for X increases from .20 to .60, her DB for NOT-X undergoes a decrease from .80 to .40. Hence there is a negative change in V-value rather than a positive one. Similarly for the other cases. So although the magnitudes of DB change are the same under each of the types of testimony, their signs must be reversed to represent changes in V-value. In addition, if we assume the truth of NOT-X, we must calculate the various contingencies using the numbers in the bottom row of the matrix, because those are the likelihoods of the forms of testimony given NOT-X. We thereby obtain the following value for the expected truth possession change if NOT-X is true:

(4.8) $ECVV(NOT-X) = .10(-.400) + .20(+.089) + .60(+.160)$
$+ .10(-.133) = +.0605.$

The point to notice is that this value is also positive. So whatever the true state of affairs, Bayesian revision of DBs together with accurate likelihoods generates an expected increase in V-value.

The general theorem may be stated as follows.

> Theorem (4.1): Suppose an agent observes the value of a certain variable (for example, the testimony of a witness), which depends probabilistically on the true answer to the question $Q(X/-X)$. Suppose the agent uses Bayesian conditionalization to update her DB vis-à-vis the question $Q(X/-X)$. Finally, suppose that her subjective likelihoods match the objective likelihoods; the likelihood ratios $\neq 1.0$; and her prior DB $\neq 1.0$ or 0. Then the objectively expected change in truth possession (V-value) vis-à-vis $Q(X/-X)$ is positive.[15]

A second and related theorem has also been proved.[16] The intuitive idea behind this second theorem can also be illustrated for testimonial cases. Not all testimony is of equal evidential weight. In particular, in place of a witness whose testimonial likelihoods are specified by the first matrix, it is evidentially better to have a witness whose objective testimonial likelihoods are more conclusive or decisive, that is, where the likelihood ratios are more extreme. To illustrate, consider a witness whose testimonial likelihoods are the following:

	$T_C(X)$	$T_N(X)$	$T_C(\text{NOT-}X)$	$T_N(\text{NOT-}X)$
X	.96	.02	.01	.01
NOT-X	.01	.01	.96	.02

This matrix describes a highly reliable witness, who will almost certainly testify truthfully (and confidently). A Bayesian reasoner whose subjective likelihoods match these objective likelihoods will have an extremely good chance of increasing her V-value about $Q(X/-X)$ by observing this witness's testimony.

Although this is an extreme case, in which the likelihood ratios for confident testimony are 96/1 and 1/96, it is intuitively obvious that even less extreme likelihood ratios could still be evidentially more probative than those

---

[15] When the likelihood ratio is 1.0, or when the prior DB is 1.0 or 0, the change in truth possession is 0; in other words, it is nonnegative though not positive. For more mathematical details, see the Appendix of Goldman and Shaked 1991*a* that appears only in its reprinted version, Goldman 1992: ch. 12. The fundamental mathematical feature of the situation that underlies the theorem is strict convexity. The proof employs Jensen's inequality.

[16] The proof originally given in the Appendix of Goldman 1992: ch. 12 is not quite adequate for this theorem. Although the proof is mathematically correct, the mathematical formulation does not exactly capture the intended conditions. The interested reader may obtain a revised proof, due to Moshe Shaked, from the author.

of the first matrix. In fact, it is generally true that more extreme likelihood ratios yield larger expected increases in truth possession than less extreme likelihood ratios. (This has been proved for two-valued variables, at any rate.) Compare the following two matrices, each describing a witness with two possible forms of testimony and associated likelihoods.

	Witness 1			Witness 2	
	T_1	T_2		T_1	T_2
X	.6	.4	X	.8	.2
NOT-X	.2	.8	NOT-X	.1	.9

The likelihood ratios associated with Witness 1 are $.6/.2 = 3$ and $.4/.8 = .5$, whereas those associated with Witness 2 are $.8/.1 = 8$ and $.2/.9 = .22$. So Witness 2's likelihood ratios are more extreme, that is, farther from 1.0, than those of Witness 1. The second theorem says that the expected increase in truth possession (or V-value) from hearing Witness 2's testimony is greater than the expected increase in response to Witness 1's testimony. For example, if the reasoner's prior DB for X = prior DB for NOT-X = .50, the expected increase in V-value from hearing Witness 1 = +.083 (whether X or NOT-X is true); whereas the expected increase in V-value from hearing Witness 2 = +.247.

The second theorem may be stated as follows.

> Theorem (4.2): Let two different variables (for example, the testimony of two different witnesses), each with two possible values, depend probabilistically on the true answer to the question $Q(X/-X)$, and let the likelihood ratios associated with one variable be more extreme than the likelihood ratios associated with the other. Suppose that an agent can observe the value of either variable and use Bayesian conditionalization to update her current DB vis-à-vis $Q(X/-X)$ based on this observation. If the conditions specified in Theorem (4.1) are met for both variables, then conditionalizing from an observation of the variable with the more extreme likelihood ratios has a greater expected increase in truth possession (V-value) than conditionalizing from an observation of the other variable.

So the practice of Bayesian reasoning with accurate likelihoods (where the specified "technical" conditions are met) has positive V-value and is a veritistically meritorious practice. It should be noted, however, that my present endorsement of Bayesian reasoning does not make me a thoroughgoing epistemological Bayesian. Some important epistemological issues are not satisfactorily resolved by Bayesianism. The theory of justification, to take a salient example, cannot be treated adequately in standard Bayesian fashion. DBs need not be *justified* even when they conform to Bayesian requirements. Assigning a DB of 1.0 to a logical truth, for example, does not ensure that the assignment is justified, because the agent might not really appreciate why the proposition is a logical truth. She might assign it probability 1.0 by mere caprice or ill-grounded authority. That would not be sufficient for justification, although it is not criticizable on Bayesian grounds.

4.4 *Estimating testimonial likelihoods*

Given the importance of accurate likelihoods (or likelihood ratios) in making Bayesian reasoning veritistically successful, the question arises whether and how the hearers of testimony can determine such likelihoods. What resources or evidence might hearers have for estimating likelihoods? Needless to say, hearers are not always fortunate enough to have good evidence concerning these likelihoods. The question is whether they *ever* have such evidence, and what the evidence would be like. I assume that, with a fixed prior, the prospect for improving one's degree of knowledge of the target proposition is better with close approximations to the likelihoods, or their ratios, than with poor approximations. (I have no mathematical proof of this, however.) So the present question is: What kinds of evidence can help attain close approximations to the likelihoods?

Although the general subject of reportage subsumes second-hand reports, third-hand reports, and so on, I continue to restrict attention to first-hand reportage: testimony about events or facts that the reporter claims to have observed, detected, or discovered himself. Friedman's route analysis suggests one classification of the sorts of elements relevant to estimating the two likelihoods, but I propose a slightly different classification with three elements: (A) the reporter's *competence*, (B) the reporter's *opportunity*, and (C) the reporter's *sincerity* or *honesty*.

A reporter's competence is his ability to detect and retain the kind of event or fact in question. This ability rests on some combination of perceptual, inferential, and memorial skills. If the proposition to which the reporter testifies concerns a common object—for example, X might be the proposition that there is beer in the refrigerator—then the relevant competence is mostly perceptual. If the proposition concerns a hard-to-identify object or relationship, considerable inferential skills may be involved. If the reporter asserts, for instance, that (he saw) a certain kind of particle pass through a cloud chamber, his inferential expertise as a physicist is crucially involved. Is he adept at discriminating *that* kind of particle from other kinds? Memory skills can be crucial if the target event occurred long ago, if the reported proposition concerns a detail that could easily be forgotten, if there is danger of confounding with other events, or danger of distortion by imagination or intense suggestion. Any evidence that a hearer has about the reporter's competence or incompetence on these dimensions is evidence that could help estimate the two likelihoods, or their ratio.

Let us look at the memory factor. Psychological studies indicate that memory for an event can be distorted by post-event occurrences, including fantasized scenarios or verbal promptings by others as to what might have happened.[17] Young children are particularly prone to be highly suggestible (Ceci and Bruck 1993). If a child or other witness is interrogated in a leading fashion prior to testifying, in a way that might prompt him to "recall" and testify to X whether or not it actually occurred, this raises the *objective likelihood* that he would so testify (even) if NOT-X was the case. So a juror who knows both the relevant psychological studies and that the witness has been suggestibly interrogated is better positioned to make an accurate estimate of the objective likelihood.

Opportunity to detect the putative fact in question is also critical. Suppose that Jones reports seeing a certain crime committed, but a hearer has independent evidence that Jones was not at the crime scene, or that his view was obstructed. If Jones was not in a position to learn the truth or falsity of X, at least not from personal observation, the hearer cannot presume that Jones is more likely to testify to X given X than given NOT-X. In other words, the ratio of the two likelihoods—TESTIMONY(X) given X / TESTIMONY(X) given NOT-X—may not be greater than 1.0.

A reporter's honesty or sincerity is also of obvious importance. Even if the reporter had both the competence and the opportunity to detect the occurrence or nonoccurrence of X, the likelihoods cannot be assessed without also considering the reporter's honesty. To assess the probability of a lie, the hearer should consider whether the reporter has an incentive to lie and, if so, the strength of that incentive. *Ceteris paribus*, the stronger the incentive to lie, the higher the probability of lying, and hence the higher the objective likelihood of TESTIMONY(X) given NOT-X. Of course, the hearer may have evidence of the reporter's sterling character. Perhaps he has a track record, known to the hearer, of speaking truthfully even when lured by strong personal motives for deception. This too is relevant in assessing the likelihood of TESTIMONY(X) given NOT-X.

The significance of track records, however, should not be exaggerated. Although Jones never lied before, perhaps he never had as strong an incentive to lie as he does now. What is relevant to the hearer is any evidence that bears on the present case: the chance that the witness would be inaccurate on *this* particular occasion, concerning the specific proposition being asserted. Similarly, Jones's past record of visual accuracy may have been achieved while

---

[17] On the first kind of distortion, see Johnson and Raye 1981, and on the second, Loftus, Miller, and Burns 1978 and Loftus, Feldman, and Dashiell 1995. For an excellent review of the literature, see Schacter 1996.

wearing glasses. If his alleged sighting of X on this occasion came under conditions of glasseslessness, this could erase the significance of the track record.

Hearers often have limited knowledge, of course, of a particular reporter. In everyday life we frequently rely on the reports of people wholly unfamiliar to us. If you arrive at an airport and the public address system announces a one-hour delay of your flight, you will typically assign a high probability to that statement (or the statement that it is delayed by *at least* one hour). But you have no knowledge whatever of the speaker's individual characteristics. (Here the speaker is delivering a report second hand; but I allow that to pass in this context.) Have you made an unreasonable probability estimate, indefensible by Bayesian standards? Not necessarily. First, you have background information about the sorts of flight information available to personnel using the public address system. Second, you have some idea of how employees are likely to be chastised or disciplined for serious errors. Third, you have general information, partly derived from knowledge of "folk psychology," about how individuals will typically respond to their job's incentive systems. Only a bizarre employee would willfully mislead the public, especially because she has nothing to gain from such misrepresentation. A simple error, of course, cannot be excluded, perhaps a verbal confusion of one flight number with another. But such slips may be infrequent enough to keep the error likelihood low. Thus, hearers may be positioned to make reasonably accurate likelihood estimates without knowing anything distinctive about the specific reporter, just by knowing the circumstances of her employment. This is a case of what Philip Kitcher calls "unearned authority" rather than "earned authority" (1993: 315 ff.), because the hearer does not calibrate the particular speaker's track record of truthfulness.

A deeper worry needs to be registered about the feasibility of making good likelihood estimates in the case of testimony. Until now I have made no distinctions among types of evidence that might support likelihood estimates. But one distinction is certainly germane: the distinction between evidence that relies on previous testimony and evidence independent of other testimony. An example of the former is when Sally judges the likelihoods concerning Jones's testimony by relying on Brown's statement that Jones is usually reliable. An example of the latter is when Sally judges the likelihoods without exploiting, directly or indirectly, any other speaker's statement. Philosophers who are skeptical about accurate assessments of testimonial likelihoods will be unimpressed by appeal to evidence based on previous testimony, because for them the veracity of such evidence itself depends on accurate testimonial likelihoods, the very problem at issue. Epistemological treatments of testimony, however, are rarely directed at likelihood assessments, because epistemologists do not generally discuss testimony in Bayesian terms. As my discussion of testimony continues, therefore, I shall drop the Bayesian framework in order to relate more smoothly to the existing philosophical literature.

4.5 *Justification of testimony-based belief*

Philosophers have been struck by how many of our beliefs are based on testimony where it is doubtful that there is any testimony-free basis for trusting that testimony. For example, how can I be justified in believing what my own name is, or who my parents are (were), or where I was born? In all these matters, I rely on testimony, either from the people who claim to be my parents, or from people who wrote and/or signed my birth certificate. I have no way to check up directly on the subject matter of any of this testimony. I can ask *others*—my (putative) grandparents, uncles, and aunts—to corroborate the testimony of my "parents." I can read newspaper listings of births from the period in question. But whatever I hear or read, it will just be more testimony. Doesn't the "regress" of testimony have to end in nontestimonial evidence, specifically, the personal observations of the reasoner?

A *reductionist* or *inductivist* approach to testimony maintains that all trust in testimony must be justifiably based on inductive inference from testimony-free evidence. Hearers must use their personal observations to check the veracity of speakers' reports and thereby establish their reliability. If a given speaker is found to be reliable enough, at least within a specified domain, the hearer is thenceforth justified in trusting her utterances in that domain on subsequent occasions. Among historical philosophers, David Hume was a clear exponent of such inductivism or reductionism:

[T]here is no species of reasoning more common, more useful, and even necessary to human life, than that which is derived from the testimony of men, and the reports of eye-witnesses and spectators . . . [O]ur assurance in any argument of this kind is derived from no other principle than our observation of the veracity of human testimony, and of the usual conformity of facts to the reports of witnesses. It being a general maxim, that no objects have any discoverable connexion together, and that all the inferences, which we can draw from one to another, are founded merely on our experience of their constant and regular conjunction; it is evident that we ought not to make an exception to this maxim in favour of human testimony, whose connexion with any event seems, in itself, as little necessary as any other. (1972: 111)

Recent writers, however, especially C. A. J. Coady, have challenged the viability of reductionism. Coady argues that Hume's notion that we rely on first-hand experience to check the reliability of testimony is misguided, because we would not be able to check the reliability of testimony if we weren't able to first detect instances of testimony. But the very detection of testimony presupposes the reliability of testimony.

This difficulty consists in the fact that the whole enterprise of [reductionism] requires that we understand what testimony is independently of knowing that it is, in any degree, a reliable form of evidence about the way the world is. This is, of course, the point of Hume's saying: "The reason why we place any credit in witnesses and historians, is not derived from any *connexion*, which we perceive *a pri-*

ori, between testimony and reality, but because we are accustomed to find a conformity between them." It is a clear implication from this that we might have discovered (though in fact we did not) that there was no conformity at all between
testimony and reality. (1992: 85)

This clear implication of Hume's theory, Coady claims, is false. We could not
possibly have discovered a total lack of conformity between truth and testimony. If there were no correlation between truth and testimony, there would
be no such thing as reports and no way of establishing the contents of alleged
reports. Hence, Hume's theory is mistaken.

One way to dispute Coady's argument is to deny that Hume's theory
implies the possibility of completely inaccurate testimony. Jack Lyons (1997)
contends that Hume is careful not to claim that there *is* no necessary connection between truth and testimony, only that it is not the case that we believe
witnesses *because of* such a connection. Furthermore, people can have inductive reasons to believe a generalization even when the generalization is necessary. One might acquire inductive evidence for the truth of the Pythagorean
theorem by measuring many right triangles even though the theorem is necessary.[18] Thus, perhaps one can be inductively justified in believing that testimony is usually reliable even if that is a necessary truth.

Coady constructs a more convincing argument, however, by pointing out
that hearers, especially young hearers, have too slim a base of personal observations to effect a global reduction of testimonial trustworthiness. Of special
interest is the fact that what is casually classified as personal observation—that
is, perceptual knowledge—commonly relies on a background theory of object
categories that is acquired in part from testimony. For example, if a person
"observes" that Russian soldiers are marching in a parade, her knowing that
they are Russian may depend on inference from her earlier reading of a newspaper report. Moreover, she knows them to be soldiers only if she possesses
that complex institutional concept, a concept that is itself probably indebted
to reliance on past testimony.[19] Though there may be some perceptual
categories that are not traceable to reliance on testimony, the foundation of
testimony-free categories and beliefs may be so minute that the project of
inductively inferring the testimony-infected remainder of our beliefs from this
meager foundation cannot succeed. At a minimum, this antireductionist conclusion has a lot going for it.[20]

Notice that Coady's challenge is a challenge about epistemic justification.
It raises the question of how people can *justifiably* accept the testimony of
speakers, not the question of how often they get *truth* from trusting testimony.

---

[18] Frederick Schmitt (1994*a*) offers a similar argument.
[19] This example and its treatment are borrowed from Elizabeth Fricker (1995: 402),
who develops a similar example presented by Coady.
[20] In Section 11.4 some conclusions for educational theory are drawn from anti-
reductionism about testimony.

The question of justification is not central to this book, so I am giving it minor billing. I do not wish to neglect it entirely, however, so this final section of the chapter examines a variety of theories in the field. I shall not argue strenuously for any particular theory. I shall simply display the fact that promising nonreductionist theories of testimonial justification abound, so there is no general reason for skepticism. Here are four nonreductionist approaches that could serve the purpose: (1) (nonreductionist) foundationalism, (2) negative coherentism, (3) proper functionalism, and (4) reliabilism.

Testimonial foundationalism assigns prima facie justification to testimonial beliefs by positing an independent "first principle," on a par with principles for perception and memory. Unlike reductionism, foundationalism does not require a hearer to have nontestimonial evidence for the reliability of testimony. Even in the absence of such evidence, testimonial belief is justified, at least prima facie justified. This kind of view was favored by Reid, and has recently been endorsed by Tyler Burge (1993). Burge advances this principle: "A person is entitled to accept as true something that is presented as true and that is intelligible to him, unless there are stronger reasons not to do so" (1993: 467). He continues: "Justified (entitled) acceptance is the epistemic 'default' position. We can strengthen this position with empirical reasons . . . But to be entitled, we do not have to have reasons that support the default position, if there is no reasonable ground for doubt" (1993: 468). A similar theory is advanced by Richard Foley (1994) under a different label: *nonegoism* (or *impartialism*, or *egalitarianism*). Foley follows Reid in suggesting that other people deserve fundamental, not merely derivative, trust in their epistemic authority. He compares this to the case of ethical nonegoism. Nonegoists accept the satisfaction of other people's interests as a fundamental value, not just as a means to satisfying their own interests. Similarly, epistemic nonegoism allows agents to grant fundamental epistemic authority to others, not only to themselves. They would not need inductive evidence of other people's reliability to be justified in accepting their reports. Trusting the reports of others could be justified, then, even when based on an innate disposition, unsupported by evidence of reliability.

A second theory is *negative coherentism*, which says that beliefs are justified as long as the believer has no reasons for doubting them (Harman 1986). In other words, beliefs are epistemically "innocent" until proven guilty. Their default condition is to be justified, a status they lose only when there is countervailing evidence. Positive evidence is not needed to justify a belief. Obviously this theory could sustain the justificational status of a young child's noninductive testimonial belief as long as she lacks evidence that the speaker is *un*reliable.

A third theory is Alvin Plantinga's (1993) *proper functionalism*. According to his theory (addressed to "warrant" rather than "justification"), a belief is warranted just in case it is produced by a faculty functioning properly in an appropriate environment, and the segment of the faculty's "design plan" governing the production of this belief is successfully aimed at truth (1993: 46). Now a faculty or tendency to trust testimony, even without inductive evidence for the reliability of testimony, might well satisfy these conditions. Reid (1970) held that we have such a faculty or principle of "credulity," which meshes with the principle of "veracity" mentioned earlier:

[An] original principle implanted in us by the Supreme Being, is a disposition to confide in the veracity of others, and to believe what they tell us . . . [W]e shall call this the *principle of credulity*. It is unlimited in children, until they meet with instances of deceit and falsehood; and it retains a very considerable degree of strength through life . . .

It is evident, that, in the matter of testimony, the balance of human judgment is by nature inclined to the side of belief; and turns to that side of itself, when there is nothing put into the opposite scale. If it was not so, no proposition that is uttered in discourse would be believed, until it was examined and tried by reason; and most men would be unable to find reasons for believing the thousandth part of what is told them. Such distrust and incredulity would deprive us of the greatest benefits of society, and place us in a worse condition than that of savages . . .

[I]f credulity were the effect of reasoning and experience, it must grow up and gather strength, in the same proportion as reason and experience do. But if it is the gift of nature, it will be strongest in childhood, and limited and restrained by experience; and the most superficial view of human life shows, that the last is really the case, and not the first. (1970: 240–1)

If Reid is right about the faculty or disposition of credulity, and right about the design plan behind this faculty, then the operation of the credulity faculty could well be an instance of proper functioning. Plantinga discusses testimonial belief in precisely Reidian terms. To fulfill Plantinga's definition, however, the faculty must operate in an appropriate environment. In this case, such an environment would be one in which speakers are disposed to tell the truth. This could well be satisfied in the actual environment, in which case the proper functioning theory would account for the warrant of testimonial belief without an inductive basis.

A fourth theory of justification that could underwrite testimonial belief without an inductive basis is *reliabilism*. This is the sort of theory I have defended elsewhere, though without attention to testimony (Goldman 1986, 1992, chs. 6, 7, and 9). In its simplest form, justificational reliabilism says that a belief is justified if and only if it is produced (and/or sustained) by a reliable belief-forming process or sequence of processes. For a testimonial belief to be justified it suffices that the general process of accepting the reports of others mostly yields truths. Accepting the reports of others is really a specific pattern of inference, where inference is construed as a process that takes some beliefs as inputs and generates new beliefs as outputs. In the testimonial case, the inputs include beliefs of the form "Person R reports X" and the outputs are beliefs of the form "X." What is required for this process to be reliable? Assuming that hearers accurately represent speakers' reports, what is further required is that those reports be generally true. So credulity achieves reliability if and only if it is exercised in an environment in which speakers' reports are generally true. If this condition is satisfied, then the (simple) reliabilist theory of justification assigns the status of "justified" to testimonial beliefs, whether or not believers have an inductive basis for regarding testifiers' reports as reliable. This is similar to the other theories I have been expounding, which also allow a testimony-based belief to be justified even if the hearer does not have enough testimony-free evidence for the general reliability of testimony. Of course, a sophisticated form of reliabilism would also accommodate "defeating" evidence, so that if the hearer has evidence *against* a testifier's credibility, she is not justified in believing that testifier's report.[21]

This section's discussion has been a digression on the topic of justification. The main result of the chapter, however, is the proof that there is a social belief-forming practice—"social" because it operates on the reports of others—with positive V-value. In saying that there "is" such a practice, I do not mean that it is actually in use. I mean that we as theorists can specify such a *possible* practice and urge people to realize or conform to it as closely as possible. This illustrates in the domain of testimony how veritistic social epistemology can identify social practices with good veritistic properties.

---

[21] Actually, two different versions of reliabilism can be distinguished and considered as rival theories of testimonial justification. One version focuses on the reliability of the inferential process occurring within the hearer. This is *intrapersonal* reliabilism. The second focuses on processes occurring within the speaker as well. This is *transpersonal* reliabilism. These versions differ in their implications when the hearer uses a reliable process in trusting the speaker's report but the speaker herself was *un*justified in believing the reported proposition, because she arrived at that belief unreliably. Transpersonal reliabilism says that the hearer's belief is unjustified because the sequence of processes that generated it—including the processes within the speaker—were not reliable in their entirety. The rationale for this approach is that the receiver's belief can be justified only if there is justification for the proposition that gets *transmitted* from the sender to the receiver. Because the speaker's belief was unjustified, there was no justification to transmit. By contrast, intrapersonal reliabilism could allow the hearer's belief to be justified even in this case, because only the hearer's belief-forming process needs to be reliable under intrapersonal reliabilism.

The concept of transmissional justification need not be confined to testimony. It could equally apply to transmission of justification within an agent; for example, transmission from premise beliefs to conclusion beliefs, or from earlier belief to later belief that is preserved through memory.

FIVE

Argumentation

5.1 *Monological argumentation*

CHAPTER 4 dealt with the most elementary type of factual discourse: simple reports of observations. Factual discourse is not confined, however, to bald reports, nor to assertions based directly on observation. Factual discourse often features more complex speech acts, in which people not only advance a factual claim but present reasons or evidence in support of it. This sort of discursive practice, argumentation, forms the subject matter of this chapter. I shall examine how different variants of argumentative practice can promote or impede veritistic ends. In contrast with Chapter 4, the emphasis is on speaker practices rather than hearer practices.

Verbal claims often articulate inference-based beliefs. The inferential grounds of a speaker's belief, however, need not always be displayed. Discourse would be long-winded and tiresome if people tried to provide all of their reasons for each of their assertions. But the practice of appending reasons or evidence is common. The credibility of the speaker's assertion often depends on his grounds, so listeners commonly want these grounds to be presented, and speakers often oblige. Thus, a speaker's utterance might take the form: "*P*; and my evidence or reasons for *P* are $R_1, \ldots, R_n$"; or, to invert the order, "$R_1, \ldots, R_n$, therefore (probably) *P*."

A set of statements or propositions schematized as "$R_1, \ldots, R_n$, therefore *P*" constitute what logicians and philosophers call an *argument*. It contains one or more premises and a conclusion, where the premises jointly provide evidential support (not necessarily conclusive) for the conclusion. If a speaker presents an argument to an audience, in which he asserts and defends the conclusion by appeal to the premises, I call this activity *argumentation*. More specifically, this counts as *monological* argumentation, a stretch of argumentation with a single speaker. Later I shall also discuss *dialogical* argumentation, in which two or more speakers discourse with one another, taking opposite sides of the issue over the truth of the conclusion. When dialogical arguers address a separate audience, not just one another, I call it *debate*. This section deals with monological argumentation.

There are other uses of the terms "arguing" and "argumentation." "Arguing" often refers simply to verbal disagreement, especially heated disagreement. If Jack vehemently asserts *P* to Jill, and Jill vehemently denies it, they would colloquially be described as arguing, or having an argument. But if neither defends his or her conclusion with any evidence or premises, this does not qualify as argumentation in my sense.

Notice that a piece of argumentation in my sense is not an argument. An argument is a set of sentences or propositions understood abstractly without reference to any speaker or audience. Argumentation is a sequence of speech acts by one or more speakers. The relation between the two is that argumentation involves the *endorsement* or *criticism* of an argument by a speaker. Proponent argumentation is a defense of the asserted conclusion by appeal to the cited premises, whereas critical argumentation is an attempt to defeat or undercut the proffered argument.[1] Admittedly, the emphasis on endorsement and criticism slightly narrows the full scope of argumentation, since arguments can also be adduced in the spirit of examination or trial rather than endorsement or opposition.[2] But I shall restrict my attention to the endorsement and critical forms of argumentation, which I take to be the fundamental types of activity.[3]

Two fundamentally different types of argumentation are *factual* and *practical* argumentation. Practical argumentation aims at decision making; it engages with the question of what to *do*. Factual argumentation is concerned with *belief*; should a proffered conclusion be believed or not? Our discussion is restricted to factual argumentation.

From the standpoint of social epistemology, monological argumentation is quite analogous to simple testimony. In each case, the speaker represents or advertises himself as a potential informant, someone who knows a certain

---

[1] It is not always clear on the surface, however, exactly what argument is being defended (or criticized). In *reductio ad absurdum* arguments, for example, the first sentence a speaker utters or displays is not something he asserts as a premise, but rather a supposition laid down for refutation. In a *reductio* the speaker's principal argument is best rendered as follows:

> Premise: The supposition that *P* implies a contradiction, *Q* & not-*Q*.
> Conclusion: Therefore, *P* is false.

This principal argument contains a "subargument," which supports the claim that *P* implies a contradiction by deriving the contradiction from *P*. The speaker should not be understood to assert each line of such a derivation; he does not, for example, mean to assert "*Q* and not-*Q*." Instead, what he asserts as premises of his subargument are statements like: "*P* implies *R*," "*R* implies *S*," and "*S* implies *Q* & not-*Q*." Even in the case of *reductio*, then, argumentation consists in defending an argument. But it is not so obvious what the defended argument's premises and conclusion are.

[2] For example, in a philosophy class a professor might say, "Consider the following possible line of argument," and proceed to formulate and examine a position without endorsing it or clearly opposing it. This is what Jack Meiland (1989) calls "argument for *inquiry*" as contrasted with "argument for *persuasion*."

[3] "Trial" argumentation is a secondary or derivative activity in the same way as trying out a new basketball maneuver during practice, or trying out a military tactic during mock combat, are secondary activities, designed to test their effectiveness in the primary sphere of application, namely, a real game or battle.

proposition (in the argumentation case, it is the conclusion) and wishes to transmit this known truth to an audience.[4] In representing himself as an informant, he not only claims to believe the asserted proposition but to believe it on a *reliable basis*, that is, by some route to belief that usually leads to truth. A witness represents himself as having observed the asserted fact, and observation is assumed to be reliable. A monological arguer asserts the proposition in question (the conclusion), and cites as his reliable basis the possession of certain evidence (his premises) that strongly support this assertion. More fully, the speaker represents himself as being in the following epistemic position: (1) he believes the asserted conclusion, (2) he believes all of the cited premises, (3) he is justified in having those beliefs, and (4) those premises lend strong support to the conclusion. If he is indeed in this epistemic position, it is (rather) likely that the asserted conclusion is true, and hence that he is in a position to be a genuine informant.

Why does this epistemic position render it likely that the conclusion is true? This claim rests on two assumptions. First, there is a link between justification and truth: if a premise belief is justified, it is likely to be true. The link between justification and truth follows from most theories of justification. It is straightforward under reliabilism, because a reliably produced belief is produced by a process that usually outputs truths. But many other theories of justification have similar implications.[5] Admittedly, the probability that *all* the premises are true will be lower than the truth probability of any one of them. But if one compares the probability of their all being true if they are believed justifiably with the probability of their all being true if they are believed unjustifiably, the former is presumably greater. The second assumption is that if the premises are true, the conclusion is likely to be true. This simply follows from the meaning of "strong support."

Like the practice of observational reporting, monological argumentation is a social activity that can increase the aggregate of knowledge or V-value. When a monological arguer *is* in the kind of epistemic situation he represents himself as being in—that is, when he satisfies the four conditions listed above— there is a substantial likelihood that his asserted conclusion is true. Let us proceed, then, on the assumption that the conclusion is, indeed, true. If audience members accept the speaker's evidence, and agree that the asserted conclusion P is inferable from this evidence, they too will adopt a belief in P. If

---

[4] Edward Craig (1990) sees a tight link between being a potential informant and having knowledge (in the *strong* sense). He tries to analyze the concept of knowledge in terms of the concept of a potential informant. This is an interesting proposal, though not entirely convincing.

[5] For reliabilism, see Goldman 1992, chs. 6, 7, and 9. Foundationalist and coherentist theories of justification also commonly hold that their favored structure of justification helps an epistemic agent arrive at truth. For a coherentist rationalization of this sort, see BonJour 1985.

they had previously withheld judgment, or rejected *P*, their switch to belief in *P* constitutes an increment in the social level of knowledge.[6]

So the practice of monological argumentation might well have veritistic merit if speakers conform to the aforementioned guidelines: they present conclusions and supporting argumentation only when they are in the advertised epistemic situation. In other words, veritistically good results are expected if the practice of argumentative discourse (in the endorsement mode) satisfies four conditions:

(1) the speaker believes the asserted conclusion;
(2) the speaker believes each of the asserted premises;
(3) the speaker is justified in believing each of the asserted premises;
(4) the asserted premises jointly provide strong support for the conclusion.[7]

To illustrate the significance of these conditions for a V-good argumentative practice, consider a perversion of argumentation that delivers veritistically disastrous results. Suppose that Oliver has not yet received his score on a certain national examination, so he neither believes that he received a score of, say, 1420, nor does he have any evidence for that proposition. However, Oliver has a strong incentive to convince his friends that he scored 1420. Perhaps he made a bet with them that he would score that high. He therefore concocts a story according to which a cousin of his, who works for the testing agency, told him over the phone that he received a 1420. In fact, he has no such cousin, and nobody told him any such thing. Oliver presents this made-up evidence to his friends, and concludes with the assertion, "I scored a 1420 on this exam." This qualifies as monological argumentation, but Oliver has violated three of the four conditions listed above: (1), (2), and (3). He does not believe his asserted conclusion, he does not believe his asserted premises, and he is not justified in believing them.

To see how this can produce veritistically negative results, consider how Oliver's friends might react to his discourse under a plausible scenario. Oliver's discourse deceptively encourages his friends to believe he is in the advertised epistemic situation of believing the conclusion, believing the premises, and being justified in believing the premises. He also encourages them to believe that the premises support the conclusion, but this much, I am assuming, is correct. Thus, they might well accept his putative evidence, agree that it

---

[6] Throughout this chapter belief will be treated in terms of the trichotomous scheme rather than the degree-of-belief scheme, in contrast with Chapter 4.

[7] A complication concerning (4) requires a little revision. Practically all nondeductive arguments in ordinary discourse are enthymemes, which omit explicit mention of premises that the speaker tacitly presupposes. Speakers are not expected to verbalize all of their premises that support the conclusion. So a better formulation of (4) would be (4'): "the asserted premises *in conjunction with tacit premises justifiably believed by the speaker* jointly provide strong support for the conclusion."

strongly supports the conclusion, and proceed to form the new belief that Oliver did score 1420. If Oliver's actual score is not 1420, their belief lowers the social aggregate of knowledge vis-à-vis the question, "What did Oliver score?" A typical friend may have antecedently believed that Oliver scored, say, in the 1250–1350 range. Assume that this belief is true. When the friend is now persuaded that Oliver scored 1420, she rejects the true proposition that Oliver scored in the 1250–1350 range. Hence, her V-value vis-à-vis the question "What did Oliver score?" is dramatically reduced.

Conditions (1)–(4) have been presented as conditions to which speakers should conform if V-value is to be promoted. But I have not *invented* these conditions. Conversational argumentation, I submit, is governed by certain "folk rules," including rules to the effect that proponent arguers should conform with conditions (1)–(4), among others. These rules, I hypothesize, are tacitly learned and represented in the minds of ordinary people, much like the rules of "proxemics," which govern the proper distance or personal space that should be allowed in everyday social interaction. Paul Grice's (1989) conversational maxims are one codification of conversational rules, although Grice gave little attention to argumentation. The rules I have just identified, however, overlap with two of his: "Do not say what you believe to be false," and "Do not say that for which you lack adequate evidence" (Grice 1989: 27). I also concur with Grice's hypothesis that conversational rules derive from a cooperative endeavor of the community; specifically, a cooperative enterprise of information sharing. According to this hypothesis, the rules of good argumentation are inspired by a communal quest for greater knowledge.

Rules for good argumentation should be distinguished from rules for good arguments, where arguments, it will be recalled, are simply sets of sentences or propositions. In logical theory arguments are considered good in either a weak sense or a strong sense. An argument is good in the weak sense if the conclusion is well supported by the premises, either deductively or non-deductively. An argument is good in the strong sense if it is good in the weak sense and all of its premises are true. Thus, the paradigm of a good argument in the strong sense is a "sound" argument, as logicians use that term.

Standards for good argumentation, however, clearly go beyond those for good arguments, in either the weak or the strong sense. The first three rules of good argumentation, which require speakers to satisfy conditions (1)–(3), are not contained in any requirements for good arguments. This is inevitable, since these rules are addressed to speakers, but an argument in the abstract sense has no associated speaker. Furthermore, in dialogical argumentation it is inappropriate for a speaker to reiterate a proposition as a premise when the opponent previously disputed that proposition. But such a premise might be part of a perfectly good argument.

I return now to characteristics of monological argumentation that might foster or impede veritistic benefits. I do not confine myself to characteristics antecedently encoded in tacit rules. We should try to identify features of argu-

mentation that can enhance veritistic outcomes, whether or not they are mandated by folk rules of argumentation. All characteristics identified in what follows are veritistically good-making features, but only some of them seem to
be embedded in tacit folk rules.

Critical to the veritistic success of proponent argumentation—at least if it
takes its normal, intended path—is the truth of the asserted conclusion. As we
have seen, truth is made (fairly) likely if the speaker meets the indicated four
conditions related to his premises and conclusion. Another important feature
is that some segment of the audience—the larger the segment the better—does
not already believe the conclusion. Although no harm is done if the entire
audience already believes the conclusion, no veritistic *gain* occurs either. As
emphasized in Section 4.1, veritistic gains accrue only by informing people of
something they do not already know, or something they positively reject. The
desideratum of being *informative*, that is, providing new information, is a general rule of conversation. Grice formulates this idea with the maxim, "Make
your contribution as informative as is required (for the current purposes of the
exchange)" (1989: 26).[8] So let us list informativeness as a fifth condition that
makes for veritistically good argumentative practice (in the endorsement
mode):

(5) At least some members of the audience to which the argumentation is
addressed do not already believe the asserted conclusion (the fewer
such members believe it, the better).

Condition (5) does not have the same status as (1)–(4), because it is not argumentatively *improper* to present an argument to an audience whose members
all believe the conclusion already. But compliance with (5) is a potentially
good-making feature of argumentative practice; and *ceteris paribus*, the greater
the degree of compliance (the fewer the members who already believe the conclusion), the greater the potential veritistic gain.

The next feature crucial to veritistic success is that the speaker's argumentation should succeed in persuading some members of the audience of the
conclusion, members who did not believe it before. The question then arises:
Which features of the argumentation and the audience combine to promote
the conclusion's aptness to be accepted by the audience? First, for argumentation to be persuasive, audience members must believe, or must be prepared
to believe, the argument's premises.[9] Acceptance of the premises can come
about in two ways: (A) audience members might antecedently believe the
premises, or (B) audience members might newly accept the premises when the

---

[8] The importance of informativeness (or relevance) is treated at length in Sperber
and Wilson 1986.

[9] Some audiences might be persuaded of a speaker's message simply by his charm or
likability, even if they don't accept his premises. But this would not count as being persuaded *by means of his argumentation*.

speaker asserts them because they trust the speaker on those subjects.[10] Even if all of the speaker's premises are believed beforehand by the audience, his argumentation can still convince them of the conclusion, because audience members may not previously have juxtaposed those premises and recognized their joint support of this conclusion.

It is possible for argumentation to help persuade a hearer of a conclusion although she rejects most of its premises. This can happen if a hearer combines, say, one of the speaker's premises, which she accepts, with some of her own prior beliefs to infer the conclusion. This, however, would be serendipitous. The normal aim of argumentation is to produce conviction in the conclusion by means of belief in *all* the asserted premises. Thus, we may list the following as a sixth condition for veritistically good argumentation:

(6) All the premises presented in the argument are credible to at least some members of the intended audience (the more such members, the better).

Conditions (5) and (6)—and other conditions to follow—should be understood as subject to the constraints of all the prior conditions. Premises that the speaker does not believe justifiably, or premises that do not jointly support the asserted conclusion, are not veritistically good choices for assertion merely because they meet condition (5) and condition (6). Each condition specifies a good-making feature of a speaker's argument only subject to the satisfaction of the earlier constraints. For example, if there are two arguments that could be endorsingly presented to the same audience, both satisfying conditions (1)–(5) but only one satisfying (6) as well, then the latter would be the (veritistically) better argument to present.

The persuasive power of argumentation depends not only on the acceptability of the premises but equally on the acceptability of the inference from the premises to the conclusion. So the speaker should not only select premises that strongly support the conclusion, but also explain this support relationship adequately to the audience. This point has been stressed by Philip Kitcher (1991). One of his illustrations concerns mathematical proofs. G. H. Hardy (1941) thought of a proof as a sequence of unadorned formulae whose connections can be recognized by the mathematical expert, with all commentary dismissed as "gas." As Kitcher points out, though, "gas" is necessary even in professional mathematics. The use of such phrases as "the strategy of the following is . . . ," or "the essential ideas of the proof are akin to those deployed in . . . ," signals the need to accommodate human cognitive limitations.

---

[10] A third possibility is that the audience might request supplementary argumentation to defend some of the asserted premises. This would invite a new piece of argumentation, whereas we are focusing on a prespecified specimen of argumentation. Concerning chains of argumentation, it is obvious that these cannot go on indefinitely. So to produce conviction, the audience must be prepared at some point to accept a premise on the speaker's say-so, if they don't already accept it.

Furthermore, a proof presentation effective for one audience (professional mathematicians, say) can be useless for others (students, mathematophobes).

The point applies, of course, much more widely than proofs in mathematics. Argumentation is veritistically better to the extent that it uses appropriate rhetorical devices to obtain the audience's comprehension of the premises–conclusion relationship. To be sure, rhetoric is sometimes used as camouflage to disguise the weakness of a premises–conclusion relationship. But the proper use of rhetoric fosters veritistic ends. Thus, we may add the following good-making feature of argumentation:

(7) The premises–conclusion relationship is displayed or explained in a fashion that promotes its comprehension by the audience.

This is something that all good teachers know.

A final point about the audience concerns the possible *defeat* of an argument by additional propositions that the audience knows or justifiably believes. To illustrate the concept of defeat, suppose Olivia endorses the following argument to Viola:

Last night's weather forecast predicted rain for today.
Therefore, it will rain today.

Viola grants Olivia's premise: last night's weather forecast *did* predict rain. Viola also agrees that this premise, taken by itself (along with general background information about weather forecasts), inductively supports Olivia's conclusion that it will rain. However, Viola also justifiably believes another proposition:

This morning's revised weather forecast predicted no rain for today.

The support that Olivia's original premise conferred on the conclusion is defeated or overridden by the addition of this new proposition (premise). A revised forecast undoubtedly reflects a more recent weather pattern, which is a better guide to today's weather than last night's pattern. When this new premise is added to the old, Viola is not justified in believing the conclusion of Olivia's argument. So Olivia's argument is *defeated* by this new premise. In important respects, of course, Olivia's endorsement of her original argument is entirely unexceptionable. In particular, it meets conditions (1)–(4). Nonetheless, with her additional information, Viola is not justified in accepting the conclusion of Olivia's argument.

My point concerning defeat is this. Even if a hearer accepts all of the speaker's premises and agrees that they strongly support the conclusion, the hearer can still reasonably decline to believe the conclusion because she (justifiably) believes some additional premise that defeats the presented argument.[11] If a speaker wishes to persuade a hearer of a certain truth, he should try to use arguments for which the hearer has no defeater.[12] Thus, we might add condition (8) as a further feature of argumentation that promotes veritistic ends:

(8) The audience has no defeater for the argument that the speaker endorses.

Conditions (5)–(8) all specify features of argumentative acts that would make them *well adapted* to their audiences (to use a popular term in argumentation theory). These are not "intrinsic" features of argumentative acts but features that relate the acts (or their contents) to their intended audiences. Such relational features make a significant difference to the persuasive power of argumentative acts, and hence to their potential for increasing V-value.

5.2 *Dialogical argumentation*

To introduce dialogical argumentation, consider someone who initially occupies the role of hearer and who possesses a defeater to an argument just addressed to her. Sticking with the weather forecast example, consider hearer Viola, who has evidence that defeats Olivia's argument in support of the conclusion that it will rain today. Viola might discharge her epistemic "duty" to herself by simply declining to believe this conclusion, or better, by adopting the belief that it won't rain today. This would probably yield better V-value for Viola's own belief system. But couldn't she do better than this as far as aggregate V-value goes? Viola could inform Olivia of the revised weather forecast, and invite her also to believe that it won't rain today. Such a speech act would be a "critical" response to Olivia's argumentation; combined with Olivia's discourse, it would constitute an instance of dialogical argumentation.

[11] John Pollock (1986: 38–9) distinguishes two types of defeaters: rebutting and undercutting defeaters. The former provide reason for denying the conclusion; the latter override the strong support relation without directly suggesting the falsity of the conclusion. The example in the text is of the rebutting sort, and that is the kind I shall usually have in mind when I discuss defeaters.

It is unclear whether a person should be said to "have" a defeater only if she is justified in believing it. A hearer will be unpersuaded by an argument even if she believes a defeating premise unjustifiably. So in the present context justification might not be regarded as essential to defeater "possession." However, it is important to the treatment of defeaters in Section 5.3 that they be true, and justification for a defeater makes it at least likely that it is true. So I shall generally assume that "possessing" a defeater involves having a justified belief in that defeater.

[12] Of course, if a speaker who is tempted to endorse argument A, with C as a conclusion, also knows or believes that an intended hearer has a defeater, D, for this argument, he (the speaker) should reconsider his belief in C and his endorsement of argument A. However, the speaker might possess a defeater D' of D: a "defeater-defeater." If so, he should select an argument A' that defuses defeater D with D'.

Notice that Viola's critical response would have an intended informative purpose. She would be trying to persuade Olivia of (what she takes to be) a truth just as Olivia was trying to persuade her of one. As long as Viola's defeating premise is justifiably believed, the new total evidence makes nonrain more probable than rain. Hence, the community of interlocutors will probably be (veritistically) better off if they believe the negation of Olivia's original conclusion rather than that conclusion. In this fashion, critical argumentation can make positive contributions to veritistic ends.

There are two other forms of critical argumentation in addition to defeater introduction. Critical argumentation can also take the form of denying the truth of one (or more) of an argument's premises, or denying the strength of its premises–conclusion relationship. To continue with the weather example, Viola might dispute the truth of Olivia's premise, because she (Viola) also heard last night's weather forecast and remembers it differently. Thus, if a hearer justifiably believes that one or more of the speaker's premises are false, it can be veritistically helpful to criticize the original argumentation by denying those premises, both to the original speaker and to the rest of the listening audience (if any).

Similar points apply to the form of critical dialogue that consists in denying the strength of the premises–conclusion relationship. If a hearer justifiably believes that, for a given argument, this relationship is weaker than its proponent contends, it is helpful if the hearer not only adjusts her credal reaction to the argument accordingly, but if she indicates the weakness of the relationship to the original speaker and the listening audience. This type of critical dialogue can also promote aggregate V-value by restraining people from believing a conclusion that may well be false (thereby increasing belief in its negation, which may well be true).

These points may be summarized as follows:

(9) Critical argumentation may challenge or rebut a speaker's argument by either (A) presenting a defeater, (B) denying the truth of some premises, or (C) denying the strength of the premises–conclusion relationship. Such criticism or rebuttal is generally veritistically beneficial, so long as it conforms with the preceding conditions, especially (1)–(4).[13]

Condition (9) is not meant to suggest, of course, that *random* challenges to people's arguments are veritistically helpful. Conformity with conditions (1)–(4) requires that a critic's denials of a proponent's premises, for example, must themselves be *justifiably* believed (see n. 13). So unless a critic is justified in believing that certain of the premises offered by the proponent are false, it

---

[13] Strictly speaking, conditions (1)–(4) must be slightly revised to fit rebuttals. Condition (2) should require a critic to believe any *denial* she makes of a premise, and condition (3) should require a critic to be justified in believing any such denial. I take these modifications for granted in the discussion that follows.

cannot be inferred from (9) that it would be veritistically beneficial to challenge these premises verbally.[14] Similarly for the other kinds of rebuttals.

As rough corollaries of (9), some other points can be made about veritistically good or bad rebuttal practices. First, rebuttals should be accurate in the sense that a critic should always represent the proponent's argument correctly, and should make only criticisms that are genuinely pertinent to that argument. It is off limits to misrepresent the proponent's premises, for example, by attacking premises that he never asserted (while implying that he did). This threatens to mislead the audience in a veritistically deleterious way, because they might lose track of the force of the real original argument. This is covered by the following principle:

(10) Rebuttals of a speaker's argument should be accurate.

When choosing between possible rebuttals (because of time or space limitations), it is better to choose more effective rebuttals over less effective ones. What determines rebuttal effectiveness? Effectiveness is a function of two variables: (i) how seriously the criticism would weaken the force of the argument, and (ii) how receptive the audience would be to the criticism. For instance, a certain premise in the original argument may be pivotal to its force. If that premise is undermined, the entire argument collapses. Another premise may be only marginally significant, in the sense that the remaining premises still give substantial inductive support to the conclusion. Other things being equal, it is better to criticize the first premise than the second. However, other things might not be equal. The listening audience might be more receptive to a denial of the less important premise than to a denial of the pivotal premise. I shall not offer a precise formula for weighing relative effectiveness, but I nonetheless propose the following principle:

(11) More effective rebuttals of a speaker's argument are to be chosen over less effective rebuttals.

Principle (11) should be understood subject to the proviso that any rebuttal is eligible only if the critic is justified in believing its assertions or denials. That is, she should not choose a rebuttal to which the audience would be highly receptive but which requires an assertion or denial for which she lacks adequate evidence, because this undermines the probability that her assertions or denials are *true* and therefore veritistically helpful.[15]

---

[14] Of course, the proponent's premises *might* be false even though the critic is not justified in believing this, so the critic's verbal challenge to the premises might be veritistically beneficial despite her lack of justification. But veritistic benefit cannot be predicted as a general rule where justification is lacking.

[15] Doesn't the fact that the audience is receptive to them constitute some indication of their truth? Why should the audience's receptivity be discounted in assessing probable truth in favor of the critic's own assessment? The critic's justification for believing her assertion or denial should take account of the audience, among other things. If, after taking account of the audience's receptivity, the critic is still unjustified in believing

We have thus far canvassed two stages of dialogical argumentation: the initial stage of argumentation, in which a proponent presents a positive argument for a conclusion, and the second stage of argumentative dialogue, in which a critic rebuts the initial argument. An alternative second stage of dialectic is where the opponent offers her own positive argument for the negation of the original conclusion, rather than a critique of the original proponent's argument. But that mode of dialectic requires no new theoretical analysis. It is adequately covered by conditions (1)–(8). We are therefore left with a final dialectical stage to be discussed: the way(s) that an original proponent should respond to a critic's rebuttal, or, in the more general case, to the rebuttals of multiple critics.

One kind of proponent response to critics is to rebut their criticisms. This introduces nothing fundamentally new; it is covered by principles (9)–(11). Good responsiveness, however, is not exhausted by rebuttals of rebuttals. That would imply that a good arguer must always defend her original position to the hilt, come what may. This may be true of formal debate, or of a lawyer's stance at trial on behalf of her client, but in ordinary conversation it is often appropriate for speakers to *retract* all or some of their previously endorsed assertions. Such retraction can often be veritistically valuable. To facilitate the discussion, I shall call the initial proponent "Peter" and the critic "Christi."

Retraction is in order when Peter's epistemic situation is changed by hearing Christi's criticisms. Changes may occur vis-à-vis any of the four circumstances cited in conditions (1)–(4). After listening to Christi's criticisms, Peter may no longer believe his original conclusion; or he may no longer believe one or more of his original premises; or he may no longer be justified in believing one or more of his original premises; or he may no longer believe, or may no longer be justified in believing, that the support relation in his original argument is so strong. In addition, if Christi adduced a new premise that defeats Peter's original argument, he may no longer be justified in believing the original conclusion, although he still satisfies conditions (2), (3), and (4) vis-à-vis the original argument. When any such changes have transpired, it may be appropriate, from the veritistic perspective, for Peter to publicly retract some of his earlier assertions, perhaps the conclusion itself.[16]

If Peter recognizes the falsity of some of his original assertions, as a result of Christi's rebuttals, why should he make a *public* retraction? Aren't veritistic ends adequately served by his silently changing his mind? Not necessarily. In the case of debate, the listening audience's credal condition is also relevant to the group's aggregate V-value. If retractions by Peter would produce more truth possession on the part of the audience, such public retractions would be

what she is tempted to assert or deny, then audience receptivity alone does not make the target rebuttal an eligible one.

[16] If Peter rejects only one of his original premises, and it plays a minor role in the argument, he may not have to abandon the conclusion.

desirable. When dialogical argumentation gets complex, it is difficult for a listening audience to track all of the claims and counterclaims. A speaker who publicly acknowledges his inability to answer certain criticisms will assist the audience in making credal revisions of their own in the direction of truth. This leads to principle (12):

(12) When a proponent's credal or epistemic situation changes as a result of criticisms of his argument, he ought to offer a public retraction of his earlier claims (especially when there is a listening audience).

Suppose, however, that the opponents' criticisms do not change Peter's mind and do not change his justificational situation, because he knows of probative replies to these criticisms. Which replies should he make, assuming limited opportunities for response? There are two factors to consider, paralleling the factors mentioned in the choice of a critic's rebuttals: (i) How seriously did each criticism weaken the persuasiveness of his argument, and (ii) How receptive would the audience be to the various responses he is contemplating? For simplicity, suppose two criticisms were offered to his argument, Z_1 and Z_2. Criticism Z_1 was a criticism of a premise, whereas Z_2 was the introduction of an alleged defeater. In both cases, Peter feels that he has probative responses, but he lacks adequate opportunity to make them both. Two factors should be considered in choosing between them. First, which criticism was more effective in dissuading the audience from his conclusion? In other words, which *needs* more rebuttal in order to revive audience belief in his conclusion? Second, which of his rebuttals has a better chance of convincing the audience? I have no general formula for balancing these factors; judicious balancing depends heavily on the opinions and inferential dispositions of the various audience members. But these are the factors that are relevant in deciding what choice of rebuttal would maximize aggregate V-value. I sum them up with the following principle:

(13) In selecting responses to critics, a justifiably undissuaded proponent should weigh both the perceived seriousness of the criticisms by the audience and the audience's comparative receptivity to the potential responses available to him.

Until now I have assumed that a proponent would respond only to criticisms previously lodged against his original argument. But this is too restrictive. Even when first launching an argument, it is frequently possible to anticipate criticisms of it. Perhaps contentions similar to one's own have appeared in ongoing debates, and they have already encountered objections. Or the style of analysis within a given discipline might make it inevitable that certain sorts of questions and worries will be raised. In these circumstances, it is veritistically desirable for the proponent to present the foreseeable or on-record objections to his premises or methodology, and to lay them to rest as well as he can. This might consist, for example, in defending the premises of his main argument with other, subsidiary arguments. This requires a series of nested arguments, which might be dubbed an *extended argumentative discourse*, rather than a single argument with a single conclusion. In science, scholarship, law, and other polemical realms, extended argumentative discourses are the norm. Scholars are expected to report existing findings and literature that form the basis of predictable objections. This should be done as part of one's initial defense of one's conclusion, not simply in subsequent responses to criticisms. Extended argumentative discourses are veritistic aids to an audience. They help an audience track lines of disagreement and mutual criticism by incorporating them into a single speech episode or document, rather than requiring the audience to locate the pertinent dialectic in widely dispersed venues. This leads me to formulate the following principle:

(14) When there are existing or foreseeable criticisms of one's main argument, a speaker should embed that argument in an extended argumentative discourse that contains replies to as many of these (important) criticisms as is feasible.

5.3 *Truth-in-evidence and the cultural climate for argumentation*

In this section I advance a general thesis about critical argumentation and the probability of acquiring truth. It has long been held by theorists of various stripes that lively and vigorous debate is a desirable thing. *Why* it is desirable is a subtle question that receives diverse answers. In keeping with the theme of this book, I address this matter from a veritistic perspective. Much of what I shall say in this section is an extension of material from the preceding two sections, but it approaches matters from a wider perspective.

I shall focus on critical argumentation that employs the *defeater* device, which may be schematized as follows. A proponent's argument features conclusion C and evidential premises R_1–R_n.

Proponent: R_1
            $\ldots$
            R_n
            Probably, C.

A defeater critic concedes that these premises render C probable, but she introduces a new premise, D, and contends that the conjunction of D with R_1–R_n renders not-C probable.

Critic: R_1

$\ldots$

R_n

D

Probably, not-C.

In all such arguments by defeat, an addition is made to the stock of (putative) evidence available to the disputants and their listening audience concerning question $Q(C/-C)$. Assume that all premises adduced by all interlocutors are true. Would it help listeners get the truth about $Q(C/-C)$ to hear all genuinely defeating criticisms that anybody can muster? I shall argue that it does.

There is a venerable principle in philosophy of science called the *total evidence principle*. I wish to postulate a veritistic variant of this principle, which may rationalize the old version of it. The old total evidence principle, enunciated by philosophers such as Rudolf Carnap (1950: 211) and Carl Hempel (1965: 64–7), concerned rationality. Its precept of rationality says that when an agent chooses a degree of credence to assign to a proposition, that degree should reflect the total evidence. It is irrational to use only a portion or proper subset of one's available evidence. Why is it preferable to use all of the evidence rather than part of it? The principle I postulate links greater evidence to a greater likelihood of getting the correct truth-value of the proposition. This postulate—call it the *truth-in-evidence principle*—runs as follows:

(TEP) A larger body of evidence is generally a better indicator of the truth-value of a hypothesis than a smaller, contained body of evidence, as long as all the evidence propositions are true and what they indicate is correctly interpreted.

The idea is as follows. Suppose that comparative support relations are sufficiently determinate that any body of evidence either supports a random hypothesis P more than its negation not-P, or supports not-P more than P, or supports them equally. Then consider two sets of evidence propositions E and E^*, where E is a proper (contained) subset of E^*. In other words, E is a body of evidence premises contained within the larger body of evidence, E^*. Principle (TEP) says that when one set of evidence propositions favors P and the other set favors not-p, the true hypothesis is *usually* the one favored by E^*, the more inclusive body of evidence. At least this holds when all the evidence propositions are true.

Consider all cases in which there are two such sets of (true) evidence. A "conforming" case is one in which the true hypothesis is the one supported by E^* rather than by E, and a "nonconforming" case is one in which the true hypothesis is the one supported by E rather than by E^*. Principle (TEP) asserts that conforming cases are more common than nonconforming cases. In other words, cases in which additional evidence proves to be misleading (points away from the truth) are the exceptions rather than the rule. I have no proof of this postulate, nor any firm view of what sort of proof it might be susceptible to, but it is an attractive methodological postulate. Moreover, it is a sort of generalization of Theorem 4.1, which says that, on average, additional evidence moves you toward truth if you interpret the evidence properly. (In the case of the theorem, proper interpretation means using Bayes' rule in conjunction with accurate likelihoods.) But (TEP) is not a mathematical consequence of that theorem.[17]

Suppose, however, that (TEP) is correct. May we derive from it the veritistic desirability of engaging in defeater argumentation? In other words, does (TEP) imply that defeater argumentation usually has positive V-value? Although I shall not attempt to prove it, I suspect that this does follow, at least when supplemented by additional assumptions and provisos. Notice first that defeater argumentation—when it is accepted, at any rate—tends to push hearers in an opposite credal direction from the original, defeated argument. Whereas the initial argument is designed to persuade hearers of C, defeater argumentation is designed to persuade hearers of not-C.[18] So if the original argumentation tended to persuade, and the defeater argumentation persuades as well, the latter will effect a large shift in belief. This will be veritistically good if and only if the conclusion urged by the defeater argumentation—not-C—is true. Will that generally be true, according to (TEP) (together with other assumptions)? Yes.

Built into (TEP) is the assumption that all the evidence propositions are true. Thus, for defeater argumentation to be veritistically desirable in virtue of (TEP), it would have to be assumed that defeater argumentation always employs true premises (and that the premises affirmed during proponent argumentation are also true). Some distance toward this condition would be traveled by assuming that critics justifiably believe whatever defeaters they assert, since justification makes truth probable. But since it does not guarantee truth, an even stronger assumption is needed to meet the conditions specified by (TEP). Another thing assumed by (TEP) is the correct interpretation of "indication," or evidential support, relations. If the veritistic value of defeater argumentation is to be established via (TEP), it is necessary that all hearers of the evidence will properly interpret the evidence. This is also a major assumption that is, obviously, not always satisfied in real-world cases. Nonetheless, it is intriguing that (TEP) plus the foregoing assumptions (and possibly others) imply that defeater argumentation has positive veritistic properties. This sug-

---

[17] This is partly because (TEP) concerns the *proportion* of cases in which new evidence indicates truth, rather than the *expectation* of increase in degrees of truth possession, which is weighted by the magnitude of increase in truth possession under various scenarios.

[18] At least this is so when the defeaters are rebutting defeaters; see n. 11. This is the kind of case I shall generally be discussing.

gests a more clear-cut rationale for vigorous critical debate in the factual arena than any others I know of.[19]

For the sake of discussion, then, let us assume that so long as arguers conform their discourse to the principles of good argumentation, defeater criticism has positive V-value. On average, it yields veritistic increases. What practices can a society or community adopt that would promote a high incidence of defeater argumentation, especially argumentation that meets the constraints on good argumentation elucidated earlier?[20] There are two general categories of practices that might encourage defeater argumentation: (1) practices that increase incentives—or decrease disincentives—for such argumentation, and (2) practices that expand opportunities for such argumentation.

In almost every culture, and especially in certain cultures, there are norms that deter critical argumentation. It is widely said that in Japanese and other Asian cultures people are encouraged to conduct their discourse so as to preserve harmony. The expression of conflict, including verbally explicit disagreement, is said to be discouraged. To the extent that this is true, it creates disincentives for critical argumentation. This claim about Japanese harmony may be exaggerated; so it has been urged by Kimberly Jones (forthcoming). Japanese discourse does permit conflict, depending on the social relationship of the interlocutors and the formal setting of the discourse. A televised debate, for example, certainly encourages verbal disagreement, and the expression of conflict is tolerated in the family more than in extra-familial relationships. Nonetheless, studies definitely reveal contrasts between different cultures in their toleration of critical discourse. Susanne Günthner (1993) found sharp differences in communicative conventions between German and Chinese students in a get-acquainted meeting. The Chinese students sought to establish a harmonious atmosphere, which restricted talk to "safe" topics on which there would be no disagreement. This was necessary to establish "facework."[21] The German students' conception of how to get acquainted was to learn people's opinions and positions, which required or tolerated debate. After the meeting, a Chinese student evaluated the Germans as too "direct," "aggressive," even "a bit offensive." The German students characterized the Chinese interlocutors as "not interesting" or "boring." It would be hasty to

---

[19] The desirability of debate and discussion in the *political* arena, which is much discussed, is a somewhat separate matter. Debate and discussion are forms of political "participation," and widespread political participation may be a desideratum in a democracy whether or not it promotes truth. This kind of rationale, however, would not apply straightforwardly across the entire factual realm.

[20] Notice that here I am inquiring into practices that would promote the deployment of another practice. This approach was already adopted in Chapter 4 and will be adopted elsewhere in the book.

[21] The Chinese "Book of Rites" is a treatise that describes the preservation of interpersonal harmony as the essential principle of Chinese rhetoric. The reader is taught to avoid disharmony and face-threatening situations. Open confrontation or an antagonistic style are said to show poor education and personal immaturity.

overgeneralize the Chinese communicative convention. The convention cited here just governs initial conversations among strangers. But most cultures place some degree of value on harmony and affiliation. To whatever extent critical debate disrupts such harmony, these cultural norms make debate a dispreferred activity.

As I have emphasized repeatedly, veritistic epistemology does not claim that truth is the supreme value, that it trumps all other values. It can certainly be maintained that harmony is more important than truth (or knowledge), and when the two conflict, let truth be damned. Veritistic epistemology takes no stance on this issue. The relative importance of truth and social harmony is for other inquiries to settle. But veritistic epistemology is interested in devices or practices that might circumvent or reduce the ostensible conflict between debate and harmony. Are there ways to encourage critical debate without threatening disharmony, at least ways to mitigate this threat?

One possibility is to reframe argumentation as a *playful* interaction (Jones forthcoming: ch. 7). By making light of an argument or dispute, hostility and tension are reduced. Of course, *factual* argumentation is less likely in any case to produce hostility and tension than practical argumentation, where the issue concerns what course of action or evaluative stance to take. But even in the domain of factual debate, when one's own discourse is criticized, people can readily feel wounded. By fostering a playful stance toward argumentation, losing an argument becomes less serious and therefore less threatening. A culture that adopts the playful stance can better promote debate without sacrificing harmony.

A playful stance toward argumentation is not equivalent to treating argumentation as a game. Indeed, games often engender a spirit of adversarialism and combat, which certainly is encountered in much argumentation. Arguers are admired for their skill, and losing an argument can be taken as a sign of inferior skill. When a high premium is placed on winning, arguers have incentives to violate rules of good argumentation—for example, to assert premises they don't believe, or for which they lack adequate evidence. It may skew their judgment of how strongly the evidence supports their favored conclusion or defeats their opponent's conclusion. Finally, a desire to win the debating match might inhibit their compliance with rules of retraction. If too much hangs on the appearance of having been right, speakers will be sorely tempted to ignore rules of retraction, to preserve the public posture of retaining their old position. This is unlikely to have positive veritistic consequences, for it could easily mislead their audience (and themselves). Playfulness is intended to have effects quite opposite to those described in this paragraph.

A second idea is to modulate styles of argumentative criticism so as to comport more easily with the values of social rapport, respect, and affiliation. According to Deborah Tannen (1990: 171), this already occurs in women's styles of talking: they use "wolf words in sheep's clothing." Tannen also cites a study by the anthropologist Penelope Brown (1990) showing how Tenejapa women in a Mayan Indian community in Mexico use apparent agreement to disagree. Another useful approach is to preach the (accurate) message that truth is hard to come by, people are highly fallible, more relevant evidence can always be found concerning (contingent) propositions, so it is no embarrassment to have other people, in different evidential situations, introduce new considerations that require abandonment of one's previous view. Mutual correction is just part of the social quest for truth. Such sober fallibilism, which is the moral of much philosophical and scientific theory as well as practice, can go some distance toward preserving otherwise fragile egos.

Leaving the category of incentives and disincentives, I turn to the category of opportunities. Here I am concerned less with face-to-face conversation than with public discourse in which channel limits imply that not all messages can be communicated. Different procedures or practices might be used to select speakers and their messages, and some might be superior to others in favoring defeater argumentation. Keeping matters brief, let me contrast three possible types of message-selection practice: (1) an *automatic turn-conferring* procedure, (2) an *ability-to-pay* procedure, and (3) a content-specific, *criticism-biased* procedure. Under an automatic turn-conferring procedure, a moderator or gatekeeper invites the next speaker according to some preordained schedule, perhaps ensuring that everyone within some preselected group has an equal speech opportunity. This is a content-neutral criterion of selection, which offers no special guarantee or likelihood that defeater argumentation or other forms of critical argumentation will transpire. The critical effectiveness of a speaker's message has no bearing on its selection, because the selection process is blind to the forthcoming message. Under an ability-to-pay or "market" procedure, selections are again made in a content-neutral way. Prospective speakers bid for the opportunity to communicate over a given channel, and the channel owner (or controller) sells the speech opportunities without screening messages for content. This procedure also offers no special guarantee or likelihood that critical argumentation, especially effective argumentation, will be featured.[22] A third type of procedure, a criticism-biased procedure, is illustrated by the publication procedures of scientific and scholarly journals. These journals do not make content-neutral publication decisions. To the contrary, articles are selected for publication precisely by and for their contents. Furthermore, such journals commonly favor critical contributions, including rebuttals of previously published arguments by defeater introduction. Critical arguments are not necessarily favored over original, nondialectical contributions, but they are favored over recapitulations of earlier views or results, which the first two message-selection criteria would permit on an equal basis. At least on the surface, a criticism-biased selection procedure fosters critical argumentation more systematically than the other two procedures, and might well be preferable on veritistic grounds.

---

[22] Market mechanisms for speech regulation will be further explored in Chapter 7.

5.4 *Fallacies and good argumentation*

Traditional argumentation theory has invested considerable effort in the study of so-called "fallacies," especially the "informal" fallacies. Philosophers and other students of argumentation have held that certain modes of argumentation are illegitimate or inappropriate in a fashion not adequately captured by formal logic. Under the credo of improving argumentative practice, many textbooks on argumentation, or "critical thinking," expose and taxonomize these fallacies, a tradition that goes back to Aristotle. One question, then, is what kind of improvement is intended? If the traditional fallacies are genuinely faulty, what kind of fault do they possess, and what kind of improvement would flow from their avoidance? My answer, of course, is a veritistic one. Fallacious patterns of argumentation are ones with no reliable tendency to issue in true conclusions. Thus, it is veritistically desirable that speakers avoid these patterns, lest they mislead hearers, and it is veritistically desirable that hearers spot these fallacious patterns, to resist believing their conclusions. Not all of the stock fallacies are genuinely fallacious. The veritistic approach can make sense of why the suspected fallacies are suspect, but can also explain why they do not always deserve their traditional disrepute.

My interpretation of several so-called fallacies will employ the principles of good argumentation presented in Sections 5.1 and 5.2. At least certain instances of fallacious patterns, I shall contend, violate rules of *argumentation*, although they do not violate rules of *argument*. The canonical fallacies are not themselves part of the folk rules of argumentation, however. They are creations of philosophers, logicians, or rhetoricians who have sought to improve argumentative practice through a kind of troubleshooting. We can make sense of this effort as part of veritistic social epistemology, even if we dispute some of the canonical claims of the fallacy-mongers.

Four so-called fallacies will be subjected here to analysis, beginning with *argumentum ad verecundiam*: appeal to authority. The classical fallacy-mongers find something amiss in arguments invoking authority, but I fail to find anything inherently wrong in the practice. Indeed, several segments of this book defend the epistemological integrity of the concept of authority and the legitimacy of sometimes relying on authority. Following Wesley Salmon (1963), we can state a standard form for arguments from authority:

> X is a reliable authority concerning P.
> X asserts P.
> Therefore, P.

Salmon suggests that this is an inductively "correct" argument, a special case of the statistical syllogism which could be rewritten as follows:

> The vast majority of statements made by X concerning subject S are true.
> P is a statement made by X concerning subject S.
> Therefore, P is true. (Salmon 1963: 64)

If Salmon is right, as I think he is, how can an accusing finger justly be pointed at arguers who appeal to authority? The problem is that speakers often invoke certain people as authorities when the speakers do not believe, or are not justified in believing, that the invoked individuals are indeed authoritative in the relevant domain. So the speakers violate condition (2) or condition (3) of good argumentation. These violations open these patterns of argumentation to a substantial likelihood of conclusion falsity. If the speaker lacks evidence that a certain individual is authoritative, the fact that this individual asserted *P* does not make it highly probable that *P* is true. The fact that some athletic hero or Hollywood star said that brand X is the best deodorant does not render it highly probable that brand X is the best deodorant, in the absence of evidence that the (vast) majority of his or her statements in this domain are true. If specific appeals to authority often violate rules of argumentation, there is merit in issuing a warning against this practice. It is unfortunate, of course, if theorists give the misleading impression that *every* appeal to authority is flawed, which is clearly unwarranted. Nonetheless, there is a genuine source of concern, as judged by norms of argumentation.

My second example is *begging the question*. The standard example of question begging is offering an argument in which the conclusion itself occurs as a premise. Intuitively this is flagrantly flawed, but wherein lies the flaw? Considered purely as an *argument*—a set of premises and conclusion—it is hard to find a flaw. A question-begging argument is logically valid, because any proposition deductively follows from itself. Furthermore, many question-begging arguments are sound, because their premises are all true. So why is there anything wrong with question-begging? To identify the flaw, let us turn from *arguments* to *argumentation*. Recall that the standard mission and virtue of argumentation is to persuade hearers of a true conclusion of which they are not antecedently persuaded. The problem of question-begging lies in its inability to achieve this effect. It cannot achieve this effect, at any rate, through a genuinely argumentative route.

According to conditions (5) and (6) of Section 5.1, argumentation should be designed to be both informative and persuasive. At least some members of the audience should be such that (A) they do not already believe the conclusion (the informability constraint) and (B) they can be persuaded of the conclusion by the credibility of the premises (the credibility constraint). When an arguer uses his conclusion itself as a premise, however, these twin constraints cannot be met. If a hearer already believes the conclusion, the informability constraint is violated. If she does not antecedently believe it, then the credibility constraint seems to be violated. Violation of the credibility constraint, however, is not so straightforward. Couldn't the proposition be credible to the hearer simply by the speaker's assertion of it? This was one mode of credibility allowed for in Section 5.1. But if the hearer is expected to accept the proposition on the speaker's say-so, why not simply *assert* the conclusion without any premises or evidence? To adduce premises for the conclusion is to advertise oneself as offering more than a simple, undefended assertion. In the case of question-begging, however, this is false advertising.

My third example is *argumentum ad hominem*, commonly explained as attacking the opponent rather than the opponent's argument. In discussing *ad hominem*, it should be assumed that the format of argumentation is debate, where two opponents address a nonspeaking audience, rather than one another. Three forms of *ad hominem* are often distinguished: the *abusive*, the *circumstantial*, and the *tu quoque*. The abusive variant consists in a direct personal attack on the opponent, typically suggesting that he is stupid, unreliable, and so forth. The circumstantial variant tries to undermine the opponent's position by suggesting that his argumentation is based only on self-interest. The *tu quoque* variant tries to show an inconsistency or discrepancy between the opponent's current position (or argumentation) and positions he has defended elsewhere. I restrict my attention to the first two variants.

Some commentators link the *ad hominem* fallacy with the so-called *genetic* fallacy. This is the alleged fallacy of criticizing a proposition, position, or argument by reference to its source, the individual who presents or defends it. This seems fallacious because the statement or position might be perfectly true or sound whatever the flaws of the speaker who defends it. It is veritistically suspect to steer the audience away from believing the opponent's conclusion without actually undermining the truth of his conclusion. If the conclusion *is* true, the *ad hominem* will prevent the audience from believing a truth, which is one kind of veritistic misadventure.

Closer analysis reveals that negative remarks about a speaker may sometimes constitute a relevant critical response to his argumentation. He may have invited the audience to accept some of the premises on his own say-so. If he did, it is highly relevant to challenge either his competence or his sincerity with respect to the premises. If he lacks authority vis-à-vis those premises, his assertion of them provides no grounds for their truth (even if he honestly believes them). If he has a vested interest in persuading people of the conclusion irrespective of its truth, then the audience is unwarranted in accepting these premises *from him*, because he might well assert them without sincere belief. Of course, these considerations would not prove the premises are false, but they would undercut the prima facie grounds for accepting them from the proponent's mouth. Thus, criticism aimed at the incompetence or self-interest of the proponent can be evidentially relevant to the truth of the premises, and hence the truth of the conclusion. People who engage in *ad hominem* argumentation rarely explain these connections, but this may be their intent, and they are simply offering enthymemes. So *ad hominem* argumentation is sometimes perfectly legitimate.

To expand on this point, consider Salmon's remarks about *ad hominem* that parallel his remarks about *ad verecundiam*. Salmon points out that "arguments against the man" often reduce to a special case of the statistical syllogism, namely one in which appeal is made to *lack* of expertise (1963: 68):

> The vast majority of statements made by X concerning subject S are false.
> P is a statement made by X concerning subject S.
> Therefore, P is false.

This is a proper inductive argument, and forms the basis of a legitimate use of *ad hominem*.

Needless to say, many other instances of *ad hominem* are not good examples of the statistical syllogism. This occurs when the negative characteristics attributed to the speaker have no probative evidential bearing on the truth of the statements he defends. In these cases, the *ad hominem* is not a legitimate critique of the opponent's argument or position, and probably deserves the "fallacy" label.

My fourth example is very brief. This is the *straw man* fallacy, the fallacy of misrepresenting an opponent's position to make it easier to attack (Kahane 1980: 78). Although sometimes this may consist in falsely attributing to the opponent statements he never made, more frequently there is no overt attribution. Instead the speaker's criticism makes sense only when construed as directed against an argument the opponent never gave. This too is no formal or logical fallacy, but there is a straightforward violation of rules of good argumentation. Specifically, it violates the responsiveness principle (10), which requires good criticisms to be accurate.

This concludes my treatment of a representative set of informal fallacies. I now wish to make some related remarks about certain precepts often given in logic and critical thinking courses. These precepts often concern both speakers and hearers, but here (for the first time in the chapter) I shall consider the hearer role, more precisely the role of doxastic agent, who considers what to believe or disbelieve based on the arguments she has heard. The basic precept behind the (alleged) *ad hominem* or *genetic* fallacy is that one should always heed the argument, not the arguer. In questioning the fallaciousness of these forms of argumentation, I have implicitly challenged this precept. Now I wish to expand the challenge and the grounds for issuing it.

Suppose you are listening to a formal debate between speakers A and B. By every standard of good argumentation you can apply, A's argument is superior to B's. How much should this incline you to accept A's conclusion? Assume you have no independent information about the debate topic. Should you be guided by the (apparent) superiority of A's argument? Not necessarily, I claim. Suppose it is a formal debate in a debating society, and the choice of sides was determined by a coin toss. In such formal debates, arguers are not expected to comply with all the standard rules of good argumentation. In particular, an arguer is not necessarily expected to believe the conclusion for which she argues. In this context, it would be sensible of you to reason as follows: "Speaker *A* made a much better case for her conclusion than speaker *B* did for his. But perhaps *A* is just the superior debater. Had the coin toss required her to take the opposite side, perhaps her argumentation would still have been superior. So I should not (firmly) accept the conclusion she actually defended." Clearly, this reasoning does not abide by the target precept: it takes the *arguer* into account as well as the *argument*. This seems entirely appropriate, so the fault lies with the precept.

Examples of this sort are easily multiplied. Suppose you again listen to speaker *A* but not in a formal debate. In this context you have every reason to believe that *A* endorses the position she defends. Suppose she argues for it brilliantly, and you can think of no effective criticisms. Should you accept her conclusion? Again, not necessarily. You may recall many past instances in which *A* argued brilliantly but was later followed by an opponent, *B*, who produced a devastating rebuttal. Or you may recall many past instances in which *A* argued brilliantly for some thesis *T*, but came back three years later and herself demolished *T*. Shouldn't you utilize past records in deciding what to believe? I certainly think so, despite the fact that they are not criticisms of the actual argument offered. It is wrong, then, to base one's belief exclusively on arguments and counterarguments encountered on the topic at hand; extrinsic facts, including ones pertaining to the arguers, may be relevant.

Perhaps I am belaboring the obvious. Perhaps it is obvious that a hearer is entitled to use all his background information in assessing the credibility of an argument's conclusion, including information about the skills of the arguers. Although this point may be obvious to some, I dwell on it because it flies in the face of precepts often given in the field of critical thinking.

5.5 *Alternative approaches to argumentation*

In this section I examine some rival approaches to argumentation, approaches that offer either different principles of good argumentation or a different, nonveritistic rationale for argumentative practices. It should be emphasized that many of these rival approaches are not committed to the total rejection of veritistic evaluation of argumentative practices. Although they approach argumentation from a nonveritistic perspective, they may nonetheless permit veritistic evaluation as a *complementary* project in the study of argumentation. In this sense, there is no decisive conflict between these approaches and mine. On the other hand, they definitely constitute contrasting orientations to the subject, contrasts that often highlight the virtues of the veritistic approach.

The first approach I consider is the *logic-of-dialectic* approach, inaugurated in recent times by C. L. Hamblin (1970, 1971). The logic-of-dialectic approach has its roots in the Platonic dialogues and in Aristotle's attempts in the *Topics* and *De Sophisticis Elenchis* to formulate rules of argumentation in a quasi-formal manner. In the Middle Ages there were numerous treatises by logicians such as Burley, Buridan, Strode, Albert of Saxony, and Paul of Venice, all dealing with a dialectical game called "Obligation." Hamblin revived this kind of approach, and has been followed by other writers such as John Woods and Douglas Walton, Nicholas Rescher, J. D. Mackenzie, and E. M. Barth and Erik C. W. Krabbe, to name a few (see, for example, Woods and Walton 1982; Barth and Krabbe 1982).

The logic-of-dialectic approach bears some resemblance to my account insofar as it studies rules for interpersonal argumentation. There are two main points of contrast between the approaches, however. First, the logic-of-dialectic approach has no official commitment to truth as the proper aim of argumentation or the basis for evaluating dialectical rules. Second, its approach has no commitment to true *belief* as an aim of argumentation, or a basis for evaluation. In fact, its leading proponents eschew the notion of belief and all other psychological concepts. They substitute for belief an externalized notion of a speaker's "commitment," where commitment is a public act, expressly distinguished from belief. Although Hamblin introduced the notion of a commitment "store" to designate the set of statements to which a speaker is committed by her sequence of utterances, Mackenzie makes it clear that such a "store" is not construed mentalistically: "A commitment store is the result of behavior; it is public, and [an arguer] has no privileged access to hers. A commitment store is no more mental than a football score or an overdraft" (Mackenzie 1989: 104); "[C]ommitment . . . must be public," because "dialectic is an empirical science" (Mackenzie 1981: 163).

Whether empiricism really requires a renunciation of "private" notions like belief need not be explored here. The pertinent point is that this renunciation excludes many of the kinds of rules we have identified as appropriate constraints on good argumentation. For example, the sincerity condition for assertion (conditions (1) and (2) of Section 5.1) cannot be expressed without the belief concept. Similarly, the antipsychologism of logic-of-dialectic precludes an audience adaptation rule like our principle (6), which makes the believability of one's premises to the audience a good-making feature of argumentation.

Nonetheless, it is conceivable that the logic-of-dialectic approach could have utility for veritistic social epistemology. It might suggest reforms in dialogical practice that would be favorable to knowledge and error avoidance. However, unless proper dialogue is constrained more tightly than current logic-of-dialectic approaches propose, the prospects are not good for pointing dialogue toward truth. Current approaches allow a speaker to retain and adopt commitments as long as (roughly) they are not inconsistent with continuing commitments. But consistency is an extremely weak constraint. There are indefinitely many consistent sets of statements, many of which contain all falsehoods. Consistency avoids the logical guarantee of error, but otherwise offers little guidance to truth. Additional constraints concerning belief and justification are needed, such as those presented earlier in this chapter, but these are foreign to the antipsychologism of logic-of-dialectic.

A second rival approach emphasizes *rational* or *justified* belief, rather than true belief, as the aim of good argumentation. According to this approach, good or successful argumentation makes it justified or rational for the audience to believe the conclusion. Roughly this approach is endorsed by John Biro and Harvey Siegel, who write:

Epistemic success is a matter of *justification*, which is in turn a matter of *rationality*: an argument succeeds to the extent that it *renders belief rational* . . . Rationality is thus at the heart of argumentation, and argumentation theory should be understood as being concerned with the ability of arguments to render beliefs rational. (1992: 96, 97)

This approach is the closest of those considered here to my own approach. Although my account has not expressly emphasized the rationality or justifiedness of hearers' beliefs, in fact the rules and principles I have adduced go a fair way toward ensuring that successful argumentation achieves this end. A speaker who complies with the conditions I have listed will only present premises he is justified in believing, and these premises will confer strong evidential support on his conclusion. A hearer of such argumentation might therefore be justified in believing both the premises and the conclusion. However, a hearer will not necessarily be justified in having these beliefs. If the hearer has solid (but misleading) evidence either of the speaker's insincerity or of his incompetence vis-à-vis his premises, then the hearer is not justified in believing them on the speaker's say-so, and therefore may not be justified in believing them at all. Consequently, she may not be rendered justified in believing the conclusion. Despite this, the speaker may have engaged in perfectly good and proper argumentation. Admittedly, the speaker in this case does not make his premises credible to *all* hearers, because at least this hearer is not persuaded by them. So the speaker's argumentation is not "ideal" as judged by my principle (6). Nonetheless, his argumentation could still conform with (6), because other hearers find the premises credible. Furthermore, (6) does not state a mandatory condition on respectable argumentation, just a veritistic desideratum. Thus, acceptable argumentation on the part of a speaker does not guarantee justified belief in his conclusion on the part of a hearer. For this reason, I would not accept Biro and Siegel's proposal to equate good argumentation with argumentation that renders a hearer's belief in the conclusion justified or rational. Finally, even if there is a general tendency of good argumentation to produce justified belief, this may not be the *ultimate* end of good argumentation. That ultimate end, as I have suggested, is true belief.

The third rival approach is the *pure persuasion* approach. This simple approach says that good argumentation is argumentation that is capable of persuading an intended audience. The provenance of this view dates back to the Greek sophists, and it has always been controversial. I have no doubt that persuasion is *relevant* to good argumentation, because argumentation cannot contribute to veritistic improvement if it fails to persuade. But persuasion helps veritistically only when the asserted conclusion is true, and the pure persuasion approach steadfastly ignores truth. If we compare this approach with the ordinary conception of good argumentation as revealed in the folk rules, it is immediately clear that it is at odds with that conception. A case in point is the example of Oliver, who manufactured the idea that a cousin had informed him that he scored 1420 on a certain national examination. Although Oliver neither believes nor is justified in believing that this occurred, he asserts it as a premise to support the conclusion that he did score 1420. Intuitively, this is a distinctly counter-normative piece of argumentation, despite the fact that it is persuasively effective. A second point of conflict concerns retraction rules. Suppose the proponent of a conclusion is faced with a critic's defeater that he cannot in turn defeat (by means of any premises he justifiably believes). Surely principles of good argumentation would encourage him, or at least permit him, to retract that conclusion. But since retraction would abandon all prospects of effectively persuading the audience (of his original conclusion), the pure persuasion approach would have to dismiss it as bad or improper argumentation. Here is another sharp conflict between this approach and the folk rules of good argumentation.

I proceed now to a fourth alternative: the *disagreement-resolution* or *dispute-resolution* approach. This view, advocated by Frans van Eemeren, Rob Grootendorst, Scott Jacobs, and Sally Jackson, says that the aim or function of argumentation is to resolve disputes. For example, van Eemeren and Grootendorst write:

[I]t is necessary for people to try to eliminate their differences of opinion . . . [E]very difference of opinion has the potential to develop into a verbally externalized *dispute* about an expressed opinion. One can only speak of a fully-fledged dispute if one language user has explicitly *cast doubt upon* the other's standpoint . . . The primary aim of interlocutors "embarking upon" a dispute of this kind is to resolve it. (1984: 1, 2)

In a similar spirit, Jacobs writes:

Conversational argument is a realization of general conversational principles adapted to the demands of a particular function—that of disagreement management. Like any rule-governed system, conversation requires regulatory mechanisms to deal with various kinds of troubles. Disagreement is one such trouble, and argument is one such mechanism for dealing with it. (1987: 229)

From my perspective, van Eemeren and Grootendorst define argumentation too narrowly, because they exclude monological argumentation in which nobody has explicitly cast doubt upon, or disagreed with, the speaker's standpoint. Jacobs appears to cover the monological case, because he says that "[a]rgument is to be found in the environment of open, implied, or projected disagreement" (1987: 229). His inclusion of merely "projected" disagreement may cover the case of monological argumentation. This is not unproblematic, however. Consider a case in which the sole hearer concedes the speaker's conclusion but the speaker proceeds to offer a *new* argument for it. Surely this is not an environment of "projected disagreement," but the speaker is still engaging in argumentation.

Let us look more closely, however, at the dispute-resolution approach. To resolve a dispute is for both parties to come to agreement. This means that either the protagonist withdraws the challenged standpoint (conclusion) or that the antagonist withdraws the objections to the standpoint (van Eemeren et al. 1993: 27). Apparently, then, the quality of different types, forms, or styles of argumentation is a function of how well they serve to resolve disagreement. The greater the effectiveness at resolving disagreement, the better the type of argumentation.

Before examining this position and its variants, notice a further feature of the Jacobs–Jackson view. They share with the logic-of-dialectic approach the idea that argumentation is a matter of overt public commitments.

> What people argue over is not so much the actual positions of the parties, but the ones that they can be held to have expressed. In making an argument, what counts are not the actual intentions and beliefs of an actor, but those that may be warrantably attributed to him. In performing a speech act, an actor is publicly committed to holding certain beliefs and intentions whether or not she actually has those intentions. Likewise, the resolution of an argument does not necessarily result in an actual consensus of opinion—only in a working consensus. (Jacobs 1987: 237)

Apparently, resolving a disagreement is a matter of reaching *publicly expressed* accord on the issue at hand, whether or not this corresponds to actual agreement in belief or opinion.

When this ingredient is incorporated into the dispute-resolution approach, however, the resulting theory faces problems. If the only goal is public accord, whatever an arguer says that promotes public agreement is normatively proper, however it may conflict with her genuine opinions or evidence. Can this be right? Suppose Peter argues sincerely for conclusion C, which Christi then disputes with a putative defeater D. Since there is now an open disagreement, both Peter and Christi should help terminate this public disagreement. *Any* argumentative speech contributing to this result should be normatively appropriate according to the dispute-resolution approach. Thus, if Peter retracted his original conclusion C, that should be a high-quality piece of argumentation. But in some circumstances this would definitely be inappropriate. Suppose that D is actually a poor objection to Peter's argument, because it really provides no substantial evidence against his conclusion; and suppose Peter recognizes this. Surely it would not be high-quality argumentation, in these circumstances, for Peter to retract his conclusion.

The van Eemeren–Grootendorst view ostensibly averts this problem, because their conception of agreement and disagreement is less purely public. Disputes involve expressed opinions; and although expression is public, opinion is still private. So I interpret the van Eemeren–Grootendorst view of dispute resolution as emphasizing genuine agreement of beliefs. Under this construal, Peter's public retraction in the preceding case would not yield resolution because he still believes *C*. Furthermore, van Eemeren and Grootendorst complicate their theory with a rationality constraint and a code of argumentative conduct for rational discussants. At least at first glance, this gives them additional resources for delimiting high-quality patterns of argumentation. They formulate the following "norm of rationality":

A language user taking part in an argumentative discussion is a rational language user if in the course of the discussion he performs only speech acts which accord with a system of rules acceptable to all discussants which furthers the creation of a dialectic which can lead to a resolution of the dispute at the centre of the discussion. (van Eemeren and Grootendorst 1984: 18)

As Biro and Siegel point out, however, the idea that rationality is captured by the mutual acceptance of rules is problematic. Suppose discussants accept a rule of argumentation that allows inferences to be based on the "gambler's fallacy." Does that make this rule of inference rational? Or suppose discussants agree to license only those arguments with an even number of premises, or agree that whoever argues the loudest has the best argument (Biro and Siegel 1992: 91). Surely their agreement on these precepts does not render these rules rational, or genuinely good rules of argumentation.

It is also questionable whether the van Eemeren–Grootendorst rules are the best set of rules according to the dispute-resolution approach. The heart of their rules is openness: granting each language user the unconditional right to advance or challenge any point of view. They exclude the possibility of taboos in rational discussions, or the immunization of points of view against criticism (van Eemeren and Grootendorst 1984: 154). Discussants must be willing to discuss—that is, ready to accept the challenges of critics and defend the views they advance. Does such openness really encourage dispute resolution? One might well suspect that openness has precisely the opposite result: the proliferation and maintenance of disagreement. To end disagreement, here is a very different but possibly more effective means. Establish a professional team of dispute settlers, and train them in all the tricks of the rhetorical trade. When a dispute arises, dispatch a member of this team to the scene and let her be the *sole* argumentative discussant; nobody else is allowed to speak. This "designated speaker," as we might call her, is encouraged, where necessary, to violate all of our previously listed rules. She may assert premises she neither believes nor is justified in believing. She may appeal to the parties' passions rather than to sound deductive or inductive principles. She may violate responsiveness rules by distorting and/or ignoring arguments against her position. When entering the scene of the dispute, her strategy is to select the side of the dispute with the most gullible discussants, those most easily susceptible of rhetorical manipulation. She will then target them for persuasion, whatever her assessment of the evidential merits of the case. This device might turn out to be the best instrument for terminating disagreement. So according to the dispute-resolution approach, it ought to be superior to the openness rules of van Eemeren and Grootendorst. But clearly this does not represent what we intuitively regard as high-quality argumentation. The trouble, as I would diagnose it, is that this argumentation scheme may be good at producing agreement but is totally inept at identifying truth. In this respect it resembles the belief-inducing pills of Section 3.1. We see, once again, how neglect of the truth-oriented mission would leave us unable to account for the standards of good argumentation tacitly understood by discussants.

SIX

The Technology and Economics of Communication

6.1 *How technology matters to knowledge*

CONSIDER all the people inhabiting the globe at a single time. Contemplate all their informational states, where "informational states" here refers to states of belief, not necessarily true beliefs. Call the entirety of these informational states the *mental infosphere*. If we are lucky, a goodly proportion of the mental infosphere consists of true beliefs, or knowledge. This, then, is the totality of human knowledge at the time in question.

However impressive this totality may be, it can undoubtedly be enlarged. First, many truths are initially known by only a single person, or only a select few. The aggregate of knowledge will be expanded if new souls are apprised (and persuaded) of these "old" truths. Second, entirely new truths may be acquired by society, items of knowledge that no individual previously possessed. These new truths may be acquired by either independent or collaborative inquiry. Communication can play a critical role in both old knowledge dissemination and new knowledge acquisition. In the former case communication is needed to transmit the knowledge-engendering messages. In the latter case, at least where collaboration is featured, communication among collaborators is essential. In general, the social advance of knowledge hinges on communication.

In Chapters 4 and 5, face-to-face speech was the default mode of communication. But face-to-face speech is only the most elementary form of human interchange, and the history of human knowledge owes a heavy debt to alternative styles and technologies of communication. Let us consider some properties of communication systems and formats, to see how more powerful and flexible systems can contribute to knowledge expansion.

Messages must be encoded and transmitted via some medium or media, such as sound waves, smoke signals, or electromagnetic radiation. One relevant property of any such medium is its scope of propagation. Natural, unamplified speech does not carry very far, so the potential audience for directly transmitted speech is always circumscribed. Smoke signals, which were used by ancient Greeks as well as native North Americans, can be seen at a greater distance, but even here the distances are only miles or tens of miles. Of course, messages can always be replicated by iterated use of the same medium. Rumors can spread great distances by word of mouth, and smoke signals can be retransmitted over hundreds of miles.[1]

Speech and smoke signals are *synchronous* modes of communication. A receiver must pick up the message (roughly) at the time it is issued, because it does not stick around afterwards. Until the invention of writing, roughly five thousand years ago, you had to be in a speaker's presence at the time of his utterance or you would miss his message. Similarly, a smoke signal is a transient event, which leaves no permanent trace. With the invention of writing, however, an *asynchronous* communication technology was introduced. Messages could be stored and read later at the receiver's convenience.

Writing also enabled messages to be delivered at great distances. Kings sent written messages by personal courier, and letters were delivered by pony express. But as long as news was hand-delivered, it traveled only as fast as people did. Speed of message propagation vastly increased with the invention of such technologies as the telegraph, the telephone, radio, and television.

The size of the reachable audience is constrained by communication technology. When books were handwritten by scribes, the process was slow and expensive. Few people could afford books, and few were in existence. The European invention of the printing press in the fifteenth century (which followed its original invention by the Chinese about 800 years earlier) led to a massive increase in the number of books produced. The nineteenth-century invention of the steam-powered press ushered in the era of the newspaper. Let us use the label *message infosphere* for the realm of encoded messages, in any medium whatever, that are in principle available for receipt or retrieval at a given time. The printing press and the steam-powered press both had enormous impact on the size of the message infosphere.

Communication technologies differ in their support of interactiveness or responsiveness. Face-to-face speech fosters bidirectionality and even multidirectionality. Speakers at a town meeting address a sizeable audience, any member of which can respond to an initial speaker's assertions. Telephonic communication also supports bidirectionality but not—at least until recently, when conference calling was introduced—multidirectionality. Network radio and television only support unidirectional message transmission. Most individuals cannot afford a television transmitter, so they cannot "return" a mes-

---

[1] Message iteration raises the problem of noise; there is no guarantee that messages will be accurately transmitted, especially when multiply iterated. I shall not probe this issue, however.

sage to a television newscaster, at least not via the very same medium. Here it is not the available technology *per se* but its cost that is decisive.

Technology is not the only facet of communication systems affecting the quantity and quality of communication opportunities. Institutions and their organization are equally important. It is not simply print technology but the institution of the scholarly library with systematic cataloging principles that has played a pivotal role in the expansion of knowledge by cultural transmission. Print technology guarantees that documents can be stored over long periods of time; so the message infosphere becomes a realm of vast proportions. But the practical usability of the message infosphere depends on organization; this is critical to the role of print in knowledge enhancement.

Consider an inquirer who hopes to benefit veritistically from the messages of others, who hopes to find answers to one or more of her questions. Does the existing message infosphere contain any stored documents with clear and reliable answers, or at least evidence that is relevant, to her questions? If so, can the inquirer find these documents? Is the message infosphere so organized that there is a good probability that relevant documents will be identified and retrieved? Alternatively, can the learner direct a query to a pertinent source, and thereby elicit a newly constructed message that gives an answer or provides relevant evidence? This is not just a matter of technology, but of informational organization. The research library traditionally performed some of these functions for the world of scholarship, but for a variety of reasons the message infosphere is an increasingly complex and changing affair, which can no longer be handled exclusively by the traditional print-dominated library.

Utopians see the Internet as a perfect fix for all informational ills. I favor a more cautious stance. Digital technology undoubtedly makes enormous contributions, but to harness its vast potential serious problems must be addressed and choices made. One business of this chapter is to assess the electronic revolution within the wider context of the social epistemic enterprise. By getting a clearer abstract picture of how communication can enhance knowledge, we shall improve our ability to assess both the current contributions of cyberspace to knowledge enhancement and the further steps that need to be taken to maximize its future contributions.

Veritistically successful communication transpires when learners receive messages that lead them to form new beliefs (or increase their degrees of belief) in true answers to questions that interest them. If messages with such potential are produced by various sources, the veritistic success of these messages depends on learners actually receiving and decoding those messages, that is, assimilating their contents. This in turn depends on there being *routes* or *paths* by which the messages travel from source to receiver. Whether a message successfully travels such a route usually depends partly on the source. A spoken message may be uttered within earshot of a targeted hearer. A written message may be mailed to the receiver's address, or placed in her office mailbox. Frequently, however, especially in the case of publicly disseminated messages, successful communication depends not only on efforts of senders but also on those of receivers. Readers decide which books and periodicals to purchase or borrow from a library. Mass media consumers decide which news or talk shows to listen to on radio or television. It often takes a confluence of efforts by sources and receivers to effect successful communication, to consummate a route from source to receiver.

Let us examine in more detail what kinds of communications, if delivered, can yield veritistic profit. The nature of these communications can be extracted from material in Chapters 4 and 5. The simplest case is one in which the communicated message contains a direct answer to some question that interests the receiver. A standard case of veritistic profit is one in which the source answers the question truly and the receiver moves from nonbelief to full belief in this answer because she trusts the source. A variant of this standard case involves degrees of belief rather than categorical belief. The receiver raises her level of conviction in the reported answer, though not necessarily to 1.0, and this constitutes veritistic improvement because the reported answer is indeed true. Such an increase in DB might be mediated by Bayesian reasoning of the sort discussed in Chapter 4.

A second category of cases are ones in which the communicated message does not contain a direct answer to a question $Q(P/-P)$ but contains a report of some evidence E that the receiver uses to answer her question $Q(P/-P)$. For example, the receiver may use evidence E to form a belief in conclusion P, or to increase her DB in P. If P is true, this will constitute a veritistic improvement. Two scenarios may be distinguished here. First, the message itself may endorse P as an inferable conclusion from E. That is, the source may both report evidence E and argue explicitly to conclusion P, an argument which the receiver accepts. Alternatively, the source may assert only E, and make no mention of P. The receiver herself initiates the inference from E to P. Under either scenario, the amount of veritistic improvement is a function of how much the receiver increases her DB in P. If E is a weighty piece of evidence for the receiver, and if the receiver's prior DB in P is not too high, the message can produce a large increase in truth possession.

As these scenarios indicate, successful communication alone does not guarantee veritistic gain; such gain depends on appropriate change in belief on the part of the receiver. Indeed, communication can even lead to veritistic loss. If communicated messages contain false but convincing reports, or if messages contain true evidence from which receivers draw false conclusions, communication breeds veritistic loss. So powerful communication systems do not supplant the necessity for accurate reportage and good reasoning. No communication technology is a panacea for knowledge improvement. Let us suppose, however, that reasoners are poised to make positive veritistic use of reports from various sources. For example, suppose that they are adept at interpreting the significance of new evidence, perhaps by having accurate likelihoods of the kind discussed in Chapter 4. Then applying the theorems of

Chapter 4, or the Truth-in-Evidence Principle from Chapter 5, we can say the following: If true evidence is publicly reported which is relevant to $Q(P/-P)$, if $Q(P/-P)$ is of interest to potential receivers, and if these receivers are disposed to interpret this evidence appropriately, then it will be veritistically beneficial (on average) for messages reporting this evidence to reach these receivers. A communication technology that facilitates receipt of such messages will be veritistically valuable. Moreover, the greater the speed and breadth of facilitation, the greater the veritistic value.

6.2 Computer-mediated communication

How does computer-mediated communication (CMC) assist the knowledge enterprise? For present purposes let us divide the knowledge enterprise into two sectors: knowledge quests by the public at large, and knowledge quests by scientists and scholars. This section is devoted to the public's use of CMC, and Section 6.3 is devoted to scholarly use of CMC. In this section I shall focus on three uses of CMC: (1) electronic mail, (2) electronic forums such as newsgroups, chat rooms, bulletin board systems, and "zines," and (3) the World Wide Web. In the next section I shall discuss electronic publishing in science and scholarship.

E-mail can be used for both one-to-one communications and one-to-many communications, as when a sender communicates with a large list-serve. In either case, e-mail's great virtue is its affordance of cheap, speedy, and efficient interactive communication with anyone (suitably equipped) in the world. Its efficiency lies partly in its asynchronous character. Receivers can read and reply to their e-mail at times convenient to them, times that may differ sharply from those of a sender living many time-zones away. These features make e-mail an ideal mode of interactive communication. What are its veritistic benefits?

Interactive communication enables an inquirer to query a potential informant on precisely the question(s) that interest(s) her. By giving inquirers speedy access to potential informants, especially friends or associates, e-mail enables people to tap sources they have reason to trust as knowledgeable on the topics in question. If you are planning a trip to the Bay Area and are concerned about local transportation when you get there, you can e-mail a Bay Area friend for transit information. If rumor has it that a French friend of yours is taking a new job, you can e-mail him directly and ask if it's true. E-mail has most of the advantages of face-to-face conversation,[2] but enables an inquirer

---

[2] It is widely noted, however, that e-mail lacks nonverbal cues present in face-to-face conversation. Ironical twists can be more ambiguous in e-mail, clouding the intent and interpretation of a message. E-mail has evolved "emoticons" partly to deal with this problem.

to elicit information promptly from well-positioned informants, regardless of their locale.

Issue-dedicated newsgroups, chat rooms, and bulletin board systems further enlarge the community from which new evidence or argumentative angles on a given topic may be acquired. Newsgroups and bulletin board systems draw people together who have no prior acquaintanceship, only a shared interest. Similarity of interests, however, may be accompanied by pertinent knowledge that can veritistically benefit participants. So these virtual communities often contribute notably to knowledge dissemination. Many internauts also praise these Net forums for their creation of global communities and subcultures, valued for their human relationships (Rheingold 1993). In addition to the intrinsic value of human relationships, such communities can also have an epistemological spinoff. A spirit of community can help regulate the quality of information flowing through the system, because it may be considered a community offense to introduce misinformation into the system.[3]

Let me turn now to the World Wide Web. The Web is often viewed as a virtual library, and the repository of innumerable documents that can redound to the knowledge benefit of almost any user. From our epistemic point of view, though, the most distinctive feature of the Web is not simply its size, though this is impressive, but its massive connectivity. This connectivity is effected by means of hypertext, a language able to connect to other text or other forms of media.[4] By clicking at one point in an on-screen text, a user is connected, often quite rapidly, to another preselected document. One virtue of this systematized connectedness is the enormous range of relevant information available at one's fingertips. From the scholar's point of view, hyperlinks resemble footnotes. They are far superior to footnotes, however, because they do not just cite related works but present them online. In theory, then, hypertext promises veritistic enhancement by making relevant evidence rapidly available to users. A second touted benefit of hypertext is the interactivity it offers to users. Each user decides what further information or details she wants to pursue, making active decisions about the search paths to be explored. Notice, however, that this interactiveness is not quite the same as a two-person conversation, because users can only activate a document's precreated links. If a document designer neglected to establish certain links because he failed to

[3] Thanks to Peter Ludlow (personal communication) for this last point. Ludlow reports that when people have tried to hoax the WELL, there has been a response of community outrage.
[4] Strictly speaking, the language is hypertext markup language (HTML), usually credited to Tim Berners-Lee, and foreshadowed by Vannevar Bush and Ted Nelson. (Nelson invented the label "hypertext.") Here and elsewhere I give scant attention to hypermedia, which incorporate multimedia into hypertext documents. This is because the special contribution of nontextual media to knowledge is quite difficult to pinpoint, and would take us into issues in the theory of representation (including mental representation) that are far from our main concerns.

anticipate certain questions or challenges, there is nothing users can do about it. By contrast, in face-to-face or electronic conversation, inquirers can address any question they like to an interlocutor, not simply trigger antecedently scripted associations. Of course, not all links are hard-coded; some calculate their target on the fly. Documents can have a dynamic quality, tailored in part to suit the user. Still, this all depends on what the designer has prepared.

Given the vastness of the Web, a major problem is how to exploit it for knowledge-enhancing purposes. You may have important information you are delighted to share with the public. But, as Paul Gilster puts it, "How could the world beat a path to your door when the path was uncharted, uncataloged, and could be discovered only serendipitously?" (1997: 163). The intended solution to the muddled state of cyberspace is search engines and autonomous agents. Search engines are supposed to assist inquirers by enabling them to track down information in the categories they desire, consummating a marriage of user and desired messages by guiding the user to the messages. Search tools like Lycos, Alta Vista, Excite, and Yahoo try to make the Internet really function like an encyclopedia or research library, whether for mundane or arcane materials. Yahoo, for example, attempts to organize the contents of the Web into a hierarchy of categories, with whose help it can fruitfully be searched.

How well do these familiar wares of CMC serve their designated purposes? Let us look at some nagging and stubborn problems facing the Internet, still viewed from our distinctive epistemic standpoint (as contrasted with the standpoint of entertainment, for example). Starting with popular newsgroups and chat rooms, just how useful are they from a veritistic perspective? That depends heavily on the trustworthiness or reliability of the information paraded by the members. According to many observers, such groups are often the incubators and amplifiers of ill-founded rumors and unreliable opinions. E-mail can also spread stories that have little relation to fact. Whether a cyberhoax or a cyberinnocent mistake, a much-publicized example in August 1997 was the wide distribution of a document allegedly given as a commencement speech at MIT by the novelist Kurt Vonnegut. Vonnegut never gave a commencement speech at MIT, nor was he the author of this funny document, which began, "Ladies and gentlemen of the class of 1997: Wear sunscreen." Instead, it was a newspaper column written by Mary Schmich of the *Chicago Tribune*. But many people were fooled—including, initially, Vonnegut's own wife.

There are two sources of concern about newsgroups, chat rooms, and the like. First, they can be a refuge for splinter groups and extremists, who want to share their views with likeminded mates. By shutting themselves off from conflicting viewpoints, communities can reinforce their own dogmas without hearing countervailing arguments. The incidence of this phenomenon unfortunately undercuts some of the veritistic rationale that is offered for user groups. User groups *can* serve as forums in which people of differing persuasions argue out their respective viewpoints. This might be expected to yield good veritistic results, in accord with the results of Chapter 5. But if such groups are only havens for likeminded souls, there will be little or no critical argumentation of the sort described in Chapter 5.[5] If cyberspace prompts people only to listen to messages that repeat their staunchest convictions, to burrow ever deeper into worldviews insulated from criticism, its net veritistic contribution may not be positive.

Narrowly selected listening is not the only veritistic threat in cyberspace. Another danger is the loosening of constraints on truth-telling that the anonymity afforded by cyberspace encourages. In face-to-face communication, a hearer knows a reporter's identity. If the report turns out to be false, it can be laid at the doorstep of the known individual. In a face-to-face community, the threat of punishment or disapproval serves as a deterrent to deliberate deceptions. On the Internet, however, sources are often wholly anonymous, or difficult to trace. "Anonymous remailers," for example, allow users to send messages without their own IDs. "Spoofing" is a practice of signing someone else's name to a message. So accountability is greatly reduced, and the threat of infojunk looms. Furthermore, since the public addressed by a source can be massively anonymous, the source may have little sentiment of responsibility toward them. In the absence of filtering mechanisms, or supervision by professionally dedicated news dispensers, reportage standards can readily deteriorate. (Some groups, however, are moderated.) Internet users also have very few clues by which to assess the accuracy or integrity of a Web page. Appearances traditionally utilized to judge a publication are no longer applicable. It doesn't take much to create a handsome Web page. Extremists defend everything from the Oklahoma City bombing to the Holocaust on finely tuned Web pages (Gilster 1997: 90).

The problem of information quality on the Net is not restricted to newsgroups or chat rooms. As the Net increasingly bulges with commercial advertising, the motivations and reliability of its messages are increasingly suspect. Americans currently consume medical information, for example, with great avidity. The Web site of Medline, a compendium of 9 million references and abstracts from medical journals, was barely put online before it was receiving one million hits a day (Stolberg 1997). Drug companies are tapping into the public's yearning for medical information. In 1996 the pharmaceutical industry spent almost $600 million advertising prescription drugs directly to patients. In August 1997, a scan of the Web uncovered 90,360 documents that match the word "asthma"; "multiple sclerosis" turned up 89,650 (Stolberg 1997). Can the lay person sift the reliable medical information from the bunk?

This worry prompted the editor of the *Journal of the American Medical*

---

[5] Furthermore, there is no guarantee that contributors to newsgroups will abide by the principles of good argumentation that, according to Chapter 5, are needed to link argumentation with veritistic advance.

Association, George Lundberg, to coauthor a cautionary editorial, pointing out that "science and snake oil may not always look all that different on the Net" (Silberg, Lundberg, and Musacchio 1997: 1244). The Net, it is argued, has become the world's largest vanity press. Anyone with a computer can become author, editor, and publisher. In such an environment, "novices and savvy Internet users alike can have trouble distinguishing the wheat from the chaff" (Silberg, Lundberg, and Musacchio 1997: 1244). Lundberg and coauthors propose a set of basic quality standards that can be developed and applied in an electronic context. The core practices they propose include the following: (1) Authors and contributors, their affiliations, and relevant credentials should be provided. (2) References and sources for all content should be listed clearly. (3) Web site "ownership" should be prominently and fully disclosed, as should any sponsorship, advertising, underwriting, commercial funding arrangements or support, or potential conflicts of interest. This should include information about arrangements in which links to other sites are posted as a result of financial considerations. Such standards, they feel, would help consumers and professionals alike make sounder judgments about the credibility or reasonableness of what they read on the Net. They are examples of "signals" of credibility that were briefly discussed in Section 4.1.

I turn next to a closer examination of hypertext. A vaunted feature of hypertext is interactivity. The reader has the feeling of charting her own course through a limitless sea of documents. But the choices available to the reader are virtually all determined, directly or indirectly, by the hypertext document's creator. The author has created hyperlinks to selected documents and omitted possible hyperlinks to others. The reader may feel that all relevant materials have authoritatively been included, but this is usually an illusion.[6] First, the document designer may have had a special agenda or angle on the subject that led him to select certain documents and deliberately omit others. Second, there may have been relevant documents of which he was simply unaware. Third, certain questions or relationships occurring to the reader may not have occurred to the author. Such selections and omissions tend to be camouflaged by hypertext, by its intimation that hyperlinks make the *whole* story potentially available (Gilster 1997: 125–35).

Nonetheless, there are two significant ways in which hypertext can be used for veritistic gain. The obvious one is provision of related information. When a current document interests a reader, documents addressing related subjects will also often interest her. At least she is potentially interested in such documents in the sense that her interest would be piqued if she were actually presented with them. That is the sort of opportunity on which hypertext capitalizes. A mere click on a link presents the additional document, which may yield knowledge *of interest* to the reader. Of course, some linked material

---

[6] Of course, the same can happen with printed texts.

may not be of interest, and readers will only discover this by testing the link. A certain amount of inquiry, therefore, is wasted, but this is inevitable in any line of investigation.

A second veritistically promising application of hypertext is to structure extended argumentative discourses (recall this notion from Section 5.2). A speaker's argument for her principal conclusion starts with some set of first-level premises. Each first-level premise, however, can be challenged. The speaker may be prepared with further arguments to support each premise, but these additional arguments would feature second-level premises that can also be challenged; and so on perhaps indefinitely. No speaker can actually defend an argument against every possible challenge, if only for reasons of time and rhetorical effect. Nor is it easy for a speaker to anticipate exactly which challenges will strike her audience as most telling or threatening. And different audience members may have different opinions about the strongest lines of criticism. Even if the speaker can anticipate the entire set of most popular challenges, and even if she has ready responses to each, it is difficult to construct a flowing, linear text that covers all these bases. In short, it is difficult to comply robustly with principle (14) of Section 5.2. Hypertext format is an ideal device to surmount this difficulty. For each challenge or objection that a hypertext author anticipates, she can create a link that leads to her answer to that objection. Readers may ignore links on premises or transitions which they accept. No reader has to explore the entire nested set of arguments prepared by the author. But the replies are all there for any interested reader to consult.

While this opportunity is definitely offered by hypertext, an opportunity that dovetails with veritistic aims, the actual use of hypertext on the Web is often quite different. Instead of leading to supporting evidence or argumentation, links often open up onto vaguely related documents. In fact, opened documents are often from remote servers for which the author bears no responsibility, which she may not endorse, and with which she has only minimal familiarity (Gilster 1997: 131–5). A hypertext compound document, then, is frequently nothing like a sustained defense of a (set of) proposition(s), with appended rebuttals to possible criticisms. It is often a mélange of texts of varying origins, the interconnectedness of which can be quite loose and disjointed. This kind of discourse structure is not notably propitious for inquiry into truth.

The critical importance of search engines and autonomous agents to the veritistic value of the Web invites lengthier analysis. (This is a domain in which applications are changing rapidly, so it is difficult to write anything that will not be out of date by the time it is published.) One of the best current search engines, Yahoo, compiles a table of contents with a hierarchy of categories chosen by numerous technicians. To see how a user might deploy Yahoo for a practical search of information, consider the following example (Hearst 1997). Suppose Aunt Alice connects to the Net to find out what kind of edible bulbs, such as garlic or onions, she can plant in her garden this autumn. If she uses Yahoo, which one of its topmost categories should she search: "Recreation," "Regional," or "Environment"? The trouble is that whichever one she chooses, the previous menu will vanish from view. If she guesses wrong about which category is most relevant, she will have to back up and try again. If the desired information is deep in the hierarchy, the process can be very slow and frustrating. Furthermore, it is a Sisyphean task to organize the entire contents of the Web, which appear far faster than they can be indexed by hand. Yahoo only lists a fraction of them. Excite and Alta Vista are more comprehensive, but that poses a new problem. Entering the string of key words, "garlic onion autumn fall garden grow" into Excite will retrieve at least 583,430 Web pages. These cannot all be browsed in a realistic time frame.

To assist with such problems, a major initiative in the information access industry is the creation of *autonomous agents*, computational entities that cooperate with a user in the service of information-gathering tasks.[7] The metaphor used is that of a personal assistant who helps a user get the job done and typically hides the complexity of its execution. For example, to assist in a search task on the Web, one might use an interface agent such as "Scatter/Gather," developed by Marti Hearst and colleagues. Scatter/Gather creates a table of contents that changes as the user gets a better understanding of what documents are available and most likely to be relevant (Hearst 1997). Suppose that Aunt Alice uses Excite and retrieves the first 500 Web pages it suggests. The Scatter/Gather system can analyze those pages and divide them into clusters based on their similarity to one another. Aunt Alice can scan each cluster and select those that appear most relevant. If she decides she likes a cluster of 293 texts summarized by "bulb," "soil," and "gardener," she can run them through Scatter/Gather again, rescattering them into more specific clusters. After several iterations, this can whittle down the set of pages to a few dozen, a more tractable number. In this fashion, refinements in search procedures can make a significant difference to knowledge quests. Another such intermediary agent is EchoSearch, which fires up parallel searches of about eight search engines, picks the "best" ten of their results, and summarizes and indexes them.[8]

Agents that assist users in information retrieval from the Internet come in many varieties: information filtering agents, off-line delivery agents, notification agents, and service agents of all assortments (Caglayan and Harrison 1997: 51–2). Information filtering agents, for example, do not identify Web sites, but use selected information sources to find *contents* of interest to a user. Filtering agents gather recent articles on selected topics and present these articles, or their gist, to the user. An example is NewsHound, a personal news

---

[7] Search engines themselves can be considered autonomous agents (or entities that deploy such agents).
[8] Thanks to Martin Fricke for the reference to EchoSearch and for other advice in this chapter.

service by San Jose Mercury News. NewsHound searches the stories in its own newspaper and in news services such as Associated Press to find articles that match a user's profile. It then delivers selected articles to the user's Internet address by e-mail. Service agents include agents that provide information about products for purchase or movies one might like to see. A species of such service agents are collaboration agents, which make recommendations based on community opinion. A collaboration agent elicits evaluations of products from a large group of users. It then recommends products to a specific user based on the evaluations of other users with similar tastes.

Many developers are working on agents that program themselves, that is, use techniques of machine learning to acquire the knowledge they need to assist users. Patti Maes explains the idea as follows.

Initially, a personal assistant is not very familiar with the habits and preferences of his or her employer and may not even be very helpful. The assistant needs some time to become familiar with the particular work methods of the employer and organization at hand. However, with every experience the assistant learns, either by watching how the employer performs tasks, by receiving instruction from the employer, or by learning from other more experienced assistants within the organization. Gradually, more tasks that were initially performed directly by the employer can be taken care of by the assistant. (1994: 32)

Maes's research demonstrates that a learning interface agent can similarly become more helpful and competent in information filtering tasks. For example, if an e-mail agent notices that a user almost always stores messages sent to a certain mailing list in a certain folder, then it can offer to automate this action the next time a message sent to that mailing list is read. Similarly, if a news filtering agent detects some pattern in the articles the user reads, it can offer similar articles to the user when it discovers them.

A method that allows agents to start from more than scratch is multiagent collaboration. When an agent does not have enough confidence in predicting its user's behavior, it asks for help from other agents assisting other users. The agent can describe a situation to peer agents and await their recommended action. When these recommendations are compared with the action eventually taken by the user, the agent can increase or decrease the level of trust it assigns to those peer agents (Maes 1994: 37).

How should search engines and software agents be evaluated for their information-processing prowess? The performance of a search engine might be measured by its *precision* or its *recall*. The precision of a search engine is the ratio of the documents relevant to a user's query that it returns over the total number of documents (both relevant and irrelevant) that it returns. Recall is the ratio of total relevant documents returned in a query to the total number of documents on the Web. These measures might have different appeal depending on one's interests. Moving to a more theoretical level, some investigators propose criteria for rating all sorts of information access technologies, including both search engines and agents. One proposed rating system constructs an analogy with optimal foraging theory in biology and anthropology. Just as different food-foraging strategies can be evaluated by determining how much energy is gained (from food) per unit of time spent foraging, so an information technology can be assessed by asking how much relevant information a user will gather with the help of that technology per unit of time it is deployed (Pirolli and Card 1995).

A much-discussed topic connected with CMCs is privacy. By making networked knowledge so easy to acquire, cyberspace may encourage *too much* knowledge, or knowledge getting into the wrong hands. Facts about an individual that ought to remain private are all too available to prying busybodies or snoops. Many aspects of computer technology, such as encryption devices, are designed to protect privacy. Important as this topic is, it does not squarely fall into the domain of epistemology as I have delineated it, because epistemology focuses on the means to knowledge *enhancement*, whereas privacy studies focus on the means to knowledge *curtailment* (at least decreasing knowledge in the hands of the wrong people). For this reason, I shall not explore this topic. I do not belittle the importance of privacy as a moral issue; it simply falls, for the most part, outside the scope of epistemology.[9]

6.3 *The economics of scholarly communication*

Though the public is massively involved in the Internet, the Net's impact on scholarly and scientific communication may ultimately be even greater. As the twenty-first century approaches, the informational demands of scientific and scholarly communities are outstripping traditional resources. Collectively, American research and teaching libraries contain almost 500 million volumes, enough to reach across the nation three times (Frye 1997). The value of these collections approaches $35 to $45 billion. Meanwhile, journal prices have soared 400 percent in the past twenty years, while the prices of books and monographs have increased 40 percent in just the past five. The problem is exacerbated by endangered books (printed on acidic, selfdestructing paper) and by the proliferation and fragmentation of scholarly disciplines, which constantly generate new journals and other publication outlets. It is doubtful that the financial resources will be available to grow, house, manage, and preserve the needed scientific and scholarly literature in the future if business is conducted as in the past. Scholarship and scholarly communication clearly

---

[9] I add the qualifier "for the most part" because of the following exception suggested by Peter Ludlow (personal communication). An agent might want to keep some of his inquiries or investigations secret from the "authorities." For example, a feminist in Iran might be interested in accessing Western writings on the topic without Iranian authorities knowing about this. So the ability to keep one's activities private can sometimes be a precondition for attaining certain knowledge.

require digital technology to come to the rescue. The cost of science and scholarship will only be sustainable, it appears, if digital technology is appropriately exploited. But will the use of such technology come at a veritistic price, or will veritistic outcomes also prosper in an electronic environment? These questions need to be explored. Let us construct a terminology and a set of categories in terms of which different scenarios can be analyzed and compared.

Any way of organizing scholarly or scientific communication will be called a communication *regime*. A regime includes both the underlying technology and the types of actors or economic entities that participate in the scheme. In the traditional ink-on-paper regime, for example, publishers and their employees (editors, copyeditors, typesetters, proofreaders, printers and binders, and marketing staff) play an intermediary role between authors and readers. Whether comparable types of actors would participate in electronic regimes is an open question.

This section focuses primarily on the *costs* of various communication regimes. In addition to cost, however, three factors should be singled out for attention when comparing alternative regimes: (1) *speed*, (2) *content quality*, and (3) *product identification*. Speed refers to the speed at which communication is effected between authors and readers. How long does it take for messages or documents created by scientists to reach their relevant audience? This is a veritistic issue insofar as the speed with which evidence and theory are communicated affects the speed at which truths are recognized and mistakes corrected.

The second category, content quality, assesses the effectiveness of the communication scheme in motivating and shaping content quality. Until now we have assumed that messages or documents are created independently of communication regimes. The latter serve only to transmit antecedently fixed messages more or less successfully or widely. But communication regimes can also influence which messages or documents get constructed. This can transpire in three ways. First, communication regimes can have an impact on incentives for investigators to conduct and report their research. Credit and prizes awarded by peers are a nonnegligible component of the motivating force behind scientific and scholarly activity, so a satisfactory communication regime must comport with attempts to assign appropriate credit; otherwise, investigators cannot be expected to produce "as much or as good" in terms of veritistically valuable findings or creations. Second, since the same information can be represented in different ways, and representational differences affect how well receivers understand and appreciate the information, communication regimes that facilitate the most perspicuous types of representation are veritistically beneficial.[10] Next, third parties involved in publishing a

---

[10] For vivid examples of how visual displays of information can facilitate understanding, see Tufte 1983, 1990.

message can help shape, improve, or polish that message, thereby influencing the quality of its content.

Finally, product identification concerns the capacity of a communication regime to ensure that interested readers locate and recognize intellectual products or documents that are evidentially appropriate to their projects and inquiries. A regime might be good at getting messages "aired" but bad at bringing readers' attention to the messages that are veritistically most beneficial to them. A superior regime would be good on both dimensions.

Scholarly disciplines differ in terms of their primary units of communication. The core scholarly units in history are books and monographs. In science, journal articles are the coin of the realm. I shall focus primarily on journals, where the most dramatic changes are now under discussion, partly because of the increased number of print journals and their soaring prices in recent years. Many new experiments and initiatives are being undertaken in the electronic publication of journals or quasi-journals. There are electronic preprint archives, electronic-only journals, and electronic versions of conventional print journals. So let us ask how scientific and scholarly communication might be transformed by e-journal publishing, and what veritistic consequences this might have.

Printed journals and magazines have been a favored form of scientific and scholarly research reporting for about three centuries, dating from the appearance of the *Journal des savants* and the *Philosophical Transactions of the Royal Society of London* in 1665. Continuation of this traditional print-on-paper style of communication, without any admixture of other styles, stands at one end of the possible alternatives that lie before us. Call this traditional communication regime R_t. At the other end of the continuum would be the publication of research articles in purely electronic form, without any print versions (other than those printed by end-users). To dramatize the contrast, we can stipulate that the opposite extreme be devoid of publishers or other intermediaries between authors and readers, implying the absence of any peer review process associated with traditional scholarly publishing. Call this communication regime R_{e-p} (electronic publishing without peer review). Obviously, many possible "mixed" regimes lie between these extremes. But let us initially examine these two for purposes of comparison.

Incarnations of R_{e-p} exist. The first automated archive for electronic communication of research information went online in 1991. This "e-print archive" in high-energy physics, called HEP-TH, began as a way of circumventing inadequacies of standard research journals, but rapidly became the primary means of communicating ongoing research in formal areas of high-energy particle theory (Ginsparg 1997). It is widely emulated in other disciplines, including astrophysics, quantum physics, superconductivity, and plasma physics. Since the mid-1970s, the primary means of communication had been a preprint system in which printed copies of papers were distributed via ordinary mail to large distribution lists. Larger high-energy physics groups typically spent between \$15,000 and \$20,000 per year on photocopy, postage, and labor costs for preprint distribution. By the mid-1980s many electronic information exchanges were taking place. Long-distance collaborations became very efficient, because revisions could be sent back and forth rapidly. Inexpensive online archives were facilitated by the development of low-cost but high-powered workstations, which enabled papers to be stored at an average cost of two cents per paper. In terms of transmission speed, the Internet runs data at rates up to 45 megabits per second—less than 0.01 of a second per paper.[11]

In 1991 Paul Ginsparg, working at Los Alamos National Laboratory, wrote software to fully automate the preprint archive. Through that software, users construct, maintain, and revise a comprehensive database and distribution network without outside supervision or intervention. They submit abstracts and research papers that are in principle suitable for publication in conventional research journals. Users subscribe to the system and receive a daily listing of titles and abstracts of new papers received. The system allows anonymous FTP access to the papers, and the World Wide Web provides an even more convenient network access.

Six months after the system's inauguration in 1991, its subscriber list encompassed most of the researchers in formal quantum field theory and string theory, and currently has over 4,000 subscribers. It was transformed from a feasibility experiment into an indispensable research tool for users. Many users report that it has effectively eliminated their reliance on conventional print journals. It costs about \$40 per year to store the totality of its papers, including figures. It is now customary in some fields served by e-print archives to reference a paper's e-print archive index number rather than a published reference. Ginsparg praises the system for some additional side benefits. It eliminates geographic inequalities by eliminating the boat-mail gap between continents, and institutes a more democratic research system in which access to new results is afforded equally to beginning graduate students and seasoned operators. Finally, it is a boon to developing countries, since the expense of connecting to an existing network is tiny compared with that of stocking and maintaining libraries (Ginsparg 1997: 49–50).

In terms of both speed and cost, this incarnation of R_{e-p} is clearly superior to R_t. But what about the factors of content quality and product identification? A principal difference between an e-print archive and a traditional journal is the absence of peer review, which could make a nontrivial difference in content quality. In conventional journal publication, publishers hire editors who validate and select the papers to be published via expert referees. Quality control is to be achieved both by excluding unsuitable documents

---

[11] These figures are governed by a variety of assumptions, of course, but the details do not concern us here.

from publication and by improving papers via suggestions from editors or referees.

Suppose that submitted papers come in four categories: (1) papers that make mistakes, that contain flat-out inaccuracies; (2) papers that are argumentatively weak in some fashion, for example, that draw poorly supported conclusions, or ignore obvious objections; (3) papers that avoid the first two types of flaws but add little new to the discipline; (4) papers that contain major new findings or theoretical reasonings, while avoiding any of the first two faults. A successful peer review process would weed out instances of the first three types and include instances of the fourth. In the absence of such a process, what will happen? Readers will have to decide for themselves, from among all papers available, which ones to read. Four possible losses, from a veritistic perspective, could result. First, unsuspecting readers might read papers of the first type and mistakenly believe their inaccurate statements. Second, insufficiently expert readers might be persuaded by conclusions in the second type of paper because (for example) they don't think of the objections that would be obvious to a more expert reader or referee. Third, readers might waste their time reading papers of the third type, with little or no veritistic gain.

A fourth worry concerns the problem of product identification. Without any way of signaling which papers would pass the test of expert review, it will be much harder for readers to identify the stronger papers. This makes it more probable that readers will fail to read some papers in the fourth category, simply because they do not get identified amid the glut of others. So the omission of peer review does appear to be a count against an R_{e-p} regime.

How do defenders of the unrefereed journal or archive respond? Replying to the alleged danger of encouraging poorly prepared material, Ginsparg argues that the instant publication to thousands of peers increases circumspection through the specter of embarrassment (1997: 52). This may be heightened by the fact that papers cannot be withdrawn (though they can be revised). Skeptics note that the threat of embarrassment might suffice for quality control in high energy physics, but it would not suffice in most disciplines. To do high energy physics at all, you have to have grants, and all grants depend on referees' endorsements. Anyone in a position to submit anything in high energy physics must be doing grantworthy research, so tighter quality control measures are not needed as much as in other research communities, where entry barriers are lower (Varian 1996: 46).

A more interesting defense of the dispensability of refereeing is the suggestion that filtering should come *after* publication rather than before it. Hal Varian points out that publishing used to be very expensive, with fixed costs for typesetting, fancy machines, skilled labor, etc. There were big costs to get the document from the manuscript into the publication stage. But now, with desktop publication, those costs are dramatically lower. When it was expensive to publish it was important to filter before publication, because it saved substantial costs. But now that it's cheap to publish, argues Varian (1996: 50), why not filter after items are published? Make items available and then let people find out which are worth looking at.

How is this to be done? One way is to utilize survey articles. Let survey writers substitute for erstwhile referees, by apprising readers of the most significant and reliable recent contributions on a given subject. Another possibility is "social filtering" systems, such as GroupLens. GroupLens matches Professor *X* to (say) ten other professors who have given similar ratings on articles they have all (or mostly) read. Then, when Professor *X* queries a title she has not yet read, the system makes a recommendation based on the article's ratings by the matching members (MacKie-Mason and Riveros 1997; Varian 1996).

These schemes might work for articles in a narrow specialty, but how could they work as a substitute for journals like *Science* or *Nature*, which publish carefully selected articles across the whole span of the sciences? If Professor *X* likes wide-ranging journals like these, how can the aforementioned devices help her? Survey articles cover recent contributions on a single topic. They do not compare articles in widely dispersed sciences, or even articles on different topics within the same science. Nor is it likely that a matching group will help. Professor *X* is likely to be matched to other people in her own field; they are the ones that have a track record of reading the same articles as *X*. But if *X* is seeking articles in several *other* fields, what is the probability that many of *X*'s matching group will have read the same such articles before *X* has read them? A system like GroupLens, moreover, only kicks in when one queries a particular article title. But if (conservatively) tens of thousands of science articles are electronically published each month, there is no guarantee that Professor *X* will query just those superior papers that will elicit enthusiastic rankings.[12]

Thus far I have discussed the value of peer review to prospective readers: it helps them solve the product identification problem. Does peer review hold any value for authors, or for the system of science and scholarship as a whole? In almost all disciplines, there is a prestige hierarchy among journals, with some known to accept only the best work in the field. In the social sciences and humanities, the most prestigious journals often reject 80 to 90 percent of submissions (Harnad 1996). This prestige hierarchy depends on a system of peer review. Although authors are typically not remunerated for their articles, greater scholarly or scientific credit redounds to authors who publish in better journals. Such credit in turn gets translated into tenure, promotion, and salary increases. The prime beneficial feature of this arrangement is that scientists and scholars are given incentives to do better work: to make more significant discoveries and to present them in well-argued discourses, so that they will be published in the higher-status journals. Such incentives tend to

---

[12] Autonomous agents might help here, however.

promote veritistic advance. Without peer review, the systems of science and scholarship would have less veritistic promise.

The danger of abandoning peer review is forcefully expressed by Frank Quinn:

People write carefully [in mathematics] because standards are high for acceptance into the literature. In turn, high standards are practical because people write carefully. This is a very beneficial equilibrium, but an unstable one, which could easily be disturbed.

A consequence of this equilibrium concerns the meaning of "publication". At present there is a relatively black-and-white distinction between published and unpublished work. This enforces standards. Authors must write carefully or remain unpublished. If there were a continuum of levels of publication, then standards would be less clear and would have less force. Authors would write to their own comfort level of quality and then negotiate the level of publication. Overall quality of the literature would decline, possibly dramatically. Unfortunately this strong published/unpublished distinction is an artifact of paper publication, and will disappear in the transition to electronic media unless it is deliberately maintained. (1995: 55)

But electronic publishing need not dispense with peer review. In fact, the most successful electronic journals still require peer review, just like their more traditional counterparts. So let us turn to communication regimes with electronic publishing plus peer review: R_{e+p}. Would R_{e+p} require the use of commercial publishers? For some people, part of the allure of electronic publishing involves a revolt against commercial presses, which are viewed as reaping profits by taking the creations of scholars and selling them back to scholars (or their repository agents, namely, libraries) without themselves adding any value to the product. Many visionaries contend that with electronic publishing, scholars and scientists can share ideas without charging each other any fees. Is this true? Is electronic publication essentially costless? Can it be made to work without subscription fees of the sort charged by commercial publishers?[13]

Since the clearest model of free electronic publishing is the e-archive discussed above, which dispenses with peer review, let us ask whether peer review itself adds much to the cost of publication. Most journal refereeing is done gratis by academics. Editors of academic journals also receive only modest remuneration, if any, from publishers. Instead, their editorial contribution to research may be recognized in the form of partial release from teaching duties. In effect, their editorial time is paid for by their institutions. Editorial and refereeing work is not free; the costs have just been traditionally shouldered by universities and other research entities. Will these entities continue to provide such support when research publication turns electronic?

---

[13] Of course, it is not only commercial presses that charge for subscriptions. Many not-for-profit learned societies maintain their existence by publishing journals which are paid for by societal dues—in effect subscriptions.

Peer review is not the only costly aspect of journal publication. Publishers also engage in such activities as copyediting and proofreading, promoting and marketing, processing of subscriptions, and handling secondary forms of distribution such as reprints, translations, microfilm or microfiche, and inclusion of articles in course packs for classroom use (J. Fisher 1996). These activities all require the efforts of employees. Admittedly, many of these responsibilities would be rendered nugatory by electronic publication. In a regime of free distribution, there would be no subscriptions to process and no fees for subsidiary rights to negotiate or collect. But quality may still require copyediting and proofreading, and effective marketing might still be needed for new journals to succeed. If entry to electronic publication is indeed so cheap, journals might proliferate and compete for contributors and readers. This may well require special skills in marketing and in preparing attractive and efficient formats. Technical publishing, moreover, makes special demands, far more than ASCII text publishing. Chemistry journals use several thousand special characters, many tables, mathematics, and graphics. It is not trivial to handle these kinds of data (Garson 1996). Other value-added features will include linking works together, powerful search engines, and customized information retrieval. Finally, the initial flush of newness concerning digital technology has lured some scholars into not-for-profit publishing ventures that they would not undertake in the print realm, and experimental startup funds have been available from universities and granting agencies. This kind of enthusiasm and these sources of funds are unlikely to last forever. It is questionable whether electronic publishing will really be so cheap once it becomes standardized (J. Fisher 1996: 235).

The dream of free scholarly exchange, moreover, may not be realistic. As Ira Fuchs (1996) emphasizes, networked information is not free. The federal subsidy for the Internet began to diminish in 1993, and institutions of higher education are being asked to absorb some of that subsidy. As demand continues to explode for the Internet, especially at peak hours, movement toward at least some usage-based fees may be inevitable. There may have to be a pricing scheme that can recover costs from those who most tax the facilities, or unbridled use will worsen the congestion. Would usage-based pricing raise users' total expenditures? Some economists argue that if the industry is competitive or effectively regulated, revenues will approximately equal costs. When faced with usage charges, frivolous uses are likely to decrease, lowering total costs. Moreover, academics will generally want text-based uses of the Internet, and these uses are tiny by comparison with multimedia. Small users, like most academics, would benefit from usage-based fees rather than flat-rate pricing, which is based on average usage of a connection (MacKie-Mason and Varian 1994: 77–8).[14]

---

[14] MacKie-Mason and Varian estimate usage prices for full recovery of the NSFNET subsidy at one dollar per person per month (1994: 80).

But scholars have not traditionally paid for their knowledge endeavors, at least if they were willing to walk to their university library and negotiate the stacks rather than purchase individual journal subscriptions. Will the electronic era change that? This depends on the lending rights and costs facing research libraries, which is another arena of change and controversy in the digital era. In addition to skyrocketing print journal prices, libraries are facing publisher proposals of expensive site licensing for electronic journals. Libraries' ability to "lend" in traditional ways is also threatened by current proposals for new copyright legislation and the murkiness of the notion of intellectual property in the electronic age.

Librarians worry that all uses of copyrighted materials will be on a licensed or pay-per-view basis only. They worry that they will be excluded from preserving and archiving intellectual resources. Publishers worry that electronic technology will open the door to large-scale unauthorized copying with just a few renegade keystrokes. They worry that under the guise of "fair use" copyright holders will lose control of their works and fail to obtain reasonable compensation (Bennett 1995: 8).

Without addressing the thorny details of this issue, let me comment on how the veritistic framework may help set standards for reasonable policy in this arena, at least vis-à-vis factual materials (as opposed to art or literature). A reasonable formulation of copyright rationale is found in the United States Constitution: Congress is empowered "to Promote the Progress of Science and useful Arts, by securing for limited Times to Authors and Inventors the exclusive Right to their respective Writings and Discoveries" (U.S. Constitution: Article 1, section 8, clause 8). Congress has attempted to fulfill this mandate by vesting in creators of such works an alienable property right, known as copyright. The current version of the statute consists in a combination of grants and limitations. The core limitation is the proviso in section 107 that "the fair use of a copyrighted work . . . is not an infringement of copyright." A chief aim of the fair use doctrine is to facilitate the dissemination of intellectual products (W. Fisher 1988). This doctrine is the basis of most scholarly and educational utilization of copyrighted intellectual materials. Another important exception, which grew out of judicial decisions, is the "first sale" rule, which allows members of the public who have purchased a copy of a copyrighted work to sell it, give it away, lend it, or even rent the copy to other people. The first sale rule promotes public access to copyrighted works by allowing libraries to lend works they have purchased to borrowers without fear of copyright infringement. Many commentators see major judicial decisions in the copyright arena as attempts to *balance* the interests of content creators and the public, some of whom are themselves content creators who wish to build on other people's works to create new works of their own.

From a veritistic standpoint, this balancing objective is eminently reasonable. As the framers of the Constitution recognized, if thinkers and investigators can earn financial rewards through the knowledge they uncover, this will promote more, and more successful, knowledge-seeking endeavors. That is a basic rationale for copyright law.[15] At the same time, society will reap the greatest benefit only if all interested parties gain access to knowledge-containing works. In principle, the concept of fair use can be used as a framework to balance these desiderata. Viewed veritistically, fair use could promote a larger aggregate of knowledge by permitting dissemination to all interested parties, especially parties who would use previous knowledge to discover or produce new items of knowledge.

The balancing of creator and user interests seemed to be tolerably well achieved in the print era. But digital technology, and conceptual issues that it triggers, threaten to unsettle this earlier stability. In the mid-1990s the National Information Infrastructure task force of the Clinton Administration drafted a white paper that could seriously undermine scholarly and educational endeavors. This document, advanced for both national legislation and as a protocol to the major international treaty on copyright, threatens to undercut fair use and first sale doctrines in the digital environment. Digital transmission of a copy of a copyrighted work would be an act of copyright infringement, and even "browsing" a work in digital form would apparently count as copyright infringement (Pamela Samuelson 1996; Jaszi 1996). These maneuvers—disguised by the document, but inferable from it—are driven by the financial interests of Hollywood copyright holders. But they would seriously erode the public side of the copyright balance. There are unquestionably many intricate issues in interpreting and applying copyright law to the networked environment. This is not the place to explore them in detail. It does not take much reflection, however, to appreciate that some forms of legislation could have serious negative repercussions for practices of scholarly and scientific communication, thereby impeding veritistic objectives.

6.4 *The economics of the mass media*

This chapter has concentrated on computer-mediated communication because, as the new technology on the block, it holds the greatest current interest and poses the most intriguing challenges. But much information is still communicated in modern society via more traditional media, and their veritistic mettle should also be explored, if only briefly and selectively. The greatest number of people still get most of their news from newspapers, mag-

---

[15] Without addressing copyright law specifically, Anthony Kronman (1978) defends the economic efficiency of assigning property rights in information, and of not requiring parties to a contract to disclose their information when acquisition of the information may have involved costly search or training. Doubts about such efficiency rationales are expressed by James Boyle (1996), but much of his treatment is difficult to follow.

azines, radio, and television. What are the veritistic properties of these media? In particular, how does the economics of the mass media affect their impact on knowledge?

The mass media are, for the most part, commercial ventures. Except for public and state-sponsored broadcasting systems, they are typically ventures that aim to turn a profit. What are their sources of revenue, and how (if at all) do these sources influence the veritistic properties of their news-distributing functions? Newspapers, of course, sell copies to readers, but they also derive a huge portion of their revenue from advertisers. Radio and television media in the United States are almost wholly advertiser-supported enterprises. (Even the Public Broadcasting System gets significant support from advertisers, although it is also maintained by government subsidy and donations from individual contributors.) Thus, all the American mass media depend heavily on commercial sponsors. In fact, as I shall proceed to show, the best way to think of these media is as selling and delivering a certain product to their advertisers, namely, the attention of their audiences.

The notion that the media are in the business of selling audiences to advertisers is not a radical doctrine. It is what American media managers themselves sometimes say, in private if not in official pronouncements. Here is one report of such a statement:

I was once at a reception with a vice president of NBC, so I took the opportunity you would all no doubt have liked to take in my place, to chastise him roundly for the low quality of his network's programs. He smiled and asked why I thought he was to blame for that. After all, what did I think the "product" of NBC TV was? I replied that it was TV programs, of course. He shook his head and informed me that it was nothing of the sort: "NBC's product is eyeballs, yours and mine, and we sell them to our advertisers. We're perfectly content to put on the screen whatever it is that will make your eyeballs adhere to it. So you get exactly what you pay for— with your eyeballs." (Harnad 1996: 103)

This thesis may be cheerfully accepted for commercial TV and radio, but does it hold for print journalism? Here is a summary of what many studies claim about the role of advertising in newspaper publishing:

Virtually all observers and economic studies appear to agree that throughout the twentieth century advertising has paid a large portion of the costs of supplying the public with newspapers. One economic study estimates that without advertisements newspapers would cost as much as five times their current price and concludes that [a newspaper free of advertisements would not be commercially viable]. Another study concluded that today's $.30 paper would sell for $1.15 if it could maintain present circulation, but since it could not maintain circulation at that price, the absence of ad revenue would [result in the extinction of the press]. Thus, for a democratic press the advertising "subsidy" may be crucial. Without advertising, the resources available for expenditures on the "news" would presumably decline, predictably leading to an erosion of quality and quantity. (Baker 1994: 8)

The author of this passage, C. Edwin Baker, does not himself agree that the viability of newspapers depends critically on advertising. But he strongly agrees that newspapers have been influenced by their advertisers just as if this dependency were true, itself an important fact for our analysis. And as the passage indicates, most people who have researched the subject believe there is a critical dependency.

Does advertisers' "subsidy" to newspapers and their pivotal role in broadcasting come at a veritistic price? How and to what extent does the information value of the reported news suffer from these economic relationships? Many students of the media concur that a veritistic price is paid. A price is exacted, according to Baker, when advertisers use their economic power to "censor" and control content. They use the incentive of advertising revenue to encourage the media to tailor message content in ways that treat their products and broader interests charitably in both news reports and editorials. They also use revenue incentives to reduce controversial elements in order to avoid offending advertisers' potential customers and to favor the middle- to higher-income audiences whose greater purchasing power advertisers value most (Baker 1994: 44). Here are some illustrations of these practices.

NBC stood up to Coca-Cola in 1970 when Coke pressured NBC to change a documentary showing Coke's offensive treatment of citrus workers in Florida. NBC broadcast the show uncensored, and the president of Coca-Cola, Inc., admitted to a congressional committee that the show was accurate. However, NBC promptly lost all its network billings from Coke. In the following eight years, NBC did not produce a single documentary on a controversial domestic issue involving an important advertiser (Baker 1994: 48; based on Brown 1979). Though censorship did not succeed in the first instance, there was a potent chilling effect.

According to many commentators, the predicted disapproval of stories stemming from fears of advertisers dissuades reporters or producers from even thinking of problematic stories. As the vice president of a large advertising agency said in testimony to the Federal Communications Commission, "There have been very few cases where it has been necessary to exercise a veto, because the producers involved and the writers involved are normally pretty well aware of what might not be acceptable" (Baker 1994: 49). A chairman of the committee on censorship of the Writers Guild of America, West, said that of those members who responded to a poll, 86 percent reported from personal experience that television censorship exists, and 81 percent believed that television presents a "distorted picture" of what is happening in the country (Baker 1994: 49).

The problem is not confined to television. There are similar reports about the rising influence of business interests on newspaper coverage. The editor and managing editor of the *Des Moines Register* resigned in protest over increasing interference in the paper's news coverage by its business office, reported in the *New York Times* as "a battle between news professionals and business executives that is raging behind closed doors at many of the country's newspapers" (Bagdikian 1997: xxiii). In 1996, a California newspaper made it official policy that any story involving a local business must be cleared by the paper's advertising department. Reporters and subeditors were told, "The . . . advertisers make it possible for us to pay our bills and meet our payroll. You might say they make your job possible" (Bagdikian 1997: xxiii–xxiv).

A salient case of media silence is on tobacco. Despite 300,000 deaths a year attributable to smoking, and despite earlier evidence of harmful effects that led the American Medical Association in 1953 to ban tobacco advertising in its journals, reports on the dangers of smoking were virtually absent for decades in those media in which tobacco companies advertise. An article in the *New England Journal of Medicine* showed statistically that the likelihood of a magazine's publishing an article about the ill effects of smoking was inversely proportional to its revenue from cigarette advertising (Warner, Goldenhar, and McLaughlin 1992).

Advertisers' concerns go beyond their own products. A 1965 memorandum on broadcast policies from Procter & Gamble stated the following: "There will be no material that may give offense, either directly or by inference, to any commercial organization of any sort." "Men in uniform shall not be cast as heavy villains or portrayed as engaging in any criminal activity." "[N]o material on any of our programs . . . [should] in any way further the concept of business as cold, ruthless, and lacking all sentiment or spiritual motivation" (Baker 1994: 55). These policies applied both to entertainment programs and to news and public affairs documentaries.

The tailoring of content to a middle- and upper-class audience is illustrated by the following quotations. Otis Chandler, head of *Times Mirror*, explained that "the target audience of the [*Los Angeles*] *Times* is . . . in the middle class and . . . the upper class." Giving more attention to minority issues, said Chandler, "would not make sense financially . . . [because] that audience does not have the purchasing power and is not responsive to the kind of advertising we carry" (Baker 1994: 68). A *New York Times* marketing executive asserted: "We make no effort to sell to the mob" (Baker 1994: 68). William Randolph Hearst III, publisher of the *San Francisco Examiner*, explained that his paper aimed "at people who are desired by advertisers, mainly in terms of purchasing power" (Baker 1994: 68).

The obvious impact of these policies is either to distort news on certain topics or to omit reportage of many facts that would interest a large segment of the public. Audience members who accept the statements or portrayals of the world as presented by the print and broadcasting media are duped on some subjects, led to false inferences by skewed presentation of evidence, or simply left in the dark on subjects that properly fall within the province of news. In short, a veritistic price is paid by the consuming public, at a minimum in lost learning opportunities.

A second economic aspect of news production that also threatens its veritistic quality is not related to advertisers. Instead it concerns the sources on

which news reporters commonly rely. As Edward Herman and Noam
Chomsky (1988) relate, the mass media are drawn into a symbiotic relationship with powerful sources of information partly because of economic necessity.[16] The media have daily news demands and news schedules that must be
met. They cannot afford to have reporters and cameras everywhere that stories
might break. Economics dictates that they concentrate their resources where
significant news often occurs, and where regular press conferences are held.
This includes government offices and business corporations and trade groups.
Government and corporate sources also have the great merit of being recog-
nizable and credible by their status and prestige. Taking information from pre-
sumptively credible sources reduces investigative expense, whereas material
from suspect sources would require careful checking and costly research.
Robert Entman (1989) similarly points to heavy reliance by reporters on accessible, familiar elites: top officials in the White House and executive branch
agencies, members of Congress and congressional staffers, representatives of
important interest groups, think-tank experts, former government officials,
and so forth. Government and business news promoters also go to great efforts
to smooth the way for news organizations. They provide media organizations
with facilities in which to gather, they provide advance copies of speeches,
they write press releases in usable language, and they schedule press conferences at hours well geared to news deadlines (Herman and Chomsky 1988:
22).

Unfortunately, the resulting symbiotic relationship between reporters, on
the one hand, and powerful officials and interest groups, on the other, can
work against the interest of truth. The media may feel obligated to carry
extremely dubious stories and to mute criticism in order to avoid offending
their sources or endangering a close relationship. It is hard to call authorities
and working partners "liars" even if they actually tell whoppers (Herman and
Chomsky 1988: 22). Sources also exploit this dependency relationship by
"managing" the media, by suggesting just the sort of "spin" on events that
favors their own interests though it may be at odds with the truth.[17]

How serious a threat to the veritistic cause are these economic aspects of
the mass media? Concentrating on the control exerted by advertisers, it might
be argued that the threat is less serious or pervasive than media debunking
suggests. First, the threat of censorship mainly applies to questions directly
affecting advertisers' interests, an inevitably narrow range of questions. On all
questions in which no advertiser has a stake, the media are free to report the
whole truth. Second, no advertiser has major sponsorship campaigns on *every*
media outlet. Even if a given advertiser deters NBC news from airing a certain

[16] Reliance on official sources is only one of five so-called "filters" discussed by
Herman and Chomsky (1988) that contribute to the propagandizing of news. A second
is the role of advertisers. I do not purport to cover all of their five themes.

[17] An attempt to model the relationship between sources and reporters and to assess
its threat to accuracy is presented in Cox and Goldman 1994.

story, it does not deter all media outlets from airing it. As long as the story can be told, the public is in a position to learn the truth. With the proliferation of media channels—print, broadcast, and electronic—the peril to the veritistic cause posed by advertising diminishes.

This response is not wholly reassuring. First, as we have seen, advertisers sometimes seek to impose large-scale constraints on programming, going far beyond their narrow interests as they might commonly be delineated. Second, even if selected media channels are unconstrained by restrictive advertisers, they may not be channels that reach a very large sector of the public. Compared to the information that *might* be made available to the total audience, advertising may be responsible for many lost opportunities, and this would constitute a veritistic loss. Third, at least in the United States there is a growing concentration of media power. According to Ben Bagdikian (1997: xii–xiii), the number of controlling firms in all of the media (daily newspapers, magazines, radio, television, books, and movies) has shrunk from fifty corporations in 1984 to about ten in 1997. Even the meaning of the word "competition" has become blurred by reality, says Bagdikian. Of the 1,500 daily newspapers in the United States, 99 percent are the only daily in their cities. Of the 11,800 cable systems, all but a handful are monopolies in their cities (Bagdikian 1997: xv).

The specter of corporate media power is one thing that inspires Internet enthusiasts to see the Net as the knight in shining armor who will save democracy in the information age. The Net is precisely where the public will be able to find truths that are censored by corporate-controlled media. There is undoubtedly some merit in this scenario. But the Internet has problems of its own as a reliable source of news, problems that keep it from being a panacea or even an unalloyed improvement over some of the traditional news media.

Professional journalism has erected standards for news reporting that go some distance toward advancing veritistic ends. (They don't help much, of course, when commercial interests at a news channel supplant reporting and editorial practices.) Professional journalists are trained to verify and corroborate their sources before going public. Or, if they cannot verify their sources but know them to be politically motivated, they will at least make the political orientation of these sources clear to readers and viewers. Material on the Net, by contrast, is not guided by any such constraints. There is nothing to keep wild rumors and unchecked stories from circulating widely and being widely accepted. Therein lies the chief danger of letting the Internet replace more traditional news outlets.

A vaunted feature of the Internet is its embodiment of free competition, the classical foil to monopoly power. But it is not clear that free competition is always optimal; nor is it clear in the present case of news reporting. A number of commentators nowadays are ruing the fact that competition among multiple news sources is lowering the traditional standards and discipline of the mainstream press. Both online gossip sheets and radio and television talk shows, they say, have spawned an information "free-for-all" that is pressuring the mainstream press to reduce its standards to a level closer to the tabloids (Scott 1998). It is by no means clear, therefore, that competition solves all problems. This issue will be examined in more theoretical terms in the next chapter.

Let me return, however, to the matter of advertising's impact on the news. Are there any institutional policies that could alleviate the situation? One type of proposal is to legally prohibit advertisers' exercise of influence. This is more easily said than done, however, as Baker remarks (1994: 99). Law is rarely effective in preventing bargaining parties from reaching outcomes that the parties find optimal. A government attempt to prevent market exchanges between advertisers and the media might be difficult to enforce. A second type of proposal is to impose a tax on advertising. Several American media commentators have proposed placing a progressive tax on advertising. As Baker points out, however, the immediate effect of such a tax would be to siphon revenue from the media and thereby reduce the impact of the press (1994: 94). Baker himself proposes a twofold approach: tax advertising and use the tax revenues to subsidize reader-generated circulation revenue. For example, the government could impose a 10 percent tax on newspapers' advertising revenue and redistribute this money back as a subsidy based on the paper's circulation revenue. The intended result of this policy would be to reduce papers' incentive to respond to advertisers and to encourage them to provide a product for which readers are prepared to pay (Baker 1994: 85–6). An additional proposal is to use a tax on advertising to fund public (noncommercial) broadcasting. This is not the place to assess these proposals in full detail. But they constitute clear attempts to institute policies that, if successful, could improve the veritistic effectiveness of the mass media.

In this chapter we have examined the impact of technological and economic structures on the set of messages created and transmitted by senders and on the set of messages actually received by interested hearers. Since the range of successfully received messages is critical to veritistic advance, technology and economics are crucial elements in the social pursuit of knowledge. In the next chapter we look at another crucial element: general policies for allocating speech opportunities.

SEVEN

Speech Regulation and the Marketplace of Ideas

7.1 *Third-party and institutional influences on speech*

CHAPTERS 4 and 5 dealt with two types of agents, speakers and hearers, whose actions and reactions shape the social quest for knowledge. Chapter 6 introduced a number of third parties in addition to speakers and hearers, agents who exert important influence on the flow of communication. Examples of such third-party agents are editors, referees, and broadcasting sponsors. These types of agents can influence the informational scene by controlling which speakers speak or which messages are broadcast over various communication channels. This "gatekeeper" function affects what messages are received by hearers or the number of hearers who receive them, and thereby impinges on information-state changes. Given the importance of gatekeepers, especially in mass communication, social epistemology must inquire into the practices available to gatekeepers and the veritistic consequences that might flow from these practices. Casting our net more widely, we should examine not only the practices of individual gatekeepers, but the fundamental institutional arrangements or frameworks that influence the dissemination of thought and ideas. Which type of framework is most conducive to veritistic ends?

Broadly speaking, gatekeeping is any kind of third-party activity that controls the production of speech or affects the dissemination of messages to possible audiences. On the facilitative side, a gatekeeper might help a speaker reach a larger audience by giving him a new or expanded forum or tool of communication. Facilitation might consist in supplying him with a megaphone, a public-address system, or an e-mail account. It might be an invitation to give the keynote address at a political convention, or to present a departmental colloquium. In each case, an opportunity is afforded that allows a speaker's

Portions of this chapter—specifically Sections 7.2 and 7.3—are substantially based on Goldman and Cox 1996. I thank Jim Cox for his collaboration on that paper. However, some minor changes have been made in the current adaptation of this material with which he might not agree.

message to be broadcast to a wider audience. On the restraining side, a gate-keeper might be a newspaper editor who declines to publish an article written by one of his reporters. Or a regulator might be an agent of the state who confiscates printed materials or threatens legal sanctions in the form of fines and imprisonment for broadcasting a certain message.

The control or influence of speech is not a single-layered phenomenon. Often there are embedded layers of regulation and metaregulation. For example, whether a writer succeeds in publishing an article in a certain magazine may depend on the decision of an editor. But the editor, let us say, works for a commercial magazine, the viability of which is regulated, so to speak, by the market. If the magazine's choice of articles leads readers and advertisers, over time, to withdraw their support, the magazine will cease publication. Finally, the continued existence of a free market for magazines depends on the state and its press policy.[1] In general, the highest layer of control is the state, so it is natural to give special attention to the state's overall policy concerning speech, although it is not necessarily more important, in every instance, than the policies and decisions of individual gatekeepers.

In considering the veritistic impact of the gatekeeping function, it is easiest to start at the lowest level, where a gatekeeper has "immediate" control over the dissemination or nondissemination of proffered messages over a given channel. Which exercises of gatekeeping functions would have good or bad veritistic consequences depends partly on the truth properties of the prospective messages and partly on the acceptance practices of the possible audiences. Wider dissemination of a true message will generally have positive veritistic consequences, at least if the expanded audience is disposed to believe its content (and does not believe it antecedently). Wider dissemination of a false message will tend to have negative veritistic consequences, again assuming an audience disposition to believe the proffered falsehood (and no pre-existing belief on their part). Thus, the simple principle that it is always veritistically good to maximize dissemination is dubious.

An example will illustrate the point. In 1980 there was a journalistic scandal in which a *Washington Post* reporter fabricated a story about an eight-year-old heroin addict; the story won a Pulitzer Prize before the fabrication was uncovered. In the scandal's aftermath it became a general rule among newspapers that reporters must share with an editor the identity of a confidential source (Goldstein 1985: 215 ff.). The resulting editorial practice is, in effect, a message-restricting practice by a certain class of gatekeepers. Editors who follow this practice will not allow a reporter's article to be published if the reporter does not share with the editor her confidential sources. This type of gatekeeping practice could well be veritistically beneficial. It might prevent

---

[1] More generally, governmental decisions determine what qualifies as legitimate market operations. Laws of property, contract, and tort produce a set of entitlements that partially define what transactions constitute legitimate market transactions.

reporters from publishing false but belief-inducing stories. If even one such restrictive gatekeeping practice is veritistically beneficial—as compared with unrestricted message dissemination—the general principle that maximal dissemination is the veritistically *best* practice would be false. Maximal dissemination might still have good V-value, but it would not be the very best speech-dissemination practice from a veritistic perspective.[2]

There is, however, a strong tradition in the freedom of speech according to which interference with the dissemination of messages is inimical to the cause of truth (that is, knowledge). The most famous early statements in this tradition are due to John Milton (1959) and John Stuart Mill (1960). Milton and Mill contended that unrestricted speech promotes the discovery and acceptance of truth better than its suppression. Their statements, of course, concerned the highest level of speech policy: governmental policy. Similarly, the First Amendment of the United States Constitution prohibits specifically *state* abridgement of free speech. Although we are interested in speech policies at all levels, the higher levels are of special concern, so they will receive the lion's share of discussion in this chapter.

It must be emphasized, however, that we are here concerned with speech policy only as viewed from a veritistic perspective. There are many alleged justifications for free speech doctrines. The truth-acquisition rationale is only one candidate among many. It is no part of this chapter's purpose to survey or evaluate the numerous rationales that have been offered for freedom of speech. To the extent that veritistic considerations are deployed to defend freedom of speech, so our reflections overlap with free speech theory. But entirely different grounds are also offered for restricting state interference in speech, for example, to promote participation in self-governance or to enhance autonomy and self-fulfillment. These grounds could outweigh veritistic considerations. I shall not investigate all types of considerations that bear on freedom of speech, nor do I seek an all-things-considered policy recommendation in the speech arena. I am only investigating veritistic consequences of speech regulation practices. Furthermore, I do not seek to explain or rationalize the U.S. Supreme Court's holdings in First Amendment matters. Whether my results are aligned with First Amendment doctrine is of marginal importance in the present context. Nonetheless, the discussion will make many points of contact with First Amendment theorizing, and it is highly rel-

---

[2] Perhaps a practice that disseminates only truths and never falsehoods—if such a practice could be realized—would be the veritistically best practice. I say "perhaps" because the outcomes partly depend on audience reactions. If audiences would not accept true messages even when disseminated, then disseminating them would not yield veritistic benefits. And if audiences would reject false messages even if disseminated, no veritistic benefit would accrue from barring their dissemination. (John Stuart Mill argued that certain types of benefits accrue from grappling with false messages, but I ignore such benefits in the present discussion.)

evant to the specifically veritistic rationale for free speech, which often goes by the name "the argument from truth."[3]

A widely invoked image in free speech theorizing is the marketplace of ideas. It is often suggested that truth has the best chance to emerge, or other values have the best chance of being achieved, if ideas are allowed to compete freely in the open market or marketplace. This approach is articulated in oft-cited historical texts. Milton wrote: "Let [Truth] and Falshood grapple; who ever knew Truth put to the wors, in a free and open encounter" (1959: 561). Competition was also invoked as the mechanism of truth determination by Justice Holmes, in a famous 1919 (dissenting) opinion: "[W]hen men have realized that time has upset many fighting faiths, they may come to believe even more than they believe the very foundations of their own conduct that the ultimate good desired is better reached by free trade in ideas—that the best test of truth is the power of the thought to get itself accepted in the competition of the market" (*Abrams v. United States* 1919: 630). This theme is echoed in a number of later Supreme Court opinions, for example, in a 1969 ruling: "It is the purpose of the First Amendment to preserve an uninhibited market-place of ideas in which truth will ultimately prevail" (*Red Lion Broadcasting Co. v. FCC* 1969: 390).[4] Frederick Schauer formulates the same idea (though without endorsement) as follows: "Just as Adam Smith's 'invisible hand' will ensure that the best products emerge from free competition, so too will an invisible hand ensure that the best ideas emerge when all opinions are permitted freely to compete" (Schauer 1982: 16).[5]

I shall refer to this group of proposals as the marketplace approach to speech policy. I believe, however, that two significantly different versions of the marketplace approach must be distinguished. The first version understands the term "market" or "marketplace" in the *literal, economic* sense, and it sees the competitive market mechanism as the kind of disciplining mechanism that promotes the discovery of truth. The second version understands the term "market" or "marketplace" *metaphorically* or *figuratively*. That is, it construes the marketplace of ideas as a market-like arena, in which debate is wide open and robust, in which diverse views are vigorously defended. This kind of debate arena may or may not result from an economic market mechanism. Under the second version, moreover, what counts is the scope of the resulting debate, not the mechanism that produces it. If a diverse set of views is vigorously aired, this qualifies as an open marketplace of ideas even when government action is required to secure this state of affairs.

The difference between these two interpretations may be highlighted by

[3] See Schauer 1982: 15–34 and Greenawalt 1989: 16–26. Schauer uses the phrase "argument from truth," whereas Greenawalt discusses the truth justification under the heading of "consequentialism."

[4] Similar ideas pervade many Supreme Court decisions, as documented by Ingber (1984: 2–3, n. 2).

[5] Since the quoted passage appears in a chapter entitled "The Argument from Truth," it is evident that by "best" ideas Schauer means *true* (or perhaps "truest") ideas.

looking more closely at the context of discussion in which the above quotation from the Supreme Court's 1969 ruling was taken, *Red Lion Broadcasting Co. v. FCC*. At issue in that case was the "fairness doctrine" of the Federal Communications Commission. When a state-licensed broadcaster presented one side of a controversial issue, it was required by the FCC to afford reasonable opportunity for presentation of contrasting views as well. At issue in the case was whether the FCC, and hence the government, was interfering with the operation of the free market by dictating policy to radio stations. Ostensibly this would conflict with the first construal of the marketplace idea. But the Court upheld the fairness doctrine, even suggesting that it was constitutionally compelled. Here the Court seemed to endorse the second version of the marketplace idea, as a fuller quotation from its holding indicates:

[T]he people as a whole retain their interest in free speech by radio and their collective right to have the medium function consistently with the ends and purposes of the First Amendment. It is the right of the viewers and listeners, not the right of the broadcasters, which is paramount. It is the purpose of the First Amendment to preserve an uninhibited marketplace of ideas in which truth will ultimately prevail, rather than to countenance monopolization of that market, whether it be by the Government itself or a private licensee. It is the right of the public to receive suitable access to social, political, esthetic, moral, and other ideas and experiences which is crucial here. That right may not constitutionally be abridged either by Congress or by the FCC. (*Red Lion Broadcasting Co. v. FCC* 1969: 390)

What is crucial, on this holding, is the fullness of the set of ideas to which the public is exposed, not the protection of an economic mechanism that might lead to assorted expressions of ideas. Unless we draw the distinction between the two contrasting conceptions of the marketplace theory, we cannot make good sense of this Court holding.

Whatever the *Red Lion* Court may have held, it seems clear that other theorizers appeal to economic theory to support the notion that an open market is the best avenue to truth. These theorizers, then, seem to endorse the first interpretation of the marketplace idea. The Holmes passage strongly hints at this, in its appeal to "free trade in ideas." Schauer's reference to Adam Smith's "invisible hand" is also a reference to economic theory. The idea is that according to economic theory, competitive markets are efficient in the sense of being maximizing institutions. Since free markets are optimal at producing and distributing goods, why shouldn't they also be optimal at producing and distributing knowledge? Indeed, there are already suggestions in the economic literature that markets are good at information dissemination or revelation. For example, there is Friedrich Hayek's idea that markets are good ways of aggregating dispersed information and making that information available to economic agents (Hayek 1948: 85–6).[6] Game theory tells us that in certain

---

[6] Hayek emphasizes, however, that the price system of the market provides limited information to each participant: only the information he needs to be able to take the right course of action, not information (for example) about the factors that have caused changes in prices.

situations sellers in a competitive market will be constrained to reveal true information about their products.[7] Third, in the public choice literature, markets are often preferred to political decision devices because of the incentives in the latter to misrepresent (Mueller 1979). Perhaps these hints generalize to a broader conclusion, namely, that a free market is an optimal institution from an information-fostering standpoint; in other words, the free market is the veritistically optimal framework for speech regulation (or, rather, deregulation). This is the first marketplace-of-ideas thesis, which I examine in the next two sections.

7.2 *Economic theory, market efficiency, and veritistic value*

7.2.A *The free market thesis*

Just what does modern economics tell us about markets? Does the economic analysis of markets really guarantee, or even suggest, that unregulated speech—or speech that is regulated only by the market—will promote veritistic value more reliably than other institutional arrangements concerning speech? I shall argue that this is not a consequence of economic theory.

In the interest of precision, let me formulate the claim I shall be disputing. I shall call the thesis "MMVV" (the Market Maximizes Veritistic Value):

(MMVV) More total V-value will be achieved if speech is regulated only by free market mechanisms rather than by other forms of regulation.

Presumably, the "free" markets that are envisaged are markets for which there is freedom of entry (and exit) for buyers and sellers and an absence of government control of prices and quantities.[8] Of course, one "other," nonmarket form of regulation is state regulation. So if there is any kind of state regulation that interferes with the market but improves the sum total of V-value, then MMVV is false.

It might seem as if we have already encountered a refutation-by-example of MMVV. Doesn't our discussion in Section 6.4 of advertisers' censorship of television programming put the kibosh on the notion that the economic market in speech has optimal characteristics? In controlling television content,

---

[7] Here I have in mind the "unraveling result," in which sellers are impelled (in equilibrium) to reveal accurate information about their product, because if they remain silent, buyers will infer it is worse than it is (Baird, Gertner, and Picker 1994: 89–109). The unraveling result only applies, however, in very special circumstances, namely, where information can be verified once it is disclosed, and where lying is sanctionable. It is doubtful how far these special circumstances generalize.

[8] Freedom of entry does not mean that market entry is costless. It means that no rent is derived from incumbency, that is, that new agents can enter at a cost which does not exceed the cost incurred by incumbents, and hence incumbents do not have a competitive advantage over potential entrants.

advertisers act as economic agents, wholly within the free market framework championed by MMVV. Doesn't the veritistic loss from their activity prove MMVV's falsity? The matter is not quite so simple or clear-cut. A free marketeer might respond by saying that although acts of censorship may indeed impede veritistic ends, the overall impact of advertisers is veritistically beneficial. Without their subsidies, far less information would be transmitted via mass communication, and this would yield far worse veritistic results. I do not endorse this reply of the free marketeer, but it does suggest that MMVV is not dead on arrival, at any rate. It should be emphasized, moreover, that MMVV is a *comparative* thesis. It does not say that free market mechanisms will yield perfect veritistic outcomes, only that they will do a better job than alternatives.

MMVV presupposes the possibility of comparing states of "total veritistic value." I have not, however, given a precise criterion for making such comparisons. I have provided a measure of aggregating knowledge (or V-value) vis-à-vis a chosen question, but I have not suggested any way of aggregating across questions. One possible way to do this, hinted at in Section 3.5, would be to weight questions in terms of their degrees of *interest*. This would presumably entail some sort of averaging of everybody's interests in each question. For reasons given in Section 3.5, however, I do not like this solution. I shall therefore leave this matter up in the air, to be resolved on future occasions. For purposes of the present discussion, a simple partial principle can often be quite helpful, a principle analogous to Pareto-superiority. If a speech act raises the aggregate level of knowledge for one or more questions and does not lower it for any other questions, then that speech act raises the total amount of knowledge or V-value. The converse holds for speech acts that lower the aggregate level of knowledge for one or more questions. Though not a fully comprehensive principle, it is sufficient for relevant comparisons in many cases. Moreover, I submit that the arguments that will be marshaled against MMVV are effective under any plausible comprehensive measure of total veritistic value. If anyone wishes to defend MMVV under some preferred measure of V-value, let such a person present that measure.

When MMVV refers to speech "regulation," I assume that it includes indirect as well as direct regulation. Indirect regulation or influence includes policies imposed by certain agents or institutions that constrain the speech-regulating activities of other agents. For example, if the federal government passes a law requiring radio and television stations to give political candidates free air time, that will presumably influence the speech-controlling activities of station managers. Those managers are the direct controllers of messages sent over their channel, but the government in this case would be an indirect regulator.

One possible way to challenge MMVV is by producing exceptions or counterexamples to it, such as the advertiser–censorship counterexample. This strategy will be utilized in Section 7.3. First, however, I want to ask what theoretical basis there is for suspecting that MMVV is correct. Proponents of MMVV suppose that there is something in the nature of market mechanisms, something that follows from the economic theory of competitive markets, that makes MMVV true. In this section it is shown, to the contrary, that economic theory has no such implication. Contrary to popular myth, economic theory lends no support to MMVV.

What is the theoretical argument for supposing that market mechanisms will maximize truth possession? No *detailed* general argument of this sort has actually been presented, but the idea, presumably, is that modern economics has demonstrated that competitive markets are the most efficient modes of social organization, the best way to organize the production and consumption of goods. Shouldn't this hold for intellectual as well as other goods? In this section I explore what economics really says about free, competitive markets and what that does or does not imply about truth acquisition.

7.2.B *Messages, products, and product quality*

To fit intellectual matters into the framework of economic theory, it must be assumed that some product is involved and there are some producers and consumers of the product. For present purposes the promising interpretation appears to be that a speaker's messages are products, a speaker is a producer, and hearers are consumers. We cannot plausibly view just any hearer of a message as a consumer of it, however. If a hearer receives a message but disbelieves its content, he hardly qualifies as a consumer of it, any more than someone who considers the purchase of a toaster but decides not to purchase it should be considered a consumer of that toaster. Only someone who *accepts* or *believes* a message—or at least increases his degree of belief in its content—should qualify as a consumer of it. Given these assumptions, MMVV might be supported or underwritten by economic theory if the theory is susceptible of an interpretation under which it implies that in a competitive market, messages will be produced and consumed in a fashion that maximizes V-value. In short, the theory must imply that the messages produced and consumed under free competition will yield a higher social aggregate of V-value than would be yielded by the messages produced and consumed under any noncompetitive conditions. Does economic theory have this implication?

One might think of it in the following way. True messages are *superior* to false messages, at least as far as intellectual matters go. So if it were generally true that competitive markets lead to the production and consumption of *superior* products, this might be directly applicable to the intellectual arena. Many people discussing the laissez-faire underpinning of economic theory seem to hint at such a general thesis. There is the Darwinian idea that competition encourages "survival of the fittest," where the "fittest" are in some sense superior or higher-quality creatures. Some such idea is also contained in the passage from Schauer quoted in Section 7.1: "Just as Adam Smith's 'invisible hand' will ensure that the *best products* emerge from free competition . . ." (emphasis added).

However, economic theory does not imply that the "best" or highest-quality products will be produced and consumed under free competition, at least where "quality" refers to some predesignated, market-independent character of the products such as truth or falsity. What economic theory actually says is that under competition the levels of outputs for each type of good will reach efficient levels, relative to the production possibilities facing producers and the preferences of consumers. This makes no categorical prediction about which types of goods will be produced in relatively greater quantities, where types of goods are antecedently classified by some specific intrinsic characteristics. There is no way, then, in which market theory implies that under competition, the messages produced and consumed will have an optimal amount of truth. To suppose that economic theory implies this is to misunderstand what it actually asserts.

7.2.C *The role of preferences*

This point may be clarified as follows. Economic theory says that a perfectly competitive market will provide consumers with an economically efficient— Pareto-optimal—allocation of commodities. This means that the commodity bundle consumers get is optimal in a way defined by their own preferences and the costs of producing the various goods in that bundle. Without reference to their preferences, however, nothing can be deduced about the particular properties of the commodity bundle that is yielded. To repeat, economics does not say that any specific types of commodities will be produced in large quantities in a competitive market. The whole idea of economic efficiency is that the system should be responsive to consumers' tastes or preferences (subject to the limits of technology), not that it should produce certain goods in comparatively large quantities no matter what people want. Thus, if consumers have no very strong preference for truth as compared with other goods or dimensions of goods, then there is no reason to expect that the bundle of intellectual goods provided and "traded" in a competitive market will have maximum truth content or V-value. If people valued falsehood, then perfect competition would provide falsehood in a Pareto-optimal way. Or, to make a more realistic assumption, if truth (knowledge) is *one* thing people value, but they are willing to substitute other commodities (such as entertainment or titillation) for truth (knowledge), then economic theory says that they will get the amount of truth such that the marginal rate of substitution between truth and these other commodities equals the marginal rate of transformation in the technology between producing truth and producing the other commodities. If consumers don't value truth very much (relatively speaking), perfect competition will efficiently ensure that they don't get very much truth as compared with other goods. (The foregoing statements presuppose the assumption that conditions of *perfect* competition are met, an assumption concerning the truth or knowledge domain that will be challenged in the ensuing discussion.[9]) What cannot be said is that competition will maximize truth acquisition under *all* circumstances, that is, no matter what consumers prefer. But that is precisely the unqualified statement that MMVV makes.

A defender of MMVV might reply to the foregoing as follows: "Granted that market regulation will not maximize V-value when people wish to substitute entertainment for truth. But won't other systems of regulation equally fail to maximize V-value when people have the same preferences? So how does the point about the role of preferences undercut the *comparative* claim of MMVV that market regulation of speech is superior to (or at least as good as) competing forms of regulation?" To answer this challenge, we may simply consider alternative modes of regulation that consist in market regulation modified by specific types of government intervention in speech. For example, consider an intervention that consists of government subsidizing public television and radio news, as it does now, thereby making it cheaper to produce and consume certain (largely) true messages or classes of messages, specifically, classes of messages that would not be produced at all under pure market practices. Then even with the same preferences initially described, some people might well acquire more true belief. To take a more extreme example, consider a system under which government suppresses certain entertainment products that people now spend their time consuming. If these products were unavailable, at least some people might choose to consume more news, with a net increase in V-value (compared with the amount of V-value attained under a pure market system, where more time is spent consuming entertainment).

These kinds of government intervention would of course interfere with market efficiency for the total set of goods. But reduction in efficiency is compatible with increasing the production and consumption of *certain* goods, in this case, true messages. The pure market promotes efficiency, but it does not follow that, for *every type* of good, the market promotes maximal production and consumption of that type of good. There are nonmarket forms of regulation, then, that seem likely to promote greater amounts of V-value, given the same set of consumer preferences. A decision to advocate or not to advocate such policies, all things considered, depends on how one balances V-value against other things (including economic efficiency). This is not an issue I try to settle here.

[9] The statements in the text also assume that truth and falsehood function like other goods or commodities, a basic premise of the argument from truth. This premise will be challenged, however, in Subsection 7.2.G below.

7.2.D *Imperfect information*

Let us now assume that efficiency would promote V-value, because people do have a strong preference for knowledge. As is well known, however, efficiency is only guaranteed under conditions of *perfect* competition, and the economic model of perfect competition is highly idealized, incorporating crucial assumptions that may not be satisfied either in general or in the case before us. The proof of the efficiency or optimality of perfect competition holds only where those assumptions are satisfied; where they are violated, optimality does not follow from competition as a theoretical proposition.

One assumption of the standard model is perfect information, that is, buyers and sellers are assumed to have accurate knowledge of market prices. If this condition is not satisfied, the "invisible hand" theoretical results concerning the market are no longer operative. This assumption is particularly relevant to the case before us for the following reason. High V-value depends on the consumption (acceptance) of true messages and the nonconsumption of false messages. Thus, consumers must be in a position to make accurate selections between true and false messages. But their ability to make such selections depends on their possession of information. The trouble is that such information, or perfect knowledge, is assumed as a *condition* of the optimal operation of the market, not as a *consequence* of the market. In the present inquiry we are asking whether the competitive market is capable of generating such knowledge; but all the theory says is that *if* there is perfect knowledge—and other conditions are met—then efficiency follows. This ostensibly throws the problem of knowledge acquisition into a different domain, prior to and independent of the market's operation.

This point can be clarified as follows. The economic theory of competition actually assumes many markets, each of which is a market for a single *uniform*, or *homogeneous*, product. This assumption is used in deriving efficiency results as follows. As long as the product is homogeneous or identical across all firms selling it, and as long as there is perfect information about the prices being charged, then each firm selling the product must sell it for the same price. For if any firm attempted to set its price at a level greater than the market price, it would immediately lose all of its customers. If any firm set its price at a level below the market price, all of the consumers would immediately come to it so that the other firms would have to match its price if they wanted to stay in business. This is how theorists derive the conclusion that a competitive market will generate a single market price. However, these inferences cannot be sustained if there is product differentiation. Under that condition, a superior variant of the product might command a higher price, so there wouldn't be a single market price for this type of product.

Notice, now, the following point about information. Unless consumers are assumed to know which particular products belong to the kind in question, they will not necessarily act in the manner specified above. Suppose, for example, that there is a uniform product-type X, say toasters, but that a certain consumer falsely believes that a particular toaster is superior in quality to the rest. Then this consumer might be willing to pay more for the particular toaster although in point of fact it is no different in quality from all others on the market. Thus, consumers' information or informability about particular (token) products must be assumed in the standard model of perfect competition. If that assumption is violated, the standard efficiency or optimality results do not follow.

This is directly relevant to the issue before us. First of all, there is a problem of specifying the product that is involved in the market for speech. If some speech messages are true and others false, the product-type *speech* is itself not a uniform, or homogeneous, product. Assume, therefore, that the unit in question is *true speech*. (This will still not yield perfect uniformity, but set that aside.) The next problem that arises is whether consumers will *recognize* instances of this product-type as such. When they are offered a true message, will they know that it is true? Not necessarily. There is no guarantee, therefore, that they will be prepared to pay prices appropriate to the product category to which a proffered specimen of speech actually belongs. If hearers cannot distinguish truths from falsehoods, speakers of truths will not be able to command higher prices for them, and hence the market for speech will not have the optimal properties it would have under perfect information.[10]

Thus, imperfect information can upset the correlation between free markets and economic efficiency, a problem studied by the economics of information. A much-cited example is the market for used cars, first investigated by George Akerlof (1970). There are many variants of the used-car example, but two can be described in general outline (for further details, see Goldman and Cox 1996: 21–3). In both cases, there is a situation of asymmetric information. An owner and potential seller of a used car knows its quality. A potential buyer, by contrast, does not know the quality of the specific car. She only knows something about the distribution of quality in the population of used cars. In the first variant, the quality of used cars is uniformly distributed, and all the buyer knows is that uniform distribution. Under these circumstances it can be shown that the equilibrium quantity of used cars traded is zero. In other words, information asymmetry causes adverse selection that is so extreme that it destroys the market. In the second variant, there are only two types of used cars: good cars and shoddy ones ("lemons"). All that the buyer

[10] The point of this paragraph is in the neighborhood of a point made by Larry Alexander (1993: 936–9). Alexander points out that purchasers of information typically agree to a price for an item (or body) of information before receiving the information, that is, before they know what it will be. My point is not only that purchasers of information do not know beforehand what messages they will receive from a source, but that once they receive a message they still may be unable to assess its truth-value correctly. They won't necessarily know whether or not it is an instance of the product-type "true speech."

knows is the proportion of good cars in the population of used cars and the proportion of lemons. Here it can be shown that good cars cannot be traded; only lemons can trade. This is a Pareto-inferior outcome characterized by zero gains from exchange of good used cars.

These examples of information asymmetry nicely illustrate that unless information is already perfect, competition *per se* does not ensure optimality, which is precisely the problem for the market in ideas. If consumers (hearers) are unable to tell by other means whether speakers' messages are true or false— good messages or lemons—mere competition cannot solve the problem, at least according to anything economic analysis offers. If hearers recognize their inability to detect message quality, they will be unwilling to pay as much for messages that in point of fact are true as they would be prepared to pay if they could tell that they are true. They need tools of truth recognition (and con- fidence that those tools are reliable) *prior to* and *independent of* the market in order for the market to be optimal. Thus, competition alone does not guaran- tee efficiency or maximization of V-value, as MMVV asserts.

7.2.E *Externalities*

Let me move now from the consequences of imperfect and uncertain infor- mation to the consequences of "externalities," which are also known to derail the usual theoretical conclusions about competitive markets. A producer's activities may impose costs, or nonzero utility effects, on people with whom the producer does not trade. A firm that produces air pollution, for example, imposes costs on people living near the firm in terms of ill health and grime. Polluters will not take these "external" costs into consideration when making production decisions. Firms will take into account only the private costs of production, not the costs to the whole society (the social cost). If the social cost were taken into account, less pollution would be generated. One way of dealing with externalities is intervention. For example, by requiring firms to obtain sufficient numbers of tradeable emissions permits to legalize their emis- sions levels, and restricting the total supply of permits, the government can prompt firms to reduce their external diseconomies in a cost-efficient way (Plott 1983; Franciosi *et al.* 1993).

Return now to our target domain, the regulation of speech, and look again at government regulation of advertising and labeling. We might consider untruthful statements as acts of "pollution," and interpret regulation of such statements as the use of government power to try to reduce such pollution. In discussions of this kind, economists frequently talk about property rights over a good being assigned to one or another party, where those rights might include conditions on the uses to which the good may be put. In the air pollution case, property rights in the air might belong to a firm, an individual, or society at large, and these property rights might be absolute or hedged in various ways. In the case of commercial advertising, one might give unconditional property rights to advertisers to put any labels they like on their products, or say anything they like about them over the public media; alternatively, one might allow advertisers only to make statements supported by scientific evidence. If advertisers are given unconditional speech rights ("nonregulation" by government), consumers will have to bear the cost of trying to ascertain whether the statements are true; otherwise they risk falling into error if the statements are lies or deception. Restricting advertisers to messages that have been certified by scientific evidence (government "regulation") will presumably reduce the incidence of false messages and consequent error on the part of consumers.

In discussion of externalities, it is often pointed out that agents who suffer costs from negative externalities might pay or "bribe" the agents creating those externalities to reduce their level of production. In the classic example, an eyeglass firm is downwind from a charcoal firm, and the charcoal in the air from the charcoal-making firm affects the precision grinding wheels of the eyeglass firm. Why shouldn't the eyeglass firm pay the charcoal firm to reduce its emissions, thereby increasing the quantity of high-quality eyeglasses that the former firm produces? Indeed, Ronald Coase (1960) has famously argued that the possibility of payments of this sort implies that firms left on their own, without governmental interference, can arrive at the efficient level of outputs (in this case, of charcoal and eyeglasses). Each will be led by the "invisible hand" to the optimal level. Similarly, why couldn't consumers pay advertisers to reduce their level of deception ("pollution"), and thereby achieve an economically efficient level of deceptive output?

As is well known, however, Coase's analysis only applies when transaction costs are zero. In this case, by contrast, it looks pretty clear that transaction costs will be positive, and indeed rather high. Even if consumers can reach a bargain with advertisers to reduce the level of deception (for a certain payment), they will not be able to enforce this agreement without paying high costs of determining whether advertisers are complying with their contract or not. This will require the consumers to determine whether the messages they are receiving are indeed truthful or deceptive, and the cost to them of doing this (in the absence of detailed knowledge about the manufacturing process, for example) may be prohibitive. Thus, transaction costs are likely to be very high, which vitiates the hope for economic efficiency.

7.2.F *Public goods*

Another commonly discussed cause of market failure is public goods (Paul Samuelson 1954). Public goods are defined in terms of two properties: nonexclusivity and nonrivalry. For most private goods, like a hamburger, people may be excluded from the benefits the goods provide. Nonexclusive goods are ones from which people may not be excluded, or not easily excluded. Once an army or navy is set up, people in the country cannot be excluded from the benefits of its protection whether they pay for it or not. Nonrival goods are goods for which benefits can be provided to additional users at zero marginal social cost. Consider one more car crossing a bridge during an off-peak period. Since the bridge is already there anyway, one more vehicle crossing it requires no additional resources.

How can public goods be responsible for market failure? In buying a public good, any one person will not be able to appropriate all of its benefits. Since others ("free riders") cannot be excluded from enjoying its benefits at no extra cost, society's potential benefits from a public good will exceed the benefits accruing to any single buyer. A single purchaser, however, will not take the potential benefits to others of the purchase into account in his/her expenditure decisions. Hence, private markets will tend to underallocate resources to public goods (Ledyard 1995).

Now messages in an open forum that enunciate truths are plausible examples of public goods. They have the property of nonexclusivity because anybody can listen in and enjoy their benefits. They have the property of nonrivalry because their benefits can be provided to additional listeners at zero marginal social cost. There is reason to expect, therefore, at least according to standard economic analysis, that a private market would tend to underallocate the resources necessary to the discovery and transmission of true messages. This suggests that the private market cannot be relied upon, all by itself, to generate as much total V-value as might be achieved by supplementing market mechanisms with other mechanisms.

7.2.G Is speech a good at all?

The preceding discussion has assumed that messages are public goods (or "bads," if false). But it is really questionable whether messages are goods or commodities at all. This was provisionally granted at the beginning of this section, but it is time for reconsideration. Commodities are normally thought of as having a producer and a consumer, or a seller and a buyer. Until now I have construed speech as involving a producer/seller and a set of consumers/buyers, but in many cases of speech this interpretation is extremely dubious. Consider billboard advertising. Here we have a speaker or message sender who is plausibly construed as a "producer," and a set of viewers who might be construed as consumers. Notice, however, that the viewers pay nothing for the right to view the message. It is not just that some people pay and others are free riders; rather, no viewers pay for the message (except, perhaps, by incurring the cost of environmental blight). More significantly, in the sense of message "consumption" relevant to our problem, namely, *belief* in the message content, there is no difference in payment between viewers who "consume" the message and those who do not. Moreover, the producer/seller of the message does not get paid for it, even by those who "consume" it. True, people who believe the message are more likely to buy the advertised item, the cost of which will partially reflect the cost of advertising. But people can believe (and therefore consume) a commercial message without buying the advertised item. It may be too expensive for them, of no interest to them, or less desirable than another brand despite what the new information reveals. Not only does the producer receive no payment for his message, he actually pays to transmit it. So the message does not seem to display the properties of a classical good at all, since the producer is not paid for "exchanging" or "trading" his message to the consumer. In fact, there seems to be no exchange or trade at all.

If messages are not goods or commodities, then there is no *market* in messages. But if there is no market in messages, then MMVV seems to lack even surface plausibility. How can market mechanisms concerning speech maximize truth possession if speech, or speech messages, involve no market mechanisms?!

One might try to save MMVV by distinguishing between messages and another class of items in the speech domain, namely, *speech opportunities*. Even if messages are not commodities, it is plausible to hold that speech opportunities are commodities, and that there is a market for them. Owners of communication forums such as billboards, radio and television stations, newspapers, and magazines, all sell space or time for commercial and political speech. Prospective speakers pay for these opportunities to display or air their messages. Moreover, speech opportunities are private goods by the criterion of exclusivity, since a would-be speaker can be excluded from the benefit of using the advertising space or time allotted to another speaker. So speech opportunities are goods, and there is definitely a market for them, whether or not messages are goods and there is a market for them.

However, is the speech-opportunity market an optimal institution in terms of aggregate V-value, as would be required to salvage MMVV? Do market mechanisms concerning speech opportunities provide the "best test," or best testing ground, of truth? This is highly dubious. Many critics of the market have pointed to "discourse inequalities," especially unequal resources among prospective speakers for the purchase of speech opportunities. Many messages that some speakers would like to transmit over the public media may not get transmitted at all because of the expense; or even if they are transmitted, they may be repeated less often and packaged less persuasively than other messages.[11] It is therefore doubtful that the market for speech opportunities is an optimal promoter of truth. This is related to the desire by marketplace "reformers" to have more regulation of the speech market rather than less. What they really seek is more regulation of the speech *opportunity* market, for

---

[11] Of course there may be other constraints on speech opportunities in addition to cost. Positions of power and influence, for example, can affect speech opportunities, especially when the latter are not sold on the open market but allocated in some other fashion.

example, by requiring broadcasters to give free air time to political candidates. I shall elaborate on this perspective below. For now we may simply note that if speech is not genuinely a good (a commodity), then the entire defense of MMVV by appeal to economic theory founders.

7.3 When and how nonmarket regulation can help

A proponent of MMVV might concede the message of Section 7.2 but remain undaunted. "Admittedly," she might say, "MMVV does not *follow* from economic theory; that much has been established. But this should not be confused with the statement that economic theory entails the *falsity* of MMVV. It does no such thing. It is quite compatible with economic theory that no system of speech regulation is as good, veritistically, as the market. In other words, MMVV may still be true, although its truth is not entailed by economic theory. And its truth is what I maintain."

Unfortunately for this MMVV proponent, Section 7.2 has already shown, or strongly suggested, that at least one system of speech regulation is better than the market, namely, a system that contains at least an admixture of nonmarket regulation. This was discussed in Subsection 7.2.C on preferences, in which it was shown how government subsidies of public television or government suppression of certain entertainment products would (under some conditions of consumer preference) produce veritistically better outcomes. These examples do not merely show that economic theory does not *imply* MMVV; they show that MMVV is false.

Let us not content ourselves, however, with just one or two examples. Let us examine a wider class of cases that seem to undercut MMVV. Keeping matters simple, we can focus on cases in two general categories. In the first category are cases of false but persuasive speech that thrives under market conditions but could be eliminated or reduced by nonmarket (especially state) practices. In the second category are cases of true messages that are not widely or prominently disseminated under market conditions. The same messages would be better disseminated under certain nonmarket policies, and so would be believed by more people. Such policies would yield veritistic gains.

There are already many governmental practices aimed at eliminating or reducing sundry types of false speech. One example is libel laws, which are clearly intended to deter potential speakers from asserting falsehoods about specified individuals or groups. On the assumption that libel laws in fact discourage many libelous statements, some of which would be believed if published, the effect of this nonmarket regulative policy is prevention of a certain mass of false belief.

It is debatable whether libel laws are optimal devices for averting false speech and hence false opinions about individuals or groups. Conceivably, market mechanisms might do better. Market mechanisms do not try to deter false statements, but offer opportunities to correct them by subsequent publication of denials or rebuttals. Given the costs of litigation, the threat of libel suits is not always very efficacious in any event. Furthermore, although statutes may provide *some* deterrence against false statements, this positive effect may be counterbalanced by the opportunities they create for chilling the exposure of truths. Wealthy individuals or groups may threaten libel litigation to deter the dissemination of true (but hard to establish) accusations, especially by speakers with more limited resources for legal engagement. This negative impact on truth promulgation may partly cancel the positive effect that antilibel statutes achieve.

On the other hand, the market mechanism of handling libelous speech through corrections and rebuttals may be comparatively ineffective. Corrections may not reach all of the original audience, and may not succeed in eradicating initially believed falsehoods. It is noteworthy that erratum notices in physics journals do not appear to be very effective in avoiding error propagation from an initially published mistake (Thomsen and Resnik 1995). Thus, I am inclined to think that libel laws, which constitute nonmarket regulation, are veritistically preferable to purely market attempts to handle the same problem.

Consider next a whole host of governmental regulations concerning speech that originated with the New Deal, as Cass Sunstein points out:

Many of the New Deal institutions actually regulate speech. The Securities and Exchange Commission (SEC) restricts what people may say when they sell stocks and bonds; it pervasively controls expression. Indeed, the SEC imposes old-fashioned prior restraints, requiring government preclearance before speech may reach the public. The Federal Communications Commission (FCC) oversees the broadcasting system under a vague "public interest" standard. It is clear that the New Dealers anticipated that the FCC would regulate the content of speech. Indeed, they sought content-based regulation as a corrective to market forces. The Food and Drug Administration (FDA) pervasively controls the labeling and communicative practices of people who sell food and drugs. Speech is one of its central targets. The National Labor Relations Board (NLRB) imposes severe restrictions on what may be said by employees, union officials, and especially employers. The Federal Trade Commission (FTC) controls unfair and deceptive trade practices. Many of those practices—indeed most of them—consist of speech. (1993: 33)

Whereas Sunstein goes on to say that these controls are aimed at promoting a well-functioning system of "free expression" (1993: 33), I would say that they are largely aimed at inhibiting false statements (or sometimes mandating true statements). Much of the FDA and FTC regulatory activity, for example, bans advertising or labeling that is false, deceptive, or misleading, where "deceptive" and "misleading" statements are ones that lead people to draw false conclusions, even if the statements are not false in themselves. This is also the purpose of SEC restrictions on what people may say when offering to sell stocks and bonds. The mere fact that these nonmarket regulatory practices exist does not prove, of course, that they are veritistically beneficial. The sorts of speech that they seek to suppress, however, are precisely the kinds of speech that are likely to be false, because speakers have powerful pecuniary motives for misrepresentation. Careful control of such speech holds out a strong promise of veritistic gain.

The next set of examples that fall under the first category are drawn from the judicial realm. First, consider laws against perjury and suborning perjury, obviously aimed at deterring witnesses from testifying falsely. If these laws succeed in deterring some potential cases of perjury, and if some of those potential pieces of perjurious testimony would, if delivered, have produced false beliefs in hearers (jurors, for example), then perjury laws are veritistically efficacious. It is hard to imagine how market regulation could duplicate this effect.

Continuing with judicial examples, we note that courts of law are highly regulated speech forums. Who is allowed to speak during a trial, and on precisely which topics, is scrupulously overseen by a judge, who determines which witnesses may testify, what questions attorneys may address to witnesses, and so forth. The rationale behind such speech governance is complex, but a substantial portion of the rationale is based on considerations of truth (Goldman 1992: ch. 11). This is explicit in the Federal Rules of Evidence (1989), which state the purpose of evidence-governing rules as follows: "These rules shall be construed to secure fairness in administration, elimination of unjustifiable expense and delay, and promotion of growth and development of the law of evidence *to the end that the truth may be ascertained* and proceedings justly determined" (Rule 102; emphasis added). The exclusion of hearsay evidence is predicated on the common-law insistence upon "the most reliable sources of information." Hearsay evidence is (allegedly) an unreliable way of getting the facts, and may lead juries toward erroneous verdicts. Not only are judges instructed to disallow "irrelevant" evidence, which cannot help the cause of truth, but even relevant evidence may be excluded "if its probative value is substantially outweighed by the danger of unfair prejudice, confusion of the issues, or misleading the jury" (Rule 403). "Prejudicing," "confusing," or "misleading" the jury invoke the prospect of producing false beliefs. Thus, the American judicial system assumes that speech regulation at trials is necessary and appropriate to further the judicial quest for truth. We may, of course, question whether all of the devices adopted by the judicial system in fact succeed in increasing the amount of (juror) truth possession. But it is plausible that *many* of them do; and since all of them are instances of nonmarket regulation, they illustrate the category we have been discussing.

The second general category consists of cases in which nonmarket regulation produces or widely disseminates truthful speech that a market framework either would not produce at all or would not disseminate so widely. There are two principal subdivisions within this category. Under the first subdivision, a nonmarket mechanism compels or mandates certain speech from a designated speaker who is not predisposed to speak on the mandated topic at all. The speaker is required to reveal or publicize things that she would prefer not to reveal or to advertise. Examples under this heading include (A) reluctant witnesses being compelled to testify at trial, (B) cigarette manufacturers being required to label their cigarette packages with warnings about the danger of smoking, and (C) government agencies being required to disclose information in their files to private citizens, under the Freedom of Information Act. In all of these cases, it is quite likely that no market mechanism would lead the knowledgeable parties to disclose or publicize their (truthful) information. Thus, nonmarket regulation has better veritistic consequences. Notice that the primary beneficiaries of compelled or mandated speech are not the speakers but the hearers. Clearly, the speakers are being made to do something involuntarily, so this is certainly not an increase in freedom for them. But veritistic evaluation is not concerned with freedom, except insofar as it contributes to knowledge. This is not to deny, of course, that freedom or autonomy is a substantial value. It just is not the value that social epistemology is concerned with. When it comes to making all-things-considered policy decisions, both kinds of values would have to be weighed and balanced. In this work, however, the spotlight focuses on the veritistic properties of practices.

The second subgroup within the second category features speakers who wish to convey their message but either lack sufficient resources for doing so in a market framework or are deterred from doing so by market considerations. Resource limitations might not entirely prevent speakers from speaking, but they might be prevented from airing their messages in prime, expensive venues that reach large audiences. This might be the situation, for example, of small-party political candidates, who cannot afford television time under a pure market arrangement. Government regulation of television networks could require the provision of speech opportunities gratis to all candidates. Thus, if small-party candidates have (new) truths to transmit that would not otherwise be heard by an audience of comparable size, and if a segment of the audience is ready to accept these truths, this nonmarket form of regulation would have positive veritistic outcomes. Of course, it could equally have negative veritistic outcomes if the speaker makes false claims that the audience accepts.

A final type of case in this category was intensively discussed in Chapter 6. This is the case of true prospective messages that newscasters, editorial writers, or documentary producers are eager to purvey through the mass media but which are censored or precluded to avoid offense to advertisers. Market mechanisms here endanger true speech, which could yield new knowledge for audience members. Any tax or other nonmarket policy considered in Chapter 6, if it succeeded in freeing message producers from these constraints, would qualify as an example of nonmarket regulation being veritistically superior to pure market regulation.

I have not proved, of course, that all of these forms of nonmarket government regulation have positive veritistic consequences. I have not *proved* that any of them does. But if even one of them does, MMVV is refuted. Its prospects, then, are pretty dim.

7.4 *The metaphorical marketplace and truth*

It is time to consider the second version of the marketplace idea. According to this view, the best way for a community to discover the truth is to ensure that a wide range of diverse views vigorously compete with one another in the public arena through critical examination. The public arena of such a debate is what is meant by the metaphorical marketplace. According to this view, if the economic market cannot be relied upon to produce such debate—and apparently it cannot—then some other mechanisms must be utilized to produce it, because this kind of social activity gives the community its best chance to obtain truth.

One component of this approach has been championed by two recent legal theorists, Owen Fiss (1987, 1991) and Cass Sunstein (1992, 1993). Both Fiss and Sunstein, who are sometimes called "new speech regulators," argue in favor of state regulation to enrich public debate, to ensure that a diverse range of positions are presented. As Fiss puts it, "The State must act as a high-minded parliamentarian, making certain that all viewpoints are fully and fairly heard" (1991: 2100). This will not necessarily be accomplished by a free (economic) market. In fact, says Fiss, noninterference "is likely to produce a public debate that is dominated, and thus constrained, by the same forces that dominate social structure, not a debate that is 'uninhibited, robust, and wide-open'" (1987: 786).[12] Sunstein also supports greater governmental activity in the interest of better speech practices. In order to promote political "deliberative autonomy," the state may properly require free air time for candidates, and may institute suitable campaign finance laws (1993: 34).

Fiss and Sunstein, however, are not full-fledged defenders of the metaphorical marketplace thesis in the form presented here. This is because neither Fiss nor Sunstein treats wide-open debate or deliberative autonomy as a means to *truth* or *knowledge*, which is, of course, my central focus. Fiss concentrates on the objective of robust debate without any further, ultimate goal, and Sunstein similarly interprets the principal aim of free speech to be the Madisonian goals of political equality and deliberative democracy, in which citizens are exposed to diverse views (1993: xvi–xx, 18–23, 51). Although these goals *could* be related to the knowledge goal, neither Fiss nor Sunstein actually draws such a connection. So leaving these two authors aside, we have to decide for our-

---

[12] The final phrase originates with Justice Brennan, in *New York Times v. Sullivan* 1964: 270.

selves whether a metaphorical marketplace constitutes a veritistically optimal speech practice.

One reason for giving credence to this idea is that it resonates with themes from Chapter 5. Didn't we learn—or at least postulate—in Chapter 5 that critical argumentation promotes veritistic outcomes? Wasn't this precisely the gist of the truth-in-evidence principle? So how can I even hesitate to grant that wide-open and vigorous debate is veritistically optimal, something that should be sought and promoted by any acceptable (high-level) speech policy?

Unfortunately, matters are not so straightforward. The truth-in-evidence principle does not entail that maximally open and vigorous debate is the best route to knowledge maximization. The general reason for this gap can be explained as follows. The second marketplace thesis asserts, roughly, that more argumentative speech is always veritistically better than less. But this approach focuses on *quantity* to the exclusion of *quality*, whereas both the truth-in-evidence principle and the Chapter 5 argumentation rules on which it builds place heavy emphasis on the quality of argumentation.

Let me spell this out more fully. The truth-in-evidence principle reads as follows:

> A larger body of evidence is generally a better indicator of the truth-value of a hypothesis than a smaller, contained body of evidence, as long as all the evidence propositions are true and what they indicate is correctly interpreted.

In Chapter 5 I appealed to this principle to endorse the veritistic desirability of defeater argumentation, but only provided that additional conditions are met. The first such condition is that all premises (evidence) asserted by speakers in the debate are true. Obviously, this is a very tough condition to meet. The second condition is that all hearers of the debate have a correct appreciation of the support relations between premises and conclusions. This is an equally tough condition to meet. Realistically speaking, where many speakers argue on a complex topic, it will rarely be the case that both conditions are met. Without the satisfaction of these conditions, however, the truth-in-evidence principle does not license an inference to the principle that more argumentative speech is veritistically better (V-better) than less.

Standards for argumentative "quality" were articulated by the rules or guidelines of Chapter 5. These rules were directed specifically at speakers, but the veritistic upshot of any argumentation always depends not only on how speakers speak—for example, whether they comply with the rules—but also on hearers' credal reactions. This is tacitly recognized by the truth-in-evidence principle. Let us see how the performance of both speakers and hearers has a bearing on veritistic prospects.

The second and third rules or guidelines of Chapter 5 jointly specify that a premise should be asserted by a speaker only if she justifiably believes it. This was rationalized on the ground that when a speaker justifiably believes a premise, it is more likely to be true than if she does not believe it justifiably. Now when different speakers engage in defeater argumentation, each adds one or more new premises to the debate (their "defeater" premise or premises) that the opponent omitted. If these premises are all true, and if the audience accepts them as true, that bodes well for veritistic advance. But if the premises are false but the audience accepts them nonetheless, that bodes ill for veritistic results. Without the assumption that the premises are true, a mere increase in the quantity of defeater argumentation does not raise the probability of veritistic advance. The same point holds for the inferential relationship between premises and conclusion, which is addressed by the fourth rule or guideline of Chapter 5. If speakers inflate the degree of evidential support that their premises confer on their conclusions but audience members are taken in by these inflations, degrees of belief in the conclusions will rise when many of those conclusions are actually false. There is nothing in the truth-in-evidence principle that suggests a good veritistic upshot from this scenario. In general, if the quantity of argumentation is increased largely through the addition of "junk" argumentation—by which I mean (1) false premises being asserted and/or (2) unwarranted inferences being drawn—there is no reason to expect an accompanying increase in V-value. Without an assurance of "quality" performance by both speakers and hearers, mere quantity of argumentation cannot be relied upon to bring the community closer to the promised land of greater knowledge.

Many of the laws and policies discussed in Section 7.3 are ostensibly aimed at deterring junk argumentation, or simple junk assertions. Libel laws are one example and regulations against advertising claims unauthenticated by scientific evidence are another. These were cited in Section 7.3 as plausible examples of state intervention in the economic marketplace that would have a veritistically beneficial effect.[13] They can equally be cited here, however, as plausible examples against the thesis that more speech is V-better than less. When it comes to false utterances that might easily persuade at least some listeners, it is veritistically preferable that those items of speech not occur. These are counterexamples to the thesis that greater speech inclusiveness always generates veritistic advance. If we look to specialized domains where the quest for truth is weighty, we find many cases where speech is scrupulously constrained, not open and unfettered. The example of courtroom procedure in Section 7.3 is a case in point. Courtroom procedure is predicated on the assumption that systematically controlled speech and evidence production is a superior route to truth revelation than a completely freewheeling enterprise. Peer review in science and scholarship is another instance of controlled speech being preferred to total inclusiveness, presumably on veritistic grounds.

[13] Although the Supreme Court has erected a two-tiered system in which a stiffer standard must be met for libeling a "public figure," it still appears that extant libel laws aim to deter false speech.

A critic might reply that I am being too protective or paternalistic toward the hearers of speech. Why assume that such hearers would always be gullible, that they would be unable to detect the falsity of the false premises that some speakers might advance? In an open debate, there would be ample opportunity for others to rebut these premises, and hearers could decide for themselves on their truth-values. Why not enable hearers to hear all sides of the debate? Doesn't that offer the greatest promise for veritistic advance? Perhaps this is (at least part of) what John Stuart Mill had in mind in speaking of "the clearer perception and livelier impression of truth produced by its collision with error" (1960: ch. 2).[14]

The critic is certainly right in rejecting the assumption that hearers are universally gullible. Still, when making speech regulation policy, it is reasonable to take the real-world dispositions of hearers into account. If hearers are disposed to believe certain categories of statements, even when the evidence or authority behind them is dubious, it may sometimes be preferable not to disseminate those statements. This is precisely what is done (in the United States) with grand jury hearings, which are legally kept secret. This is because the sorts of charges and pieces of testimony presented to grand juries are often of a questionable and shaky nature. Since the public may well be inclined to place undue credence in such charges, even if rebutted, the proceedings of grand juries are not supposed to be divulged to the public. This makes eminently good sense.

A second problem with Mill's "collision" defense of the metaphorical marketplace is that more speech in the marketplace does not guarantee that each hearer will actually observe and mentally "process" this collision. In other words, there is a problem of *equal hearer attention*. The mere fact that more viewpoints are expressed or broadcast in some public forum does not ensure that more of these will receive even roughly equal attention by potential listeners. Diversity of speech does not guarantee diversity of reception. When a glut of messages fills the airwaves, listeners may increasingly tune in only those messages they want to hear and filter out those they don't. So even if speech policy (or speech technology) succeeds in opening the airwaves (or fiber-optic cables) to a wider range of speaker opinions, that is no guarantee that people will actually track the dialectical merits of the countervailing arguments, and observe a collision of viewpoints. This problem was identified in Section 6.2 in connection with electronic newsgroups and bulletin board systems. It is another reason why more speech is not a surefire means to more knowledge.

A third problem is that speakers on different sides of a debate do not always have equal incentives for pressing their viewpoint. People with commercial interests in persuading customers of certain propositions have much greater incentive to speak on those subjects often, "loudly," and in slickly packaged

---

[14] Thanks to Brad Thompson for pressing this point in class discussion and writing.

formats, even if their messages are false or misleading. Speakers with opposing viewpoints on the same propositions may have a lesser stake in the dissemination of those opposing views. If both sides are allowed to speak as much as they wish, even the stream of messages directed at hearers will not be evenly balanced.

This raises a crucial point of vagueness or ambiguity in the second marketplace thesis. When it lauds the openness and diversity of a speech arena, does it mean to refer to speech *tokens* or speech *types*? If a certain viewpoint has already been expressed in some forum, does it enlarge the marketplace to have additional repetitions (tokens) of it by other speakers (or the same speaker), either in the same or another forum? Or does it suffice for the openness of a marketplace that each type of viewpoint be represented at least once? It seems obvious that the persuasive impact of a given viewpoint is likely to be affected by how frequently and saliently it is aired. So defenders of the metaphorical marketplace theory might wish to count tokens rather than types. Does this lead to the conclusion that a marketplace is fully open only if every viewpoint is expressed an equal number of times? Is government speech policy a failure if it fails to bring about this scenario?

I have disputed the second marketplace thesis that more speech is always V-better than less. But even if that claim were true, we would be left with the question of how to realize or effectuate an open market for ideas. The second version of the marketplace idea, unlike the first, does not address the question of mechanisms. It only specifies a condition to be attained, not how to attain it. As we saw earlier, some defenders of the metaphorical marketplace advocate government action to help create it. But it is unclear how far the government should be allowed to go. Moreover, these defenders of the metaphorical marketplace are primarily concerned with political speech, and the proper treatment of nonpolitical speech is left largely unaddressed. In any case, since we have rejected the notion that the metaphorical marketplace is veritistically optimal, it is pointless to explore precisely what mechanisms would realize it.

Having repudiated both versions of the marketplace idea, we are left without any grand or simple solution to the problem of speech regulation. Unfortunately, I have no candidate of similar simplicity to propose in their place. But having broached the question of what legitimate role the state should play in speech policy, it is appropriate to examine some standing proposals in this area as they appear in First Amendment jurisprudence. Whether or not these policies were designed for veritistic purposes, we may still ask how well they serve veritistic ends.

7.5 *State regulation and metaregulation*

There are two levels of governmental speech policy. At the first level there is statutory and regulatory policy. At the second level, at least in the American political structure, there is a Constitutional provision (enforced by judicial review) that constrains actions taken by government at the first level. This is metaregulation.

Why should there be metaregulation of the state's first-level speech regulation? The historical worry about state regulation of speech is twofold: First, is the state *competent* to make regulation decisions in the interest of truth? Is the state in a good position to determine which messages are true or false, or which speech contexts or speech arrangements are likely to produce more V-value than others? Second, there is the question of *interests*. Can the state be relied upon to make regulation decisions based solely—or even primarily—on the welfare (veritistic or otherwise) of society? Doesn't the state or its officials have their own narrow interests to protect? To put speech regulation in the hands of the state is like putting the henhouse in the hands of the fox.

Beginning with competence, it is always difficult to estimate the consequences of any prospective law or policy. Most people would probably agree that copyright laws in the past have served the veritistic interests of society by providing incentives for intellectual discoveries. In the era of cyberspace, however, it is extremely difficult to predict the veritistic outcomes of alternative copyright policies. As we saw in Chapter 6, government may well have dubious ideas about optimal copyright policies (and their proposals may be warped by political interests, which goes beyond the competence question). A tolerably clear example of government ineptitude was the FCC's fairness doctrine. Broadcasters were required to give equal time to opposing viewpoints when they aired controversial material. This was intended to enhance and enrich public debate, possibly with veritistic ends in mind. But most observers say that the actual result of the fairness doctrine was a diminution in public debate. The threat of FCC suits simply discouraged broadcasters from airing controversial material in the first place. The policy had a chilling effect precisely opposite to the one intended.

Worries about state interests are an even more pervasive feature of metaregulation thinking. This type of worry can be illustrated by reflecting on a central distinction in First Amendment jurisprudence: the distinction between *content-based* versus *content-neutral* restrictions.

Content-neutral restrictions limit communication without regard to the message conveyed. Laws that prohibit noisy speeches near a hospital or ban billboards in residential communities are examples of content-neutral restrictions. Typically, these are laws that prohibit speech in terms of its time, place, or manner. Content-based restrictions limit communication because of the message conveyed. These include laws that forbid the hiring of teachers who advocate the violent overthrow of government, or outlaw the display of the swastika in certain neighborhoods. In assessing the constitutionality of content-based restrictions (at least of "high-value" speech, e.g., political speech), the Supreme Court employs a very stringent standard. In an oft-quoted dictum, the Court announced that "above all else, the First

Amendment means that government has no power to restrict expression because of its message, its ideas, its subject matter, or its content" (*Police Department v. Mosley* 1972: 95). The Court has invalidated almost every content-based restriction that it has considered in the past thirty years or more—at least outside the realm of low-value speech (Stone 1987: 48). Content-neutral restrictions are treated more leniently or sympathetically.

A number of reasons have been given to explain the Court's strict standard for content-based restrictions. Of interest here is one discussed by Geoffrey Stone (1987): the "improper motivation" explanation. The idea is that communication should not be prohibited merely because public officials disapprove of, or disagree with, the speaker's views. As a corollary of this, the government may not restrict expression because it might be embarrassed by publication of the information disclosed. Clearly, this rationale for a strict standard against content-based restrictions fits the concern about self-oriented government interests that could yield regulatory abuse.

From the perspective of regulating the regulators, how useful is the content-based/content-neutral distinction? The worst abuses of regulatory power take the form of banning or censoring certain messages entirely, messages that are threats to the state or which the state dislikes for various reasons. A very stringent standard against content-based restrictions seems well designed to confront this kind of danger. Content-neutral restrictions, by contrast, are usually much less abusive, since they only bar speech in certain forums or on certain occasions. The same messages speakers desire to transmit may be communicated via other channels. However, content-neutral restrictions can still constrict expression, even quite dramatically, as the following hypothetical law illustrates: "No person may make any speech; distribute any leaflet; publish any newspaper, magazine, or other periodical; operate any radio, television, or cable system; or engage in any other form of public communication" (Stone 1987: 58). Such a law is content neutral, but it would cripple the transmission of information. Thus, content-neutral restrictions are hardly innocuous, and it is appropriate that they be judicially constrained. It must be shown that governmental interests in proposing a content-neutral restriction could not be served by less intrusive means. Content-based restrictions, however, face even more severe standards.

From a purely veritistic point of view, is there reason to respect the distinction between content-based and content-neutral regulation? Does a special bias against content-based regulation serve veritistic ends? We have seen ample reason for expecting government to be especially *tempted* and perhaps *prone* to engage in content-based restriction, and to that extent the bias against content-based restriction may make sense. But what about veritistic considerations? Which type of restriction is more threatening from a veritistic standpoint? Are content-based restrictions generically more threatening to information dissemination and hence to be avoided on veritistic grounds? One reason to resist this conclusion is that content-neutral restrictions are not so innocuous, even when they are of limited scope. It is true that content-neutral restrictions do not (generally) keep a speaker from expressing his viewpoint altogether. Nonetheless, they may substantially reduce the size of the audience that receives the speaker's message. If the audience precluded from reception is precisely the audience most likely to be persuaded by it, and if the message is in fact true, then the restriction could mean a significant veritistic loss. So even content-neutral restrictions of limited scope can be veritistically serious, and their impact should not be minimized.

The veritistic desirability of precluding content-based restrictions depends on exactly how that notion is understood. Let us distinguish two senses of "content-based." Let us call a law or policy that regulates a class of speech acts by specifying a particular content a *content-specific* policy. A speech-regulating law or policy that mentions no particular content but requires for its application a reference to content will be called a *content-related* policy. It seems plausible to me that content-specific restrictions should be resisted, but content-related restrictions might well be veritistically promising.

Before illustrating the promise of content-related restrictions, let us first consider another side to the question of how to metaregulate the state's regulation policies. Frederick Schauer (1997) has pointed out that when one worries about how far regulators should be trusted, one needs to attend not only to regulator "pathologies" but also to speaker pathologies.[15] Political regulators are obviously tempted to try to suppress the spread of information that is harmful or embarrassing to them. It is appropriate for second-order constraints to anticipate this pathology. But it is also common wisdom that speakers often have interests that tempt them to distort or misrepresent the truth. This holds for commercial advertisers, political speakers who support or oppose certain candidacies, and so forth. A veritistically effective metaregulation framework must be concerned to balance the interest-distorting pathologies of speakers against the interest-distorting pathologies of regulators. In earlier eras, when communication styles and technologies were less advanced, it might have sufficed to let the principle *caveat emptor* hold sway. Listeners would know when a speaker had a stake—for example, a financial stake—in distorting the facts, and they would adjust their trust in the message accordingly. But in our age, with its sophisticated communication technologies and practices, clever speakers hide their stake in the persuasive success of their messages. When a Web surfer reads an item about some medicine on the Web, there may be few if any clues about whether the source is related to the manufacturer, or stands to profit from the acceptance of the message. In short, the reader may have no easy way to discover whether this is an interest-driven message or an impartial one. That greatly compounds his difficulty in assessing its trustworthiness.

---

[15] Audience pathologies, I would add, should also be included in the list.

Under these circumstances, a law requiring revelation of a speaker's identity and financial interests in the content of the message, whenever there are such interests, could be very helpful from a veritistic perspective.[16] Does such a law qualify as content neutral? It does not prohibit or constrain speech in terms of time, place, or manner, the usual marks of a content-neutral restriction. But it is not content specific either, since it does not constrain messages identified in terms of particular contents. Nonetheless, it is content related, because it constrains any message in which the speaker stands to profit from the persuasive success of its contents. Similarly, consider the policy of restricting commercial advertisements to claims that have been scientifically substantiated. This is not a content-specific restriction since it specifies no particular contents. But it is a content-related restriction since it excludes types of contents based on their evidential properties. Having drawn the distinction between content specificity and content relatedness, it looks as if content specificity should indeed make a speech restriction highly suspect, but content relatedness seems unobjectionable.

I have not proposed a grand solution to the problem of how speech should be regulated (or deregulated) for the sake of veritistic ends. It has sufficed for present purposes to place this central issue squarely on the agenda of social epistemology and to illustrate how the issue intersects with longstanding discussions in the free speech arena.

---

[16] This kind of proposal was reported in Section 6.2, but it could be broadened considerably beyond the domain of the Internet.

PART THREE

Special Domains

EIGHT

Science

8.1 Science as convention or "form of life"

THIS chapter begins a series of four domain-specific chapters, each examining the veritistic dimensions of social practices within a specific arena of social life. According to orthodoxy, the institution of science quintessentially aims at knowledge or truth acquisition, so it is a natural place to start. As we saw in Chapter 1, however, postmodern critics repudiate science as a bona fide route to truth. Even among mainstream philosophers of science, many are skeptical of the claim that science succeeds in, or even aims at, delivering truth, especially "theoretical" truth. The first five sections of the chapter, therefore, are devoted to ground-clearing operations: rebutting critics who deny that a veritistic analysis of science is appropriate, or who doubt that such an analysis can support the epistemic authority of science. Only later in the chapter will I turn to more positive analyses of science from a social perspective.

A central theme of social constructivism is that no social practice should be enshrined as a privileged way of getting at truth. No practice can lay claim to universal, timeless, or context-free validity. Social constructivists and other postmodernists seek to demystify or deconstruct science's epistemic authority. One route to demystification is to argue that science is just a highly elaborate set of social conventions—a "discursive formation" (Foucault) or "form of life" (Wittgenstein)—which arose in a particular historical setting and captured the loyalty of our culture, but which has no intrinsic claim to epistemic superiority. Translated into our terminology, this position implies that science is veritistically no better than other practices, despite the special reputation it enjoys. I shall begin, therefore, with one popular development of this theme, a historical analysis of the seventeenth-century origins of modern science presented by Steven Shapin and Simon Schaffer (1985).

Shapin and Schaffer recount Robert Boyle's defense of the experimental philosophy and his debates on this subject with Thomas Hobbes. In Shapin and Schaffer's view, Boyle and Hobbes propounded competing "language games" or "forms of life," and Boyle's was victorious. Intrinsically, however, each proposed form of life is merely a set of conventions, neither having more veritistic validity than the other. Of course, Boyle's experimental approach claimed to establish certain "matters of fact" through witnesses observing the outcome of an experiment. But this was just Boyle's way of *defining* "matter of fact," according to Shapin and Schaffer; it is not a way of discovering convention-independent truth. More elaborately, Shapin and Schaffer analyze Boyle's experimental program in terms of three "technologies": (1) a *material technology* embedded in the construction and operation of a scientific instrument (for example, the air pump); (2) a *literary technology* by means of which the phenomena produced by the instrument were made known to people who were not direct witnesses; and (3) a *social technology* that incorporated the conventions experimental philosophers should use in dealing with each other and considering knowledge claims (Shapin and Schaffer 1985: 25). In the third category, and worthy of special attention here, was the requirement that witnessing an experimental phenomenon be a public, collective act. In science, as in criminal law, Boyle insisted, the reliability of testimony depended upon its multiplicity:

For, though the testimony of a single witness shall not suffice to prove the accused party guilty of murder; yet the testimony of two witnesses, though but of equal credit . . . shall ordinarily suffice to prove a man guilty; because it is thought reasonable to suppose, that, though each testimony single be but probable, yet a concurrence of such probabilities, (which ought in reason to be attributed to the truth of what they jointly tend to prove) may well amount to a moral certainty, i.e., such a certainty, as may warrant the judge to proceed to the sentence of death against the indicted party. (Quoted in Shapin and Schaffer 1985: 56)

Shapin and Schaffer construe the requirement of public witnessing as a "convention," which establishes something that the group *calls* a "matter of fact": "[E]xperimental knowledge production rested upon a set of *conventions* for generating matters of fact and for handling their explications" (1985: 55). In other words, social practices created or constituted factual matters; they didn't reveal or uncover them. This familiar doctrine of social constructivism is one we encountered in Chapter 1, and I believe that its merits were adequately exploded there. Furthermore, there is no sound reason to attribute this approach to Boyle himself. As the above-quoted passage indicates, Boyle does not contend that multiple witnessing necessarily *constitutes* or *entails* an experimental fact, only that it warrants belief in such a fact "to a moral certainty." It is obvious that group witnessing can in principle be erroneous; there could be, for example, a mass hallucination. Thus, the true state of affairs in nature is not *defined* by what multiple witnesses jointly concur in observing. Nor did Boyle endorse that late twentieth-century form of constructivism.

Was Boyle right, however, in thinking that multiple witnessing is an instrumentally good practice for getting truth? A good case can be made that he was. Indeed, a fairly plausible application of Bayes' Theorem shows that getting a true fact "to a moral certainty" is more likely via the concurring testimony of multiple witnesses than via the testimony of a single one of those witnesses.

More precisely, in my terminology, the practice of relying on multiple-witness testimony has more positive veritistic value than the practice of relying on single-witness testimony.

The primary sort of scientific fact in question here is whether a scientific instrument, like an air-pump, does or does not undergo a certain observable change. If third parties are to place their credence in witnesses to the event, are they better off appealing to a single witness or to multiple concurring witnesses? Under some reasonable assumptions, many witnesses are better than one. Consider a series of possible cases in which a third party uses Bayesian conditionalization upon hearing concurring reports from one or more witnesses. Assume she starts in each case with the same prior probability for the experimental outcome, and assume that all witnesses, individually, have—and are believed to have—the same level of credibility. Finally, assume that each witness is more credible than not, that is, it is more likely that a witness will testify to X if X does occur than if X does not occur. Using notation similar to that of Chapter 4, let X be the target event, let $T_1(X)$ be testimony by a single witness that X occurred, $T_2(X)$ be testimony by two witnesses that X occurred, and so forth. Since we are assuming that each witness's testimony has positive probative value, this means that the likelihood ratio concerning $T_1(X)$ exceeds unity. That is,

$$\frac{p(T_1(X)/X)}{p(T_1(X)/\text{NOT-}X)} > 1.$$

Suppose we further assume that the testimony of each pair of witnesses is mutually independent. (The independence assumption may not be so safe, though Boyle tried to promote independence by preaching against the influence of powerful authorities over others.) Then the likelihood ratio of increasing numbers of witnesses will be more extreme than the likelihood ratio for a single witness. To be concrete, let $p(T_1(X)/X) = .6$ and $p(T_1(X)/\text{NOT-}X) = .2$. Then the likelihood ratio for a single witness, R_1, is $.6/.2 = 3$. This implies that a Bayesian third party, upon hearing a single witness testify to X, will revise upward her confidence in the truth of X. Depending on her assessment of the prior probability of X, however, this will presumably not reach anything like "moral certainty." Suppose now that two or more witnesses testify, witnesses with the same likelihoods as one another. Then we get the following numbers. The likelihood ratio for two witnesses, R_2, is $.6^2/.2^2 = .36/.04 = 9$; the likelihood ratio for three witnesses, R_3, is $.6^3/.2^3 = .216/.008 = 27$; the likelihood ratio for four witnesses, R_4, is $.6^4/.2^4 = .1296/.0016 = 81$; and so on. Conditionalizing with these very high likelihood ratios will lead to posterior probability assignments very close to 1, unless the agent's prior for X is extremely low. Thus, Boyle's talk of a "moral certainty" is pretty much on target.

Furthermore, if the third party has accurate likelihood estimates about the witnesses, she is objectively likely to achieve greater truth possession (V-value) under the multiple witness scenario than under the single witness scenario. This follows from Theorem 4.2 of Chapter 4. Recall that according to that theorem, a Bayesian reasoner's average increase in truth possession—when using accurate likelihoods—is greater with more extreme likelihoods than with less extreme likelihoods. Thus, although Boyle did not have a precise proof of the veritistic merit of his multiple-witnessing practice, it is indeed quite defensible, at least under the various assumptions I have listed. Moreover, we don't need the independence assumption to get this result. As long as the likelihood ratio is greater for multiple-witness scenarios than for single-witness scenarios, the multiple-witness practice is veritistically superior.

A second feature of Boyle's experimental philosophy stressed by Shapin and Schaffer was its exclusivity. Although experiments were to be conducted in a "public space," frequently the Royal Society's assembly rooms, not everyone was admitted as a witness. This issue was an especially sore point for Hobbes, who was himself conspicuously and deliberately excluded. In practice, Hobbes observed, the place where the experimentalists meet is not public, and the experiments are available to be witnessed only by a self-selected few. The space occupied by the Gresham experimentalists had a "master" who decided who could come in and who could not. "Hobbes himself was the sort of philosopher who on no account ought to be admitted to the experimental companionship, for he denied the value of systematic and elaborate experimentation" (1985: 72). In fact, Boyle's view of who was eligible to be a reliable witness was strongly influenced by considerations of Restoration respectability and politics. He often listed his experimental spectators, and described them, for example, as "those excellent and deservedly famous Mathematics Professors, Dr. *Wallis*, Dr. *Ward*, and Mr. *Wren* . . ., whom I name, both as justly counting it an honour to be known to them, and as being glad of such judicious and illustrious witnesses of our experiment" (1985: 58). Boyle also forged alliances on grounds of political expediency, for example, an alliance with the clergy, who themselves were interested in producing and controlling assent in matters of spirit. Thus, in the view of Shapin and Schaffer, experimental science of this period was really "a tightly organized, well-insulated coterie, jealous of its prerogatives and hostile toward outsiders who intrude without proper credentials" (Gross and Levitt 1994: 63). In a later book, Shapin (1994) expands on this picture with an account of how, in seventeenth-century England, only aristocrats or gentlemen were accorded the status of reliable and trustworthy reporters.

Some of Shapin and Schaffer's historical interpretations are open to dispute. Was the Royal Society as rigid and intolerant as Shapin and Schaffer imply? It did exclude Hobbes from the circle of the scientific elect, but Hobbes, after all, rejected the experimental philosophy. Moreover, the Society demonstrated a willingness to accept some of Boyle's opponents. Christian Huygens was a staunch opponent of Boyle, but he was elected a Fellow of the Royal Society (1985: 250).[1]

Finally, even if Boyle chose some of his authorities badly, in purely epistemic terms, two questions remain. First, is this feature of Boyle's experimental philosophy essential to the continuing practice of science? If not, then this may be a mere historical accident or curiosity, or at most a feature of the political requirements for getting scientific practice respected and adopted in seventeenth-century England. It may say little about the continuing practice of science in later centuries and in our own time. Second, is it obvious that a practice of "credentialism" is inimical to veritistic interests? Granted that it is in conflict with pure egalitarianism, it does not follow that it is necessarily in conflict with veritistic concerns. Perhaps a properly applied practice of credentialism would promote rather than hinder veritistic ends. Nothing Shapin and Schaffer say demonstrates otherwise.

8.2 A political–military account of science

Science-studies writers would hasten to retort that the political character of science is as central today as it was historically. Shapin and Schaffer remark: "He who has the most, and the most powerful, allies wins" (1985: 342). This is certainly intended as a comment on contemporary as well as seventeenth-century science. Exactly what moral should be drawn, however, from the presence of "political" tactics in science, whether historical or contemporary? Suppose we grant Shapin and Schaffer's contention that Boyle's victory over Hobbes was a political victory, in the sense that politics was instrumental in winning friends for scientific practice (à la Boyle). Does this fact challenge the veritistic merits of science? The intrinsic merits of a practice are not necessarily affected by the steps taken to implement or achieve recognition for it. A little politics may be needed to obtain financial backing for the local opera company, but that need not affect the artistic merits of opera, nor turn it into a branch of politics. Suppose, however, that scientific practice is not merely *facilitated* by politics, but just *is* politics through and through. Surely that would challenge the veritistic *bona fides* of science. Surely science would have no truth-leaning tendency if its practitioners merely engaged in a fancy form of intellectual politicking! This more radical thesis about science is also endorsed by a goodly number of science-studies students, and demands our attention. Perhaps its leading exponent is Bruno Latour, as formulated in Latour 1987.

Latour focuses on what produces persuasion or conviction in science. When controversies arise in science, how are they settled? When disagree-

---

[1] Thanks to Seungbae Park for this observation.

ment becomes intense, says Latour, hard-pressed dissenters will quickly allude to what others wrote or said, as the following imaginary conversation illustrates:

Mr. Anybody (as if resuming an old dispute): Since there is a new cure for dwarfism, how can you say this?
Mr. Somebody: A new cure? How do you know? You just made it up.
— I read it in a magazine.
— Come on! I suppose it was in a color supplement . . .
— No, it was in *The Times* and the man who wrote it was not a journalist but someone with a doctorate.
— What does that mean? He was probably some unemployed physicist who does not know the difference between RNA and DNA.
— But he was referring to a paper published in *Nature* by the Nobel Prizewinner Andrew Schally and six of his colleagues, a big study, financed by all sorts of big institutions, the National Institute of Health, the National Science Foundation, which told what the sequence of a hormone was that releases growth hormone. Doesn't that mean something?
— Oh! You should have said so first . . . that's quite different. Yes, I guess it does.
(Latour 1987: 31)

As Latour proceeds to explain, Mr. Anybody's opinion can be easily brushed aside, so he enlists the support first of a newspaper article and ultimately of a new set of "allies": a journal, *Nature*; a Nobel Prize author; six coauthors; and granting agencies. Now Mr. Anybody must be taken seriously, since he is no longer alone: "a group, so to speak, accompanies him. Mr. Anybody has become Mr. Manybodies!" (1987: 31)

This appeal to higher and more numerous allies, Latour points out, is a species of argument from authority. He says that it is derided by philosophers and scientists alike because it creates a majority to impress the dissenter even though the dissenter might be right. Science, he says, is seen as the opposite of the argument from authority, because a few might win over the many because truth is on their side. Galileo contrasted real science with rhetoric, which Galileo mocked and derided:

But in the physical sciences when conclusions are sure and necessary and have nothing to do with human preferences, one must take care not to place oneself in the defence of error; for here, a thousand Demosthenes and a thousand Aristotles would be left in the lurch by any average man who happened to hit on the truth for himself. (Drake 1970: 71)

Early modern physicists were anxious to remove science from the realm of authority. Latour is right, though, to challenge their claim that argument from authority has no place in science. As a descriptive matter, scientists do invoke the authority of others in their citations. Science is an importantly social and collective affair, not an individualist one. Latour provides a political or military metaphor for scientific controversy, in which the assemblage of alliances is crucial.

In practice, what makes Mr. Somebody change his mind is exactly the opposite of Galileo's argument. To doubt that there is a cure for dwarfism, he at first has to resist his friend's opinion plus a fake doctor's opinion plus a newspaper. It is easy. But at the end, how many people does he have to oppose? Let us count: Schally and his coworkers plus the board of the New Orleans university who gave Schally a professorship plus the Nobel Committee who rewarded his work with the highest prize plus the many people who secretly advised the Committee plus the editorial board of *Nature* and the referees who chose this article plus the scientific boards of the National Science Foundation and of the National Institutes of Health who awarded grants for the research . . . For Mr. Somebody, doubting Mr. Anybody's opinion takes no more than a shrug of the shoulders. But how can you shrug off dozens of people whose honesty, good judgment and hard work you must weaken before disputing the claim? (1987: 32–3)

Similarly, referring to the weightiness of technical papers full of references, Latour says:

The number of external friends the text comes with is a good indication of its strength . . . The effect of references on persuasion is not limited to that of "prestige" or "bluff." Again, it is a question of *numbers*. A paper that does not have references is like a child without an escort walking at night in a big city it does not know: isolated, lost, anything may happen to it. (1987: 33)

Latour's emphasis on numbers in scientific controversy suggests two things: first, that scientific *speakers* marshal the largest number of allies that they can, and second, that scientific *hearers* are persuaded by numbers. (The speaker practice is presumably predicated on their belief that numbers will impress hearers.) If these claims are correct, could science possibly succeed in getting truth? How can mere numbers point toward truth? In politics, allies or resources propel a candidate to victory independent of his or her merit. Similarly, according to the intimated account, allies and resources in science achieve persuasion independent of the rational merit of a claim, or its probability of truth, or even the hearers' judgments of these matters.

Before assessing the descriptive accuracy of this political approach and its veritistic implications, let us give it a clearer formulation:

(PT$_1$) The persuasive force of a scientist's claim is a function of the number of allies marshaled on its behalf.

Obviously, (PT$_1$) is too simplistic to be descriptively accurate, and Latour does not endorse precisely this form of the political approach. First, not every ally counts equally; some are more impressive than others. Second, there are different ways to deploy allies and paralyze one's enemies to increase one's persuasiveness. Latour puts it as follows:

It would be possible to go much further in the Byzantine political schemes of the context of citations. Like a good billiard player, a clever author may calculate shots with three, four or five rebounds. Whatever the tactics, the general strategy is easy to grasp: do whatever you need to the former literature to render it as helpful as possible for the claims you are going to make. The rules are simple enough: weaken your enemies, paralyze those you cannot weaken . . ., help your allies if they are attacked, ensure safe communications with those who supply you with indisputable instruments . . ., oblige your enemies to fight one another . . .; if you are not sure of winning, be humble and understated. These are simple rules indeed: the rules of the oldest politics. (1987: 37–8)

We might translate these additional elements into the following, more refined, version of the political approach:

(PT$_2$) The persuasive force of a scientist's claim is a function of his relatively effective deployment of a weighted number of allies against a weighted number of enemies.

By adding a weighting of the allies (by authority or reputation) as well as the effectiveness with which they are deployed against the enemies, (PT$_2$) provides a more plausible descriptive account than (PT$_1$). But even if (PT$_2$) were correct, would it puncture the epistemic pretensions of science?

I answer to the contrary, and the groundwork for this answer may be laid by initially examining (PT$_1$). Even if (PT$_1$) were correct in saying that persuasion varies with the number of allies, there might be a deeper, epistemic explanation of this phenomenon. Hearer-scientists might believe that the most reliable indicator of the truth of a controverted scientific statement is the number of (qualified) scientists who affirm it as compared with the number of (qualified) scientists who dispute it. In other words, the relative number of allies and enemies might be taken as a measuring rod of the truth of the claim. This is quite different from supposing that the sheer force of numbers psychically commands assent in the way that a military force overwhelms an opposition or a plurality of votes spells victory at the polls. In the military and political cases, the outcome has nothing to do with persuading anybody of (what they take to be) a truth. But if numbers win in science, it might be because the scientific audience believes that greater numbers are *evidence* for the truth of that side's view. Latour's political–military account does nothing to undermine this possibility.

A similar epistemic account might be provided to explain (PT$_2$), if the latter is in fact correct. Start with the weights associated with greater authority or reputation. A plausible definition of "authority" is someone whose opinion within the relevant domain is likely to be right, or true. If scientists consider someone an authority, they consider him a likely source of truth on the subject. So if they are persuaded by appeal to one or more such authorities, it could easily be because they seek to form a true opinion on the disputed subject and believe that more numerous or more reliable authorities are better guides to truth than fewer or less reliable authorities. This would be an epistemic explanation, of the kind developed in some detail by Philip Kitcher (1993: ch. 8).

Turn next to the various tactics described by Latour in quasi-military terms:

deploy your allies as skillfully as possible, weaken your enemies, and so forth. These colorful metaphors are all descriptive of various argumentative tactics: use selected claims of your allies as premises to support your own claims, criticize the premises of your enemies with which they try to undermine your claims, and so forth. Perhaps the reason these tactics have persuasive prospects is precisely because they affect the audience's perception of the likely *truth* of your claims. Well-supported claims are more likely to be believed than poorly supported claims; failure to rebut your opponents' criticisms induces doubt about the truth of your claims, whereas defeat of those criticisms eliminates such doubts. Latour's strategical advice makes sense precisely on the assumption of an epistemic account of persuasion, one that depicts scientific audiences as truth seekers.

Let us next ask whether Latour is right to ascribe such a dominant role to authority in scientific persuasion. The notion that scientists are persuaded by the "vector sum" of the voices behind an idea looks just too simplistic, and skepticism about it is supported from research on persuasion generally. An influential model of persuasion is due to Richard Petty and John Cacioppo (1986a, 1986b). Petty and Cacioppo suggest that message receivers process messages quite differently in different contexts or on different occasions. Sometimes they engage in peripheral or shallow processing, employing a simple decision rule to decide whether to accept the message, for example, whether they find the communicator likable, or credible, or—I add—whether the communicator invokes an impressive list of allies. On other occasions they engage in more "elaborate" processing; for example, they pay close attention to the presented message, carefully scrutinize the arguments it contains, devise or recall similar arguments from memory, and so forth. It seems plausible to assume that scientists, especially when they are considering an article of scientific importance in their own specialty, engage in elaborate processing, which is likely to include details of the presented argument and not simply the social or professional status of the communicators and their supporters. This suggestion is further supported by the findings of other sociologists of science. Stephen Cole (1992: 51) points out that Watson and Crick's model of DNA was quickly accepted by others despite the fact that when their brief paper was published in *Nature* they were young scientists without any significant reputation. Another study by Cole (1992: ch. 6) suggests that evaluations of scientific grant applications are not strongly influenced by "political" characteristics of the applicant such as personal prestige or departmental rank, but seem to reflect the judged quality of the proposal itself. So there is little reason to suppose that scientists are persuaded exclusively by "political" considerations, and ample reason to suspect that an epistemic or truth-seeking model is a better approximation.

To summarize, even if Latour's political–military account of scientific persuasion were correct as far as it goes—hearers are indeed persuaded by the weight of authorities—this is fully compatible with an epistemic or truth-seeking account as well, because authorities can be relevant to the search for scientific truth. At the same time, there is suggestive evidence that mere authority or prestige is not the sole factor in scientific persuasion. An epistemic model of persuasion, then, is compatible with all the evidence adduced so far. The epistemic account sketched above does not guarantee that science will succeed in getting the truth. Even if scientists are persuaded by what they *presume* to be reliable authorities and good arguments, those authorities may not be so reliable, nor the arguments so good. Nonetheless, the epistemic account presents a very different image of scientific persuasion than the muckraking political account sketched by Latour and others.

8.3 *Biases and interests*

In the two preceding sections I have hovered close to some of the debunking arguments of veriphobes described in Chapter 1. In this section I revisit the fifth postmodern criticism of veritistic epistemology posed in that chapter: truth is humanly unattainable because all putatively truth-seeking practices are corrupted by biases or self-serving interests. Here I mainly address the charge that truth is unattainable because fundamental biases are built into the human psyche. Of course, this charge is not leveled at the truth prospects of science alone; it is a more sweeping claim. But if it is right, it holds for science as well. So this is as good a place as any to inspect its credibility.

In assessing the threat of distorting interests, we must first distinguish between the interests of speakers and the interests of hearers. Undoubtedly speakers often speak out of personal advantage. When it suits their interest to say something they know to be false, there is a nonnegligible danger they will say it anyway. The existence of scientific fraud shows that even scientists are not immune from this disease. This in itself, however, does not demonstrate universal dupery. Deception is guaranteed only if hearers have no way of telling when to distrust communicators, and as a blanket contention that is extremely dubious. The threat of distortion by interests, then, is more serious if it is located in hearer-believers rather than speakers. But isn't this an equally serious threat? Don't scientists have their own interests and biases, and couldn't these inescapably imperil the prospects for scientific truth acquisition?

Two kinds of biases are commonly distinguished in the cognitive psychology literature: "hot" and "cold" biases. Hot biases stem from desires, motivations, interests, or emotions. Cold biases reside in purely cognitive, intellectual processes. Postmodernists typically emphasize the former as insidious threats to truth and accuracy, but readers of psychology and cognitive science may be more familiar with threats from "cold" biases. Charges of "illusion" and "irrationality" have been leveled at our native inferential procedures, and if these charges are right, they might dim the prospects for truth attainment quite apart from the possibility of hot biases.

Before proceeding, I want to stress a point made in Section 1.7 about the argument from bias. None of the psychological literature on biases suggests that people are wholly incapable of forming veridical beliefs. Most of it contends that native cognitive heuristics just don't coincide with normatively appropriate procedures. People do not make all and only sound deductive inferences; their naive procedures for making probability estimates do not match those of Bayesian statistics; and so forth. This hardly establishes—nor does it purport to establish—that they have zero capacity for accurate belief formation. Indeed, other segments of cognitive science confirm that people are extremely accurate in their beliefs. Healthy mechanisms of perception and memory show remarkable facility at accurate object recognition and event retention; people learn to do arithmetic with substantial accuracy; and the capacity to master the syntax of a novel language is an amazing and yet-to-be-fathomed property of the young child's brain.

Let me now survey a few of the best-known examples of so-called inferential biases or "illusions," most prominently due to Amos Tversky and Daniel Kahneman (Kahneman and Tversky 1973; Kahneman, Slovic, and Tversky 1982; Tversky and Kahneman 1983; Nisbett and Ross 1980). I shall then review some recent challenges suggesting that charges of "bias" may be exaggerated. Three of the most salient biases treated in the literature are (1) the overconfidence bias, (2) the conjunction fallacy, and (3) the base-rate fallacy.

Overconfidence is studied with questions of the following sort:

> Which city has more inhabitants: (a) Hyderabad, or (b) Islamabad?
> How confident are you that your answer is correct?
> 50% 60% 70% 80% 90% 100%?

The subject chooses what she believes is the correct answer and then rates her confidence that the answer is correct. After many subjects answer many questions, the experimenter counts the answers in each of the confidence categories that were actually correct. The typical finding is that where subjects indicated a 100 percent confidence, the relative frequency of correct answers was only about 80 percent; where subjects indicated a 90 percent confidence, the relative frequency of correct answers was only about 75 percent; and so on (Lichtenstein, Fischhoff, and Phillips 1982).

The initial demonstration of the "conjunction fallacy" was with problems of the following sort:

Linda is 31 years old, single, outspoken and very bright. She majored in philosophy. As a student, she was deeply concerned with issues of discrimination and social justice, and also participated in antinuclear demonstrations. (Tversky and Kahneman 1983: 299)

Subjects were asked which of two alternatives was more probable:

> Linda is a bank teller (T).
> Linda is a bank teller and is active in the feminist movement (T&F).

Eighty-five percent out of 142 subjects chose T&F. Tversky and Kahneman argue that this is incorrect because the probability of a conjunction of two events, such as T&F, can never be greater than that of one of its constituents.

Kahneman and Tversky presented base-rate neglect in the following famous demonstration. A group of students had to solve the engineer–lawyer problem:

A panel of psychologists have interviewed and administered personality tests to 30 engineers and 70 lawyers, all successful in their respective fields. On the basis of this information, thumbnail descriptions of the 30 engineers and 70 lawyers have been written. You will find on your forms five descriptions, chosen at random from the 100 available descriptions. For each description, please indicate your probability that the person described is an engineer, on a scale from 0 to 100. (Kahneman and Tversky 1973: 241–2)

A second group of students received the same instructions and the same descriptions, but were told that the base rates were 70 engineers and 30 lawyers (as opposed to 30 engineers and 70 lawyers). Kahneman and Tversky found that the mean response in both groups was essentially the same, and concluded that base rates were largely ignored, contrary to proper probabilistic considerations.

One systematic challenge to the import of these findings has been launched by Gerd Gigerenzer (1991). Gigerenzer's critique is two-pronged. First, he claims that the Tversky–Kahneman approach assumes a uniquely correct normative theory of probability, but there is no consensus about this normative matter or the proper interpretation of the probability calculus. Specifically, Gigerenzer argues that most of the Tversky–Kahneman claims assume that single events can be assigned probabilities, whereas this is denied by probability "frequentists." Second, Gigerenzer presents experimental evidence showing that when subjects are given analogous tasks that are formulated or are interpretable in frequentist terms, they perform vastly better than on the original tasks.

Starting with the overconfidence phenomenon, Gigerenzer first argues that probability theory is not violated if one's degree of belief in a single event is different from the relative frequency of correct answers one generates in the long run. So he suggests that what should be examined is people's estimated relative frequencies of correct answers and the true relative frequencies of correct answers. He carried out this experiment with colleagues, asking subjects to answer several hundred questions of the Islamabad–Hyderabad type and then having them estimate their relative frequencies of correct answers. The overconfidence phenomenon, he reports, *disappeared*. Estimated frequencies were practically identical with actual frequencies, with even a small tendency towards underestimation. Similar results were obtained when subjects estimated the relative frequencies of correct answers in each confidence category.

Concerning the conjunction fallacy, Gigerenzer first points out that, for a frequentist, the Linda problem has nothing to do with probability theory, because subjects are asked for the probability of a single event, not for frequencies. He proposes instead that the problem be posed in a frequentist mode, such as the following:

> There are 100 persons who fit the Linda description. How many of them are:
> (a) bank tellers,
> (b) bank tellers and active in the feminist movement?

When the experiment was conducted in this fashion by Fiedler (1988), the conjunction fallacy largely disappeared. In Fiedler's first experiment, for example, only 22 percent of the subjects given the frequency version violated the conjunction rule as compared with 91 percent of the subjects given the single-event version. When presented in frequentist terms, it appears, subjects have a far more accurate grasp of probability.

What about alleged base-rate neglect? Here Gigerenzer cites studies that support subjects' greater conformity with Bayesian reasoning when it is clearly indicated that random sampling is involved. For example, Gigerenzer, Hell, and Blank (1988) made subjects aware of random sampling in the engineer–lawyer problem by having them draw each description blindly out of an urn. In this condition subjects were closer to Bayesian predictions than to base-rate neglect (also see Nisbett *et al.* 1983). Other evidence also suggests that people's capacity to appreciate the relevance of base rates is a good deal stronger than initially supposed. Jonathan Koehler (1996) offers a wide survey of the literature, and concludes that the base-rate fallacy has been oversold. When base rates are directly experienced in trial-by-trial outcome feedback, for example, their impact on judgments increases. Manis *et al.* (1980) provided subjects with 50 yearbook pictures of male students and asked them to predict their attitudes about two legislative issues. After each prediction, some subjects were told that 20 percent of the targets favored the proposed legislation; other subjects were told that 80 percent of the targets favored the legislation. The influence of the feedback on base-rate usage was quick and dramatic. After viewing 20 pictures, subjects who experienced the 80 percent base rate were more than twice as likely to predict that a target person favored the proposed legislation than subjects who experienced the 20 percent base rate.

There has been a tendency to overemphasize base rates in normative assessment, even from a Bayesian standpoint, as Koehler points out (1996: 12). Although base rates should influence prior probabilities, they need not be the same. Prior to hearing the daily weather forecast, your estimate that it will snow tomorrow would rightly be based on much more information than the relative frequency for snow on this day in previous years. It should take into account such factors as yesterday's temperature, cloud formation, and so on. In such cases it is quite inappropriate to use an available base rate as one's prior probability. As Maya Bar-Hillel points out (1990), a prospective surgical patient who has been told that Surgeon *A*'s patient-mortality base rate is twice as high as that of Surgeon *B* might still reasonably believe that the probability of death is greater with Surgeon *B*. Surgeon *A*'s higher mortality rate might simply reflect a larger number of dangerous cases *A* has undertaken.

The foregoing discussion does not refute the heuristics-and-biases approach root and branch; it only shows that the magnitude, prevalence, and seriousness of such biases may have been exaggerated. Even if we concede the existence of cognitive biases, however, it remains to be seen how deleterious they are to scientific activity. One philosopher of science, Miriam Solomon (1992), not only suggests that cognitive bias is not fatal to science, but that such biases can sometimes produce *good* scientific results. Solomon argues that in one historical case, the case of continental drift, the use of cognitive heuristics such as salience and belief perseverance actually had a positive impact on the course of research. (Salience is the tendency to give disproportionate weight to vivid evidence, and belief perseverance is the tendency of old beliefs to persist in the face of counterevidence.) Different groups of scientists who studied the continental drift hypothesis in the twentieth century reacted differently to accumulating bodies of evidence. They gave greater weight to their own prior hunches and to new evidence that was more salient for them because it emerged from their own investigations. Solomon contends that the net upshot for the scientific community was that more diverse research avenues were pursued and this distribution of research effort ultimately served the community well. Of course, this type of success story is presented for only this specific episode in the annals of science. The general moral I would draw, however, is that it is premature to conclude that cold cognitive biases are inevitably fatal to the veritistic mission of science.

What about "hot" biases? In the philosophical literature, an extreme position on this question is called "doxastic voluntarism," the notion that one can *choose* to believe or disbelieve by a simple act of will. Historically endorsed by Descartes, it is nowadays quite controversial, and the reasons are straightforward. Begin with perceptual belief. When confronted in broad daylight with a desert landscape, you cannot "will" the belief that an ocean is there instead. Similarly with inferences. You might dearly hope that your favorite team won the championship last night, but if the morning paper reports a defeat, you naturally infer that they did indeed lose; you cannot abort this inference by a mere act of will. From a veritistic point of view, this is a good thing. If beliefs were readily molded by desires, this would threaten the ratio of true to false beliefs because desires are not systematically aligned with reality.

Despite the resistance of belief to *direct* voluntary control, both folk wisdom and research psychology suggest that there is such a thing as wishful thinking. This is relevant to science as well, since there is talk aplenty in science studies of the "contamination" of science by "interests." Science studies contains few detailed treatments (if any) of how, exactly, desires or preferences might influence beliefs, but it behooves us to consider what psychological research says on the subject.

Much of the psychological evidence that people sometimes believe what they want to believe concerns people's assessments of their own abilities. The average person believes extremely flattering things about him or herself, things that do not stand up to objective analysis, as Thomas Gilovich (1991) summarizes in a review of the literature. For example, a large majority of the public think that they are more intelligent, more fair-minded, less prejudiced, and more skilled behind the wheel of an automobile than the average person. This is known as the "Lake Wobegon effect," after Garrison Keillor's community where "the women are strong, the men are good-looking, and all the children are above average." A survey of one million high-school seniors found that *all* students thought they were above average in terms of ability to get along with others, 60 percent thought they were in the top 10 percent, and 25 percent thought they were in the top 1 percent (Gilovich 1991: 77). A survey of university professors found that 94 percent thought they were better at their jobs than their average colleague (Cross 1977).

The efficacy of the wish to believe is not confined to self-serving beliefs. In one study, subjects who preferred to believe that capital punishment is an effective deterrent to murder found support for such a belief in an equivocal body of evidence; those who preferred to believe it is not an effective deterrent found support for their position in the same body of evidence (Lord, Ross, and Lepper 1979). A study of the public's reaction to the Kennedy–Nixon debates in 1960 revealed that pro-Kennedy people thought Kennedy had won the debates and pro-Nixon people thought Nixon had won (Sears and Whitney 1973).

What mechanisms underlie the generation of wish-fulfilling beliefs? There is growing consensus among psychologists in the field that motivational influence on beliefs arises from subtle ways of searching and processing evidence. Gilovich explains it as follows:

When we prefer to believe something, we may approach the relevant evidence by asking ourselves, "what evidence is there to support this belief?" If we prefer to believe that a political assassination was not the work of a lone gunman, we may ask ourselves about the evidence that supports a conspiracy theory. Note that this question is not unbiased: It directs our attention to supportive evidence and away from information that might contradict the desired conclusion. Because it is almost always possible to uncover *some* supportive evidence, the asymmetrical way we frame the question makes us overly likely to become convinced of what we hope to be true. (1991: 81)

Ziva Kunda and her students found evidence that our preferences lead us to test hypotheses slanted toward confirmation in just this way. In one study, participants were led to believe that either introversion or extroversion was related to academic success. Those who were led to believe that introversion was predictive of success thought of themselves as more introverted than those who were led to believe that extroversion was associated with success. When asked to recall autobiographical events relevant to introversion/extroversion, those who were led to believe in the importance of introversion recalled more incidents of introversion, whereas those led to believe in the value of extroversion recalled more incidents of extroversion. By establishing a preference for one of these traits, the ease of generating evidence consistent with that trait was facilitated (Kunda and Sanitioso 1989).

People's preferences can influence not only the *kind* of information they consider but the *amount.*

When the initial evidence supports our preferences, we are generally satisfied and terminate our search; when the initial evidence is hostile, however, we often dig deeper, hoping to find more comforting information or to uncover reasons to believe that the original evidence was flawed. By taking advantage of "optional stopping" in this way, we dramatically increase our chances of finding satisfactory support for what we wish to be true. (Gilovich 1991: 82, reporting Diaconis 1978)

There is a limit, however, to the extent that "massaging the evidence" can determine beliefs; objectivity constrains the belief-formation process. This is argued forcefully by Kunda:

[P]eople motivated to arrive at a particular conclusion attempt to be rational and to construct a justification of their desired conclusion that would persuade a dispassionate observer. They draw the desired conclusion only if they can muster up the evidence necessary to support it . . . People will come to believe what they want to believe only to the extent that reason permits. Often they will be forced to acknowledge and accept undesirable conclusions, as they appear to when confronted with strong arguments for undesired or counterattitudinal positions. (Kunda 1990: 482–3)

For example, in the introversion–extroversion study, changes in self-concepts were constrained by prior knowledge. The subjects who were predominantly extroverted to begin with viewed themselves as less extroverted when they believed introversion to be more desirable, but they still viewed themselves as extroverted. Further evidence for such constraints was found in a study in which subjects were preselected for extroversion or introversion (Sanitioso, Kunda, and Fong 1990). Both groups viewed themselves as more extroverted when induced to believe that extroversion was beneficial than when induced to believe that introversion was beneficial. But in all conditions the extroverts still viewed themselves as considerably more extroverted than the introverts viewed themselves.

Further evidence of constraints on desire-driven belief is readily found in science, the prime area of our concern. Peter Galison comments on a team of particle physicists who were forced by the evidence to relinquish their view that there are no "neutral currents," although they had a great deal riding on this claim:

[I]t is stunning to reread Cline's memorandum . . . that began with the simple statement, "At present I do not see how to make this effect go away." With those words, Cline gave up his career-long commitment to the nonexistence of neutral currents. "Interest" had to bow to the linked assemblage of ideas and empirical results that rendered the old beliefs untenable. (Galison 1987: 258)

Kunda also emphasizes that people can be motivated to arrive not only at a particular, directional conclusion but at an accurate conclusion. Certain studies demonstrate that manipulations designed to increase motives for accuracy eliminate or reduce cognitive biases. Kruglanski and Freund (1983) found that subjects motivated to be accurate (because they expected to be evaluated, expected to justify their judgments, etc.) showed less of a primacy effect in impression formation, less tendency to use ethnic stereotypes in their evaluations of essay quality, and less anchoring when making probability judgments. If scientists are motivated for accuracy, they too will presumably engage in better styles of reasoning. Peer pressure from other scientists provides precisely such an incentive, since scientists are constantly asked to justify their judgments to others.[2]

Furthermore, as Gilovich emphasizes, scientists utilize a set of formal procedures that help guard against biases from desire and preference. Control groups and random sampling, for example, help them avoid using incomplete and unrepresentative data. So it is unwarranted to conclude that truth or accuracy is simply beyond the reach of human cognition, and especially unwarranted to draw this conclusion for science. Motivation-driven reasoning has a robust reality, but there are limits to the epistemic damage it can inflict, especially on science.

Let me emphasize the point that science has no free ride to the truth, and that biases of various sorts can and do operate in science. In addition to the cold and hot biases already reviewed in this section, science studies calls attention to ways in which values and cultural perspectives sometimes guide the framing of hypotheses and the gathering of evidence. One prominent set of stories comes from the history of primate research. About forty years ago pri-

---

[2] Peer pressure for justification does not guarantee, of course, that scientists will abandon whatever initial biases they may bring to a problem. It does place constraints, however, on the public defenses they can offer of biased conclusions, and these constraints can be expected to have impact on their private reasoning as well. But, it may be asked, does argument crafted to respond to scientific peers really provide any inoculation against bias? In support of skepticism about reason, Hilary Kornblith (1998) contends that the more detailed and carefully crafted the argument, the greater the suspicion that rationalization, and hence bias, is at work! This strikes me as unduly pessimistic. Careful craftsmanship in argument production, I suspect, is mainly due to participation in strictly norm-governed activities of public justification, of which science is a paradigm. It remains to be shown that higher levels of care are correlated with higher levels of bias. Kornblith has no empirical evidence for this. It should be noted, incidentally, that the style of skepticism Kornblith advocates in this paper is not *total* skepticism. His version of skepticism about reason admits that rational belief is not only possible, but often actual.

matologists began studying savanna baboons in the hope that they might
illuminate the life of our human ancestors. Baboon troops are very male-
dominated; they also form shifting alliances with other males to get better
access to females. Primatologists concluded that the males' behavior was the
crucial determinant of social cohesion, and inferred that this is the paradigm
of all primate social life. This inference was undoubtedly abetted by culture-
imbued assumptions about aggressive males. Later, however, primatologists
recognized that they have to study every individual in a troop, not just the
biggest, most aggressive, or most salient. They then amassed examples of other
types of primates in which females as well as males maintain social cohesion,
and cooperation rather than aggression is the rule (Smuts 1985; Strum 1987).
Similarly, beginning in the 1940s, the standard biologist's view on sexual
selection was that males are prone toward promiscuity but females are coy and
choosy—a strikingly Victorian perspective. This was initially rooted in studies
on *Drosophila*, which were extrapolated to nature at large (Hrdy 1986). It took
studies by *women* primatologists to discover that female primates commonly
solicit males other than their so-called harem leaders. Female langurs, for
example, will leave their natal troops to travel temporarily with all-male bands
and mate with males there (Hrdy 1986).

   These stories from the history of primatology suggest that extrascientific
perspectives can guide and sometimes warp the course of science, but they
hardly support total skepticism about the prospects of science. For one thing,
the observations and generalizations about baboon troops and *Drosophila*
were not inaccurate. The problem lay in rash generalizations from inadequately varied samples of evidence. Successful science often does require individuals with different perspectives to frame and investigate new hypotheses;
and in some sectors of science, such as primatology, fruitful hypotheses may
stem from scientists' personal experience arising from gender and even empathy. But, to repeat, none of this shows that science is incapable of finding
truth, or even that it has a greater propensity toward falsehood than alternative (nonscientific) ways of learning about nature.

8.4 *The theory ladenness of observation*

The next two challenges to scientific objectivity I shall consider originate
within the mainstream of philosophy of science, the first being the so-called
"theory ladenness" of observation. Science's alleged access to truths of Nature
rests critically on observation, or perception. The empirical method presumes
that careful, disciplined observation can get Nature to disclose its secrets. But
can science legitimately rest so securely on observation? This is what the doctrine of theory ladenness challenges. The core contention of theory ladenness
is that observation is infected with, contaminated by, or "shot through and
through" with the observer's theoretical commitments. There is no such thing

as pure, unadulterated perception. What an observer perceives is not simply a function of the stimuli that impinge on his receptors, but of the theoretical views that he brings to the perceptual act.

Such themes are found in the writings of two theory-ladenness proponents, Thomas Kuhn and Nelson Goodman. Kuhn writes: "[P]aradigm changes . . . cause scientists to see the world of their research-engagement differently . . . It is as elementary prototypes for these transformations of the scientist's world that the familiar demonstrations of a switch in visual gestalt prove so suggestive" (Kuhn 1962: 110). "What a man sees depends both upon what he looks at and also upon what his previous visual–conceptual experience has taught him to see" (Kuhn 1962: 112). "[A]fter the assimilation of Franklin's paradigm, the electrician looking at a Leyden jar saw something different from what he had seen before . . . Lavoisier . . . saw oxygen where Priestley had seen dephlogisticated air and where others had seen nothing at all" (Kuhn 1962: 117). "Practicing in different worlds, the two groups of scientists [who accept competing paradigms] see different things when they look from the same point in the same direction" (Kuhn 1962: 149). Nelson Goodman cites psychological research in support of theory ladenness. In the "phi phenomenon," where two spots of light are flashed a short distance apart and in quick succession, the viewer normally *supplements* the stimuli and sees a spot of light moving continuously along a path from the first position to the second (Goodman 1978: 15–16). Artists make frequent use of the observer's tendency to supplement or "fill in":

[A] lithograph by Giacometti fully presents a walking man by sketches of nothing but the head, hands, and feet in just the right postures and positions against an expanse of blank paper; and a drawing by Katharine Sturgis conveys a hockey player in action by a single charged line. That we find what we are prepared to find (what we look for or what forcefully affronts our expectations), and that we are likely to be blind to what neither helps nor hinders our pursuits, are commonplaces of everyday life and amply attested in the psychological laboratory. (Goodman 1978: 14)

What is the intended epistemological moral of the theory-ladenness doctrine, assuming it is true? At least two distinct morals might be distinguished. The first is that observation is not a neutral arbiter among competing theories, because scientists of different theoretical persuasions will tend to make different observations. If theory T_1 predicts observation O, a scientist who accepts T_1 will see (or judge that) O. If theory T_2 predicts observation O', a scientist who accepts T_2 will see (or judge that) O', where O and O' are incompatible. Thus, observation will be incapable of settling their theoretical disagreement, of choosing between their theoretical frameworks. Another version of this moral stems from a variant formulation of theory ladenness which denies a "theory-neutral observation language" (Feyerabend 1962). If different theories have wholly disjoint observational vocabularies, adherents of different theories will not agree on what is observed. So how can observation force rival theorists to agree on theoretical matters?

From my veritistic perspective, failure of agreement is not the central problem. The central problem is the threat to truth. If observation is infected by theory, what reason is there to expect observation to yield truths? Commitment to a false theory could lead to mistaken observations; the reliability of observation is threatened by the intrusion of theoretical allegiances. Since I am primarily interested in the veritistic properties of observation, it is the second possible moral that chiefly concerns me. But let me look briefly at the problem of reaching agreement.

We must first distinguish questions about observational judgments versus questions about observational experience itself (assuming these are distinguishable). If scientists come to an experiment with different theoretical concepts, they may classify what they see in different (and incompatible) terms; some of their observational judgments will differ. Is there any way to resolve this difference? In general, scientists can retreat to more minimal and unproblematic categorizations of what they see. They can turn to descriptions of the events in more narrowly visual terms (Kitcher 1993: 226–7; Shapere 1982; Pinch 1985). Commonality of judgments is to be expected using these more neutral categories, as long as experiences themselves do not diverge. Proponents of theory ladenness may retort, however, that perceptual experience itself will differ as a function of each perceiver's theoretical background. Is this right? Is the theory-ladenness doctrine, so construed, psychologically accurate?

Jerry Fodor (1984) challenges theory ladenness on psychological grounds. Many defenders of theory ladenness, such as Kuhn, Goodman, and Russell Hanson, invoked New Look psychology of the 1950s. Fodor argues that the contentions of New Look psychology are dubious. Is it true that what one knows or believes always shapes what one sees? Consider the Müller-Lyer illusion, says Fodor, in which one of two parallel lines looks longer than the other although actually they are of equal length. Even if the viewer is familiar with the figure, and *knows* that the lines are equal, the one line still *looks* longer than its mate. In other words, "theoretical" knowledge does not prod the visual system into changing the appearance it produces. Thus, appearances are not shaped willy-nilly by theoretical beliefs. Another of Fodor's examples also addresses the New Look claim that expectations shape perception. As a matter of theoretical expectation, nobody would *expect* a lecturer to say, in the middle of a philosophical discourse, "Piglet gave Pooh a stiffening sort of nudge, and Pooh, who felt more and more that he was somewhere else, got up slowly and began to look for himself." Despite the theoretical improbability of such an utterance, one would still hear and understand it if it were made. Contrary to New Look psychology, we don't hear only what we expect to hear. Thus, there is no reason to hold that someone with a theoretical allegiance will never perceive or observe anything that conflicts with his theory's predictions.

Fodor concedes that observation is a matter of "inference," and background information is utilized as "premises" by perceptual systems. But on Fodor's (1983) view perceptual systems are *modular*, which implies that the range of information to which the system has access is highly restricted. In his terminology, modular systems are "informationally encapsulated." Perceptual systems do not have access to knowledge contained in the "central system," which is where scientifically acquired theories would be lodged. According to Fodor, then, a correct psychology does not support the theory-ladenness doctrine.

Although Fodor's examples are instructive, the psychology of observation is an enormously complicated subject, and not everyone agrees with Fodor's views. In particular, most cognitive scientists recognize such phenomena as "top-down" processing, context effects, priming effects, and the impact of stored knowledge on perception. Consider subjects in a speech-shadowing experiment who are required to repeat aloud what they hear as accurately and with as little delay as possible. When distortions are introduced in the latter portion of a word—as in pronouncing *cigaresh* for *cigarette*—shadowers will frequently restore it to its proper pronunciation (Marslen-Wilson and Welsh 1978). In other words, they will incorrectly hear—or at least report hearing—*cigarette*. This looks like a case in which "theoretical" knowledge infects perception.

What is unclear, however, is under what precise stimulus and perceiver conditions such errors occur. In the previous example, the stimulus is heard very briefly, the distortion occurs at the end of the word only, and the task demands require attention to many other stimuli and very swift responses. There is no reason to suppose that comparable errors will occur under all stimulus conditions, no matter what the temporal parameters are, for example. This is particularly relevant to the issue of scientific observation. Scientists, after all, can arrange for types of observation that minimize the probability of perceptual error. Certain types of scientific data, for example, are photographs or instrument printouts that can be examined by observers quite leisurely and circumspectly. Needless to say, scientists with different theoretical beliefs may still disagree about the disputed *causes* of observed marks, tracks, or features in photographs or printouts they examine. But in terms of more primitive, less contentious, types of descriptions of these observable objects, there can be extensive agreement and accuracy.

Science also has another way to dodge the threat of theory-tainted observation: conduct experiments in a *blind*—or "double blind"—fashion. If an observer is ignorant of the conditions of an experiment—exactly what manipulations have been performed—she cannot use her theory to form expectations about the experimental outcome. The theory has no way of contaminating her observation of the outcome. So even if expectations are capable of shaping perceptions to fit their image, blinding the observer to the experimental manipulations circumvents the danger. In many sectors of science today, such a stratagem is intensively utilized. Thus, the theory-laden-ness doctrine does not constitute a fundamental and unavoidable obstacle to observational accuracy in science.

8.5 *Underdetermination of theory*

Theory ladenness is one of two doctrines that have cast serious doubts over the prospects for scientific objectivity. The second of these doctrines is the underdetermination of theory. Even if scientific observations are granted objectivity, what objective methodology is there for inferring the truth of any particular theory? Proponents of underdetermination claim that there is no methodology for inferring particular theories from the data, or even for favor-ing one theory over another. W. V. Quine (1953, 1960) has claimed that theor-ies are so radically underdetermined by the data that a scientist can, if he wishes, hold on to *any* theory he likes "come what may." This conclusion has led sociologists of science and their followers to draw strong conclusions about the role of nonepistemic factors in science. Mary Hesse (1980: ch. 2) and David Bloor (1981) have claimed that underdetermination shows the neces-sity for bringing social factors into the explanation of theory choice—on the grounds that evidential considerations are demonstrably insufficient to explain these choices. Harry Collins (1981) has claimed that underdetermi-nation lends credence to the view that the world does little if anything to constrain our beliefs about it. These conclusions, however, are entirely unwar-ranted, as amply demonstrated by Larry Laudan's (1990) critique of the under-determination doctrine. I can do no better than review selected highlights of Laudan's critique.

Quine has been the leading exponent of the underdetermination thesis, but he has really offered two distinct doctrines. The weaker doctrine is a *non-uniqueness thesis*. It holds that, for any theory *T* and any body of evidence sup-porting *T*, there is at least one rival (that is, contrary) theory to *T* that is as well supported as *T*. This weak doctrine, however, is compatible with the nonrela-tivist view that, for many pairs of theories, one is better supported than the other. A much stronger and more influential thesis Quine suggests is the *egal-itarian thesis*: Every theory is as well supported by the evidence as any of its rivals. Quine nowhere explicitly formulates the thesis in precisely this form, but Laudan argues that many of his pronouncements presuppose it. The egal-itarian thesis is essentially equivalent to what Laudan calls the *equirationality of all theoretical systems*, which he formulates as follows:

> (ER) It is rational to hold on to any theory whatever in the face of any evid-ence whatever.

This is strongly implied in the following famous passage: "Any statement can be held true come what may, if we make drastic enough adjustments elsewhere in the system" (Quine 1953: 43).

As Laudan shows, however, Quine nowhere provides an exhaustive examination of possible rules of rational theory choice with a view to showing them impotent to decide between all pairs of theories. The principal argument, which Quine derives from Pierre Duhem, is that a threatened statement or theory can always be immunized from recalcitrant evidence by making suitable adjustments in our auxiliary theories. The failure of a prediction falsifies only a block of theory as a whole, a conjunction of many statements. The failure shows that one or more of those statements is false, but it does not show which. The underdetermination theory in this guise, which Laudan calls *Quinean underdetermination*, is formulated as follows:

(QUD) Any theory can be reconciled with any recalcitrant evidence by making suitable adjustments in our other assumptions about nature.

Laudan's main point about (QUD)—an important point—is that (QUD) drops any reference to the *rationality* of theory choices. It is doubtless possible to jettison a whole load of auxiliaries in order to save a threatened theory (where "save" means "make it logically compatible with the evidence"). But Quine does not establish the reasonableness or rationality of doing so, as (ER) demands. Saving a threatened theory by abandoning the auxiliary assumptions once needed to link it with recalcitrant evidence comes at a price. If we give up those beliefs without replacement, we not only abandon an ability to say anything whatever about the phenomena that produced the recalcitrant experience; we also give up the ability to explain all the other things which those now-rejected auxiliaries enabled us to give an account of—with no guarantee that we can find alternatives that will match their explanatory scope. As Laudan concludes, "[I]f it is plausible . . . to hold that scientists are aiming . . . at producing theories with broad explanatory scope and impressive empirical credentials, then it has to be said that Quine has given us no arguments to suppose that any theory we like can be doctored up so as to win high marks on those scores" (1990: 276).

A recurring problem with Quine's various endorsements of underdetermination is that they seem to hold only under purely "deductivist" approaches to empirical support. As Laudan rightly insists, however, that is an unjustifiably restricted vision of what a scientific method might be like. Quine assumes that if two theories enjoy precisely the same set of known confirming instances, they must have the same empirical or evidential support. But this is not necessarily so. According to Bayesianism, for example, rival theories sharing the same known positive instances, or deductive consequences, are not necessarily equally well confirmed, because the two theories might begin with different prior probabilities. Many other principles of rational theory choice might also introduce further distinguishing features.

After arguing the weakness of the underdetermination doctrine, Laudan
also shows how unrelated that doctrine is to any thesis about social factors in
science. Writers like Hesse and Bloor apparently think that since deduction
underdetermines theory choice, scientists must supplement deduction with
social rather than logical factors. But why suppose that everything is either
deductive logic or sociology? Why couldn't some form of inductive or abduc-
tive reasoning—neither of which is purely logical or social—be causally
responsible for theory choices? For our purposes, then, there are two major
upshots. First, no rationality-threatening version of the underdetermination
thesis has been persuasively defended. Second, even if the underdetermination thesis were right, it would imply nothing about the role of social factors
in science.

8.6 *Scientific realism and the veritistic superiority of science*

The preceding sections defused a variety of challenges to a veritistic analysis
of science. This section clarifies my own approach by comparing and contrasting it with related approaches in philosophy of science. I am attracted to
standard forms of realism in philosophy of science, but I am also sensitive to
the difficulties and intricacies of attempting to defend realism over antirealism in satisfactory detail. Given the limitations of space, I am going to defend
a more modest doctrine, one which is nonetheless suited to the veritistic message of this volume.

What is scientific realism? An initial formulation of the position, which he
calls "naive," is suggested by Bas van Fraassen:

The picture which science gives us of the world is a true one, faithful in its details,
and the entities postulated in science really exist: the advances of science are discoveries, not inventions. (1980: 7)

This formulation has the right flavor, but the position it describes would satisfy few philosophers, as van Fraassen points out. For one thing, it saddles the
scientific realist with the belief that today's theories are correct, which few
philosophers of science would endorse. Maybe science is only moving toward
the truth and hasn't reached it yet; perhaps the growth of science is a process
of endless self-correction. It does capture the tenor of realism, however, to
characterize scientific theory as a story about what there really is and as an
enterprise of discovery rather than invention. As this suggests, however, it
seems better to describe scientific realism as a view about the *aims* of science,
not its actual success—present or future—in achieving these aims. Van
Fraassen therefore offers the following formulation of scientific realism:

Science aims to give us, in its theories, a literally true story of what the world is
like; and acceptance of a scientific theory involves the belief that it is true.
(1980: 8)

Van Fraassen himself rejects realism even under this "aim" construal. He appears to accept it insofar as scientific theories are concerned solely with observable events. Insofar as they make statements about unobservables, however, he says that science does not aim at truth, merely at "empirical adequacy".

Science aims to give us theories that are empirically adequate; and acceptance of a theory involves as belief only that it is empirically adequate. (1980: 12)

He calls his version of antirealism "constructive empiricism." Notice that he does not deny that the meanings of scientific theories transcend the observables; nor does he deny that such theories are literally true or false. He only denies that science is concerned with their (full) truth or falsity. Instead, he says, science is only concerned with the observable (empirical) consequences of a theory. Now the observable consequences of a theory—the "phenomena" it implies—will in general be quite vast. They will not be exhausted by the phenomena actually observed now or even at some future time. So to say that science is concerned to have theories that "save the phenomena" still ascribes a very difficult project to science; it is no trivial matter to formulate a theory with observable implications that are wholly correct. Moreover, van Fraassen ascribes to science an aim that is quite veritistic, in my sense. To accept a theory, he says, is to believe that it is empirically adequate. A belief that a theory is empirically adequate, then, is either true or false: either all its observable implications are correct or they are not all correct. So van Fraassen ascribes to science the aim of helping its practitioners believe certain truths, namely, truths about the empirical adequacy of theories. This aim is certainly different from the one posited by scientific realism, but it is still a veritistic aim.

As indicated earlier, I am a wholehearted scientific realist; but the project of veritistic epistemology, applied to science, does not require scientific realism. The project can proceed quite cheerfully in tandem with van Fraassen's brand of antirealism. Veritistic epistemology could ask how well science works, and how it might be improved, in generating knowledge about empirical adequacy. For this reason, the project of veritistic evaluation should not be equated with, or restricted to, scientific realism.

I conclude, then, that science has truth-oriented aims, whether or not the truths extend beyond the observable or are restricted to observables. Are science's aims *exclusively* truth-oriented? Philosophers of science would hasten to identify other virtues of theories: simplicity, explanatory power, and so forth. I suggest that these items are best treated, not as virtues separate from and additional to truth, but as demarcating *kinds* of true propositions that science is especially interested in finding. Let me explain.

Science does not ask the same questions as other branches of inquiry. It mainly seeks to uncover natural laws, causal and explanatory relations between events, and so on. This does not imply, though, that science has interests other than truth. It just means that science is interested in true answers to a special class of questions, questions about lawful relations, explanatory relations, causal relations, and so forth. Science seeks answers to such questions as "What are the causes of cancer?" and "What caused the extinction of the dinosaurs?" In each case it seeks true answers to these questions. The same holds for simplicity and explanatory power. Science is particularly interested in finding answers to the questions, "What theory explains such-and-such a set of phenomena?" "What is the simplest theory that would explain X, Y, and Z?" and so forth. This is how I would incorporate the so-called "supraempirical virtues" within a veritistic framework.

Another reason philosophers shy away from truth is their conviction that science rarely gives us *exact* truth, at best only *approximate* truth (e.g., Cartwright 1983). So some philosophers think we should give an account of science in terms of an aim slightly different from truth, namely, "approximate truth," or "verisimilitude." Unfortunately, it has proved difficult to give a satisfactory definition of verisimilitude (Popper 1972; D. Miller 1974; Niiniluoto 1982; Tichy 1978; Oddie 1986). I propose to re-express this idea in a slight, though significant, variant. Although scientists aim to believe genuine truths, they recognize that the statements they typically formulate, especially lawlike formulas, are not precisely true. They do not, however, actually *believe* those statements. The sort of proposition they typically believe is not one expressed by a formula "F," but one with the content "F, to some approximation," where the kind and range of approximation varies with the problem and context of application. Since the approximation qualifier is often suitably chosen, the believed propositional content is often actually true, not just "approximately true." Moreover, there is no need to define a special notion of approximate truth, distinct from truth, to account for the aims or achievements of science.

Thus far I have argued that science's *aim* is veritistic. What about its success in achieving this aim? Does science have any special capacity or power to lead inquirers toward truth, any superior veritistic quality, virtue, or authority? The postmodern chorus intones "No," of course. Science has no special epistemic authority. What does veritistic epistemology say? At its starting point, veritistic epistemology is not committed to the veritistic superiority of science. Veritistic epistemology seeks to evaluate or assess the veritistic properties of many practices or clusters of practices, and it begins from a stance of theoretical neutrality toward these sundry practices. The business of veritistic epistemology, to be sure, is to give better grades to some practices than to others. But it is not committed *at the outset* to the principle that science must get high grades. A sketch of how veritistic epistemology can examine the practice of science is illustrated in the remainder of the chapter. I shall give reasons that support the (relatively) superior veritistic quality of science, at least for several of its subpractices. My analysis will not suggest, however, that science cannot be improved. On the contrary, identification of possible weaknesses or modes of improvement is an important dimension of veritistic epistemology. Before turning to such details, though, let me be more specific about the sense in which science might be a "superior" set of cognitive practices, or might have a certain epistemic "authority."

As we saw earlier, few philosophers of science would wish to claim that science has cognitive authority in the sense that it *now* has true theories. Even the claim that most observational predictions of current science are true might be met with skepticism. A more popular line is to hold that, even if the sciences have only a modest amount of truth right now, they are gradually making *progress* toward truth. As time goes on, mature sciences move closer and closer to theoretical truth. This kind of doctrine has been defended by Hilary Putnam (1978), Richard Boyd (1983), Michael Devitt (1984), and Philip Kitcher (1993), among others. Larry Laudan (1981) calls it "convergent realism." I find this an attractive claim about science (especially in the version told by Kitcher), but it too is somewhat precarious. Laudan (1981) has posed some serious problems for existing versions of convergent realism, and it is not feasible to explore this controversy here.

I propose, therefore, to advance a more cautious thesis as the most tenable formulation of the epistemic authority of science. Instead of making categorical or absolute claims about the veritistic success of science, or its rate of veritistic improvement, I shall restrict my defense of science to its *comparative* veritistic performance: how well it performs, or has performed, in comparison with rival, nonscientific practices that try to tackle the same questions. So the thesis I shall endorse may be called the thesis of *comparative scientific superiority*.

(CSS) Scientific practices are veritistically better than any set of non-scientific practices available to human beings for answering the sorts of questions that science seeks to answer.

Thesis (CSS) is admittedly pretty vague, owing in part to the vagueness of the term "scientific." Some practices, both actual historical practices and merely possible ones, might be hard to classify as clearly scientific or clearly nonscientific. But vague statements are not worthless. There is sufficient clarity concerning what qualifies as scientific and nonscientific that (CSS) is a significant doctrine, the truth of which is worth examining.

There is another dimension of vagueness in (CSS), however, that complicates matters. Since science, historically speaking, is really a succession of evolving practices, precisely which scientific practices does (CSS) claim to be superior to which nonscientific ones? Several refinements of (CSS) are possible. The strongest version would say that even the worst scientific practices are veritistically superior to the best nonscientific ones. A weaker version would say that the best scientific practices are superior to the best nonscientific ones. Even focusing on just the weaker version, at least two interpretations are available, one focusing on historically actual practices and a second focusing on possible practices. In other words, (CSS) might mean (A) that the best actually used scientific practices are better than the best actually used nonscientific practices, or (B) that the best possible scientific practices are better than the best possible nonscientific practices. For most purposes, I prefer the best/best and actual/actual interpretation. That is: the best actual scientific practices are veritistically superior to the best actual nonscientific practices. But I reserve the right to examine different interpretations as the context dictates.

The domain restriction in (CSS) warrants emphasis. (CSS) does not assert that science is more reliable in its domain than nonscientific practices are in theirs. Suppose, for example, that introspection is a nonscientific practice.[3] It could well turn out that introspection's accuracy vis-à-vis conscious states is higher than science's accuracy about theoretical physics. This assumed fact would not constitute a counterexample to (CSS), however, because introspection is not veritistically superior to science at answering questions about the fundamental nature of the physical universe. The domain restriction is critical. Science investigates some of the most complex questions humans try to answer, so it would be unfair to downgrade it for having a worse track record than nonscientific methods if the latter are only applied to, and perhaps are only applicable to, much easier questions.

8.7 *The case for scientific superiority*

What defense can be given of (CSS)? Debates among philosophers and historians of science often concentrate on science's most sophisticated dimension: its theoretical posits. I think that the case for (CSS) can partly be made in that arena. Although changes in theoretical posits cannot always be interpreted as progress, as Laudan stresses (1981),[4] there are certainly large and important periods of veritistic progress. Philip Kitcher makes important responses to Laudan's alleged "confutation" of convergent realism by focusing attention on specific *parts* of theories that contributed to success or error (1993: 141–9). The assessment of science's veritistic merits in the theoretical domain, however, is a tricky business, and transcends the scope of this work.

Fortunately, a defense of (CSS) does not require a demonstration of science's superiority to nonscience in the theoretical domain. It will suffice that science is merely *noninferior* to nonscience in that domain, and this seems

---

[3] I argue elsewhere (Goldman 1997) that introspection may well be a scientifically legitimate practice. This suggestion can be ignored, however, for purposes of the present illustration.

[4] For example, Laudan points to the various aether theories of the 1830s and 1840s. They were highly successful in empirical terms, but—at least by our present lights—they did not constitute veritistic progress in the theoretical domain, because their central theoretical posits, the various types of aether, do not exist. The theoretical term "aether" refers to nothing (Laudan 1981: 26 ff.).

like a fairly easy case to make. Historically, what did nonscience produce by way of widely accepted theoretical posits, both entities and causal powers? First, there were the strange beasties of yore: elves, gremlins, leprechauns, nymphs, ghosts, and the like. Then there were the agents of witchcraft and sorcery. Next there were astrological theories about the causal impact of the stars on human affairs.[5] Finally, there were deities of many, many kinds, in each and every culture. Atheistic readers will grant straightaway that beliefs in those deities constituted rampant falsehood. Theistic readers should be reminded that even if they are right in believing that *their* God exists, they are unlikely to cede truth to past theistic beliefs in *rival* deities: the posited gods of the ancient Greeks, the Norse gods, the tribal gods of the Canaanites, and so forth. So when it comes to nonscientifically posited unobservables, the track record of nonscience is surely not superior to that of science.

However, I shall not push my case for overall scientific superiority on a marked superiority in the theoretical sphere. The "demonstrable" superiority of science comes in a more prosaic terrain. Although science's loftiest endeavors and principal research targets often concern theoretical propositions, a more homely set of propositions is also of interest to science: singular predictions of observable events. Consider predictions about such mundane matters as tomorrow's weather, the next eclipse of the sun, how to avoid contracting a certain disease, and whether a nuclear reaction will be started under specifiable conditions. In all such cases, there is little doubt that people who deploy appropriate scientific methods have vastly better track records of belief than people who lack such methods (and cannot appeal to others who do possess them). Meteorologists are not perfect predictors of the next day's weather, but surely their beliefs—or degrees of belief—about the weather, when based on all available information, are veritistically superior to those of lay people. A layperson, of course, can listen nightly to meteorologists and arrive at equally good predictive beliefs (or DBs) without personally using scientific methods. The layperson's beliefs, however, are derivative from scientific practices, and their accuracy owes as much to science as the accuracy of the meteorologists' beliefs. Similarly, medical researchers and practitioners can predict with considerable reliability whether a given vaccine will or will not prevent a recipient from contracting a certain disease, and the correctness of their beliefs is undoubtedly attributable to scientific practices. Prior to scientific medicine, knowledge of successful prevention techniques was woefully impoverished. Nonscientific methods simply did not yield many true answers to questions like "What treatment would prevent or cure disease *D*?" Science has provided

---

[5] Admittedly, it is not so clear that astrology falls on the nonscience line of the boundary, since it owes its origins to Aristotelian science. From the perspective of modern belief systems, however, it should be classified as nonscience, since it is no longer treated as even a *candidate* scientific theory. Alchemy is omitted here because it was plausibly a science throughout the period during which it was entertained.

vastly more true answers. Even if laypersons also believe, for example, that a certain type of vaccine will prevent polio, their knowledge obviously derives from science. Similarly, correct predictive knowledge of the next solar eclipse, or the date that a comet will return, is based on scientific knowledge that was simply unavailable prior to modern scientific astronomy.

These simple and obvious kinds of knowledge understandably breed popular recognition of science's veritistic superiority. It is a mistake to let philosophically abstruse questions about theoretical frameworks or referential success obscure these mundane areas of scientific superiority. No doubt, high rates of knowledge of singular predictive statements are often closely intertwined with knowledge about theoretical entities and lawful regularities. But we need not enter the debate about these matters to establish science's superiority. Since science is assuredly no worse than nonscience in matters of theory, and is transparently better than nonscience in generating accurate observable predictions on many topics, its overall track record is clearly superior. How can (CSS) seriously be doubted?

8.8 *Sources of scientific success*

Which facets of science that distinguish it from nonscience are responsible for its veritistic superiority? This is not so easy to say. I begin with a rough catalogue of practices that distinguish science from nonscience, and take some passing shots at which of these are the principal determinants of science's (comparative) veritistic success. This again is a topic that deserves lengthier treatment; mine will, perforce, be abbreviated. One reason for this is that not all veritistically significant practices of science are *social* practices, and given the emphasis of this book, more detailed attention will be devoted to them.

Here is a short list of some central facets or dimensions of science that seem veritistically significant:

(1) An emphasis on precise measurement, controlled test, and observation, including a philosophy, organon, and technology for more and more powerful observation.

(2) A systematic and sophisticated set of inferential principles for drawing conclusions about hypotheses from observations of experimental results.

(3) The marshaling and distribution of resources to facilitate scientific investigation and observation.

(4) A system of credit and reward that provides incentives for workers to engage in scientific research and to distribute their efforts in chosen directions.

(5) A system for disseminating scientific findings and theories as well as critical assessments of such findings and theories.

(6) The use of domain-specific expertise in making decisions about dissemination, resource allocation, and rewards.

Perhaps the most distinctive feature of empirical science is its requirement that belief be founded on precise measurement and careful test, rather than old wives' tales, Scripture, or the unsubstantiated opinions of dubious authorities. The Fellows of the early Royal Society, as we saw, established the philosophy of observation and experiment as a hallmark of science. Here is a list of their early experiments, designed to test a number of old wives' tales:

Experiments of destroying *Mites* by several fumes; of the equivocal Generation of *Insects*; of feeding a *Carp* in the Air; of making insects with Cheese, and Sack; of killing Water-Newts, Toads, and Slowworms with several Salts; of killing Frogs, by touching their skin, with Vinegar, Pitch, or Mercury; of a Spiders not being inchanted by a Circle of *Unicorns-horn*, or Irish Earth, laid round about it. (Sprat 1958: 223)

Who would deny that careful measurements and observational tests provided a better basis for believing or disbelieving these old wives' tales than naive trust and credulity? This is a simple illustration of the veritistic superiority of science over at least one nonscientific practice (though perhaps not the best practice nonscience has to offer).

Another critical feature of science, part and parcel of its investment in observation, is the invention, calibration, and utilization of ever more powerful and accurate instruments of observation. A classic example is the telescope, which in Galileo's hands led to the discovery, among other things, of the moons of Jupiter.[6] Contemporary science, of course, is awash with instrumentation. Medical science uses microscopes, gastroscopes, colonoscopes, and so forth to observe cells and organs not otherwise perceivable. Neuroscience uses PET scans, CAT scans, and MRI technology to observe brain activity. Particle physics employs accelerators to observe the behavior of small particles when they collide. Does anyone seriously contend that knowledge would be better served by dispensing with this instrumentation and relying on unassisted eyes and ears?

Notice that even the self-styled demystifiers of science, the social constructivists, themselves engage in observation to try to establish their accounts of science. To take a noted example discussed in Chapter 1 (Latour and Woolgar 1986), Latour himself entered a scientific laboratory to *observe* what scientists do there. In other words, he and his coauthor adopted the field research methods of scientific ethnologists in order to study what transpires in biological science. Their own practice, then, belies their avowed contention that science has no better way to establish truth than nonscience. They implicitly concede

---

[6] For detailed discussion of how the reliability of the telescope was established, including its use in terrestrial observation, see Hacking 1983: ch. 11 and Kitcher 1993: 227–33.

that scientific observation is a sounder way to establish an account of science than any nonscientific, nonobservational methodology.

It may be replied that Latour and Woolgar simply did what it takes to persuade their audience. Since their audience was enamored of science, they adopted scientific methods in order to convince them. Their practice isn't committed to the view that observations establish any truth about science. Indeed, they themselves write: "In a fundamental sense, our own account is no more than *fiction*" (1986: 257). But is this assessment of their own work entirely candid and plausible? Surely not. Why go to all the work of visiting the Salk Institute, making observations, and recording notes over a lengthy period of time if the intent was to write fiction? Moreover, don't they want their audience to believe that *their* social constructivist stories about science are more accurate than the stories told by realists? If their observations are not intended to provide good evidence for the truth of their stories, their extended argumentation based on that evidence is thoroughly misleading and disingenuous.

Science also includes what I called an "organon" for observation, which includes principles for *what* to observe and how to *describe* what is observed. The latter includes different types of scaling methods and measurements. The former includes choices of observational subject matter depending on the kind of scientific inquiry conducted. In experimental studies the investigator may want to know whether a certain "dependent variable" causally depends on a certain "independent variable." The experimenter manipulates the independent variable in the experiment and observes the effect on the dependent variable. In this kind of inquiry, the methodology is to make observations on two separate groups: the experimental group and the control group, the latter being a group to which the experimenter's manipulation is not applied.

The rationale for these kinds of manipulations and observations is linked, of course, to the kinds of licensed or unlicensed inferences to conclusions about hypotheses. Thus, observational methodology is closely connected with inferential practices, our second category of scientific practices. For example, only by comparing the properties or responses of an experimental group with a control group can one be in a position to draw a scientifically licensed inference of causal relevance between the independent and dependent variables. Nonscientific practice is replete with conclusions about causal efficacy that are not based on comparative evidence about control groups. This is a significant area in which its veritistic colors pale by comparison to those of modern scientific practice.

Another example outside of science is to draw inferences from samples to populations where the properties of the sample do not provide strong evidence for the conclusion about the population. Nonscientific inference, for example, does not heed appropriate warnings about sample size, or the importance of a *random* rather than a *biased* sample. Here again the practices of nonscientific inference have poorer veritistic properties.

Further instances of fallacious nonscientific practices are readily adduced, borrowing extensively from Ronald Giere (1979: ch. 8). Consider the confidence ancient Greeks apparently had in the Delphic oracle. Giere formulates the hypothesis they accepted as: "The oracle is a future-seeing system; that is, it has special powers that enable it to see the future." What was a typical test of this hypothesis that produced confidence in it? In a typical case a rich man might have asked the oracle whether his family would continue to prosper or not, and the reply might have been, "I see grave misfortune in your future." If, a year later, the only son and heir had fallen into a well and drowned, that would have been regarded as a fulfillment of the prediction. The trouble is that the prediction was very indefinite. The nature of the misfortune was unspecified and so was the time it would occur. If anybody were to pick a rich Greek family at random and make a similar prediction, it would not be unlikely that something bad would befall it at some later time. So such a prediction could easily be made even by a system without future-seeing powers. Thus, the fulfillment of the prediction doesn't raise the probability that the oracle is such a system. This pitfall is readily avoided with the help of scientific methodology, but nonscientific practice falls prey to fallacious reasoning of this sort.

Another example drawn from Giere is the faith people often place in certain contemporary "seers" like Jeane Dixon. Several of Dixon's biographies argue that her powers are proved by her many past successes. Dixon regularly issues whole sets of predictions at the beginning of a year. The predictions concern all types of subjects, especially those dealing with famous people in entertainment, politics, and the arts. For example, it is claimed that Dixon "predicted" the assassination of John Kennedy (actually she said that he would die in office). Ordinary reasoners might be impressed by the fulfillment of just one or a few of her predictions. That might suffice to convince them that she is a "seer," even if most of her predictions are wrong. But couldn't anyone, even a person with no special prophetic powers, make such a long list of predictions with a high probability that a few would come true? If so, then the observed fulfillment of a few of Dixon's predictions should not raise the probability of her being a genuine seer. This would be obvious to anyone trained in scientific practice, and would therefore keep such a reasoner from gullibly accepting a false conclusion.

At this juncture the reader might expect me to articulate the general features of scientific reasoning that make it superior to nonscience. Unfortunately, that is a difficult task. In both traditional philosophy of science and the foundations of statistics, the issues are complex and highly controversial. Traditional confirmation theory features many rival entrants, including the hypothetico-deductive method, Popper's "corroboration" approach, the bootstrapping approach, eliminative induction, and Bayesianism. No single view has received a clear majority, and some views do not readily lend themselves, at least under standard treatments, to veritism. For example, most defenses of Bayesianism in the literature take a subjectivist approach, and do not appeal to veritistic virtues in my sense.

The situation might seem different for statistical theory, because statistical practices are deeply institutionalized in many parts of science—especially the life sciences, psychology, and the social sciences. However, the precise methods and their rationale are open to debate. The standard textbook treatments of classical statistics are a hybrid of the Fisherian and Neyman–Pearson frameworks, but actually the Fisherians and the followers of Neyman–Pearson disagreed quite strongly about their methods, and regarded their pure forms, at least, as incompatible (Gigerenzer *et al.* 1989). The veritistic properties of statistical practices are also difficult to assess because of certain ambiguities in statistical theory. For example, standard statistical treatments of hypothesis-testing talk about "rejecting" the null hypothesis and "accepting" another hypothesis. But what exactly is "acceptance"? Neyman denied that to accept a hypothesis is to regard it as true, or to believe it. At most it means to *act* as if it were true (Gigerenzer *et al.* 1989: 101). But if this interpretation is used, it is unclear what implications statistical practice has for veritistic success, since veritistic success, by definition, involves beliefs or degrees of belief. Another problem is that contemporary Bayesians and others offer serious critiques of classical statistics, or at least of the theoretical rationales offered for classical statistics (Howson and Urbach 1989: chs. 5–8). None of this implies that the employment of statistical methods by statistical practitioners does not result in vastly better beliefs and degrees of belief as compared with wholly non-scientific reasoning on the same topics. I certainly do not mean to denigrate statistical methods in favor of naive or statistically unsophisticated reasoning. It is difficult, however, to marshal philosophically unchallengeable "proofs" of the good veritistic properties of statistical methods without getting into thorny issues.

8.9 *The distribution of scientific research*

I turn now to the social dimensions of science, where two types of questions will be pursued. First, do the social practices of science make positive or negative contributions to its veritistic achievements? Even if science is veritistically superior to nonscience, as I have contended, this might be despite its social practices rather than because of them. The social ingredient in science might contaminate its search for truth, might be an impediment to truth, even if science manages to transcend it. Second, among rival social practices, which ones are better than others from a veritistic point of view? Four topics will be addressed with these questions in mind: (1) How can an optimal distribution of research effort in a scientific community be achieved? (2) If scientific research is driven by prospects of credit rather than knowledge, how badly does this impede the veritistic goals of science? (3) How should editors of science journals decide which articles to publish? (4) Can authority be used effectively in science?

At the beginning of Section 8.8, I placed six types of scientific practices on the agenda, the last four of which are social. The first of those four practices is what I examine next, the marshaling and distribution of resources to facilitate scientific investigation and observation. Clearly, scientists need resources to conduct their observations carefully and systematically. Precise instruments of observation are expensive, and clinical studies often run for years and encompass thousands of subjects. So science needs financial support, and this must come from society, whether through public or private avenues. The practice of raising and distributing such funds is a social practice. Granted the veritistic superiority of science, however, it hardly needs further argument to show that any successful practice for the funding of scientific research is at least somewhat beneficial, or beneficial on average, for veritistic ends. This should suffice to dispel the notion that any and every social practice contaminates veritistic ends.

The trickier question concerns the optimal distribution of research funding, which is closely connected to the problem of optimal distribution of research methodologies. The latter is an issue that has been fruitfully addressed by Kitcher (1990; 1993: ch. 8). Kitcher introduces the topic with an illustration inspired by the quest for the structure of DNA.

Once there was a very important molecule (VIM). Many people in the chemical community wanted to know the structure of VIM. Method I involved using X-ray crystallography, inspecting the resultant photographs and using them to eliminate possibilities about bonding patterns. Method II involved guesswork and the building of tinker-toy models. (1990: 11)

If the community's goal is to fathom the structure of VIM as quickly as possible, how, asks Kitcher, should the use of the two methods be distributed among the available scientists? It might be that the chances that an individual would discover the structure of VIM using method I were greater than the chances that that individual would discover the structure by using method II. It does not follow, however, that the optimal distribution of community effort is to have *all* chemists use method I. On the contrary, it is likely to be better to diversify efforts, so that some chemists use method I and some use method II. But how, exactly, is such diversity to be achieved? More generally, what is the community optimum distribution of labor in different circumstances, and how (if at all) can it be achieved?

M. Ross Quillian (1994) presents a similar example. In 1894 there was great interest in developing an understanding of flight. There were two general ways that the problem could be researched. Researchers might devote their energy to studying the animals that fly: birds, bats, flying insects. They might try to identify the distinctive features of such creatures. A second research methodology might attempt to construct devices that fly. With hindsight the second problem-solving method can be recognized as more successful. But should the scientific community of the late nineteenth century have invested *all* of its energy in that direction?

Kitcher provides a helpful analysis of the situation. Suppose that each problem-solving method is associated with a probability function, $p(n)$, representing the (objective) chance that the method will deliver a correct answer (within some time interval t) if n workers use that method. Assume further that any proposed answer is recognizably either correct or incorrect. N workers are available for distribution between the available methods (in the present case, we assume, two methods). The community optimum (CO) distribution is given by having n workers use method I and $N - n$ workers use method II where the numbers n and $N - n$ are chosen so as to maximize the following formula:

$$(8.1) \quad p_1(n) + p_2(N - n) - \text{prob (both methods deliver)}.$$

Kitcher discusses some natural properties of the function $p(n)$, in particular, how the probability of success depends on the number of workers invested in a method. He then proceeds to show that there are definitely cases in which the CO-distribution would not have everyone use method I, nor everyone use method II, but have a *mix* of methods I and II. That is, it maximizes the probability of discovery to have some workers pursue method I while others pursue method II.

Kitcher worries, however, whether the CO-distribution in these cases is realizable. If a monarch were in charge of science, who assigned each scientist to a method, such a monarch could ensure that scientists are appropriately allocated to the different methods. But if each scientist chooses his or her preferred method independently, there is danger of overconcentration on a single method. In particular, says Kitcher, if each scientist has purely epistemic ends, and only cares about her chances of following a method that yields the answer, she is apt to choose the one with the highest intrinsic chance (objective probability) of yielding the answer. But if all scientists know which method has the best chance of yielding the answer, they will all choose that method, and there will be no beneficial diversification of labor. This is what Kitcher calls a "discrepancy" between the CO-distribution and what is *individually rational* (IR); in short, it is a CO–IR discrepancy.

Kitcher finds a "solution" to the problem of CO–IR discrepancies in the prospect of scientists' having "baser" motives than purely epistemic ones. If scientists seek private ends, such as winning a much-coveted prize, they will choose methods a little differently. A scientist might switch to an intrinsically inferior method, one with a lower intrinsic probability of yielding the answer, when fewer people are trying that method. If each person pursuing a given method has an equal chance of winning the prize, you might have a better chance of winning by joining a small number pursuing an inferior method than by joining a much larger group pursuing a superior method. Thus, the prospect of egotistical or "sullied" scientific motives might solve the problem of CO–IR discrepancies.

I take no exception to this proposal as *one* possible solution to the problem of research distribution. But other solutions are also possible, to which Kitcher gives scant attention. First, Kitcher oddly ignores the fact that although there is no science "monarch," there are centralized agencies whose decisions powerfully influence the allocation of research efforts. These are the funding agencies, both governmental and extragovernmental.[7] Very little of modern science can be conducted without funding, and as long as individual scientists at least propose to use different methods, funding agencies are in a position to encourage diversity by financially supporting it. Centralized decision making is one part of the larger social practice that determines the allocation of research effort.

Two additional factors of a decentralized nature also contribute toward diversification. First, scientists do not always agree in their estimates of the probability that a given method will yield an answer. Indeed, it is quite typical for scientists to have widely dispersed estimates of a particular method's utility or fruitfulness, depending on a variety of background assumptions. This alone might guarantee a substantial diversity of research paths. Moreover, this would suffice to effect a division of labor even if scientists have purely epistemic goals, and only wish to pursue (what they regard as) the most probable route to an answer. In short, CO–IR discrepancies can be avoided without depending on "sullied" motives.[8]

Differences in skills, training, and available equipment are other factors that might lead even decentralized planning toward diversification. Pursuit of method I may require a bundle of skills or a type of instrumentation that scientist *S* simply does not have. So although method I may have the highest probability of success (when pursued by practitioners with appropriate skills and equipment), *S* will not pursue it. She may instead pursue method II, despite its lower probability of success. Thus, differences in specialization, training, and resources can suffice for a division of labor, again without dependence on sullied motives (Giere 1988: 213–14).

Since funding decisions are obviously a critical factor in the overall direction of scientific research, let us focus on different possible practices of funding agencies. Critics of centralized planning in general might think it best to minimize the influence of central granting agencies. Let scientists decide on their own what research methods to pursue, just as entrepreneurs decide autonomously which investments to make. The cases are not parallel, however, because veritistically valuable scientific research may not be profitable,

---

[7] Kitcher has a *very* brief mention of funding research (1993: 305), but this is not explicitly connected with solving the division-of-labor problem.

[8] Kitcher does mention this possibility, but only in a late section of a lengthy discussion (1993: 374 ff.).

or not immediately profit-making. Society wants to support some of this research anyway, and the question is which research to support. Could central planning be minimized by having granting agencies randomize their decisions? Simply flip coins to decide whose research proposals to fund? Nobody seriously supposes that randomization is the way to maximize veritistic goals. So alternative policies must be considered.

Assuming there is an adequate supply of competent researchers ready to pursue each method, if funded, the main problem for an agency is how to allocate grants so as to maximize the probability of finding an answer (within some time interval t). Kitcher has already provided an algebraic formula for determining this allocation. (Actually, things are a bit more complicated. If workers have different skills and specialties, they may not be transferable across methods, as Kitcher assumes. Second, one method may be more expensive per worker than another. Existing funds might cover N workers using one method, but could not support as many as N workers using a more expensive method. Here I shall ignore these complications.) The principal question confronting an agency is what values to assign to the probabilities of success for each method. The problem is that different investigators will have different subjective estimates of these probabilities, and the funding agency must decide whose estimates to trust, or how to "average" the divergent estimates. Fundamentally, this becomes a question of judging degrees of authority among scientists in the field. The problem of authority attribution will be tackled in Section 8.12.

An excellent illustration of the problem can be given with a slight change in focus. Instead of considering only rival *methods* for possible funding, consider also rival *hypotheses*. Researchers typically have different opinions about which of various hypotheses (or categories of hypotheses) will truly answer a given scientific question. Assume that at a particular time none of the hypotheses in the field has been investigated sufficiently to establish its truth or falsehood "definitively," although some hypotheses are regarded as highly improbable by certain investigators. Assume further that each grant applicant proposes to test a particular hypothesis. No proposed test will be relevant to *all* hypotheses; each would support or refute just the tested hypothesis (and its negation). Thus, the agency must decide which of the many floated hypotheses are most worth testing.

To be concrete, consider competing views about which types of therapies will cure or alleviate certain medical conditions: conventional therapies or so-called "alternative" medical treatments. For any type of condition, the question medical science seeks to answer is: "What therapy would cure or alleviate this condition?" Proponents of traditional medicine assign extremely low probabilities to hypotheses asserting the effectiveness of alternative therapies. Proponents of alternative medicine assign them much higher probabilities. The question is whether grants should be given to test the efficacy of alternative treatments. Since medical science is chiefly interested in treatments that *do* work, it would not typically want to fund testing procedures merely to establish that they don't work. So it should consider the prior probability of the treatment's efficacy. (An exception here is when patients are already employing a given treatment; then it may be important to establish definitively its worthlessness, or its bad side effects.) Another issue is whether an applicant who proposes to conduct tests is properly trained for the job, that is, capable of using methods that will provide solid evidence about the treatment's efficacy. This is a contentious issue in this area, because people who wish to test alternative medical treatments are usually proponents of such treatments, and they sometimes lack credentials for conducting traditional kinds of clinical tests.

This is an area of active controversy, partly because in 1991 the United States Congress set up an Office of Alternative Medicine in the National Institutes of Health (Kolata 1996*a*). This office awarded a million-plus dollar grant, for example, to a professor of nursing with a doctorate in education, who thinks that magnets can soothe chronic pain. This hypothesis draws guffaws from leading scientists, who say that this could work only if laws of physics were violated. Another proponent of alternative medicine was awarded a grant of almost a million dollars to conduct a study involving 1,500 to 2,000 people, looking at whether alternative medical treatments can help patients with HIV. She planned to follow HIV patients who use alternative therapies for a year, asking them to report what they are taking and how their disease is progressing. This plan was criticized by an expert on clinical trial design, who said that such a study would be of no value at all because no control group was to be used. The experience of the grant recipient was also questioned, because the largest clinical trial she had ever conducted previously involved thirty people. One member of the Office's advisory council regarded their entire grant review process as highly unusual, saying that if it had been conducted strictly by scientists, probably nothing would have been funded. Most of the advisory council members, however, were themselves practitioners of alternative medicine, or strong believers in it. Indeed, this whole office was a project of a certain Senator who himself used alternative therapies and was then the chairman of the Senate Appropriations Committee.

The question here is whether the National Institutes of Health is choosing an optimal distribution of research efforts for identifying effective treatments given its total funding. (I am assuming, perhaps counterfactually, that the same total funds would be available to NIH even if the special Office of Alternative Medicine had not been established.) Traditional scientists claim that grants to practitioners of alternative therapies constitute a poor allocation of research efforts, partly because the hypotheses they pursue have low probabilities of being right and partly because the grant-winning researchers do not use good methods, that is, methods capable of detecting effective treatments. These views are disputed, of course, by proponents of alternative medicine. The question is: whose views should be heeded? That is essentially a question of how to settle disputes about authority, a question I defer to the final section of the chapter (I do not promise to deliver there a full theory of authority settlement).

8.10 *The drive for credit*

The preceding section broached the question of how science is affected by different motives for scientific activity. Of critical interest is whether "impure," nonepistemic motives of scientists might interfere with science's institutional aim of finding truth. That there is no necessary conflict can readily be appreciated from technological applications of science. A scientist may be motivated to make a scientific discovery because she stands to profit from its technological use. This profit motive, however, need not conflict with a veritistic motivation; in fact, discovering truths may be an essential means to profitable technological application. A marketable product or device is typically one that consistently performs in a specified fashion. So the scientist must find a way to design a product that *will* consistently perform that way. The scientist must *accurately* identify some compound, structure, or mechanism that reliably produces a desired response or effect. So finding truth is often a means to the goal of profit, not something at odds with it. A profit motive can *discipline* one's search for truth rather than distort it. (This is not to deny, of course, that truth distortion, especially in the form of lying, can also be a means to profit in many circumstances.)

Not all science, however, is aimed at technological application, and even when technological uses are foreseen in the distance, pure scientists may not expect to benefit from them. There is another kind of nonepistemic motive, however, that scientists might be described as pursuing, namely, credit, respect, or honor from their scientific colleagues. Nobel Prizes are the highest form of such honor, but respect and credit of a more routine sort are also regularly sought. Credit, however, is not the same as truth or knowledge. If scientists are credit-motivated, might that not distort their search for truth or knowledge?

Realistically, I suspect, scientific research is driven by twin motives, the desire for personal scientific knowledge and the desire for credit. The desire for personal knowledge stems partly from sheer curiosity and partly from its use in the conduct of research. Scientists are not oblivious, however, to the credit desideratum. Some amount of scientific credit, after all, is normally a precondition for job maintenance, and larger amounts of credit often conduce to a higher salary, a better job, and/or greater personal satisfaction. Granted, then, that real scientists' research decisions are driven by a combination of motives, we may nonetheless seek to understand how these motives tilt research toward greater or lesser amounts of knowledge generation. For this purpose it helps to construct analytic models, some which assume pure knowledge motivation and some which assume pure credit motivation. By comparing the consequences of these assumptions, one can illuminate the impact of the two types of motives. I shall proceed in this spirit.

A model that assumes the pursuit of credit requires some complementary assumption about how scientists assign or award credit for research. If we are to determine how an investigator, V, will act if she pursues credit, we must make some assumption about how her research activities or results would elicit varying amounts of credit. A cynical possible assumption is that scientists give credit to others only to promote their own careers. Suppose investigator V publishes a certain research result. Under the cynical assumption, creditor C will give it high marks if it supports his (C's) own scientific position, will give it low marks if it cuts against his position, and will ignore it if it neither supports nor conflicts with his position. This is surely an unduly cynical picture. Instead let us make the following, more realistic, assumption, one that is still slightly crude but analytically instructive. Assume that peers assign credit to an investigator V as a function of how much knowledge they think they gain from V's research. If potential creditor C reads a research paper by V that does not affect his probability distribution (DBs) over the hypotheses by even one iota, then he doesn't learn anything from V's paper and does not think he has learned anything (at least vis-à-vis the primary hypotheses in the field). So C assigns zero credit to V for that paper. On the other hand, if the paper persuades him to raise his subjective probability (DB) dramatically for a particular hypothesis, then he feels he has learned something important from the paper. So he gives V an amount of credit proportional to his change in DB. Assume that V's paper argues for hypothesis H. Then the amount of credit C confers on V is proportional to the amount of increase in C's subjective probability for H that results directly from V's paper. Some of this credit might be retracted if C later reads cogent-seeming critiques of V's paper, but I set such subsequent developments aside (see Goldman and Shaked 1991a). Assume, then, that this is the standard credit-assignment procedure, and that investigators know that it is.

How would such a credit-assignment procedure affect the research choices and veritistic outcomes under the two scenarios we set out to examine, namely, (1) where the researcher is knowledge-driven, and (2) where the researcher is credit-driven? I examine these scenarios with the help of the model developed in Chapter 4 for Bayesian reasoners. Assume that scientific peers are all Bayesians, and are known to be such by investigator V. V has a choice between two experiments or tests to perform, both of which are relevant to the truth of two competing hypotheses, H_1 and H_2. To fit Theorem 4.2 and the Bayesian framework, assume that H_1 and H_2 are exhaustive. Here is an example of a pair of tests that fit the specifications I have in mind (based on Salmon 1990).

Suppose a physician does an X-ray for diagnostic purposes. H_1 is the hypothesis that the patient has a particular disease and H_2 is the hypothesis that he doesn't. There are two possible observable outcomes, E and not-E, where E is a certain appearance on the film. From long medical experience it may be known that E occurs in 90 percent of all cases in which the disease is present, but only 15 percent of all cases in which the disease is absent. In other words, the objective likelihood of observing E if the disease is present is .90, the objective likelihood of observing E if the disease is absent is .15, and these are the subjective likelihoods used by practitioners. Here is a matrix describing the likelihoods:

	E	not-E
H_1	.90	.10
H_2	.15	.85

Now we know from Theorem 4.1 that if this X-ray test is performed, if the result is observed, and if Bayesian reasoning is applied, there will be an expected increase in degree of knowledge (V-value) concerning the question of whether the patient has the disease. This expected increase will occur for any prior—other than 0 or 1.0—that the practitioner or a colleague might have.

Now assume that there is a second test—call it a Y-ray test—that the physician might administer instead. (In real medical practice, both tests might be performed; but let us proceed on the assumption that only one can be performed.) Here the observable effects are F and not-F, and the objective likelihoods are given below.

	F	not-F
H_1	.99	.01
H_2	.10	.90

Intuitively, the second test is the more "decisive" test, as reflected in the fact that its likelihood ratios are more extreme than the likelihood ratios for the first test. As we know from Theorem 4.2, moreover, the expected increase in truth possession from the second test is greater than the expected increase in truth possession from the first test (for the same priors). Thus, if a physician is only interested in the increase in knowledge—and not, for example, in cost—the second test should be chosen in preference to the first.

Administering an X-ray test, of course, is not a standard example of a research experiment. But suppose that a researcher is in a parallel situation to the one involving the physician. She can choose between two experiments that bear on scientific hypotheses H_1 and H_2, where the likelihoods are accurately known and are as specified in the foregoing matrices. Then a purely *knowledge*-driven investigator, who appreciates the theorems we have presented, would choose to perform the second experiment, and the expected knowledge increase associated with this experiment is indeed higher than that associated with the first experiment. Thus, a purely knowledge-motivated investigator in this kind of case would make a veritistically preferable research choice.

What about a credit-motivated investigator who is confronted with the same choice and the same information? Would she also make the veritistically preferable research choice? A credit-motivated investigator does not care which experiment is likely to yield the greatest increase in truth possession. She only cares about the magnitudes of DB changes that her prospective creditors will undergo, whether or not those changes are in the direction of truth. Does the second experiment always have expected DB changes that are greater than the expected DB changes associated with the first experiment? Not always, but usually. For some possible priors held by the investigator and by her prospective creditor—where the latter priors are assumed to be known by the investigator—the first experiment would be chosen (Goldman and Shaked 1991a). But these are fairly extreme and presumably unusual conditions. There are possible cases, then, in which a credit-motivated investigator would choose a veritistically *inferior* experiment; hence credit motivation sometimes has worse veritistic upshots than knowledge motivation. Usually, however, the choice under credit motivation would coincide with the choice under knowledge motivation.

What I have presented, of course, is a very special case. It hardly proves that the veritistic prospects of credit motivation are almost always as good as those of knowledge motivation. It can, however, be considered a further counter-example—in addition to Kitcher's—to the debunking notion that credit motivation invariably has markedly deleterious effects on quests for scientific knowledge.

8.11 *Scientific publication*

Suppose that an editor of a major science journal, such as *Science* or *Nature*, construes his or her charge as trying to publish articles that will maximally increase scientific knowledge within the scientific community. How should the editor discharge this responsibility? Although many rejected articles will no doubt be published elsewhere, it simplifies matters to think of the editor's decision as determining whether the research described in the article reaches the community at all. The aim, then, is to choose, for each journal volume with a fixed page limit, a set of articles that is maximally informative to the community. Actual science journal editors, of course, may not restrict themselves to purely informational or veritistic concerns. They may be mindful of potential technological applications of research, or of its social and political significance. For purposes of epistemology, however, we may highlight the purely veritistic desiderata. Surely this is *one* dimension, perhaps the most important dimension, of a science editor's mandate.

A journal like *Science* or *Nature* publishes articles in many areas of science, so choices among all competing submissions have something to do with the relative "significance" of articles to their respective fields. This introduces factors that lie outside my framework, so I shall not address them squarely. One possible way of dealing with them is to consider the total number of scientists who will read and become informed by each of two competing submissions. *Ceteris paribus*, a more "significant" article will reach and inform more scientists, and will thereby produce a greater increase in aggregate knowledge across the scientific community than an article that reaches fewer scientists. But number of readers does not wholly capture the significance dimension.

Setting aside the breadth-of-impact question, how can two articles be compared by an editor for expected veritistic value? Let us focus on articles that report experiments or observational studies, and let us assume that all scientists are Bayesian reasoners. Thus, they will respond to reported experimental outcomes by Bayesian conditionalization. The choice facing an editor, however, is somewhat different from the choice examined in the previous section, in which a researcher chooses between two experiments. First, the researcher choosing between experiments does not know what the outcome of the experiment will be; she chooses "prospectively." The editor, by contrast, considers articles reporting experimental outcomes; he chooses "retrospectively." Second, in the type of case analyzed in the previous section, both experiments concern the same pair of rival hypotheses. Thus, anyone who learns about either experiment would update, or conditionalize, from the *same priors*. The editor, on the other hand, tries to choose among experimental reports on entirely different subjects, where even one and the same reader would have different priors. This complicates the editor's task.

Let us examine these differences in further detail. First, consider a test between two hypotheses, H_1 and H_2, where there are four possible outcomes: W, X, Y, and Z. Suppose that the matrix below gives the subjective likelihoods of all scientists that might potentially read about the test's outcome (but the numbers are not necessarily the objective likelihoods).

	W	X	Y	Z
H_1	.1	.2	.3	.4
H_2	.4	.2	.3	.1

Viewed prospectively, this is a potentially valuable test, since if either outcome W or outcome Z occurs, a Bayesian reasoner will revise his probability vis-à-vis H_1 and H_2 fairly substantially. (The exact amount of revision, of course, depends on the reasoner's priors.) If the actual outcome of the experiment turns out to be either X or Y, however, then it will have no cognitive impact at all, because the subjective likelihood ratio in each of those cases is 1.0. Upon learning of either X or Y, a Bayesian reasoner will not make the slightest change in his probability assignment for H_1 or H_2. Although this experiment might be a (pretty) good test to *perform*, viewed prospectively, if it is performed and the outcome is either X or Y, it is not such a good test outcome to *report* or *publish*. Learning of outcome X or Y, under the specified assumptions, could not increase the readership's knowledge (about H_1 or H_2). So a veritistically oriented editor will not wish to publish an article reporting either of these outcomes. She will prefer any other submission that promises to yield a veritistic increase.

What are the best submissions to choose, then? Are they the ones that would produce the most dramatic changes in probabilities (DBs)? The editor could identify these submissions if she knows, or can estimate, both the priors and the subjective likelihoods of the readers. From this information, plus knowledge of Bayes' Theorem, the most "impactful" articles can be identified. But remember: the editor aims to produce the greatest increases in *knowledge*, and the greatest changes in belief may not be the greatest increases in knowledge. Suppose, for example, that readers unwisely have an extreme likelihood ratio associated with a given outcome, so if that outcome occurs, which is favorable to hypothesis H_1, they dramatically increase their subjective probability for H_1. (Suppose their priors for H_1 are low.) Nonetheless, H_1 might be false. If it is, they will all have dramatically decreased their knowledge, not increased it.

What is an editor to do? Here is one proposal, which appeals to the opinions of authorities. Given our assumptions, an editor should want to know whether a hypothesis favored by an impactful test outcome is true or false. So let the editor consult the best authorities she can in the field of the reported experiment. If, in light of all previous background knowledge plus the favorable recent test outcome, most authorities think that the favored hypothesis is true (that is, their posteriors for that hypothesis are greater than .50), then the editor should regard the expected probability increase for that hypothesis as an increase in *knowledge*. If, on the other hand, most authorities still think that the favored hypothesis is false (their posteriors for that hypothesis remain below .50), then the editor should regard the expected probability increase for that hypothesis as an increase in *error*, hence a decrease in knowledge. This would imply that the editor would choose not to publish this report.

Intuitively, however, this proposal seems wrong. Suppose that, according to a typical authority, the reported test outcome should raise a scientist's DB in hypothesis H_1 from .15 to .45. That is a pretty dramatic change in the credibility assigned to H_1, but it still leaves the recommended posterior below .50. So according to the foregoing proposal, the test outcome should not be reported, because that would only tend to produce a higher DB in a falsehood. This recommendation, however, seems intuitively misguided. We would normally think that a test outcome of the sort described is just the kind of thing a science editor should consider very favorably for publication.

The problem, I think, is that we have been looking at the *short-term* knowledge state of the scientific community rather than its *long-term* knowledge state. The long-term knowledge state will depend not simply on the results of this test, but possibly on a much longer series of tests. However, the relevant segment of the scientific community needs to decide which future tests are worth performing, and this means deciding which hypotheses are most worth testing. In general, it is more reasonable to test credible hypotheses, ones with a serious chance of being true, than long-shot hypotheses. If this is right, scientists in the field need to know how credible each contending hypothesis currently is. In particular, any substantial change in their level of credibility should be brought to the scientists' attention. So any test outcome that warrants a comparatively large revision in credibility is an outcome with a strong claim for publication. This implies that the test outcome described in the previous paragraph, which warrants a revision from .15 to .45, would definitely be a strong contender for publication.

Notice my phrase "warrants a comparatively large revision in credibility." The mere propensity of an ordinary (Bayesian) scientist-in-the-street to change his DB for H_1 from, say, .15 to .45 given the test outcome does not guarantee that this would be an *appropriate*, or *warranted*, change. It would be a warranted change only if the subjective likelihood estimates generating such a change are reasonably accurate estimates. So an editor should want to know, not simply whether publication of a certain test outcome would produce a large DB change among readers, but whether this magnitude of change would be appropriate. This is another topic on which she might reasonably consult her authorities, in their capacity as referees. Authorities would employ their own likelihoods to decide how big a change would be warranted by the test outcome reported in the target paper. The editor should use these (comparatively) authoritative likelihoods rather than those of the average scientist-in-the-street, or those endorsed by the investigator-author of the submitted article. Here, then, is another important role for authorities in the publication-decision process.

Let me illustrate how authorities can and should be used to assess the probative value of a test outcome by assessing the likelihoods associated with that outcome. I present a concrete illustration involving observational studies in epidemiology (Taubes 1995). Epidemiologists select a group of individuals afflicted with a particular disorder—for example, cancer—then identify a control group free of the disorder, and compare the two, looking for differences in lifestyle, diet, or some environmental factor. What blunts the edge of such studies, however, are possible biases or confounds. Confounding factors are the hidden variables in the population being studied, which can easily generate an association that may be real but does not represent a *causal* connection, which is what the epidemiologist is seeking. For example, the researcher may find a higher incidence of cancer among high alcohol consumers than among low alcohol consumers. But this association does not guarantee that alcohol consumption is a cause of cancer. People who drink also tend to smoke, boosting their risk of cancer. So smoking is a confound that the researcher's data may not reveal, and in general it is not transparent what the confounds may be. A study published over a decade ago found coffee drinking to be linked with pancreatic cancer, but that finding has not been replicated (Taubes 1995). The study corrected for smoking, which often accompanies heavy coffee-drinking, but only for smoking during the five years before the cancer was diagnosed. The researchers might have done better to ask their subjects about smoking habits a full twenty years before diagnosis.

One value of authorities in assessing an epidemiological study of this sort is that they may know what confounds are serious possibilities for that study. Knowledge of such confounds may then be translated, for purposes of Bayesian analysis, into estimates of likelihoods. The competing hypotheses that interest an epidemiological researcher can be illustrated as follows:

H_1: High alcohol consumption is a *cause* of cancer.
H_2: High alcohol consumption is not a cause of cancer.

Suppose, then, that a researcher has found a certain incidence of high alcohol consumption in a population of cancer patients and a much lower incidence in a control group. Call these comparative data D. For D to have probative force for H_1 under a Bayesian analysis, the likelihood of finding D given H_1 must be higher than the likelihood of finding D given H_2. Such a difference in likelihoods is what would be claimed, implicitly or explicitly, by a researcher who submitted this research for publication. An expert, however, might challenge this alleged likelihood difference on grounds of a possible confound. High alcohol consumption might be linked with cancer even if it is not a *cause* of cancer, but is merely correlated with smoking which *is* a cause of cancer. In other words, once the possible smoking confound is considered, the likelihood of finding D given that high alcohol consumption is not a cause of cancer (H_2) is substantially raised. That likelihood might rise so much, in fact, that it might be as large, or almost as large, as the likelihood of finding D given that high alcohol consumption is a cause of cancer (H_1). Thus, the probative force of the data would be eliminated or vastly reduced. This is just the sort of evidential assessment an editor seeks from a referee.

8.12 *Recognizing authority*

In two of the last three sections we have seen how prominent a role authority can play in science. I do not interpret such prominence, of course, as a basis for debunking science; on the contrary, as I have shown, proper deployment of genuine authorities can promote science's veritistic success. Nonetheless, there is a fundamental conundrum about the use of authority: how are people to tell who is an authority, and how good an authority, in a given domain? The problem is hardly trivial, because those who seek to use authorities—program officers of funding agencies, for example, or editors of journals—are often novices in the target domain. How is a novice to identify an authority?

He might ask *other* authorities, but this just pushes the problem back one step further: how can he identify *them* as authorities on the authorities?

The root problem, evidently, is the problem of *direct* identification of an authority by a novice. Is this possible? Let us begin by defining what it means for someone to be an authority in a subject. I presume that being an authority, or expert, is a comparative matter. Someone is an authority in a subject if he or she has *more* knowledge in that subject than almost anybody else. Thus, we might define an authority in roughly the following terms:

> Person *A* is an authority in subject *S* if and only if *A* knows more propositions in *S*, or has a higher degree of knowledge of propositions in *S*, than almost anybody else.

This allows for the possibility of several authorities or experts in the same subject, but not very many. There is a penumbra of vagueness here that the definition respects. Instead of restricting the definition to actual knowledge, one might expand it to cover potential knowledge. Authorities typically have certain intellectual skills needed for answering questions on a given topic even if they haven't already found those answers. Such skills may be even more significant for expertise than already attained knowledge. I shall take this amendment for granted in what follows, without building it into the official definition.

Consider a judge, *J*, who wishes to determine (directly) whether a candidate authority, *A*, really is an authority in a given subject. Assume that judge *J* himself is not an authority, but wishes to determine whether *A* is. If *A* is an authority, he will know things—perhaps many things—that *J* does not know. If *J* himself does not know them, however, how can he tell that *A* does? Suppose *A* claims to know proposition *P*, and *J* does not (antecedently) believe *P*. Should *J* credit *A* with knowledge of *P*? If *J* does not already believe *P*, there are two possibilities (restricting ourselves to categorical belief rather than degrees of belief): either *J* believes not-*P*, or he has no opinion. In either case, why would *J* credit *A* with knowing *P*? If *J* believes not-*P*, he should certainly not credit *A* with knowing *P*. If he has no opinion about *P*, he could credit *A* with knowledge on the basis of pure faith, but this would hardly count as *determining* that *A* knows that *P*. Although he could place blind trust in *A*, this would not be a reliable way of determining authority. Moreover, he cannot follow this policy systematically. If two people, *A* and *A'*, each claims to be an authority, and *A* claims to know *P* while *A'* claims to know not-*P*, how is *J* to decide between them when he himself has no opinion?

The first crucial step in solving the problem is to give it a *temporal* dimension. Although *J* cannot credit *A* with knowing something *now* that *J* does not know now, he can certainly credit *A* with knowing things *before* he, *J*, knew them. *J* can determine that there are many propositions in the target domain such that *A* knew them at a time when *J* was either ignorant about them or in error. This would provide *J* with evidence for the conclusion that *A* has some skills or basis of knowledge in the subject area that exceed his own. This would support the further conclusion that A probably has additional knowledge that he, J, lacks. If, moreover, there is no comparably large set of propositions that J knew before A knew them—in other words, if there is no symmetry in their bodies of relative knowledge and ignorance—then J has grounds for inferring that A has superior authority in this subject.

Let me provide some simple scenarios of how such determinations of authority can transpire. There are many circumstances in which J can personally verify something that A previously asserted, but which J did not initially believe. For instance, A might assert at time t that St. Paul is the capital of Minnesota, a proposition which J, at t, either denies or doubts. At A's encouragement, J either flies to Minnesota and finds the capitol in St. Paul, thereby personally verifying the truth of the asserted proposition, or he consults an uncontestedly reliable encyclopedia or atlas and verifies its truth. At the later time t', then, J knows it. So he is now in a position to concede, not only that it is true, but that A knew it before he (J) did. So that is one item to chalk up to A's greater geographical authority, at least at that earlier time. Evidence for such authority would mount if A proved right in similar test cases where J verified the asserted propositions.

A slightly more complex illustration concerns propositions about the repair or treatment of malfunctioning systems, such as automobiles, air conditioners, economies, or organisms. In each such case, J might personally verify that the system in question is malfunctioning in a specified respect. The question is addressed to both A and J: How can the system be repaired? Suppose J has no ideas at all in which he places much credence. By contrast, A says that if the system is given treatment T, it will return to normal within a certain time interval.[9] Upon hearing this proposal, J either has no opinion or denies that T will "work." Treatment T is then applied to the system—which J verifies— and at some later time within the specified interval, the system returns to normal—which J also verifies. J has now verified that the proposition A asserted is true. Thus, J must concede that A knew this proposition (truly believed it) at a time when J himself did not know it. Once again, this provides J with evidence of A's greater authority in the target domain. After all, how could A have known the relevant "treatment" proposition beforehand without having a fund of domain-relevant knowledge that J himself lacked (and presumably still lacks)?

In the foregoing cases J observationally verifies the truth of A's assertion, thereby obtaining evidence of A's authority. This is not the only fashion, however, by which such evidence can be obtained. Another route is through argumentation. At time t, A asserts proposition P and J denies it. A then proceeds to adduce premises that strongly support P. Either J admits the truth of all the

---

[9] I formulate the proposition in purely conditional terms, so that it does not entail causal efficacy on the part of T. The latter would be harder to verify.

premises to begin with, or he verifies all premises that he does not antecedently believe. Furthermore, *J* knows of no propositions that defeat *A*'s argument for *P*. So, at time *t'*, *J* becomes persuaded of the truth of *P*. He is thereby justified in believing that *A* knew something at an earlier time that he himself did not know. If this happens on many occasions, for propositions in the target domain, and there are no occasions, or fewer occasions, on which the reverse occurs, then *J* has ample evidence of *A*'s superior authority.

We have thus far discussed ways by which *J* can determine that *A* has authority superior to his own. What about comparing the relative authority of two competing candidates, each of whom might be more knowledgeable than *J* is? The strategies are substantially the same as those already identified. If *A* and *A'* both claim to be authorities in domain *D*, *J* can pose various questions to them. The interesting cases are those in which they offer conflicting answers. To decide who is right (without appeal to yet another authority), *J* can use either of the strategies discussed earlier: observational verification or argumentation. The case of observation is straightforward: simply look to see who is right. The case of argumentation is a little different. *J* must listen to their opposing arguments and decide which is strongest, or who does the best job in rebuttal and counterrebuttal. As we saw in Chapter 5, successful argumentation is an indicator of truth, so although the method of argumentation is hardly an infallible algorithm for determining who is right, it is certainly helpful. A judge is not consigned to blind trust.

Our discussion shows that radical doubts about novice recognition of authorities are unwarranted. Such radical doubts have been expressed by John Hardwig:

[I]f I am not in a position to know what the expert's good reasons for believing p are and why these are good reasons, what stance should I take in relation to the expert? If I do not know these things, I am also in no position to determine whether the person really is an expert. By asking the right questions, I might be able to spot a few quacks, phonies, or incompetents, but only the more obvious ones. For example, I may suspect that my doctor is incompetent, but generally I would have to know what doctors know in order to confirm or dispel my suspicion. Thus, we must face the implications of the fact that laymen do not fully understand what constitute good reasons in the domain of expert opinion. (1985: 340–1)

The critical point Hardwig ignores is the possibility of knowing *that* a specialist is an expert without knowing *how* or *why* he is an expert, just as it is possible to know *that* an instrument or piece of equipment is reliable without knowing how it works. As we have seen, expertise or authority can be demonstrated to novices through observational verification. The novice can determine that an automobile mechanic prescribed successful repairs, or that a physician described a successful treatment for a malfunctioning kidney. Without knowing the expert's reasons for predicting the success of these treatments, the novice can reasonably infer that the candidate expert must have had such reasons. There must have been additional knowledge underlying the correct selection of a treatment. The successful treatment *might* have been fortuitous, but that is unlikely; it is dramatically unlikely if the specialist displays similar success on many occasions. Thus, the existence of expertise can be inferred although the novice remains ignorant of the substantive ground of that expertise.

Although I have emphasized the possibility of observational verification in the establishment of authority, the process of authority determination will typically proceed at a level somewhat removed from observation, especially in science. A candidate authority may display knowledge of certain facts that the judge "verifies," but verification may consist in substantial amounts of inference rather than observation. In other words, in testing for expertise, a judge need not restrict himself to facts of an observational sort before conceding superior knowledge to the candidate. I have emphasized observational verification because that is the most perspicuous case, not because it is the most common sort of case for establishing authority in science.

Once the possibility of direct determination of authority is demonstrated, it is obvious that authority recognition need not be restricted to direct recognition. Once *J* establishes that *A* is an authority, he can appeal to *A*'s opinions to help him decide whether another person is an authority. It is not a trivial matter to amalgamate one's total information, both direct and indirect, to assess someone's level of expertise. I do not offer a general theory of how this should be done. What I take myself to have shown is that authority recognition by novices is not fundamentally impossible, that the "conundrum" of authority recognition by novices is soluble at the basic level.[10]

---

[10] It must be conceded that solving this fundamental conundrum is not a panacea for problems of authority attribution, especially at the frontiers of science. At the frontiers, it is very difficult to pinpoint an outcome that can serve as an uncontroversial "verification."

NINE

Law

9.1 *Truth and legal adjudication*

THIS chapter switches the focus of veritistic evaluation to the law. The law features highly codified systems and procedures in which multiple players interact to produce certain judgments, namely, verdicts. Since one of the central aims of these procedures, I shall argue, is to produce true or accurate judgments, it is natural to evaluate existing procedures along the veritistic dimension. This is the appropriate task, at any rate, for social epistemology. Are current systems and procedures optimal from a veritistic standpoint? If not, what changes might yield improvements?

Notice that I am speaking of *judgments* rather than *beliefs*, although belief-producing practices are my standard object of veritistic appraisal. The reason for this deviation is that the palpable outputs of legal deliberations are not private beliefs but public judgments of guilt and innocence, liability or non-liability. It is therefore smoother to conduct the chapter's discussion in terms of judgments. This departure from the book's main framework is minor because legal judgments normally issue from beliefs of the trier of fact. When judgments are mentioned, beliefs are not far from the picture. Like beliefs, moreover, judgments are things that can be true or false, accurate or inaccurate.

The problem of adjudication, at least in the form I shall address it, is the problem of *applying* the law to particular cases under dispute. How should legal systems channel the flow of evidence and information about particular cases so as to produce suitable judgments about those cases? To highlight this problem, the adjudication issue needs to be separated from other issues in the legal sphere, and the status of the judgments in question needs to be carefully examined.

For present purposes I take it as given that the body politic has arrived at certain laws or statutes, that a certain history of case law is in place, and that certain canons of legal interpretation are entrenched. Whether these laws and so forth are good from a moral point of view is not up for present discussion. The question of their goodness falls into the realm of general moral and political philosophy, which transcends the scope of this book. I shall assume that the job of an adjudication system is to apply whatever laws are "on the books" (and constitutionally legitimate).[1] If those laws are bad, they should doubtless be changed. But it is not the job of the adjudication system as such to effect that change. In endorsing this division of labor, I am not denying the possible appropriateness of juror nullification. It might sometimes be morally right for jurors to undercut an existing statute by refusing to apply it even in a clear case. My point is, first, that adjudication systems should not be designed on the assumption that the laws to be applied will be morally or politically wrong. Second, remedies for bad legislation should primarily be addressed at the legislative level, not at the enforcement level. But this issue will not be pursued here.

When seeking to apply the law to particular cases, either criminal or civil cases, two kinds of factors must be considered by the adjudicator (or adjudicative system): (1) What are the *material* (nonlegal) *facts* of the case? and (2) What is the *legal basis* for classifying this case under the target category or categories? A prosecutor or plaintiff claims that the case falls under some legal category, for example, a criminal offense of type O, or a civil tort of type T. The legal basis for such a claim would consist in a variety of legal factors, for example, statutes, common law, judicial precedents, canons of interpretation, and patterns of reasoning that enable people to see analogies or similarities across cases. An adjudicator will seek to decide the case by determining whether the legal basis warrants the alleged classification in virtue of the material facts.

Now in order to defend the veritistic, or truth-oriented, approach to adjudication, I need to show that some relevant truths and falsehoods are in play. To begin, I freely help myself to the assumption that there are certain "material" truths and falsehoods. These truths have their status independent of any knowledge of them by the adjudicative body. Such truths might include, for example, that the defendant started a certain fire, or that the defendant was aware that a certain drug he manufactured had specified side effects. The existence of such facts is relevant to whether the case is *really* an instance of arson or an instance of gross negligence. Of course, whether or not the actions of the defendant realize some category of criminal offense or civil wrong depends not only on the material facts of the case—what acts were committed by the defendant, and what was his state of mind—but on the definitions of the pertinent legal categories. That is why the adjudicator must take into account both the material facts and the legal basis.

Unlike most discussion in the philosophy of law, my attention will be mainly directed to the problem of identifying material facts. In other words, the fact-finding dimension of adjudication will occupy center stage. For purposes of this chapter, then, attention might conceivably be restricted to the question of how various aspects of adjudication procedures affect the fact

---

[1] By "laws" I here refer to what H. L. A. Hart (1961) calls "primary rules." Rules of adjudication can also be laws, but these would be what Hart calls "secondary rules."

finder's success or failure at identifying the relevant material facts. There is a difficulty, however. Juries never make formal pronouncements concerning the material facts they identify. Their formal verdicts are restricted to "guilty" or "innocent" (on such-and-such counts) and "liable" or "nonliable" (for such-and-such harms). So it is natural to ask about the truth or falsity of their verdicts. A group of twelve jurors might all differ from one another in their detailed beliefs about the material facts. The legal system is mainly concerned, however, about the accuracy of their official, collective verdict. Since the verdicts concern "legal facts" in some sense, not purely material facts, we must inquire into what makes verdicts true or false.

A sporting analogy will be helpful. When a baseball umpire calls a pitch a strike or a ball, or when he calls a runner safe or out, the verdict is based on two sorts of factors. First, there are recognized standards or criteria for what counts as a ball and a strike, and what counts as being tagged out. These standards or criteria are analogous to the legal basis for a verdict. Second, there is a question about the target physical events. Where did the pitch travel in relationship to home plate and the batter's body? Was any part of the runner's body touching a base when the runner was tagged? These physical events or facts are analogues of the material facts in the legal setting. Now let us turn to the verdict and the question of whether there is an associated "fact" that makes it true or false. I want to say—what it seems entirely natural to say—that in most cases there is a determinate fact as to whether a pitch is a strike or a ball, or whether a runner is safe or out. In nonborderline cases, the physical facts are (metaphysically speaking) determinately on one side or other of the relevant zone of demarcation. A pitch well above the batter's head, or three feet wide of the plate, is determinately a ball. In such cases, and closer ones as well, a certain verdict is definitively *merited* or *deserved*. If an umpire calls it differently, he makes a mistake. The pitch was really a ball, even if it is called a strike. The runner was really out, even if he is called safe. In short, there are facts—the runner being out, the pitch being a ball—with which an umpire's verdict is either aligned or misaligned; there are facts that make his verdict either correct or incorrect. I shall call such facts *merit facts*, because they are the sorts of facts that merit a particular judgment, even if that judgment is not the one issued by the authorized judge in the case.[2] Merit facts are not identical with physical facts; they "arise from" a combination of physical facts and normative criteria.

Merit facts contrast with what I shall call *judgment facts*. If an authorized umpire calls a runner out, then from the point of view of the game, that runner *is* out. It is recorded as an out, and this record is what affects the progress and official outcome of the game. So this sort of judgment fact is terribly

---

[2] If the reader prefers "desert" facts to "merit" facts, that substitution can be made throughout. Another possibility is "entitlement" facts; but "entitlement" is appropriate only for positive classifications, not negative ones, and both need to be covered here.

important. But it should not be confused with a merit fact; nor does the undoubted existence and importance of judgment facts subvert the existence of merit facts. Indeed, merit facts and judgment facts can coexist even if, in an obvious sense, they conflict. There might be a fact that the runner is "really" safe (a merit fact) although there is also a fact that he is called out (a judgment fact).

It would be foolish to insist that in every play of a game, there is a determinate merit fact. Baseball observers would probably agree that some pitches are so close to the edge of the strike zone that they could properly be called either strikes or balls, even if there were perfect agreement on the precise path of the pitch. Indeed, different umpires (permissibly) seem to have different zones of interpretation, and there are said to be different (tacit) customs of interpreting the strike zone in the American and National Leagues. Given this amount of vagueness, it is plausible that a certain subset of pitches do not fall clearly into either category (even given the true path of the ball). So the class of merit facts concerning baseball pitches may not enjoy perfect determinacy.

All of the foregoing remarks, I want to say, apply mutatis mutandis to the realm of law, although the law has vastly greater complexity than baseball. By analogy with baseball, however, I hold that there are legal "merit facts" concerning guilt or innocence, liability or nonliability. These merit facts are determined, or warranted, by the material facts of the case (what the defendant actually did or failed to do, what circumstances actually obtained, and so forth) and by the legal basis of the case. If an adjudicator issues a judgment that accords with such a merit fact, the judgment is true or correct. If the adjudicator issues a contrary judgment, it is wrong or incorrect.[3] I do not claim that *all* legal cases are of this sort. "Hard" cases may well be indeterminate. In hard cases, even the totality of the material facts (as known from a God's-eye view) and the relevant legal considerations may not clearly warrant one unique judgment rather than another. For my purposes, however, total determinacy is not necessary. In fact, even a comparatively modest amount of determinacy will suffice, as will be explained below.

The extent of, and basis for, determinacy or indeterminacy in the law are questions that lie at the center of raging disputes in legal philosophy and jurisprudence. I believe I can stay neutral on many of these disputes.[4] (A good thing, too, since this territory is well beyond the plausible reach of this book.)

[3] There is a view in the law, sometimes associated with Legal Realism, which holds that "the law is what judges say it is." In distinguishing between merit facts and judgment facts I am assuming that this view is mistaken. It should be pointed out, however, that it is probably wrong to attribute this view to Legal Realists, at least to *all* Legal Realists. Perhaps it is attributable to Felix Cohen and Jerome Frank, but not to most of the other Legal Realists (Brian Leiter, personal communication). See Leiter 1996.

[4] In particular, I want to stay neutral as between different approaches to the philosophy of law that allow for at least partial legal determinacy, such as (1) legal positivism (or conventionalism), (2) the natural law theory, and (3) the Dworkinian theory of law. My approach is consistent, I believe, with any of these approaches.

But some discussion of this terrain is unavoidable, to clarify where my claims fit within a large literature on these subjects.

Following Jules Coleman and Brian Leiter (1995), three possible sources of legal indeterminacy may be identified: (1) global semantic skepticism, (2) gaps in the law, and (3) conflicts or contradictions in the law. Global semantic skepticism claims that language in general is thoroughly indeterminate; there are no objective facts that make sentences mean one thing rather than another. If semantic skepticism were true, legal language would inherit its global indeterminacy. Few philosophers of language, however, hold such a strong global position. There are, to be sure, great unsettled debates over the sources of (determinate) meaningfulness, but only a minority would deny entirely that there is (ever) such meaning.[5] I shall proceed on the majority view that rejects global semantic skepticism.

The other two arguments for legal indeterminacy are specific to the law. The "gap" argument claims that legally binding sources for dispute resolution may be in short supply. Existing statutes, standards, and interpretive resources may not suffice to cover novel cases. At least they may be too weak to warrant a unique outcome. H. L. A. Hart (1958) argued that in such cases, judges must exercise discretionary authority, but there is no correctness prior to the exercise of such discretion. Gaps can arise when statutes or general legal principles suffer from ambiguity, or are open to nonequivalent verbal formulations. Such ambiguity may resist attempts at resolution by appeal to (for example) legislative intent. But as Kent Greenawalt (1992) points out, although different formulations may imply different outcomes for *some* imaginable and perhaps actual situations, many activities will be either excluded under all plausible formulations or included under all plausible formulations. For example, every plausible formulation of the statutory crime of theft will exclude the ordinary act of scratching one's nose (Greenawalt 1992: 36).

The argument from conflicts or contradictions says that sometimes the law is genuinely contradictory, so that each of two conflicting conclusions about a given case could legitimately be drawn.[6] Here too there would be no uniquely correct outcome. One response to the conflict worry is that conflicting norms can sometimes be ordered in their importance. It is not clear, however, that there is a common scale of importance against which conflicting legal norms or values can always be compared. Some degree of incommensu-

---

[5] W. V. Quine (1960) is a prominent semantic skeptic, but most current theorists would say that his semantic skepticism rests on an untenable form of behaviorism. Saul Kripke (1982) might also seem to be a semantic skeptic. But Kripke is better interpreted as simply denying that meaning can arise from individual behavior or mental states. He seems to admit that it arises from some sort of communal facts. Perhaps a clearer example of a current semantic skeptic is Stephen Schiffer (1987).

[6] For example, Joseph Singer writes: "legal reasoning is indeterminate and contradictory. By its own criteria, legal reasoning cannot resolve questions in an 'objective' manner" (1984: 6).

rability may reign among legal values (Coleman and Leiter 1995: 227).[7] So some amount of indeterminacy seems inescapable.

Defenders of *strong* determinacy in the law, such as Ronald Dworkin and Michael Moore, would resist these conclusions. At least in Dworkin's early writings (Dworkin 1967, 1977), he suggested that even in "hard" cases there is a correct answer to be discovered.[8] Moore, a defender of natural law theory, also seems to espouse this position (Moore 1985, 1989; see also Brink 1985). Strong determinacy is compatible with the project of this chapter, but by no means required. All I require for the tenability of my project is the rejection of total indeterminacy.

The principal current theorists who endorse total indeterminacy belong to a family of three approaches: Critical Legal Studies (CLS), Feminist Jurisprudence, and Critical Race Theory.[9] But their attacks on legal determinacy, apart from the points already discussed here, involve disputes on topics unrelated to the present focus. Their criticisms of legal determinacy, for example, are frequently intertwined with attacks on legal "liberalism." Unfortunately, it is quite doubtful that there is any unified doctrine that comprises legal liberalism, or that determinacy needs to be associated in any way with liberalism (Coleman and Leiter 1995: 203–11). At any rate, this chapter is not committed to any doctrine called "liberalism." My framework is not opposed to liberalism; it is just neutral vis-à-vis the usual views associated with philosophical liberalism.

Another concern of the so-called "Crits" is the lack of "objectivity" in the law. The term "objectivity" has many meanings. Under one of its meanings, to say that our current system lacks objectivity is to say that it is not very good at producing accurate judgments.[10] This denial of objectivity is perfectly compatible with everything I say in this chapter. The chapter by no means assumes or maintains that the American adjudication system, or any other existing adjudication system, gets a high score on the veritistic dimension. My project of veritistic evaluation assumes that there are some legal truths that an adjudication system should *aim* to reveal, but it does not assume that this or that system is actually effective at revealing these truths. So some contentions advanced by the Crits do not concern determinacy, and some are not at odds with views adopted here.

A few more words are in order about the implausibility of total indeterminacy. Debates in legal philosophy and jurisprudence tend to center on hard

---

[7] On the topic of value incommensurability, see Raz 1986 and Anderson 1993.

[8] For an application of Dworkin's line of reasoning to various indeterminacy arguments, see Kress 1989. A semantic framework that might support strong objectivism is presented in Stavropoulos 1996.

[9] Representative writings of these movements include the following: Kennedy 1976 and Unger 1975 (Critical Legal Studies), Bell and Bansal 1988 (Critical Race Theory), and Minow 1987 (Feminist Legal Theory).

[10] This would not be a favored way of expressing a CLS position, but it is strongly intimated by various strands of the CLS literature.

cases, perhaps because they pose the most pressing theoretical issues. Hard cases are also the bread-and-butter of lessons in law schools, again because they raise the most interesting issues for understanding of the law. Finally, hard cases are the ones that appellate courts take on their docket, and are widely reported when decided. All this attention to hard cases may create a false impression in people's minds: the impression that most, or even a substantial proportion of, legal cases are difficult to decide (given all the facts). I suspect that this is false. Many if not most cases are dull and obvious, at least if the material facts are known. The threat of indeterminacy simply does not arise. Greenawalt's case of scratching one's nose is a good example. Would anybody maintain that Jennifer's act of nose scratching *equally* warrants being classified as an instance of theft as it warrants being classified as nontheft? I trust not. So it is certainly a determinate case of a legal merit fact: in scratching her nose, Jennifer is innocent of committing theft. Presumably there are innumerable cases of this type, not just a handful.[11] This is enough to get my project off the ground.

It is important to distinguish between *metaphysically* easy and *epistemologically* easy cases. If all the material facts of a case are "given," metaphysically speaking, it may be straightforward how it ought to be classified. But this does not mean that it is epistemologically easy to determine what those facts are. In particular it may not be easy for the legal trier of fact to make this determination. Witnesses to the crucial material facts may no longer be alive, or what witnesses there are may be disposed to hide or distort the facts. So metaphysically easy cases may be epistemologically hard to decide. The whole point of this chapter is to consider which systems or procedures of fact finding are epistemologically superior. The metaphysical/epistemological distinction might also be applied to legal facts, in addition to material facts. Although there may be decisive reasons in the law (precedents, lines of legal argumentation, and so forth) for adjudicating a case one way rather than another, these reasons may not be apparent to a random judge. A judge may have an epistemologically difficult judicial task even if, metaphysically speaking, the law is determinate. But this chapter—unlike most philosophy of law—is not directed at these jurisprudential issues. It is directed primarily at selecting systems of material fact finding.

To introduce my project more fully, return again to the baseball realm. In baseball the epistemological task of classifying relevant plays in a game is a task assigned to umpires. But which individuals should be appointed or hired as umpires? What criteria should be used in hiring decisions? First, a candidate should know the rules of baseball in considerable detail. Second, his visual acuity should enable him to discriminate, *inter alia*, subtly different paths of projectiles. Obviously, these desiderata are relevant to the task of ren-

---

[11] Several writers cite the prevalence of easy cases as a reason for rejecting the thesis of total indeterminacy, including Ken Kress (1989), Lawrence Solum (1987), Frederick Schauer (1985), and Kenney Hegland (1985).

dering accurate verdicts about baseball plays. The better his eyesight and knowledge of the rules, the better an umpire he will be, *ceteris paribus*. I add *"ceteris paribus"* because there are other desiderata for an umpire. An umpire should be cool but firm in tight situations, he should work collegially with other umpires, and so forth. So judgmental accuracy is not the only important trait in an umpire; but it is a crucial trait.

Analogously, it is a vital and central desideratum of a legal adjudication system that it promote the rendering of accurate verdicts. No system can be perfect, in part because parties to law suits are commonly prone to deception, and deception is hard to detect. Nonetheless, accuracy is certainly to be sought, as far as is feasible and subject to other constraints. Returning to the case of the umpire, how should we measure a candidate umpire's accuracy? Suppose we have an independent test for balls and strikes (perhaps an optical scanner). But also suppose, as was allowed earlier, that some pitches are genuinely—metaphysically—indeterminate vis-à-vis the ball/strike category. This indeterminacy does not endanger the assessment of a candidate's accuracy. We may simply ignore indeterminate cases and measure the candidate's accuracy by his score on determinate ones. We can do the same, in theory, in the law. Insofar as we concentrate on accuracy, what we seek in an adjudication system is one that promotes correct verdicts in determinate cases. Indeterminate cases may simply be ignored. This is why the application of social epistemology to legal adjudication is conceptually in the clear even if there is (metaphysical) indeterminacy. None of this guarantees, of course, that it is easy to figure out what degrees of accuracy various adjudication systems will promote. But figuring that out is social epistemology's proper task in the legal domain, however difficult a task it may be.

9.2 Alternative criteria of a good adjudication system

My emphasis on the veritistic criterion for a good adjudication system is supported by at least one official document of the American legal system: the Federal Rules of Evidence. Rule 102 of the Federal Rules reads:

These rules [of evidence] shall be construed to secure fairness in administration, elimination of unjustifiable expense and delay, and promotion of growth and development of the law of evidence to the end *that the truth may be ascertained* and proceedings justly determined. (Emphasis added)

Although this passage invokes further desiderata such as time, cost, and justice in addition to truth, it clearly makes truth determination one of the core objectives. Nonetheless, many people might resist the weight I am giving to the truth-finding desideratum. Adjudication systems, they might say, are devices for resolving disputes, and it remains to be shown that accuracy is the most important criterion for a good dispute-settling system. Certainly there are other candidate criteria that deserve consideration. Three alternative criteria will therefore be examined: (1) *fairness* or *impartiality*, (2) *acceptability to the parties*, and (3) *evidence responsiveness*.

Before turning to these alternatives, let us draw a distinction between two kinds of disputes: *interest-based* disputes and *merit-based* disputes (Perritt 1984).[12] Interest-based disputes are ones in which people have conflicting interests but no external standard by which to resolve this conflict. For example, two friends may agree to spend the evening together, but one prefers to see a film and the other prefers to play cards. There is no external standard by which to resolve this disagreement. In a merit-based dispute, one party claims to merit certain treatment because of something done by the other party, something allegedly covered by an external standard. For example, the first party might claim to merit a certain award because the second breached a contract, or acted tortiously. All legal disputes are of this second, merit-based, kind. Only for this class of disputes do I favor a truth-oriented approach. But this encompasses all legal disputes.[13]

Does any alternative constitute a satisfactory approach to legal, merit-based disputes? Let us begin with fairness or impartiality, by first asking what fairness or impartiality consists in. Perhaps impartiality means not giving either party *any* advantage or edge over the other in resolving the dispute. Is this really a plausible aim of an adjudication system? Consider a suit in which one side knows of numerous witnesses to a critical event who are all prepared to support its contention concerning that event, whereas the other side has no witnesses to support its account of the matter. This arises because what actually transpired in that event fits the contention of the first side, as every witness to it would be prepared to attest. Now any adjudication system that allows the testimony of witnesses—in contrast with possible adjudication systems that would disallow witnesses altogether—gives an edge or advantage to the first party. A witness-permitting system makes it more likely, in this case, that the first side will win. Is this a count against such a system? Surely not. If a party gains an "advantage" in a dispute-resolution procedure simply as a byproduct of being in the right, that is unobjectionable. If a procedure renders it more likely that one party will win because of its merit, that is no flaw of the procedure.

Another way of clarifying the "no advantage" idea is to say that each party to a dispute must have an equal chance of winning, no matter what features it might have. But this implies that flipping a coin to decide who wins should be an adequate procedure. A moment's reflection indicates that this is an

---

[12] Perritt uses the terminology "rights disputes" rather than "merit-based disputes."

[13] In cases of genuine indeterminacy, the external standard does not cover the cases unambiguously. This does not mean that they are not legal disputes. Legal disputes are ones that invoke external standards and presume the possibility of a resolution by reference to such standards. That such a presumption fails for certain disputes does not prevent them from being legal disputes.

absurd system for settling legal disputes. Do we want a system that gives a defendant—no matter what he has actually done—a 50–50 chance of being judged guilty, or innocent? Should a totally innocent person have a 50 percent chance of losing a frivolous civil suit that might be brought against him? This would obviously encourage suits for large damages against random parties, even when plaintiffs have suffered no harm at all, much less harm caused by the named defendants. If a plaintiff could win half of her suits, on average, no matter what events have transpired, she would be sitting pretty (as long as she were not named as defendant in an equal number of suits). Such an adjudication system would obviously be a disaster.

A dispute-resolution system, then, should not be impartial in the sense of equalizing chances of winning. Parties who *merit* victory in virtue of the material facts should be favored by the system, and parties who do not should be disfavored. Similar remarks apply to a popular metaphor that conveys the impartiality theme, the metaphor of "a level playing field." It is unclear what, exactly, this metaphor means. Does a level playing field imply that each player has an approximately equal prospect of winning? If that is the meaning, then a level playing field is not a good feature of an adjudication system, for the reasons given above.

It might be replied that procedural fairness or impartiality does not require giving *no* advantage to any party; it just requires giving no *unfair* advantage to any party. But what does an *unfair* advantage consist in? That is precisely what a fairness approach must explain, and so far we have no viable explanation.

Shall we define an "unfair" advantage as an advantage that accrues to a party in virtue of some features *other* than its merit? The fairness criterion might then be construed as saying that a system should not favor any party *except* in virtue of their merit-determining properties (or indicators thereof). Only merit-determining properties should tilt the system in one's favor, should influence the outcome of the dispute. But this is just another way of saying that the system should be designed to generate accurate, merit-reflecting judgments, which is precisely what the truth-oriented approach maintains. On this interpretation, fairness or impartiality is not a rival of the veritistic approach to dispute resolution; rather it is a tool for achieving truth determination.

Let me spell this out more fully. A system should treat parties impartially on all dimensions irrelevant to the determination of merit facts, precisely to enable the merit facts to shine through and be decisive. Except where race, gender, ethnicity, and so forth are themselves material facts (for example, in a civil rights action, or in a criminal case where they are necessary for identification purposes),[14] they are irrelevant to, and totally unreliable indicators of, the material facts in legal cases. That is why systems should be impartial with respect to these features, and many others. So the correct appeal of the impar-

---

[14] Thanks to Brian Leiter for suggesting the relevant qualification here.

tiality idea can be fully explained only within the framework of a veritistic criterion of dispute resolution.

The next alternative to consider is the acceptability of a system to the parties. Like impartiality, mutual acceptability has intuitive appeal. But considered as either a necessary or a sufficient condition of a system's adequacy, the proposal faces serious problems. The problems can best be exposed by carefully considering the *reasons* parties might have for accepting or rejecting a dispute-resolution system.

Suppose parties accept a given adjudication system because they believe it is veritistically effective. Does this suffice to make this system a good one? Imagine that although the parties *believe* in the veritistic virtues of the system, their confidence is misplaced. It is actually a veritistic disaster, and many alternative systems would be better. If we (some group of theorists) know this, and know that the ordinary citizens are deluded on this score, should we still regard the system as good? This scenario is not fantastic. There can be culturally generated myths about the truth-generating properties of systems. (There might be such a myth about the adversarial system in Anglo-American culture.) Does the existence of the myth make the system a good one? I don't think so. If verdicts regularly go astray, as judged by the veritistic criterion, this misfortune is not much ameliorated by misguided public acceptance of the system.

Even if general acceptance is not sufficient for a system's worth, it might be necessary. Is this so? Before answering, consider possible reasons for rejecting a system. Given a choice, a tortfeasor might reject a certain system for settling a suit against him because he knows he is legally in the wrong and fears that the system would reveal this fact. This reason for rejecting a system should not count against its worth. So party acceptability of a system, *tout court*, is not a necessary condition of a system's adequacy.

Instead of deeming a *system's* acceptability as a criterion of its worth, let us consider the acceptability of its *outcomes* as the criterion of worth. A system is good, under this proposal, if it frequently generates outcomes (settlements) that both parties find acceptable. The problem with this proposal is that one might accept an outcome not because she thinks it is merited but because she despairs of doing any better under the system. She might view the system as corrupt and insensitive to her situation, but she lacks the bargaining power to do better outside the system. So she accepts the outcome as the best of a bad situation. For this reason, outcome acceptability is not a compelling criterion of system adequacy.[15]

---

[15] I do not mean to suggest that a system's acceptability has *no* good-making features. Clearly, the acceptability of a dispute-resolution system can help preserve the stability and maintenance of the enterprise that it serves, and that is often a good-making feature. What I am saying is that mere acceptability does not suffice for justice; it is not *all* an adjudication system should aim for. Thanks to David Golove for urging these points on me.

The third alternative to veritism is evidence responsiveness. According to this proposal, a legal adjudication system is good insofar as it induces adjudicators to align their verdicts with the evidence they receive. Although an evidence-responsive verdict will sometimes coincide with the truth, it need not do so. The current proposal points out that our legal system requires fact finders to make decisions based on the evidence. Why isn't this the appropriate criterion of system worthiness?[16]

Viewed from within our legal system, there is no question that jurors must base their decisions on the evidence they receive. An evidence-based decision is a proper one, even when it contravenes the merit fact of the case (which the evidence may not reveal). But this viewpoint is an "internal" one, a viewpoint appropriate to a certain role-player in the system (a juror). The question we are presently pursuing is "external" to any given adjudication system. It looks at whole systems and compares them with rivals. When such an external stance is taken, we cannot appeal to an internal component of a system as a criterion. We first need a criterion appropriate to the choice of a system, and a component already built into one system (or even several systems) is inappropriate. We can make sense of evidence responsiveness, however, if verdict accuracy is taken as our external criterion. Verdict accuracy rationalizes the desideratum of evidence responsiveness because evidence responsiveness is the best general means of achieving accuracy, though it sometimes goes astray.[17]

In endorsing the accuracy criterion, some might suppose that I am ignoring the true and proper aim of adjudication, namely, justice. What is the relationship between accuracy and justice? Two senses of justice need to be distinguished: *substantive legal justice* and *procedural justice*. Substantive justice in matters of adjudication consists in judgments or decisions about a person

[16] This proposal bears a straightforward similarity to the evidentialist theory of justified belief, as presented, for example, by Richard Feldman and Earl Conee (1985).

[17] At this juncture a distinction must be drawn between different senses of legal "merit." A certain party might merit victory in a given case relative to the "metaphysical" facts of that case. For a variety of reasons, however, she might not have managed to produce sufficient evidence—as judged by the applicable standard—to warrant victory in that case. Indeed, a judge might even dismiss the case for insufficient evidence. Although in one sense this litigant "merited" victory, in another sense she did not. The sense in which she did not merit victory is merit *relative to the existing and applicable standards of evidence*. I would call this second sense of "merit" a *system-internal* sense of "merit." The first sense of "merit"—the one I work with throughout the text—might be called a *system-external* sense of "merit." (Notice that system-external merit, in the intended sense, is external only to the *adjudication system*, not to the system of *substantive* laws. Whether or not a party has system-external merit does depend on what laws are in place.) When one is operating within a given adjudication system and taking its procedures for granted, the system-internal sense of "merit" should be heeded. But when one is designing adjudication systems, considering revisions in existing adjudication systems, or comparing adjudication systems (which is our present mission), the system-external sense of "merit" is crucial. That is why, except for this note, the chapter focuses on the system-external sense of "merit."

that accord with her (legal) merit or desert. Thus, there is no conflict at all between accuracy and substantive legal justice.[18] Essentially, they amount to the same thing. Procedural justice is another matter. A judgment or decision is procedurally just if it results from the application of a proper procedure.

What is a "proper" procedure? We might distinguish between a thin and a thick sense of "proper procedure." In the thin sense, a token procedure is proper if it comports with the accepted or customary procedure followed in the system. In the thick sense, a customary procedure itself might not be proper, because it violates some external standard for procedural rightness. What is that external standard? As previously argued, an appropriate standard would be the accuracy standard. A procedure is good and proper to the extent that it promotes accurate judgments.[19] In the thick sense of propriety, then, even procedural justice makes some reference to the accuracy desideratum. Notice, however, that whichever sense of propriety is adopted, a distinction remains between substantive and procedural justice. A given decision by a court can be procedurally just but substantively unjust if it results from a customary and generally accurate procedure that errs on that particular occasion.

The criterion of verdict accuracy requires slight refinement if it is to mesh with the Anglo-American tradition in criminal law. The evidence standard of "beyond reasonable doubt" is imposed in the criminal law because certain kinds of verdict errors are regarded as more serious than other kinds: convictions of the innocent are worse errors than acquittals of the guilty. What this shows is not that truth determination is the wrong criterion of system goodness, but that one category of truths—the truths of innocence—is weighted more heavily than another category of truths—the truths of guilt. With this weighting element acknowledged (for the criminal realm), the veritistic criterion is precisely on track.

I have called the veritistic criterion a "central" or "fundamental" criterion for the evaluation of adjudication systems. I do not say, however, that truth is the *only* relevant value. Other values include speed, cost, and the nonviolation of independent legal rights of the role-players (parties, witnesses, jurors, and so forth). By "independent" rights, I mean rights flowing from sources other than the adjudication system itself (or its rationale). If a proposed adjudication system entails or risks the violation of certain rights, it might properly be rejected despite its exemplary truth-conducive properties. The difficult problem is to say how the truth-getting value should be *weighted* as compared with

[18] But does substantive legal justice coincide with moral justice? If not, shouldn't the latter be pursued instead of accuracy? This is a vexed question, which cannot be addressed here at length. My inclination, however, is to say that adjudication systems cannot reasonably be burdened with the task of securing moral justice; legal justice is a hard enough task to fulfill.

[19] Use of an accuracy-promoting procedure might not be *sufficient* for procedural justice, however. It may also be necessary that the procedure in question be customary and predictable as well. To judge a case by an ad hoc, completely unanticipated, method would not qualify as procedurally just even if the method were generally accurate.

these other values. This is not a problem I shall try to settle. It falls outside the scope of social epistemology. It is enough for my purposes to show, as I believe I have shown, that truth is a primary or central value in legal adjudication. Any adjudication system that fails badly on the veritistic dimension has a strong count against it. This suffices to get the program of social epistemology through the door. It shows that social epistemology has important work to do in this territory, even if it does not get the final word on the subject. Any "all-things-considered" choice among adjudication systems or their components must involve more than veritistic considerations. But veritistic considerations do have pride of place, and they are the ones on which I shall concentrate.

9.3 *Truth and the Bill of Rights*

Some people might take exception to the suggestion that truth deserves "pride of place" among the desiderata of adjudication. Other factors are so weighty, they might argue, that painting truth into the foreground distorts the picture. When we read the (American) Bill of Rights, don't we see a picture in which certain defendant rights and privileges handily trump the search for truth? Doesn't this indicate that an emphasis on truth is off the mark, even granting that social epistemology does not purport to encompass all dimensions of evaluation?

As a preliminary point, notice that social epistemology is not wedded to the constitutional or legal heritage of any one political entity. Social epistemology is universal. When applied to the law, it is not uniquely concerned with *American* legal institutions, although I cite these disproportionately out of personal familiarity. The United States Constitution has no privileged position in our deliberations, unlike deliberations that transpire in American courts or American law schools. If the U.S. Constitution did not support an adjudicatory emphasis on truth, that would not sink my theoretical ship. In point of fact, though, a strong case can be made that it does support this emphasis. Even the Bill of Rights, properly interpreted, helps justify the view that the truth goal deserves substantial priority or weight.

My defense of this contention will be heavily based on Akhil Reed Amar's (1997) treatment of the criminal procedure aspects of the Fifth and Sixth Amendments.[20] Amar combines Constitutional history with textual interpretation to support the centrality of the truth goal. He also criticizes a number of twentieth-century Supreme Court decisions in this area and makes several new proposals for criminal procedure. Some of Amar's work in this territory is fairly controversial, especially particular doctrines he advocates for contemporary criminal procedure. But I think we can separate Amar's claims about

[20] Amar also analyzes Fourth Amendment jurisprudence, but it is less directly relevant to my concerns.

the historical role of truth seeking from his claims about the merits of more recent Supreme Court jurisprudence. Only the former are relevant here.

Begin with the Fifth Amendment clause on self-incrimination:

No person . . . shall be compelled in any criminal case to be a witness against himself.

On its face, this privilege compromises the search for truth. Since the law regularly relies on witnesses to obtain the truth, why not use a criminal defendant as such a witness, if truth is the paramount aim? Since the testimony of other witnesses is sometimes compelled, why not that of a criminal defendant? So it seems as if the Fifth Amendment gives higher priority to factors other than truth.

Amar considers several possible rationales for the self-incrimination privilege that he plausibly dismisses. One frequently cited rationale is the psychological cruelty of the so-called cruel trilemma: without the privilege, the defendant would have to choose among self-accusation, perjury, or contempt (see *Murphy v. Waterfront Commission* 1964; *Miranda v. Arizona* 1966). But, observes Amar (1997: 65), our justice system has no such scruples about compelling answers from a civil litigant. Nor does the system object to forcing people, even in criminal cases, to testify against friends and relations (except spouses), despite the potential pain. Finally, there is no trilemma if one is innocent and says so. So under this interpretation, only the guilty would be beneficiaries of the privilege. No other criminal procedure provision of the Bill of Rights, Amar argues, is designed to give *special* protection to the guilty.

Another interpretation of the self-incrimination clause is that it protects a special zone of mental privacy (*Murphy v. Waterfront Commission* 1964: 55). Again Amar argues that this does not fit. Civil litigants and witnesses must often testify concerning highly private, highly embarrassing matters, for example, in divorce cases. If the Bill of Rights were intended to protect a special, private zone, why not extend this to civil as well as criminal cases? Furthermore, under Court interpretations, immunity dissolves the self-incrimination privilege. Once a witness is given immunity, she can be forced to testify about anything in the private zone. This does not fit with the idea that a private sphere must be maintained.

A third possible foundation of the clause is "noninstrumentalization." Government disrespects a person when it uses him as a means of his own destruction (Rubenfeld 1989; Luban 1988).[21] This explanation does not work, says Amar, because the government "uses" persons as witnesses all the time, whether they are willing or not. It is a general duty of citizenship to serve as a witness when necessary to enforce the laws. Second, if there were a general prohibition against the government using a person against himself, why may it do so in civil prosecutions? Third, the government is allowed to force an

---

[21] Luban writes: "making me the active instrument of my own destruction signals the entire subordination of the self to the state" (1988: 194).

arrestee to submit to photographing, fingerprinting, and voice tests whose results may be introduced in a criminal court (*Schmerber v. California* 1966). If these instrumental uses are permissible, why is using testimony so different, asks Amar (1997: 67)?

The answer Amar proposes is a truth-based one: "Truth is a preeminent criminal procedure value in the Bill of rights: most procedures were designed to protect innocent defendants from *erroneous* conviction. Especially when pressured, people may confess—or seem to confess—to crimes they did not commit" (1997: 84). If the prospect of an unreliable (inaccurate) confession on the witness stand today seems improbable, Amar reminds us that from 1789 until well into this century many innocent defendants in noncapital cases could not afford lawyers and were not furnished lawyers by the government. If forced to take the stand, they could be bullied or bamboozled by a prosecutor into agreeing to things that would wrongly seal their fate. This increases the plausibility that avoidance of this scenario was indeed on the minds of the framers.[22]

Let us turn to the Sixth Amendment, which reads:

In all criminal prosecutions, the accused shall enjoy the right to a speedy and public trial, by an impartial jury of the State and district wherein the crime shall have been committed, which district shall have been previously ascertained by law, and to be informed of the nature and cause of the accusation; to be confronted with the witnesses against him; to have compulsory process for obtaining witnesses in his favor, and to have the Assistance of Counsel for his defence.

The deep principles underlying the Sixth Amendment, Amar argues, are the protection of innocence and the pursuit of truth. A speedy trial protects the innocent person from prolonged punishment in pretrial detention. It also helps ensure that the accuracy of the trial itself will not be undermined, as might occur if a delayed trial causes the loss of exculpatory evidence (Amar 1997: 90). The publicness of the trial is also intended to protect an innocent person from an erroneous verdict of guilt. Prosecution witnesses may be less willing to lie or shade the truth with the public looking on. Bystanders can bring missing information to the attention of court and counsel. Counsel, confrontation, and compulsory process are also designed as engines by which an innocent person can make the truth of his innocence visible to the jury and the public (Amar 1997: 90).[23]

---

[22] Amar points out that concern with the unreliability of a defendant's in-court testimony was expressed by the Supreme Court a century ago in one of its earliest self-incrimination opinions: "It is not every one who can safely venture on the witness stand though entirely innocent of the charge against him. Excessive timidity, nervousness when facing others and attempting to explain transactions of a suspicious character, and offenses charged against him, will often confuse and embarrass him to such a degree as to increase rather than remove prejudices against him" (*Wilson v. United States* 1893: 66).

[23] The public aspect of the trial suggests that a premium is placed not only on the jury producing a true verdict but on the public's believing its truth. This is not a point I shall be stressing, but it is obviously compatible with the veritistic approach.

The relationship between the publicness of a trial and the discovery of truth was highlighted as early as 1685, when Solicitor General John Hawles put the point as follows: "[T]he reason that all trials are public is, that any person may inform in point of fact, though not subpoena'd, *that truth may be discovered* in civil as well as criminal cases. There is an invitation to all persons, who can inform the court concerning the matter to be tried, to come into the court, and they shall be heard" (Hawles 1811: 460; emphasis added). Truth was equally stressed by William Blackstone: "This open examination of witnesses *viva voce*, in the presence of all mankind, is much more conducive to the clearing up of truth, than private and secret examination . . . [A] witness may frequently depose that in private, which he will be ashamed to testify in a public and solemn tribunal" (1765: 3/373).

The ability to compel witnesses to testify on one's behalf is also dedicated to the truth goal. In the words of the Supreme Court, "The right to offer the testimony of witnesses, and to compel their attendance, if necessary, is in plain terms the right to present a defense . . . to the jury *so it may decide where the truth lies*" (*Washington v. Texas* 1967: 19; emphasis added).

The right to counsel, argues Amar, is again one of the tools that an innocent party needs to convince the jury (truly) of her innocence. Trials are commonly filled with technical lawyer's law—for example, the rules of evidence. Without expert assistance, the accused may be unable to exercise her rights effectively to cross-examine prosecution witnesses and present her own evidence and witnesses (Amar 1997: 139).

Amar summarizes his view as follows:

Truth and accuracy are vital values. A procedural system that cannot sort the innocent from the guilty will confound any set of substantive laws, however just . . . A Constitution proclaimed in the name of We the People should be rooted in enduring values that Americans can recognize as *our* values. Truth and the protection of innocence are such values. Virtually everything in the Fourth, Fifth, and Sixth Amendments, properly read, promotes, or at least does not betray, these values. (1997: 155)

Amar's critics contend that he ignores many considerations. Carol Steiker (1994), for example, argues that Amar's "originalism" fails to bring the Constitution—specifically, the Fourth Amendment—into tune with our times. In the modern context of professional police forces, which did not exist at the time of the framers, the exclusion of evidence from illegal searches assumes an importance it did not have in colonial times. But Steiker does not really dispute Amar's historical claim that truth was a paramount concern in the framing of the Fourth, Fifth, and Sixth Amendments. At most she says that other pressing values outweigh that of truth determination in the regulation of searches and seizures. Nothing I advocate is incompatible with this conclusion.

Similarly, although Yale Kamisar (1995) criticizes Amar's views on Fifth

Amendment issues, he does not really dispute the importance of truth or reliability, especially its historical importance:

To be sure, the "voluntariness" test *started out* as a rule protecting against the danger of untrustworthy confessions. It is also true that for a long time thereafter the rule that a confession was admissible so long as it was "voluntary" was more or less an alternative statement of the rule that a confession was admissible so long as it was free of influence that made it unreliable or "probably untrue." (1995: 937)

Kamisar contends that unreliability is no longer the sole or even principal reason for excluding coerced or involuntary confessions. The main concern is impermissible police interrogation methods. Even if Kamisar is right about this, it just shows, once again, that truth is not the only desideratum, a point I fully acknowledge. I would formulate the point as follows. Avoiding or deterring impermissible police methods is a *side constraint* on our adjudication system. Evidence may be excluded if that side constraint is violated. But the existence of such a side constraint should not belie the fact that the overarching goal of the system is truth determination.

For these reasons, the project of veritistic epistemology seems to accord quite well with the spirit of the American Constitution. The Constitution aside, however, it is questionable whether the specifics of the American adjudication system are optimal means to truth determination. Even ignoring provisions of the system that reflect extraveritistic side constraints, how effective is the Anglo-American system from a veritistic point of view? That question will occupy us for the rest of the chapter.

9.4 *Common-law vs. civil-law traditions*

Modern adjudication systems are elaborate institutional structures. Labor is often divided among agents who uncover the evidence, agents who argue over the implications of the evidence, agents who issue verdicts on the evidence, and agents who oversee the entire process. Since the ultimate outcomes of a system hinge on the types of inter-agent transactions permitted and encouraged by the system, this is prime territory for social epistemology. The variety of possible adjudication systems is obviously legion, and some of these systems can be expected to outstrip others in their propensity to reach the truth. This signals a natural domain for veritistic epistemology.

In Western legal history, there are two broad traditions of adjudication: the common-law (Anglo-American) tradition and the civil-law (Continental) tradition. These are sometimes referred to, respectively, as the "adversary" system and the "inquisitorial" system. The latter designations are rather unfortunate. Though the common-law system is indeed adversarial, its adversarial character is only one of its distinguishing marks. The term "inquisitorial" is unfortunate because of its misleading connotations. So I shall avoid "inquisitorial" entirely, and I shall use the term "adversarial" only to label one dimension of common-law adjudication, not the tradition as a whole.

One possible project for the epistemology of adjudication is to compare the veritistic merits of the common-law system and the civil-law system as whole systems. This project makes sense, since each system has its own integrity, with some of its features complementing other features of that system. For example, certain exclusionary rules in the common-law system may be rationalized by the role of lay juries in that system. It might make sense, therefore, to make a comparative evaluation of two entire systems. This is *global* evaluation. On the other hand, from the vantage point of possible reform, it may not be in the cards that an entire adjudication system or tradition would be replaced or exchanged for another. Procedural change usually happens piecemeal. So it would be nice to know how well each procedure, or each small group of procedures, functions in the search for truth. My strategy will be to combine the global and the local. I shall engage in global evaluation by making a provisional case for the veritistic superiority of the Continental, or civil-law, system. But some of the discussion will focus on the local level, looking at selected components of the American system that could be improved without wholesale redesign.

Let me begin by reviewing some of the principal differences between the common-law and civil-law traditions. I draw substantially on the work of John Langbein (1985) and Mirjan Damaska (1997). A chief difference between the common-law and civil-law traditions consists in the composition of the trier of fact, or decision maker. In the common law it is a lay jury;[24] in the Continental tradition it is a professional judge or board of judges. In recent times, however, Continental systems have added lay judges to supplement the professional ones, at least in criminal cases.

A second major difference between the traditions is that the bench, in the Continental system, doubles as investigator and as trier of fact. In other words, the court rather than partisan lawyers takes the main responsibility for gathering and sifting evidence. In a German civil suit, for example, the suit commences with a complaint filed by the plaintiff's lawyer. The complaint narrates the key facts, asks for a remedy, and proposes means of proof for its main factual contentions. The defendant's answer follows the same pattern. But neither plaintiff's nor defendant's lawyer will conduct a substantial search for witnesses or other evidence. Digging for facts is primarily the work of the judge. Similarly, the judge serves as the examiner-in-chief, and interrogates each witness. Counsel for either party may pose additional questions, but counsel are not prominent as examiners. After the court takes testimony or other evidence, counsel may comment, making suggestions for further proofs or advancing legal theories. So counsel do play a role in the proceedings, but

---

[24] Of course, even in the common-law system, parties can waive trial by jury.

their role is definitely subsidiary to that of the court. Counsel do not interrogate witnesses, and indeed the very concepts of "plaintiff's case" and "defendant's case," as distinct stages of the proceeding, are unknown. Furthermore, although a German lawyer will discuss the facts with his client, and will nominate witnesses whose testimony might be helpful, the lawyer will stop at nominating. A lawyer will never have out-of-court contact with a witness, which would be regarded as a serious ethical breach. If such contact were revealed to the judge, it would cast that party's case in substantial doubt.

The common-law system, especially the American version, contrasts quite markedly in the role of counsel. Lawyers are responsible for all the main initiatives and conduct of the case. In pretrial they engage in preparation of witnesses and other evidence, and at trial their battle dominates both interrogation and argumentation phases of the proceedings. This is what marks the common-law system as an adversary system. The judge is largely a referee, who enforces conformity with legal requirements by restricting the introduction of evidence, constraining counsel's argumentation, and the like. The main burden of action, however, is shouldered by the lawyers of the parties, and unlike the Continental system, the trier of fact remains essentially passive.

Other differences also attend the central role of the court under the Continental system versus partisan counsel under the common-law system. In the American system, partisan control includes the selection and preparation of expert witnesses. Each side typically has its own expert witnesses, who are often subject to abusive cross-examination. This practice typically amazes European jurists. In the Continental tradition experts are selected and commissioned by the court. Indeed, in the German system, experts are not even called "witnesses." They are regarded as "judges' aides."

One other institutional contrast is worth highlighting. This is the mass and density of evidentiary rules in the common-law system (Damaska 1997).[25] This maze of evidentiary rules departs in large measure from the methods of factual investigation employed in general social practice. A large class of "exclusionary" rules bars certain types of evidence from reaching the trier of fact, though these same types of evidence would cheerfully and blithely be regarded as probative in everyday life. The hearsay rule is perhaps the most prominent of this class of rules. This peculiarity of the common-law system is worth examining, although it has no obvious relationship to the adversarial character of that system.

What kind of methodology should be deployed in addressing questions of veritistic quality? Empirical studies of each system's accuracy, or purely theoretical analysis? Obvious problems confront the prospect of empirically

---

[25] Damaska identifies a number of other important contrasts between the two traditions, which I pass over because they have no discernible (to me) veritistic ramifications.

investigating a system's reliability. Some might say that we can never be in a better position to judge the facts of a case than the fact finder who actually worked on the case. But this does not seem right. The public often knows about certain evidence excluded from the jury. It may therefore be in a better position than the jury to judge the facts of the case. Second, new evidence or new technologies can convincingly demonstrate the inaccuracy of earlier verdicts. DNA techniques have recently established the innocence of persons convicted of murder before DNA techniques were available. Furthermore, certain types of experimental studies can make contributions toward estimates of accuracy. For example, as Gordon Tullock points out (1980: ch. 3), information about jury disagreements can be used to infer minimum error rates. An empirical research group in England arranged to have a regular jury impaneled and a second jury drawn from the jury list to listen to the same case (McCabe and Purves 1974). Afterward, both juries deliberated and voted. In 7 of the 28 cases studied in this fashion—a quarter of the total—the two juries disagreed. In these cases, as Tullock points out, one of the juries must have been wrong. Thus, at least one-eighth of the 56 juries were mistaken. This is only a minimum error rate, of course, since whenever two juries agreed, they might both have been wrong.

Although this methodology yields some information about error rates, it does nothing to address the probable sources of error. It offers few clues about which features of the adjudication procedure might be responsible for error. Since that is the prime target of my investigation, the methodology I pursue will be rather different. Most of my discussion will proceed by means of theoretical analysis. A number of issues, however, would definitely benefit from new empirical research, and I shall occasionally sketch how such research might be conducted. At present, however, the range of empirical research that addresses the veritistic questions I am asking is fairly limited.

9.5 Exclusionary rules

One feature of the common-law system that invites veritistic scrutiny are its many exclusionary rules. Recall from Chapter 5 our truth-in-evidence principle. The truth-in-evidence principle says that a larger body of evidence—true evidence, at any rate—is generally a better indicator of the truth-value of a hypothesis than a smaller, contained body of evidence, as long as the implications of the evidence for the hypothesis are properly interpreted. In other words, adding true evidence to an already given body of evidence will generally help a cognitive agent assess the truth of a hypothesis, at least if the significance of the evidence is properly interpreted. This principle seems to speak against withholding any true item of evidence from the trier of fact. Exclusionary rules are veritistically suspect.

What are the possible rationales for exclusionary rules? They fall into two categories: veritistic and extraveritistic rationales. Extraveritistic rationales appeal to considerations other than truth: rights, interests, or values of a different sort. As discussed earlier, the practice of excluding illegally obtained evidence is meant to deter police and other officials from making illegal searches or seizures. Rule makers presumably recognize that judgmental accuracy may be sacrificed by excluding illegally obtained evidence. But this veritistic concern is simply trumped, in their eyes, by other values. Since I fully admit the possible legitimacy of this maneuver, and since I offer no principle for balancing veritistic and extraveritistic values, I shall not pursue this kind of rationale further.

Other cases of exclusionary rules, however, lend themselves to veritistic rationales. Designers of evidentiary rules may think that truth will actually be promoted by excluding certain types of evidence rather than admitting them. To explain the plausibility of this approach, start first with what the U.S. Federal Rules of Evidence say about "relevant" evidence. Relevant evidence is defined as "evidence having any tendency to make the existence of any fact that is of consequence to the determination of the action more probable or less probable than it would be without the evidence" (Rule 401). As Richard Lempert (1977) points out, this definition lends itself to the following probabilistic interpretation. Evidence is *ir*relevant to a hypothesis when it makes that hypothesis neither more probable nor less probable than it would be without that evidence. This will hold when the evidence was just as likely to occur if the hypothesis were true as if it were false. When these likelihoods are the same ($p(E/H) = p(E/\text{not-}H)$), their ratio is 1.0. That is when evidence is irrelevant. By contrast, an item of evidence is relevant when the likelihood ratio for that item differs from 1.0. In terms of the Bayesian model explained in Chapter 4, when the likelihood ratio is either greater or less than unity, there will be some probative impact of the new evidence on the hypothesis in question (so long as the prior is neither 0 nor 1.0). Suppose, for example, that the fact finder in a criminal trial receives evidence that the perpetrator's blood, shed at the crime scene, was type A. Suppose that the fact finder also knows that the defendant's blood is type A, and 50 per cent of the remaining suspect population has type A blood. This information implies that the likelihood of this evidence (= the perpetrator's blood is type A) if the defendant were the perpetrator is 1.0, and the likelihood of this evidence if someone else committed the crime is .50. Thus, the likelihood ratio in question is (1.0/.50), or 2.0, clearly different from unity. This evidence, then, is relevant evidence, for it should make a difference to the fact finder's probability estimate of the defendant's guilt. In particular, it should raise that estimate above what it was prior to receipt of this evidence.

The general principle of the Federal Rules of Evidence is that relevant evidence should be admitted. A number of exceptions, however, are added. Rule 404, for example, excludes character evidence (to incriminate a defendant) even when it is relevant. Similarly, Rule 410 excludes evidence of withdrawn guilty pleas, even when such evidence is relevant. And Rule 403 says: "Although relevant, evidence may be excluded if its probative value is substantially outweighed by the danger of unfair prejudice, confusion of the issues, or misleading the jury . . ."

How could relevant evidence mislead the jury? Lempert suggests a straightforward answer, which comports nicely with our discussion of Chapter 4. Relevant evidence might mislead the jury because the jury might *misestimate* the likelihoods, and hence the likelihood ratio. If the jury's estimate of the likelihoods is substantially different from their true value, this could lead to an inappropriately large or inappropriately small revision in their estimate of guilt. To use the terminology of Chapter 4, the fact finder can be misled if their subjective likelihoods differ markedly from the objective (true) likelihoods. This is precisely why it might be reasonable to exclude certain categories of evidence, for example, withdrawn guilty pleas, from jurors. Jurors might be prone to see certain types of evidence as more weighty or less weighty than they really are, by misestimating the likelihood ratio.

How is all this related to the goal of truth? As Theorem 4.1 established, when Bayesian reasoners correctly estimate likelihoods (when their subjective likelihoods match the objective likelihoods), their reasoning on new evidence tends to push their degree of belief in the hypothesis toward greater knowledge (or truth possession). Its effect is veritistically positive. But when reasoners *mis*estimate the objective likelihoods, no such increase in knowledge or truth possession can be assured (even as probable). So in cases where there is a distinct danger of the fact finder misestimating the likelihoods, there is reason to worry. This is how a veritistic rationale for certain exclusions can be constructed.

Several problems, however, face this type of rationale. To warrant exclusion on this ground, rule designers should have information or evidence about two things: (1) the true likelihoods in the relevant class of cases, and (2) the likelihood estimates that fact finders—especially jurors—are prone to make. Without such evidence, it would seem, rule designers would lack grounds for claiming, or suspecting, that fact finders will *mis*estimate the true probabilities. Do rule designers really have such evidence? Do they have hard base-rate facts, for example, about the proportion of guilty defendants who entered and then withdrew a guilty plea, or about the proportion of innocent defendants who entered and then withdrew a guilty plea? Do they have hard information about likelihood estimates jurors would be prone to make about such scenarios? In both cases, rule designers clearly lack such hard evidence.

Perhaps they do not need hard base-rate facts, however, to make reasonable surmises that jurors would be prone to misestimate the relevant likelihoods. Maybe judicial experience would suffice to establish, for example, that innocent defendants sometimes get bamboozled into entering guilty pleas, which they subsequently withdraw after ample consultation with counsel. Furthermore, they may have adequate experience with inexperienced jurors to know that the latter are not equipped with the same background knowledge to appreciate how this can happen. Hence, the jurors will underestimate the relevant likelihood.

If this difference in knowledge or experience is what separates jurors from rule designers, however, why not admit evidence of a withdrawn guilty plea and let the defense counsel give the kind of information rule designers have to the jury? Perhaps that would rectify their propensity to misestimate the likelihood.

Next, we should be careful in applying Theorem 4.1 to the present set of problems. That theorem says that new evidence generates an expected increase in truth possession (or knowledge) when the reasoner uses accurate likelihoods. But failure to have perfectly accurate likelihoods does not guarantee an expected *decrease* in truth possession. We simply do not have precise mathematical results to report about what can be expected to happen when inaccurate likelihoods are employed. When the subjective likelihood ratio is at least in the same direction (greater than unity or less than unity) as the true likelihood ratio, perhaps there will also be a general tendency for knowledge to increase. In that case, the argument from misestimation in favor of exclusion would be very weak indeed. The relevant choice here, after all, is not between giving evidence to jurors with perfectly accurate likelihoods versus giving evidence to jurors with inaccurate likelihoods. The relevant procedural choice is between giving evidence to jurors with admittedly inaccurate likelihoods versus not giving them evidence (of this sort) at all. The latter choice is what the present exclusionary rule mandates. It is far from clear that this is the veritistically preferable choice. All things considered, then, the veritistic rationale for exclusion—the misestimation rationale—rests on shaky ground.

Finally, we should remind ourselves that part of our mission is to compare the common-law system with the civil-law system, in which there are no purely lay juries that serve as fact finders. If the inability of lay juries to make accurate likelihood estimates vis-à-vis certain types of objectively probative evidence forces a lay jury system to throw out those types of evidence, that is a major count against it. Certainly it is a major count against such a system when evaluated veritistically. If the Continental system uses these types of evidence without incurring gross misestimates of likelihoods, that is an important factor in its favor as compared with the common-law system.

9.6 *Adversary control of proceedings*

The next component of the common-law system to be examined is its much-debated adversarial component. Under the common law, partisan counsel play a crucial role in both pretrial and trial phases. Critics of the adversarial approach, as we shall see, claim to detect basic truth-distorting flaws at both stages.

Before inspecting the alleged flaws, let us ask whether the adversary system has any virtues from a truth-oriented perspective. Veritistic virtues are often claimed on its behalf. The best way for the court to discover the facts, it is said, is to have each side strive as hard as it can in a keenly partisan spirit, to bring to the court's attention the evidence favorable to that side. Then let the neutral trier of fact decide on the basis of all the evidence. It does not matter that each counsel is biased; these biases will cancel each other out. As long as the trier of fact is neutral, the truth goal will be served.

Our own discussion in Chapter 5 might be invoked in support of this view. Engaging in critical argumentation was there shown (or conjectured) to have veritistically desirable consequences, at least when certain conditions are met. What better exemplifies the spirit of critical argumentation than the adversary system in the law?

Unfortunately, not all that attorneys do in a partisan spirit counts as "arguing." In effect, certain lawyerly activities create or change the evidence rather than simply interpret or debate it. These dimensions of their activities may hide or camouflage the truth rather than bring it into clearer focus, and the effects of these activities cannot easily be overturned or rebutted by the arguments of opposing lawyers.

A critical part of the lawyer's pretrial activity is to coach witnesses, and this can shape (or "misshape") the evidence in two ways.

Every sensible lawyer, before a trial, interviews most of the witnesses. No matter how scrupulous the lawyer, a witness, when thus interviewed, often detects what the lawyer hopes to prove at the trial. If the witness desires to have the lawyer's client win the case, he will often, unconsciously, mold his story accordingly. Telling and re-telling it to the lawyer, he will honestly believe that his story, as he narrates it in court, is true, although it importantly deviates from what he originally believed. So we have inadvertent but innocent witness-coaching . . . [T]he contentious method of trying cases augments the tendency of witnesses to mold their memories to assist one of the litigants, because the partisan nature of trials tends to make partisans of the witnesses. (Frank 1949: 86)

Thus, coaching by counsel can affect the substantive content of witness testimony. Second, coaching can affect the style of a witness's testimony, thereby making a material difference to how a jury views that testimony.

The lawyer . . . seeks to . . . hide the defects of witnesses who testify favorably to his client. If, when interviewing such a witness before trial, the lawyer notes that the witness has mannerisms, demeanor-traits, which might discredit him, the lawyer teaches him how to cover up those traits when testifying . . . In that way, the trial court is denied the benefit of observing the witness's actual normal demeanor, and thus prevented from sizing up the witness accurately. (Frank 1949: 83)

In these activities, lawyers do not merely argue over a fixed body of evidence;

they are actually engaged in manufacturing evidence, evidence slanted toward their client. The evidence is manufactured in the sense that the specifics of what and how the witness testifies are different from what they would be without the lawyer's intervention. While an opposing lawyer can, in principle, rebut misleading arguments an initial lawyer presents, an opposing lawyer cannot undo testimony that is presented to the court. He might try to produce additional evidence that runs in a contrary direction, for example, by getting an adverse witness to contradict himself. But once we realize that lawyers in the adversary system actually (help to) produce certain details of the testimony, rather than merely argue over it, the original justification rooted in adversarial debate is revealed as a distorted picture of the actual situation.

Similar remarks apply to the activity of cross-examination.

As you may learn by reading any one of a dozen or more handbooks on how to try a law-suit, an experienced lawyer uses all sorts of stratagems to minimize the effect on the judge or jury of testimony disadvantageous to his client, even when the lawyer has no doubt of the accuracy and honesty of that testimony. The lawyer considers it his duty to create a false impression, if he can, of any witness who gives such testimony. If such a witness happens to be timid, frightened by the unfamiliarity of court-room ways, the lawyer, in his cross-examination, plays on that weakness, in order to confuse the witness and make it appear that he is concealing significant facts. (Frank 1949: 82)

In effect, the adversary system permits a lawyer to intentionally *mislead* the jury. Although the lawyer knows or believes that an adverse witness is telling the truth, he can purposefully elicit behavior from the witness that will incline the jury to think, falsely, that the witness is unreliable, untrustworthy, or insincere. On its face, this lawyerly practice conflicts with Rule 403, which recommends the exclusion of evidence that threatens to mislead the jury. Nonetheless, it is a practice that the adversary system readily encourages.

An opposing lawyer, of course, also has opportunities for cross-examination, and opportunities on "re-direct" to rehabilitate his own witness. However, he cannot undo the testimony and manner of testimony that the previous lawyer has elicited. The battle, then, is not simply a contest for argumentative superiority, but a contest for manipulative superiority. Who can make the witness *appear* in a light more favorable to his client? Although argumentative superiority may be disposed to point toward truth, there is little reason to believe that superior manipulative skill is positively correlated with truth.

These questionable features of the common-law system contrast sharply with those of the Continental system. In the latter tradition, lawyers neither coach witnesses outside the trial nor interrogate witnesses at trial. All interrogation is conducted by judges. This averts the veritistically dubious activities by partisan lawyers we have just been discussing. Attorneys for each party may suggest questions to the court to be asked of witnesses, enabling them to extract important information from witnesses. But it is neutral judges who actually pose the questions.[26]

The adversary system is sometimes referred to as the "fighting" or "sporting" approach to justice, insofar as it promotes a lively contest between the attorneys for each side. The kinds of features recently identified, moreover, lead many commentators to suspect that trial outcomes depend heavily on the relative skills of the rival lawyers. To the extent that this suspicion is correct, this is a real threat to the search for truth. There is no reliable correlation between a party being in the right and that same party having the superior attorney, or team of attorneys. In fact, the correlation between being right and having the superior attorney may well be close to zero.[27] If the correlation is indeed zero, and if superiority of attorneys is a decisive factor in determining trial outcomes, this is probative evidence that the system fares poorly at getting the truth. To dramatize the point, suppose that counsel superiority is the *sole* factor determining the outcome, and there is zero correlation between rightness and counsel superiority. Then the system will reach true verdicts only about half of the time!

Is the suspicion that trial outcomes heavily depend on lawyerly skill correct? How decisive a factor is lawyerly skill? If we supplement skill with other types of relevant resources for hire, such as number of attorney hours expended, and use of private investigators to dig for favorable witnesses and evidence, many people would say that superior legal resources usually do spell victory, at least in complex civil litigation. It is debatable, however, whether this generalization holds across the board. At any rate, we would need more evidence before condemning the adversary system as a veritistic washout.

Is there any way to obtain more evidence on this issue? In principle, experimental manipulations might be designed to shed some light, but details of such possible manipulations are admittedly problematic. Before spelling out an idea, let me present some background on other experiments in the legal sphere. Research on jury behavior has often been conducted with mock juries. For example, to study the effect of such factors as jury size and decision rule, Hastie, Penrod, and Pennington (1983) conducted manipulations with mock

[26] Are judges in the Continental system really neutral? One of the frequently alleged flaws of the Continental system is that judges all have a similar background as agents of the state and therefore bring a certain systematic bias to the courtroom. But the Continental system no longer uses exclusively professional judges as triers of fact. At least in criminal cases, lay judges supplement professional ones. This brings decision makers into the system with different backgrounds and presumably different biases.

[27] Cynics might contend that there is even a negative correlation, at least in civil suits. Wealthier parties hire more skillful lawyers, and wealthier parties are usually in the wrong; so says the cynic. I am not prepared to go this far—though some types of class action litigation, such as tobacco litigation, certainly tempt one in this direction. An optimist might reply that contingency fees ameliorate the situation to some degree. Even citizens with meager resources can hire an expensive lawyer on a contingency fee basis if they have a clear-cut and lucrative case. (Thanks to Holly Smith for this last observation.)

juries. Working from the transcript of a real trial, they filmed a reenactment of the trial using professional actors, a police officer, a judge, and two attorneys. The trial film was shown to several mock juries, which varied in size and decision rule (unanimity versus less-than-unanimity). Differences between the juries were then analyzed by social scientists who had observed their deliberations and verdicts.[28]

The manipulation I am contemplating would be harder to arrange. We want the same case to be handled by two different pairs of lawyers (or pairs of attorney teams), in order to compare the two outcomes. It is not only the trial proceedings that would be of interest, but out-of-court activities as well. It would not be easy to run the same initial case materials through different lawyers. For example, a potential plaintiff witness who had previously been interviewed by one lawyer would not be the "same" person if he had to go through it again with a second lawyer. He might have been affected by the first interview. Furthermore, since the only independent variable of interest is the two lawyer-pairs, it would be desirable to "control" the jury. That is, the same jury or an equivalent jury should deliberate after each of the two trials, to make sure that jury differences do not contribute to differences of outcome. If it is the same jury, however, their second run through the trial would be massively influenced by the first. The alternative is to use a different but "equivalent" jury the second time. But how is "equivalence" to be ensured? Jury composition would have to be carefully controlled for, which would be extremely difficult.

These wrinkles are practical experimental difficulties I do not know how to surmount. In *thought*-experimental terms, however, it is reasonably clear what we want to know. If two different lawyers were given the same case to try, and if they worked with an equivalent judge and jury, would the outcome be the same or different? In how many cases would permuting or inverting the relative skills and resources of the lawyers produce different outcomes? If it were a significant percentage of cases, that would be a sobering fact about the veritistic properties of the adversary system.

Of course, one would want to run not just a single manipulation of this kind but numerous manipulations, across a spectrum of cases ranging from lopsided to tight. In lopsided cases, the known material facts and legal status may be so overpowering that even the weakest attorney for one side could not lose the case and even the most talented for the other could not win it. The fact that *this* outcome would not reverse under attorney changes is not particularly reassuring, however, because there may be plenty of nonextreme cases in which outcomes would reverse. So we should not choose only this sort of case to study. Nor should we choose only tight cases, in which attorney switches could easily spell the difference. This too might be an unrepresentative

---

[28] One reason for the choice of mock juries was that observers would not have been permitted in real jury deliberations.

scenario, which might magnify our worries beyond reason. We would need to experiment with a range of cases to see how many such cases would permit attorney switches to change the outcome.[29] Though obviously expensive, this would be an eminently worthy series of experiments to run.

Absent experiments of this kind, one must appeal to judgments of well-placed observers of the system. Such judgments provide little comfort to defenders of the adversary system. It is widely remarked, for example, that defenses mounted by public defenders commonly fall short of the quality of defense that better-paid attorneys would provide, either because of the former's relative inexperience or because their heavy case loads restrict the amount of time they devote to each case. Affluent clients, moreover, evidently believe that more time spent by more expert attorneys makes a nonnegligible contribution toward the probability of victory, because well-heeled corporations are prepared to spend seemingly limitless amounts of money on the most expensive lawyers. If these items of common lore are correct, they suggest that lawyerly resources make a substantial difference to legal outcomes. Given our previous reasoning, it follows that the adversary system, in which outcomes often hinge on superior legal resources, is relatively poor for veritistic purposes. The much-diminished role of counsel under the Continental system looks better in this regard.

9.7 Discovery and secrecy

This section continues an assessment of the adversary system, at least indirectly, but it focuses on a special problem of getting relevant evidence before the trier of fact. We have already emphasized the importance to truth determination of getting relevant evidence before the fact finder. If critical evidence somehow gets hidden from the fact finder, that may seriously if not conclusively impair the truth-getting project. The task of uncovering evidence in criminal cases belongs largely to government investigators (police), which falls outside our purview. But sometimes the adjudication system itself assumes the task—as it should—of getting evidence before the fact finder. Often the extraction of evidence is problematic, and a system's success in addressing this problem speaks significantly to its truth-getting powers.

This section concentrates on how to get parties to disclose evidence relevant to their case. Attention will be confined to civil litigation, where disclosure and discovery issues comprise an increasingly large and time-consuming chunk of pretrial activity. Before 1938, in American law, each party to a lawsuit could keep the other side in the dark concerning what evidence it planned

---

[29] There is also the problem of *which* attorney switches to make. Should we only make switches between the most and the least talented attorneys? Or should intermediate examples be chosen to participate?

to introduce at trial, or what experts it planned to utilize. The discovery rules that were incorporated into the Federal Rules of Civil Procedure in 1938 were intended to end the practice of "trial by ambush," by providing parties with procedures for obtaining pretrial disclosure of evidence that was in the possession of their opponents. Revisions were subsequently made in 1980, 1983, and 1993. However, there continue to be complaints of discovery abuse by attorneys and their clients. Lawyers routinely "make specious objections, withhold documents, reinterpret questions asked of their clients, ignore those parts of questions they would rather not answer, and twist the common meaning of language to avoid disclosing documents" (Nader and Smith 1996: 102). Stonewalling can help big corporations win a war of attrition, because their opponents often lack the financial resources to continue the litigation.

The analysis of the problem that follows is based on Talbott and Goldman 1998, of which William Talbott is the principal author. Two types of problems about evidence disclosure can be usefully separated. Let us first distinguish *positive* versus *negative* evidence that a party may possess. Positive evidence is evidence that can assist a party's cause if presented to the trier of fact. Negative evidence is evidence that would hurt its cause. The first problem of evidence disclosure is that each party, if allowed to do so, would prefer to keep (at least some of) its positive evidence secret until the time of trial. That would keep the opposing side from developing an effective rebuttal. Since 1938, parties have been required to disclose beforehand the documentary evidence, expert witnesses, and so forth that they plan to introduce at trial. Attorneys may also make discovery requests of their opponents to extract documents or other evidence that they suspect are relevant, and the rules require compliance with applicable requests. The problem of positive evidence disclosure is tolerably well solved by the discovery rules, because positive evidence is evidence that a party will introduce at trial. If it did not disclose that evidence earlier, the omission will be apparent when it introduces that evidence at trial.[30] The problem of negative evidence, however, is far more intractable.

Given two opposing parties, A and B, B would like to have any evidence in A's possession that is negative for A. Evidence negative for A is positive for B, and hence in B's interest to know about. At the same time, A will be strongly motivated not to disclose negative evidence in its possession, especially highly probative evidence. Since negative evidence is precisely what party A will not itself present at trial, it has a better chance of keeping that evidence secret, even when this violates the disclosure rules.[31] If company A's internal memos

---

[30] Of course, the party can allege that it did not possess or know of the evidence at the earlier time. But that claim will often be hard to support.

[31] The 1993 amendment to the Federal Rules of Civil Procedure requires a party to provide to other parties "a copy of, or a description by category and location of, all documents, data compilations, and tangible things in the possession, custody, or control of the party that are relevant to disputed facts alleged with particularity in the pleadings" (Rule 26(a)(1)(B)).

would damage its case, it will not present these memos at trial, and there is no straightforward way such evidence will get into *B*'s hands, and hence before the fact finder, unless *A* discloses them. It serves *A*'s interests, then, to "duck" or "dodge" *B*'s discovery requests that would cover such documents.[32]

A good illustration of the problem, discussed by Talbott and Goldman, was a product liability suit in the State of Washington.[33] A suit against Fisons Corporation claimed that an asthma medication manufactured by the defendant had caused severe brain damage in a young child to whom the medication was administered while she was suffering from a viral infection. One month before trial an anonymous "Good Samaritan" leaked to the attorneys for the child a "smoking gun" document, an earlier letter from the defendant manufacturer that had been sent to only a small number of physicians. The letter referred to "life-threatening toxicity" of the key ingredient of the medication in children with viral infections. The document proved that Fisons knew its medication had a potentially lethal defect and yet continued to market the drug without warning most doctors. Moreover, this document had not been disclosed by the defendant during the formal discovery process, despite the fact that there were discovery requests that appeared to ask for just such a record. After this disclosure by the Good Samaritan, the defendant settled the child's product liability claim for $6.9 million, and paid an award of approximately $1 million to the child's doctor. A Good Samaritan leak, of course, cannot be expected in the ordinary course of events. It is clear from the monetary damages that Fisons ultimately paid that it stood to lose a great deal by disclosing the "smoking gun" document, and therefore decided against disclosure. This kind of nondisclosure seems to be quite common where large damages are at stake. A lot of "discovery games" take place surrounding such evidence, in which attorneys for defendants who don't want to disclose certain evidence try to dodge the necessity of production through various stratagems, or try to "hide" a disclosed document by burying it amid thousands or even millions of pages of other documents.

Given the financial incentive some parties have to hide negative evidence, even rules that imply an obligation of disclosure may fail to ensure compliance. Talbott therefore proposes two types of changes in the existing discovery rules that could alleviate the situation.[34] First, he proposes constraints on legitimate responses that lawyers may make to discovery requests, constraints

---

[32] Of course, there is a danger of getting caught red-handed concealing something where there is a lot of paper floating around that could provide clues to suppressed documents. So parties do have some incentive to release damaging memos. But this does not undercut the basic point that lawyers can and do conceal negative evidence.

[33] *Washington State Physicians Insurance Exchange & Association v. Fisons Corporation* (1993). This case is also discussed, along with similar ones, by Nader and Smith (1996: 121–8).

[34] These proposals should be credited to Talbott (rather than Talbott and Goldman) because they originate with him. For details, see Talbott and Goldman 1998.

that would limit the legitimate ducking and dodging that now abounds. Second, he proposes changes that would severely sanction attorneys who assist or counsel their clients to avoid disclosure. Only serious sanctions aimed at lawyers, he argues, can create appropriate incentives to counteract built-in incentives against disclosure. The goal of accurate verdicts calls for such a system of penalties.

Talbott and Goldman acknowledge that such a system would undermine to some degree the unalloyed adversarial ethos in which every attorney zealously pursues the interests of his client, and is expected to refrain from aiding the opposition in any fashion. Disclosing negative evidence does, clearly, assist the opposition. But this compromise of the extreme adversarial ethos seems necessary to maximize truth determination, and is already implied by the discovery rules currently in place.[35] Recognition that the adversarial ethos is working badly in this important area of litigation seems to be slow in coming, but it can be found among some commentators. Stuart Taylor, Jr. (1994) writes: "I fear [that] the discovery process has been clogged by a culture of evasion and deceit that accounts for much of its grotesque wastefulness, and the adversary system has been perverted from an engine of truth into a license for lawyerly lies."

The next set of legal practices I wish to discuss falls somewhat outside the main thrust of this chapter. Although these practices can affect the accuracy of verdicts, their immediate effect is to prevent information arising during litigation from being revealed to the public. This sort of concealment can impair truth determination in other trials, or prevent meritorious cases from being brought to trial. But it also has an impact on public ignorance, which is of veritistic concern.

Two kinds of practices that produce such concealment or secrecy are *confidential settlements* and *vacatures*.[36] In a confidential settlement, the sued party pays damages on condition that the facts of the case and the amount of the settlement be kept a secret. A vacature is an agreement, approved by the presiding judge after trial, to "vacate" the result, which has the legal effect of voiding it as if it never occurred. Vacatures are usually accompanied by a confidential settlement, in which the parties agree to a court order sealing the records of the trial. Such practices are popular among corporations settling product liability suits, because they are worried that other people injured by

---

[35] At least it is implied when the civil discovery rules are combined with the American Bar Association's *Model Rules of Professional Conduct* (1995). Rule 3.4(d) of the *Model Rules* says: "[A lawyer shall not] in pretrial procedure . . . fail to make reasonably diligent effort to comply with a legally proper discovery request by an opposing party." So the *Model Rules* already require attorneys to do certain things that "assist" an opposing party. The only remaining question is how far the system should go in requiring such "assistance."

[36] My discussion follows that of Nader and Smith 1996: ch. 2. Also see Hare, Gilbert, and ReMine 1988.

their products (or their lawyers) will be more inclined to sue if they learn of the current settlement and the evidence produced in the context of that suit. They may also want to conceal from the public the dangerous characteristics of their product. Plaintiffs are often prepared to agree to these confidentiality provisions because they need the money being offered in the settlement.

Ralph Nader and Wesley Smith (1996: 73) recount the story of the Ford Pinto and its notorious fuel tank design that caused minor collisions to result in fuel tank ruptures and fires. General Motors also had fuel tank troubles. General Motors' lawyers managed to keep this damaging information secret, however. When they were sued by victims of fuel tank fires, GM disclosed documents and agreed to settlements only under confidentiality agreements. In a 1983 trial in Kansas, the judge agreed to seal the court transcript and exhibits even though the proceedings had taken place in a public courtroom.

The obvious solution is for courts to refuse to accept most confidential settlements, or for legislatures to prohibit or curtail such settlements. Judges must review and approve proposed settlements, and the law must be prepared to enforce them. One measure of the envisaged type was adopted by the Texas Supreme Court in 1990, which amended the state's court rules to create a presumption that all court records are to remain open (Nader and Smith 1996: 95). Several other states have enacted similar court rules. Also in 1990, Florida adopted an antisecrecy law, the Sunshine in Litigation Act. This law prohibits courts from entering orders that conceal a public hazard or information about a public hazard. It also makes any agreement to conceal a public hazard unenforceable. Washington State passed a similar law in 1993. Here are examples, then, in which one facet of the adjudication system is reformed with an eye to increasing public knowledge. Though not primarily aimed at improving verdict accuracy, these examples are clear illustrations of applying veritistic social epistemology to the legal realm. However, these are examples of "local" changes, within the common-law tradition, rather than of global changes.

9.8 *Expert testimony*

The role of experts in science was broached in Chapter 8. In the law too the proper handling of testimony from scientific experts is a pressing and sensitive issue. Whose expert testimony should be admitted at trial, and how should such admission or exclusion decisions be made? These are crucial questions in contemporary American legal theory, and they fall quite naturally into social epistemology. Two factors have recently contributed to the centrality of these questions: first, the rapid growth of product liability litigation, with its frequent appeal to scientific evidence, and second, a recent and controversial Supreme Court decision on scientific testimony.

As far back as 1858, the Supreme Court foresaw the problems now before us. It also worried about the court and the jury's ability to assimilate and evaluate expert testimony: "[E]xperience has shown that opposite opinions of persons professing to be experts may be obtained to any amount," and cross-examination of all these experts is virtually useless, "wasting the time and wearying the patience of both court and jury, and perplexing, instead of elucidating, the questions involved."[37] In 1897 the Supreme Court decided to limit cross-examination of experts. It said that once an expert gives his opinion, the court should take it or leave it. It would be "opening the door to too wide an inquiry to interrogate him as to what other scientific men have said upon such matters, or in respect to the general teachings of science thereon, or to permit books of science to be offered in evidence."[38] In other words, whatever a qualified witness said was okay.

This highly permissive stance was turned on its head in *Frye v. United States*, decided in 1923 by a Federal Court of Appeals. The issue in contention in *Frye* was whether a lie detector test would be admitted as evidence. The trials court refused to admit it, on the grounds that there was not yet a scientific consensus about the validity of this new method. In other words, the standard set by *Frye* for scientific testimony was that such testimony should incorporate principles and methods *generally accepted* by the relevant scientific community. The Court of Appeals agreed, and the general acceptance standard became the dominant approach for seventy years. The standard had the effect of excluding a lot of "junk science"—patently absurd testimony by witnesses of dubious authority.

In 1975, however, the Federal Rules of Evidence were signed into law. Rule 702 governed testimony by experts: "If scientific, technical, or other specialized knowledge will assist the trier of fact to understand the evidence or to determine a fact in issue, a witness qualified as an expert by knowledge, skill, experience, training, or education, may testify thereto in the form of an opinion or otherwise." A question arose whether the more liberal Rule 702, which says nothing about "general acceptance," superseded *Frye*. Some courts went with *Frye*, others with the Rules.

Against this background we find the stunning 1983 decision concerning *Barefoot v. Estelle* (see Gianelli 1993). This began as a capital murder case in Texas. In the penalty phase, the prosecution offered psychiatric testimony concerning Thomas Barefoot's future dangerousness. One psychiatrist, Dr. James Grigson, without ever examining Barefoot, testified that there was a "one hundred percent and absolute chance that Barefoot would commit future acts of criminal violence." Barefoot challenged the admission of this evidence on constitutional grounds due to its unreliability. In an amicus brief to the Court, the American Psychiatric Association stated that the "large body of research in this area indicates that, even under the best of conditions, psychiatric predictions of long-term future dangerousness are wrong in at least

---

[37] Quoted in Angell 1996: 125; Angell also cites Loevinger 1995.
[38] Quoted in Angell 1996: 125.

two out of every three cases." The brief also noted that the "unreliability of these predictions is by now an established fact within the profession" (Gianelli 1993: 113; also see Gianelli 1994: 2020). Nonetheless, the Supreme Court rejected Barefoot's argument, saying:

> The rules of evidence generally extant at the federal and state levels anticipate that relevant, unprivileged evidence should be admitted and its weight left to the factfinder, who would have the benefit of cross-examination and contrary evidence by the opposing party . . . We are not persuaded that such testimony is almost entirely unreliable and that the factfinder and the adversary system will not be competent to uncover, recognize, and take due account of its shortcomings. (*Barefoot v. Estelle* 1983: 898–9)

Thomas Barefoot was executed in 1984 (partly) on the basis of junk science.

In 1993 the Supreme Court settled the issue of whether the Federal Rules of Evidence supersede *Frye* by saying that they do. In *Daubert v. Merrell Dow Pharmaceuticals* (1993), the Court viewed the Federal Rules as "relaxing" the traditional barriers to testimony, and as rejecting the "austere" standard of *Frye*. On the other hand, the *Daubert* opinion said:

> That the Frye test was displaced by the Rules of Evidence does not mean, however, that the Rules themselves place no limits on the admissibility of purportedly scientific evidence. Nor is the trial judge disabled from screening such evidence. To the contrary, under the Rules the trial judge must ensure that any and all scientific testimony or evidence admitted is not only relevant, but reliable.

The Court went on to mention four illustrative factors that trial judges might use in reviewing the admissibility of purportedly scientific testimony: (1) whether the theory or technique in question can be or has been tested, (2) peer review and publication of the theory or technique, (3) the known or potential rate of error, and (4) general acceptance of the methodology or technique. In short, the Court suggested some flexible criteria for guiding trial judges in their role as "gatekeeper" of scientific testimony.

Daubert is often described as being a compromise. On the one hand, it clearly intended to liberalize the admission of scientific testimony as compared with *Frye*. On the other hand, it does instruct judges to exercise supervision of proffered testimony, appealing in part to reliability. The message of *Daubert*, however, seems confusing and ambiguous, and subsequent decisions have reinforced the impression of ambiguity. When the Supreme Court itself acted, after *Daubert*, in a landmark case concerning silicone breast-implant litigation, it ostensibly approved the loosest and least scrupulous of gatekeeping functions. But an important recent decision of a Circuit Court concerning breast-implant litigation, also under the aegis of *Daubert*, observed quite tight criteria for testimonial admissibility. These wide fluctuations are worth examining in some detail.

In 1991 a federal jury in San Francisco awarded the plaintiff Mariann Hopkins $7.34 million in a breast-implant case against Dow Corning. (A subsequent case won a verdict of $25 million.) At the trial, much was made of secret documents discovered earlier at Dow Corning, which cast the company in a bad light. Neither these documents, however, nor any other evidence offered at trial, went reliably to the question of whether there is a causal link between breast implants and the rare disorder from which Hopkins allegedly suffered, namely, mixed connective tissue disease.[39] At that time, no epidemiological study showed any increased risk of connective tissue disease (or related diseases) from breast implants. Epidemiological studies conducted since then have also failed to find any such increase of risk. Partly under the influence of the much-publicized Hopkins award, the Food and Drug Administration banned silicone breast implants in 1992.[40] The FDA ban was followed by a tidal wave of litigation. In the next two years, more than 16,000 breast-implant lawsuits, brought by over a thousand lawyers, were filed in federal and state courts. The Hopkins decision reached the Supreme Court in 1995, after its *Daubert* opinion had been issued. In *Hopkins* the respondent (Dow Corning) claimed that the Appeals Court, acting after *Daubert*, had failed to abide by the *Daubert* criteria of admissibility. Yet the Supreme Court let stand the Hopkins decision in 1995. How this squares with *Daubert* itself is puzzling. *Daubert* had concerned the question of whether the antinausea drug Bendectin had caused birth defects. After the Supreme Court opinion, the Appeals Court decided that the testimony by plaintiffs was inadmissible, because expert opinion indicated that no epidemiological studies had found Bendectin to be a risk factor for human birth defects. So extremely similar scientific issues were handled dramatically differently.

A new breast-implant decision in 1996 complicates the picture still further (Kolata 1996b). A Federal District judge in Oregon, applying *Daubert* criteria, dismissed seventy breast-implant claims very similar to that of Hopkins. Expert testimony that plaintiffs wished to introduce was challenged by the defense on the grounds that it was not based in science. Exercising his gatekeeping function under *Daubert*, Judge Robert Jones asked a panel of four disinterested scientists to advise him on the plaintiffs' evidence. After four days of hearings in which the independent panel questioned the experts offered by plaintiffs and defense, Judge Jones decided that none of the proffered plaintiff testimony was of sufficient quality to be presented in court. The testimony was criticized on the grounds that it failed to establish a probability that implants cause disease. Here the impact of *Daubert* was to screen out allegedly scientific testimony quite meticulously. If upheld, this decision would run in

---

[39] For an excellent history and analysis of breast-implant litigation and its scientific context, see Angell 1996.

[40] It was relevant that neither Dow Corning nor other manufacturers had conducted tests establishing the safety of silicone breast implants. But they were not required to do so originally because the product was already on the market when the FDA received authority to require tests for new products. Breast implants had originally been approved under a "grandfathering" clause.

the opposite direction from the "liberalization" policy of evidence admission that seemed to be heralded by *Daubert*.

Let us tarry no further over the delicate issue of *Daubert* interpretation. *Daubert* aside, what practice(s) for admitting or excluding proffered scientific testimony would be veritistically best? We can approach the question from the local or the global perspective. The local perspective would confine the possible answers to ones that fit the common-law adversarial tradition. The global perspective would entertain the possibility that the best solution lies within the Continental tradition.

In the adversarial tradition, faith is placed in the idea that competing partisan testimony presented to the fact finder will optimize the search for truth. This idea was endorsed in the *Daubert* (1993) opinion itself:

> Respondent expresses apprehension that abandonment of "general acceptance" as the exclusive requirement for admission will result in a "free-for-all" in which befuddled juries are confounded by absurd and irrational pseudoscientific assertions. In this regard respondent seems to us to be overly pessimistic about the capabilities of the jury, and of the adversary system generally. Vigorous cross-examination, presentation of contrary evidence, and careful instruction on the burden of proof are the traditional and appropriate means of attacking shaky but admissible evidence.

Our own discussion in Chapter 5 would seem to support this perspective. Wasn't it demonstrated in Chapter 5 that critical argumentation promotes the search for truth? So if one party's expert witnesses offer pseudoscience, or simply poor-quality science, the opposing party's witnesses can rebut the former's contentions.

Unfortunately, as we have noted previously, Chapter 5 did not demonstrate the simple principle that critical argumentation always promotes truth. The veritistic value of critical argumentation was only defended subject to two important qualifications, both of which are probably violated in the instance under discussion. First, it was assumed that the *premises* used by the arguers are all true. This is a very stringent condition to meet in general, and it is obviously doubtful for the case of scientific testimony. For example, an expert witness might assert (or presuppose) as a premise that effects found in studies of experimental animals, for example, rats, apply to humans as well. But that statement may well be false. Second, the veritistic power of critical argumentation was advanced only subject to the condition that the audience for the argumentation correctly interprets the evidential support relations between the premises and conclusions asserted by the speakers. This condition is almost surely not met when a lay jury is confronted with technical scientific testimony. Perhaps *some* jurors, *some* of the time, draw correct probabilistic conclusions from the mass of scientific statements produced by both sides. But it is unlikely that lay jurors can generally be expected to make suitable inferences on arcane and sophisticated topics, where even substantial education and training do not always suffice to produce understanding. So we have no general guarantee, from considerations of the adversary process or critical argumentation, that truth will tend to emerge.

In fact, a very different scenario seems all too likely. Presented with conflicting arguments from highly credentialed "experts," it is easy for the confused juror to perceive the intellectual merits of the two sides as a deadlock.[41] To the naive juror, the ostensible credentials of opposing experts may seem equally impressive, and the subtleties of their arguments are too impenetrable to dictate a preference. Since the jury must render a decision, the apparent "parity" of argumentative strength may incline jurors to choose on the basis of nonintellectual factors, for example, the personal appeal of the opposing experts, or the party that elicits more sympathy. These types of factors, however, have no reliable correlation with the merit facts of the case, so their impact tilts away from accuracy rather than toward it.

To assess the genuine probative force of proffered testimony, it is natural to turn to someone of relatively greater knowledge or expertise. This is what *Daubert* does in enjoining judges to serve as gatekeepers. But do judges have the requisite metaexpertise, that is, the expertise to judge scientific expertise? In receiving the *Daubert* case on remand from the Supreme Court, Judge Kozinski of the Ninth Circuit Court spoke of a "complex and daunting task" facing judges in a post-*Daubert* world (quoted in Kesan 1996: 2001). Judges, after all, are not typically well educated in science. Judge Jones pursued an exemplary strategy in identifying four independent scientists of exceptional qualifications to serve as proxy gatekeepers. But can all judges be relied upon to do their jobs so well? Will judges in all jurisdictions obtain high-quality specialists?

The legal system could plausibly enlist the help of established scientific organizations, as several commentators have suggested, for example, Marcia Angell (1996: 205). Reputable experts could be recommended to courts by organizations like the National Academy of Sciences, the American Association for the Advancement of Science, or more specialized scientific societies. These could be used to assist judges in exercising their gatekeeping function.

More radical reforms might also be proposed. One is to replace juries with judges as triers of fact in tort cases. Other countries do not use juries in civil cases. We should consider eliminating them at least for tort cases, where issues commonly become technical and arcane.

Another radical reform would be to retain juries but adopt the Continental practice—mentioned in Section 9.4—of having neutral, court-selected experts testify at trial. In other words, partisan expert witnesses might be largely replaced by neutral expert witnesses. Partisan specialists could not be replaced entirely, since parties should be allowed to introduce results of tests that they

---

[41] In a nationwide survey of 800 people who served on civil and criminal juries, 89 percent reported that paid experts were believable (see Kesan 1996: 1988).

themselves conducted. In a criminal case, the prosecution's criminologist could testify concerning what blood samples were taken, what analyses were done, and what the results of these analyses were. Similar testimony could be introduced in civil cases. The scientific *interpretation* of these results, however, should be confined to neutral expert witnesses. Party specialists would not be permitted to testify about the import of the test results for the facts under dispute, or on the scientific reliability of those types of tests. That would be the province of neutral experts. Actually, the current Federal Rules of Evidence (Rule 706a) already allow judges to appoint expert witnesses of their own, but this is rarely done. The present proposal is to make this standard practice, and have it replace party-selected scientific experts (except those who have conducted case-pertinent tests).

Those habituated to the adversarial tradition might find court-appointed expert witnesses discomfiting, since they would introduce an element of chance or randomness into the picture. If your side has conducted a test, which your specialists view as probative, you may have no way of telling beforehand (or before pretrial depositions) how a court-appointed expert will testify concerning that test. Wouldn't this threaten the ability of counsel to prepare its case?

Granted, court-appointed experts would emerge as an unpredictable element from each party's perspective. But is this objectionable or unparalleled? Isn't this precisely the situation parties face in the selection of *judges*, who decide matters of *law*? Judges are assigned to cases by lot. Parties have no inkling, before a judge is selected, what legal judgments this "expert" will render in their case. The proposal for scientific witnesses is a perfect parallel. Before knowing the identity of court-appointed scientists, parties may be unable to predict what scientific judgments they will have to contend with. But why is this objectionable? On the contrary, assuming that court-selected experts are at least as knowledgeable and definitely less biased than party-selected experts, this practice seems well designed to improve the accuracy of verdicts. How different the early outcomes of tobacco litigation might have been if jurors never received testimony from tobacco-hired "experts"!

Why favor the extreme step of replacing party experts with court-selected experts? Why won't the screening practice of judges like Judge Jones have a comparable effect? A judge can use independent experts as advisors to screen the admissibility of party-selected testimony, without overturning or revamping the adversarial tradition of party-selected witnesses. The trouble I find with this advisory use of independent experts is that their only function is to assist the judge in deciding between admission or exclusion of partisan-prepared testimony. Exclusion of testimony, however, is a fairly drastic step, which should not be undertaken lightly. It calls for clear and precise criteria of exclusion, which are extremely difficult to formulate, as the *Daubert* opinion itself illustrates. The necessity for such criteria can be happily circumvented if courts do not make decisions about which testimony is "sufficiently" scientific. If neutral experts are chosen from a professionally approved list of candidates, scientific soundness will be guaranteed as far as the current state of science allows, and the threat of partisanship will be greatly diminished.[42]

9.9 Juries

The lay jury is a prominent distinguishing mark of the common-law as opposed to the Continental system, so one might expect it to figure prominently in my discussion. In fact, however, my treatment of it will be fairly brief. One reason for brevity is that the core rationale for the lay jury may be extraveritistic. Jury service may be seen as an important facet of self-government, as a bulwark against central authority, and as a means to educating the citizenry. Since these kinds of considerations fall outside the veritistic dimension of adjudication, they are not prime targets for my comparatively narrow agenda. However, if lay juries were abysmal on the accuracy dimension, maybe these extraveritistic considerations would be trumped. So the veritistic properties of juries must not be ignored. Furthermore, the institutional options are not exhausted by either lay juries, on the one hand, or professional judges, on the other. In many Continental systems, the trier of fact, especially in criminal cases, is a panel composed partly of professional judges and partly of ordinary citizens. This option might honor the extraveritistic values but with less cost in veritistic value (assuming for the sake of argument that lay juries are somewhat less accurate). Second, as mentioned in Section 9.8, we might drop lay juries for certain categories of litigation, like torts, without abandoning lay juries entirely. This choice might be grounded partly on veritistic grounds: specialized knowledge may be required more in tort cases than in criminal cases.

How can the accuracy of lay juries be investigated? An approach cited in Section 9.4 is to compare two juries' verdicts on one and the same case. Where there is disagreement, one of the juries must be wrong. Another approach is to compare the jury's verdict with the one the presiding judge would have rendered if she had been the trier of fact. This approach was adopted by Harry Kalven, Jr. and Hans Zeisel (1966), in their much-admired study of the American jury. When judge and jury disagree, we cannot, of course, conclude that the jury was wrong. But this kind of study indicates the magnitude of difference to be expected between lay and professional triers.

---

[42] Won't a list of professionally approved scientists still include some with a partisan stance? If the judge chooses from this list, might not her own biases determine her choice of experts? Can partisanship really be avoided, then, by court-selected experts? To avoid these threats to neutrality, one could adopt the practice of selecting an expert witness (or panel of such witnesses) by *lot*. As the canonical method for selecting judges to try cases, why not extend it to expert selection as well?

Kalven and Zeisel surveyed judges' opinions in 3,576 criminal cases. Ignoring a complication, the outcomes are presented in the following table (from Kalven and Zeisel 1966: 58, table 12).[43]

		JURY		
		Acquits	Convicts	Total Judge
JUDGE	Acquits	14%	3%	17%
	Convicts	19%	64%	83%
	Total Jury	33%	67%	100%

Focusing on the four cells excluding the totals, the agreement cells are the upper left and lower right cells, and the disagreement cells are the upper right and lower left cells. As there indicated, judge and jury agreed in 78 percent of the cases and disagreed in 22 percent of the cases.[44] Is 22 percent a serious percentage of cases? I am inclined to think so, at least if the errors are heavily weighted in one direction; but others might disagree. Furthermore, as Kalven and Zeisel explain, the class of cases studied are the tighter or more difficult cases, since they are the cases in which the defendant chose to go to trial rather than offer a plea. Presumably, pleas are offered in more one-sided cases, on which judge and jury would have agreed. So the total percentage of prospective disagreement that can be inferred is lower than 22 percent.

The implications of this study are limited by at least two factors. First, no immediate inference can be drawn as to how the errors were distributed. The data are compatible with judges erring as often as, or more often than, juries, so the veritistic inferiority of juries cannot be inferred. Second, this study covered only criminal cases, and was conducted in an era when sophisticated modes of evidence, such as DNA analysis, were less frequent. It is possible that the intricacy of contemporary tort litigation, and even that of contemporary criminal trials, might yield greater discrepancies between judges and juries than Kalven and Zeisel found. New studies should be executed in the contemporary setting before firm conclusions are drawn.

Other approaches to studying juries may shed light on their probable veritistic qualities. In Hastie, Penrod, and Pennington's (1983) detailed analysis of jury behavior, for example, jurors were given memory tests for information from the trial. Jurors seemed to perform remarkably poorly, the authors report.

Memory on the eight fact items tested appeared to run at a rate of about 60 percent accuracy for information directly stated in testimony . . . Performance on the

---

[43] The complication is that juries "hung" in some of these cases, whereas judges always rendered "guilty" or "not guilty" judgments. So there were some noncomparabilities. By consolidating the "hangings" in a natural way, however, Kalven and Zeisel obtain the figures shown in the table.

[44] Disagreement is massively in one direction, with juries less inclined to convict than judges. But I shall not explore this issue.

judge's instruction memory questions were even lower, less than 30 percent accurate on questions about material stated directly in the judge's final charge, such as the elements of the legal definition of second degree murder. (1983: 80)

This kind of finding does not inspire confidence about verdict accuracy.[45]

Other aspects of the jury system can also be approached from the veritistic perspective. The whole manner of jury selection—including voir dire and peremptory challenges—poses many interesting questions. Is a prospective juror's voting behavior predictable in virtue of socioeconomic status, past experiences, political persuasion, and so on, as jury consultants like to claim? If some such characteristics are good predictors of post-trial voting, this may suggest that the facts of the case are less weighty than they ought to be in determining verdict outcomes. This might bear on possible reforms of current procedures. For example, some legal analysts recommend eliminating peremptories altogether. But if certain types of jurors would be inclined to vote a certain way independent of the merit facts of the case, that "biased" kind of juror is a threat to verdict accuracy, and a peremptory dismissal might make good veritistic sense. Peremptory challenges can also be used, however, to dismiss jurors who would be all too good at tracking the merit facts. This speaks against the desirability of peremptories, from a veritistic perspective. So possible jury-selection reforms and other "local" reforms of the jury system deserve far more attention than they can be given here.

Finally, I return to the "global" dimension of our analysis: the comparison of the common-law and civil-law traditions. There are many salient respects, we have seen, in which the common-law system seems to be veritistically inferior to the Continental one. Although better empirical research needs to be done, this inferiority thesis is the tentative conclusion that emerges from our reflections. I have not, of course, given much attention to the alleged weaknesses of the Continental system. One of these commonly attributed weaknesses (mentioned in n. 26) is that judges, being a particular class of bureaucrats, have a particular perspective on society that might bias some of their judgments.[46] Another criticism is that Continental judges—unlike attorneys in the Anglo-American system—have insufficient incentives to investigate the evidence on each side of a case with the right amount of depth and energy. Obviously, these factors must be assessed before coming to any firm conclusion about the relative veritistic merits of the common-law and civil-law systems. Finally, one has to consider how the veritistic dimension should be weighted in comparison with the extraveritistic dimensions. But given the

---

[45] However, the memory performance of all jurors taken together leaves more room for optimism (Hastie, Penrod, and Pennington 1983: 81). A forgetful juror can be reminded of certain items by other jurors.

[46] Inclusion of lay judges on the panels of criminal cases might dilute this worry about the Continental system, because the professional judges would be exposed to lay opinions.

importance of the veritistic criterion, as defended in Section 9.2 especially, it would be very significant to find, as my preliminary explorations here suggest, that the common-law system is veritistically inferior to the Continental one.

TEN

Democracy

10.1 *Knowledge and the nature of voting*

INSTITUTIONS as well as individuals have a stake in knowledge. The satisfaction of institutional goals often requires occupants of selected institutional roles to obtain certain types of knowledge. This point was illustrated in Chapter 9, where it was argued that the aims of the law make it important for factfinders to render accurate judgments about cases they adjudicate. In this chapter it is suggested that the successful functioning of democracy, at least *representative* democracy, depends on the acquisition of certain types of knowledge by particular actors or role-players. After identifying the critical types of knowledge, I explore the social practices or policies that would encourage their acquisition.

Since this is not a book-length treatment of political theory, some broad assumptions will have to be made about democracy without detailed defense. For example, I shall assume that the essence of democracy is rule of the people for the people by means of voting. Given the centrality of voting, voters' knowledge is the first place to look for forms of knowledge that are central to democracy. What is the connection between voting and knowledge (or belief)? According to one view of voting, a vote is the expression of a *preference*. A preference, however, is not the sort of thing that can be true or false, accurate or inaccurate. So this conception of voting offers no straightforward clue to the sort of knowledge that voters in a democracy ought to have. According to a second conception of voting, to vote for X is to make a *statement* or express an *opinion* of a certain sort. Since statements or opinions are precisely the kinds of things that can be true or false, this provides an inviting framework for a knowledge-oriented investigation. Let us therefore carefully consider this approach, often called the *cognitive* or *statemental* theory of voting.

How, precisely, should this view be formulated? In particular, what is the propositional content of an act of voting? One version of the cognitive theory says that voting for X is making a statement to the effect that X constitutes, or accords with, the common interest or the general will. Perhaps the first expression of this idea is found in Rousseau:

When in the popular assembly a law is proposed, what the people is asked is . . . whether it is in conformity with the general will, which is their will. Each man, in giving his vote, states his opinion on that point; and the general will is found by counting votes. When therefore the opinion that is contrary to my own prevails, this proves neither more nor less than that I was mistaken, and that what I thought to be the general will was not so. (1973: 250)

This sort of cognitive theory has recently been endorsed by David Estlund (1990) and discussed seriously by Jules Coleman and John Ferejohn (1986) and Joshua Cohen (1986). This kind of approach, moreover, seems to be presupposed by the Condorcet "jury theorem" (to be discussed below), which relates the judgmental competence of a collective body to the judgmental competence of its members. The rough idea is that the aggregate of votes by a large body of voters has a strong propensity to be accurate, or correct, if each voter has even a slight propensity toward correctness. This entire approach is predicated on the idea that voting involves a judgment that can be accurate, or true, an approach that would be congenial to the epistemic project before us. For our project could then adopt the simple (though not unproblematic) postulate that democracy succeeds when voters have true, or accurate, opinions about what is in the common interest.

Nonetheless, the approach I shall develop does not rest on a cognitive theory of voting. I resist this tempting theory—tempting in the context of my project—because there are serious problems with the cognitive theory, as pointed out by Thomas Christiano (1995).[1] First, there seem to be many cases where it is most unnatural to interpret a vote as a statement about the common interest. Suppose a group of people wish to take a sightseeing trip together, but they must first agree on where to go. A good way to decide where to go is to take a vote and see which destination is most popular. Here it is natural to encourage everyone to vote on the basis of his or her own interest. Must each vote nonetheless be interpreted as a statement that the voted-for destination is the *group's* preferred destination? That is highly implausible. Sally may know antecedently that most members of the group prefer, say, Yosemite to Yellowstone, even though she prefers Yellowstone. When she votes for Yellowstone, must we still interpret her vote as a statement that the group's interest is to go to Yellowstone? That would be absurd.

This case suggests a revision in the statemental approach to voting. The approach might say that votes are sometimes statements about the common interest and sometimes statements about the voter's own interest. There are two problems with this suggestion. If different voters make statements on different topics, how does it make sense to aggregate their diverse statements as one does in counting votes? Aggregation seems to make sense (as Estlund urges) only if the statements are on the same topic. Furthermore, if voters

[1] Not all of the criticisms that follow are voiced by Christiano, but many of them are, and all are influenced by his discussion.

might be making different statements, isn't it important to find out which statement each intends to make before counting votes? But in fact it is unnecessary to determine what statements voters mean to be making, if any, in order to legitimately count up their votes.

Finally, voting cannot simply consist in making a statement that something is (say) in the common interest, because not every such statement counts as a vote. People who have no vote on a given subject—because they live in a different district, or do not belong to the relevant organization—can make statements about the common interest to their heart's desire without thereby voting. Having a vote means having a certain type of entitlement or power, as Christiano points out. This is not captured by the cognitive or statemental view. Of course, people also have powers to make statements; but not everybody with the power to make a statement of the proposed sort has voting power. As Christiano puts it (1995: 410), to have a vote in a certain body or community is to have a certain type of *resource*, a resource that enables one to influence that body's collective decisions in a manner specified by certain rules. To cast a vote is to exercise the power, or to expend the resource. Christiano's resource view is a much more attractive account of the nature of vote possession and voting acts than the cognitive or statemental view. (The latter does not even offer an account of vote possession.) But nothing in the remainder of my discussion really hinges on this account, or any other specific account, of the nature of voting.

10.2 *Voting and information as studied by political science*

If the importance of knowledge to democracy is not directly implicated in the nature of voting itself, how can we identify the role that knowledge ought to play in a well-functioning democracy? Some insight into this question might be gleaned by a look at the study of political information in political science. For at least fifty years, political scientists and other social scientists have been studying political information. Perhaps their findings, and their ruminations on these findings, will alert us to the proper role of knowledge in a democracy.[2]

One principal and consistent finding by American political scientists is that ordinary American citizens have a minimal, even abysmal, knowledge of textbook facts about the structure of American government, the identity of their elected officials, and fundamental facts about contemporaneous foreign policy. Various surveys in the 1970s, for example, indicated that only 52 percent of American adults knew that there were two U.S. senators from their state; only 46 percent could name their representative in Congress; and only 30

---

[2] My summary of these findings is based substantially on a summary by Larry Bartels (1996).

percent knew that the term of a U.S. House member is two years. In 1964 only 38 percent knew that the Soviet Union was not a member of NATO, the alliance of Western European and North American countries directed against the Soviets (Page and Shapiro 1992: 9). These and other facts have led public opinion research to be dominated by the paradigm of "minimalism": the view that mass publics display "minimal levels of political attention and information," "minimal mastery of abstract political concepts," "minimal stability of political preferences," and "minimal levels of attitude constraint" (Sniderman 1993: 219).

More recent research has often departed from this litany of minimalism, painting a more optimistic portrait of mass publics. Even in 1966, V. O. Key defended what he called the "perverse and unorthodox argument . . . that voters are not fools" (1966: 7). Several books published in the early 1990s follow Key's lead in revising the older portrait of ordinary citizens, including Popkin 1991, Sniderman, Brody, and Tetlock 1991, and Page and Shapiro 1992. Common to these books and many other works is the theme that ordinary citizens, either individually or collectively, are able to make sense of their political world despite their lack of detailed information about ideologies, policies, and candidates.

There are three main strands to the more optimistic picture. One strand is the idea of a two-step flow of communication from relatively attentive and well-informed "opinion leaders" to the public at large (Berelson, Lazarsfeld, and McPhee 1954; Katz and Lazarsfeld 1955). This approach suggests that ordinary citizens who pay little attention to the details of politics learn what they need to know to make suitable votes by listening to the opinions of experts or news junkies. A second strand suggests that citizens might be adept at using bits and pieces of information at their disposal to mimic the choices they would make *if* they were fully informed. They can use *cues* and *information shortcuts* to arrive at the same answers more informed citizens arrive at. Cues such as party identification (Robertson 1976) and retrospective evaluations of the economy (Fiorina 1981) have been interpreted as efficient information shortcuts for "cognitive misers." Even Gerald Ford's ignorance of how to eat a tamale has been offered as a sound basis for voters to make inferences about his policy positions (Popkin 1991: 3, 111). Hispanic voters in Texas took Ford's ignorance to betray a lack of familiarity with their whole culture, which may indeed have had implications for his political position. Richard McKelvey and Peter Ordeshook are quite categorical in praising the reliability of appropriate cues: "Cues can provide more than approximations: They provide, under appropriate assumptions, all the information that is required to identify a preferred candidate"(1986: 934). A detailed study of voters confronting complex California ballot initiatives on insurance reform confirmed this idea. When uninformed voters were simply apprised of the insurance industry's official position on a particular proposition, they were likely to emulate the voting behavior of relatively well-informed voters (Lupia 1994).

A third ground for optimism is the presumed beneficial effect of aggregating many imperfect individual judgments into a collective judgment. The logic of the argument is derived from Condorcet's "jury theorem," which demonstrates mathematically that the probability of a correct majority vote on a binary choice in a group of modestly (and equally) well informed individuals increases substantially as the size of the group increases (Condorcet 1994). In an electorate consisting of N individuals voting independently, if the probability of a correct choice by each individual voter is p, the probability P of a correct majority choice (for N odd) can be much greater than p. For example, when $p = .55$, an electorate of $N > 70$ is sufficient to produce $P > .80$. In mass electorates, values of p even slightly greater than .5 produce values of P approaching 1.0. (Similarly, for $p < .5$, the probability of correct majority choice decreases with N in the same fashion.) A number of political scientists have used Condorcet's logic to argue that aggregate election outcomes may reflect much more collective enlightenment than the level of information possessed by individual voters (N. Miller 1986; Wittman 1989; Converse 1990; Page and Shapiro 1992).

These optimistic assessments, however, are questionable and problematic, as Larry Bartels (1996) has argued. Starting with the aggregation rationale for optimism, Bartels makes the crucial point that the Condorcet jury theorem only applies when individual judgments are probabilistically independent of one another. In other words, individual errors must be truly "random," with an expected value of zero and no correlation across voters. But this assumption is extremely implausible. If one uninformed voter is inappropriately swayed by a rhetorical flourish in a televised debate or advertisement, a second voter is likely to be swayed in the same direction, rather than the opposite direction. If one uninformed voter is influenced by systematic biases in press coverage of the campaign, another uninformed voter who is influenced by such biases is likely to be influenced in the same direction. Thus, errors will not simply "cancel out" no matter how large the electorate may be.[3]

Second, Bartels designed a study to test the hypothesis that uninformed voters successfully use cues and information shortcuts to behave *as if* they were fully informed. Hypothetical "fully informed" vote choices were imputed to individual voters using the observed relationship between political information and vote choices for voters with similar social and demographic characteristics. It was then determined whether uninformed voters actually voted in Presidential elections the same way as these fully informed imputations. The results were negative. At the individual level, the average deviation of actual vote probabilities from hypothetical "fully informed" vote probabilities was about ten percentage points. In the electorate as a whole,

---

[3] Bartels points out that formal models of correlated individual choices confirm the intuition that modest positive correlation reduces the efficacy of statistical aggregation modestly, and severe positive correlation reduces it severely (for $p > .5$). See Berg 1993.

these deviations were significantly diluted by aggregation, but by no means eliminated. Incumbent presidents did almost five percentage points better than they would have if voters had in fact been "fully informed," and Democratic candidates did almost two percentage points better.

Are average deviations of this magnitude large or small? Bartels suggests the following perspective. If every voter simply behaved randomly—voting for each candidate half the time—the resulting average deviation from "fully informed" voting probabilities would be on the order of 20 percentage points. Thus, the information voters bring to bear in Presidential elections reduces the average magnitude of their deviations from a hypothetical baseline of "fully informed" voting by about 50 percent. Thus, they do significantly better than they would by chance, but significantly less well than they would with complete information, despite the availability of cues and shortcuts.

At this point in time, then, it is highly debatable how effective cues and shortcuts are. In order to settle this issue, it seems crucial to ask: What kinds of knowledge (or information) is it essential that voters should have? Unless we can specify antecedently the kinds of facts that are criterially important for voters to have, how could anybody determine whether cues and shortcuts are effective means to knowing those facts or not? What, exactly, are cues and shortcuts supposed to be effective indicators *of*? This is a prior question that political scientists seem not to have answered, or even tried to answer. The category of "fully informed" used by Bartels and others is simply the category of top rating given by interviewers to respondents who answer the interviewer's political questions. But do these high ratings constitute, or correlate with, the kind of political knowledge it is *important* for respondents to have? Perhaps comparatively good knowledge of the answers to *these* interview questions is compatible with ignorance of really crucial political information! This problem needs further attention. To answer it, we need to examine the aims or goals of democracy, in order to decide what type of knowledge is required (if any) for democratic processes to satisfy those aims or goals.

In what follows, then, I try to specify a *core* type of political question, one that voters in a representative democracy should answer correctly if the democracy is to function optimally. Once this core type of question is specified, we can consider which social practices help or hinder voters in getting correct answers to these questions.[4]

10.3 *Core voter knowledge*

Let us begin with a simple model of the aim and structure of representative democracy. Assume first that the job of elected officials or representatives is to

---

[4] Not all democratically relevant knowledge is knowledge by *voters*, but core knowledge for voters is where I begin.

achieve the citizens' goals or aims. In other words, the people's ends or aims are what democracy is supposed to promote. In representative democracy, however, there is a division of labor. Ordinary citizens are not expected to devise or execute the best political means to the achievement of their ends; that is what representatives are hired to do. The job of ordinary citizens is simply to select the officials who will do the best job (in the political sphere) at achieving the electorate's ends.

The ends of ordinary citizens can be of two basic sorts: egoistic or altruistic. A person's total set of ends can therefore be some composite of self-oriented states of affairs and collectivistically oriented states of affairs. In other words, a citizen's ends might include not only the advancement of his own personal situation but also the advancement of justice and equity in society. Whatever a citizen's fundamental ends, it is assumed that he or she votes for electoral candidates on the basis of his or her estimate of how well the competing candidates would perform in achieving that voter's ends.

To simplify our analysis, the following additional assumptions are made. First, it is assumed that each potential voter will vote. The problem of whether it is rational to vote (given the low probability that a single vote will swing the election) is ignored. Second, it is assumed that candidates have a single dominant motive in their political activity, namely, to win the election—and perhaps future elections as well. Third, in the first stage of our analysis, it is assumed that each election is a two-way race; that is, there are only two candidates per election. Multicandidate elections pose much greater analytical problems than two-candidate elections, so I begin with the simpler, two-candidate case.

Let us now look more carefully at the citizens' goals or ends. The result of a candidate being elected and holding office for a given term, let us suppose, is a large and complex combination of outcomes. Call such a combination of outcomes an *outcome set*. The actual outcome set that results from the winner's conduct in office is only one of indefinitely many possible outcome sets. All of these possible outcome sets are mutually exclusive, inasmuch as each outcome set differs from every other outcome set with respect to at least one outcome. Each possible outcome might be conceptualized as the value of some variable, where variables might be illustrated (in gross terms) by the level of employment (E), the cost of living (L), the form and quality of health care (H), the crime rate (C), the quality of the environment (V), and so forth. Each outcome set is a combination of values of these sorts of variables.[5] Thus, the outcome sets might be described in the following format:

---

[5] These examples all feature variables concerning aggregate conditions of the social unit. Perhaps it is more realistic to assume that voters' preferences primarily feature outcomes concerning their own personal welfare, for example, their own income or their own taxes. If so, those types of outcome variables may be readily substituted for the ones in the text.

$$OS_1 = \{E_{73}, L_{47}, H_{131}, C_{39}, V_{252}\}$$
$$OS_2 = \{E_{125}, L_{93}, H_{58}, C_{83}, V_{17}\}$$
$$OS_3 = \{E_{21}, L_{98}, H_{55}, C_{102}, V_{61}\}$$

And so forth.

I shall not try to settle exactly which elements should constitute outcomes in an outcome set. Roughly, however, these may be conceptualized as "intrinsically" valued outcomes, at least for purposes of the present analysis. Each voter is assumed to have a preference ordering over the outcome sets. Thus, for each pair of outcome sets, a voter either prefers the first to the second, prefers the second to the first, or is indifferent between them. I do not assume that a voter has actually thought about a full outcome set in any detail, or explicitly compared it to other outcome sets. The preference orderings in question may be conceived of as *dispositions* on the part of voters to prefer various outcome sets to others, which would be manifested if the voter actually contemplated the choices in question.

Suppose that official F is elected and serves in office for the specified term. Consequent on her conduct of office (plus other things), outcome set OS_{73} actually results. Further suppose that if F's electoral opponent F^* had been elected instead, the latter's conduct of office would have produced a different outcome set, OS_{345}. Then if voter V rank-orders OS_{73} above OS_{345}, then F was a better official *for voter V* than F^* would have been, that is, better *from V's point of view*.

Obviously, the outcomes that flow from an official's term of office are a function of more than just that official's conduct. They are a function of numerous other contextual factors. Lump all of these other factors under the heading "the State of Nature." In the case of the Presidency, the State of Nature includes the initial state of the economy and the forces impinging on it, the technological state of the country, the occurrence of natural disasters, the actions of foreign officials (who, for example, declare or threaten to declare war), the actions of Congresspersons and other domestic officials, and so forth. All such conditions constrain what the holder of an office accomplishes, no matter what his or her policies and competences may be. Even Presidents cannot personally control what transpires during their term of office, and the same point holds for any other elected official.

Although nobody single-handedly determines exactly what results from his or her term of office, it is reasonable to assume that there are differences, if only minor differences, between the two outcome sets that would result from any two different candidates' holding office. As long as a given voter is not indifferent between the outcome sets that the respective candidates would produce, it makes a genuine difference to the voter which one is elected. Of course, a voter may not know beforehand which candidate would, if elected, produce a better outcome set from his or her point of view. But that is precisely the question—the central question—that a voter needs to ponder in deciding how to vote.

Let us therefore call the following question the *core voter question*:

(CVQ) "Which of the two candidates, C or C', would, if elected, produce a better outcome set from my point of view?"

Each core voter question has two possible answers:

Answer C: Candidate C would produce a better outcome set (from my point of view).

Answer C': Candidate C' would produce a better outcome set (from my point of view).

Strictly speaking, there is a third possible answer: "The outcome sets that would be produced by the two candidates are indifferent (from my point of view)." But this answer has such a low probability of being true that I shall ignore it in what follows.

I assume that for each core voter question, one of the two possible answers is true and the other is false. In other words, I am assuming that the subjunctive (or counterfactual) proposition that constitutes the answer is determinately either true or false, whether or not anybody knows the particular truth-value. At the time of voting, neither candidate yet occupies the office for which both are running. One of them, of course, could be the current incumbent, who occupies the office during the present term. For the target term of office, however, neither candidate has yet acted in an official capacity, nor produced any outcomes. All official actions and outcomes that are being contemplated for the present vote lie in the future. Nonetheless, I assume that each candidate, if elected, *would* act in a fashion so as to produce a certain outcome set. Candidates themselves may not know beforehand how they will act in every detail, especially since they cannot foresee all the contingencies under which they will have to make decisions. Still, whether they know it or not, they would produce a certain outcome set if elected. Moreover, the two outcome sets that the respective candidates would produce are ones over which each voter has a preference ordering. Hence, ignoring indifference, one of the answers to a voter's core question is true and the other is false, for each voter.

The picture I am assuming has a highly deterministic flavor, which some might find objectionable. Let me therefore mention two ways in which this picture might be modified without seriously compromising the main conclusions I wish to draw. A first softening of the deterministic picture is to withdraw the assumption that each candidate, if elected, would produce a *unique* outcome set and to substitute the assumption that each candidate would produce some outcome set within a smallish *range* of outcome sets. As long as every outcome set in the range that C might produce is preferred by voter V to every outcome set in the range that C' might produce, answer C is true; and as long as every outcome set in the range that C' might produce is preferred by V to every outcome set in the range that C might produce, answer C' is true. This would suffice for my purposes.

A second way of softening the deterministic picture is to offer an explicitly probabilistic picture. In this picture one assumes that there is an (objective) probability p that C would produce a better outcome set for V than C', and a probability $1 - p$ that C' would produce a better outcome set for V than C. In other words, there is a probability p that answer C is true and a probability $1 - p$ that answer C' is true. These assumptions should suffice to analyze patterns of veritistic success or failure in a larger class of elections, which is all that really interests me. For example, if V believes that answer C is true, and the probability is .9 that answer C is true, then we can say that in ten elections of a similar sort where V has a similar belief, V will be right approximately nine times out of ten. For purposes of assessing information processes in veritistic terms, this kind of analytic picture might well suffice. To keep matters clear and simple, however, the initial deterministic picture is preferable. I shall therefore work with that picture, although readers are invited to substitute either of the alternatives I have expounded if that makes them more comfortable.

In a particular election, then, we assume that one of the answers to voter V's core voter question is true and the other is false. If V believes the true answer, V has core *knowledge* (in this election). If V believes the false answer, V has core *error*. If V has no opinion, V has core *ignorance*. Alternatively, we could say that V is, respectively, *informed*, *misinformed*, or *uninformed* on the core question. The first classification system employs the trichotomous belief classification system. But we can easily substitute the classification system of degrees of belief, which introduces a desirable element of realism. Obviously voters are often quite unsure which candidate would produce the best outcome set for them, so their opinion state might be represented anywhere on the unit interval.

In saying that a voter "knows" the answer to the core question, I am, of course, continuing to use the term "know" in its weak sense, in which it means simply: truly believe. In the strong sense of "know," which is usually thought to include a justification condition, it is much more difficult for voters to "know" the answer to a core question. To have strong knowledge, they would need substantial justification for their core belief, and such justification may be hard to come by. However, although such justification may well be desirable, I shall show that certain significant consequences for democracy logically follow from widespread core knowledge even in the weak sense of "knowledge," so we need not concern ourselves with core knowledge in the strong sense.

In a two-candidate election, where it is assumed that potential voters will vote, it is also reasonable to assume that if V believes that C would produce a better outcome set than C', then V will vote for C; and conversely if V believes that C' would produce a better outcome set than C. In short, V's vote will accord with his or her core belief. The same holds if V has a degree of belief greater than .50 for either core answer, at least if we make a further simplifying assumption. Since there are only two candidates, even a slim difference in V's degree of belief in answer C as compared with answer C' suffices. As long as there is some difference (implying that one of the degrees of belief is greater than .50), V will vote for the candidate in whom V places greater confidence of a better outcome set. Strictly speaking, this is not true. Voter V might have a higher degree of belief in answer C than in answer C' but think there is a slight probability that candidate C' would produce a vastly better outcome set than candidate C. This could induce V to vote for C'. To help keep matters simple, our model will neglect this kind of possibility.

In having either a belief or a degree of belief (DB) in a core answer, a citizen need not have any very specific or detailed conception of the precise outcome set that either candidate would produce. Obviously, each outcome set is enormously complex and detailed, and hardly anyone, much less an ordinary citizen, would be able to give anything approaching an exhaustive description of an actual outcome set. But believing an answer to a core voter question does not require a voter to have a detailed conception of the outcome sets each candidate would produce. All that is required is that the voter believe (or have a DB in) a *comparative* proposition: either the proposition, "The outcome set C would produce would be better (by my lights) than the outcome set C' would produce," or the proposition, "The outcome set C' would produce would be better (by my lights) than the outcome set C would produce." Neither proposition specifies a particular outcome set, so it is not implausible that someone should believe such a proposition (even believe it categorically).

It is obvious that beliefs or DBs in answers to core questions do not come "out of the blue." They invariably are the product of other beliefs, or at least impressions and/or images of the two candidates. Beliefs in core answers may be the products of beliefs about the two candidates' past records, their policy platforms and promises,[6] their ideologies, their personalities, skills, and political competences, their debts to interest groups, and so forth. In focusing on core voter beliefs, I do not mean to slight the importance of these other beliefs. On the other hand, I contend that the importance of all these other beliefs lies in their impact on the voter's core opinion. Even if the other beliefs are all true, it will be unfortunate if the voter forms an erroneous belief on the core question. And even if the other beliefs are all false, a crucial part of the democratic process will be well served if the voter's opinion on the core question is true.

---

[6] Some models of electoral competition assume that citizens compare the platforms of the candidates and vote for the one whose platform is preferred, for example, McKelvey 1975 and Kramer 1977. My model does not exclude the possibility that core beliefs are based on comparisons of platforms (or promises), but it definitely is not committed to this assumption.

10.4 *The democratic value of core voter knowledge*

Under my assumptions, to repeat, a voter's belief in a core answer is either true or false. For any voter's core question (relative to a given office that is up for election), the voter has either knowledge or error or ignorance vis-à-vis that question. It should be emphasized that each voter has a distinctive core question. The question, "Which candidate would be better by *my* lights?" asked by voter Smith is a different question from "Which candidate would be better by *my* lights?" asked by voter Jones. The two questions could have different, noncorresponding true answers. Thus, each core voter question must be indexed to a particular voter. I shall now show that democracy is successful, in a certain sense, when the electorate has *full core knowledge*. By full core knowledge I mean a situation in which every voter knows the true answer to his or her core question. "Knowledge" of a truth means either categorical belief in it or a DB greater than .50.

Since we are dealing with two-candidate elections and ignoring ties (highly improbable scenarios in large elections), in each election some candidate wins a majority of votes. Call the winner of a given election C^*. What can be deduced about the winner under the assumption of full core knowledge? First, those voters who voted for C^* believed (or had a DB greater than .50 in) the core answer "C^* would be better than C by my lights." This just follows from the assumption that people vote in accordance with their core belief plus the fact that full core knowledge implies that everybody has a core belief (not simply a DB of exactly .50). Next consider the fact that full core knowledge implies that each voter's core belief is *true*. This implies that all voters who voted for C^* held the *true* belief that C^* would (will) be better than C in terms of their preference orderings. By hypothesis, however, the group that voted for C^* was a majority. Hence, as a consequence of majority rule, full core knowledge guarantees that a majority of citizens will get their more preferred outcome set of those available. This is a good or successful result from the standpoint of democracy's goals.

Recall our earlier endorsement of the commonplace dictum that democracy is government both of the people and for the people. A plausible interpretation of the idea that democracy is *for* the people is that democracy aims to effect outcome sets that are relatively preferred by a majority of the electorate (or as large a plurality as possible). This is precisely what is achieved under full core knowledge, at least relative to the specific candidates running for office and the outcome sets each would produce if elected.

The foregoing shows that, under majority vote in a two-candidate election, full core knowledge *guarantees* that a majority of voters get their more preferred outcome set. I now wish to show that the same consequence is not guaranteed under any different assumption about core knowledge. Let us start at the opposite end of the continuum. Consider a scenario of *full core error*, in which every voter believes the false answer to his or her core question. There the electorate is guaranteed to elect a candidate who produces a worse outcome set than the rival candidate would have produced. Whichever candidate wins a majority of the votes, the assumption of full core error implies that that majority was mistaken in thinking that this candidate would do better by their lights than the opponent. Thus, all of the voters comprising that majority will be worse off with the election winner than they would have been with the (actual) loser.

Consider next a situation of *full core ignorance*, in which all voters have "no opinion" (degree of belief = .50) about their core question. Assume that when voters have no opinion, they cast their ballots randomly. That is, for each of the two candidates, the probability is .50 that a citizen will vote for that candidate. Under these conditions, the chances are 50/50 that the voters will choose the worse candidate, even under a system of majority rule.

Granted that full core error and full core ignorance do not guarantee choice of the better candidate, one might speculate that this result could be guaranteed by something short of *full* core knowledge (knowledge by *all* voters). For example, if a majority of voters have core knowledge, won't that suffice to guarantee the indicated good result? No, it won't. To illustrate, suppose that in an electorate of 1,000 voters 60 percent have core knowledge and 40 percent have core error. It is possible for such an electorate to choose the wrong candidate. Let Jones be the better choice for 400 members of the electorate, and Smith the better choice for the remaining 600. Then the democratically "good" result would be a victory for Smith. But that need not transpire. All 400 voters for whom Jones is the better choice might know that he is and vote for him. They might be joined by 200 voters who mistakenly believe that Jones is better for them as well. (*Ex hypothesi*, there are 400 voters who have core error, so there is ample room for this scenario.) In this fashion, Jones can be elected despite the fact that he is the worse candidate for a majority. So 60 percent core knowledge is not enough to produce the "right" result. In fact, nothing short of 100 percent core knowledge *guarantees* the "good" result. To help convince the reader of this, consider a case in which, in a 1,000-voter electorate, 99 percent have core knowledge and 1 percent have core error in a given election. Candidate Smith is better for 501 voters and Jones is better for 499 voters. Jones, the worse candidate, can still win. Suppose that core error resides exclusively among those voters for whom Smith is really better. All 499 voters for whom Jones is better vote for Jones, and they are joined by two voters who mistakenly think that Jones is better for them. This suffices to give Jones, the worse candidate, a majority.

Although it takes full core knowledge to *guarantee* a democratically good result, high levels of core knowledge can make a democratically good result highly *probable*. With a high level of core knowledge, it requires a very lopsided distribution of error among the remaining voters to tip the election to the worse choice, and in general such a lopsided distribution is unlikely.[7] My main conclusion, then, is that core knowledge promotes democratically "successful" results, and greater core knowledge is always better.

I have assumed that it is a good or valuable result from the standpoint of democracy that a majority gets its preferred outcome set. This might be challenged. Suppose that the majority-preferred outcome set involves slavery, or some other serious infringement of liberties. Is this still a democratically good result? Here it would be appropriate to qualify the posited principle in the following way: A majority getting its preferred outcome set is desirable from the standpoint of democracy *subject to appropriate constitutional constraints* (or constraints that *should* be handled at the constitutional level).[8] The need for this qualification indicates that democratic procedures alone do not ensure justice. This point is widely appreciated and unsurprising. So it is not being suggested that democratic "success" is the only significant value to be sought in the political domain. I assume only that it is one substantial value, and try to show how its achievement is contingent upon certain veritistic accomplishments.

Another objection to the principle of majority preference, even with the foregoing qualification, is that a losing minority might have a more *intense* preference than the majority, which might make the majority's victory unfortunate all things considered. The claim of a more intense preference might be right in the following sense. Call the outcome set that the winning candidate will produce OS_W, and call the outcome set that the losing candidate would have produced OS_L. The intensity of preference that the losers have for OS_L as compared with OS_W might be greater than the intensity of preference that the winners have for OS_W as compared with OS_L. Unfortunately, democracy cannot be expected to solve all problems of social choice, and the problem of preference intensity is one of those that democracy may well be unequipped to handle. (Perhaps this is one reason why certain problems must be addressed

---

[7] Similarly, if a lower bound is set on the margin of victory, some level of core voter knowledge short of 100% can guarantee the "good" result, as Mark Wunderlich has pointed out (personal communication). If we continue to consider a 1,000-voter electorate, but stipulate that the winner gets at least 52 percent of the vote (520 votes), then 99 percent core knowledge guarantees the good result. Since 99 percent core knowledge leaves at most 1 percent having core error, only 10 voters, at most, vote incorrectly. So at least 510 of the winner's votes must be correct, guaranteeing the good result. In general, where the winning candidate receives M percent of the vote and E is the percentage of voters with false core beliefs (or core ignorance), a successful outcome is ensured as long as $(M - E) > 50$ percent. Since particular margins of victory cannot generally be assumed, however, the more core knowledge exists in the electorate, the better off it is.

[8] I am indebted to James Cox for this formulation. The point here might also be expressed in terms of John Rawls's distinction between "higher law" and "ordinary law" (Rawls 1993: 231). As Rawls formulates it, ordinary legislation is the expression of the ordinary power of Congress and of the electorate. Higher law binds and guides this ordinary power. One might say that I am concerned here with democracy at the ordinary level.

at the constitutional level.) As acknowledged earlier, it is not being claimed that democracy solves all problems of social choice, only that insofar as democracy can solve such problems, it needs the help of core knowledge. Majority rule *per se*, unaccompanied by core knowledge, cannot be counted upon to achieve even the sorts of ends that might reasonably be sought from democracy.[9]

I take myself to have proved, then, that core voter knowledge is critically valuable for the realization of democratic ends. What follows from this about other kinds of voter knowledge? Nothing *follows* concerning other types of political knowledge on the part of voters. It remains an open question whether various other types of voter information are helpful or unhelpful, essential or inessential, for reaching democratic goals. Do voters have to know what a candidate's past track record consists in, or what interest groups have contributed to her campaign? These may well be useful things to know, because they might help voters determine the true answer to their core questions. But it is possible that they can answer their core questions correctly without such information.

Although our discussion to this point gives no clue about how important or unimportant these other types of information are, it does provide a benchmark for assessing the importance of all such forms of knowledge. They are all valuable to the extent that they contribute to core voter knowledge. This point

---

[9] The general idea that majority rule can be rationalized or justified in a consequentialist fashion, by its tendency to satisfy people's preferences, is found elsewhere in the social choice literature. A version of this idea was proposed by Douglas Rae (1969). Rae considered an anonymous individual who belongs to a generic political "committee" (or legislature) and who wishes to "have his way" as often as possible, by securing the collective adoption of policies he likes and the defeat of proposals he dislikes. Rae pointed out that for a committee of n members, and where a decision rule specifies the minimum number of members required to impose a policy, there are n possible decision rules. One rule is that n members must agree (unanimity), a second is that $n - 1$ members must agree, and so forth. Rae speculated that the optimal decision rule would be the bare majority rule. This proposal was proved as a theorem by Michael Taylor (1969), and Taylor's proof was generalized by Philip Straffin, Jr. Straffin used the following criterion: A "best" decision rule should maximize the average, over all members, of the probabilities that the collective decision will agree with an individual's decision. Thus, the aim of a good decision rule is to have members "get their way" as much as possible. Then, under Rae's assumption that each player will vote in favor of a proposal with probability p, for some p between 0 and 1, Straffin proved that majority rule is uniquely best among all "symmetric" rules when the number n of members is odd, and one of the two best rules when n is even. My remarks on the "success" of democracy are in the same general spirit as the Rae–Taylor–Straffin approach, because "success" in my terminology involves at least a bare majority "getting their way."

Nothing in the Rae–Taylor–Straffin approach, of course, addresses the value of what I have called core voter knowledge. But this is because Rae, Taylor, and Straffin are discussing *direct* democracy, whereas I am discussing *representative* democracy. If the Rae–Taylor–Straffin approach were applied to the problem of representative democracy, it would again become clear that no good decision rule, such as majority rule, by itself guarantees that a large number of members will "get their way." If their votes are predicated on false assumptions about the consequences of choosing this or that representative, even majority rule will not serve their interests.

is highly significant. The study of political information has heretofore lacked a clear criterion for the importance or unimportance of different types of voter knowledge. I suggest that conduciveness to core voter knowledge is an appropriate criterion.[10] Similarly, the desideratum of core voter knowledge establishes a clear benchmark by which to assess various practices that influence the circulation of political information and disinformation among voters. Such practices should be assessed by their encouragement or discouragement, their facilitation or obstruction, of core voter knowledge.

10.5 *Improving core information*

Let us call the criterion of conduciveness to core voter knowledge the *CVK criterion*. An obvious problem with the CVK criterion, as any practicing social scientist will quickly observe, is the methodological difficulty in applying it. We can only determine the degree to which practices meet this criterion, it would appear, if we can determine the proportion of people who actually attain or fail to attain core voter knowledge in various elections. But how can we determine that? How can we determine in even a single case whether a voter's core belief in a particular election is core knowledge or core error, that is, whether her core belief is true or false? Assume we can adequately fix the voter's preferences over a relevant range of outcome sets (although this is not wholly unproblematic terrain).[11] How, then, do we determine which candidate would produce a preferable outcome set from this voter's standpoint? If we allow ourselves the luxury of time, and attempt only retrospective assessments, we could wait and see which outcomes the election winner actually produces during his or her term in office.[12] But how do we determine what the loser *would* have produced if elected?

This is, no doubt, a difficult problem, but before addressing it I want to emphasize why its difficulty should not deter us from making the core voter question our focus of inquiry. In everyday life we constantly confront choices that pose the question: Which option would produce the best outcome set? In buying a new or used automobile, one must predict and compare the outcomes that would flow from each possible purchase. Which car would be more pleasurable to drive? Which would incur greater repair costs and inconve-

---

[10] In the final section of the chapter, however, I consider a slightly different perspective.

[11] Some political scientists have found evidence of massive instability over time in voters' preferences (Almond 1960). Other investigators, however, downplay and reject the myth of voter capriciousness (Page and Shapiro 1992).

[12] Unfortunately, even this is tricky, since relevant effects of someone's tenure in office may still occur years after that term of office. I intend my model to include such remote effects; or at least I don't specifically wish to exclude them. The causal influence of an official's actions, however, will usually decrease at more remote times.

nience? Which would last longer? Analogously, a young academic starting out in her field may be offered two academic positions, and she must try to predict and compare the outcomes that would flow from each option. Would she secure tenure in Department X? In Department Y? Which set of colleagues would prove more helpful and congenial? How well would she enjoy living in each locale? In each case, after the choice is made and time has passed, one may know (many of) the outcomes of the option actually chosen. But the outcomes of the forgone choice(s), and hence the comparisons between the options, are more difficult to determine.

In all such cases, like the voting case, the critical question one wants to answer is the "core" comparative-outcome question: Which choice would produce an outcome set that is preferable to me?[13] No doubt this core question is difficult to answer correctly. It is even difficult to determine the correct answer retrospectively. Nonetheless, this is the *appropriate* question to ask at the time of choice, and a reasonable one to ask later. If one is misinformed or prevented from getting knowledge pertinent to this kind of question, at the time of choice, one may feel justifiably annoyed. If a dealer misrepresents the mileage of a used car a customer is considering, the customer's decisional information is clearly compromised. If the young academic has little chance of earning tenure in one of the positions because her research orientation does not match the desired profile, that is information she would like to have before making her choice. Such pieces of information are relevant to the core comparative-outcome questions critical to the agents' choices. However difficult it is to answer these core questions, or even to know afterwards what the correct answer was, they are the right questions to focus on. It would be wrong to substitute other questions merely because they are easier to answer. That would be acting like the drunk who searches for his lost keys under the street lamp because the light is good rather than down the block where he actually dropped them.

Since one should not evade core questions, and since these involve counterfactuals, let us pay some explicit attention to counterfactuals. Two issues on this topic should be distinguished. First there is the semantic question: What does a counterfactual proposition *mean*? A great deal of philosophical literature addresses this problem, but I don't think we need go into it here.[14] The second and more important question for us is: How can one empirically determine the truth-value of a counterfactual? When a counterfactual proposition asserts something about the sequence of events that would have unfolded if

---

[13] There is an issue of whether the appropriate preference ordering is the one the agent has at the time of choice or the one(s) that would be developed over time (possibly different ones under different choice scenarios). Since I am assuming no change in preference ordering for the political situation, I ignore this issue.

[14] The leading work on this subject is Lewis 1973, but there is no consensus that Lewis's theory is correct.

some initial event had occurred, a standard procedure is to apply known *laws of nature* to infer subsequent events from the hypothetical initial ones. If I wonder what would have happened to my watch had I released it in midair, I apply the law of gravitation to the hypothetical release and infer that the watch would have fallen. The inference would be different, of course, if the watch were hypothetically released in gravity-free space. In principle, the same kind of procedure might be used to determine the relevant counterfactuals in electoral outcome questions. If we knew dynamical laws of history and the complete initial political circumstances, we might predict the outcome sets that a political figure would have produced had he been elected.[15] But even the best experts do not know such dynamical laws, at least no precise laws of this kind. This does not mean that wholesale skepticism or pessimism is in order. Despite the absence of precise laws, experts may make reasonably plausible judgments with the help of *ceteris paribus* (other things equal) generalizations.[16] The point, then, is that counterfactuals in this terrain are not entirely intractable. What I shall stress here, however, is a different point. It is possible to make progress in this territory even without firm knowledge of counterfactuals in *particular cases*.

Theoretical considerations can warrant the conclusion that many voters answer their core questions falsely without knowing which particular voters err in which particular races. Similarly, theoretical considerations might indicate that certain patterns of political communication impede high levels of core voter knowledge without indicating which particular voters go wrong on which occasions. Thus, it is possible to make proposals for policy improvements without achieving full-scale counterfactual knowledge in the political domain.[17]

Here is how theoretical considerations might help. The Center for Responsive Politics reported that in 1996 those candidates who spent the most money on their campaigns won in about 90 percent of the House races and in about 80 percent of the Senate contests. Unless there is a very high correlation between candidates who spent the most money and those who would have produced the best outcome sets for a majority of voters, quite a few voters must have voted for candidates who were not the best *for them*. If we continue

---

[15] Actually, even knowledge of such laws might not suffice for highly accurate predictions in this terrain, because the number of relevant initial conditions for application of these laws would be vast, and it is virtually impossible to know all these conditions.

[16] Political scientists have recently begun to appreciate the importance of counterfactuals for their discipline, as reflected in Philip Tetlock and Aaron Belkin 1996a. This volume addresses the problem of making counterfactual judgments in history and social science. Tetlock and Belkin 1996b proposes a set of criteria for distinguishing plausible from implausible counterfactual conjectures across a range of applications.

[17] The situation here is analogous to one discussed in Section 9.4. If different juries render opposite judgments concerning the same trial, we can conclude that *one* of the juries was mistaken, even if we cannot identify the particular jury that was in error.

to assume that ballots are cast on the basis of core beliefs, then the "mistaken" ballots were cast on the basis of false core beliefs. To be more specific, if there was a zero correlation between being the higher-spending candidate and being the "better" candidate—that is, the one who would have been best for a majority of voters—then in approximately half of the House races won by bigger spenders (45 percent of the total) the "worse" candidate was elected.[18] This does not mean, of course, that *all* voters who voted for a "worse" but winning candidate made a mistake. Perhaps only a small percentage of those who voted for the winner supported somebody who was worse *for them*, based on a mistaken core belief. Nonetheless, there must have been enough such voters to carry the day. Thus, if we are right in suspecting that the two traits of spending more and being the "better" candidate are not highly correlated, there must be a substantial number of misled voters. We don't have to know *who* they are to draw this conclusion.

These considerations not only suggest that there is substantial core voter error; they also suggest possible ways of combating such error. These ways include public financing of elections and limits on campaign contributions from individuals or interest groups. The rationales for these much-discussed proposals are not wholly veritistic, but they are (or can be) partly veritistic. A nonveritistic rationale is that interest group contributions tend to influence candidates to move their policies in the direction of their contributors. Public financing allows candidates to be more independent of interest groups (Baron 1994). A veritistic rationale would run as follows. Each candidate sends messages to voters with an eye to persuading them that he or she is "better" for them. Each tries to cancel or override the messages of the opponent, by attacking the image, record, and policies of the opponent and deflecting the opponent's attack on their own image, record, and policies. The comparative message advantage, however, heavily depends on the money available for tailoring and broadcasting the messages. Both message experts and television advertising time are expensive. Hence, differences in financial resources are readily translated into differences in persuasive power, even when the persuasion obscures the true answer to each voter's core question. Reducing differences in campaign financial resources would presumably reduce the extent of *misleading* persuasive power.

Additional analysis can suggest other potential sources of core voter error or ignorance, as well as possible policies that might alleviate the situation. In the remainder of this section I examine such sources and policies. I make no claims of novelty for my suggestions. Here, as elsewhere in the book, I want to show how veritistic analysis can be undertaken and what it looks like in broad contours. I leave refinements and major innovations to others. In some

---

[18] I am assuming that all the races were effectively two-candidate races, although many of them undoubtedly featured additional candidates.

cases, moreover, I shall be content to call attention to already adopted policies. Even policies already in place can illustrate how policy choices can be
guided by the veritistic perspective, and specifically by the benchmark of core
voter knowledge.

To assess which practices and policies might be tweaked to improve core
voter knowledge, let us first identify the players and institutional structures
that figure prominently in the flow of political information. Studying their
roles and the possible barriers they erect to core voter knowledge may alert us
to feasible changes that could increase core voter knowledge. Here is a classification of the principal players and institutional structures:

(1) Voters
(2) Candidates and officials
  (A) Elected
  (B) Appointed
(3) Third parties
  (A) Political parties
  (B) Interest groups
  (C) The press
(4) Institutional structures
  (A) The basic structure of representation
  (B) Rules governing campaigns and the disclosure of campaign-related
      events
  (C) Rules governing nomination procedures
  (D) Debates and other deliberative events

Voters are obviously the principal players in the electoral process, and the
ones whose behavior and thinking is most intensively studied under the heading of political information processing. Clearly, voters' thought and behavior
patterns are among the principal causes of their own core knowledge, error, or
ignorance. Since the pioneering work of Anthony Downs (1957) it is generally
assumed that most citizens or voters expend little energy in acquiring political information. Since the costs of learning the details of political issues outweigh the benefits for the average citizen, Downs argued that most citizens
will be "cognitive misers" in political matters. This led to the cognitive "shortcut" view summarized in Section 10.2. For the most part, theorists and policy
advocates assume that the basic information-seeking practices of voters cannot be easily changed, and they look elsewhere for alterations or innovations
in practices that could improve voter information. I shall mainly follow this
approach, but first I shall briefly examine two hypothesized shortcuts voters
engage in, how those shortcuts can lead voters astray, and how (at least in one
case) the situation might be ameliorated.

One shortcut or pattern that may characterize voter behavior is a tendency
to listen to trusted, like-minded sources and to ignore or avoid countervailing
or conflicting sources of political information. People who like Rush

Limbaugh's line are far more likely to tune him in than those who despise it. People are more likely to attend a political rally for a candidate they antecedently favor than for one they antecedently oppose. People may find it downright unpleasant and disagreeable, as Michael McKuen (1990) points out, to engage in political conversation with others of the opposite persuasion. The result, however, is that people rarely hear arguments on the other side of an issue, and this could easily lead to core voter error. The candidate you initially favor may not really be in your interest, but you might not find this out if your principal sources of political information are similarly slanted or biased.

A reasonably innovative idea that *might* improve the situation is James Fishkin's (1991) proposal for a "national caucus." The idea is to assemble a national sample of the citizenry, a cross-section of the electorate, for several days. These "delegates" would interact in person with the major candidates (at the primary election stage, for example) and would debate the issues in depth with the candidates and with one another. The delegates would then be polled on their preferences, and their opinions would be given coverage in the media. Since the delegates would be drawn from different sectors of the population, like-minded members of the population would be prone to trust their "representatives," who resemble them. But these representatives would have benefited from a richer and more diverse array of information, including the sorts of countervailing considerations that ordinary citizens rarely encounter. This could help everyone achieve greater core knowledge.

A second hypothesized shortcut that voters use in making their decisions is "retrospective voting." According to this hypothesis, advanced by John Ferejohn (1986) among others, when a voter is confronted with a choice between an incumbent and an opponent, she simplifies her decision problem by simply asking how well the incumbent has performed during his current term in office. More precisely, she asks how well off she is as a result of this incumbent's current tenure. There is evidence that supports the intensive use of this shortcut. If an incumbent administration has been successful in promoting economic growth and avoiding major wars, it will tend to be rewarded at the polls, no matter how attractive the policy positions of the opposition (Ferejohn 1986: 7; Page and Jones 1979). Essentially, voters find a threshold utility level so that if their current utility is below that level, they will vote against the incumbent; if their current utility is above the threshold, they will vote to reelect the incumbent.

On the surface, this looks like a decision rule that violates our model's assumption, namely, that the proximal cause of a voter's choice is a *comparative* belief about the two candidates. Retrospective voting seems to ignore the nonincumbent altogether. However, we can incorporate the retrospective voting rule into our model by construing it as a kind of simplifying postulate, or rule of thumb, to answer the core voter question: "If the outcome of the incumbent's past term of office is *good enough*, the incumbent will also produce a better outcome in the next term than would the nonincumbent. If the past outcome is not good enough, the reverse holds." Using this rule of thumb, the voter's retrospective belief about incumbent performance determines her answer to the core question.

Spelled out in terms of this postulate, it is obvious how the retrospective voting shortcut can go wrong, construed as a way to answer the core question. The main problem is that however well the incumbent has performed during the past term of office, the challenger might do even better the next time around. Conversely, even if the incumbent performed unsatisfactorily during the last term, the challenger might do even worse if elected for the next term. Moreover, the retrospective approach takes an exceedingly simplistic view about the causal role of the incumbent. The voter attributes her utility level to the performance of the incumbent, without adequately considering the context, or "State of Nature." Perhaps the economy was humming along quite autonomously, and *no* President would have ruined it. Conversely, perhaps an enemy power was bent on war, and no President could have prevented it (short of intolerable capitulation). Finally, the retrospective approach is applicable only to chief executives, indeed, perhaps only Presidents, since no single legislator, nor any mayor or governor, can plausibly be held responsible for a typical voter's overall utility level.

I have no particularly innovative remedies or melioratives for the retrospective voting practice. It is evident from the previous paragraph what additional types of information should supplement belief about one's current utility level in order to arrive at a true core belief. Whatever can be done to supply voters with this additional information, and get them to use it, would be veritistically beneficial.[19]

I turn next to the behavior of candidates and elected officials, as well as the parties that endorse them. It is generally assumed, especially in the economic approach to politics, that the sole aim of candidates is to win election. Similarly, it may be assumed that this is the sole aim of parties, to have their endorsed candidates win. Perhaps it is unduly cynical to assume that this is everyone's *sole* aim, but it seems to be a sufficiently central aim that we won't go too far afield with that assumption. Finally, this may also be a controlling aim of elected politicians' performance in office. Strategies of action are adopted that will help them be viewed as the best choice for a majority come next election time. Obviously, this assumption cannot explain everything. It cannot account for the behavior of an American President in his second term of office, since he cannot stand for re-election. But setting aside term limits,

---

[19] Many proponents of the retrospective voting technique see it as a device to "discipline" and control officials, as a solution to the problem of "principals" controlling their "agents" (Ferejohn 1986; Fiorina and Shepsle 1990). I am not considering the technique from this point of view, however, simply from the veritistic standpoint, specifically the standpoint of core voter knowledge.

the assumption that future electoral victories are a principal if not dominant goal seems not unreasonable—and certainly widespread in the field.

Given this assumption, candidates will have an incentive to communicate to the electors whatever they think will persuade a majority that they are the preferable candidate, whether or not these communications are *true* or *accurate*. The candidate will try to embellish his own record or image, distort that of the opponent, hide from the public whatever facts would hurt his persuasive effort, and so forth. Of course, he will only make claims and charges that he feels will be credible, at least to a targeted segment of the electorate. But in general he will be prepared to misinform or underinform voters in a variety of ways if these messages would contribute to victory. Some types of underinformation provision may be relatively innocuous, such as a Congressperson failing to inform his constituency how much he dislikes doing constituency work back in his district (Ferejohn 1990: 9). Other tempting acts of deception or misinformation may be much more serious. Only countervailing forces, such as the risk of losing support if his claims are proved to be untrue, or if his promises are later broken, will deter a candidate from making false or misleading claims. (Actually, numerous studies show that victorious Presidential candidates keep, or try to keep, the vast majority of their campaign promises, at least those directly under their control. But this does not show that they would be unwilling to break their promises if it would not hurt them in later elections.)

Similar assumptions apply to political parties, and, we might now add, to *interest groups*. When an interest group believes that candidate *C* is the better candidate for its interests, it will devote resources toward convincing (other) voters that *C* is better for the latter as well, even when such a belief (indexed to those voters) is false. So here are additional message sponsors, beyond the candidates themselves, who are prepared to disseminate potentially misleading messages—messages that could easily produce false core beliefs. The messages themselves need not be false in any material way. They may contain no misstatement of fact. They might merely paint an appealing portrait of candidate *C* while camouflaging his commitment to unmentioned policies that are actually quite harmful to some of the targeted voters' interests. What policies or practices can counteract these forces that incline toward core voter error?

Of course, the opposition forces will always attempt to counteract these tendencies. But how can the playing field be groomed, not merely to make it *level* (as is usually advocated), but tilted toward beliefs in *true* core answers? Some steps have already been taken in this direction, and it is instructive to see how these steps can be understood in terms of the centrality of core voter knowledge, even if that wasn't their explicitly stated intent.

A straightforward step, now quite obvious, was surprisingly taken in the United States only in 1990 at the suggestion of the prominent journalist David Broder. This was the proposal to start "Ad Watch" coverage of political advertisements, in which reporters examine campaign ads for truthfulness and realism, trying to expose smears and misrepresentations.[20] Another current proposal is to apply truth-in-advertising laws to campaign commercials. One might require a message to accompany a commercial saying, "Warning: The opinions expressed here are not those of any candidate for office but are paid for by Corporation *X* which last session employed 87 lobbyists on Capitol Hill, received $640 million in tax breaks, and got exempted from 237 government regulations." Such a proposal is similar in spirit to campaign reform laws passed during the "sunshine era" of the 1970s, laws requiring candidates to disclose campaign contributions and expenditures. If voters learn that a candidate has been significantly supported by certain interest groups, inferences can be drawn about some of the policies this candidate is likely to favor, and these conclusions can help voters determine whether this candidate is the best one *for them*. In other words, it can help them answer their core question accurately.

As is evident from these examples, people have been engaged in veritistic social epistemology in the political sphere for some time, though not under this theoretical label. Indeed, my mission in this book is not to create an entirely novel enterprise, but rather to systematize, make explicit, and provide theoretical foundations for an enterprise that people in many areas of social life already recognize as important. In the political sphere, numerous historical philosophers have commented on the need for citizen information. For example, Rousseau discussed the fact that since people can be deceived, it is necessary to make people see things as they are, to point out to them the right path which they are seeking, to provide guidance and increase public knowledge (Page and Shapiro 1992: 391). John Stuart Mill, Thomas Jefferson, and John Dewey also emphasized the need for public education to promote the aims of democracy (Page and Shapiro 1992: 391–2).

Thus far I have emphasized the danger of deceptions being perpetrated in the context of electoral campaigns. But the problem of inaccurate information equally pervades the ordinary conduct of political affairs. At the national level, the study of such deception has focused in recent decades on the conduct of American foreign policy. Many past foreign policy deceptions have been widely discussed in recent years, including Kennedy's alleged "missile gap," Johnson's disinformation about the Tonkin Gulf incident that started the Vietnam War, innumerable cover-ups of covert CIA activities, Reagan's hiding of Iran–Contra activities, and so forth.

Some political analysts see this pattern of problems as a natural outgrowth of the basic relationship between electorates and their elected officials, the so-called *principal–agent* relationship (Fiorina and Shepsle 1990; Spiller 1990). People commonly delegate certain tasks to others, as when people retain lawyers to write their wills, contractors to build their houses, mechanics to

---

[20] This innovation is credited to Broder by James Fallows (1996: 254).

repair their cars, and teachers (or school systems) to educate their children. All such contexts feature informational asymmetries, since the delegating principals cannot monitor everything their agents do, and they may also lack the agents' expertise. This gives rise to opportunities, as well as incentives, for agents to hide some of their actions from the principals. In the political sphere, the electorate may be viewed as a collective principal, which jointly "hires" its elected officials to conduct political affairs on its behalf. But officials have many incentives and opportunities to hide some of their activities from the principal.

Given the endemic problems of political agency, institutions need to be developed to counteract or reduce the amount of informational asymmetry. The Freedom of Information Act was one major initiative in this direction, allowing citizens access to information from federal agencies that document their activities. This is another example of a practice designed for veritistic ends that exemplifies the mission of veritistic social epistemology.

Other proposals that go even deeper into the institutional structure of political representation are also advocated on informational grounds. One is the proposal that the system of single-member district representation be replaced by *proportional representation*.[21] In a single-member district system of representation, the society is divided up into geographical districts from which a legislator is elected by a majority or plurality. In a proportional system, legislators are elected to represent points of view in proportion to the number of citizens who endorse those points of view. Under a party list version of proportional representation, a number of parties are put up for election to seats in a legislature. Parties acquire seats in proportion to the number of votes they receive throughout the country. The crucial feature of proportional representation, for present purposes, is that (A) it tends to encourage a multiparty system, and (B) a multiparty system encourages a greater articulation of platforms and programs. As Christiano puts it,

Parties tend to develop much more specific and distinctive packages of proposals under this system than under the single-member district system. The latter encourages vagueness and ambiguity on important issues as well as complete neglect of many issues. Each party must attempt to appeal to a much larger base of individuals with a much greater diversity of views in order to win an election. The consequence is not an increase in the complexity of programs but rather an increase in attempts to finesse issues of great importance to constituents so as not to offend other constituents. This practice leads to ambiguity and vagueness in the formulation of all programs. (1996: 231)

The proffered rationale for proportional representation, then, is an increase in information provided to voters about each party's program. Obviously, it is anticipated that this will increase voters' accuracy in assessing the comparative value of the different parties for them.

---

[21] My discussion of this topic follows that of Christiano 1996: 224–40.

10.6 *Democracy and the press*

The discussion has concentrated until now on candidates and voters. Only passing attention was given to a crucial type of intermediary in the flow of political information, namely, journalists and reporters. The press plays such a pivotal role in political information processing, however, that it deserves a section unto itself.

Ideally, I suggest, the press should comprise a set of experts who would report, interpret, and explain political events in a way that serves the veritistic interests of voters, especially their interest in core voter knowledge. Since ordinary citizens cannot be expected to acquire such knowledge entirely on their own, and since successful democracy depends on their acquiring such knowledge, the responsibility of promoting and facilitating this knowledge naturally falls to the press. The situation is not unlike the filtering of medical information to patients. Laypersons are not generally competent to understand or assess "raw" medical information, such as the significance of a certain diagnostic test outcome. Thus, physicians or other technically trained experts should explain and interpret such information to patients. The press can be expected to play a similar role in the political sphere. As matters presently stand, however, there are two major impediments to an adequate fulfillment of this role by the press. First, the press is primarily a collection of private enterprises that aim at profits, and this aim often conflicts with veritistically optimal practices. Second, the personnel comprising the press are not, by and large, suitably trained to advance veritistic ends as much as possible.

The main deficiency of the (American) press I shall highlight—following the lead of many observers—is its style of reportage and commentary. This style is attributable to the two impediments cited above: the profit motive and inadequate training. To increase profits, commercial television networks try to appeal to the largest audience possible, and they believe that the route to popularity is an emphasis on the competitive or game-like nature of electoral campaigns, or even the ordinary conduct of governmental business. As Thomas Patterson (1993) puts it, election-related information is consistently interpreted within a *strategic game schema*, a framework according to which candidates compete for advantage. Television and the print media give disproportionate attention to how well the game is being played, or who is winning the horserace. Increasingly less interpretation is presented within a *policy schema*, which focuses on the citizens' task of choosing leaders and governmental policies. The game schema is presumably favored because of its supposed allure to readers or viewers. Another reason it might be favored, as James Fallows suggests, is because journalists simply do not have the right tools to engage in policy analysis.

Journalists are not required to have any systematic training in history, the liberal arts, natural sciences, or sociological and economic analysis. Yet they have largely displaced the scholars with such training from the role of "public explainers," who put in context the events of the day. (1996: 150)

Patterson provides evidence that the press has become increasingly horse-race oriented since 1960. A random selection of election stories on the front page of the *New York Times* revealed a gradual change over the period from 1960 to 1992. In 1960 about 54 percent of the stories were framed in policy terms and 46 percent in strategic game terms. In 1992, by contrast, about 15 percent were framed in the policy schema and 85 percent in the game schema (Patterson 1993: 73–4). Journalistic coverage has also drastically reduced reportage of what candidates or officials actually say, utterances that are important to the electorate's understanding of policy issues. In 1960 the *New York Times* devoted an average of 14 front-page lines to continuous quotes or paraphrases of candidates' statements. In 1992 the average had fallen to 6 lines (Patterson 1993: 75–6). In 1968 the average length of a "sound bite" of a presidential candidate in a television news story was 42 seconds—where a sound bite is a block of uninterrupted speech. By 1988 the 42-second sound bite had shrunk to less than 10 seconds (Patterson 1993: 74).

Television is also obsessed with stories about conflict and adversarialism, to the detriment of genuinely important stories about agreement and conciliation. Fallows tells about President Clinton's trip to Russia in 1995. When a senior economic official began to talk to correspondents about a clever economic/strategic deal the administration had worked out with the Ukraine, the life went out of their eyes. Then one of the reporters said, "Look, we have a rule here. 'No conflict, no story.' If you get Bob Dole to attack this deal, then we can write about it. Otherwise, forget it" (Fallows 1996: 164).

It would be a mistake to suppose that the strategic game schema yields *no* helpful information for citizens trying to answer their core voter questions. This schema includes analyses of how a candidate's statements or positions emerge from his (or his advisors') strategic calculations. To the extent that such analyses correctly reveal the candidate's true thoughts and commitments, they may legitimately raise questions about the candidate's longer-term intentions, and how his policies might change under shifting political vicissitudes. All this can definitely be germane to answering core voter questions. By and large, however, such discussion—often no more than speculation and conjecture on the commentator's part—simply serves to distract attention from the fundamental policy issues. By continually displacing deeper discussion of policies, this journalistic obsession deprives viewers of the kinds of information that are maximally helpful from the perspective of answering core voter questions correctly. Other dimensions of the game strategy schema are even more unfortunate substitutes for policy analysis and evaluation. Reportage on who is winning, as revealed by the latest polls, is of minimal value to citizens trying to answer their core voter questions. This kind of information might be worth something in a multicandidate election; voters might like to know if a candidate has such a slim chance of winning

that a vote for him would be "wasted." But it is of little value in a two-candidate race.[22] It is mainly informative to citizens in a "spectator" mode, not in
the mode of political participants. But democracy's success depends on suitably informed participation, not idle spectatorship.

Are there prospects for improvement from the press? Journalists have been
known to respond to pleas for greater civic responsibility. Criticized for being
too uncritical in the Reagan years, American journalists subsequently became
more adversarial. So perhaps the kinds of criticisms leveled above, which echo
what many observers have been saying, will succeed in inducing the press to
improve their practices. It may be unrealistic, however, to set expectations
very high for the commercial press. This is all the more reason to give strong
support to publicly supported radio and television, where one already finds
the Public Broadcasting System doing the most responsible and commendable
job from the perspective I have been presenting.

10.7 *Multicandidate elections*

Until now the discussion has been confined to two-candidate elections. How
do things change when we move to multicandidate elections? It is difficult to
demonstrate a tight connection between core voter knowledge and democratic "success" in multicandidate elections, but that is largely because there
is great unclarity or indeterminacy in what *counts* as success in multicandidate
elections. If it were clear what results "ought" to flow from voters' preferences
in multicandidate elections, then we could trace the exact contribution of core
voter knowledge toward such results. But because voting theory is notoriously
problematic as soon as one turns to multialternative voting, one cannot say,
uncontroversially and in full generality, what counts as a "good" result.

The fundamental problem is that there are numerous nonequivalent decision procedures or voting methods, and it is not clear which is right. While all
agree on a winner when some alternative is most preferred by a majority, they
do not agree on a winner when no such alternative exists. To illustrate, con-

---

[22] There are two ways that horserace information might be helpful to a voter, even
in a two-candidate election. First, as Thomas Christiano points out, skill at winning an
electoral horserace may be an indicator of the sorts of political skills needed for office
as well. Second, as David Copp points out, in Congressional elections there are districts
other than the voter's own distinct, and his voting decision might reasonably be
affected by information about how the votes will go in those other districts. For
example, someone might initially prefer the Republican candidate in his own district.
But if he learns through horserace coverage that Congress will be dominated by
Republicans, he might think it important to keep a few Democrats in Congress to moderate potential Republican excesses. Thus, horserace information can legitimately influence one's own voting choices, even when the latter are steered exclusively by an eye
to outcomes.

sider the following three election methods: (1) *plurality criterion*, (2) *pairwise comparison*, and (3) *runoff procedure*. Under the first method, an alternative is selected if a plurality of voters rank it highest. Under the second method, an alternative wins if a majority prefers it to each of the other alternatives in pairwise comparisons. Under the third method, if no alternative is top-ranked by a majority, the two top-ranked alternatives from a first ballot are advanced to a second one, and the majority winner of the second ballot is selected.

These three methods can yield three different winners even in the very same case (Saari 1994: ch. 1). Suppose a departmental party is to be held, and to save money only one beverage will be served. The fifteen department members have the following preferences over the three alternatives: beer, wine, and milk (where ">" denotes "is preferred to").

> For six members: milk > wine > beer
> For five members: beer > wine > milk
> For four members: wine > beer > milk

Under the plurality criterion, milk would be the winner, because six members rate it at the top. Under the pairwise comparison method, wine would be the winner, because wine is preferred to beer by ten members (those in the first and third groups) and wine is preferred to milk by nine members (those in the second and third groups). Under the runoff procedure, beer would be the winner, because milk and beer survive the first ballot, and in the second ballot beer is preferred to milk by nine members (those in the second and third groups). When three such respectable-looking methods yield such widely divergent results, it should begin to be apparent that the notion of a "correct" winner is quite unclear.

This problem carries over to the situation of representative democracy. Let $OS(C_1)$, $OS(C_2)$, and $OS(C_3)$ be the outcome sets that would be produced by candidates C_1, C_2, and C_3 respectively. Suppose that there is a fifteen-member electorate whose preference orderings mirror those of the department members described in the previous paragraph. If C_1 is elected and produces outcome set $OS(C_1)$, does that mean that democracy has "succeeded"? By the plurality criterion, the answer is "yes," but by the two other criteria, the answer is "no." So what counts as success, or a democratically "good" result, is indeterminate in multicandidate situations.

Perhaps this approach is too pessimistic, however. To justify the importance of core voter knowledge, we might hope to get along without determining a uniquely correct decision procedure. Perhaps we could content ourselves with observing that, if we apply as a criterion of correctness whatever procedure is in fact in use, core voter knowledge is helpful under that procedure. For example, suppose that the plurality criterion is actually in use by a given organization or polity. Then in the preceding case, we would take the best outcome set to be $O(C_1)$, because a plurality of six members rank that outcome topmost.

Will the actual procedure (the plurality method) result in this best outcome set being obtained? Not necessarily. In particular, if the six members do not *know* that C_1 will produce a better outcome set for them than C_2 or C_3, they may not vote for C_1. But if they do know that C_1 will produce a better outcome set for them than the other two candidates, they will vote for him. Thus, it might be contended that core voter knowledge is useful under the plurality method even in multicandidate voting, and similarly useful under any other chosen method.

Unfortunately, although the foregoing conclusion seems roughly right, the analysis conducted for two-candidate voting does not carry over straightforwardly to multicandidate voting. This is because *strategic* voting complicates multicandidate voting. Strategic voting is casting a ballot in a way that misrepresents one's genuine preferences. What leads people to vote strategically is that no voter individually determines the winner; it is determined by many people's votes. If V knows (or believes) that her most-favored alternative (or candidate) will lose because not enough other people favor it, and if she might obtain her second-favored alternative rather than her least-preferred alternative, she might vote for the second-ranked alternative rather than the topmost one. (This does not arise in two-candidate elections because the second-preferred alternative is also the least-preferred one.) In the beverage example, the five-member second group, expecting that their favored alternative, beer, will lose out to milk under a plurality procedure, may all decide to vote for wine, their second-most-preferred alternative. This vote might be expected to combine with the wine votes from the third group to push wine into the victory column, thereby obtaining the second group's second-most-preferred alternative rather than their least-preferred one (milk). Thus, a person's knowing that an alternative (or candidate) X is best for them does not guarantee that they will vote for X in a multialternative election. So it isn't clear just how helpful such knowledge is.

But perhaps core voter knowledge still helps, even when strategic voting is employed. Consider the representative-democracy analogue of the beverage example, in which strategic calculations lead the second group to vote for candidate C_2, correctly believing that, if elected, he would produce their second-ranked outcome set. This might be a democratically good result, because it is better for that group that they obtain their second-ranked outcome set rather than their third-ranked outcome set. So core voter knowledge might still be good from a democratic point of view. The trouble is that if the second group votes strategically, the first group no longer gets their most-preferred outcome set, which would be the "right" result under the plurality criterion. So it is not unambiguous that core knowledge leads to a democratically optimal result. Nor is it clear that it leads to a "wrong" result, however, because the outcome set produced by C_2 is deemed right by at least one criterion, the pairwise comparison criterion.

In any case, the problems that arise from strategic voting might be blamed—if blame is in order—on the existence of strategic knowledge rather than on core knowledge. Certainly strategic knowledge (at least *partial* strategic knowledge) can grossly distort election results. To illustrate this, consider a popular voting procedure among voting theorists, the *Borda Count* method. Under the Borda Count method, each voter ranks all candidates rather than voting for just one. Zero is assigned to the lowest-ranked candidate, one to the next, and so on. With n candidates, a voter's highest-ranked selection receives $n - 1$ votes from that voter. A winner is determined under the Borda Count method by adding the votes for each candidate from all voters. Now suppose that a fifteen-member department has an election to choose a new chair, where there are three candidates: Abbott, Boyce, and the old Chair (Saari 1994: 7). The actual preference orderings of the members are distributed as follows:

> Seven members: Abbott > Boyce > Chair
> Seven members: Boyce > Abbott > Chair
> One member: Chair > Abbott > Boyce

If everyone voted their genuine preferences, Abbott would be elected under the Borda Count. Abbott would receive $(7 \times 2) + (7 \times 1) + (1 \times 1) = 22$ votes; Boyce would receive $(7 \times 1) + (7 \times 2) + (1 \times 0) = 21$ votes; and Chair would receive $(7 \times 0) + (7 \times 0) + (1 \times 2) = 2$ votes. Suppose all members know this actual set of preference orderings. Facing the prospect of defeat, Boyce's supporters decide to vote strategically, by voting as though they preferred Boyce > Chair > Abbott, thereby giving Abbott only 15 votes rather than 22. (Of course, Chair would then get nine, they expect.) Abbott's supporters, however, anticipate this maneuver, so each of them marks their ballots as Abbott > Chair > Boyce. This reduces Boyce's total to only 14. But it raises Chair's total to 16. So Chair wins the election, despite the fact that only one person actually ranks him topmost!

This illustrates how strategic voting sometimes leads to highly perverse results. Notice, however, that this example does not feature *perfect* strategic knowledge. Apparently, Abbott's supporters did not clearly think through the result of their manipulation, or they would have recognized that Abbott would still not win. Moreover, Boyce's supporters did not anticipate the counter-maneuver by Abbott's supporters, or they would not have acted as imagined. So although partial strategic knowledge may yield perverse results, it is not clear that total strategic knowledge would do so. In any case, I am not committed to the idea that *strategic* knowledge is such a good thing for democratic purposes. I have only argued that *core* knowledge is a good thing. That is much harder to demonstrate in multicandidate elections, for the reasons we have examined, but it has not been shown wrong either. Given the morass of complications, I leave further analysis of the multicandidate case to other occasions, or other writers.

10.8 *Other types of beneficial knowledge*

My preoccupation with core voter knowledge is not meant to suggest that this is the only kind of knowledge that is valuable for democratic ends. In this closing section, I briefly consider two other possibilities: (A) knowledge by other role-players in a democracy, and (B) other types of knowledge on the part of voters.

Although I began the chapter by remarking that institutions typically need various role-players to attain appropriate kinds of knowledge, our analysis of democracy has thus far addressed only the knowledge requirements for voters. What about other role-players, such as elected officials and their advisors? It takes but little reflection to recognize that a more successful democracy can be achieved by relatively more knowledgeable officials and advisors. Suppose that the best (majority-preferred) outcome set that would be produced by any candidate in a given race is outcome set OS_{200}. This is not an *ideal* outcome set for the voters, however, because many conceivable outcome sets would be preferred to OS_{200} by a majority. In this situation it would be nice to have an even better candidate in the field, someone who would produce an outcome set preferable to OS_{200}.

What would it take for someone occupying the same office in the same State of Nature to produce a better outcome set? Often it would take superior knowledge, either personal knowledge by the elected official or knowledge by her advisors and the officials she appoints. Without detailing the many types of knowledge that might be useful, let us lump them together under the heading "office-related knowledge." Other things being equal, a political and educational system that gets people into office who have (or acquire) more office-related knowledge, the better off that system will be. Of course, knowledge alone is not sufficient. Knowledge can be used to achieve an office-holder's personal ends in place of public ends. But if equally good intentions are assumed, superior knowledge is preferable to inferior knowledge. So whatever can be done both to educate potential candidates and to nominate the better educated (or more knowledgeable) among them will be beneficial from the standpoint of democracy. At least this is beneficial so long as voters can recognize those nominees who are best in terms of their preference orderings, which is again the issue of core voter knowledge.

What method of selecting nominees will best achieve this end? It is instructive to examine some historical changes in practices, again in the United States. Before 1968 the system of nominating Presidential candidates was dominated by party leaders. In the aftermath of the 1968 elections, the system was changed to a system of popular primaries. According to many observers, however, this "reform" is unsatisfactory, because citizens are forced to choose at the primary stage when they inevitably know very little about the candidates. Ordinary citizens are not well positioned to make an informed choice at the nominating stage, and many good potential nominees have been forced to drop out for insubstantial reasons (such as Edmund Muskie in the 1972 Democratic primary race). Several observers (Patterson 1993, for example) therefore urge a return to something like the older system, in which party leaders play the crucial role in the nominating process. Leaders are far more knowledgeable than citizens about the qualities of potential nominees, and they could therefore perform the nominating task much better.

Notice that this tactic permutes the usual way of addressing knowledge problems. Instead of assuming that a certain class of agents will execute a given task and figuring out how to give those agents more task-related knowledge, the current proposal starts with an assumption about which class of agents is destined to have more task-related knowledge and proposes to re-assign the task to that class of agents.[23] The current proposal takes the locus of superior political knowledge for granted—namely, party leaders rather than ordinary citizens—and seeks to redesign the institutional structure accordingly. It aims to ensure that the right role-players have the right knowledge by changing the identities of role-players rather than by changing levels of knowledge.

Will nominees selected by party leaders really perform better in terms of voters' preference orderings? Patterson argues that party leaders are at least as adept as voters themselves in selecting nominees with high voter acceptability (1993: 228). In the twenty years before the primary reforms, when party leaders chose nominees, only one major-party Presidential nominee was perceived more negatively than positively by the electorate. In the twenty years after the reforms, almost half of the nominees have been so viewed.[24] Moreover, as E. E. Schattschneider has commented: "The parties do not need laws to make them sensitive to the wishes of the voters any more than we need laws compelling merchants to please their customers" (1943: 60).

I turn now to a different kind of knowledge it might be important for voters to have, not *core* knowledge. According to the model of representative democracy pursued throughout the chapter, the primary job of officials is to respond to the citizenry's goals, where goals are expressed in terms of outcomes. The specific policies or means for achieving these outcomes are the responsibility of elected officials. Officials can do their jobs perfectly well even when they pursue policies at variance with the wishes of the public, as long as the executed policies achieve a high level of the public's *outcome*

---

[23] This general possibility was suggested by Mark Wunderlich.

[24] Some caution is needed in interpreting this finding, I would urge. As indicated earlier, press coverage has turned more adversarial in recent years, and campaigning has become more negative. These factors alone might account for greater negative perceptions of candidates in the second twenty-year period. The difference in voter acceptability might not result from a difference in quality of nominees produced by party leaders versus open primaries respectively.

preferences.[25] On this view, officials need not be responsive to voters' policy preferences, only to outcomes preferences. Core voter knowledge was identified as crucial to democracy in virtue of its contribution to outcome attainment, not policy approval.

In point of fact, though, elected officials in America do tend to respond to their constituencies' policy sentiments. As Benjamin Page and Robert Shapiro put it: "When Americans' policy preferences shift, it is likely that congruent changes in policy will follow" (1983: 189). Is this a good thing? Not necessarily, at least when judged by an outcomes standard. If citizens' policy preferences are ill informed, official conformity with those preferences may lead to dispreferred outcomes. Thus, either officials should be less swayed by citizens' policy preferences, or those preferences had better be well informed. Admittedly, an official may not be in a position to ignore his constituency's policy preferences, given his interest in re-election. In assessing an elected official, voters may not wait until outcomes have occurred. (In any case, many pertinent outcomes postdate the term of office.) Voters may be powerfully influenced by their own views of whether adopted policies are destined to "work." However mistaken these opinions may be, voters may base their voting decisions on them nonetheless. So officials may be forced to respond to voter policy preferences. It will not promote good outcomes, however, if these policy preferences are actually poor instruments for achieving preferred outcomes. It follows that *policy*-related knowledge on the part of citizens can be more important than I have hitherto asserted. Until now I have only insisted that citizens must have *core* knowledge if democracy is to succeed. Whether core knowledge requires policy-related knowledge was left up in the air. But if officials are disposed to accede to the public's policy preferences, outcome success will be contingent on the public's possessing policy knowledge as well.[26] This sets a substantially higher epistemic standard for the public to meet than the core knowledge standard.

It is time to sum up. In this chapter I have identified the main type of knowledge that is critical to the task of voters, and I have surveyed some of the principal practices and changes in practices that may increase this type of knowledge. I have shown how democracy's success hinges on social practices that advance the prospects for accurate political opinion.

---

[25] Of course, certain policies might be ones that voters regard as intrinsically objectionable. If so, they deserve to be placed in the category of "outcomes." In general, however, a reasonable distinction can be drawn between policies considered as mere means and their outcomes. I assume such a distinction here.

[26] An ignorant public cannot reasonably expect officials *both* to conform with their policy preferences *and* to conform with their outcome preferences. To say that this is unreasonable, however, is not to say that they don't expect it.

ELEVEN

Education

11.1 *Goals, methods, and interests*

THE fundamental aim of education, like that of science, is the promotion of knowledge. Whereas science seeks knowledge that is new for humankind, education seeks knowledge that is new for individual learners. Education pursues this mission in several ways: by organizing and transmitting pre-existing knowledge, by creating incentives and environments to encourage learning, and by shaping skills and techniques that facilitate autonomous learning and steer inquiry toward truth. This veritistic conception is a traditional picture of what education is all about, one aligned with an "Enlightenment" conception of epistemology. Despite popular critiques of the Enlightenment view, the veritistic model is still the best available, one that fits all stages of education from lowest to highest. Admittedly, knowledge and knowledge-dedicated skills are not the sole educational goals. Education in studio art or music performance, for example, is not primarily concerned with propositional knowledge or with skills for acquiring propositional knowledge. But propositional knowledge is, nonetheless, education's most pervasive and characteristic goal.

It is easy to misconstrue the implications of the veritistic or Enlightenment model. It might appear to follow from this model, for example, that the right way to teach is to pour the wine of truth into waiting vessels. But this oft-criticized approach is by no means implied by veritism. The veritistic conception *per se* only specifies goals; it is neutral, at least at first, about pedagogical means to these goals. If the traditional "stand and deliver" method of teaching is a comparatively poor way to help pupils acquire knowledge, so be it. Other techniques must be chosen to achieve veritistic ends. Didactic instruction is especially unlikely to be adequate for training students in knowledge-acquiring skills. Such skills may be better taught by carefully guided practice rather than explicit precept. I caution the reader, therefore, not to draw unwarranted inferences about good methods of teaching from the veritistic model of educational ends.

Teaching methods aside, two questions naturally leap forward from the veritistic conception of education. First, which pieces or domains of knowledge should education help people acquire? Which of the generally acknowledged truths should educators try to teach, or otherwise produce cognizance of? Second, when the truth is a matter of lively controversy in a given domain, how should it be decided which contents to teach? Who should decide how hotly contested subjects should be taught, and what criteria or guidelines should be followed?

Let me begin the discussion of the first question by recalling some pertinent details of the basic veritistic framework. At first glance our framework tells us that veritistic advance only occurs when someone acquires belief in a truth, or increases her degree of belief in a truth, that *interests* her. So one ostensible constraint is that education should center on matters that interest students.[1] The careful reader, however, will recall that when the topic of interests was addressed in Section 3.5, several senses of "interest" were distinguished, and the knower's own interests were not the only ones said to be relevant. Interests of the communities or institutions to which knowers belong were also deemed relevant. These factors are quite pertinent to issues in education.

Three senses of "interest" were discussed in Section 3.5. First, a question can interest an agent in the sense that she has an aroused curiosity or concern about it. Second, a question can be of interest to an agent in a dispositional rather than an occurrent sense. A question might be one that *would* interest someone if she were to consider or contemplate it; for example, if it were called to her attention and perhaps made vivid. Third, a question can be of interest to an agent in a more deeply dispositional sense: she would have an aroused concern about it if she learned some additional facts she does not currently know. There are many things that people have an interest or "stake" in learning although they do not realize it themselves. This is particularly true of children. Many types of knowledge will be useful to them later in life, a fact they do not yet appreciate. If they *were* to learn and understand the utility of these types of knowledge, however, they would be interested (in the first sense) in acquiring them. Presumably schools should not restrict themselves to subject matters that antecedently interest students, that is, interest them in the first sense of "interest." Schools may dedicate themselves to teaching things that are *in* the students' interest, albeit not yet so recognized by the students. Of course, it may be difficult to motivate students to learn subjects for which they have no aroused curiosity. Arousing such curiosity would then be a pedagogical necessity. But this is more a question of educational means than of ends. It is not a constraint on the truths to be taught that students have a *prior* aroused interest in learning them.

Finally, it is legitimate for schooling systems, at least public systems, to appeal to the public's interest in deciding what children should be taught. Clearly it is in the public interest for the citizenry to be informed about com-

[1] The role of interest in education was emphasized, of course, by John Dewey; see Dewey 1913; 1916: ch. 10. A more recent statement of a Deweyan view is Arnstine and Arnstine 1987.

municable diseases and known methods of avoiding contagion. A public educational system might properly insist on teaching such things to children even if they lack any initially aroused interest in learning them. Other things may be included in the curriculum because they are essential to the exercise of a citizen's duties in a democratic society.

These reflections provide some initial baselines by which curriculum choices might be made under a veritistic rationale. They are not terribly specific or determinate, nor are they intended to be. A theory of education, at least at the philosophical level of the present approach, should not be expected to give detailed content prescriptions for all types of schooling. There are many different educational enterprises, and no general philosophy of education can reasonably prescribe curricula for all such enterprises. What is plausibly taught in the primary grades of a public school system might have little or no relation to what is plausibly taught to adults in a nursing school or a business college.

Furthermore, nothing in the veritistic approach assumes that the only or best way to promote knowledge acquisition by students is for teachers to select beforehand the truths to be learned. Teachers may promote knowledge acquisition by posing questions to which students must find answers. The teacher may or may not know the answers antecedently. Even if she does know the answers, she may not wish to transmit them directly as opposed to letting the students learn the answers for themselves. This is a crucial part of education insofar as education includes the training of students in knowledge-acquiring skills. They should learn to discover truths on their own, not simply to receive them from teachers. However, it is inappropriate under veritism for teachers to recommend or inculcate methods of inquiry that are known or believed to lead to wrong answers.[2] If the aim of learning is to learn truths, as veritism maintains, then educators should try to train students in truth-acquiring methods. At a minimum students should be trained in those methods thought to be better at truth acquisition than other available methods. Virtually all methods are fallible, of course. But anyone who deliberately trains students in methods believed to be unreliable—or markedly less reliable than other methods—abjures the mission of education according to veritism. It is one role of education to train the younger generation (at appropriate stages of intellectual preparedness) in the best methods society has produced for learning new truths. Given the comparative superiority of science at answering the sorts of questions it addresses (as argued in Chapter 8), the importance of science education becomes obvious.[3]

[2] Here some qualification is in order to admit methods that lead to only approximately correct answers. I shall take such a qualification "as read" without trying to be more specific.
[3] Who should decide what are the best methods that society has produced? Which methods are the best methods is not always uncontroversial. I address this question in Section 11.5 below.

What about domains of thought and discourse that do not admit of truth and falsity? Are they to be excluded from education altogether? First of all, I have already indicated that knowledge is not the exclusive goal of education. The arts have values of their own, even if they do not partake of veritistic value. So activities should not be excluded from the educational sphere simply because no truths are involved. In many domains, of course, it will be controversial whether truth is at stake or not. Does poetry, or literature more generally, aim at truth (and sometimes succeed in this aim)? In these matters an educator need not take a firm stance. At a minimum, it is appropriate to teach the fact *that some people maintain* that these domains are truth evaluable, or, more plausibly, that some people maintain that such-and-such literary works express such-and-such truths. Even if it turns out that literary works do not express truths, because they make no truth-evaluable statements, it is still a truth that many readers or critics claim to find truths in these works. Here it is useful to distinguish primary and secondary judgments within a given subject matter. In the literary domain, for example, a statement of the form, "Novel N expresses truth T" is a primary statement. A corresponding secondary statement would be "Commentator Bernstein says that novel N expresses truth T." A literature teacher who herself is uncertain about the cognitive status of literature might not be prepared to assert primary statements in this domain, but she could comfortably assert secondary statements, many of which would be uncontroversially true.

It might be objected that it isn't worth teaching the truth of secondary statements unless they are evidence for the truth (or falsity) of the primary statements contained within them. If primary statements in a given domain lack truth-values, why bother to teach secondary statements of that domain?[4] Two replies are in order here. First, in the case of novels there may be no truth of the matter as to whether novel N *expresses* a particular factual statement T, but even if T is only *suggested* by N, it may itself be a truth that is worth learning. So there is potential veritistic value to be acquired. Second, the way that readers interpret or react to literature is itself an essential part of what should be learned about literature. So the sorts of facts reported by secondary statements are an integral aspect of the subject matter, not a purely peripheral aspect that is unworthy of being taught.

I return now to domains in which truth and falsity have unquestioned applicability. Assume that there is a superabundance of uncontroversially known truths, and that the interests factor places only weak constraints on

---

[4] Thanks to Tim Bayne for posing this possible objection. It should be noted that the kinds of primary statements I mean to be discussing here are statements to the effect that a given literary work expresses a truth *about the real world*, for example, about human character. It is relatively uncontroversial (at least among philosophers) that literary works can express truths about *fictional* worlds, for example, that Arthur Conan Doyle's stories express truths about the fictional world of Sherlock Holmes.

the selection of topics. Does veritism imply anything more about *which* truths should be in a curriculum, at least a curriculum for children in public schools? A small segment of a suitable curriculum might be inferred by taking a page from John Rawls. Rawls introduced the notion of "primary goods" (1971: 62), defined as things that have a use whatever a person's rational plan of life. Analogously, we may introduce the notion of educationally "fundamental" knowledge, defined as knowledge that is likely to be useful whatever other types of knowledge a person wishes to acquire. Are there any items that fit this description, or fit it pretty closely? Yes. Whatever types of knowledge a person wishes to acquire, literacy is likely to be useful in acquiring such knowledge.[5] So knowledge that makes a person literate (in some language or other) qualifies as educationally fundamental. That kind of knowledge, at a minimum, should be included in the curriculum. This conclusion manifestly accords with the actual practice of virtually every primary education system in the world.

11.2 *Veritism and multiculturalism*

Although I have extracted a few curricular morals from the veritistic approach and shall try to extract some more in later sections, I do not wish to claim that curricular conclusions can be drawn in great profusion from veritistic premises. On the contrary, I shall be at pains to insist that veritism is not nearly as constraining as its critics might suspect or allege.

Consider the contemporary issue of multiculturalism in education. It might be supposed that veritism is the antithesis of multiculturalism because veritism is committed to educational "essentialism," which favors a core curriculum.[6] Doesn't veritism amount to espousing the "tyranny of Truth" (with a capital "T"), which is the heart of essentialism? No. Many mistakes or unwarranted inferences are contained in these interpretations. The alleged association between veritistic epistemology and a core curriculum does not hold, and the appearance of such an association must be corrected.

The spirit of essentialism is succinctly expressed in the following argument from Robert Maynard Hutchins: "Education implies teaching. Teaching implies knowledge. Knowledge is truth. The truth is everywhere the same. Hence education should be everywhere the same" (1936: 66). The first several premises of this argument, a few quibbles aside, seem to be correct. Education implies teaching; teaching, at least in part, is the conveying of knowledge; and knowledge is truth (more precisely, knowledge entails truth). What about the

---

[5] This needs to be amended to read, "for *most* types of knowledge a person wishes to acquire." There may be some categories of knowledge that are not promoted by mastery of written words.

[6] The term "essentialism" is borrowed from Gutmann 1992*b*: 3–24.

fourth premise, that truth is everywhere the same? This raises some technical issues about propositions, but let us restrict discussion to propositions devoid of indexical or demonstrative elements like "I," "you," "here," or "now." Then I would agree that for any specified proposition P, its truth-value is the same at all times and places. (*Beliefs* about a proposition's truth-value may vary over time, but the truth itself does not vary over time.) Does the truth of all four premises commit us to the truth of the conclusion, that education should be everywhere the same? No, because the conclusion does not follow from the premises. The reason is simple. There are many truths. Although each of them is true at all times and places, it does not follow that each should be taught at all times and places. Being true may be a necessary condition for being taught (ignoring the necessity for approximations and simplifications), but it is not a sufficient condition. That leaves open the possibility of teaching different truths at different times and places, contrary to the idea of essentialism.

Hutchins's conclusion might be interpreted as following from his premises if the premises were somehow taken to imply that the entire totality of truths should be taught everywhere. Certainly one possible reading of the fourth premise, "*the truth* is everywhere the same," is that there is a single totality of truths. But even if we grant the premise so understood, Hutchins would need a further premise to the effect that each item in this totality should be taught everywhere, and that is dubious in the extreme. On a more plausible interpretation of the original premises, it is not implied that every truth should be taught, merely that everything to be taught should be true. This is fully compatible with the idea that the particular subset of truths to be taught may be relativized to locale, culture, and context. A school in one cultural niche should teach one subset of the truths, while a school in a different cultural niche should teach another subset of the truths.

Some essentialists, no doubt, maintain that the truths of morality and human nature are found in certain classical works of the European tradition, and perhaps only in those works. If you hold that position, and you hold that the truths on those topics should be taught everywhere, then you get the doctrine that a certain canon should comprise the curriculum. This doctrine does not follow, however, from the objectivity of truth, or from objectivity conjoined with the view that education should teach truth. These are compatible with the idea that truths are found in works from many different traditions, so that no particular tradition should monopolize the curriculum.

Furthermore, even if a particular tradition did contain more truths than other traditions, it would still be an important truth for students to learn that there are many traditions (Wolf 1992: 75–85). In a society as diverse as America it is particularly important to teach about such diversity. The range of distinctive values, experiences, and perspectives that accompany different identities comprise an important set of facts or truths. All students, whether they recognize it or not, have an interest in learning such truths; and society has an interest in those truths being learned. Moreover, it is not only in an ethnically diverse country such as the United States that diversity should be taught. Everyone is a citizen of the world, and in our dramatically shrinking globe everyone can expect to interact with others of different backgrounds and historical experiences. A well-educated person must be trained for world citizenship, a point appreciated and stressed by the Greek and Roman Stoics (Nussbaum 1997). So educational multiculturalism need not stand in conflict with veritistic epistemology. Teaching the sorts of material that multiculturalism advocates—that such-and-such values and perspectives are held by such-and-such cultures, because of their historical experiences—is compatible with teaching only truths. There are, of course, radical versions of multiculturalism that preach the enshrinement of cultures at the price of imperiling or obscuring the truth. Veritism parts company from those permutations of multiculturalism.

There are many other possible ways to defend the appropriateness of (moderate) multiculturalism in the curriculum. One way is to argue, as does Charles Taylor (1992), that people's self-identities are bound up with their self-images, which are in turn a function of how others see them. Multicultural curricula would help prevent the growth of demeaning self-images that threaten members of historically dominated or marginalized groups. Similarly, Harvey Siegel defends multiculturalism on moral grounds: "[I]t is wrong, morally wrong, to treat students (or anyone else) in ways which harm them; it is wrong to fail to treat students with respect; it is wrong to treat students in such a way that their ideas, and their cultures, are not taken seriously" (1997: 143). These moral types of rationale for multiculturalism complement my epistemic type of rationale; the two need not compete.

Other types of rationale for multiculturalism, however, are more apt to conflict with a veritistic rationale. Many writers, especially postmodernists, defend multiculturalism by appeal to a kind of relativism. Respecting other cultures, according to such writers, involves respecting their epistemologies as equally valid or legitimate. To insist on the superiority of one's own Western or Enlightenment epistemology would be cultural imperialism. Since the hallmarks of Enlightenment epistemology are standards like truth, reason, and justification, these standards cannot be invoked under relativism. Thus, relativism is incompatible with veritism.

In reply to this defense of multiculturalism, I first challenge the claim that non-Western cultures have no concept of or commitment to truth in their epistemologies. As argued in Section 1.7, truth is a goal for humankind across history and culture. Diverse cultures have certainly differed on the best methods for arriving at truth, as Westerners have differed among themselves, but that does not mean that they reject or ignore truth as a goal. The conception of education as a knowledge-producing enterprise, in the truth-entailing sense of "knowledge," is not a piece of Western imperialism.

Next let us look more carefully at the relativist or postmodern claim that respecting other cultures involves respecting their epistemologies as equally valid or legitimate. Granting the moral imperative of *respecting* the views of others, the question arises whether this means regarding their views as having equal merit as one's own. As Siegel points out (1997: 151), this is not an appropriate construal. Respecting the views of others should involve taking them seriously, recognizing that many people accept them, seeing what can be said for them, and allowing them to challenge one's own view. But it does not necessarily mean agreeing with them. As we saw in Chapter 5, a hearer might reasonably decline to accept a speaker's view even if she (the hearer) grants that the speaker has some good reasons for it. The hearer may simply think that she has good defeaters of that view. So it is not illegitimate to employ Enlightenment epistemology even in the context of multiculturalism.

Furthermore, Enlightenment epistemology is required for postmodernism even to get its defense of multiculturalism off the ground. When the postmodernist claims that other cultures deserve respect, she makes a moral claim, a claim endorsed as *true* and *justified*. But this already presupposes the Enlightenment concepts of truth and justification (Siegel 1997: 145). Such a claim also clashes with postmodernism's rejection of universalism and "totalizing metanarratives." In endorsing the universal moral claim that other cultures deserve respect, postmodernists undercut their own oft-repeated strictures against universalizing (Siegel 1997: ch. 10). Thus, whereas multiculturalism is defensible from a veritistic and Enlightenment standpoint, it cannot be successfully defended from a postmodern one.

11.3 *Postmodernism and collaborative learning*

Curricular multiculturalism is not the only educational moral that is drawn nowadays from postmodern epistemology. Another such moral is the desirability—indeed, imperativeness—of certain types of instructional methodology. Some educational theorists, for example, advocate the collaborative or cooperative style of learning as the only desirable method of learning, and advocate this by appeal to postmodern philosophy. A clear representative of this approach is Kenneth Bruffee (1993), who repeatedly invokes the writings of Rorty, Kuhn, and Latour and Woolgar in support of this approach. Since it helps to have a specific proponent on which to focus, I shall focus on Bruffee, though he is not alone in defending these ideas.

Let me say at the outset that I do not denigrate the value of collaborative learning in education. Undoubtedly it is often valuable for students to work together in discussion groups, exchanging ideas and trying to solve problems collectively. Mutual engagement can be a useful means to knowledge. But Bruffee elevates collaboration into much more than a means; he regards it as the essence of education, for reasons inspired by postmodern epistemology. As a veritist, I reject this type of rationale for collaborative learning, as well as the notion that this is the only proper conception of teaching, as Bruffee maintains. Cooperative learning unquestionably has its benefits; but it should not replace the goal of knowledge acquisition, in the truth-linked sense of "knowledge." This goal is indeed intended to be replaced under Bruffee's post-modern approach.

Bruffee's rejection of a veritistic conception of knowledge is indicated early on:

> Most of us, including most college and university teachers, assume a foundation (or cognitive) understanding of knowledge. Knowledge is an entity that we transfer from one head to another—for example, from a teacher's head to a student's or from a staff member's head to the head of the boss. Collaborative learning assumes instead that knowledge is a consensus among the members of a community of knowledgeable peers—something people construct by talking together and reaching agreement. (1993: 3)

To begin with, there are unfortunate flaws in this formulation. Defining "knowledge" as "a consensus among . . . *knowledgeable* peers" (my emphasis) involves a flagrant circularity. The important issue, however, is Bruffee's social constructivist account of knowledge, according to which knowledge is simply consensus. As my previous arguments in this book suggest, the consensus view is wrong on two counts. First, consensus is not a necessary condition for knowledge. Knowledge can be acquired by individual observation, as when you open your blinds on a winter's morning and see that snow has fallen. When you see the snow and recognize it as such, you know that snow is on the ground. You don't need to consult others and reach a consensus before acquiring knowledge. This possibility is explicitly denied by Bruffee: "[W]e construct and maintain knowledge not by examining the world but by negotiating with one another in communities of knowledgeable peers" (1993: 9).

Second, contrary to Bruffee, community consensus is not sufficient for knowledge. In 1997 a California-based cult called "Heaven's Gate" committed mass suicide, apparently in the belief that the nearby comet Hale–Bopp would transport them to heaven. Did their communal consensus qualify their belief as knowledge? Surely not. Is communal consensus, then, really all that education should aim at? No. Finally, the first-quoted passage disputes the notion that knowledge can be transferred from one head to another. But what exactly is wrong with the idea that your knowledge of the snowfall can be passed from you to another member of your household who hasn't yet observed it?

Bruffee claims that all education is essentially collaboration because he holds that education is essentially reacculturation. This idea became vivid in his own teaching career as an English professor when his institution, Brooklyn College, adopted open admissions in 1970. Teaching students with few basic skills or cultural background for higher education convinced him that the largest problem they faced was one of accommodating to the alien cultures, first the cultures of other students and second the culture of the "literate," the professors. Students had to cross boundaries from their own local culture to other students' cultures and then to the academic culture. He extrapolates from this idea to all higher education. Even the learning of mathematics is reacculturation, namely, learning the culture of mathematicians. He explicitly rules out the idea that education should involve the attempt to teach students truths:

> Teachers do not tell students what the "right" answer is in consensus-group col-laborative learning, because the assumption is that no answer may be absolutely right. Every "right" answer represents a consensus for the time being of a certain community of knowledgeable peers: mathematicians, historians, chemists, sociol-ogists, or whatever. (1993: 47)

Indeed, the notion of rightness or correctness, according to Bruffee, is simply acceptability to a specified community. Echoing the views of Rorty (1979), Latour (1987), and Vygotsky (1978), he defines "correct" as "what is accept-able in the community that the [learner] aspires to enter" (Bruffee 1993: 120).

If education is merely acculturation, a serious problem arises. Why should colleges and universities hire mathematicians, historians, chemists, and soci-ologists to staff their courses? Why should students pay considerable sums of money to attend courses taught by these individuals? Each represents a certain community, to be sure, but why select representatives of *those* communities? Street gangs are also communities, indeed, communities whose languages and conversational practices it would take some effort to learn. Why shouldn't col-leges and universities hire gang members, presumably at lower salaries, to replace traditional faculty, and let the students acculturate to gang culture? What would be lost? On a veritistic view, the answer is clear. On Bruffee's view, it would just be the exchange of one set of cultures for another, with no ob-vious criterion for preference.

In some passages, Bruffee hints at such a criterion. An answer given to a question, he says, can have different degrees of authority. "[T]he authority of the answer depends upon the size of the community that has constructed it and the community's credibility among other, related knowledge communit-ies" (1993: 47). So his possible reply to the problem posed above is that acad-emic communities have greater authority than street gangs because of their size, or because of their greater credibility among related knowledge com-munities. But in fact mathematicians might be outnumbered by street gang members; if they are not outnumbered now, they might be in the future. Should colleges replace mathematicians with street gang members as soon as the former are outnumbered? What about credibility level? The credibility of rock stars might actually be as high in their "related knowledge communities" as the credibility of sociologists in theirs. Does that mean that each culture group is equally suitable for teaching positions in higher education?

The obvious difference between genuine academics and gang members is that the former possess types of knowledge, in the veritistic sense of "know-ledge," that the latter lack. People's interest and society's interest in such knowledge is the reason that the proposed replacement would be unsuitable. The veritistic approach not only explains quite naturally why mathematicians are preferable educators to gang members; it also explains why (other) flagrant perversions of education are indeed perversions. Obliteration of historical truths was characteristic of Soviet education under Stalinism. By Bruffee's criterion, however, there was nothing obviously wrong with Stalinist education. The Soviet educational establishment was highly "authoritative" in Bruffee's sense: it was large in size and it was credible to related knowledge communities (other Communist communities).

Can traditional academic disciplines really be defended by reference to truth? Such a claim will not go unchallenged. Perhaps the truths of mathematics can pass, but virtually all other disciplines are on slippery ground. The empirical sciences are all admitted to be fallible. Yesterday's scientific truths may be overturned by today's evidence, and when it comes to humanistic fields, few would feel secure in offering a truth-invoking rationale. Do professors of literature or professors of philosophy really know more truths (in the subjects they teach) than people outside their communities?

In response to this challenge, we need to recall from Section 11.1 the distinction between primary and secondary judgments in a field. In the sciences, primary judgments are the scientific hypotheses that serve as the focal targets of investigation. The truth-values of these hypotheses are indeed difficult to determine. Today's experimental findings often defeat those of yesterday, suggesting different truth-values for the hypotheses than the ones previously assigned. But now consider the secondary judgments in a science. Secondary judgments would include statements describing the pieces of evidence and arguments thus far accumulated that bear on a given hypothesis, for example, the experimental results or the theoretical considerations that tilt for or against it. At a minimum such secondary propositions are things that authorities in the field will know, even if they don't know the truth-value of the hypothesis itself. Secondary propositions of this sort are propositions on which experts will commonly agree, and on which candidates for doctorates in the field will be examined. Similarly, in a field like philosophy one would be hard pressed to show that professors in the field know the truth about primary theses such as nominalism in metaphysics, contractarianism in political philosophy, or reductionism in the philosophy of mind. Surely they do know, however, the reasons adduced by various philosophers for and against these primary theses. Propositions describing these reasons (and the persons who advanced them) comprise the secondary judgments of the field. Substantially accurate knowledge of such secondary propositions is a feature that does distinguish professors from philosophical neophytes. To acquire credentials in philosophy, one must demonstrate knowledge—true belief—of suitable secondary propositions. Ph.D. candidates who commit serious errors in attributing positions and rationales for positions to historical or contemporary philosophers will find it hard to obtain their degrees. In general, then, there is a range of facts about which academics must have (veritistic) knowledge to qualify as experts, and those without training in the field will typically lack such knowledge. So a crucial knowledge difference distinguishes members of academic communities from nonmembers. Given the truth-in-evidence principle postulated in Chapter 5, we may also expect people with better knowledge of secondary propositions (evidence propositions) to have more knowledge of primary propositions. But that further conclusion is inessential to the position being advanced at the moment.

Finally, when Bruffee tells us in his final chapter exactly what should be taught in his preferred nonveritistic, non-"foundational" curriculum, he contradicts the very core of his position. Here is a quotation typical of that chapter:

[The] goal [of the curriculum] is to help students come to terms with cultural pluralism by *demonstrating* that knowledge is not a universal entity but a local one, constructed and maintained by local consensus and subject to endless conversation. (1993: 192; emphasis added)

In saying that the curriculum should *demonstrate* that knowledge is not a universal entity, Bruffee clearly implies that it is a philosophical truth that knowledge is not a universal entity. What else but a truth could be "demonstrated"? And why should it be a central goal of the curriculum to teach this to students if it isn't true? Should an entire curriculum be dedicated to teaching a philosophical lie, error, or deception? Evidently, Bruffee thinks that this philosophical proposition and others like it are not lies or falsehoods at all. He presents them as truths. (Other passages speak repeatedly of helping students "discover" such philosophical propositions. Like "demonstrate," "discover" is a truth-implying verb.) But insofar as Bruffee's recommended curriculum is predicated on certain alleged philosophical truths, this conflicts with his own repudiation of truth as a relevant consideration.

It might be replied that truth is not meant to figure in Bruffee's vindication of his curriculum. Consensus is the only matter of importance. There is no consensus, however, on the philosophical propositions Bruffee favors (about the nature of knowledge). Most philosophers who teach epistemology—certainly in the English-speaking centers of philosophy such as Britain, North America, Australia, and New Zealand—would reject these philosophical assertions. At a minimum, many would dissent, which suffices to avert a consensus. If it is replied that mainstream epistemologists are outnumbered by believers in postmodernism, I reiterate my rejoinder that legitimate cognitive authority is not proportional to a community's size.

Bruffee's defense of collaborative learning does not rely exclusively on postmodern or social-constructivist philosophy. He also cites some empirical findings that support the educational superiority of collaborative or cooperative methods. For example, he cites the work of Uri Treisman, who followed Asian-American students around the Berkeley campus to try to discover why they tended to excel at mathematics and science. Treisman discovered that they moved in packs and were continually engaged in conversation about their work. African-American and Hispanic students, by contrast, were largely isolated from one another. So Treisman changed the way in which Berkeley's remedial mathematics and science program was organized. He gave African-American and Hispanic students a place to study collaboratively. Lo and behold, many of Treisman's remedial students soon became B and A students.

This kind of finding, I agree, is appropriate support for the technique of collaborative learning (though Treisman's research apparently did not involve controlled experimentation of the most desirable sort). It suggests the instrumental value of collaborative learning, which I acknowledged at the outset to be potentially efficacious. Notice, however, that Treisman utilized a success criterion totally at odds with Bruffee's postmodernism. The criterion of success is earning Bs or As, presumably a sign of knowledge in the veritistic sense. Moreover, earning an A or a B is an accomplishment that in principle can be attained by individualized study. It does not essentially require study with other students. Treisman's work only suggests that collaborative study is a good means to individual veritistic knowledge. It does not hinge on, or hint at, the rejection of the veritistic conception. Since Bruffee's postmodern message is the debunking of veritistic knowledge, his appeal to Treisman's work is misplaced.

A good deal of other research has also examined the effectiveness of cooperative learning, and it suggests a more qualified picture than would be gleaned from Bruffee's salesmanship. The success of cooperative learning techniques depends critically on the specific classroom tasks that are utilized. The situation is instructively reviewed and analyzed by Robert Slavin (1990, 1992).

Slavin points out, first of all, that the effectiveness of cooperative learning techniques must be measured by reference to the learning that takes place in individuals. There is little doubt that in many tasks, such as carrying heavy loads or solving difficult problems, helping one another can lead to a better *group product*. Children working alone will not solve as many problems as children working together (especially with no time limit); pooled knowledge will improve the group's output. But this does not demonstrate improved learning by each group member. A group productivity measure does not indicate anything one way or another about individual learning. Cooperative tasks often involve diffused responsibility. Individuals may be rewarded even if they themselves make little contribution. For example, in laboratory science groups in which a single lab report is produced, some students may do the minimum and leave others to pick up the slack. Group productivity does not signal learning on the part of these freeloaders.

To ensure that all participants benefit from a cooperative learning activity, one must pay attention to both task structure and incentive structure. Slavin illustrates this point with a sixth-grade class studying a unit on European geography. Four or five students work as a team to learn the locations of the major European countries. After studying together, each takes a quiz separately, and the average score of the team determines whether or not they all get a certain reward. This task emphasizes individual accountability, in that the group's success depends on the learning of each group member. But there is also an incentive to cooperate, in that each will earn a reward if the group as a whole does well.

There are many perspectives among educational theorists on the question of why and under what circumstances cooperative learning may be effective. Slavin discusses several such perspectives but I shall mention only two. Slavin's own favored perspective focuses on motivation, which can be enhanced via tasks with cooperative incentive structures. When team members' outcomes depend on one another's behavior, as in the European geography task, this motivates students to engage in behaviors that help the group to be rewarded. The group incentive induces students to encourage suitable goal-directed behaviors—and hence learning—among their teammates. In this case, there can be gains in learning even if students do not actually help one another or even work together.

Another perspective on the gains that accrue from cooperative learning is the cognitive elaboration perspective. Research in cognitive psychology has long held that cognitive restructuring or elaboration of material improves memory retention. One of the most effective means of elaboration is explaining the material to someone else. Indeed, research on peer tutoring has found achievement benefits for the tutor as well as the tutee. Similarly, Dansereau (1985) found that learning is facilitated when students play roles of "recaller" and "listener." Two students read a section of text, and then the recaller summarizes the information while the listener corrects errors, fills in omitted material, and thinks of ways to remember the main ideas. On the next section, the students switch roles. Both recallers and listeners learn more than students working alone, but the recaller learns even more than the listener.

Clearly, there are many ways in which suitably structured cooperative tasks can benefit learning. There is no need, however, to link the rationale for cooperative techniques to postmodern or social constructivist philosophy. Given the fundamental problems with these philosophical movements (at least in their more radical forms), educational theorists should think twice before hitching their wagons to these stars. But that does not mean abandoning the legitimate value of cooperative educational techniques.

11.4 *Critical thinking, trust, and pedagogy*

The previous section was largely devoted to an educational approach rooted in anti-Enlightenment epistemology. I now wish to jump to the opposite end of the epistemological spectrum. A possible criticism of educational veritism must be considered from the perspective of traditional epistemology. Many mainstream epistemologists hold that the crucial epistemic aim is not *true* belief, but warranted, justified, or rational belief. Epistemologists of this persuasion might apply this conception to the realm of education. Students should be taught to form opinions on the basis of good reasons, by critical reflection on the available evidence. If this yields truth, all well and good; if not, epistemic ideals will still have been reached. The trouble with veritism, some epistemologists might say, is that it invites the educational system to concern itself exclusively with getting facts into pupils' heads, without worrying about whether those facts are believed for good or bad reasons. Perhaps this consideration is what leads a number of philosophers of education to emphasize critical thinking in the curriculum (for example, Scheffler 1973; Ennis 1962; McPeck 1981; Paul 1984; Siegel 1988).

A good initial statement of this approach is given by Harvey Siegel:

A learner is, if she is successfully educated, expected to come to know many things. The "items of knowledge" a learner is expected to come to know are tremendously diverse, from simple "facts" to complex theories. Such facts and theories, moreover, are to be understood as well as known. It is not enough simply to know (in the sense of being able to repeat) the axioms of Euclidean geometry, for example; the learner is expected to understand them as well . . . Such knowledge and understanding demands, among other things, a proper understanding of the relevance of reasons and rules of inference and evidence. Without understanding the way in which (for example) the parallel line axiom offers a reason for taking the angle-side-angle theorem to be true, the learner cannot be said to understand fully either the axiom or the theorem . . . To understand the role of reasons in judgment is to open the door to the possibility of understanding conclusions and knowledge-claims generally. And, as we have seen, the ability to recognize the importance of and properly assess reasons is a central feature of critical thinking. Here, then, is the way that critical thinking is relevant to the epistemology of education. (1988: 43–4)

I am very sympathetic to some form of critical-thinking approach, but this is not incompatible with veritism. Unlike many critical-thinking advocates (such as Siegel), I do not see critical thinking as an epistemic end in itself. Critical thinking or rational inference is a useful *means* to the fundamental epistemic end of true belief. It is a crucial skill that should be developed in cognizers to help them attain true belief. Acknowledging an important role for critical thinking in education, then, is no admission of any flaw in veritism. It can be seen as merely an elaboration of veritism's implications. I shall say more about this later in the section.

First, however, I want to consider a possible scope limitation to the good reasons approach to education. A good bit of actual teaching consists of teachers "telling" things to students, that is, making statements or assertions without supporting reasons, evidence, or argument. Should students be expected to believe these statements? If students are generally unjustified in believing such statements, should the educational system discourage teachers from making them? This question belongs to the general problem of the epistemology of testimonial belief, which was briefly surveyed in Section 4.5. Not only students but all sorts of hearers encounter unsupported assertions or "testimony" from speakers. Under what circumstances are they justified in believing these statements? The good reasons approach would presumably answer with something like the following principle:

> (GR) A hearer is never justified in believing what a speaker (baldly) asserts unless the hearer has good, independent reasons to trust the speaker on that occasion.

Opposed to this precept of good reasons is a principle of unsupported trust, which can be formulated as follows:

> (UT) Sometimes a hearer is justified in believing what a speaker (baldly) asserts simply because the speaker asserts it, even if the hearer lacks good, independent reasons to trust the speaker on that occasion.

What might lead an epistemologist to endorse this limited thesis of unsupported trust? (I call it "limited" because it only says that *sometimes* hearers are justified in believing speakers' assertions in the absence of good, independent reasons to trust them.) Unsupported trust might be defended by appeal to the falsity of reductionism about justified testimonial belief. Reductionism asserts that a hearer is justified in believing speakers' assertions if and only if the hearer has good reasons to trust the speaker, reasons that do not ultimately rest on testimony itself but instead rest wholly on perception, memory, and so forth. As we saw in Section 4.5, some philosophers reject reductionism, on the grounds that hearers rarely have good testimony-free reasons for trusting testimony. If reductionism is therefore rejected, a further choice must be made. One option is to turn skeptical about testimonial belief, contending that people are rarely justified in believing items of testimony precisely because people rarely have testimony-free evidence for its reliability. Alternatively, one could defend widespread justification for testimonial beliefs on the grounds that extratestimonial grounds for testimony's reliability are not needed to confer justification on testimonial beliefs. The second option implies (UT). It implies that at least on some occasions one is entitled to trust a speaker's testimony (assertion) without good reasons, that is, without good, independent reasons of a testimony-free kind.

How does this apply to education? As noted, teachers commonly expect students to accept at least some statements that they do not support with evidence. Indeed, teachers (like other people) cannot give reasons for absolutely everything they assert, since reason giving must somewhere come to an end. One cannot defend every premise of every argument with further premises, on pain of infinite regress. To be sure, students might *have* reasons for trusting a teacher even if the teacher does not *state* those reasons. But is it even necessary that students should possess independent reasons for trusting their teachers? That is what (GR) implies. Principle (GR), however, is contradicted by (UT). If (UT) is embraced in light of the failure of testimonial reductionism, teachers might legitimately expect students to believe their assertions even in the absence of good, independent reasons to trust them. This kind of approach suggests a definite limitation on the good reasons approach to education. Admittedly, (UT) does not specify *teachers* as among the speakers whose assertions may justifiably be believed in the absence of evidence for their reliability. But if (UT) is correct, why should it not apply to teachers?

A plausible way to soften the trust position is to qualify it as follows, a position suggested by Tyler Burge (1993) and Elizabeth Fricker (1994).

(QUT)   A hearer has a presumptive epistemic right to believe what a speaker (baldly) asserts even without positive independent reasons for trusting the speaker on this occasion. This presumption is defeated, however, if the hearer has negative evidence that renders the speaker's assertion untrustworthy.

If a hearer has reasons for doubting the speaker's sincerity or competence in the present context, this defeats the presumption in favor of trust. But the presumptive right to believe does not require positive, testimony-free reasons for trusting the speaker.

If negative evidence can overturn the presumption, it is natural to ask whether hearers are always required to monitor a speech situation for defeating evidence. This question is posed by Fricker (1994). Is a hearer obliged to look for, to be on the alert for, defeating evidence? Are her critical faculties always to be engaged in seeking, or being on guard for, the defeat of trustworthiness? Fricker initially answers this question affirmatively: "[T]he thesis I advocate . . . is that a hearer should always engage in some assessment of the speaker for trustworthiness. To believe what is asserted without doing so is to believe blindly, uncritically. This is gullibility" (1994: 145). This position is in the spirit of an unqualified critical-thinking approach.

In a later discussion, however, Fricker appears to soften her claim. She distinguishes between the "developmental" and "mature" phases of the reception of testimony. "Simply-trusted testimony plays an inevitable role in the causal process by which we become masters of our commonsense scheme of things" (1995: 403). In other words, young children cannot be expected to monitor for defeating evidence while they are still acquiring the kinds of common-sense knowledge that can be used to defeat presumptions of trust. This softer position seems to me more plausible. Notice, however, that when it is applied to the educational context, it cuts against a universal application of the critical-thinking approach. Very young children, at least, should not be expected or trained to monitor a teacher's utterances for untrustworthiness. Teachers' statements can be justifiably believed via unsupported trust, and it is not unreasonable for the educational system to expect young children to accept such statements without first subjecting them to critical scrutiny.

We have found reasons, therefore, to reject the most stringent form of a critical-thinking approach. But this leaves plenty of room to applaud the merits of critical thinking. Indeed, the veritistic value of critical thinking was already presaged by material in Chapter 5. True, Chapter 5 focused on the argumentative practices of speakers rather than the credal reactions of hearers or learners. But many speaker-directed rules discussed in Chapter 5 presupposed the ability of hearers to appreciate the force of arguments and counter-arguments. No veritistic improvement can be expected from speakers' argumentative messages unless hearers make appropriate credal responses to them. This assumes the ability and propensity of hearers to engage in critical thinking: to recognize the evidential weight of premises, to appreciate the reduction in net evidential weight effected by defeating evidence, and so forth. Indeed, the truth-in-evidence principle enunciated in Chapter 5 heralded greater prospects for truth only on the assumption that the total evidence is "correctly interpreted." Correct interpretation transpires only if those who assess the evidence are good critical thinkers. So we have already laid the foundations for endorsing the educational value of training in critical thinking. There is a nontrivial question of exactly which types of instructional materials best promote the acquisition of critical-thinking skills. This issue will not be addressed here.

Critical thinking is not only a matter of mental responses to others' speech. Students should also develop skills in crafting their own argumentative speech and writing. As indicated in Chapter 5, all participants in a social discourse can profit veritistically when each member contributes her personal knowledge to the public debate and shows its relevance to the issues in question. Speaker participation in communal argumentation under the aegis of rules like those of Chapter 5 will advance the cause of truth. So the development of speaking and writing skills in this genre is an educational imperative.

Another skill closely intertwined with critical thinking is the active search for new evidence that potentially conflicts with the old. A critical thinker does not rest content with evidence she has personally unearthed, or with evidence reported by her own friends, mentors, and allies. A good critical thinker seeks exposure to the opinions of opponents, and takes their counter-arguments seriously. This too should be part of training in critical inquiry.

The educational importance of critical thinking flows quite naturally from one of education's chief goals formulated at the beginning of the chapter: to shape skills that assist inquiry into truth. Skills at interpersonal argumentation are precisely such techniques. So education takes a page out of one of our earlier lessons in social epistemology. Are there additional applications of social epistemology to education? Definitely.

Chapters 6 and 10 established social epistemology's concern with the veritistic properties of communication technologies and practices of public discourse (especially, in the case of Chapter 10, political discourse). Social epistemology's findings in these domains have significant educational applications. A truth seeker in the information age must negotiate all sorts of treacherous communicational terrain, full of hazards of every kind. Whose words should be trusted over the Internet? Which political messages deserve relatively greater credence or trust? To what sources can a citizen turn to help appraise the intentions behind this or that political message? Guidance in "media literacy" properly belongs in the information-age classroom, as many schools have already decided. Veritistic social epistemology can provide a framework for identifying the assortment of communicational practices with which budding truth seekers need to be acquainted.

11.5 *Curricular content and epistemic authority*

In this final section I confront a pressing issue in educational theory and practice, an issue briefly introduced in the first section of the chapter. How should the content of textbooks and other curricular materials be determined? What authorities should be consulted and what criteria should be used in making such choices? These issues lurk near the surface of the recent culture wars on the American educational scene. Partial answers may flow fairly naturally from the veritistic perspective, but the thorniest theoretical problems in this terrain are not trivial to resolve.

The issues were all too vividly illustrated by a heated mid-1990s dispute between backers of traditional United States history and proponents of new or revisionist history. A federal project was funded to develop National History Standards to guide the teaching of history in secondary schools. Even before the proposed standards were released to the public, they were attacked by a former head of the National Endowment for the Humanities, Lynne Cheney, and later condemned in a 99–1 vote by the U.S. Senate. Revisionist ideologues, Cheney proclaimed, had hijacked the project to pursue their revisionist agenda. Conservative polemicists led by Rush Limbaugh amplified Cheney's charges and tried to turn the history standards debate into a cause célèbre. People at other positions on the political spectrum also leveled criticisms of the proposals. Ultimately, a revised version of the standards won general acceptance.[7]

The first point to be stressed under the veritistic conception is that the preeminent aim of education is the learning of truths, at least what society is best able to identify as truths at the time in question. Values distinct from truth or knowledge are undoubtedly advocated in the educational sphere: for example,

---

[7] A history of the debate, together with a history of similar controversies over history textbooks in the twentieth century, is provided by three leading developers of the history standards, Gary Nash, Charlotte Crabtree, and Ross Dunn, in their book *History on Trial: Culture Wars and the Teaching of the Past* (1997). For an instructive review of this book, see Wilentz 1997.

the value of patriotism. But this value has no place within a veritistic conception. Of course, I have frequently conceded that knowledge is not the only
human value, and in many institutional contexts the value of knowledge may
be trumped by other values. In education, however, knowledge takes prece-
dence over other values such as *amor patriae*. To the extent that the conserva-
tives' attack on the history standards was propelled by patriotism pure and
simple, their arguments had no merit under veritism.

A second problem with patriotism as an educational precept is that it is
hard to swallow under a universal educational philosophy. American conser-
vatives may champion the teaching of patriotism in America, but would they
endorse the inculcation of patriotism in all countries at all times? Would they
approve of it for Stalin's or Mao's Communism, for Hitler's Nazism, or for any
other regime they find politically objectionable? Would they endorse the
notion that educational establishments under these regimes, or under later
regimes in the same countries, should distort or suppress historical truth in
the interest of patriotic pride? Should Japan hide the truth about its role in the
Second World War? Should German schools be silent about the Holocaust in
the name of patriotic pride? Should Russian youngsters remain ignorant of
Stalin's massacres?

Not all disputes over educational content can be framed as truth versus
patriotism, or some other non-truth-linked value. Traditionalists will typically
insist that the materials they want included in a history curriculum are not
falsehoods but truths. Assuming they are right, the question is: *which* truths
should be taught? Another bitterly contested episode concerning history
involved an exhibit at the Smithsonian's Air and Space Museum commemo-
rating the dropping of the first atomic bomb on Hiroshima. Veterans groups
complained about the curators' plan to ask visitors to consider the moral and
political dimensions of Truman's decision to drop the bomb and to look at
photographs of charred women and children in Hiroshima. In the veterans'
eyes, this would arouse the idea that the Japanese were victims rather than
aggressors in the Second World War. As revisions were made in the script, some
politicians insisted that the Air Force veterans should have veto power over
the way the story was told. Ultimately the exhibit was canceled and the
exhibit director was forced to resign his post as director of the Air and Space
Museum. The main issue under controversy was not whether the curators were
presenting falsehoods in depicting the victims of Hiroshima. The question was
whether to present *those* truths to the public. Since a museum exhibit of this
kind is undoubtedly an educational event, it illustrates how the choice *among*
truths often plagues the selection of historical materials.[8]

---

[8] This is not to deny that some of the claims in the projected text for the
Smithsonian exhibit might be challenged in terms of truth-value. The University of
Arizona historian Michael Schaller, who was involved with a group of historians in lob-
bying for retention of the exhibit, nonetheless had reservations about the planned text

Can veritism say anything useful about this nagging problem? One point that flows from the veritistic framework is that the greatest V-value accrues when people's false beliefs are shaken by new information, or when they are informed of things they previously did not suspect. Much less V-value accrues, if any, when antecedent true beliefs are simply refreshed through the reiteration of previously digested information. Thus, to the extent that Smithsonian visitors were to have been presented with fresh historical information, that might have had greater V-value than the depiction of previously familiar material. Similarly, if primary or secondary school pupils have an image of George Washington and other Founding Fathers as pillars of moral rectitude, learning the truth that many of them were slaveholders can produce a significant rise in V-value. If we make no comparisons of relative importance among propositions, but focus only on the magnitude of veritistically positive changes in credal states, learning surprising facts will have more V-value than learning unsurprising facts.

A case might certainly be made for the greater veritistic significance of more *important* truths, but it is difficult to construct a satisfactory and precise measure of importance. Truths describing general patterns are, plausibly, more important than truths describing single incidents. Similarly, truths that provide explanations for events (especially large-scale events) are, plausibly, more important than truths with little or no explanatory significance. It is doubtful, however, that these suggestions account for all dimensions of importance. A remaining question is whether importance can be fully quantified in an *interest-independent* way. If importance is heavily a function of interests, one historical truth can be counted as more important than another only relative to the interests of specified individuals or groups. This might not be a bad conclusion. Perhaps the choice of what historical truths to teach should be a function of the interests of various groups and individuals.

Sometimes, however, there is an overriding societal interest in teaching certain categories of truths. Citizens cannot adequately discharge their duties if they do not know baseline civics, such as how a bill becomes law, or what basic civil rights are conferred by the Constitution and its Amendments. The necessity for such pieces of knowledge makes a case for at least a modest core curriculum. But it does not resolve more subtle issues in the choice of curricular materials.

Should truth be admitted, however, as even one constraint on educationally appropriate content? Defenders of new history sometimes side with

---

(Schaller, personal communication). For example, the text relied on postwar statements by figures such as General Eisenhower that questioned the use of the bomb against a nearly beaten enemy. It is not at all clear, however, that such sentiments were voiced to President Truman before August 6. Moreover, recent Japanese scholarship suggests that American decision makers may have been correct in their belief that hardline Japanese militarists were inflexible and that only something so novel and dramatic as the atomic bomb would convince them and the Emperor to seek plausible peace terms.

postmodern philosophies in rejecting the ideas of truth and objectivity, retreating to the "situated," the "relative," and the "contextual." This kind of veriphobia, as I argued in Chapter 1, is ill founded and ill advised. Why cede the high ground of truth to traditionalists such as Lynne Cheney (1995)? New history is founded on careful research, which makes as good a claim as traditional history to unearth historical truths. New history may reveal previously unexamined aspects or dimensions of events such as the writing of the Constitution or the Spanish–American War, and there may be truth in each of these aspects and dimensions.[9]

Philosophical confusion often frightens people away from truth. The fact that historical claims are open to revision and subject to debate does indicate that such claims are never certain or "absolute" (in one sense of the latter term). But the epistemic status of "not certain" or "revisable" does not imply the metaphysical status of "not objectively true." Very few propositions, if any, are certain or unrevisable. This does not mean that only these few are true. "Not certain" means that a proposition *could* be overthrown by further evidence, not that it *will*. Being revisable or uncertain does not prevent a proposition from "fitting" the relevant portion of reality and hence being true. Only misbegotten epistemology hoodwinks people into a rejection of truth. Substantive claims of sound history should not be compromised by the worship of false philosophies.

I have been emphasizing the point that there are many truths concerning any complex set of events. This can make the choice of truths to be taught a difficult one. But what about cases in which different parties swear allegiance to incompatible, or contradictory, propositions? How should content decision makers decide which propositions to include in textbooks or other curricular materials? Who is to be trusted or consulted? Let us turn here to subjects in addition to history. What about materials in mathematics, physics, or biology?

Controversies over which propositions are true are unlikely to arise for mathematics or physics taught in primary and secondary schools. Agreement among experts will be pretty pervasive, and decision makers will not face the problem currently before us. There are intense debates over which mathematical skills should be taught, but there is little controversy at these levels as to which mathematical propositions are true. In biology, by contrast, there are serious debates—though not primarily among scientists—over the teaching of evolution. Here we have an instructive example for social epistemology. When the vast majority of biologists endorse some form of evolutionary theory as

---

[9] What exactly is "new history"? There is no agreed-upon answer. "New history" may refer to social, cultural, or economic history as opposed to political history. But there is also "new" political history: history that thrives on examining politics and power in an expanded context, for example, by examining power relations between and among groups previously ignored.

true, while other self-styled experts such as creation scientists dispute its truth, how should schools respond?[10]

One formula for dealing with such situations is: "[T]each the conflicts" (Graff 1992). When people disagree, all sides should be given equal time in the classroom, and students can decide for themselves. One problem with this principle arises when there are more than two sides to an issue. Suppose there are seven, or seventeen, competing views. Should all sides really receive equal time in the classroom? Apart from limits of time, there is a clear danger that students will be confused. Is it really possible to have a fair and complete presentation of the relevant philosophical issues about the nature of science and scientific evidence in a high school classroom? If society has good reason to pick out one of the competing propositions as true, why shouldn't that one be taught exclusively? On the other hand, when is society in a position to pick out a single rival hypothesis as true if experts, or self-styled experts, disagree? How should content decision makers decide in the name of society which putative experts to trust the most?

Philip Kitcher (1982) argues forcefully that scientific creationism has no scientific merits. He divides scientific claims into three major categories: (1) those that are best justified by the evidence, (2) those that are less well justified than some rivals, but merit our attention because they resolve some outstanding puzzles, and (3) those that have nothing going for them given the available evidence. Kitcher places scientific creationism (the scientific defense of special creation) in the third category, and I am inclined to agree. But Kitcher, after all, is just one thinker. Why should content decision makers heed him? Should they count numbers, then? Should a majority view always get exclusive billing in the classroom? That would be a total renunciation of the "Teach the conflicts" maxim, which has considerable initial appeal. But what counts as sufficient numerical support to warrant a place in the classroom? Does a single supporter of a given view entitle it to (equal?) classroom time? If one is too few, how large must a minority be? And what about the fact that millions of ordinary Americans are believers in special creation, possibly a more numerous group than the disbelievers? How is their greater numerosity to be balanced against the greater expertise of biologists?

To begin with, numbers should not count; at least not numbers of people with no expertise in the subject. The tougher question is how to gauge expertise. This problem was visited in Section 8.12, where two ways of judging

---

[10] Federal courts in the United States have ruled unconstitutional some state laws requiring creationism to be given equal time in the classroom. A Louisiana statute to this effect was struck down in 1985 by a federal appeals court. However, this decision was based on the fact that the principal or primary effect of the statute advanced religion, and fostered an excessive entanglement with religion. The legal status of laws concerning religion is specific to the creationism example and does not generalize to other content decisions in education. So I downplay the legal aspect of creationism laws for present purposes.

comparative authority were proposed. If novices can directly verify some of the claims of competing authorities, they can use these verifications to assess the candidates' comparative authoritativeness. This is unlikely to be applicable, though, to the evolution versus creationism dispute. The second proposed way to assess comparative authoritativeness is to assess the respective quality of the parties' argumentation. The judge (decision maker) should listen to the rivals' opposing arguments, and decide which is strongest, or who does the best job in rebuttal and counterrebuttal. This procedure definitely can be applied to the dispute in question. Supplementary procedures can also be applied. First, the judge can assess the parties' argumentative credentials on topics related to the disputed one. Let the biologists and creationists debate a sector of biology slightly removed from the targeted one and see how they fare in argumentation. Who knows more and who can rebut the other more successfully? Second, let others with established expertise in neighboring branches of science assess the authoritativeness of the rivals. Using this bundle of techniques, a novice or neutral judge can reach a conclusion about which of two disputants is more likely to be right. When the judgment decisively favors one party over another, it is inappropriate to air the losing position in the classroom. (That is what I would expect in the creationism case.) In other cases, a decisive choice between the disputants may be impossible. The viewpoints may have approximately equal evidential or argumentative merit. In that case, equal time in the classroom may be appropriate, assuming that time permits and students have the intellectual maturity to profit from hearing the dispute.

The motto that might be extracted from the foregoing discussion is: "Respect duly established expertise." I do not, however, wish to underestimate the fallibility of experts and authorities, nor to counsel blind acceptance of their opinions. In some fields even the most expert individuals, comparatively speaking, are highly fallible. These are fields in which precise knowledge is simply scarce. Education itself may be such a field when it comes to pedagogical techniques. The opinions of educational authorities should undoubtedly be respected in pedagogical matters, but parents should not refrain from questioning researchers and educators in these matters. Although the latter may be more knowledgeable about existing research than parents, the research itself may be far from conclusive.

Indeed, there is a general reason why the public should reserve a healthy dose of skepticism for the new ideas of researchers and practitioners in a field—any field, not just education. Researchers and practitioners have a built-in incentive to promulgate their own innovations: innovation is what earns them kudos and recognition. The "tried and true" does not attract much attention. Researchers and practitioners want to show the public that they can make advances in their field, and are therefore prone to exaggerate the promise or proven effectiveness of their new ideas and methods. This might account for the record of faddishness that suffuses the field of education.

This chapter is far from the final word on the social epistemology of education. But I do take it to establish the importance of social epistemology to the philosophy of education. As in science, law, politics, and all other sectors where information is critical to society, social epistemology should be a guiding force. At the edge of the twenty-first century, the age of information has not merely dawned; it is reaching its zenith. Veritistic social epistemology has an important role to play in this era.

BIBLIOGRAPHY

Abrams v. United States (1919). 250 U.S. 616.

Ackerman, Bruce (1989). "Why Dialogue?" *Journal of Philosophy*, 86: 5–22.

Akerlof, George (1970). "The Market for 'Lemons': Quality Uncertainty and the Market Mechanism." *Quarterly Journal of Economics*, 84: 488–500.

Alexander, Larry (1993). "Trouble on Track Two: Incidental Regulations of Speech and Free Speech Theory." *Hastings Law Journal*, 44: 921–62.

Almond, Gabriel (1960). *The American People and Foreign Policy*. New York: Praeger.

Alston, William (1989). "Epistemic Circularity," in *Epistemic Justification*. Ithaca, NY: Cornell University Press.

—— (1993). *The Reliability of Sense Perception*. Ithaca, NY: Cornell University Press.

—— (1994). "Belief-Forming Practices and the Social," in Schmitt 1994*b*.

—— (1996). *A Realist Conception of Truth*. Ithaca, NY: Cornell University Press.

Amar, Akhil Reed (1997). *The Constitution and Criminal Procedure: First Principles*. New Haven, Conn.: Yale University Press.

American Bar Association (1995). *Model Rules of Professional Conduct*. Chicago, Ill.: American Bar Association.

Anderson, Elizabeth (1993). *Value in Ethics and Economics*. Cambridge, Mass.: Harvard University Press.

Angell, Marcia (1996). *Courts on Trial: The Clash of Medical Evidence and the Law in Breast Implant Cases*. New York: Norton.

Appleby, Joyce, Hunt, Lynn, and Jacob, Margaret (1994). *Telling the Truth about History*. New York: Norton.

Aristotle (1924). *The Works of Aristotle*, vol. 8: *Metaphysics*, trans. W. D. Ross. Oxford: Clarendon Press.

Arnstine, Donald, and Arnstine, Barbara (1987). "Teaching Democracy Through Participation: The Crucial Role of Interest." *Educational Forum*, 51: 377–92.

Austin, J. L. (1950). "Truth." *Proceedings of the Aristotelian Society*, supp. vol. 24: 111–28.

Axelrod, Robert (1984). *The Evolution of Cooperation*. New York: Basic Books.

Ayer, A. J. (1963). "Truth," in *The Concept of a Person and Other Essays*. London: Macmillan.

Bagdikian, Ben (1997). *The Media Monopoly*. 5th edn. Boston, Mass.: Beacon Press.

Baird, Douglas, Gertner, Robert, and Picker, Randal (1994). *Game Theory and the Law*. Cambridge, Mass.: Harvard University Press.

Baker, C. Edwin (1994). *Advertising and a Democratic Press*. Princeton, NJ: Princeton University Press.

Baker, Gordon, and Hacker, Peter (1985). *Wittgenstein, Rules, Grammar, and Necessity*. Oxford: Blackwell.

Barefoot v. Estelle (1983). 463 U.S. 880.

Bar-Hillel, Maya (1990). "Back to Base Rates," in R. M. Hogarth and H. J. Einhorn, eds., *Insights in Decision Making*. Chicago, Ill.: University of Chicago Press.

Barnes, Barry, and Bloor, David (1982). "Relativism, Rationalism, and the Sociology of Knowledge," in Martin Hollis and Steven Lukes, eds., *Rationality and Relativism*. Cambridge, Mass.: MIT Press.

Baron, David (1994). "Electoral Competition with Informed and Uninformed Voters." *American Political Science Review*, 88: 33–47.

Bartels, Larry (1996). "Uninformed Votes: Information Effects in Presidential Elections." *American Journal of Political Science*, 40: 194–230.

Barth, E. M., and Krabbe, E. C. W. (1982). *From Axiom to Dialogue*. Berlin: Walter de Gruyter.

Bell, Derrick, and Bansal, Preeta (1988). "The Republican Revival and Racial Politics." *Yale Law Journal*, 97: 1609–21.

Benhabib, Seyla (1992). "Models of Public Space: Hannah Arendt, the Liberal Tradition, and Jürgen Habermas," in C. Calhoun, ed., *Habermas and the Public Sphere*. Cambridge, Mass.: MIT Press.

Bennett, Douglass (1995). "Fair Use in an Electronic Age: A View from Scholars and Scholarly Societies," in Michael Matthews and Patricia Brennan, eds., *Copyright, Public Policy, and the Scholarly Community*. Washington, DC: Association of Research Libraries.

Berelson, Bernard, Lazarsfeld, Paul, and McPhee, William (1954). *Voting: A Study of Opinion Formation in a Presidential Campaign*. Chicago, Ill.: University of Chicago Press.

Berg, Sven (1993). "Condorcet's Jury Theorem, Dependency Among Jurors." *Social Choice and Welfare*, 10: 87–95.

Biro, John, and Siegel, Harvey (1992). "Normativity, Argumentation and an Epistemic Theory of Fallacies," in Frans van Eemeren and Rob Grootendorst, eds., *Argumentation Illuminated*. Dordrecht: Foris Publications.

Blackstone, Sir William (1765). *Commentaries on the Laws of England*.

Block, Ned (1995). "How Heritability Misleads about Race." *Cognition*, 56: 99–128.

Bloor, David (1976). *Knowledge and Social Imagery*. Boston, Mass.: Routledge & Kegan Paul.

—— (1981). "The Strengths of the Strong Programme." *Philosophy of the Social Sciences*, 11: 199–214.

Boghossian, Paul (1990). "The Status of Content." *Philosophical Review*, 99: 157–84.

BonJour, Laurence (1985). *The Structure of Empirical Knowledge*. Cambridge, Mass.: Harvard University Press.

Boyd, Richard (1983). "On the Current Status of Scientific Realism." *Erkenntnis*, 19: 45–90.

Boyle, James (1996). *Shamans, Software, and Spleens*. Cambridge, Mass.: Harvard University Press.

Brandom, Robert (1994). *Making it Explicit*. Cambridge, Mass.: Harvard University Press.

Brink, David (1985). "Legal Theory, Legal Interpretation, and Judicial Review." *Philosophy and Public Affairs*, 17: 105–48

Brower, Bruce (1996). "The Epistemic Contract." Unpublished manuscript. Philosophy Department, Tulane University.

Brown, Les (1979). "Sponsors and Documentaries," in John Wright, ed., *The Commercial Connection: Advertising and the American Mass Media*. New York: Dell Publishing Company.

Brown, Penelope (1990). "Gender, Politeness, and Confrontation in Tenejapa." *Discourse Processes*, 13: 123–41.

Bruffee, Kenneth (1993). *Collaborative Learning: Higher Education, Interdependence, and the Authority of Knowledge.* Baltimore, Md.: Johns Hopkins University Press.

Burge, Tyler (1993). "Content Preservation." *Philosophical Review*, 102: 457–88.

Caglayan, Alper, and Harrison, Colin (1997). *Agent Sourcebook.* New York: Wiley Computer Pub.

Carmines, Edward, and Kuklinski, James (1990). "Incentives, Opportunities, and the Logic of Public Opinion in American Political Representation," in Ferejohn and Kuklinski 1990.

Carnap, Rudolf (1950). *Logical Foundations of Probability.* Chicago, Ill.: University of Chicago Press.

Cartwright, Nancy (1983). *How the Laws of Physics Lie.* New York: Oxford University Press.

Ceci, Steven, and Bruck, M. (1993). "Suggestibility of the Child Witness: A Historical Review and Synthesis." *Psychological Bulletin*, 113: 403–39.

Chafe, Wallace L., and Nichols, Johanna (1986). *Evidentiality: The Linguistic Coding of Epistemology.* Norwood, NJ: Ablex.

Chalmers, Alan (1990). *Science and Its Fabrication.* Minneapolis, Minn.: University of Minnesota Press.

Cheney, Lynne (1995). *Telling the Truth: Why our Culture and Our Country Have Stopped Making Sense—and What We Can Do About It.* New York: Simon & Schuster.

Christiano, Thomas (1995). "Voting and Democracy." *Canadian Journal of Philosophy*, 25: 395–414.

—— (1996). *The Rule of the Many.* Boulder, Colo.: Westview Press.

Coady, C. A. J. (1992). *Testimony.* Oxford: Oxford University Press.

Coase, Ronald (1960). "The Problem of Social Cost." *Journal of Law and Economics*, 3: 1–44.

Cohen, Joshua (1986). "An Epistemic Conception of Democracy." *Ethics*, 97: 26–38.

Cole, Stephen (1992). *Making Science: Between Nature and Society.* Cambridge, Mass.: Harvard University Press.

Coleman, Jules, and Ferejohn, John (1986). "Democracy and Social Choice." *Ethics*, 97: 6–25.

—— and Leiter, Brian (1995). "Determinacy, Objectivity, and Authority," in Andrei Marmor, ed., *Law and Interpretation.* Oxford: Clarendon Press.

Collins, Harry (1981). "Stages in the Empirical Programme of Relativism." *Social Studies of Science*, 11: 3–10.

Condorcet, Marie Jean Antoine Nicolas Caritat, Marquis de (1994). "An Essay on the Application of Probability Theory to Plurality Decision-Making" (1785), in *Condorcet*, extracts trans. and ed. Iain McLean and Fiona Hewitt. Brookfield, Vt.: Edward Elgar.

Converse, Philip (1990). "Popular Representation and the Distribution of Information," in Ferejohn and Kuklinski 1990.

Corlett, J. Angelo (1991). "Epistemology, Psychology, and Goldman." *Social Epistemology*, 5: 91–100.

Cox, James, and Goldman, Alvin (1994). "Accuracy in Journalism: An Economic Approach," in Schmitt 1994b.

Craig, Edward (1990). *Knowledge and the State of Nature.* Oxford: Clarendon Press.

Cross, K. Patricia (1977). "Not *Can* but *Will* College Teaching Be Improved?" *New Directions for Higher Education*, 17: 1–15.

Damaska, Mirjan (1997). *Evidence Law Adrift*. New Haven, Conn.: Yale University Press.

Dansereau, Donald (1985). "Learning Research Strategy," in J. Segal, S. Chipman, and R. Glaser, eds., *Thinking and Learning Skills: Relating Instruction to Basic Research*, vol. i. Hillsdale, NJ: Erlbaum.

Daubert v. Merrell Dow Pharmaceuticals (1993). 113 S. Ct. 2786.

David, Marian (1994). *Correspondence and Disquotation*. New York: Oxford University Press.

Davidson, Donald (1980). *Essays on Actions and Events*. Oxford: Clarendon Press.

De Groot, Morris (1974). "Reaching a Consensus." *Journal of the American Statistical Association*, 69: 118–21.

Derrida, Jacques (1976). *Of Grammatology*, trans. G. Spivak. Baltimore, Md.: Johns Hopkins University Press.

Devitt, Michael (1984). *Realism and Truth*. Princeton, NJ: Princeton University Press.

de Waal, Frans (1996). "The Biological Basis of Behavior." *Chronicle of Higher Education*, 42/40: B1, B2.

Dewey, John (1913). *Interest and Effort in Education*. New York: Macmillan.

—— (1916). *Democracy and Education*. New York: Macmillan.

—— (1938). *Logic: The Theory of Inquiry*. New York: Holt.

—— (1957). *Reconstruction in Philosophy*. Boston, Mass.: Beacon Press.

Diaconis, Persi (1978). "Statistical Problems in ESP Research." *Science*, 201: 131–6.

Downs, Anthony (1957). *An Economic Theory of Democracy*. New York: Harper.

Drake, Stillman (1970). *Galileo Studies: Personality, Tradition and Revolution*. Ann Arbor, Mich.: University of Michigan Press.

Dretske, Fred (1969). *Seeing and Knowing*. London: Routledge & Kegan Paul.

—— (1981). *Knowledge and the Flow of Information*. Cambridge, Mass.: MIT Press.

Dreyfus, Hubert, and Rabinow, Paul (1983). *Michel Foucault: Beyond Structuralism and Hermeneutics*, 2nd edn. Chicago, Ill.: University of Chicago Press.

Dummett, Michael (1976). "What is a Theory of Meaning? II," in Gareth Evans and John McDowell, eds., *Truth and Meaning*. Oxford: Clarendon Press.

Dworkin, Ronald (1967). "The Model of Rules." *University of Chicago Law Review*, 35: 14–46.

—— (1977). *Taking Rights Seriously*. Cambridge, Mass.: Harvard University Press.

Earman, John (1992). *Bayes or Bust?* Cambridge, Mass.: MIT Press.

Ennis, Robert (1962). "A Concept of Critical Thinking." *Harvard Educational Review*, 32: 81–111.

Entman, Robert (1989). *Democracy Without Citizens: Media and the Decay of American Politics*. New York: Oxford University Press.

Estlund, David (1990). "Democracy without Preference." *Philosophical Review*, 99: 397–424.

Etchemendy, John (1988). "Tarski on Truth and Logical Consequence." *Journal of Symbolic Logic*, 53: 51–79.

Fallows, James (1996). *Breaking the News: How the Media Undermine American Democracy*. New York: Pantheon.

Farber, Daniel, and Sherry, Suzanna (1997). *Beyond All Reason: The Radical Assault on Truth in American Law*. New York: Oxford University Press.

Federal Rules of Evidence for United States Courts and Magistrates (1989). St. Paul, Minn.: West.

Feldman, Richard, and Conee, Earl (1985). "Evidentialism." *Philosophical Studies*, 48: 15–34.

Ferejohn, John (1986). "Incumbent Performance and Electoral Control." *Public Choice*, 50: 5–25.

—— (1990). "Information and the Electoral Process," in Ferejohn and Kuklinski 1990.

—— and Kuklinski, James, eds. (1990). *Information and Democratic Processes*. Urbana, Ill.: University of Illinois Press.

Feyerabend, Paul (1962). "Explanation, Reduction and Empiricism," in Herbert Feigl and Grover Maxwell, eds., *Minnesota Studies in the Philosophy of Science*, vol. iii. Minneapolis, Minn.: University of Minnesota Press.

Fiedler, K. (1988). "The Dependence of the Conjunction Fallacy on Subtle Linguistic Factors." *Psychological Research*, 50: 123–9.

Field, Hartry (1986). "The Deflationary Conception of Truth," in Graham MacDonald and Crispin Wright, eds., *Fact, Science and Morality*. Oxford: Blackwell.

—— (1994a). "Deflationist Views of Meaning and Content." *Mind*, 103: 249–85.

—— (1994b). "Disquotational Truth and Factually Defective Discourse." *Philosophical Review*, 103: 405–52.

Fine, Arthur (1996). "Science Made Up: Constructivist Sociology of Scientific Knowledge," in P. Galison and D. Stump, eds., *The Disunity of Science*. Stanford: Calif.: Stanford University Press.

Fiorina, Morris (1981). *Retrospective Voting in American National Elections*. New Haven, Conn.: Yale University Press.

—— and Shepsle, Kenneth (1990). "A Positive Theory of Negative Voting," in Ferejohn and Kuklinski 1990.

Fisher, Janet (1996). "Traditional Publishers and Electronic Journals," in Robin Peek and Gregory Newby, eds., *Scholarly Publishing: The Electronic Frontier*. Cambridge, Mass.: MIT Press.

Fisher, William, III (1988). "Reconstructing the Fair Use Doctrine." *Harvard Law Review*, 101: 1659–1795.

Fishkin, James (1991). *Democracy and Deliberation: New Directions for Democratic Reform*. New Haven, Conn.: Yale University Press.

Fiss, Owen M. (1987). "Why the State?" *Harvard Law Review*, 100: 781–94.

—— (1991). "State Activism and State Censorship." *Yale Law Journal*, 100: 2087–2106.

Flax, Jane (1990a). *Thinking Fragments: Psychoanalysis, Feminism, and Postmodernism in the Contemporary West*. Berkeley, Calif.: University of California Press.

—— (1990b). "Postmodernism and Gender Relations in Feminist Theory," in Linda Nicholson, ed., *Feminism/Postmodernism*. New York: Routledge.

Fodor, Jerry (1983). *The Modularity of Mind*. Cambridge, Mass.: MIT Press.

—— (1984). "Observation Reconsidered." *Philosophy of Science*, 51: 23–43.

Foley, Richard (1994). "Egoism in Epistemology," in Schmitt 1994b.

Foucault, Michel (1978). *The History of Sexuality*. New York: Pantheon Books.

—— (1979). *Discipline and Punish*, trans. A. Sheridan. New York: Vintage Books.

Franciosi, Robert, Isaac, R. Mark, Pingry, David, and Reynolds, Stanley (1993). "An Experimental Investigation of the Hahn-Noll Revenue Neutral Auction for Emissions Licenses." *Journal of Environmental Economics and Management*, 24: 1–24.

Frank, Jerome (1949). *Courts on Trial*. Princeton, NJ: Princeton University Press.

Fraser, Nancy, and Nicholson, Linda (1990). "Social Criticism without Philosophy," in Linda Nicholson, ed., *Feminism/Postmodernism*. New York: Routledge.

Frazer, J. G. (1959). *The Golden Bough: A Study in Magic and Religion*, abr. and ed. T. Gaster. New York: S. G. Phillips.

Fricker, Elizabeth (1994). "Against Gullibility," in B. K. Matilal and A. Chakrabarti, eds., *Knowing from Words*. Dordrecht: Kluwer.

—— (1995). "Telling and Trusting: Reductionism and Anti-Reductionism in the Epistemology of Testimony." *Mind*, 104: 393–411.

Friedman, Richard (1987). "Route Analysis of Credibility and Hearsay." *Yale Law Journal*, 96: 667–742.

Frye v. United States (1923). 293 F. 1013 (D.C. Cir.).

Frye, Billy (1997). "Universities in Transition: Implications for Libraries," in Lawrence Dowler, ed., *Gateways to Knowledge*. Cambridge, Mass.: MIT Press.

Fuchs, Ira (1996). "Networked Information Is Not Free," in Robin Peek and Gregory Newby, eds., *Scholarly Publishing: The Electronic Frontier*. Cambridge, Mass.: MIT Press.

Fuller, Steve (1988). *Social Epistemology*. Bloomington, Ind.: Indiana University Press.

Galison, Peter (1987). *How Experiments End*. Chicago, Ill.: University of Chicago Press.

Garson, Lorrin (1996). "Can E-Journals Save Us?—A Publisher's View," in Meredith Butler and Bruce Kinga, eds., *The Economics of Information in the Networked Environment*. Washington, DC: Association of Research Libraries.

Geach, Peter (1960). "Ascriptivism." *Philosophical Review*, 69: 221–5.

Gianelli, Paul (1993). "'Junk Science': The Criminal Cases." *Journal of Criminal Law and Criminology*, 84: 105–27.

—— (1994). "Daubert: Interpreting the Federal Rules of Evidence." *Cardozo Law Review*, 15: 1999–2026.

Giere, Ronald (1979). *Understanding Scientific Reasoning*. New York: Holt, Rinehart, & Winston.

—— (1988). *Explaining Science*. Chicago, Ill.: University of Chicago Press.

Gigerenzer, Gerd (1991). "How to Make Cognitive Illusions Disappear: Beyond 'Heuristics and Biases'," in W. Stroebe and M. Hewstone, eds., *European Review of Social Psychology*, vol. ii. New York: Wiley.

—— Hell, Wolfgang, and Blank, Hartmut (1988). "Presentation and Content: The Use of Base Rates as a Continuous Variable." *Journal of Experimental Psychology*, 14: 513–25.

—— Swijtink, Zeno, Porter, Theodore, Daston, Lorraine, Beatty, John, and Krüger, Lorenz (1989). *The Empire of Chance: How Probability Changed Science and Everyday Life*. New York: Cambridge University Press.

Gilbert, Margaret (1989). *On Social Facts*. New York: Routledge.

Gilovich, Thomas (1991). *How We Know What Isn't So*. New York: Free Press.

Gilster, Paul (1997). *Digital Literacy*. New York: Wiley.

Ginsparg, Paul (1997). "First Steps Toward Electronic Research Communication," in Lawrence Dowler, ed., *Gateways to Knowledge*. Cambridge, Mass.: MIT Press.

Goldman, Alvin (1970). *A Theory of Human Action*. Englewood Cliffs, NJ: Prentice-Hall.

—— (1976). "Discrimination and Perceptual Knowledge." *Journal of Philosophy*, 73: 771–91.

—— (1978). "Epistemics: The Regulative Theory of Cognition." *Journal of Philosophy*, 75: 509–23.

—— (1986). *Epistemology and Cognition*. Cambridge, Mass.: Harvard University Press.

—— (1987). "Foundations of Social Epistemics." *Synthese*, 73: 109–44.

—— (1991). "Epistemic Paternalism: Communication Control in Law and Society." *Journal of Philosophy*, 88: 113–31.

—— (1992). *Liaisons: Philosophy Meets the Cognitive and Social Sciences*. Cambridge, Mass.: MIT Press.

—— (1994a). "Argumentation and Social Epistemology." *Journal of Philosophy*, 91: 27–49.

—— (1994b). "Psychological, Social, and Epistemic Factors in the Theory of Science," in D. Hull, M. Forbes, and R. Burian, eds., *PSA 1994*. East Lansing, Mich.: Philosophy of Science Association.

—— (1994c). "Action and Crime: A Fine-Grained Approach." *University of Pennsylvania Law Review*, 142: 1563–86.

—— (1995a). "Social Epistemology, Interests, and Truth." *Philosophical Topics*, 23: 171–87.

—— (1995b). "Education and Social Epistemology," in Alven Neiman, ed., *Philosophy of Education 1995*. Urbana, Ill.: Philosophy of Education Society.

—— (1997). "Science, Publicity, and Consciousness." *Philosophy of Science*, 64: 525–45.

—— and Cox, James (1996). "Speech, Truth and the Free Market for Ideas." *Legal Theory*, 2: 1–32.

—— and Shaked, Moshe (1991a). "An Economic Model of Scientific Activity and Truth Acquisition." *Philosophical Studies*, 63: 31–55. Expanded version in Goldman 1992: ch. 12.

—— —— (1991b). "Results on Inquiry and Truth Possession." *Statistics and Probability Letters*, 12: 415–20.

Goldstein, Tom (1985). *The News at Any Cost: How Journalists Compromise Their Ethics to Shape the News*. New York: Simon & Schuster.

Goodman, Nelson (1978). *Ways of Worldmaking*. Indianapolis, Ind.: Hackett Publishing Company.

—— (1984). *Of Mind and Other Matters*. Cambridge, Mass.: Harvard University Press.

Gould, Stephen Jay (1981). *The Mismeasure of Man*. New York: Norton.

Graff, Gerald (1992). *Beyond the Culture Wars: How Teaching the Conflicts can Revitalize American Education*. New York: Norton.

Greenawalt, Kent (1989). *Speech, Crime and the Uses of Language*. New York: Oxford University Press.

—— (1992). *Law and Objectivity*. New York: Oxford University Press.

Grice, Paul (1989). *Studies in the Way of Words*. Cambridge, Mass.: Harvard University Press.

Gross, Paul, and Levitt, Norman (1994). *Higher Superstition: The Academic Left and its Quarrels with Science*. Baltimore, Md.: Johns Hopkins Press.

Grover, Dorothy (1992). *A Prosentential Theory of Truth*. Princeton, NJ: Princeton University Press.

—— Camp, Joseph, Jr., and Belnap, Nuel, Jr. (1975). "A Prosentential Theory of Truth." *Philosophical Studies*, 27: 73–125. Reprinted in Grover 1992.

Günthner, Susanne (1993). "The Negotiation of Dissent in Intercultural Communication—An Analysis of Chinese–German Conversation," paper presented at the International Pragmatics Association conference, Kobe, Japan.

Gupta, Anil (1993). "Minimalism," in James E. Tomberlin, ed., *Philosophical Perspectives*, 7: *Language and Logic*. Atascadero, Calif.: Ridgeview.

382   *Bibliography*

Gutmann, Amy, ed. (1992*a*). *Multiculturalism and the "Politics of Recognition."* Princeton, NJ: Princeton University Press.
—— (1992*b*). "Introduction," in Gutmann (1992*a*).
Habermas, Jürgen (1984). *The Theory of Communicative Action*, 2 vols., trans. T. McCarthy. Boston, Mass.: Beacon.
—— (1990). *Moral Consciousness and Communicative Action*. Cambridge, Mass.: MIT Press.
—— (1996). *Between Facts and Norms*. Cambridge: Polity.
Hacking, Ian (1983). *Representing and Intervening*. New York: Cambridge University Press.
Hamblin, C. L. (1970). *Fallacies*. London: Methuen.
—— (1971). "Mathematical Models of Dialogue," *Theoria*, 37: 130–55.
Harding, Sandra (1991). *Whose Science? Whose Knowledge?* Ithaca, NY: Cornell University Press.
—— (1992). "After the Neutral Ideal: Science, Politics, and 'Strong Objectivity'." *Social Research*, 59: 567–87.
Hardwig, John (1985). "Epistemic Dependence." *Journal of Philosophy*, 82: 335–49.
Hardy, G. H. (1941). *A Mathematician's Apology*. Cambridge: Cambridge University Press.
Hare, Francis, Gilbert, James, and ReMine, William (1988). *Confidentiality Orders*. New York: Wiley.
Harman, Gilbert (1965). "The Inference to the Best Explanation." *Philosophical Review*, 74: 88–95.
—— (1986) *Change in View*. Cambridge, Mass.: MIT Press.
Harnad, Steven (1996). "Implementing Peer Review on the Net: Scientific Quality Control in Scholarly Electronic Journals," in Robin Peek and Gregory Newby, eds., *Scholarly Publishing: The Electronic Frontier*. Cambridge, Mass.: MIT Press.
Hart, H. L. A. (1958). "Positivism and the Separation of Law and Morals." *Harvard Law Review*, 71: 593–629.
—— (1961). *The Concept of Law*. Oxford: Oxford University Press.
Hartsock, Nancy (1983). "The Feminist Standpoint: Developing a Ground for a Specifically Feminist Historical Materialism," in Sandra Harding and Merrill Hintikka, eds., *Discovering Reality*. Dordrecht: D. Reidel.
Haslanger, Sally (1993). "On Being Objective and Being Objectified," in Louise Antony and Charlotte Witt, eds., *A Mind of One's Own: Feminist Essays on Reason and Objectivity*. Boulder, Colo.: Westview Press.
—— (1995). "Ontology and Social Construction." *Philosophical Topics*, 23: 95–125.
Hastie, Reid, Penrod, Steven, and Pennington, Nancy (1983). *Inside the Jury*. Cambridge, Mass.: Harvard University Press.
Hauser, Marc (1996). *The Evolution of Communication*. Cambridge, Mass.: MIT Press.
Hawkesworth, Mary (1989). "Knowers, Knowing, Known: Feminist Theory and Claims of Truth." *Signs: Journal of Women in Culture and Society*, 14: 533–57.
Hawles, Sir John (1811). "Remarks on Mr. Cornish's Trial," in *Howell's State Trials*. London: Hansard
Hayek, Friedrich A. (1948). *Individualism and Economic Order*. Chicago, Ill.: Chicago University Press.
Hearst, Marti (1997). "Interfaces for Searching the Web." *Scientific American*, 176/3: 68–72.
Hegland, Kenney (1985). "Goodbye to Deconstruction." *Southern California Law Review*, 58: 1203–21.

Heider, Eleanor (1972). "Universals in Color Naming and Memory." *Cognitive Psychology*, 3: 337–54.

Hempel, Carl (1965). "Inductive Inconsistencies," in *Aspects of Scientific Explanation*. New York: Free Press.

Herman, Edward, and Chomsky, Noam (1988). *Manufacturing Consent: The Political Economy of the Mass Media*. New York: Pantheon Books.

Herrnstein, Richard, and Murray, Charles (1994). *The Bell Curve: Intelligence and Class Structure in America*. New York: Free Press.

Hesse, Mary (1980). *Revolutions and Reconstructions in the Philosophy of Science*. Brighton, Sussex: Harvester Press.

Horgan, Terence (1995). "Review of Truth and Objectivity." *Nous*, 29: 127–38.

Horton, Robin (1982). "Tradition and Modernity Revisited," in Martin Hollis and Steven Lukes, eds., *Rationality and Relativism*. Cambridge, Mass.: MIT Press.

Horwich, Paul (1990). *Truth*. Oxford: Blackwell.

—— (1992). "Theories of Truth," in J. Dancy and E. Sosa, eds., *A Companion to Epistemology*. Cambridge, Mass.: Blackwell.

—— (1993). "Review of Wright's 'Truth and Objectivity'." *Times Literary Supplement*, July 16: 28.

—— (1996). "Realism and Truth," in James Tomberlin, ed., *Philosophical Perspectives*, 10: *Metaphysics*. Atascadero, Calif.: Ridgeview.

Howson, Colin, and Urbach, Peter (1989). *Scientific Reasoning: The Bayesian Approach*. La Salle, Ill.: Open Court.

Hrdy, Sarah (1986). "Empathy, Polyandry, and the Myth of the Coy Female," in R. Bleier, ed., *Feminist Approaches to Science*. New York: Pergamon Press.

Hume, David (1972). *Enquiries Concerning Human Understanding and Concerning the Principles of Morals* (1777), ed. L. A. Selby-Bigge, 2nd edn. Oxford: Oxford University Press.

Hutchins, Edwin (1996). *Cognition in the Wild*. Cambridge, Mass.: MIT Press.

Hutchins, Robert Maynard (1936). *The Higher Learning in America*. New Haven, Conn.: Yale University Press.

Huyssen, Andreas (1986). *After the Great Divide: Modernism, Mass Culture, and Postmodernism*. Bloomington, Ind.: Indiana University Press.

Ingber, Stanley (1984). "The Marketplace of Ideas: A Legitimizing Myth." *Duke University Law Review*, 1984: 1–91.

Jacobs, Scott (1987). "The Management of Disagreement in Conversation," in Frans H. van Eemeren, Rob Grootendorst, J. A. Blair, and C. A. Willard, eds., *Argumentation: Across the Lines of Discipline*. Dordrecht: Foris.

Jaggar, Alison (1983). *Feminist Politics and Human Nature*. Totowa, NJ: Rowman & Allanheld.

James, William (1975). *Pragmatism* (1907). Cambridge, Mass.: Harvard University Press.

—— (1909). *The Meaning of Truth*. Cambridge, Mass.: Harvard University Press.

Jaszi, Peter (1996). "Taking the White Paper Seriously," in Patricia Brennan, ed., *Copyright and the NII*. Washington, DC: Association of Research Libraries.

Johnson, M. K., and Raye, C. L. (1981). "Reality Monitoring." *Psychological Review*, 88: 67–85.

Jones, Kimberly (forthcoming). *The Myth of Harmony: Conflict Discourse in Japanese*. Norwood, NJ: Ablex.

Kahane, Howard (1980). *Logic and Contemporary Rhetoric*, 3rd edn. Belmont, Calif.: Wadsworth.

Kahneman, Daniel, and Tversky, Amos (1973). "On the Psychology of Prediction." *Psychological Review*, 80: 237–51.

— Slovic, Paul, and Tversky, Amos, eds. (1982). *Judgment under Uncertainty: Heuristics and Biases*. Cambridge: Cambridge University Press.

Kalven, Harry, Jr., and Zeisel, Hans (1966). *The American Jury*. Boston: Little Brown.

Kamisar, Yale (1995). "On the 'Fruits' of *Miranda* Violations, Coerced Confessions, and Compelled Testimony." *Michigan Law Review*, 93: 929–1010.

Katz, Elihu, and Lazarsfeld, Paul (1955). *Personal Influence*. Glencoe, Ill.: Free Press.

Kennedy, Duncan (1976). "Form and Substance in Private Law Adjudication." *Harvard Law Review*, 89: 1685–1778.

Kesan, Jay (1996). "An Autopsy of Scientific Evidence in a Post-Daubert World." *Georgetown Law Journal*, 84: 1985–2041.

Key, V. O., Jr. (1966). *The Responsible Electorate: Rationality in Presidential Voting, 1936–1960*. Cambridge, Mass.: Harvard University Press.

Kim, Jaegwon (1993). *Supervenience and Mind*. New York: Cambridge University Press.

Kirkham, Richard (1992). *Theories of Truth*. Cambridge, Mass.: MIT Press.

Kitcher, Philip (1982). *Abusing Science: The Case Against Creationism*. Cambridge, Mass.: MIT Press.

— (1990). "The Division of Cognitive Labor." *Journal of Philosophy*, 87: 5–22.

— (1991). "Persuasion," in Marcello Pera and William Shea, eds., *Persuading Science: the Art of Scientific Rhetoric*. Canton, Mass.: Science History Publications.

— (1993). *The Advancement of Science*. New York: Oxford University Press.

Koehler, Jonathan (1996). "The Base Rate Fallacy Reconsidered: Descriptive, Normative and Methodological Challenges." *Behavioral and Brain Sciences*, 19: 1–17.

Kolata, Gina (1996a). "In Quests Outside Mainstream, Medical Projects Rewrite Rules." *New York Times*, June 18: A1, A16.

— (1996b). "Judge Dismisses Implant Evidence." *New York Times*, December 19: A1, A14.

Kornblith, Hilary (1993). "Epistemic Normativity." *Synthese*, 94: 357–76.

— (1998). "Distrusting Reason," in P. French, T. Uehling, and H. Wettstein, eds., *Midwest Studies in Philosophy*, vol. xx. Notre Dame, Ind.: University of Notre Dame Press.

Kosslyn, Stephen (1980). *Image and Mind*. Cambridge, Mass.: Harvard University Press.

Kramer, G. (1977). "A Dynamical Model of Political Equilibrium." *Journal of Economic Theory*, 16: 310–34.

Kress, Ken (1989). "Legal Indeterminacy." *California Law Review*, 77: 283–337.

Kripke, Saul (1982). *Wittgenstein on Rules and Private Language*. Cambridge, Mass.: Harvard University Press.

Kronman, Anthony (1978). "Mistake, Disclosure, Information and the Law of Contracts." *Journal of Legal Studies*, 7: 1–34.

Kruglanski, A., and Freund, T. (1983). "The Freezing and Unfreezing of Lay Inferences: Effects on Impressional Primacy, Ethnic Stereotyping, and Numerical Anchoring." *Journal of Experimental Social Psychology*, 19: 448–68.

Kuhn, Thomas (1962). *The Structure of Scientific Revolutions*. Chicago, Ill.: University of Chicago Press.

— (1977). *The Essential Tension*. Chicago, Ill.: University of Chicago Press.

Kunda, Ziva (1990). "The Case for Motivated Reasoning." *Psychological Bulletin*, 108: 480–98.

—— and Sanitioso, R. (1989). "Motivated Changes in the Self-Concept." *Journal of Experimental Social Psychology*, 25: 272–85.

Lammenranta, Markus (1996). "Reliabilism and Circularity." *Philosophy and Phenomenological Research*, 56: 111–24.

Langbein, John H. (1980). "Torture and Plea Bargaining." *The Public Interest*, 58: 43–61.

—— (1985). "The German Advantage in Civil Procedure." *University of Chicago Law Review*, 52: 823–66.

Latour, Bruno (1987). *Science in Action*. Cambridge, Mass.: Harvard University Press.

—— and Woolgar, Steve (1986). *Laboratory Life: The Construction of Scientific Facts*, 2nd edn. (Originally published 1979 with the subtitle *The Social Construction of Scientific Facts*.) Princeton, NJ: Princeton University Press.

Laudan, Larry (1981). "A Confutation of Convergent Realism." *Philosophy of Science*, 48: 19–49.

—— (1990). "Demystifying Underdetermination," in C. Wade Savage, ed., *Minnesota Studies in the Philosophy of Science*, vol. xiv. Minneapolis, Minn.: University of Minnesota Press.

Ledyard, John (1995). "Public Goods: A Survey of Experimental Research," in J. Kagel and A. Roth, eds., *The Handbook of Experimental Economics*. Princeton, NJ: Princeton University Press.

Lehrer, Keith, and Wagner, Carl (1981). *Rational Consensus in Science and Society*. Dordrecht: D. Reidel.

Leiter, Brian (1996). "Legal Realism," in Dennis Patterson, ed., *A Companion to Philosophy of Law and Legal Theory*. Oxford: Blackwell.

Lempert, Richard (1977). "Modeling Relevance." *Michigan Law Review*, 75: 1021–57.

Lewis, David (1973). *Counterfactuals*. Cambridge, Mass.: Harvard University Press.

Lewy, Casimir (1947). "Truth and Significance." *Analysis*, 8: 24–7.

Lichtenstein, Sarah, Fischhoff, Baruch, and Phillips, L. D. (1982). "Calibration of Probabilities: The State of the Art to 1980," in Kahneman, Slovic, and Tversky 1982.

Loevinger, L. (1995). "Science as Evidence." *Jurimetrics Journal*, 35: 153–90.

Loftus, Elizabeth, Feldman, Julie, and Dashiell, Richard (1995). "The Reality of Illusory Memories," in Daniel Schacter *et al.*, eds., *Memory Distortion: How Minds, Brains and Societies Reconstruct the Past*. Cambridge, Mass.: Harvard University Press.

—— Miller, David, and Burns, Helen (1978). "Semantic Integration of Verbal Information into a Visual Memory." *Journal of Experimental Psychology: Human Learning and Memory*, 4: 19–31.

Longino, Helen (1990). *Science as Social Knowledge*. Princeton, NJ: Princeton University Press.

Lord, Charles, Ross, Lee, and Lepper, Mark (1979). "Biased Assimilation and Attitude Polarization: The Effects of Prior Theories on Subsequently Considered Evidence." *Journal of Personality and Social Psychology*, 37: 2098–2109.

Luban, David (1988). *Lawyers and Justice: An Ethical Study*. Princeton, NJ: Princeton University Press.

Lupia, Arthur (1994). "Shortcuts Versus Encyclopedias: Information and Voting Behavior in California Insurance Reform Elections." *American Political Science Review*, 88: 63–76.

Lyons, Jack (1997). "Testimony, Induction, and Folk Psychology." *Australasian Journal of Philosophy*, 75: 163–78.

Lyotard, Jean-François (1984). *The Postmodern Condition: A Report on Knowledge*. Minneapolis, Minn.: University of Minnesota Press.

McCabe, Sarah, and Purves, Robert (1974). *The Shadow Jury at Work*. Oxford: Blackwell.

McKelvey, Richard (1975). "Policy Related Voting and Electoral Equilibrium." *Econometrica*, 43: 815–43.

—— and Ordeshook, Peter (1986). "Information, Electoral Equilibria, and the Democratic Ideal." *Journal of Politics*, 48: 909–37.

Mackenzie, Donald (1981). *Statistics in Britain: 1865–1930, The Social Construction of Scientific Knowledge*. Edinburgh: Edinburgh University Press.

Mackenzie, J. D. (1981). "The Dialectics of Logic." *Logique et Analyse*, 94: 159–77.

—— (1989). "Reasoning and Logic." *Synthese*, 79: 99–117.

Mackie, J. L. (1977). *Ethics: Inventing Right and Wrong*. New York: Penguin.

MacKie-Mason, Jeffrey, and Riveros, Juan (1997). "Economics and Electronic Access to Scholarly Information," paper presented at the Conference on Economics of Digital Information and Intellectual Property.

—— and Varian, Hal (1994). "Some FAQs about Usage-Based Pricing," in Ann Okerson, ed., *Scholarly Publishing on the Electronic Networks*. Washington, DC: Association of Research Libraries.

MacKinnon, Catharine (1989). *Toward a Feminist Theory of the State*. Cambridge, Mass.: Harvard University Press.

McKuen, Michael (1990). "Speaking of Politics: Individual Conversational Choice, Public Opinion, and the Prospects for Deliberative Democracy," in Ferejohn and Kuklinski 1990.

McPeck, John (1981). *Critical Thinking and Education*. New York: St. Martin's Press.

McTaggart, J. M. E. (1921). *The Nature of Existence*, vol. i. Cambridge: Cambridge University Press.

Maes, Patti (1994). "Agents that Reduce Work and Information Overload." *Communications of the ACM*, 37/7: 31–40.

Maffie, James (1995). "Towards an Anthropology of Epistemology." *Philosophical Forum*, 26: 218–41.

Manis, Melvin, Dovalina, Ismael, Avis, Nancy, and Cardoze, Steven (1980). "Base Rates Can Affect Individual Predictions." *Journal of Personality and Social Psychology*, 38: 231–48.

Marslen-Wilson, W., and Welsh, A. (1978). "Processing Interactions and Lexical Access During Word Recognition in Continuous Speech." *Cognitive Psychology*, 10: 29–63.

Meiland, Jack (1989). "Argument as Inquiry and Argument as Persuasion." *Argumentation*, 3: 185–96.

Mill, John Stuart (1960). "On Liberty" (1859), in *On Liberty, Representative Government, The Subjection of Women*. New York: Oxford University Press.

Miller, David (1974). "On the Comparison of False Theories by their Bases." *British Journal for the Philosophy of Science*, 26: 178–88.

Miller, Nicholas (1986). "Information, Electorates, and Democracy: Some Extensions and Interpretations of the Condorcet Jury Theorem," in Bernard Grofman and Guillermo Owen, eds., *Information Pooling and Group Decision Making*. Greenwich, Conn.: JAI.

Miller, Richard (1995). "The Norms of Reason." *Philosophical Review*, 104: 205–45.

Miller, Warren, and Stokes, Donald (1963). "Constituency Influence in Congress." *American Political Science Review*, 57: 45–56.

Milton, John (1959). "Areopagitica, A Speech for the Liberty of Unlicensed Printing" (1644), in E. Sirluck, ed., *Complete Prose Works of John Milton.*

Minow, Martha (1987). "Law Turning Outward." *Telos*, 73: 79–100.

Miranda v. Arizona (1966). 384 U.S. 436.

Moore, Michael (1985). "A Natural Law Theory of Interpretation." *Southern California Law Review*, 58: 277–398.

—— (1989). "The Interpretive Turn in Modern Theory: A Turn for the Worse?" *Stanford Law Review*, 41: 871–957.

Mueller, Dennis C. (1979). *Public Choice.* Cambridge: Cambridge University Press.

Murphy v. Waterfront Commission (1964). 378 U.S. 52.

Nader, Ralph, and Smith, Wesley (1996). *No Contest: Corporate Lawyers and the Perversion of Justice in America.* New York: Random House.

Nash, Gary, Crabtree, Charlotte, and Dunn, Ross (1997). *History on Trial: Culture Wars and the Teaching of the Past.* New York: Knopf.

New York Times v. Sullivan (1964). 376 U.S. 254.

Nicholson, Linda (1990). "Social Criticism without Philosophy: An Encounter between Feminism and Postmodernism," in Linda Nicholson, ed., *Feminism/Postmodernism.* New York: Routledge.

Niiniluoto, Ilkka (1982). "What Shall We Do with Verisimilitude?" *Philosophy of Science*, 49: 181–97.

Nisbett, Richard, and Ross, Lee (1980). *Human Inference.* Englewood Cliffs, NJ: Prentice-Hall.

—— Krantz, David, Jepson, Christopher, and Kunda, Ziva (1983). "The Use of Statistical Heuristics in Everyday Inductive Reasoning." *Psychological Review*, 90: 339–63.

Nitzan, S., and Paroush, J. (1982). "Optimal Decision Rules in Uncertain Dichotomous Choice Situations." *International Economic Review*, 23: 289–97.

Norris, Christopher (1988). *Deconstruction and the Interests of Theory.* London: Pinter.

Nozick, Robert (1981). *Philosophical Explanations.* Cambridge, Mass.: Harvard University Press.

Nussbaum, Martha (1997). *Cultivating Humanity: A Classical Defense of Reform in Liberal Education.* Cambridge, Mass.: Harvard University Press.

Oddie, Graham (1986). *Likeness to Truth.* Dordrecht: Reidel.

Onyewuenyi, I (1991). "Is There an African Philosophy?" in T. Serequeberhan, ed., *African Philosophy: The Essential Readings.* New York: Paragon House.

Oruka, H. Odera (1990). *Sage Philosophy: Indigenous Thinkers and Modern Debate on African Philosophy.* New York: E. J. Brill.

Orwell, Geroge (1949). *Nineteen Eighty-Four.* New York: Harcourt, Brace.

Page, Benjamin, and Jones, Calvin (1979). "Reciprocal Effects of Policy Preferences, Party Loyalties, and the Vote." *American Political Science Review*, 73: 1071–89.

—— and Shapiro, Robert (1983). "Effects of Public Opinion on Policy." *American Political Science Review*, 77: 175–90.

—— —— (1992). *The Rational Public.* Chicago, Ill.: University of Chicago Press.

Patterson, Thomas (1993). *Out of Order.* New York: Knopf.

Paul, Richard (1984). "Critical Thinking: Fundamental to Education for a Free Society." *Educational Leadership*, 42: 4–14.

Peek, Philip (1991). "African Divination Systems: Non-Normal Modes of Cognition," in Philip Peek, ed., *African Divination Systems: Ways of Knowing.* Bloomington, Ind.: Indiana University Press.

Peirce, Charles (1931–5) *Collected Papers*, vols. i–vi, ed. Charles Hartshorne and Paul Weiss. Cambridge, Mass.: Harvard University Press.

Perritt, Henry Jr. (1984). "'And The Whole Earth Was of One Language'—A Broad View of Dispute Resolution." *Villanova Law Review*, 29: 1229–59.

Petty, Richard, and Cacioppo, John (1986*a*). *Communication and Persuasion: Central and Peripheral Routes to Attitude Change*. New York: Springer.

—— —— (1986*b*). "The Elaboration-Likelihood Model of Persuasion," in L. Berkowitz, ed., *Advances in Experimental Psychology*, vol. xix. New York: Academic Press.

Pickering, Andrew (1984). *Constructing Quarks: A Sociological History of Particle Physics*. Chicago, Ill.: University of Chicago Press.

Pinch, Trevor (1985). "Theory Testing in Science—The Case of the Solar Neutrinos." *Philosophy of Social Science*, 15: 167–88.

Pinker, Steven (1994). *The Language Instinct: How the Mind Creates Language*. New York: Morrow.

Pinnick, Cassandra (1994). "Feminist Epistemology: Implications for Philosophy of Science." *Philosophy of Science*, 61: 646–57.

Pirolli, Peter, and Card, Stuart (1995). "Information Foraging in Information Access Environments," in ACM/SIGCHI, *Human Factors in Computing Systems: Mosaic of Creativity*. New York: Association of Computing Machinery.

Plantinga, Alvin (1993). *Warrant and Proper Function*. New York: Oxford University Press.

Plott, Charles R. (1983). "Externalities and Corrective Policies in Experimental Markets." *Economic Journal*, 93: 106–27.

Police Department v. Mosley (1972). 408 U.S. 92.

Pollock, John (1986). *Contemporary Theories of Knowledge*. Savage, Md.: Rowman & Littlefield.

Popkin, Samuel (1991). *The Reasoning Voter*. Chicago, Ill.: University of Chicago Press.

Popper, Karl (1972). *Objective Knowledge*. Oxford: Clarendon Press.

Putnam, Hilary (1978). *Meaning and the Moral Sciences*. Boston, Mass.: Routledge & Kegan Paul.

—— (1981). *Reason, Truth and History*. New York: Cambridge University Press.

—— (1994). "Sense, Nonsense, and the Senses: An Inquiry into the Powers of the Human Mind." *Journal of Philosophy*, 91: 445–517.

Quillian, M. Ross (1994). "A Content-Independent Explanation of Science's Effectiveness." *Philosophy of Science*, 61: 429–48.

Quine, Willard van Orman (1953). "Two Dogmas of Empiricism," in *From a Logical Point of View*. Cambridge, Mass.: Harvard University Press.

—— (1960). *Word and Object*. Cambridge, Mass.: MIT Press.

—— (1971). *Philosophy of Logic*. New York: Harper & Row.

—— (1987). *Quiddities: An Intermittently Philosophical Dictionary*. Cambridge, Mass.: Harvard University Press.

Quinn, Frank (1995). "Roadkill on the Electronic Highway: The Threat to the Mathematical Literature." *Notices of the American Mathematical Society*, 42: 53–6.

Rae, Douglas (1969). "Decision-Rules and Individual Values in Constitutional Choice." *American Political Science Review*, 63: 40–53.

Ramsey, F. P. (1978). *Foundations: Essays in Philosophy, Logic, Mathematics and Economics*, ed. D. H. Mellor. London: Routledge & Kegan Paul.

Rasmusen, Eric (1989). *Games and Information*. Oxford: Blackwell.

Rawls, John (1971). *A Theory of Justice*. Cambridge, Mass.: Harvard University Press.
—— (1993). *Political Liberalism*. New York: Columbia University Press.
Raz, Joseph (1986). *The Morality of Freedom*. Oxford: Clarendon Press.
Red Lion Broadcasting Co. v. FCC (1969). 395 U.S. 367.
Reid, Thomas (1970). *An Inquiry into the Human Mind*, ed. Timothy Duggan. Chicago, Ill.: University of Chicago Press.
—— (1983). *Inquiry and Essays*, ed. Ronald Beanblossom and Keith Lehrer. Indianapolis, Ind.: Hackett.
Rescher, Nicholas (1973). *The Coherence Theory of Truth*. Oxford: Oxford University Press.
—— (1977). *Methodological Pragmatism*. Oxford: Blackwell.
Rheingold, Howard (1993). *The Virtual Community: Homesteading on the Electronic Frontier*. Reading, Mass.: Addison-Wesley.
Robertson, David (1976). "Surrogates for Party Identification in the Rational Choice Framework," in Ian Budge, ed., *Party Identification and Beyond*. London: Wiley.
Rorty, Richard (1979). *Philosophy and the Mirror of Nature*. Princeton, NJ: Princeton University Press.
—— (1991). "Solidarity or Objectivity?" in *Objectivity, Relativism, and Truth*. New York: Cambridge University Press.
Rosenberg, Jay (1980). *One World and Our Knowledge of It*. Boston, Mass.: D. Reidel.
Roth, Paul, and Barrett, Robert (1990). "Deconstructing Quarks." *Social Studies of Science*, 20: 579–632.
Rousseau, Jean-Jacques (1973). *The Social Contract and Discourses* (1762), trans. G. D. H. Cole, rev. J. H. Brunfit and John C. Hall. London: J. M. Dent & Sons.
Rubenfeld, Jed (1989). "The Right of Privacy." *Harvard Law Review*, 102: 737–807.
Russell, Bertrand (1912). *The Problems of Philosophy*. Oxford: Oxford University Press.
Saari, Donald (1994). *The Geometry of Voting*. Berlin: Springer.
Sainsbury, R. M. (1996). "Crispin Wright: Truth and Objectivity." *Philosophy and Phenomenological Research*, 56: 899–904.
Salmon, Wesley (1963). *Logic*. Englewood Cliffs, NJ: Prentice-Hall.
—— (1990). "Rationality and Objectivity in Science *or* Tom Bayes Meets Tom Kuhn," in C. Wade Savage, ed., *Scientific Theories*. Minneapolis, Minn.: University of Minnesota Press.
Samuelson, Pamela (1996). "The Copyright Grab." *Wired*, 4/1: 134–8, 188, 190–1.
Samuelson, Paul A. (1954). "The Pure Theory of Public Expenditure." *Review of Economics and Statistics*, 36: 387–9.
Sanitioso, R., Kunda, Z., and Fong, G. (1990). "Motivated Recruitment of Auto-biographical Memory." *Journal of Personality and Social Psychology*, 59: 229–41.
Sapir, E. (1921). *Language*. New York: Harcourt, Brace, & World.
Sartwell, Crispin (1992). "Why Knowledge is Merely True Belief." *Journal of Philosophy*, 89: 167–80.
Schacter, Daniel (1996). *Searching for Memory*. New York: Basic Books.
Schaller, Susan (1991). *A Man Without Words*. New York: Summit Books.
Schattschneider, E. E. (1943). *Party Government*. New York: Holt, Rinehart & Winston.
Schauer, Frederick (1982). *Free Speech: A Philosophical Enquiry*. New York: Cambridge University Press.
—— (1985). "Easy Cases." *Southern California Law Review*, 58: 399–440.

Schauer, Frederick (1997). "Discourse and Its Discontents." *Notre Dame Law Review*, 72: 1309–34.

Scheffler, Israel (1973). *Reason and Teaching*. London: Routledge.

Schiffer, Stephen (1987) *Remnants of Meaning*. Cambridge, Mass.: MIT Press.

Schmerber v. California (1966). 384 U.S. 757.

Schmitt, Frederick (1994a). "Socializing Epistemology: An Introduction through Two Sample Issues," in Schmitt 1994b.

—— ed. (1994b). *Socializing Epistemology*. Lanham, Md.: Rowman & Littlefield.

—— (1995). *Truth*. Boulder, Colo.: Westview.

Scott, Janny (1998). "For the Media, an Unsavory Story Tests Ideals and Stretches Limits." *New York Times*, February 1: 1, 17.

Searle, John (1983). *Intentionality: An Essay in the Philosophy of Mind*. New York: Cambridge University Press.

—— (1995). *The Construction of Social Reality*. New York: Free Press.

Sears, D. O., and Whitney, R. E. (1973). "Political Persuasion," in I. deSola Pool, ed., *Handbook of Communication*. Chicago, Ill.: Rand McNally College Publishing Co.

Sellars, Wilfrid (1963). "Empiricism and the Philosophy of Mind," in *Science, Perception and Reality*. New York: Humanities Press.

Shapere, Dudley (1982). "The Concept of Observation in Science and in Philosophy." *Philosophy of Science*, 49: 485–525.

Shapin, Steven (1994). *A Social History of Truth*. Chicago, Ill.: University of Chicago Press.

—— and Schaffer, Simon (1985). *Leviathan and the Air-Pump: Hobbes, Boyle and the Experimental Life*. Princeton, NJ: Princeton University Press.

Shapley, Lloyd, and Grofman, Bernard (1984). "Optimizing Group Judgmental Accuracy in the Presence of Interdependence." *Public Choice*, 43: 329–43.

Shaw, R. (1991). "Splitting Truths from Darkness: Epistemological Aspects of Temne Divination," in Philip Peek, ed., *African Divination Systems: Ways of Knowing*. Bloomington, Ind.: Indiana University Press.

Shepard, Roger, and Metzler, Jacqueline (1971). "Mental Rotation of Three-dimensional Objects." *Science*, 171: 701–3.

Siegel, Harvey (1988). *Educating Reason: Rationality, Critical Thinking, and Education*. New York: Routledge.

—— (1997). *Rationality Redeemed? Further Dialogues on an Educational Ideal*. New York: Routledge.

Silberg, William, Lundberg, George, and Musacchio, Robert (1997). "Assessing, Controlling, and Assuring the Quality of Information on the Internet." *Journal of the American Medical Association*, 277: 1244–5.

Singer, Joseph (1984). "The Player and the Cards: Nihilism and Legal Theory." *Yale Law Journal*, 94: 1–70.

Slavin, Robert (1990). *Cooperative Learning: Theory, Research and Practice*. Englewood Cliffs, NJ: Prentice-Hall.

—— (1992). "When and Why Does Cooperative Learning Increase Achievement? Theoretical and Empirical Perspectives," in Rachel Hertz-Lazarowitz and Norman Miller, eds., *Interaction in Cooperative Groups: The Theoretical Anatomy of Group Learning*. New York: Cambridge University Press.

Slezak, Peter (1991). "Bloor's Bluff: Behaviorism and the Strong Programme." *International Studies in the Philosophy of Science*, 5: 241–56.

Smuts, Barbara (1985). *Sex and Friendship in Baboons*. New York: Aldine.

Sniderman, Paul (1993). "The New Look in Public Opinion Research," in Ada

Finifter, ed., *Political Science: The State of the Discipline II*. Washington, DC: American Political Science Association.

—— Brody, Richard, and Tetlock, Philip (1991). *Reasoning and Choice*. Cambridge: Cambridge University Press.

Sokal, Alan (1996*a*). "Transgressing the Boundaries: Towards a Transformative Hermeneutics of Quantum Gravity." *Social Text*, 46, 47: 217–52.

—— (1996*b*). "A Physicist Experiments with Cultural Studies." *Lingua Franca*, 6/4: 62–4.

Solomon, Miriam (1992). "Scientific Rationality and Human Reasoning." *Philosophy of Science*, 59: 439–55.

Solum, Lawrence (1987). "On the Indeterminacy Crisis: Critiquing Critical Dogma." *University of Chicago Law Review*, 54: 462–503.

Sommers, Frederic (1994). "Naturalism and Realism," in Peter French, Theodore Uehling, Jr., and Howard Wettstein, eds., *Midwest Studies in Philosophy*, vol. xix. Notre Dame, Ind.: University of Notre Dame Press.

—— (1997). "Putnam's Born-again Realism." *Journal of Philosophy*, 94: 453–71.

Spence, A. Michael (1974). *Market Signaling*. Cambridge, Mass.: Harvard University Press.

Sperber, Dan, and Wilson, Deirdre (1986). *Relevance: Communication and Cognition*. Oxford: Blackwell.

Spiller, Pablo (1990). "Agency and the Role of Political Institutions," in Ferejohn and Kuklinski 1990.

Sprat, Thomas (1958). *History of the Royal Society* (1667). London: Routledge & Kegan Paul.

Stavropoulos, Nicos (1996). *Objectivity in Law*. Oxford: Clarendon Press.

Steiker, Carol (1994). "Second Thoughts about First Principles." *Harvard Law Review*, 107: 820–57.

Stich, Stephen (1990). *The Fragmentation of Reason*. Cambridge, Mass.: MIT Press.

Stolberg, Sheryl (1997). "Now, Prescribing Just What the Patient Ordered." *New York Times*, August 10, 4: 3.

Stone, Geoffrey (1983). "Content Regulation and the First Amendment." *William and Mary Law Review*, 25: 189–252.

—— (1987). "Content-Neutral Restrictions." *University of Chicago Law Review*, 54: 46–118.

Straffin, Philip, Jr. (1977). "Majority Rule and General Decision Rules." *Theory and Decision*, 8: 351–60.

Strawson, P. F. (1950). "Truth." *Proceedings of the Aristotelian Society*, supp. vol. 24: 129–56.

—— (1964). "A Problem about Truth—A reply to Mr. Warnock," in George Pitcher, ed., *Truth*. Englewood Cliffs, NJ: Prentice-Hall.

Strum, Shirley (1987). *Almost Human: A Journey into the World of Baboons*. New York: Random House.

Sunstein, Cass (1992). "Free Speech Now." *University of Chicago Law Review*, 59: 255–316.

—— (1993). *Democracy and the Problem of Free Speech*. New York: Macmillan.

Talbott, William, and Goldman, Alvin (1998). "Games Lawyers Play: Legal Discovery and Social Epistemology." *Legal Theory*, 4: 93–163.

Tannen, Deborah (1990). *You Just Don't Understand*. New York: Morrow.

Taubes, Gary (1995). "Epidemiology Faces Its Limits." *Science*, 269: 164–9.

Taylor, Charles (1992). "The Politics of Recognition," in Gutmann 1992*a*.

Taylor, Michael (1969). "Proof of a Theorem on Majority Rule." *Behavioral Science*, 14: 228–31.

Taylor, Stuart, Jr. (1994). "Sleazy in Seattle," *The American Lawyer*, 16/5: 74–9.

Tempels, P. (1969). *Bantu Philosophy*. Paris: Présence Africaine.

Tetlock, Philip, and Belkin, Aaron, eds. (1996a). *Counterfactual Thought Experiments in World Politics*. Princeton, NJ: Princeton University Press.

—— —— (1996b). "Counterfactual Thought Experiments in World Politics: Logical, Methodological and Psychological Perspectives," in Tetlock and Belkin 1996a.

Thomsen, M., and Resnik, D. (1995). "The Effectiveness of the Erratum in Avoiding Error Propagation in Physics." *Science and Engineering Ethics*, 1: 231–40.

Tichy, Pavel (1978). "Verisimilitude Revisited." *Synthese*, 38: 175–96.

Tong, Rosemarie (1989). *Feminist Thought: A Comprehensive Introduction*. Boulder, Colo.: Westview.

Tufte, Edward (1983). *The Visual Display of Information*. Cheshire, Conn.: Graphics Press.

—— (1990). *Envisioning Information*. Cheshire, Conn.: Graphics Press.

Tullock, Gordon (1980). *Trials on Trial*. New York: Columbia University Press.

Turner, V. (1975). *Revelation and Divination in Ndembu Ritual*. Ithaca, NY: Cornell University Press.

Tversky, Amos, and Kahneman, Daniel (1983). "Extensional versus Intuitive Reasoning: The Conjunction Fallacy in Probability Judgment." *Psychological Review*, 90: 293–315.

Unger, Roberto (1975). *Knowledge and Politics*. New York: Free Press.

van Eemeren, Frans H., and Grootendorst, Rob (1984). *Speech Acts in Argumentative Discussions*. Dordrecht: Foris.

—— —— Jackson, Sally, and Jacobs, Scott (1993). *Reconstructing Argumentative Discourse*. Tuscaloosa, Ala.: University of Alabama Press.

van Fraassen, Bas (1980). *The Scientific Image*. Oxford: Clarendon Press.

Varian, Hal (1996). "The Economics of the Internet and Academia," in Meredith Butler and Bruce Kinga, eds., *The Economics of Information in the Networked Environment*. Washington, DC: Association of Research Libraries.

von Frisch, Karl (1967). *The Dance Language and Orientation of Bees*. Cambridge, Mass.: Harvard University Press.

Vygotsky, L. S. (1978). *Mind in Society: The Development of Higher Psychological Processes*, ed. Michael Cole *et al.* Cambridge, Mass.: Harvard University Press.

Warner, Kenneth, Goldenhar, Linda, and McLaughlin, Catherine (1992). "Cigarette Advertising and Magazine Coverage of the Hazards of Smoking." *New England Journal of Medicine*, 326: 305–9.

Washington v. Texas (1967). 388 U.S. 14.

Washington State Physicians Insurance Exchange & Association v. Fisons Corporation (1993). 858 P. 2d 1054 (Wash.).

Wilentz, Sean (1997). "Don't Know Much About History." *New York Times Book Review*, November 30: 28, 31.

Willett, Thomas (1988). "A Cross-Linguistic Survey of the Grammaticization of Evidentiality." *Studies in Language*, 12: 51–97.

Wilson v. United States (1893). 149 U.S. 60.

Wilson, W. Kent (1990). "Some Reflections on the Prosentential Theory of Truth," in J. Michael Dunn and Anil Gupta, eds., *Truth or Consequences*. Dordrecht: Kluwer.

Wittgenstein, Ludwig (1922). *Tractatus Logico-Philosophicus*. London: Routledge.
—— (1969). *On Certainty*, trans. G. E. M. Anscombe and G. H. von Wright. New York: Harper.
Wittman, Donald (1989). "Why Democracies Produce Efficient Results." *Journal of Political Economy*, 97: 1395–1424.
Wolf, Susan (1992). "Comment," in Gutmann 1992*a*.
Woods, John, and Walton, Douglas (1982). "Question-Begging and Cumulativeness in Dialectical Games." *Nous*, 16: 585–605.
Woolgar, Steve (1988). *Science: The Very Idea*. London: Tavistock.
Wright, Crispin (1992). *Truth and Objectivity*. Cambridge, Mass.: Harvard University Press.
Wright, Larry (1995). "Argument and Deliberation: A Plea for Understanding." *Journal of Philosophy*, 92: 565–85.
Wynn, Karen (1992). "Addition and Subtraction by Human Infants." *Nature*, 358: 749–50.

INDEX OF NAMES

GENERAL INDEX

Breinigsville, PA USA
21 July 2010
242112BV00002B/3/A